The Language of Fashion

DICTIONARY AND DIGEST

of Fabric, Sewing and Dress

BY MARY BROOKS PICKEN

AND THE EDITORIAL AND RESEARCH STAFF
OF THE MARY BROOKS PICKEN SCHOOL

A History of Textiles and Weaving

A textile or cloth is a flexible woven material consisting of a network of natural or artificial fibres, often referred to as 'thread' or 'yarn'. Yarn is produced by spinning raw fibres of wool, flax, cotton, or other material to produce long strands. Textiles are then in turn, formed by weaving, knitting, crocheting, knotting, or pressing fibres together (felt). The words 'fabric' and 'cloth' are used in textile assembly trades (such as tailoring and dressmaking) as synonyms for textile. However, there are subtle differences in these terms in specialized usage. Textile refers to any material made of interlacing fibres. Fabric refers to any material made through weaving, knitting, spreading, crocheting, or bonding that may be used in production of further goods (garments, etc.). And finally, Cloth may be used synonymously with fabric but often refers to a finished piece of fabric used for a specific purpose (e.g., table cloth).

The word 'textile' comes from Latin, textilis, meaning 'woven' (from textus, the past participle of the verb texere, 'to weave'). From ancient origins, the production of textiles has altered almost beyond recognition however. Industrialisation and the introduction of modern manufacturing techniques have changed both the working methods – speed and scale, and the end product itself. For some types of textiles though; plain weave, twill, or satin weave, there is little difference between the ancient and modern methods. Textile production has been evidenced as early as Neolithic times. In 2013, linen cloth was found at the 'Çatalhöyük' site (Turkey), dated at around 700 BCE. Another fragment has been found in Fayum (a city in middle Egypt), dated to about 5000 BCE. Flax was the predominant fibre in Egypt at this time (3600 BCE), hugely popular in the Nile Valley, though wool became the primary fibre used in other cultures around 2000 BCE.

Emerging from these early examples, weaving has developed into an enormous industry. Essentially, weaving is a method of fabric production in which two distinct sets of yarns are interlaced at right angles to form a fabric. Other techniques include: knitting, lace making, felting and braiding. The longitudinal threads are called the 'warp' and the lateral threads are the 'weft' or 'filling'. (Weft, or woof is an old English word meaning 'that which is woven.') Cloth is usually woven on a loom, a device that holds the warp threads in place while filling threads are woven through them. The way that these warp and filling threads interlace with each other is called 'the weave'. The majority of woven products are created with one of three basic weaves: 'plain weave' (strong and hard-wearing, used for fashion and furnishing fabrics, with a simple criss-cross pattern), 'satin weave' (which typically has a glossy surface and a dull back, characterized by four or more weft yarns floating over a warp yarn, or vice versa) and finally, 'twill' (a pattern of diagonal parallel ribs - in contrast with a satin and plain weave).

Before the Industrial Revolution (1760-1840), weaving was a manual craft and wool was the principal staple. In the great wool districts a form of factory system was introduced, but in more rural areas weavers worked from home on a putting-out system. The wooden looms of that time were either 'broad' or 'narrow'; broad looms were those too wide for the weaver to pass the shuttle through the shed, necessitating employing an assistant (often an apprentice). This ceased to be necessary after John Kay invented the flying shuttle in 1733 however. The flying shuttle essentially involved a box, at either end of the loom, which caught the shuttle at the end of its journey, and propelled the shuttle on its return trip. This massively sped up the process of weaving, consequently resulting in a shortage of thread and a surplus of weaving capacity! The problem was largely solved with the opening of the Bridgewater Canal in June 1761, allowing cotton to be brought into Manchester, an area rich in fast flowing streams that could be used to power machinery.

Edmund Cartwright was the first to attempt to mechanise weaving. He built a factory at Doncaster and obtained a series of patents between 1785 and 1792. Cartwright later sold these to the Grimshaw brothers of Manchester, but their Knott Mill mysteriously burnt down the year afterwards. Whatever the process, woven 'grey cloth' - the end-product of weaving, was then sent to 'finishers', where it was bleached, dyed and printed. Natural dyes were originally used, with synthetic dyes coming in the second half of the nineteenth century (the need for these chemicals was an important factor in the development of the chemical industry too). Up until this point, all textiles were made from natural fibres; animal substances such as wool or silk, plant based materials such as cotton, flax or jute, and mineral sources, such as asbestos and glass fibres. In the twentieth century however, these were supplemented by artificial fibres made from petroleum.

Today, the textile industry is thriving, creating many sub-industries – such as those purely devoted to colouring or patterning the woven material. Many famous fashion designers, such as Armani, Gianni Versace and Emilio Pucci have relied on textile designs to set their fashion collections apart; easily recognisable by their signature print driven designs. In properly printed fabrics the colour is bonded with the fibre, so as to resist washing and friction. This can be done by stencils, wood-blocks, engraved plates, rollers or silkscreens. Woodblock printing, still used in India and elsewhere today, is the oldest of these dating back to at least 220 CE in China. Most commonly however, textiles are dyed all over, with fabrics now available in almost every colour. Coloured designs can be created by simple printing, weaving together fibres of different colours (tartan or Uzbek Ikat), adding coloured stitches to finished fabric (embroidery), creating patterns by resist dyeing methods, tying off areas of cloth and dyeing the rest (tie-dyeing), or drawing wax designs on cloth and dyeing in between them (batik).

Textiles have been a fundamental part of human life since the beginning of civilization. As has been evidenced, the methods and materials used to make them have expanded enormously, but the function of fabric itself has largely remained the same! The history of textile arts is also the history of international trade, as silks were brought from China to India, Africa and Europe, whilst Tyrian purple dye was an important trade good in the ancient Mediterranean. We hope this book inspires your own journey into textiles and weaving. Enjoy.

THIS BOOK AND YOU

THIS book provides you with a quick and ready reference for about 8000 words in "the language of fashion" — words associated primarily with wearing apparel and accessories and whatever goes into the making of them. Most of these words are not easily available elsewhere, as they are not usually to be found in the dictionary of average size. When they are in the dictionary, they are not always defined from a fashion point of view; and they are not assembled in groups for comparison or quick reference.

You who would know fashion and use it to express beauty and charm in your own clothes will find a study of this book invaluable. It will enable you to become familiar with the history of fashion. It will illuminate your reading of articles on fashion, and the advertising of fashion merchandise. And in planning your own clothes, it will help you to understand what goes with what and why, and to use fashion to your personal advantage.

Among other special advantages of this book, these may be noted: It includes the important stitches, laces, embroideries, and weaves you might be interested to know about, describing them so that you will recognize them at once; and in many cases you will be able actually to do the stitches from the illustrations. It defines fabrics and leather, generally specifies which garments and articles they are suitable for, and occasionally lists the qualities of the materials as they affect their choice for wear. It groups the different kinds of furs, and indicates which are real furs and which are imitations. You will find the book particularly helpful, for example, when you see something advertised and would like to find out the essential details. Hundreds of types of garments are given, making it easy for you to identify the important feature of a silhouette, and often to know something of its origin.

This book should prove an inspiration to those who desire to make a fancy-dress costume or to dress a pageant or play; for, when there are illustrations and definitions of costumes, enough information is often available for the development of those costumes. Every historical costume, being representative of a period or type, is suitable to wear for fancy dress.

INCREASE YOUR FASHION VOCABULARY

The language of fashion provides the everyday talk of many women — when shopping, when describing something seen or advertised or reported. One can make her talk more accurate and far more picturesque if she knows a silhouette or color or texture or design, knows what it is related to and also something of its history.

It is hoped that this book will increase the vocabulary of many, make fashion talk more interesting and the reading of fashion material in the press more understandable and therefore exciting.

Fashion writers should find this book an inspiration. It should help them to make comparisons of fashion garments and to write descriptions that will make word pictures for their readers. People in the trade, manufacturers and designers, should also find its illustrations and definitions useful, especially in helping them find appropriate names for articles they design or create. Often they

FOREWORD

can take from the old a word that describes the article they have created, change it in some way to make it modern, or find a new way to spell it. The spelling of even ordinary words is often changed for copyrighted names and trade-marks.

This book is no larger than the average novel; yet it carries in its pages the story of mankind. Fashion has always been influenced by the mode of transportation, the architecture of the period, and the customs of the people. Prosperity and poverty are recorded in the fashions of the ages; likewise, frugality and extravagance.

Fashions have been named for men and women, for leaders, and for painters of note or vogue; and inventions have also had a part in contributing to the language of fashion. Very few fashions or items of dress have actually originated in America and practically all of these in the last half century. Dr. Paul Nystrom lists some of these in his book, "Economics of Fashion," among them: the bungalow apron, jumper, middy blouse, Gibson Girl waist, the boyish form silhouette, union suits, rubber heels for shoes, health shoes, styles in nurses' uniforms, and the slide fastener.

Names come quickly into use in fashion. This book aims to cover the majority of important ones of the past, but can not anticipate the future. When the name of a living person influences fashion, study that person's pictures in the press, actually see the garment or article illustrated. If a historic character influences the fashions, then by all means see pictures of this person in history books. If the work of a painter influences colors or decoration or silhouette, study the works of the painter and see for yourself the items that are in vogue at the moment.

KEEP THIS BOOK AT HAND

Fashion writers delight in unusual words, making it desirable for the average person to be able to look up these words as she reads. When you read about fashions, keep this book at hand and use it. It will prove a boon because you can quickly find the definition of any word that is new to you or one the full meaning of which you are not sure.

Work to use familiar words more discreetly and new words correctly. You will be delighted with your speech, and you will find all fashions more interesting.

HOW TO USE YOUR BOOK

If you want to look up the meaning or the spelling or the pronunciation of a word, simply look for it as you would in the average dictionary. Every word is listed alphabetically; and it is printed in black type (called bold face) so that you can find it quickly. The pronunciation follows the word, as explained in detail hereafter. No word is capitalized unless it should always be spelled with a capital letter. When an entire word in the definition is printed in capital letters, it means that you can also find a definition under that word, listed alphabetically or in a group.

When there is more than one meaning, each is numbered. The sense in which the word is generally used in the world of fashion is given first — which is not necessarily the most common usage otherwise. Indeed, we omit the most common usage when it has no bearing on our subject. The origin of the word is given if the story is unusually interesting.

For many French words we give both the masculine and the feminine forms. The latter is often indicated only by a final *e*, but sometimes by a further change in the last syllable, as, for example: *blond*, a fair man, and *blonde*, a fair woman; *brunet*, a dark man, and *brunette*, a dark woman; *masseur*, a man who massages, and *masseuse*, a woman who massages. Foreign words that appear within the definitions are printed in italic, which is a lighter type.

FOREWORD

GROUPS

Types of garments, similar or related articles and parts of dress, silhouettes, fabrics, raw materials, elements of design, details of construction, and the like have been assembled in groups for the purpose of reference, study, and comparison. If you are a student or a teacher, or if you are engaged in selling or in writing, designing, illustrating, or any other type of fashion work, you will be especially interested in the groups of which there are over 100 listed in the table of contents.

If a word belongs to one of the groups, it is listed and defined as an individual word; and the name of the group follows the definition, printed in capital letters and preceded by the word *See*. If you look it up under the group name, you will find the word as part of the group. Individual words, group names, and words within groups are always listed alphabetically.

Gainsborough hat, for example, is listed alphabetically under the letter *G*; a brief description of the hat is given; and the definition is followed by the words *See* HATS, as a cross reference to the group. Under the word HATS, different types of hats are listed. In this group, *Gainsborough h.* is given a more complete definition. The word *hat* is represented by *h.* — as one-letter abbreviations such as *b.* for blouse and *l.* for lace are customary when a group name is repeated as part of the term that is being defined.

Words in groups are usually more fully defined; and the groups and the definitions within the groups have a definite advantage for those who are especially interested in the study of fashion. If you merely want to look up the meaning of a word quickly, however, or the spelling or pronunciation, you do not have to refer to the group, as you will find the individual listing adequate for your purposes.

Cross references are also given in groups that are related to other groups, as boots and shoes and slippers are related, for instance, and hats and caps and bonnets.

ILLUSTRATIONS

There are around 600 illustrations in this book. The illustrations of stitches, weaves, laces, garments, and all other groups are generally assembled within the group for pictorial comparison. This is a convenience for those wishing to study one subject or to obtain information about hats, for example, or collars, shoes, weaves, or stitches.

PRONUNCIATION

The pronunciation of words not only varies throughout the world, but even in different parts of the United States. Many words are pronounced in two or more ways, and authorities are not always agreed upon which pronunciation is preferred. In this book, as a rule, we have limited ourselves to one pronunciation, the one most often preferred. A second pronunciation is given only if the accent can fall on different syllables; or if different spellings are given and the pronunciation is affected by the spelling; or if the word has recently been taken from a foreign language — if it is French, for example — and may be given the English or the French pronunciation. If no pronunciation is given, pronounce the word just as it looks — the most obvious way.

As pronunciation varies with time, we naturally have chosen the pronunciations that prevail at the present time. The pronunciation is given in parentheses immediately after the word that is being defined. The way a word is spelled is not always a guide to how it is pronounced, as the sound of a letter varies in different words. Notice, for example, the difference in the sounds of *a* and *o* and *e* when you say the words *art* and *fate, ton* and *note, be* and *pen*. For the pronunciation, therefore, we have had to respell the words in a manner to indicate the sound values.

FOREWORD

We have used two different guides to pronunciation. First comes the type customarily employed in dictionaries, which makes use of what are called phonetic symbols. For the benefit of those who have not yet become familiar with phonetic symbols, we have added a second guide, separated from the first by a semicolon (;). In this we have used the letters of the alphabet for the respelling so as to indicate the sound value in simple and familiar forms. The word is divided, but not necessarily into syllables. The divisions are not separated by hyphens or an accent mark, the division on which the emphasis falls being indicated by italic type. The division *are*, which appears frequently in the secondary pronunciations, should be pronounced as it is in the word *fare*.

PHONETIC GUIDE TO PRONUNCIATION

The first guide to pronunciation divides the word into syllables separated by hyphens (-) or by the accent mark ('), the latter denoting the syllable on which the emphasis falls. Phonetic symbols are used because a phonetic symbol always represents the same sound, unlike a letter of the alphabet, which may have as many as four different speech values, as will be seen in the Key to Pronunciation. The key has been made as simple as possible, and has been designed to make use of the fewest symbols possible. You will observe that it consists chiefly of vowels, as variation occurs mostly in vowel sounds. Familiarize yourself with these symbols. Know immediately when you see the symbol ā, for example, that you pronounce it like the *a* in *fate*. For your convenience, the key words are repeated at the bottom of each page so that when you look up a word you can find the pronunciation of the symbols, if necessary, without having to turn back to this key.

The pronunciation is preceded by the abbreviation *Sp.* or *F.* if the word is Spanish or French. There are many foreign words in the language of fashion, chiefly French, because France has a profound influence on fashion. As you know, every language has its own individual characteristic pronunciations. Sounds that are never used in English can not be accurately represented by English words and the phonetic symbols derived from them. We give an explanation of how to pronounce some of the most frequently recurring foreign sounds, but we have not gone into the more intricate points of foreign pronunciation.

KEY TO PRONUNCIATION

ā — *fate*
ă — *fat*
à — *dance* (between ă and ä)
ä — *art*
ē — *me*
ĕ — *met*
ē — *her, fur, sir*
ê — *there, fare, wear*
ī — *ride*
ĭ — *rid*
ō — *note*
ŏ — *not*
ô — *corn, warm*
ōō — *food*
ŏŏ — *foot*
ū — *cute*
ŭ — *cut*
ü — as the French *sur, curé*. (Say ē with lips in ō shape.)
ow — *now, thou*

ŋ — as the *n* in *finger* (before pronouncing the g). Imparts nasal sound to preceding vowel rather than having a separate sound of its own.

ə — short, unstressed sound, as the last syllable of *villa;* second syllable of *element, filament.* Indicates slurring of vowel sound in unaccented syllable.

ñ — as the ny in *canyon*, ñ in Spanish *señor*.
zh — as the *z* in *azure*, *s* in *pleasure*.

STUDY THE KEY TO PRONUNCIATION

Simple words have been chosen for the key so that when you say them correctly you will know what sound is represented by the symbol. When you look up a word, say the

FOREWORD

pronunciation so that by hearing it you will become familiar with the preferred form and feel completely at ease when you use the word in conversation.

As we have said before, pronunciation varies throughout the world; and possibly you do not pronounce the letter *a* differently when you say the key words, for example: *fat, fate, dance, art*. In each word, however, *a* should have a decidedly different sound. You can train your ear by paying attention to the speech of word-conscious persons with whom you come in contact and by listening carefully to those noted for their diction who speak in the pulpit, on the platform, on the radio, on the stage and screen. Remember that our education does not end when we leave school. It should continue throughout our life. By keeping alert and interested in what is going on about us, we can enjoy a fuller, richer life. Knowing words, their full meanings as well as their correct pronunciation, can become a fascinating worth-while hobby.

WHEN SPELLING VARIES

Some words may be spelled in two or more ways, each of which is correct, but one of which is usually preferred. With the preferred form, we give the variant spellings, each preceded by the word *or*, as in *pajama or pyjama*.

In some cases where the variant spelling is commonly used by many, we list the variant also in its alphabetical place so that you can readily find the word under the form with which you are familiar. If we had listed the word only under the preferred form — *filibeg*, for instance, and you were looking for *philibeg* — you might think that the word was not included in the book.

The definition of a word is given only under the preferred spelling. To save space, as you will see, we do not repeat the definition. You will know where to find it, however, because after every variant we give the preferred spelling in capital letters.

Some words, as they appear in fashion news cabled from abroad and in magazine and newspaper articles, are often given a spelling which varies from the authentic form. *Burunduki*, for example, the Siberian chipmunk, is frequently spelled *barunduki; gillie*, the laced sports shoe, frequently appears as *ghillie*.

NEW WORDS AND OLD

Spoken language is a living thing, subject to change. New words come into being as the need arises; old words drop out or are used in a different sense. This is particularly true of the language of fashion, which is being continually influenced by what is happening daily throughout the world. All articles of apparel have a relationship to other countries and to the past, which usually gives them their name.

An event of international importance may bring a little-known part of the world into the news of the day, and this in turn may affect the current fashions; or the popularity of a period play on the stage or screen or of a "best seller" novel may bring about the widespread revival of fashions of other days. So we have included in this book not only the fashion names that are in current usage, but even fashion terms from past eras. These are important not only for their bearing on the past, but for what they may mean in the future — there are modern versions of the wimple and the snood, for example, and the hoop skirt. Many of the words given will be found in the literature of the seventeenth, eighteenth, and nineteenth centuries — more, perhaps, in the latter.

COLOR

Some words are important in the fashion world for a season or more, but do not survive. This is especially noticeable with regard to colors. Each season, different shades have their vogue under new names. The more ephemeral have been omitted from this book; but we have included some color names, such as *Alice blue*, that have been more lasting. As a rule, new colors are given names that will bring the color to mind. Hindenburg Gray, for example, was like the color of the ill-fated zeppelin; Queen Blue is the soft, medium-blue color favored by Queen Elizabeth of England.

TRADE-MARKS

Industry has made its own definite contribution to the language of fashion, chiefly in words coined for use as trade-marks or as the names of fabrics or accessories or articles of apparel. In the definitions in this book, wherever possible, we state which words belong in this category, such as *Bakelite* and *Plaskon*, the trade names for certain synthetic compositions.

Popular trade-marks or copyrighted names become an everyday part of fashion vocabulary, and their use throughout this book does not in any way affect the validity of their trademark or copyright. *Zipper* is one such popular word. Although it was patented by a rubber manufacturer as the name of an overshoe to be worn in wet weather (which was fastened by a slide fastener), the word *zipper* is now widely used for the slide fastener itself, whether used on overshoes, baggage, garments, or accessories.

Mary Brooks Picken wishes to express her deep appreciation for the splendid coöperation of the following, who have helped her to make this book complete, helpful, and interesting: *Artists:* C. Florence Valentine, Marie Struve, Jean Powers. . . . *Research and Editing:* Kathleen Masterson, Treva Wampler, June Sumner, Joyce Brindley, Elizabeth McCleary, Pauline Foster, Evelyn Boatwright, Theresa Brakeley, Harriet Hastings.

CONTENTS
ACCORDING TO GROUPS

	PAGE
Belts	7
Bindings	8
Blouses	9
Bobs	9
Bodices	10
Bonnets	10
Boots	11
Bows	12
Bracelets	13
Braids	13
Buckles	15
Bustles	16
Buttons	16
Buttonholes	16
Canvas	18
Caps	18
Capes	22
Checks	25
Coats	28
Collars	31
Color	33
Combs	34
Cottons	37
Crepes	38
Cuffs	40
Dots	43
Dress & Dresses	44
Dyeing	47
Embroideries	48
Eyelets	53
Fabric	53
Fancy Dress	53
Fashion	55
Fasteners	56
Feathers	56
Finishing	57
Flannels	58
Furs	60
Ginghams	65
Gloves	66
Godets	66
Goods	67
Handbags	69
Hats	70
Heels	75
Hems	76
Hoods	77
Hoops	78
Hose	78
Jackets	81
Knitting	85
Knots	86

	PAGE
Laces	86
Leathers	92
Lengths	94
Linens	95
Masks	98
Necklaces	102
Necklines	102
Needles	103
Nets	103
Patterns	108
Pearls	109
Pins	111
Plackets	112
Plaits	113
Pockets	114
Prints	116
Rayon	119
Ribbons	121
Rings	121
Sashes	124
Satins	124
Scissors	125
Seams	126
Serges	127
Shears	128
Shirts	128
Shoes	129
Silhouettes	131
Silk	133
Skirts	134
Sleeves	135
Slips	137
Slippers	137
Sport Clothes	139
Stitches	141
Straws	148
Stripes	149
Suits	149
Sweaters	150
Taffetas	151
Tapes	152
Threads	153
Tucks	157
Vamps	160
Veils	160
Velvets	161
Weaves	163
Wigs	165
Wool	166
Wraps	167
Yarns	169

THE LANGUAGE OF FASHION
DICTIONARY AND DIGEST OF FABRIC, SEWING, AND DRESS

A

aal (äl; ahl). Dye, red in color, obtained from root of East Indian shrub.

aba or **abba** (ä′bə; ah ba). 1. Square Arab mantle. See WRAPS. 2. Cloth woven from hair of camels, goats, etc. Used for shawls aba mantle.

abaca (ä-bə-kä′; ah ba kah). Fiber from leaf stalk of banana, commonly used in Philippines for making cordage, coarse fabrics, straw hats. Native name for Manila hemp.

abalone (ăb-ə-lō′nē; ab a lo ne). Shellfish, iridescent shell of which is used for inlay, buttons, beads, ornaments. Commonly called ear shell.

abb. 1. Warp yarn. Term used by weavers. 2. Inferior part of fleece around edge.

abbé cape (F. à-bā; a bay). Tiered shoulder-cape. See CAPES.

abbot cloth. Rough, canvas-like drapery material in basket weave. Usually of cotton. Similar to MONK'S CLOTH.

abbreviate (ă-brē′vĭ-āt; a bree vi ate) or **abbreviated** (ă-brē′vĭ-āt-ĕd; a bree vi ate ed). Shortened or relatively short.

abnet (ăb′nĕt; ab net). Long scarf or sash, usually of linen or linen mixture. Worn by Jewish priests.

abolla (à-bŏl′ə; a bahl a). Ancient Roman cloak. See WRAPS.

abrasion (ə-brā′zhən; a bray zhun). The wearing down by friction of parts of the surface of a textile to form a design.

absinthe (ăb′sĭnth or F. ăb-săNt; ab sinth or ab sant). Light yellowish-green shade, color of the liqueur.

absorbent cotton (ăb-sôr′běnt; ab sor bent). Cotton batting without any oils. Used chiefly for medical purposes. See COTTON.

academic costume (ăk-ə-dĕm′ĭk; ak a dem ik). Characteristic dress worn by faculty, students, and graduates of colleges and universities, and by those on whom honorary degrees have been conferred. Costume varies with rank. Consists of long gown, generally black, with long, full sleeves; sometimes a hood draped across shoulders; and a cap or MORTARBOARD. Color of hood denotes academic degree held by wearer. Costume also worn on official occasions by lawyers, clergy, etc.

acajou (F. á-kà-zhōō; a ka zhoo). French word for mahogany color.

acca. Medieval fabric made of silk mixed with gold threads. Probably made in Syria and named for Acre, Syrian seaport.

accent. Emphasis or prominence given to line or decorative color in costume.

accessory (ăk-sĕs′ə-rĭ; ak sess a ri). Article of apparel that completes the costume, such as shoes, gloves, hats, bags, jewelry, neckwear, belts, boutonnières, scarfs; in trade usage, also negligees, corsets, lingerie, etc.

accolé (ăk-ə-lā′; ak a lay). Entwined around or encircling the neck; collared; also, joined, touching, or overlapping, especially at the neck. Used of designs on coats-of-arms, shields, etc.

accordion plaits (ə-kôr′dĭ-ən plēts or plāts; a cor dee un pleets or plates). Straight, narrow plaits. See PLAITS.

accroche-cœur (F. à-krôsh kẽr; a krosh cur). French term meaning little flat curl of hair worn at temple; kiss-curl.

Acele. Trade name for a brand of rayon. See RAYON.

acetate rayon. One of the three types of rayon now manufactured commercially in the U.S.A. See RAYON.

acock. Turned up; at an angle; cocked.

active sports clothes. Clothes suitable for active participants in sports events. For types, see SPORTS CLOTHES.

acton. Jacket worn as part of armor. See JACKETS.

adamas (ăd′ə-măs; add a mass). Very hard precious stone, often a diamond. Used in gem cutting.

adaptation. Garment similar to an original model, yet having definite changes.

adonize (ăd′ō-nīz; add o nize). To dress up, beautify, dandify.

adorn. To ornament, decorate; to add to the effect.

afghan (ăf′găn; af gan). Soft, wool blanket, usually knitted or crocheted. Used as coverlet or worn as wrap.

afghan-stitch. Simple crochet stitch which produces plain pattern. Same as TRICOT-STITCH. See STITCHES.

afternoon dress. Costume for daytime social functions. See DRESS.

agabanee (ăg-ə-bä′nē; ag a bah nee). Silk-embroidered cotton fabric, made especially in Syria.

agal (ăg′ăl; ahg ahl). Decorative fillet usually made of two thick woolen cords wound with gold and silver threads. Worn by Arabs over the KAFFIYEH, to hold it on the head.

agamid (ä-gä-mēd′; ah gah meed′) or **aga** (ä′gä; ah gah). Strong inner bark of a Philippine plant. Used for making coarse cloth and rope.

agate (ăg′ĕt; ag et). Striped or cloudy variety of chalcedony, or quartz. Used as ornament on accessories.

aggrape (à-grăp′; a grap). Obsolete type of clasp, buckle, hook and eye. See AGRAFFE.

16th Century Aglets

aglet (ăg′lĕt; ag let) or **aiglet** (ăg′lĕt; aig let). Metal sheath or tag at end of a shoe-lace or ribbon tie, to facilitate threading. Much used in 16th and 17th century costume. Later, any ornamental pendant; sometimes a small image. Also written aiguillet. From French word aiguille, meaning needle.

agnelin (F. àñ-ə-lăN; an y lanh). French word for lambskin having wool left on in dressing.

agraffe or **agrafe** (à-grăf′; a graf). Metal fastening device, consisting of a lever and an eyelet. Used on early armor and costumes. From early Norman word aggrape, meaning clasp, buckle, or hook and eye, as used on medieval armor. Still in use in 18th century.

agréments (F. à-grā-mäN; a gray monh). French word for trimmings, ornaments.

aigrette or **aigret** (ā-grĕt′; ai gret). 1. Upright tuft of feathers or plumes of egret, or heron. See FEATHERS. 2. Something resembling feather aigrette, as a cluster of jewels.

aiguille (à-gwēl′ or F. ā-gwē; ai gweel or ai gwee). French word meaning needle.

aiguille à reprises (F. à rə-prēz; ah re preez). French word for darning needle.

aiguille à tricoter (F. à trē-kō-tā; ah tree ko tay). French word for knitting needle.

aiguillette (ā-gwĭ-lĕt′ or F. à-gwē-yĕt; ai gwil let or ai gwee yet). Aglet or ornamental tag; also, trimming of looped cords, as on military and naval uniforms.

aile (F. ăl; ale). French word meaning wing.

ailes de pigeon (F. ăl də-pē-zhôN; ale de pee zhonh). Powdered side curls, as formerly worn by men. French term meaning pigeon's wings.

ailette (F. ā-lĕt′; ai let). Protective shoulder plate of forged iron or steel. Worn as part of medieval armor. Original form of the epaulet, the wide, ornamented shoulder.

Air-conditioned. Trade name applied to cottons treated by chemical process to remove fuzz and thereby increase porosity.

airplane cloth. Firm-textured cloth in plain weave, originally made of unbleached linen for airplane wings. Since World War, made of cotton in varying weights and colors. Used for light-weight luggage, sports and work shirts, etc.

à jour or **ajour** (F. à zhōōr; ah zhoor). Drawn work or other open work. French term meaning pierced or showing light through.

alabaster (ăl′ə-băs-tẽr; al a bass ter). 1. Fine-grained, translucent mineral substance, used for small statues, lamps, etc. May be white or various delicate

---

fāte, făt, dănce, ärt mē, mĕt, hẽr, thêre rīde, rĭd nōte, nŏt, côrn, fōōd, fŏŏt cūte, cŭt, cūré now fin(g)ger villa(ə) señor pleas(zh)ure

alacha   2   **antique**

tints. **2.** Having texture or nearly-white color of alabaster.
alacha (ȧ-lä′chä; ah lah chah). Lightweight Oriental fabric of silk or cotton.
alamode (ăl′ȧ-mōd; *al* a mode). Thin, light-weight, glossy silk fabric. Formerly used for making scarfs, hoods, etc.
à la mode (F. ȧ lȧ mōd; ah lah mode). French phrase meaning in fashion or according to the fashion.
alaska (ȧ-lăs′kȧ; a *lass* ka). **1.** Overshoe. See BOOTS. **2.** Yarn made of cotton and wool. See YARNS.
Alaska sable. Incorrect term for skunk fur. No longer legal in advertising. See FURS.
Alaska sealskin. Fur of Alaska seals. Usually dyed brown or black. See FURS.
alb or **alba.** Long white vestment with long close sleeves, and girdle. Worn by clergy, usually over cassock and amice. Name derived from Latin *tunica alba*, meaning white tunic, secular garment worn before 9th century.
albatross (ăl′bȧ-trŏs; *al* ba tross). Soft, light-weight, woolen material with slightly creped surface, similar to bunting. In plain or fancy weave, usually in light colors. Named for the bird because fabric resembles its downy breast. Used for negligees, dresses, warm nightgowns, infants' wear.
Albert crepe. Silk and cotton crepe. See CREPES.
Alençon lace (F. ȧ-lôṅ-sôṅ; a lonh sonh). Needle-point lace with solid design on net ground. See LACES.
alépine (F. ȧ-lā-pēn; a lay peen). French word for BOMBAZINE.
alesan (ăl′ȧ-săn; *al* a san). Light, creamy brown color, or CAFÉ AU LAIT.
Algerian stripe (ăl-gē′rĭ-ăn; al *jeer* i an). Cream-colored fabric with alternate stripes of rough knotted cotton and of silk, woven in imitation of Moorish cloth.
Alice blue. Medium light blue, having very slight greenish cast. Favorite color of Alice Roosevelt (Longworth), worn by her when in the White House.
alliance (F. ȧl-lē-äṅs; al lee ahnce). French word for wedding ring.
alligator. Skin of the water reptile. See LEATHERS.
all-in-one. Foundation garment or corselet consisting of girdle and brassière, usually with or without a pantie.
allongé (F. ȧ-lôṅ-zhā; a lonh zhay). French word meaning lengthened, elongated, outstretched.
allover. Covering entire surface; also, fabric completely covered with a design, such as lace. See LACES.
alma. Silk dress fabric in diagonal twill weave. Usually made in black for mourning purposes.
almuce (ăl′mūs; *al* muce). Medieval hood like a cowl. See HOODS.
alnage (ăl′nĭj; *al* nij). Formerly, English measurement of cloth by the ell, or 45 inches.
aloe fiber. Soft hemp-like fiber of fleshy-leaved century or similar plant. Used for cloth, lace, embroidery, etc. Also called *bowstring hemp*.

aloe lace. Fragile lace of aloe fibers. See LACES.
aloe thread embroidery. Embroidery of aloe fibers. See EMBROIDERIES.
alpaca (ăl-păk′ȧ; al *pack* a). **1.** Hair of the Peruvian alpaca. See WOOL. **2.** Smooth, thin, wiry fabric having cotton warp and alpaca or other worsted filling. Similar to and sometimes called *mohair* and *brilliantine*. Used for linings, men's and women's summer suits. **3.** Fabric, usually of cotton and rayon, so called because of wiriness.
alpargata (Sp. äl-pär-gä′tȧ; ahl par *gah* ta). Coarse, low-priced Spanish shoe. See SHOES.
alpine hat. Soft felt hat. See HATS.
amaranth (ăm′ȧ-rănth; *am* a ranth). Purple tinged with red, so called because like one shade of flower of same name.
amazone or **habit d'amazone** (F. ä-bē dȧ-mȧ-zôn; a bee dam a zone). French term meaning riding-habit.
amber. **1.** Hard, translucent substance, found in the soil. Cloudy amber is yellowish in color; clear amber is a sparkling brown. Used for beads, ornaments, accessories, etc. **2.** Yellowish or brown color of amber.
ambergris (ăm′bēr-grēs; *am* ber greece). Waxy substance of white, grayish, yellow, black, or variegated color, found floating in the ocean in certain tropical regions, or obtained from its source, the sperm whale. Used in the manufacture of perfume and formerly also in cooking.
amener des modes (F. ȧm-nā dā mŏd; am nay day mody). French expression meaning to bring in fashions.
American badger. Coarse, long-haired, creamy white fur with black band just below tip. Used for trimmings. See FURS.
American Broadtail. Trade name for processed baby lamb. See FURS.
American cloth. In British usage, sturdy enameled cloth—oilcloth, for example. Used in the household; also, for traveling cases, toilet accessories, etc.
American mink. Brown, durable fur of American wild or ranch-bred mink. See FURS.
American opossum. Long-haired, fairly durable, gray fur of American opossum. See FURS.
American sable. Baum marten. Silky, brown, fairly durable fur. See FURS.
amethyst (ăm′ĭ-thĭst; *am* i thist). **1.** Clear purple or bluish-violet stone used in jewelry. **2.** Violet shade, having more red than blue.
amice (ăm′ĭs; *am* iss). **1.** Rectangular piece of linen worn by clergy as Mass vestment, originally over the head, now about the shoulders. **2.** Furred hood. See ALMUCE under HOODS.

Ecclesiastical
Amice

amictus (ȧ-mĭk′tŭs; a *mick* tus). Toga or any cloak-like outer garment. Worn by ancient Romans.
Amish costume (ä′mĭsh; *ah* mish). Plain habit worn by the Amish women of the Mennonites. Consists of plain gathered skirt, basque, and bonnet, usually in dull black and without ornament. All Amish garments are tied on, no modern fasteners of any kind being used.
amulet (ăm′ū-lĕt; *am* you let). Object, usually small piece of stone, bone, metal, etc., worn by the superstitious as protection against evil or bad luck. Common in earlier days; still worn as ornament in some parts of U. S.
anadem (ăn′ȧ-dĕm; *an* a dem). Garland; chaplet; wreath; fillet. Worn on the head as ornament.
anaglyph (ăn′ȧ-glĭf; *an* a glif). Ornament in low relief, as a cameo. Opposite of INTAGLIO.
anamite (ăn′ȧ-mīt; *an* a mite). Natural, unbleached, natural color of twine.
angel skin. Dull, waxy, smooth, gardenia-like finish given to certain fabrics, such as crepe, lace, or satin. Also called *peau d'ange*.
angel sleeve. Long, loose, flowing sleeve See SLEEVES.
angelus cap. Type of peasant handkerchief cap. See CAPS.
Angleterre edge or **edging** (F. äṅg-glȧ-tĕr; ong gla tare). Needle-point edging on braid or cord, made with one line of loops.
Anglo-Saxon embroidery. Ancient outline embroidery. See EMBROIDERIES.
Angora. **1.** Wool of the Angora goat. See WOOL. **2.** Fine, soft, fuzzy fabric made of Angora wool.
aniline or **anilin** (ăn′ĭ-lĭn; *an* i lin). Colorless oily compound, used as base of coal-tar dyes.
ankle boot. Boot of ankle height. See BOOTS.
ankle length. Length of dress or other garment reaching to anklebone. See LENGTHS.
anklet. **1.** Ornament worn around the ankle. **2.** Short hose reaching to ankle.
Anne Boleyn costume. Costume of 16th century as worn by Anne Boleyn, one of the wives of Henry VIII. See FANCY DRESS.
annulet (ăn′ū-lĕt; *an* you let). Small ring, especially as used in decoration.
antelope. **1.** Soft leather made from antelope skins. See LEATHERS. **2.** Short-haired coat of small brown African deer. See FURS.
antelope-finish suede. Sueded leather resembling antelope. See LEATHERS.
anti-crease. Chemical process of finishing fabric to prevent wrinkling. See CREASE-RESISTANT.
antimacassar (ăn-tĭ-mȧ-kăs′ẽr; ant i mȧ *kass* er). Covering or tidy, used to protect back, arms, and headrest of sofas, chairs, etc. Originally, to prevent soiling by macassar hair oil, much used during 19th century.
antique (ăn-tēk′; an *teek*). **1.** Of another age; applied to any garment or accessory made in ancient style; as, antique jewelry. **2.** Used derisively of a gar-

antique lace

ment that is old-fashioned, antiquated, out of style. **3.** Applied to silk woven, printed, or watered with an indistinct design.
antique lace. Darned bobbin lace. See LACES.
Antwerp pot lace. Rare bobbin lace with pot of flowers in design. See LACES.
apparel. Clothing of all sorts; also to clothe or attire. Term applied to the apparel industry, which makes ready-to-wear.
appenzell (ăp-ĕn-tsĕl'; ap en *tsell*). Type of drawn-work embroidery. See EMBROIDERIES.
appliqué (F. à-plē-kà; ap li kay). Decoration laid on and applied to another surface, as band or separate design of petals, leaves, figures, etc. Used on lace, fabric, and leather. French word meaning applied or put on.
appliqué embroidery. Motif or design applied by means of stitches; usually fabric applied, to fabric. See EMBROIDERIES.
appliqué-stitch. Any stitch used in applying pieces to a background. See STITCHES.
apricot (ā'prĭ-kŏt; *ai* pri cot). Color between red-orange and yellow-orange, ▸like that of ripe apricot fruit.
apron. **1.** Article of dress worn over clothing to protect or adorn it. Extends from waistline or shoulders, and is usually tied on by strings. Made of fabric, leather, or other material. Late in 16th century, became article of full dress; in colonial times, made of fine lace, worn with formal costumes; late in 18th century, worn almost floor length. **2.** Part of shoe upper covering instep.
apron check. Gingham with even checks, popular for aprons. See GINGHAMS.
apron dress. Dress having apron-like skirt, tied at waist and open in back. See DRESSES.
apron tunic. Long or short open ornamental tunic worn apron-fashion. See TUNIC, 2.
aquamarine (ăk-wa-ma-rēn'; ak wa ma reen). **1.** Variety of beryl used as semi-precious stone. Comes in blue, blue-green, or green color. **2.** Clear, light, green-blue color.
arabesque (ar-a-bĕsk'; ar a *besk*). Intricate design showing flowers, foliage, figures, etc., composed of interlaced lines in scroll effect. Usually made with cords, stitchery, or applied and outlined pieces.
Arabian (a-rā'bĭ-an; a *ray* bi an). Having characteristic features of Arabian dress, general type of which consists of loose, wide trousers, covered by ankle-length robe; loose, coat-like outer garment; square mantle; rich, colorful fabrics, and embroidery; slippers or sandals; kerchief headdress for men; veil for women.
Arabian embroidery. Elaborate Oriental embroidery. See EMBROIDERIES.
Arabian lace. Coarse, dark needle-point lace. See LACES.
araneum lace (a-rā'nĭ-ŭm; a *ray* ni um). Same as ANTIQUE LACE. See LACES.

arc. Any part of the line that is used in forming a circle.
arctic. High, waterproof overshoe. See BOOTS.
arctic fox. Fur of arctic fox, either white or blue. See FURS.
arctic wolf. Coarse, durable fur of white wolf. See FURS.
ardoisé (F. ăr-dwä-zā; ahr dwah zay). French word meaning slate-colored.
argent (F. ăr-zhän; ahr zhonh). French word for silver.
Argentan lace (ăr'jĕn-tăn; *ahr* jen tan). Alençon type of lace, bold in design. See LACES.
argentine (ăr'jĕn-tēn; *ahr* jen teen). Substance of silvery luster made from fish scales. Used in making imitation pearls.
argentine cloth. Glazed tarlatan to open-weave cheesecloth, glazed to make it dust-proof.
arisard (ăr'ĭ-särd; *ar* i sard). Tunic-like garment girdled at waistline. Formerly worn by women in Scotland.
arm band. Band of cloth worn around the arm; especially, band worn on sleeve for mourning or identification purposes.
Armenian lace. Narrow, scalloped, knotted, needle-made lace. See LACES.
armet (ăr'mĕt; *ahr* met). Hinged helmet snugly shaped to the head, closing neatly over chin and neck.
armhole. Hole in garment for the arm; line on which set-in sleeve is sewn to garment; measurement where arm joins body.
armil. Obsolete term for bracelet.
armilausa (ăr-mĭ-lô'sa; *ahr* mi *law* sa). Medieval cloak. See WRAPS.
armlet. **1.** Ornamental band worn on upper arm; distinguished from bracelet worn on lower arm. **2.** Small, short sleeve. See SLEEVES.
armor. Covering for the body, usually metal, formerly used as protection in battle.
armozeen or **armozine** (ăr'mə-zēn; *ahr* mo zeen). Heavy plain corded silk fabric. Used in 16th century and following for dresses and waistcoats; later used chiefly for scholastic and clerical robes. Also spelled *armazine, amazeen*.
armscye (ärm'sī; *arm* sigh). Opening for a sleeve; obsolete term for armhole.
armure. **1.** Stiff, richly embroidered dress material woven plain, striped, ribbed, or with small fancy design, sometimes in two colors. Made of silk, wool, cotton, rayon, or combinations of fibers. Used for linings, skirts, suits. From French *armour*, meaning armor; so called because design suggested chain armor. **2.** Drapery fabric in Jacquard weave with raised satin figure on rep or twill ground. Made of silk, cotton, wool, rayon, or mixture.
arras (ăr'as; *ar* as). **1.** Tapestry inwoven with figures and scenes, needle- or loom-made. So called because first made at Arras, France. **2.** Type of bobbin lace. See LACES.
arrasene embroidery (ăr-a-sēn'; *ar* a *seen*). Type of chenille embroidery. See EMBROIDERIES.
array. To clothe or dress, especially in

impressive attire; to adorn. Also, such attire.
arrowhead. Satin-stitch made with twist to form arrows as stays on tailored garments at joining of coat collars and lapels; at corners of pockets and pocket laps; at ends of seams, tucks, plaits, and machine stitching.

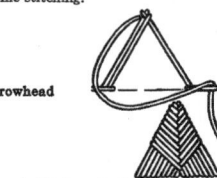

Arrowhead

arrowhead-stitch. Series of stitches resembling arrowheads. See STITCHES.
artificial leather (ăr-tĭ-fĭsh'al; ahr ti *fish* al). Cotton cloth, treated to imitate leather. See LEATHERS.
artificial silk. Imitation of silk, made synthetically. Illegal to sell such an imitation in U. S. under name *artificial silk*.
art linen. Various plain-woven linens or linen imitations used chiefly for embroidery. See LINENS.
art needlework. **1.** Materials for needlework, such as stamped goods, designs, linens, threads, etc. **2.** Store department selling supplies for all types of needlework.
artois (F. ăr-twä; ahr twah). Long, loose cloak. See WRAPS.
art silk. Type of finely woven silk on which one paints or embroiders.
art ticking. Same as regular ticking, but with printed design. See TICKING.
ascot (ăs'cət; *ass* cot). **1.** Broad neck-scarf, usually double. Tied so that ends come horizontally on each side of knot, then cross diagonally. Worn by men and fastened with scarf-pin. **2.** Double scarf that is informally looped under the chin. Worn by men and women. Named for Ascot Heath, in England, the scene of horse races frequented by fashionable English people.

Man's Ascot Tie

Assisi embroidery (ä-sē'zē; a *see* zee). Type of cross-stitch embroidery. See EMBROIDERIES.
assure (F. à-sūr; a sur). French word meaning woof or texture.
astrakhan or **astrachan** (ăs'tra-kan; *ass* tra can). **1.** Heavy fabric knitted or woven with a deep-pile surface of curled loops to resemble caracul fur. **2.** Name formerly used for caracul fur. See FURS.
asymmetric (ă-sĭ-mĕt'rĭk; a si *met* ric) or **asymmetrical.** One-sided, not sym-

atelier

metrical or balanced; often, down much more on one side than the other.

atelier (F. ȧ-tĕl-yā; a tell yay). Large dressmaking establishment, particularly one of the famous French dressmakers. French word meaning workroom or studio.

atours (F. ȧ-tōōr; a toor). French word meaning dress, apparel, ornaments, etc., worn by women.

atrous (ā'trŭs; ai truss). Black.

attaché case (F. ȧ-tȧ-shā; a ta shay). Brief case or traveling case, sometimes fitted with writing or toilet accessories. Carried by attachés.

attachments. Sewing-machine appliances for hemming, tucking, quilting, pinking, binding, braiding, etc. Some are called by trade name, *Fashion Aids*.

attar. Perfume obtained by distilling flower petals, chiefly rose.

attifet (F. ȧ-tė-fȧ; a tee fay). French word meaning: **1.** Ornament for head. **2.** Small 16th century bonnet having point over forehead.

attire. Complete costume or clothing, especially rich, ornamental dress; also, to dress in such clothing.

auburn (ô'bẽrn; aw bern). Dark copper-brown shade with golden cast; generally used of hair.

Aubusson-stitch (F. ō-bü-sôn; o boo sonh). Vertical canvas stitch; same as REP-STITCH. See STITCHES.

au fait (F. ō fĕ; o fay). French phrase meaning expert, skilled, thoroughly conversant. Literally, to the fact or act. Incorrectly used for *comme il faut*, meaning proper, in good form.

au fond (F. ō fôṅ; o fonh). French phrase meaning fundamentally, essentially; literally, at the bottom.

august (ô'gŭst; aw gust). To turn brown or tan, make sunburned.

au naturel (F. ō nȧ-tü-rĕl; o na too rel). French phrase meaning in or according to a natural manner or condition; also, in the nude.

aune (F. ōn; own). Old French measure of 45 inches. Used for fabric.

aureate (ô'rĭ-ĕt; aw ree et). **1.** Golden or yellow-gold in color. **2.** Of or like gold in resplendence.

auricomous (ô-rĭk'ȧ-mŭs; aw rick a mus). Golden-haired; used of anything making the hair golden in color.

aurulent (ô'rōō-lĕnt; aw roo lent). Golden in color.

Australian opossum. Fairly long, durable fur of the phalanger, shading from light brown underfur to silvery gray on top. See FURS.

automobile veil. Large protective veil formerly worn by women when motoring. See VEILS.

Ave Maria lace (ä'vȧ mä-rē'ȧ; ah vay mah ree a). Narrow DIEPPE POINT LACE. See LACES.

awning cloth or **stripe.** Heavy cotton fabric in plain or twill weave, often woven with yarn-dyed stripes. Used for awnings, lawn umbrellas, etc.

Ayrshire embroidery (ĕr'shẽr; air sher). Small-patterned eyelet type of embroidery. Same as MADEIRA. See EMBROIDERIES.

azure (ăzh'ẽr; azh er). Indeterminate shade of blue, variously applied to color of clear deep-blue sky, of lapis lazuli, etc.; actually, synonym for blue.

B

babiche (bȧ-bēsh'; bah *beesh*). Thong, cord, or thread made of rawhide, gut, etc. Name derived from American Indian word.

baboosh (bȧ-bōōsh'; bah *boosh*) or **babouche** (F. bȧ-bōōsh; bah boosh). Heelless slipper of Turkish origin. See SLIPPERS.

babushka (bȧ'bōōsh-kȧ; *bah* boosh ka). Hood tied under the chin. See HOODS.

baby. In the fur trade, term used to describe smaller and usually finer and softer skins of a species, not necessarily referring to age of animals. See FURS.

baby bonnet. Dainty, lacy bonnet, usually beribboned, for infants. See BONNETS.

baby bunting. Sleeping bag like large, loose envelope, having attached hood. Worn by infants, especially outdoors.

baby deer. Rare, short-haired, blue-gray fur of young Alaskan deer. See FURS.

baby flannel. Either soft cotton or light wool flannel, suitable for infants. See FLANNELS.

baby lace. Any narrow, dainty lace. See LACES.

baby Louis heel. Low Louis XV heel. See HEELS.

Babypads. Trade name for absorbent paper made in imitation of fabric, for use inside infants' diapers.

baby pin. Miniature bar pin. See PINS.

baby ribbon. Extremely narrow pastel or white ribbon. See RIBBONS.

baby sash. Ribbon sash tied with bow at back. See SASHES.

baby skirt. Little, short, plaited or flared skirt. See SKIRTS.

Baby Stuart cap. Baby's close-fitting, shirred cap, with narrow chin band. See CAPS.

back comb. Hair comb worn at back. See COMBS.

backed. Used of fabric having two-ply or double warp or weft; as, cotton-backed fabric.

back-filled. Used of fabric with excessive sizing. See FABRIC.

background. **1.** That part of fabric, picture, or photograph which forms a setting for the design. **2.** Used of a dress simple enough to set off decorative accessories.

backing. That which forms back part; especially, back structure, consisting of extra warp, weft, or both, in fabric having more than one kind of warp and weft; also, supporting warp in pile fabric; a support for a flimsy fabric.

back-stitch. Hand stitch resembling machine-stitch. See STITCHES.

back-stitch embroidery. Outline embroidery done with back-stitch. See EMBROIDERIES.

backstrap. **1.** Strap at back of handbag for carrying it. Sometimes used as name of bag. See HANDBAGS. **2.** Pull strap on shoe or boot.

badger. Coarse, long-haired, durable fur of the badger. See FURS.

bag. **1.** Sack, pouch, or other container of varying shape and size for carrying articles. See HANDBAGS. **2.** (Plural) In England, baggy trousers.

bagatelle (băg-ȧ-tĕl'; bag a *tell*). Trifle; something of no importance.

baggage. Trunks and heavy luggage of a traveler.

baggy. Bulging; shapeless; hanging without form; as, baggy sleeves or blouse.

bagheera (bȧ-gē'rȧ; ba *gee* ra). Fine, uncut pile velvet. See VELVETS.

bag sleeve. Sleeve full at top. See SLEEVES.

bague (F. bȧg; bahg). French word for ring.

baguette (F. bȧ-gĕt; ba get). Rectangular in shape; as, baguette diamond. French word meaning rod or small stick.

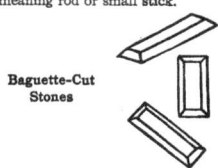

Baguette-Cut Stones

bag wig. Wig having back hair enclosed in bag. See WIGS.

baize. Coarse, open-weave fabric with long nap, usually of wool. Dyed in various solid colors. Also spelled *baise* and *bayes*.

baju (bä'jōō; *bah* joo). Short, loose, light jacket. See JACKETS.

Bakelite (bā'kȧ-lĭt; *bay* ka lite). Trade name for synthetic composition. Used for buttons, buckles, household accessories; ornaments for apparel accessories.

baku or **bakou** (bä'kōō; *bah* coo). Fine, light-weight straw. See STRAWS.

bal (băl; bal). **1.** Heavy, ankle-high shoe. Short for BALMORAL. See SHOES. **2.** French word for ball or dance.

balandran (bȧ-lăn'drȧn; ba *lan* dran) or **balandrana** (bȧ-lăn'drȧn-ȧ; ba *lan* dran a). Wide medieval wrap. See WRAPS.

balayeuse (F. bȧ-lȧ-yẽz; bah lah yuz). Ruffle sewn inside bottom of woman's skirt to protect it. Same as DUST RUFFLE. French word meaning sweeper.

balbriggan (băl-brĭg'ȧn; bal *brig* an). Cotton fabric having fine machine-knit surface, often with fleeced back. Used for underwear, hosiery, sweaters, etc. So called because similar to unbleached hosiery fabric made at Balbriggan, Ireland.

baldric (bôl′drĭk; *bawl* drick). Belt, band, or sash worn regalia-fashion for decoration or usefulness; formerly to support sword, bugle, etc. Same as BANDOLEER.

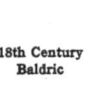

18th Century Baldric

baleine (F. bȧ-lĕn; ba len). French word for whalebone.
balerino. Dust ruffle. See BALAYEUSE.
balibuntal. Variant spelling of BALIBUNTL. See STRAWS.
baline (F. bȧ-lēn; ba leen). 1. Coarse fabric of cotton or wool. Used in packing. 2. Fabric of hemp or jute. Used for stiffening in upholstery.
Balkan blouse (bôl′kȧn; *bawl* kan). Blouse gathered into a hip band. See BLOUSES.
ball dress. Elaborate evening gown. See DRESSES.
ballerina costume (băl-a-rē′nȧ; bal a ree na). Short, full-skirted BALLET COSTUME. See FANCY DRESS.
ballet costume (băl′ā; *bal* lay). Full, usually short skirt on basque bodice. See FANCY DRESS.
ballet slipper. Light-weight, heelless dancing slipper. See SLIPPERS.
balibuntl or **balibuntal** or **balibuntal** (băl′ĭ-bŭn-tl; *bal* i bun tl). Fine, smooth straw. See STRAWS.
ball park blue. Light violet blue color. See COLOR.
balloon sleeve. Very full sleeve, usually in a close-fitting basque. See SLEEVES.
balmacaan (băl-mȧ-kăn′; bal ma can). Loose, flaring overcoat. See COATS.
Balmoral (băl-mŏr′ȧl; bal *mor* al). 1. Striped or figured woolen petticoat, worn as part of costume, with dress looped up to show it. Also, fabric used for petticoat. 2. (Not capitalized) Front-laced shoe, called BAL for short. See SHOES. 3. Scotch cap. See CAPS.
balteus (băl′tĭ-ŭs; *bal* ti us). 1. Girdle worn regalia-fashion by ancient Romans. 2. Girdle worn by ecclesiastics. Also spelled *baltheus*.
bambin hat (băm′bĭn; *bam* bin). Hat having halo effect. See HATS.
ban. Cotton fabric like fine muslin, made in East Indies of fiber from banana leaf stalks.
banal (bā′nȧl or F. bȧ-nȧl; *bay* nal or ba nal). Trite; commonplace; with no individual taste or interest.
band. 1. Strip of fabric used to hold, ornament, or complete any part of garment or accessory. 2. (Plural) Two front flaps on collar worn by ministers. Also called *Geneva bands*. 3. In 16th and 17th centuries, wide ornamental collar or ruff. See COLLARS.
bandanna (băn-dăn′ȧ; ban *dan* a). Large kerchief worn decoratively as neck- or head-piece. Originally, large brightly colored handkerchief with spots or figures made by tie-dyeing. From Hindu word *bandhnu* for this method of dyeing.

bandbox. Medium-small, light-weight box, usually round, for hat or other article of apparel. Originally for holding ornamented bands worn in 16th and 17th centuries.
bande (F. bȧnd; bahnd). French word for BAND.
bandeau (băn-dō′; ban *doe*). 1. Narrow brassière, uplift, or "bra." 2. Strip, usually made of covered buckram or wire, attached to side or back of hat to adjust size or fit or to give height. 3. Narrow band or fillet encircling head, as diadem of flowers.
bandeau top. Slip top made as bandeau. See SLIPS.
bandelet or **bandelette** (băn′dȧ-lĕt; *ban* da let). Any little band or fillet.
bandle linen. Homemade Irish linen. See LINENS.
bandoleer or **bandolier** (băn-dō-lēr′; ban do *leer*). Broad band, belt, or scarf worn over one shoulder and under other. Originally worn by soldiers. From French word *bandoulière*, meaning shoulder-belt.
bandore (băn-dōr′; ban *dore*). 18th century name for veiled headdress worn by widows.
bandoulière (F. bän-dōō-lyêr′; bonh doo lyair). French word for BANDOLEER.
band-string. Ribbon, cord, etc., often finished with tassels or decorated with jewels. Used in pairs to tie 16th and 17th century ruffs or bands.
bang. Front hair cut short and worn down over forehead or curled on top of head. Colloquially, bangs.
bangkok (băng′kŏk; *bang* cock). Fine, light-weight straw used for hats. See STRAWS.
bangle. 1. One of ornamental pendants on bracelet or necklace. 2. Type of bracelet. See BRACELETS.
banyan or **banian** (băn′yȧn; *ban* yan). Loose wrap worn in 18th century. See WRAPS.
bar. 1. To stitch across from one side to other, or cross threads so made. Used to strengthen, as at ends of buttonhole; to trim or finish, as at end of seam; to take place of an eye, as in loop form. 2. Joining thread thrown across open space in needle-point lace. See also BRIDE, PEARL, LEG, TIE.
barathea (băr-ȧ-thē′ȧ; bar a *thee* a). Fine, soft fabric, closely woven in small diaper or bird's-eye design, often with silk warp and worsted filling or cotton warp and silk filling. Used for dresses, light-weight suits.
barb. Cloth, covering the throat and extending from chin to upper chest; usually part of headdress. Formerly worn by women mourners and others; now worn by some nuns. Often of plaited linen.
barbe (F. bȧrb; barb). Small, short lace scarf or lappet. Worn around head or neck.
barbette (băr-bĕt′; bar *bet*). Strip of linen worn under chin and over head with flat coif. Worn in 13th century.

barcelona (bär-sȧ-lō′nȧ; bar sa *lo* na). Kerchief of twilled silk in black, solid colors, checks, and fancy designs. Worn around head or neck, or carried in hand. So called because originally made at Barcelona, Spain.
barefoot sandal. Backless, low-cut shoe. See SHOES.
barège (F. bȧ-rĕzh; ba rezh). Sheer, gauze-like fabric of wool combined with silk, cotton, etc. Used for veils, dresses. So called from Barèges, France, where originally made.
bar-fly apparel. Any apparel suitable for wear at a cocktail bar.
barmskin or **barmcloth.** English terms for leather apron. So called from barm, meaning the lap.
barondukí (bär-ȧn-dū′kĭ; ba ron *du* ki). Misspelling of burunduki, for *burun duchy*, plural of Russian word *burunduk*, meaning chipmunk. See BURUNDUKI under FURS.
Baronette satin. Trade name for high-luster rayon fabric. See SATINS.
baroque (bȧ-rōk′; ba *roke*). 1. Irregularly shaped; especially used of a pearl. 2. Fantastic in style, grotesque, exaggerated; said of the over-ornate in architecture, furniture, furnishings, dress.
bar pin. Elongated brooch, usually slender. See PINS.
barracan (băr′ȧ-kăn; *ba* ra can). Coarse, strong, thick fabric made of wool and goat's hair. Used in Eastern countries for mantles and other wraps. Also called *barragon*.
barré (F. bȧ-rā; ba ray). Having stripes, bars, or ribs running crosswise, from selvage to selvage.
barrel heel. Heel of nearly cylindrical shape. See HEELS.
barret (băr′ĕt; *ba* ret). Medieval cap. See CAPS.
barrette (bȧ-rĕt′; ba *ret*). Bar clip for keeping hair in place or for decoration, worn especially by young girls. In colonial days, hair-clasps of various metals, often set with pearls, worn to keep back hair in place.
barrister's wig (băr′ĭs-tẽrz; ba *riss* terz). Wig of full-bottomed type worn by English lawyers. See WIGS.
barrow or **barrow-coat.** Warm swaddling wrap for infants, drawn in at neck and bottom.

Type of Barrow-Coat

barry or **barrie.** Obsolete term for underskirt or petticoat.
barvel or **barvell** (bär′vĕl; *bar* vel). Large, coarse, leather apron. Worn by workmen, especially fishermen.
bas (F. bä; bah). French word for stocking. Ribbed or open-work stocking

āte, făt, dánce, ärt mē, mĕt, hẽr, thêre rīde, rĭd nōte, nŏt, côrn, fōōd, fŏŏt cūte, cŭt, cūré now fin(ŋ)ger villa(ȧ) señor pleas(zh)ure

basané

called *bas à cotes* or *à jour;* woolen stocking, *bas de laine;* and silk stocking, *bas de soie.*
basané (F. bȧ-zȧ-nā; ba za nay). French word meaning sunburned, bronzed, or tanned.
Basco (băs′kō; *bass* co). Trade name for linen-like finish given to cotton damask.
baseball shoe. Shoe worn by baseball players during a game. See SHOES.
basic color. The color of a basic dress or coat or both, or a suit, which is the principal color of the costume. With it may be worn accessories of one or more colors to give accent and variety.
basic dress. Simple, classic type of dress, accessories for which can be varied. See DRESSES.
basin (F. bȧ-zăṇ; ba zanh). French word for cotton fabric resembling dimity.
basinet (băs′ĭ-nĕt; *bass* i net). Small, shallow, close-fitting helmet with or without visor, often pointed on top, shaped somewhat like a basin.
basket cloth. Fabric in basket weave.
basket filling-stitch. Embroidery stitch worked like darning. See STITCHES.
basket-stitch. Embroidery stitch resembling series of overlapping cross-stitches. See STITCHES.
basket weave. Plain weave with two or more yarns used as one. See WEAVES.
basque (F. băsk; bask). Bodice closely fitted by seaming from shoulder to waist, with or without short skirt-like continuation. Typical of bodice worn by Basque peasants. French word meaning short skirt, as on bodice or jacket; originally on doublets. See BODICES.
Basque beret. Round, flat cap. See CAPS.
basque costume. Same as BALLET COSTUME. See FANCY DRESS.
basquine (F. bȧs-kēn; bass keen). Ornamental outer petticoat worn by Basque and Spanish peasant women.
bassinet (băs′ĭ-nĕt; *bass* i net). Wicker basket used as a baby's crib. Has hood-like covering over one end, as in cradle or perambulator, and is usually draped with light fabric.
bast. Woody fiber of various plants used in weaving, including FLAX, RAMIE, JUTE, HEMP.
basting (bāst′ĭng; *baist* ing). Large, easy stitches used to hold fabric in place temporarily. See STITCHES.
basting cotton. Cotton thread used for basting. See THREADS.
bat or **batt.** Woman's heavy, low shoe. See SHOES.
bate. In leather manufacturing, to steep in a bath, as is done with hides.
bateau neck (F. bȧ-tō; ba toe). Boat-shaped neckline, high in front and back, pointed at shoulders. See NECKLINES.
Bath coating. English name for light-weight, long-napped woolen fabric. Originally used as coating; now used for infants' blankets, petticoats, etc. Named for Bath, England.
bathing cap. Rubber or waterproof cap. See CAPS.
bathing suit. Garment or garments designed for wear in water. See SPORTS CLOTHES.

bathrobe. Full-length coat-like garment. Worn before and after bathing and as dressing gown.
bath slipper. Slipper or sandal to slip on before and after bathing. See SLIPPERS.
bâti (F. bȧ-tē; bah tee). French word meaning basting or tacking.
batik (bä′tĕk, băt′ĭk, bȧ-tēk′; *bah teek, bat ik,* or ba *teek*). Method of applying color designs to fabric. See DYEING. Also, the fabric so decorated.
batiste (bȧ-tēst′; ba *teest*). 1. Soft, sheer, cotton or linen fabric of plain weave, made in white and delicate colors. Finer weaves used for handkerchiefs, lingerie, dresses, blouses, neckwear, clothing for small children; coarser weaves, for linings. Probably named for its inventor, Jean Baptiste, of Cambrai. 2. Light-weight, all-wool fabric with even warp and weft, thinner than challis, like fine nun's veiling. Called *wool batiste, tamise cloth;* lightest weight called *chiffon batiste.* Used for dresses, negligees. 3. Sheer, washable silk fabric, plain or figured, similar to silk mull. Also called *batiste de soie.* Used for summer dresses, inexpensive dress foundations.
batswing. Soft, napped, woolen or cotton fabric, usually taupe. Used in England for coats and other garments. Originally, woven in tubular form for seamless petticoats.
Battenberg lace (băt′ən-bẽrg; *bat* en berg). Coarse form of Renaissance lace. See LACES.
batting. Cotton or wool in sheets or rolls. Used for warm interlinings, quilts, puffs.
battlemented (băt′l-mĕnt-ĕd; *bat* l ment ed). Embroidery, applied trimming, cut-out border, etc., giving, with indented lines, effect of battlements in ancient fortresses.
batuz work. Embroidery with attached metal plates. See EMBROIDERIES.
batwing sleeve. Long, shaped sleeve. See SLEEVES.
baudekin (bô′də-kĭn; *baw* da kin) or **baldachin** (băl′də-kĭn; *bal* da kin). Rich fabric of gold warp and silk filling, introduced from East by Crusaders. Often brocaded, embroidered, jeweled. Used first as canopy or drapery for royal throne; later, for garments of nobility. Now, term used for any luxurious fabric with gold threads.
baum marten (bowm; bowm). Dark brown fur of pine or beech marten. See FURS.
bautta (bä-ōōt′tȧ; bah *oot* tah). Hooded cloak. See WRAPS.
Bavarian lace. Simple bobbin lace. See TORCHON under LACES.
bavette (F. bȧ-vĕt; ba vet). French word for bib.
bavolet (F. bȧ-vō-lȧ; ba vo lay). 1. Rustic French cap. See CAPS. 2. Trimming on back of hat or bonnet.
bayadere (bä-yȧ-dēr′; bah ya *deer*). Striped crosswise in multicolor design. Also, fabric so striped or stripe of such design. See STRIPES.
bazaar (bȧ-zär′; ba *zar*). Market place; group of shops or stalls, also fair, where

beck

goods are assembled for sale; especially fancy wares, odd knickknacks, etc.
beach sandal. Sandal for beach wear. See SHOES.
beachwear. All clothes or accessories designed for wear on beach or in water.
bead. Perforated ball or cylinder or other shape, in any size or material, strung on thread or wire, or attached to fabric for decoration; also, to apply beads or beading.
beading. 1. Lace-like edging made of loops; also, open-work trimming through which ribbon may be run. 2. Beads applied as trimming in allover pattern or design.—**seam b.** Narrow insertion used to join seams and finish edges. Also called *veining* and *entre deux.*
beading needle. Needle used for beading. See NEEDLES.
bead work. Beads sewn in design to fabric or leather; the art of sewing beads in design.
beam. 1. Part of loom consisting of wooden cylinder used for winding warp before weaving. Also, cylinder for rolling cloth as woven. 2. In leather trade, frame or sloping board used for working skins in tanning. Also, to stretch cloth over; to wind yarn on; to dress hides on.
bear. Fur, or pelt, of various types of bear. See FURS.
bearer. Roll of padding worn to distend skirt. See HOOPS.
bearskin. 1. Tall, black fur cap. See CAPS. 2. Pelt of a BEAR. See FURS. 3. Heavy, shaggy woolen cloth. Used for overcoats.
beau monde (F. bō môṅd; bo mond). French phrase for the fashionable world; society.
Beauvais embroidery (F. bō-vā; bo vay). Multicolored embroidery. See EMBROIDERIES.
beaver (bē′vẽr; *bee* ver). 1. Soft, brown, durable fur of beaver. See FURS. 2. Man's tall hat. See HATS. 3. One of various fabrics. See BEAVER CLOTH. 4. Piece of medieval armor attached to helmet or breastplate, protecting lower part of face.
beaver cloth. 1. Soft-finished, thick-napped woolen fabric. Originally made in England to resemble beaver fur. Used for overcoats and uniforms. 2. Pile fabric similar to hatter's plush. Used for millinery. 3. Heavy, napped cotton cloth. Used for work clothes, athletic clothes.
beaver-dyed cony (kō′nĭ; *co* ni). Processed rabbit fur. See FURS.
beaverette. Beaver-dyed cony or rabbit fur. See FURS.
beaverkin. Small beaver hat. See HATS.
beaverteen. 1. Twilled cotton cloth with uncut, looped warp threads forming pile. 2. Variety of fustian of coarse twilled cotton, having nap, first dyed, then shorn.
beaver top. Shoe with soft upper. See SHOES.
beck. Pendant tip or lappet on medieval headdress, falling like a beak over center of forehead. Worn during 15th century.

fāte, făt, dȧnce, ärt mē, mĕt, hẽr, thêre rīde, rĭd nōte, nŏt, côrn, fōōd, fŏŏt cūte, cŭt, cũre now fin(ṇ)ger villa(ȧ) señor pleas(zh)ure

Bedford cord. Sturdy fabric in rib weave, with raised lengthwise cords. May be all wool, silk, cotton, rayon, or combination of these. Similar in appearance to plain PIQUÉ, except that piqué is usually cotton. First made in America at New Bedford, Massachusetts. Used for dresses, suits, skirts, riding habits, children's coats.

bedizen (bē-dīz'n; be *diz* en). To overdress or dress up in gaudy finery.

bed jacket. Short jacket for wear when sitting up in bed, or for shoulder warmth when sleeping. See JACKETS.

bedraggled (bē-drăg'ld; be *drag* ld). Soiled, ragged, rumpled, or otherwise unattractive.

bedroom slipper. Soft slipper, usually bright in color. See SLIPPERS.

bed socks. Soft, warm socks; usually ankle-high; often knitted. Worn in bed for warmth in winter. See HOSE.

beefeater's hat. Brimmed hat worn as part of the medieval uniform of the British Yeomen of the Guard, often called *beefeaters*. See HATS.

bee-gum hat. Man's silk hat. See HATS.

beer jacket. Straight box jacket. See JACKETS.

beetling. Pounding fabric to give flat surface. Process used on table damask in addition to calendering.

beetroot. Dark red shade of the beet.

beggar's lace. Type of torchon lace. See LACES.

begird (bē-gĕrd'; be *gerd*). To bind with girdle or band.

beige (F. bāzh; bayzh). **1.** Pale tan shade, color of undyed, unbleached yarn. **2.** Originally, fabric of undyed, unbleached wool. French word meaning natural.

bejewel (bē-jū'ĕl; be *jew* el). To ornament or decorate with jewels.

belaced (bē-lāsd'; be *laced*). Edged or decorated with lace.

belcher. Scarf or necktie of garish color. Originally, blue neckcloth marked with white spots having blue centers. Named for Jim Belcher, English pugilist.

Belgian lace. ANTWERP, BRUSSELS, MECHLIN, and VALENCIENNES laces. See LACES.

bell-boy or **bell-hop cap.** Pillbox cap. See CAPS and HATS.

bell-boy or **bell-hop jacket.** Short, fitted jacket. See JACKETS.

Bellmanizing. Trade name of process for treating cotton fabrics to give them permanent crisp finish without starch or other temporary dressing.

bellows tongue. Wide, folding tongue of blucher or various work shoes and boots, stitched in place at each side to keep boot or shoe watertight.

bell-shaped hoop. Hoops of graduated sizes fastened one above the other, with largest at bottom and smallest at top. See HOOPS.

bell skirt. Circular-cut, lined skirt. See SKIRTS.

bell sleeve. Full sleeve, flaring at bottom. See SLEEVES.

belly doublet (d ŭb'lĕt; *dub* let). Doublet having stuffed or padded front. See PEASECOD.

BELTS
belt. Strap or band encircling waist, usually fastened by buckle, clasp, button, etc. Belts usually named from manner in which worn—as, cross-belt, shoulder-belt, etc.; or from purpose for which used—as, army-belt, cartridge-belt.

garter b. A band, usually of elastic, that goes around the waist and has supporters attached.

marguerite (mär-gə-rēt'; mar ga *reet*). Waistband or belt with plastron at front, often laced, and tabs at back. Popular in 19th century.

Sam Browne b. Broad leather band worn around waist, with light strap over right shoulder. Named for British army officer.

sanitary b. A belt, usually of elastic, that has tabs to which a sanitary napkin may be attached.

suspender b. Belt combined with shoulder straps or braces.

waist b. Belt worn around waistline, especially as distinguished from military belt worn over one shoulder.

wampum b. (wăm'pəm; *wahm* pum). Belt made of wampum or colorful shell beads. Worn by North American Indians.

zonar (zō'när; *zo* nar). Belt formerly worn by Jews and Christians of the Levant, as mark distinguishing them from Moslems.

zoster (zŏs'tēr; *zoss* ter). Belt or girdle worn in ancient Greece, especially by men.

belt buckle. Fastening of belt. See BUCKLES.

belting. **1.** Material used for making belts. **2.** Belts, collectively. **3.** Short for BELTING RIBBON. See RIBBONS.

belting ribbon. Stiff grosgrain ribbon. See RIBBONS.

Bemberg. Trade name for a brand of rayon yarn. Also applied to fabrics made from this yarn and garments made from the fabric. See RAYON

bench-made. Applied to shoes made at shoemaker's bench. Shoes made entirely by hand now comparatively rare.

bend. Right or left half of BUTT, or hide covering animal's hindquarters.

bengal (bĕn'gôl; *ben* gawl). One of various fabrics made in Bengal, India; especially, thin silk and hair fabric, and striped muslin-like fabric.

bengaline (bĕng'gə-lēn; *beng* ga leen). Corded fabric, similar to poplin but heavier, with warp threads, usually of silk, completely covering crosswise ribs of worsted, cotton, rayon, or silk. Used for coats, suits, dresses, trimming.

Bengal stripe. Gingham-like cloth woven with colored stripes. So called because originally from Bengal, India, name referring only to pattern.

benjamin (bĕn'jə-mĭn; *ben* ja min). Close-fitting overcoat. See COATS.

benjy. **1.** Straw hat. See HATS. **2.** British slang term for waistcoat.

benn. Scottish term for colored silk sash.

benny. Short for BENJAMIN, an overcoat. See COATS.

berdash or **burdash** (bēr'dăsh; *bur* dash).

Type of sash or neckcloth. Worn by men about 1700.

beret (F. bĕ-rā; be ray). **1.** Round, soft cap; as, BASQUE BERET. See CAPS. **2.** Adaptation of Basque beret shape in hats. See HATS.

beretta (bĕ-rĕt'ə; be *ret* a). Medium-large draped beret. See HATS.

berger (bēr'jēr; *bur* jer). Curl of hair at nape of neck, hanging to shoulder. Fashionable in late 17th and 18th centuries.

beribboned (bē-rĭb'ənd; be *rib* und). Decorated with ribbons.

Berlin canvas. Coarse square-meshed fabric. See CANVAS.

Berlin wool. Fine worsted yarn. See YARNS.

Berlin work. Allover embroidery done in Berlin wool. See EMBROIDERIES.

Bermuda fagoting. Fagoting on wrong side of fabric. See FAGOTING under STITCHES.

berrettino (bĕr-rĕt-tē'nō; be ret *tee* no). Cardinal's skull-cap. See CAPS.

bertha. Deep, cape-like collar. See COLLARS.

beryl (bĕ'rĭl; *bare* ill). Natural mineral substance found in hexagonal prisms; usually green or bluish-green, but also white, pink, yellow. Used as precious stone; varieties include aquamarine, emerald, morganite.

bespangle (bē-spăng'gl; be *spang* gl). To decorate with spangles or other glittering ornaments.

Bessarabian lamb (bĕs-ə-rā'bĭ-ən; bess a *ray* bee an). Coarser-haired, cross-bred type of Persian lamb. See FURS.

Bethlehem headdress. Red cap shaped like cut-off cone, decorated with coins and often with embroidery; worn with white veil attached at back and metal chain hanging loosely under chin. Worn by women of Bethlehem, Palestine, for many centuries. Adapted in modern women's hats. See HATS.

between needle. Short sewing needle, often used for hand quilting. See NEEDLES.

bezel (bĕz'ĕl; *bez* el). Face or upper faceted part of a cut stone.

bezette or **bezette** (bə-zĕt'ə; be *zet* a). Linen rags saturated with coloring material and used for dyeing. From Italian word *pezetta*, meaning piece of cloth dyed red.

bias (bī'əs; *by* as). Line taken, in folding or cutting material, diagonally across warp and woof threads.—**true b.** In fabric, a diagonal line running at angle of 45 degrees to selvage. Unlike other garments are sometimes cut on true bias to prevent sagging, twisting, riding up, and to insure better wear. Binding cut on true bias is easy to apply, especially on curved edges.

bias binding. Narrow bias with edges folded in for ease in applying. See BINDINGS.

bias slip. Slip cut on bias of the fabric. See SLIPS.

bib. **1.** Small collar. See COLLARS. **2.** Piece of cloth worn by children over front of bodice as protection when eating. **3.** Part of apron above waist.

bib and tucker. Colloquial term for clothes, attire. One's best bib and tucker means one's best clothing. Originally, garments worn by women. See BIB under COLLARS. See TUCKER.
bibelot (bĭb′lō or F. bē-blō; *bib* lo or bee blo). Trinket or small decorative article.
bicorn or **bicorne** (bī′kôrn; *by* corn). Two-cornered hat. See HATS.
bicycle bal. Sports shoe laced far down toward toe. Originally designed for bicycling. See SHOES.
Biedermeier, (bē′dẽr-mī-ẽr; *bee* der my er). German style of furniture of the period 1815-48, comparable to the Empire style in France, but less ornate. Applied in fashion to dress styles worn during the Biedermeier period.
bietle (bē′tl; *bee* tl). Deerskin jacket worn by American Indian women. See JACKETS.
bifurcated (bī′fẽr-kāt-ĕd; *by* fur cate ed). Divided into two branches; forked. Term applied to divided skirts.
biggin. Close-fitting cap, sometimes of mesh. See CAPS.
biggonet (bĭg′ə-nĕt; *big* o net). Cap or biggin. See CAPS.
bijou (F. bē-zhōō; bee zhoo). Jewel or trinket, especially of delicate or elegant workmanship.
bijouterie (bē-zhōō′tə-rē or F. bē-zhōōt-rē; bee *zhoo* ta ri or bee zhoo tree). Jewelry or trinkets, collectively.
biliment. Ornament or decorative part of a woman's dress; especially headdress or its jeweled ornament. Sometimes gold lace ornamented with jewels worn in 16th century. See LACES.
billycock or **bilicock.** Round-crowned hat. See HATS.
binary color (bī′nə-rĭ; *by* na ri). Secondary color. See COLOR.
Binche lace (F. bănsh; bansh). Flemish bobbin lace. See LACES.
bind. To enclose an edge in a bias binding or band, for decoration, extra strength, or protection.
binder. 1. Sewing-machine attachment for applying bias binding to fabric edge. 2. Anything which binds, as a band, cord, fillet.

BINDINGS

binding. 1. Double or single fold of bias fabric; also, ribbon, tape, etc., used to bind edge. Ready-made bias binding is available in white in sizes 3 to 13, and in colors in several widths. No. 3 is the narrowest; 13, the widest. No. 5 is of a size to fit the sewing-machine binder and is therefore made in a wide range of colors, as well as black and white. 2. Edging around the top of a shoe, usually of grosgrain.
bias b. Ready-made binding having edges turned in, ready for application.
cotton b. Same as BIAS BINDING.
seam b. Narrow ribbon-like strip of fabric which comes ready-made, 6 or 9 yards long, silk or cotton, in black, white, and colors. Used for finishing edges, especially skirt hems. Silk type resembles light-weight, soft taffeta ribbon.

bind off. Knitting term meaning to drop stitches to make an edge.
bingle. Hair cut short enough to be above nape of neck. See BOBS.
binnogue (bĭn′ŏg; *bin* og). Headdress formerly worn by peasant women in Ireland.
bird of paradise feathers. Colorful plumes of male bird of paradise. See FEATHERS.
bird's-eye. 1. Geometric pattern of small diamond shapes, each having center dot resembling bird's eye. Woven into cotton or linen fabrics on dobby machine. 2. Cotton or linen cloth in characteristic weave; filling yarns loosely twisted for more absorbency. Cotton used for diapers, etc.; fine linen used for towels.
biretta (bĭ-rĕt′ə; bi *ret* a). Square ecclesiastical cap. See CAPS.
birrus or **byrrus** (bĭr′əs; *bir* us). 1. Ancient hooded wrap. See WRAPS. 2. Coarse, thick, woolen cloth. Used for outer garments by poor people during Middle Ages.
bishop. Type of bustle worn by American colonists. See BUSTLES.
bishop's lawn or **bishop cotton.** Fine lawn, as used for bishop's sleeves. Also called *Victoria lawn.*
bishop sleeve. Sleeve full at bottom. See SLEEVES.
bishop's purple or **bishop's violet.** Deep blue-red color.
bistre (F. bēstr; beestr) or **bister** (bĭs′tẽr; *bis* ter). Dark brown, color of pigment made from wood soot.
bizarre (bĭ-zär′; bi *zar*). Extravagantly odd, unusual, or showy.
black. Hue so dark that no color can be seen in it.
black fox. Fur of red fox during rare color phase. See FURS.
black muskrat. Fur of muskrat having black back. See FURS.
black work. Embroidery of black stitches on white fabric. See EMBROIDERIES.
Blake. Shoe sewn by special process. See SHOES.
blanc (blängk or F. bläṅ; blank or blonh). French word for white. In French trade usage, everything that is bleached.
blancard (blăng′kẽrd; *blank* erd). Strong French fabric woven of partly blanched linen yarn. Made at Rouen in 18th century.
blanch. To remove color or make white; bleach.
blanket. 1. Piece of woven fabric in plain or twill weave, often thick, usually wide, made of wool, cotton, or mixture. Used as bed covering, robe, etc. Name derived from ancient white or undyed woolen cloth, called *blanchet,* made in Beauvais, France. 2. Length of fabric from which to cut a garment.
blanket-stitch. Single-purl edge finish. See STITCHES.
blanket-stitch couching. Type of couching done with blanket-stitch. See COUCHING under EMBROIDERIES.
blanket-stitch seam. Two edges of fabric joined in an open seam by means of blanket-stitch. See SEAMS.

blanket or **carpet wool.** Same as MISCELLANEOUS WOOL. See WOOL.
blatta. Formerly, purple or purple fabric.
blazer. Light-weight sports jacket. See JACKETS.
blazer stripe. Bright-colored stripe. See STRIPES.
bleaching. 1. Process of making fabrics white or lighter, or more susceptible to dyes, often by chemically removing natural pigment. See GRASS BLEACHING. 2. Process for removing yellowish tinge of all white furs. Often used on less expensive dark furs before dyeing. See BLEACHING under FURS.
blend. Merging of colors or lines to shade or tone into one another.
blending. Dyeing of the surface hairs of paler furs to make them more attractive. Also called *tipping, topping,* and *feathering.* See BLENDING under FURS.
bleu (F. blė; bluh). French word for blue.
blind-stitch. Concealed stitch. See STITCHES.
blistered. 1. Having raised spots, as if covered with blisters. Term used of crepe fabrics. 2. Formerly, having slashed openings through which showed contrasting color or material, typical of 16th century doublets, breeches, sleeves.
block. 1. To shape or re-shape by using mold or block; as, to block a hat. Also, mold or frame so used, or resulting shape of hat. 2. Formerly, support for wig.
block colors. Colors as applied in block printing. See PRINTING under DYEING.
blocked lapin (F. lá-păṅ; la panh). Lapin fur sheared, dyed, and put together in effect of squares. See FURS.
block pattern. Basic size pattern. See PATTERNS.
block printing. Process of printing fabric from engraved or carved blocks. See PRINTING under DYEING.
blond or **blonde.** 1. Person having flaxen, golden, light auburn, or yellowish-brown hair; blue, gray, hazel, or brown eyes; and fair complexion. 2. Color, slightly darker and grayer than beige.—**brunette b.** Person having light chestnut or auburn-brown hair; hazel, gray, blue-gray, or brown eyes; and medium complexion.—**Titian b.** (tĭsh′ən; *tish* an). Person having reddish hair; blue-gray or brown eyes; medium or clear-white complexion, varying color.
blonde lace. Silk bobbin lace. See LACES.
blonde net. Washable cotton net. See NETS.
bloomer. Pantaloon type of garment, closed by elastic above or below knee. Worn by women and children as undergarment; also, with or without overskirt for athletic games. Named for Mrs. Amelia Jenks Bloomer, American dress reformer of early 19th century, who first wore gathered trousers.
bloomer dress. Child's dress with matching bloomers. See DRESSES.
bloom side. In leather trade, hair side of hide.
blotch. Indistinct or obscure in outline or coloring; said of printed fabrics.

BLOUSES

louse. 1. Loose waist or bodice of various types extending from neckline to waistline or below. Worn inside or outside separate skirt. See also, BASQUE, BODICE, SHIRT, SWEATER. 2. Long, loose smock, with or without belt, worn by English workmen and by French and Russian peasants. 3. To form a drooping bulge or fulness.
Balkan b. (bôl'kən; *bawl* kan). Blouse with full, loose sleeves, gathered into wide band around top of hips. So named because it came into fashion in 1913 during Balkan war.
bluey. Shirt or blouse, usually blue, of Australian bushman.

Bolero Blouse, 1926   Sash Blouse, 1917

bolero b. Long-waisted blouse, having an overlapping section that forms a bolero. Popular in 1926.
camisa b. (kə-mē'zə; ka *mee* za). Embroidered waist or bodice with large, flowing sleeves. Spanish word for shirt. Worn by women in Philippines.
casaque (F. kȧ-zȧk; ka zack). French word for woman's loose blouse.
casaquin (F. kȧ-zȧ-kaṅ; ka za kanh). Woman's waist or blouse, usually fitted to the figure.
choli or **cholee** (chō'lē; *cho* lee). Short-sleeved bodice or short blouse, not reaching to skirt, low at throat, usually of cotton. Worn by Hindu women.
dressing sacque. Dressy blouse, wrist length, loose at the waist, usually unbelted. Worn especially for dress-up at home in early part of 20th century.
garibaldi (găr-ĭ-bôl-dĭ; ga ri *bawl* di). Shirtwaist copied from high-necked, bloused shirt with full sleeves.

19th Century Camisa Blouse   Gibson Waist, Early 1900's

gaucho b. (gow'chō; *gow* cho). Full blouse gathered at waistline, with full sleeves gathered at wristband, as worn by Gauchos, or South American cowboys.

Gibson waist. High-necked shirtwaist, usually tailored, having long sleeves set in with fulness, often having plait over each shoulder, as worn in portraits of women by Charles Dana Gibson.
guimpe (F. gămp; gamp). Short blouse,

Type of Balkan Blouse   Middy Blouse, 1920's

often with sleeves. Usually worn with pinafore type of dress.
huipil or **huepilli** (Sp. wī-pēl' or wē-pē'lyē; wi *peel* or we *peel* ye). Sleeveless blouse or piece of cotton cloth with opening for head. Worn by Mexican Indian and peasant women. Inherited from Aztecs.
middy b. Loose, unbelted, hip-length blouse with sailor collar. Copy of blouse worn by midshipmen ("middies") or cadets in U. S. Navy.
overblouse. Blouse that is not tucked inside skirt at waist, but worn outside. Length below waist varies with fashion.
peek-a-boo waist. Shirtwaist made or partly made of eyelet embroidery or sheer fabric. Fashionable in late 19th and early 20th centuries.
pierrot (pē'ĕr-ō; *pee* er o). Woman's waist with low-cut neck and sleeves, popular in 18th century. SEE PIERROT COSTUME under FANCY DRESS.
Russian b. Loose, long-sleeved blouse

Step-In Blouse, 1920's

extending below hips, usually belted.
sash b. Blouse crossed in front like a surplice, with attached sash pieces forming a girdle.
shirtwaist b. Waist similar to a man's shirt in plainness of cut and style. Worn by women and girls, with or without a tailored skirt. More often called *tailored blouse.*
step-in b. Blouse of any type attached to step-ins. Keeps blouse from riding up and provides panties.
tuck-in b. Any blouse worn with end tucked inside skirt at waist.
blouse coat. Coat with upper part slightly bloused, usually with kimono sleeves. See COATS.

blucher (bloo'chēr; *blue* cher). High laced shoe. See SHOES.
blue. Primary color of many tints, tones, and shades, from palest blue to midnight.
bluebonnet. Scottish cap of tam o' shanter type. See CAPS.
blue fox. Smoky blue fur of arctic fox. See FURS.
blue-green. Color between blue and green.
bluet (blū'ĕt; *blue* et). Plain fabric, usually cotton or wool, of blue color.
bluey. Shirt or blouse of Australian bushman. See BLOUSES.
bluing or **blueing.** 1. Preparation used in rinsing water to keep white fabric white by counteracting with a bluish tint the yellowish tinge acquired from age or fading. 2. A rinse for white or gray hair.
blunt. Short, thick needle used in tailoring. See NEEDLES.
blunt scissors. Scissors with ends rounded instead of pointed. See SCISSORS.
boa (bō'ə; *bo* a). Soft, fluffy neck-piece, rounded in effect. Usually made of feathers or tulle or lace, etc.
boarded leather. Leather in which surface is artificially broken up into close, parallel creases. See LEATHERS.
boater. Straw hat with straight brim and a ribbon band. See HATS.
boat neck. Same as BATEAU. See NECK-LINES.

BOBS

bob. 1. Hair cut short, not reaching below nape of neck. 2. Knot of hair; formerly, bob wig. See WIGS.
bingle. Hair cut short enough to be above nape of neck.
boyish b. Hair cut short and trimmed fairly close to head as in a man's haircut. Worn by many women from 1925 to 1930. Popularized by the British actress, Beatrice Lillie. Also called *mannish haircut.*

Boyish Bob, 1926   Irene Castle Bob

Dutch b. Haircut in which hair is cut straight around back from lobe of one ear to the other and usually banged in front.
Irene Castle b. Hair cut, worn back off the forehead, and loosely waved over ears, in the manner introduced and made popular by Irene Castle, the famous dancer who first made bobbed hair fashionable just before the World War.
long b. Hair that has been cut, but is long enough to roll under in one large curl at back.

bobs (continued)

page boy b. Long bob, with hair worn almost straight except for slight curl under at ends.
shingle. Hair cut close to the head, especially in back, showing the natural contour of the head.
wind-blown b. Irregular haircut brushed so as to make the hair in front appear as though blown forward by the wind.
bobbin. Thread carrier used in lace-making, spinning, weaving, and also in sewing machines.
bobbinet (bŏb-ĭ-nĕt′; bob i *net*). Net with six-sided meshes. See NETS
bobbin lace. Untied mesh made on pillow design with bobbins. See LACES.
bob wig. Short wig. See WIGS.
bocasine (bŏk′ȧ-sĭn; *bock* a sin). Woolen fabric similar to fine buckram.

BODICES

bodice (bŏd′ĭs; *bod* iss). 1. Waist of woman's dress. 2. Originally, tight-fitting waist; also, wide laced girdle extending from bust to waist. 3. Obsolete term for corset or stays, sometimes called *bodies* or *pair of bodies*.

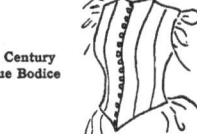

19th Century Basque Bodice

basque b. (F. básk; bask). Closely fitted bodice. See BASQUE.
cardigan b. Short, buttoned-down-the-front bodice, usually without belt. Similar in effect to cardigan.
corset b. Usually formal bodice or waist part, so draped or shaped as to follow the corset line. Often in color contrasting with the skirt.
jersey (jẽr′zĭ; *jer* zi). Skintight, untrimmed bodice of knitted silk or wool; buttoned in front. Popular in 1880's.
Watteau b. (wŏ-tō′; wot *toe*). Bodice with low square or round neckline; short, deeply ruffled sleeves; and many ribbon bows.
bodice top. Straight top of slip. See SLIPS.
bodkin. 1. Blunt needle with large eye, used for lacing ribbon or tape through lace, beading, or other part of garment. See NEEDLES. 2. Implement with sharp point at one end for punching holes in cloth. 3. Decorative, stiletto-shaped hairpin.
body clothes or **body linen.** Underclothing.
body coat. Close-fitting coat. See COATS.
body lining. Lining, as in a coat, extending to waist or just below.
Bohemian lace (bō-hē′mĭ-ȧn; bo *he* an). Bobbin lace with braid-like effect. See LACES.

boiled-off silk. Silk with natural gum removed. See DEGUMMING. See SILK.
boiled shirt. Shirt with starched bosom. See SHIRTS.
Boilfast color. Trade term applied to threads guaranteed fast. See COLOR.
boina (boi′nä; *boy* nah). Woolen cap. See CAPS.
bois de rose (F. bwä dȧ rōz; bwah da rose). Shade of softly grayed red. French term for rosewood.
bolero (bō-lĕr′ō; bo *lare* o). Short jacket of Spanish type. See JACKETS.
bolero blouse. Long-waisted blouse having an overlapping section that forms a bolero. See BLOUSES.
bolero hat. Boxy hat worn by Spanish dancers. See HATS.
Bolivia cloth (bō-lĭv′ĭ-ȧ; bo *liv* i a). Soft, all-wool pile fabric, medium to heavy weight, velvet-like in feel. Tufts of pile usually in diagonal or vertical rows. Used for coats, suits.
boll (bōl; bole). Pod of plant, especially of cotton, which contains the fibers.
bolt. 1. Complete length of cloth from loom, rolled or folded, varying in length from 30 yards to 100 or more. 2. Roll of ribbon approximately 10 yards long.
bolting cloth. Stiff, transparent fabric in leno weave, like very fine canvas. Made of finely spun yarn—wool, silk, linen, hair, etc. Used for stencils, fancy work, wig and toupee foundations. So called because originally made for bolting or sifting meal and flour.
bombards. Loose, baggy, padded breeches, as worn by American colonists.
bombast. Padded or stuffed; also, soft material used as stuffing. Originally, cotton or cotton wool. From Old French *bombace*, meaning cotton or padding.
bombazet or **bombazette** (bŏm-bȧ-zĕt′; bom ba *zet*). Thin, smooth-finished worsted fabric in plain or twill weave. Used for dresses, coats.
bombazine (bŏm-bȧ-zēn′; bom ba *zeen*). 1. Fine, plain or twilled English fabric; usually having silk warp and worsted filling; sometimes, cotton and wool. Dyed in piece. Usually made in black for mourning apparel. Also called *bombazin*, *bomberzeen*, or *bombax*. 2. Obsolete term for raw cotton.
bombé (F. bôṅ-bā; bonh bay). Rounded out; bulged; puffed up in convex shape. Used in dressmaking, embroidery, upholstery.
bombycine (bŏm′bĭ-sĭn; *bom* bi sin). Made of silk; also, silk yarn or fabric.
bonanza (bȧ-năn′zȧ; bo nan za). Anything highly successful or easily worked or having unusual value.
bone lace. Same as BOBBIN LACE. See LACES. So called because original bobbins were of bone.
bon goût (F. bôṅ gōō; bonh goo). French term for good taste.
boning. Whalebone, featherbone, or steel, covered or uncovered. Used for stiffening seams and edges, especially in corsets and dress bodices.
bonnaz (bō-năz′; bo *nahz*). Machine embroidery. See EMBROIDERIES.

BONNETS

bonnet. Head covering, with or without front brim; typically worn on top and back of head, leaving forehead and covered, and tied under chin. So calle from coarse medieval cloth, bonne derived from Hindu *banat*, of which hat or hoods were made in 14th century For other types of headgear, see HAT! CAPS, HOODS.

Bonnet, 1865

baby b. Lacy or daintily trimmed fabric covering for infant's head, extending from nape of neck to forehead, and covering ears; tied with fabric strings o ribbons under chin.
cabriolet (F. kȧ-brē-ō-lā; ka bree o lay). Bonnet suggesting shape of carriage top or cab's hood; sometimes tied under chin; similar to Kate Greenaway bonnet. Named for cabriolet or cal with forward or poke top.

Cabriolet, 1810

19th Century Coal Scuttle Bonnet

capote (F. kȧ-pōt; ka pote). Mid-Victorian type of bonnet having tie strings. Worn by women and children.
coal scuttle b. Bonnet with stiffened brim and flat back, resembling coal scuttle. Popular in mid-19th century.
cottage b. Bonnet of particular shape fashionable in England during early 19th century.
Easter b. Any type of new spring hat; usually worn for first time on Easter Sunday. Now seldom a bonnet.
hive. Kind of bonnet, usually of straw, shaped to resemble a beehive.
Indian b. Ornamental headdress, usually of long feathers, as worn by North American Indians. Not a bonnet in the usual fashion sense.
Kate Greenaway b. Children's bonnet of type illustrated by Kate Greenaway; in style of Empire period, with a ribbon band, and a frill around face.
poke b. Bonnet with small crown at back, having wide, rounded front brim projecting from top of head beyond face. Worn as hat.

fāte, făt, dánce, ärt mē, mĕt, hẽr, thêre rīde, rĭd nōte, nŏt, côrn, fōōd, fŏŏt cūte, cŭt, cûrē now fin(g)ger villa(ȧ) señor pleas(zh)ure

bonnets

Quaker b. Small, close-fitting, plain bonnet of prescribed characteristics;

Poke Bonnet, 1846

made of the fabric of the dress, and worn by women of the Quaker faith.
Salvation Army b. Black, straw, off-the-face bonnet trimmed with midnight blue ribbed silk. Brim is lined with blue silk, either plain or shirred. Has chin tie, which fastens with bow at side. Blue band around bonnet lettered with Salvation Army name. Uniform bonnet of the Salvation Army often adapted by fashion for women's hats, similar in silhouette but made in all hat materials and colors.
scoop b. Woman's bonnet, long and narrow in front like a scoop.

Salvation Army Bonnet.

(Adaptation, 1938)

slat b. Bonnet with brim reinforced with slats of cardboard or light-weight wood.
sunbonnet. Bonnet of fabric or straw having wide brim, generally stiffened, often with a ruffle around the front and sides as protection from sun; usually having short cape-like portion in back to protect neck. Worn informally outdoors.

Mid-19th Century Slat Bonnet

Early 19th Century Sunbonnet

bon ton (F. bôṇ tôṇ; bonh tonh). French phrase for fashionable style; the elite of society.
book cloth. Any of several fabrics, usually cotton, specially woven for book coverings. Used also as stiffening and interlining in collars, etc.
book linen. Firm linen or cotton fabric, often with sizing. See LINENS.

11

BOOTS

boot. 1. Footwear extending above ankle. In America, boot usually means top boot, extending well up calf of leg or higher. In England, boot means high-cut shoe, as distinguished from slipper, pump, oxford. Properly, boot means high-cut shoe of any height. **2.** Part of stocking between foot and top.

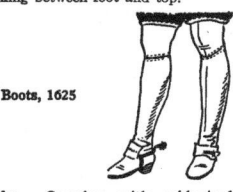

Boots, 1625

alaska. Overshoe with rubberized cloth top and rubber sole.
ankle b. Boot extending to ankle.
arctic. High, waterproof overshoe, usually of cloth and rubber, fastened with one or more buckles.
blucher (blōō'chēr; *blue* cher). Mid-leg boot or shoe distinguished by type of quarters, or side part from heel to vamp. See SHOES.
bootee (bōō-tē'; boo *tee*). Boot having short leg. For men, usually made with elastic gore over ankle or with laced front. For infants, usually knitted and tiny or half-leg length.
bootikin. Small boot.
bottekin (bŏt'ə-kĭn; *bot* e kin). Small boot, variously decorated, usually fancy.
bottine (F. bŏ-tēn; bot teen). **1.** Small boot of fine quality for women. **2.** Half or low boot. Type of buskin or legging.
brodequin or **brodekin** (brōd'kĭn; *brode* kin). Type of half boot or buskin once worn by women.
bucket top. French fall (crushed top) boot with top fulness greatly exaggerated.
buskin (bŭs'kĭn; *buss* kin). Boot extending half-way to knees, laced with cord or ribbon. Worn in ancient Greece, chiefly by actors. Also see SHOES.

Early Greek Buskins

carriage b. Lined boot, usually of fabric, often fur-trimmed. Worn by women in winter over ordinary shoes or slippers as protection against weather. Originally worn only in carriages to keep the feet warm; later, in automobiles; more recently, on the street. Some carriage boots are made large enough for both feet to slip into when in an automobile.
cavalier b. High, soft leather boot

boots

with flaring top, as worn with 17th century cavalier costume. Also see SLIPPERS.

Cavalier Boots, 1625

cothurnus (kŏ-thēr'nŭs; ko *ther* nus). Buskin or half boot, especially one with thick soles. Worn by ancient Greeks and Romans as part of theatrical costume.
cowboy b. Boot with high, fancy top, usually decorated with stitching; high, Cuban heel to prevent foot slipping from stirrup when riding horseback. Type of boot worn by cowboys.
finnesko (fĭn'ĕs-kō; *fin* ess ko) or **finnsko.** Boots made from tanned skin of reindeer and worn with fur side out. Worn by Arctic travelers.
French fall b. Leather boot with high top wide enough to crush down. Worn in colonial America.

17th Century French Fall Boots

gamashes (gə-mǎsh'ĕz; ga *mash* es). High boots worn in late 17th century. Also spelled *gamoshes* and *gramashes*.
gum b. High, protecting, rubber boot.
half boot. Boot extending short way above ankle.
Hessian b. (hĕsh'ən; *hesh* an). Knee-high boot, usually decorated at top with tassel. Worn in 19th century after being introduced into England by Hessians.
high-low. Boot reaching just over ankle, laced to top.
hip b. Fishing boot, usually of rubber, extending almost to hips. Used in fishing, etc.
hunting b. Laced boot with waterproof sole, usually blucher-cut and having bellows tongue. Used when hunting and for general rough outdoor wear.
jack b. Large, heavy, all-leather boot, reaching above knee. Worn by cavalry during 17th and 18th centuries.
jockey b. Type of top boot with cuff and often tassel at top, worn by children. See TOP BOOT.
kamik (kä'mĭk; *kah* mick). Sealskin boot worn by Eskimos.
larrigan. Knee-high boot with moccasin foot. Used by lumbermen, trappers.
leg b. Boot, without lacing, reaching some distance above ankle.

āte, făt, dânce, ärt mē, mĕt, hēr, thêre rīde, rĭd nōte, nŏt, côrn, fōōd, fŏŏt cūte, cŭt, cûré now fĭn(ŋ)ger villa(ə) señor pleas(zh)ure

boots

boots (continued)
lumberman's overs. Combination felt boots over which rubber arctics are worn.
napoleon b. (nə-pō'lĭ-ən; na *po* li un). Top boot, designed by Napoleon. Popular in mid-19th century.
pac or **pack.** Above-the-ankle shoe or half boot of moccasin type, worn by lumbermen.
Polish (pō'lĭsh; *po* lish). Women's front-laced shoe or boot, five or more inches high from heel seat to top. Said to have originated in Poland.
Russian b. Calf-high boot with leather top or cuff, sometimes having tassel in front.
skitty b. British dialect term for heavy half boot that laces up front.
startup or **startop** (stärt'ŭp; *start* up). Kind of buskin worn by country people in 16th and 17th centuries.
storm b. Leather shoe, often waterproofed, cut extra high, well above ankle. Designed for women's use in bad weather.
thigh b. Boot with upper part extending over thigh.
top b. High, solid-legged or laced boot, usually of leather or rubber. Used for riding, hunting, fishing, and other sports.

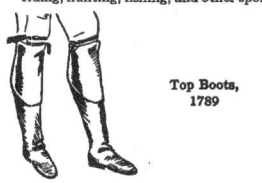

Top Boots, 1789

water b. Watertight, high boot. Worn in deep water, chiefly by fishermen.
Wellington (wĕl'ĭng-tən; *well* ing ton). 1. Loose, square-topped boot reaching above knee in front. Worn by men for riding. 2. Similar boot, shorter, worn by men under trousers. Properly called *half Wellington*.

bootee (boo-tē'; boo *tee*). Boot having short leg. See BOOTS.
bootery. Retail shop selling shoes.
boot hook. Long, metal hook with T handle across top to enable one to pull on riding boots by bootstraps.
boot-hose. 1. Long, heavy hose, leggings, or spatterdashes. Formerly worn in place of boots. 2. Hose made to wear with boots.
bootikin. Small boot, gaiter, or legging. See BOOTS.
boot jack. V-shaped board or frame. Used in pulling off boots.
bootlace. Fabric tape or leather string used to fasten boot.
bootstrap. Loop attached inside top of boot at back or side; used in pulling boot on.
boot top. 1. Top or upper part of boot, especially if flared and decorative. 2. Formerly, lace ruffle worn to hide top of boot.
boot tree. Device put inside boot or shoe when not in use, to keep its shape.

Bo Peep costume. Shepherdess costume for character in nursery rhyme. See FANCY DRESS.
bordé (F. bôr-dā; bor day). French word meaning edged or bordered.
bordeaux (F. bôr-dō; bor doe). Claret color; clear, deep, ruby-red shade of wine made from Bordeaux grapes.
border. Outer part or outside edge, usually ornamental; strip or stripe around or near edge; also, to make such a border.
bordered fabric. Fabric woven or printed with a border that is used as trimming or finish in making a garment. See FABRIC.
bordure (F. bôr-dür; bor dure). Edging, edge, or border of cloth; also, selvage.
boroso leather (bō-rō'sō; bo *ro* so). Kind of sharkskin. See LEATHERS.
bosom (bŏŏ'zm; *boo* zum). Front part of garment covering the breast.
bosom knot. Bow of colored ribbon. See BREAST KNOT.
bosom shirt. Shirt having a starched, plaited, or tucked bosom, often of different fabric from that of the shirt. Also, small partial shirt, as a vestee, gilet, or the like. See SHIRTS.
boss. Any protuberant part, usually ornamental, of same or different material, as knob, stud, pad. Also, to ornament with bosses; to stuff out, emboss, stud.
Boston bag. Small piece of luggage, usually of soft leather, pouch-like in shape, having handle at each side of top opening. Carried by hand.
Botany wool (bŏt'ə-nĭ; *bot* a ni). Fine merino wool. See WOOL.
bottekin (bŏt'ə-kĭn; *bot* a kin). Small boot. See BOOTS.
bottier (F. bô-tyā; bo tyay). One who deals in shoes or boots, especially of fine quality. French word for shoemaker.
bottine (F. bô-tēn; bot teen). Small boot of fine quality. See BOOTS.
bottu (bŏt'tōō; *bot* too). Mark, as dot on forehead, worn in India for decoration or to indicate sect.
bouchette (boo-shĕt'; boo *shet*). Large breastplate buckle. See BUCKLES.
boucle (F. boo-klā; boo clay). Woven or knitted so that surface has looped or knotted appearance. Applied to fabric used extensively for sports suits. French word for curled or, literally, buckled.
boudoir (F. boo-dwär; boo dwar). Lady's private room to which only intimates are admitted.
boudoir cap. Cap to cover the hair; worn by women in the boudoir. See CAPS.
bouffant (F. boo-fäɴ; boo fonh). Puffed-

Bouffant Skirt, 1930's

out, full, flaring, as in bulging drape of skirt or sleeve. From French word *bouffer*, meaning to swell.
bouffette (F. boo-fĕt; boo fet). French word for bow made of ribbon or other material; also, a tassel.
boughten (bô'tn; *baw* ten). Purchased; bought at store as distinguished from made at home. Not good usage.
bouillon (F. boo-yôɴ; boo yonh). French word meaning flounce or puff on a dress.
boulevard heel (boo'lə-värd; *boo* le vard). High, covered heel of Cuban type but lighter. See HEELS.
bound buttonhole. Buttonhole with fabric- or braid-bound edges. See BUTTONHOLES.
bound seam. Seam finished with bias binding. See SEAMS.
bouquet (F. boo-kā; boo kay). Bunch of flowers or cluster similar in appearance, as of precious stones.
Bourbon cotton (boor'bŭn; *boor* bun). Fine quality of cotton. See SEA-ISLAND COTTON under COTTONS.
bourdon (F. boor'dn or F. boor-dôɴ; *boor* dun or boor donh). Net lace having corded edge. See LACES.
bourette or **bourrette** (F. boo-rĕt; boo ret). Yarn of various fibers having unevenly spaced nubs or knots; also, fabric with uneven surface woven from such yarn. Originally, method of weaving in which loops were thrown to surface of cloth.
bourré (F. boo-rā; boo ray). Stuffed or wadded. Frequently used of quilted articles; also, of padded embroidery.
bourrelet or **bourlet** (F. boor-lā; boor lay). Wreath-like rounded cloth pad or helmets or as turban; similar padded roll worn as part of coif, worn by women in 14th century.
boutonnière (F. boo-tô-nyêr; boo ton yare). Flower or small bouquet worn in buttonhole; also, any small bouquet of real or artificial flowers. French word for buttonhole.

BOWS

bow (bō; bo). Two or more loops of ribbon, cord, fabric, etc., held together by tying or tacking or by means of a clip.
Cadogan b. (cə-dŭg'ən; ca *dug* an). Small, square bow tied at the nape of the neck to hold curls of long bob back from the face. Worn below hat brim. Named for Cadogan, British general (1675–1726), from the style of hairdress worn by men in his period, contemporary with Louis XIV and Louis XV in France.
pump b. Same as TAILORED BOW.
tailored b. Flat, stiff bow, as used on

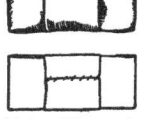

Tailored Bow

pumps and tailored hats. Often made of grosgrain ribbon.

bowknot (bō′nŏt; *bo* not). Ornamental slipknot made by doubling ribbon, cord, fabric, etc., into one or more loops, usually tied so as to leave ends free to draw loops easily through knot.
bowler (bōl′ẽr; *bole* er). British term for man's derby. See HATS.
bowstring hemp. Plant fiber used in making cloth, etc. See ALOE FIBER.
bow tie. Tie worn in a BOWKNOT.
box cloth. Coarse, thick melton cloth, usually buff color. Used for riding habits, etc.
box coat. Squared, loose coat. See COATS.
box leather. Leather finished so that close creases run in two directions. See LEATHERS.
box plait. Plait with edges turned in opposite directions. See PLAITS.
box toe. In shoe manufacturing, a piece of buckram or leather cut to pattern and placed between lining and upper of the tip to make the toe hold its shape.
boxy silhouette (sĭl-ōō-ĕt′; sil oo *et*). Squared silhouette of straight skirt worn with box coat. See SILHOUETTES.
boyang (bō′yăng; *bo* yang). Band around trouser leg below knee. Worn by laborers.
boyish bob. Hair cut short and trimmed reasonably close to head. See BOBS.
boyish-form silhouette. Straight, uncorseted figure popular in the 1920's. See SILHOUETTES.
bra or **bras** (brä). Short for BRASSIÈRE. Breast girdle.
brabant (brə-bănt′; brah *bant*). Type of sturdy linen fabric formerly made in Brabant, French Netherlands.

BRACELETS

bracelet. Ornamental ring, band, or chain for wrist or arm. Worn by women; now seldom worn by men.
bangle b. Ornamental circlet of gold, silver, glass, or other material. First worn by women of East Indian countries; now worn with sportswear, often several at a time. Returns to fashion at regular intervals, each time with a new type of pendant—animals, coins, or hearts, Cupids, and other sentimental tokens.
charm b. Bracelet having pendant charms or amulets attached.
love b. Large link bracelet, often made up of hearts, Cupids, etc.
slave b. 1. Bracelet made of several narrow rings, usually metal. 2. Single broad, solid band, usually of metal and close-fitting.

bracelet cuff. Cuff of metal, lace, ribbon, or other material, wider than average bracelet. Worn around wrist. See CUFFS.
bracelet sleeve. Sleeve reaching below elbow. See SLEEVES.
bracelet tie. Ankle-strap shoe. See SHOES.
bracer. Guard for arm or wrist. Worn in archery, fencing, etc. In ancient armor, called *brassart*.
braces. British term for suspenders, or straps to hold up trousers.

braconnière (F. brȧ-kô-nyêr; bra con yare). Short skirt of overlapping hoop-like steel plates. Worn as part of 16th century armor.
bragas (brä′gäs; *brah* gahs). Spanish term for pair of loose, wide breeches.
braguette (F. brȧ-gĕt; brah get). Piece of ancient armor, similar to CODPIECE.

BRAIDS

braid. 1. Narrow cord-like strip of flat tape woven of silk, wool, linen, etc., for trimming, binding, designs, outlines, etc. Varieties of braids usually named for use or appearance. Also, to weave or intertwine to form a braid; also, to trim with braid. 2. Band or ribbon for the hair, or plait of real or artificial hair. 3. To plait the hair into a braid. 4. Narrow tape-like strip woven or made with bobbins, in variety of designs and weights, and used to form more solid parts of motifs in lace.

Coronation Braid   Soutache Braid

Military Braid   Rick Rack Braid

cannetille (F. kȧn-tē; can tee). Lace-like braid of gold or silver thread.
coronation b. (kŏr-ə-nā′shən; cor o *nay* shun). Firmly woven, highly mercerized, filled cotton cord or braid, alternately thick and narrow. Used in couching and to outline pattern in embroidery or lace.
finishing b. Narrow, plain-woven braid, with decoration of simple embroidery stitches.
hercules b. (hẽr′kū-lēz; *her* cue leez). Heavily corded worsted braid, varying from ⅜- to 4-inch width. Used for trimmings.
hole b. Tape-like braid used in lace, made with bobbins, having small holes at regular intervals in plain ground.
lacet (lăs′ĕt; *lass* et). Type of braid woven of silk or cotton in various widths, often with looped edge. Used for edging, trimming, combined with tatting or crochet.
ladder b. Bobbin-made braid with open stitches crossed by bars giving ladder-like effect.
middy b. Narrow, finely plaited braid. Used to trim middy blouses; also, as a piping or seam finish on tailored dresses and coats.
military b. Flat braid of diagonal twill weave, in various widths and colors and in all fibers. Used for bindings, trimmings, braids, and ornaments.
orris (ŏr′ĭs; *or* iss). General term for all types of galloon, especially upholstery braids.
pigtail b. Small, round, closely woven braid. Used for trimming.
rat-tail b. Tubular silk braid re-

sembling rat's tail. Used for trimming.
rice b. Braid similar to coronation, but smaller in size, with thick parts spaced to give appearance of grains of rice. Used in trimming and in crochet laces.
rick rack b. Flat, woven braid in zig-zag form. Made in cotton, silk, rayon, and wool, in various sizes and many colors. Used for trimming.
Russian b. Same as SOUTACHE.
soutache b. (F. sōō-tȧsh; soo tash). Narrow, flat, decorative braid. Used chiefly to sew ornamental designs on garments.
stickerei (stĭk′ẽr-ī; *stick* er eye). Braid of even weave, having embroidered, scalloped, or notched edge.
straw b. Braid from ¼ inch to 3 inches wide, used in manufacture of straw hats. Largely imported. Finer straws come from South America, Italy, Switzerland; cheaper kinds, from China, Japan.

braided-band-stitch. Embroidery stitch. See STITCHES.
braiding. 1. Applying braid in designs to fabric, by hand or machine. 2. Plaiting three or more cords of fabric, ribbon, braid, or leather together, or three or more strands of hair, to form a braid.
braiding foot. Sewing-machine attachment for applying braid, silk twist, etc., in rows, scrolls, monograms, motifs.
braid work. That part of the making of bobbin lace which consists of making the braids. See BRAID, 4.
braies (brāz; braiz). Roman breeches. Worn during 1st and 2nd centuries, in addition to tunic; first brought from Asia by Gauls. Short braies worn by Emperor Augustus beneath toga, probably as protection against cold. Forerunner of pantaloons.
Brandenburg. 1. Ornamental loop or frog, usually of braid. Worn on garment in place of other fastener and for decoration. 2. Facing of embroidery on military coat, usually of parallel bars. Named for Brandenburg, Prussia.
brassard (brăs′ẽrd; *brass* erd). 1. Badge worn on arm. 2. BRASSART.
brassart (brăs′ẽrt; *brass* ert). Medieval armor for upper or whole arm. Also called *demibrassart*.
brassière (brȧ-zîr′ or F. brȧ-syêr; bra zeer or brass yare). Close-fitting undergarment shaped to support bust. Also called *bra*, *uplift*, *bandeau*.
braw. Scottish word meaning well-dressed; also, fine, brave, handsome.
braws. Scottish word meaning fine clothes.
breadth. 1. Width—opposite of length; measurement of fabric from selvage to selvage. 2. Term used by painters to indicate wealth of color.
breast. 1. The bosom; the part of clothing covering the bosom. 2. Forward surface of the heel. See HEEL BREAST.
breasting. In shoe manufacturing, the sole leather that turns away from the sole and is shaped to cover the front surface of the heel. Used on French or other covered wooden heels. See HEEL BREAST.

fāte, făt, dȧnce, ärt, mē, mĕt, hẽr, thêre, rīde, rĭd, nōte, nŏt, côrn, fōōd, fŏŏt, cūte, cŭt, cûré, now fin(ṇ)ger villa(ə), señor pleas(zh)ure

breast knot or bosom knot. Dainty bow, usually of colored ribbon. Formerly worn on bosom of dress; highly fashionable during 18th century.
breastpiece. Piece of fabric worn over front of bodice, as bib, chemisette, plastron.
breastpin. Ornamental pin. See PINS.
breastplate. 1. Part of defensive armor, made of plate metal, covering breast. 2. Formerly, vestment of Jewish high priest.
brede (brēd; breed). Obsolete term for braid or embroidery; to braid, plait, intertwine.
bredstitch or **bredestitch** (brĕd′stĭch; breed stitch). Old embroidery stitch. See STITCHES.
breech. 1. Breeches; or to clothe with breeches. 2. Short, coarse wool from hind legs of sheep or goat. See WOOL.
breechcloth or **breechclout.** Loincloth. Chiefly worn by savage or semicivilized people. Worn by India's crusader, Gandhi, in 20th century.
breeches (brĭch′ĭz; brich es). Garment covering hips and thighs.
breloque (F. brĕ-lŏk; bre loke). Charm, seal, or ornamental trinket, especially as worn on watch chain.
bretelle (F. brĕ-tĕl; bre tell). Decorative suspender-like shoulder-strap extending from waist-belt in front over shoulders to waist-belt at back. Embroidered ones popular with European peasantry.

20th Century
Bretelles

Breton (brĕt′ən or F. brĕ-tôṅ; bret on or bre tonh). Hat with upward rolling brim. See HATS.
Breton lace. Net with embroidered design. See LACES.
Breton work. Ancient chain-stitch embroidery done by Breton peasants. See EMBROIDERIES.
brick color. Any of various shades of reddish yellow or dull red likened to the color of red bricks.
brick-stitch or **brickwork.** Blanket-stitch or flat embroidery stitch arranged in brick formation. See STITCHES.
bridal lace. Type of reticella lace. See LACES.
bridal veil. Wedding veil. See VEILS.
bride. 1. Loop, bar, or tie, as made in needlework. 2. Slender warp or weft thread connecting parts of design in lace having no net ground. 3. Bonnet string. 4. Married woman, until first wedding anniversary.
bride lace. Ribbon of lace formerly given and worn at weddings, usually to bind sprigs of rosemary.
bride picotée (F. brēd pē-kō-tā; breed pee ko tay). Six-sided buttonholed bar having 3 or 4 purls.

briefs. Woman's undergarment similar to drawers but shorter, shaped with crotch, fitting legs snugly.
brier-stitch (brī′ẽr; bry er). Type of feather-stitching. See STITCHES.
brigandine (brĭg′ən-dĭn; brig an din). Medieval coat of mail, usually made of metal plates sewn together on fabric or leather.
brilliant. 1. Diamond or other stone cut with many facets to give brilliancy. 2. Imitation diamond. 3. Cotton fabric woven with geometric figures, often in color.
brilliantine (brĭl′yən-tēn; bril yan teen). 1. Fine, lustrous, wiry, durable fabric in plain or twill weave with cotton warp, worsted or mohair filling. Superior to alpaca, with higher luster. Used for dresses, linings, etc. 2. Oily dressing to give sheen to natural hair.
brim. Extended rim of hat, as distinguished from crown.
brimmer. Hat with broad brim. See HATS.
brin. 1. Stout fabric of linen or linen and cotton. 2. One of sticks of a fan.
brindled (brĭn′dld; brin dld). Streaked; having indistinct spots or stripes on dark background; unattractive; lacking in color or line.
briolette (F. brē-ō-lĕt; bree o let). Pear-shaped or oval-cut diamond or other stone, with surface cut in long triangular facets.
bristle (brĭs′l; briss l). Short, coarse, very stiff hair.
British warm. Heavy overcoat. See COATS.
Brittany or **Brittany cloth** (brĭt′ə-nĭ; brit a ni). Cotton or cotton and linen fabric made in Brittany, France.
broach. Same as BROOCH. See PINS.
broadbrim. Wide-brimmed hat. See HATS.
broad chain-stitch. Same as SQUARE CHAIN-STITCH. See STITCHES.
broadcloth. 1. Fine, wool, closely woven, napped and calendered fabric in plain or twill weave, usually twilled back. Better grades have gloss and a velvet feel. Used for dresses, suits, skirts, coats. Originally so named for exceeding usual 29-inch width. 2. Closely woven fabric in plain weave, of cotton, silk, rayon, or mixtures. Has light crosswise rib because filling yarn is heavier than warp with less twist. Resembles fine poplin. Used for men's shirts, women's and children's sports and tailored dresses, pajamas.
broadloom. Woven on wide loom, especially silks and carpets.
broad silk. Any silk fabric more than yard wide, as distinguished from ribbon and 18-inch silk.
broad-stitched seam. Same as top-stitched seam, with additional row of stitching on each side of seam line. See SEAMS.
broadtail. Pelt of stillborn, unborn, or very young Persian lambs, having lustrous moiré effect. See FURS.
broadtail cloth. Pile fabric with markings resembling broadtail fur.

brocade (brō-kād′; bro cade). 1. Jacquard-weave fabric having interwoven allover design of raised figures, usually flowers, foliage, etc., with pattern emphasized by contrast of surfaces in weave or by contrasting colors. Made of various foundation materials, in varying weights; often having silk, silver, or gold threads, sometimes all three, introduced into weft. Used for dresses, wraps, draperies, etc. Also, to weave patterns into fabric or to work in a design. 2. Loosely, fabric having raised design similar to brocade.
brocaded. 1. Having designs woven in relief on foundation fabric of contrasting weave. 2. Loosely, embroidered or ornamented with raised pattern, as in brocade.
brocade embroidery. Stitchery on brocaded fabrics. See EMBROIDERIES.
brocatel or **brocatelle** (F. brŏk-ə-tĕl; brock a tell). Heavy, figured fabric with Jacquard pattern in raised effect, higher than in brocade. Woven with two sets of yarns forming silk face on linen back. Highly fashionable before 18th century. Used for drapery and upholstery.
broché (F. brō-shā; bro shay). Woven with raised figure; also, to weave with raised figure; also, fabric of silk or silk and rayon with pile that forms raised design. French word meaning embossed or figured.
brochette (F. brō-shĕt; bro shet). Small BROOCH. See PINS.
brodé (F. brō-dā; bro day). French word meaning embroidered.
brodequin or **brodekin** (brŏd′kĭn; brode kin). Ancient half boot. See BOOTS.
broderie (F. brŏd-rē; brod ree). Embroidery or ornamental design or decoration resembling embroidery. French word for embroidery.
broderie anglaise (äṅ-glāz; anh glaze). Same as MADEIRA. See EMBROIDERIES.
brogan (brō′gən; bro gan). Heavy work shoe. See SHOES.
brogue. 1. Heavy, trimmed oxford. See SHOES. 2. (Plural) Obsolete term for trousers or hose.
broigne (broin). Medieval garment consisting of metal rings or plates sewn on leather or fabric. Worn as part of defensive armor.
broken check. Irregular check, as in fabric design. See CHECKS.
broken twill weave. Variation of regular twill. See WEAVES.
brolly. British colloquial term for umbrella.
bronze. Reddish-brown shade, ranging from warm yellow to greenish tones.
bronzed. Having appearance of bronze; browned or sunburned.
brooch (brōch; broach). Large ornamental pin. See PINS.
brother-and-sister mode. Fashion for dressing brothers and sisters in matching styles.
brown. Any of various dark, dusky, or tawny colors composed of red and yellow, usually containing black.
brown holland. Linen cloth, unbleached or partly bleached. See HOLLAND under LINENS.

Bruges lace (F. brüzh; broozh). Fine tape bobbin lace. See LACES.
brune (F. brün; brune). French word for brunette.

Brother-and-Sister Clothes

brunete (F. brü-nĕt; bru net). Early woolen fabric of good quality, dyed in various colors. Popular in 13th century, and later for tunics, pantaloons, stockings. Named for ancient town in Normandy, Brunete, where first made.
brunet or **brunette**. Person with complexion and hair and eyes that are dark or medium dark.—**florid b.** Person with black or dark brown hair, black or brown or gray eyes, and dark complexion with high coloring.—**olive b.** Person with dark brown or black hair, clear brown or black eyes, dark complexion, and very red lips.—**pale b.** Person with black or dark brown hair, brown or gray or blue eyes, and fair skin.
brunet blond or **brunette blonde**. Person with light or auburn hair, hazel or gray or blue-gray or brown eyes, and medium complexion. See BLOND.
brunswick (brŭnz'wĭk; bruns wick). 1. Close-fitting riding coat. See COATS. 2. (Capitalized) Color having a metallic look; as, Brunswick black or blue or green, which are dark colors having a Japan finish. 3. Obsolete fabric in twill weave, probably German in origin.
brushed wool. Napped woolen fabric, usually containing long, silky, mohair fibers. Used for sweaters, scarfs, trimming.
Brussels lace. Machine-made net with appliquéd design. See LACES.
buck. 1. Short for BUCKSKIN. See LEATHERS. 2. Suds in which cloth or yarn is soaked, as for bleaching, or clothes are washed. Also, cloth or clothes so treated. Also, to wash, soak, steep, or boil in suds or lye.
bucket tops. Wide-topped boots. See BOOTS.
Buckingham lace (bŭk'ĭng-əm; buck ing am). Old bobbin lace having fine clear ground. See LACES.

BUCKLES

buckle. 1. Device consisting of a frame, usually metal, covered or uncovered, and one or more teeth, chapes, or catches. Used for fastening and decoration. Also, to fasten with a buckle. 2. Crisp curl of hair, as in wigs worn in colonial times.
belt b. Buckle usually serving double purpose of fastening and decorating belt of garment.

bouchette (bōō-shĕt'; boo shet). Large buckle. Used in medieval armor to fasten breast-plate.
fermail (fĕr'māl; fer mail). Ancient buckle or clasp.
shoe b. 1. Decorative buckle used as ornament on shoes, usually pumps. 2. Small buckle used for fastening shoe strap.
stock b. Formerly, buckle for holding a neck stock in place.

Bucko. Trade name for reversed calf. See LEATHERS.
buckram (bŭk'rəm; buck ram). Two-ply, coarse, stiff, open-weave fabric filled with glue sizing. Used for stiffening or foundation purposes in clothing, millinery, shoes. Name derived from Bokhara, where cloth was first made as foundation for special floor covering.
buckskin. 1. Soft, strong leather. See LEATHERS. 2. (Plural) Breeches made of buckskin. 3. In western U. S., purse made of buckskin. 4. Creamy white, closely woven woolen cloth. Also called *buckskin cloth*.
buff. 1. Light, brownish-yellow shade, color of buffalo leather. 2. Buffalo skin. See BUFFSKIN under LEATHERS. 3. Coat of buff leather. See COATS. 4. To polish to a velvety surface.
buffalo cloth (bŭf'ə-lō; buff a lo). Woolen fabric having shaggy pile, as used for heavy lap robes, called *buffalo robes*.
buffcoat. Coat of buff leather. See COATS.
buffin. Coarse woolen fabric, popular in England during 16th and 17th centuries for clothing. So called from resemblance to buff leather.
buffon (bŭf'ən; buff on) or **buffont** or **buffant** (bŭk'ənt; buff ant). Article of neckwear, usually of gauze, linen, or lace. Worn around neck, puffed out over bosom, pouter-pigeon fashion. Popular in late 18th century.

18th Century Buffont

buffskin or **buff leather**. Leather prepared from buffalo or other skins. See LEATHERS.
bugle (bū'gl; bue gl). Tube-like bead of glass, jet, or composition. Used for trimming, especially hanging from an edge.
built-up. 1. Extended or added to; as, built-up shoulders or built-up waist. See SLIPS. 2. Made of several sections fastened one to other; as, built-up heel. See HEELS.
Bulgarian embroidery (bŭl-gâr'ĭ-ən; bul gay ri an). Bright-colored Oriental embroidery. See EMBROIDERIES.

bullion embroidery (bōōl'yŭn; bool yun). Ancient embroidery of gold wire. See EMBROIDERIES.
bullion lace. Heavy gold or silver lace. See LACES.
bullion-stitch. Decorative stitch having outer thread twisted around central one. See STITCHES.
bumper brim. Hat having a tubular brim, of varying size. See HATS.
bun. Roll or coiled knot of hair on any part of head.
bundle-stitch. Parallel stitches tied together at center. See STITCHES.
bungalow apron. Simple, straight-line, kimono-sleeve dress designed as a substitute for a house dress. See DRESSES.
buntal (bōōn-tăl'; boon tahl). Fine, white Philippine fiber, used in making ballibuntl, bangkok, and other straws.
bunting. 1. Soft, thin, cotton or wool fabric in plain open weave. Used for flags, decorations. 2. Garment for infants. See BABY BUNTING.
bur or **burr**. 1. Small lump or burl, as formed in fabric; also, to remove burs. 2. Waste threads removed in preparation of raw silk.
Burano lace (bōō-rä'nō; boo rah no). Needle-point lace, similar to Alençon. See LACES.
buratto lace (bōō-rät'tō; boo raht toe). Filet type of lace. See LACES.
burden-stitch. Flat couching. See STITCHES.
bure (bûr or F. bür; bure). 1. Ancient, strong, loosely woven cloth. Used in early and medieval times for garments. Originally, called *burah*, heavy and coarse, worn by Roman slaves and by peasants of Gaul; later, lighter in weight, softer. Burian, same cloth, used for covering tables, chests, etc.; also called *bureau*, which later developed into name of piece of furniture. 2. Brown color with red-yellow cast.
bureau (F. bü-rō; bure ro). 1. Ancient, coarse, heavy cloth, first called *burian*. See BURE. 2. Low chest of drawers for the bedroom, usually having mirror attached to it or hung above it.
burgoigne (bĕr-goin'; bur goyn). Front part, next to hair, of 18th century headdress.
burgonet (bĕr'gə-nĕt; bur go net). Lightweight helmet with a visor, resembling a morion but having cheek-pieces, sometimes nose-piece. Worn during Middle Ages.
burgundy (bĕr'gŭn-dĭ; bur gun di). Dark bluish-red shade, color of red wine produced in Burgundy, France.
buri (bōō-rē'; boo ree). Fiber from unopened leaf stems of Philippine talipot palm. Used in making straw hats.
buriti (bū'rĭ-tĭ; bue ri ti). Leaf fiber from Brazilian palm. Used in making straw hats.
burka (bōōr'kä; boor kah). Voluminous, shroud-like garment covering entire body from top of head to feet, having eye-holes or strips of lace for the wearer to see through. Worn by Mohammedan women.
burl. Kink in thread; knot or lump in woven fabric; also, to pick knots, burs,

fāte, făt, dánce, ärt mē, mĕt, hẽr, thêre ride, rĭd nōte, nŏt, côrn, fōōd, fŏŏt cūte, cŭt, cûré now fin(ŋ)ger villa(ə) señor pleas(zh)ure

burlap

loose threads, etc., from cloth before finishing.
burlap. Coarse, plain-woven, canvas-like fabric, usually made of jute or hemp. Low grades used for gunny sacks, wrapping furniture; firmer quality used for curtains. Also called *gunny*.
burlet. Kind of coif or hood.
burnet. 1. Variant spelling for brunete, medieval fabric. 2. Obsolete term for dark brown color.
burnish. To polish or shine metal, leather, etc., especially by means of friction.
burnoose or **burnous** or **burnus** (bẽr-nōōs'; bur *noose*). Cloak with hood. See WRAPS.
burnsides. Side whiskers. So called because originally worn by General A. E. Burnside. Usually called *sideburns*.
burnt almond. Yellow-red or bright brown color.
burnt-out print. Print design made by burning out one fiber in parts of fabric made of two different fibers. See PRINTS.
burrah (bẽr'ä; *bur* ah). Cotton fabric in plain weave, often striped. Worn by East African natives.
burunduki (bōō-rən-dŭ'kē; boo run *due* kee). Siberian chipmunk fur. See FURS.
busby (bŭz'bĭ; *bus* bi). 1. Tall fur cap. See CAPS. 2. Large, bushy wig. See WIGS.
bushel (bŏōsh'əl; *boosh* el). To mend, repair, or alter garments.
bushelman or **busheler.** Person, usually tailor's assistant, who repairs clothes.
bush jacket or **coat.** Belted, hip-length jacket. See JACKETS.
busk (bŭsk or bōōsk; busk or boosk). 1. Thin strip, as of whalebone, steel, wood, worn in front of corset for stiffening. 2. Obsolete term for corset.
buskin (bŭs'kĭn; *buss* kin). 1. Ancient half boot. See BOOTS. 2. Modern gored shoe. See SHOES. 3. (Plural) Gold-threaded silk stockings worn by Roman Catholic priests, abbots.
buss (bŏōs; booss). To dress, array. Chiefly Scottish.
Buster Brown collar. Large, starched collar that fits close to the neck. Front corners often rounded. See COLLARS.
bust forms. Device worn inside the brassière to fill out a flat bust. Made of rubber, silk, lace, or other material and molded to the form of the breast

Bust Extender, 1909.

Bust Forms, 1938

bust length. Length of sleeve which comes a little lower than halfway between armhole and elbow, in line with the bust line. See LENGTHS.

bustian (bŭs'chən; *buss* chan). Obsolete cotton fabric. Once used for waistcoats, vestments, etc.

BUSTLES

bustle (bŭs'l; *buss* l). Pad or frame worn below waist at back to distend skirts. Began about 1870 as connecting link between panniers. Compare HOOPS.

19th Century Bustle Silhouette

bishop. Formerly, kind of bustle filled with horsehair. So called by American colonists.
crinoletta (krĭn-ō-lĕt'ə; crin o *let* a). Cylindrical device of whalebone or steel, often covered with flounces, worn as bustle in late 19th century.
tilter. Petticoat bustle like a TOURNURE, except that shirring containing springs is separate piece of material; adjusted to figure by means of belt.
tournure (F. tōōr-nûr; toor nure). Petticoat bustle made by placing steel springs in shirring across back of petticoat and tying the ends together with tape across front.

bustle-back. Having exaggerated fulness at back of skirt.
bustle silhouette. Silhouette having exaggerated back fullness directly below waistline. See SILHOUETTES.
butcher's linen (bŏōch'ẽrz; *booch* erz). Bleached crash. See LINENS.
butt. Hide or skin covering hindquarters of animal, thicker, sturdier than rest. When severed, right and left halves called BENDS.
butterfly headdress. Headdress worn in latter half of 15th century, in which hair was enclosed in one or two stiff, projecting, ornamented cases pushed toward back of head. These helped to support large, transparent veil folded into wings, which were held out widely at sides by means of wires.

BUTTONS

button. Piece of bone, metal, glass, or any composition, of various shapes, having shank or holes by means of which it is sewed to garments. Used for fastening and for trimming. Also, to fasten or secure with buttons.
composition b. Button made of synthetic material, such as Plaskon or Bakelite.

covered b. Button of any shape, with or without shank, covered with fabric which matches or contrasts with that of garment.
crochet b. Button mold covered with crochet and finished off to serve as a button.
overall b. Button, usually of metal, that is applied to overalls by means of a special machine.
pearl b. Button in round, flat, or other shape, usually made of mother-of-pearl. Used for trimming as well as for fastening.
shank b. Button with a projecting piece on underside by means of which it is attached to material.
shell b. Button composed of two pieces, hollow inside, sometimes covered with fabric.
shoe b. Button used for fastening shoe. Usually thought of as small round shank button of beady appearance.
tops. Buttons made decorative only on top, with fabric or metal or glass, etc., and having shank on underside for sewing button in place.

BUTTONHOLES

buttonhole. Slit to fit a button, cut in a garment and then bound or finished with buttonhole-stitch. Also, loop for a button.
bound b. Buttonhole not finished with buttonhole-stitch, but having edges bound with fabric or braid instead.
diagonal b. Buttonhole that runs on a slant.
horizontal b. Buttonhole that runs crosswise.
loop b. Loop of crochet, cord, self-fabric, or the like, serving as a buttonhole and usually attached to an edge.
simulated b. Imitation buttonhole which has no slit cut in fabric, but is worked with buttonhole-stitch. For decoration, not use.
vertical b. Buttonhole that runs straight up and down.
worked b. Tailored buttonhole having edges finished with tailored buttonhole-stitch.

buttonhole bar. Cross-threads covered with buttonhole-stitch or over-and-over-stitch. Used to stay ends of buttonhole or seam; or to make loop to serve as an eye for a hook.
buttonhole cutter. Tool used to cut buttonholes for tailored garments, cutting buttonhole complete at one operation.
buttonhole eyelet. Eyelet overcast and worked with single purl-stitch. See EYELETS.
buttonhole gimp. Small, firm cord, 1/8 inch in diameter, wound with silk thread. Used by tailors to strengthen buttonholes around opening; secured by buttonhole-stitches.
buttonhole scissors. Scissors with screw for regulating length of cutting blade. See SCISSORS.
buttonhole-stitch. Stitch with double purl. See STITCHES.

buttonhole tied-stitch. Open-seam stitch used to join ribbons. See STITCHES.
buttonhole twist. Strong, closely twisted thread used for working buttonholes. See THREADS.
buttonhook. Hook for drawing buttons through buttonholes; used chiefly when buttoning shoes.
button mold. Mold in shape of button, made of wood or bone or composition, to be used on garment as a button after being covered with self-fabric or crochet.
button-tab crotch. Crotch formed by fabric strip fastened with a button. See CROTCH.

buyer (bī'ēr; *by* er). Man or woman who buys for manufacturer or for one or more departments of store. Person is usually responsible for the department for which he buys.
bycocket or **bycoket** (bī-kŏk'ĕt; by *cock* et). Medieval and Renaissance hat. See HATS.
byrnie (bēr'nĭ; *bur* ni). Ancient coat of linked mail.
byssus (bĭs'ŭs; *biss* us) or **byssin** (bĭs'ĭn; *biss* in). Ancient, fine fabric of linen, cotton, or silk; especially cloth made from fine flax fiber; probably the cloth used to wrap Egyptian mummies.
Byzantine (bĭz'ən-tēn; *bis* an teen). Of

the style of costume worn in Byzantine Empire, 5th and 6th centuries, characterized by three types of garment, worn alike by men and women: (1) Short, girdled tunic with long, tight sleeves; (2) dalmatica, full-length garment with wide sleeves; (3) long wrap of rich material embroidered in two squares. Richness of ornament and style of embroidery influenced later French and Russian dress.
Byzantine embroidery. Appliqué of bulky fabrics. See EMBROIDERIES.
Byzantine-stitch. Canvas stitch worked in diagonal zigzag pattern. See STITCHES.

C

caam (kăm; kahm). Heddles of loom.
cabaan or **caban** (kə-bän'; ca *bahn*). White fabric scarf. Worn by Arabs over shoulders.
cabana (kȧ-bä'nȧ; ca *bah* na). Small hooded shelter; often, a small beach house or bathhouse. Term applied in fashion to clothes suitable for wear on the beach, usually bright, colorful, active sports clothes.
cabas (F. kȧ-bä; ca bah) or **caba** (kä'bə; *ca* ba). Reticule or woman's work bag or basket, usually flat in shape.
cabasset (F. kȧ-bä-sā or kăb'ə-sĕt; ca bah say or *cab* a set). Open-faced helmet, shaped like high-crowned hat, with narrow, straight brim. Used in 16th century.
cabbage. Left-over pieces of cloth, as kept by tailors or dressmakers after cutting out garments; also, to cut off and keep such pieces.
cabbage-tree hat. Woven fiber hat. See HATS.
cable cord. Cotton cord composed of several softly twisted strands; available in several sizes in black, white, or natural. Used for corded pipings, shirrings, trimmings, etc.
cable net. Net with coarse, open mesh. See NETS.
cable-stitch. Embroidery stitch similar to chain-stitch. See STITCHES.
cabochon (F. kȧ-bō-shôn; ca bo shonh). 1. Stone cut in round, convex shape, unfaceted; also, this shape. 2. Small piece of dome-shaped buckram used as foundation in construction of ribbon flowers and other millinery ornaments.

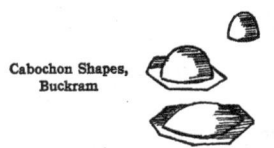

Cabochon Shapes, Buckram

cabretta leather (kȧ-brĕt'ə; ca *bret* a). Skin of cabretta, a hair sheep, finished and used like kid. See LEATHERS.
cabriolet (F. kȧ-brē-ō-lā; ca bree o lay).

Bonnet suggesting shape of cab's hood. See BONNETS.
cabron (F. kȧ-brōn; ca bronh). French word for kidskin.
cache-peigne (F. kȧsh-pĕñ; cash pane). Trimming, as band of flowers, on underside of hat brim, usually at back. French expression for hair ornament worn to conceal comb.
cachet (F. kȧ-shā; ca shay). Seal or stamp of approval. French word for seal or stamp.
cack. Infant's shoe. See SHOES.
caddie or **caddy.** Slouch hat. See HATS.
cadeau (F. kȧ-dō; ca doe). French word for gift.
cadenette (F. kȧd-nĕt; cad net). 1. Braids of hair at each side of face. Worn in 18th century by French soldiers. So called for Marshal Cadenet in 17th century. 2. Lovelock.
cadet blue (kə-dĕt'; ca *det*). Dark grayish-blue color.
cadet cloth. Sturdy woolen fabric, bluish-gray. Used for uniforms in boys' military schools.
cadet gray. Definitely grayed blue color.
cadge. Obsolete term meaning to bind edge of garment.
cadis or **caddis** (kăd'ĭs; *cad* iss). 1. Ancient, coarse, simply-woven woolen cloth, between flannel and bure. Made in Provence since time immemorial. 2. Narrow, tape-like, worsted fabric for bindings. Also spelled *cades*.
Cadogan bow (cə-dŭg'ən; ca *dug* an). Small, square bow worn to hold curls of long bob back from the face. See BOWS.
café au lait (F. kȧ-fā ō lā; ca fay o lay). Light, creamy brown, the color of fresh coffee with cream in it.
caffa. 1. Rich silk fabric used in 16th and 17th centuries. 2. Painted cotton fabric formerly made in India.
caffoy or **cafoy** (kăf'oi; *caff* oy). Fabric similar to damask. Used for hangings in 18th century.
caftan or **kaftan** (kăf'tăn; *caf* tan). Long, coat-like garment fastened with long sash, having extra long sleeves. Usually of cotton or silk and cotton mixture in gay stripes. Worn by higher and middle classes throughout eastern Mediterranean countries.

cage. In fur trade, revolving wire drum for shaking sawdust from furs after drumming.
calamanco (kăl-ə-măng'kō; cal a *mang* co). Glossy woolen fabric in satin weave, plain or striped, resembling camel's hair cloth.
calash (kə-lăsh'; ca *lash*). Hood made on hoops. See HOODS.
caldron or **cauldron** (kôl'drən; *cawl* drun). Reddish old-copper or brown color, having red-yellow cast; redder than HENNA.
Caledonian brown (kăl-ə-dō'nĭ-ən; cal e *doe* ni an). Dull reddish-yellow color.
calendering. Finishing process consisting of passing fabric between heated steel rollers to give a smooth, glazed, or watered surface; unpatented processes not permanent. Moiré is calendered.
calf leather or **calfskin.** Soft leather made from skins of young cattle. See LEATHERS.
calico (kăl'ĭ-kō; *cal* i co). 1. In U. S., plain-woven cotton cloth printed with figured pattern on one side. Originally, fine fabric, comparatively new at time of Civil War when cost was 75¢ per yard for 18-inch width; now made from cheaper grade of cotton, highly sized. Largely replaced by percale. Also called *cotton print*. Used for house dresses, aprons, etc. 2. In England, plain white cotton cloth. So called for Calicut, India, where cotton textiles were first printed.
Californian embroidery. 1. Primitive stitching with animal substances. 2. Leather stitchery, braiding, etc. See EMBROIDERIES.
California top. Collapsible top of an automobile. Not to be confused with HOLLYWOOD TOP. See SLIPS.
caliga (kăl'ĭ-gə; *cal* i ga). 1. Ancient Roman military shoe. See SHOES. 2. Stocking worn by bishops.
calk (kôk; cawk) or **calker.** Metal plate with sharp points worn on sole or heel of shoe, boot, or clog to prevent slipping on ice. In colonial America, clog having spiked sole. Also, metal used on heel or sole to give longer wear.
calotte (kə-lŏt'; ca *lot*). Tiny, close-fitting cap. See CAPS.

calpac (kăl'păk; cal pack). Large, black, Oriental cap. See CAPS.
calyx-eyed needle (kā'lĭx; kay lix). Self-threading needle. See NEEDLES.
calzoneras (Sp. kăl-sa-nā'räs; cahl so nay rahss). Trousers buttoned at each side, as worn in Mexico.
camaca or camoca (kăm'a-ka; cam a ca). Ancient, rich, heavy fabric of silk or silk and cotton; often figured, sometimes plain. Made in 14th century in Greece and Isle of Cyprus.
camail (kà-māl'; ca mail). Chain-mail hood or neck guard worn with armor, especially one attached to helmet.
camauro (kä-mow'rō; cah mow ro). Formerly, pope's cap. See CAPS.
cambaye (kăm-ba'; cam bay). Lightweight cotton cloth made in Bengal and other parts of India. So called because exported from Cambay.
cambresine (kăm-brĕ-zēn'; cam bre zeen). Fine linen fabric named for Cambrai, France.
cambric (kăm'brĭk; came brick). 1. Fine, closely woven, white or yarn-dyed warp cotton fabric in plain weave, with gloss on right side. Used for aprons, underwear, shirts. Also called *cotton cambric* and *cambric muslin*. 2. Thin, stiff, plain-woven, glazed cotton fabric in white and solid colors; loses glaze in laundering. Used for linings, fancy dress costumes, dressmakers' trial models, inexpensive chintz. 3. Fine, smooth, white fabric of linen in plain weave. Used for blouses, collars, cuffs, shirt bosoms, napkins, doilies, etc. First made in 14th century at Cambrai, France.
cambric muslin. Same as CAMBRIC, 1.
camel (kăm'ěl; cam el). Medium light brown color.
camelin or cameline (kăm'a-lĭn; cam e lin). Ancient fabric of camel's or goat's hair, first made in the Levant during 13th century.
camel's hair. Long, silky hair of camel, spun into textiles for coats, overcoats, automobile blankets, etc.
camel's hair cloth. Thick, warm, lightweight coating fabric usually in twill weave with high glossy finish, made entirely or partly of camel's hair, mohair, or, in cheaper grades, of cow-hair. Usually in light tan shade.
camel's hair shawl. Shawl made in part of camel's hair.
cameo (kăm'ē-ō; cam ee o). Any of several stones delicately carved in relief to show design, often woman's head, usually in white against background of shell-pink or other contrasting color. Worn by women as ornamental brooch, ring, pendant, etc.
cameo silhouette. Outline of costume giving etched effect. See SILHOUETTES.
camicia (ka-mē'chä rōs'ě; cah mee chah roce sah). Red shirt, such as worn by Garibaldi, the Italian patriot. See SHIRTS.
camisa (kä-mē'zȧ; ca mee za). Embroidered waist, having large, flowing sleeves. See BLOUSES. Spanish word, also meaning shirt or chemise.
camise (ka-mēs'; ca *meece*). Loose, light-

weight shirt, smock, or tunic. Originally called *sherte* and worn next to skin by early Saxons. After Norman invasion, name changed to Old French *camise;* and it became outer garment decorated with embroidery, especially when worn by nobility. Now worn by Orientals and called *kamis.*
camisole (kăm'ĭ-sōl; cam i sole). 1. Underbodice, often lace-trimmed, usually with straight top and shoulder straps of ribbon, lace, or self-material. First worn as corset cover. 2. Kind of jacket or jersey. See JACKETS. 3. Short negligee jacket. See JACKETS.
camisole neckline. Neckline like that of a camisole top slip, straight above the bust line, with straps over the shoulders. See NECKLINES.
camisole top. Type of top used on slips and other garments, as in a camisole, which is finished straight across and has straight shoulder straps. See SLIPS.
camlet (kăm'lět; cam let). 1. Fine, closely woven, nearly waterproof fabric. First made in Asia, probably of camel's hair. Later made in Europe of wool, silk, or both, sometimes with hair. Much used by American colonists for cloaks, petticoats, hoods, etc. Also spelled *chamlet.* 2. Garment of this fabric.
campaign wig. Very full wig with curls at top and sides. So called because the average man used a wig only when making public appearances. See WIGS.
Canadian embroidery. Primitive work with porcupine quills and thongs. See EMBROIDERIES.
canary yellow. Brilliant, slightly reddish yellow, similar to plumage of the bird.
cancan dress. Type of dress worn originally by the cancan dancers in Paris, France, in the middle nineties. Consists of basque bodice with exaggerated sleeves; long, full, plain skirt; and many ruffled petticoats. See DRESSES.
candlewicking. 1. Tuftings of threads to give a napped surface to fabric, usually in form of design. See CANDLEWICK EMBROIDERY under EMBROIDERIES. 2. Thick, soft, cotton thread. See THREADS.
candlewick needle. Thick needle. See NEEDLES.
candy stripe. Stripe like those in stick candy. See STRIPES.
caned. Stiffened with haircloth. Applied to full-length skirts worn by 19th century women just after discard of hoopskirts.
canepin (F. kȧn-păṅ; can panh). French word for kidskin. See LEATHERS.
canezou (F. kȧn-zōō; can zoo). Woman's jacket. See JACKETS.
cangan (kăng'gȧn; *cang* gan). Coarse cotton fabric made in China.
canions (kăn'yŭnz; *can* yunz). Ornaments worn at knees, attached to stockings or breeches. Originally, decorative extension of trunk hose, usually in form of horizontal folds below knees. Formerly called *cannons.*
cannelé (F. kȧn-lā; can lay). Woven in grooves, having fluted surface; also, such a weave, as in rep; also, fabric so woven, creased, or sewn.

cannequin (kăn'a-kĭn; *can* e kin). White cotton fabric from East Indies. Popular from 16th to 18th century.
cannetille (F. kȧn-tē; can tee). 1. Gold or silver metal thread. See THREADS. 2. Braid of gold or silver thread. See BRAIDS.
cannon curl. Cylindrical or round curl worn horizontally.
cannons. Ornamental garters or fasteners for breeches. See CANIONS.
canotier (F. kȧn-nō-tyā; ca no tyay). Straight-brimmed hat. See HATS.
canroy. Calendering machine to remove lint from cotton fabrics.
Canton crepe. Slightly ribbed crepe. See CREPES.
Canton flannel. Stout, absorbent, cotton flannel. See FLANNELS.
Canton linen. Crisp, linen-like fabric. Same as GRASS CLOTH.
cantoon. Cotton fabric corded on one side, usually having satiny finish on other. Obsolete.

CANVAS

canvas. Heavy, strong, plain-woven fabric of linen, cotton, silk, or mixture; soft-finished or highly sized. Used for interlinings, for art needlework, and for stiffening coats, skirts, facings, etc.; heavier grades used for seamen's clothing, sails, tents, mailbags, etc. Name from Latin *cannabis,* meaning hemp. A painting is often spoken of as a canvas.
Berlin c. Coarse fabric with square mesh formed by paired threads; originally, of silk, but made later of other fibers also. Used in canvas work.
cross-stitch c. Stiff, open-weave fabric, heavier than tarlatan, available in different sizes of mesh. Used for cross-stitch designs.
Java c. Type of canvas of loose, even, basket type of weave; used as foundation for embroidery, especially of cross-stitch type.
leviathan c. (le-vī'a-thǎn; le vy ath an). Coarse, open, double canvas used as ground for embroidery of the type of Berlin work.
penelope c. (pa-něl'o-pě; pe *nell* o pe). Double-thread canvas like Berlin canvas, used for needle tapestry work.
single c. Canvas woven in plain open weave, one thread over and one under. Used for canvas embroidery.

canvas embroidery. Wool embroidery on canvas. See EMBROIDERIES.
canvas shoe. Tennis or sports shoe. See SHOES.
canvas stitch. Type of cross-stitch, or other stitch used in canvas embroidery. See STITCHES.
canvas work. Same as CANVAS EMBROIDERY. See EMBROIDERIES.

CAPS

cap. 1. Close-fitting head covering, without complete brim; usually of soft material, and sometimes with visor. 2. Headdress worn to indicate particular order, rank, or dignity. For other types of headgear, see BONNET, HAT, HOOD.

fāte, făt, dânce, ärt mē, mět, hêr, thêre rīde, rĭd nōte, nŏt, côrn, fōōd, fŏŏt cūte, cŭt, cürè now fin(ŋ)ger villa(a) señor pleas(zh)ure

angelus c. Type of peasant handkerchief cap such as worn by the women in the famous painting, "The Angelus," by Millet (1814–75).
Baby Stuart c. Baby's close-fitting, shirred cap, with narrow chin band. Original type of baby cap.

Angelus Cap

Cap with Flaps, 1525

17th Century Baby Stuart Cap

balmoral (băl-mŏr'ɘl; bal *mor* al). Flat Scotch cap of tam-o'-shanter type, with round projecting top.
barret (băr'ĕt; *ba* ret). Small flat cap similar to biretta. Worn during Middle Ages by soldiers and Roman Catholic priests.
Basque beret (F. básk bĕ-rā; bask be ray). Round, flat, close-fitting cap of soft woolen fabric, as worn by Basque peasants.

Basque Beret

bathing c. Close-fitting cap of rubber or rubberized fabric worn to keep hair dry when swimming.

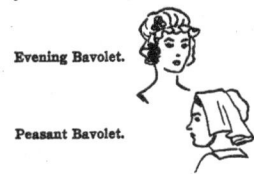

Evening Bavolet.

Peasant Bavolet.

bavolet (F. bȧ-vō-lā; ba vo lay). Head covering in rustic cap form. Worn mostly by French peasant women, untrimmed. In more elaborate form, worn as theater cap under large hats.

Bearskin 1938

bearskin. Tall, black fur cap, especially military headdress worn by Foot Guards of British army.
bell-boy or **bell-hop c.** Pill-box cap, usually trimmed with braid or buttons. Worn by hotel call-boys.

Bell-Boy Cap

beret (F. bĕ-rā; be ray). See BASQUE BERET.
berretino (bĕr-rĕt-tē'nō; ber ret *tee* no). Scarlet skull-cap worn by cardinals. Italian word, derived from BIRETTA.
biggin (bĭg'ĭn; *big* in). Close-fitting cap worn by young children and sometimes by adults in France and America before 1700. More recently adapted in snood effect and made of mesh. Corruption of French *béguin*, meaning cap as first worn by certain devout persons or Béguines.

Biggin

biggonet (bĭg'ɘ-nĕt; *big* o net). Woman's cap or biggin, often having earpieces.
biretta (bĭ-rĕt'ɘ; bi *ret* a). Square cap having three or four projections on top radiating from center, often finished

Priest's Biretta

with pompon. Officially worn by Roman Catholic ecclesiastics, and by some European university professors.

Kin to trencher or mortarboard worn by scholars in America.
bluebonnet. Broad, flat cap of blue fabric, usually wool, of tam-o'-shanter type. Worn in Scotland.
boina (boi'nä; *boy* nah). Type of round, woolen cap. Worn by Spaniards.
boudoir c. (bōō'dwăr; *boo* dwar). Cap with gathered crown, usually edged with ruffle. Made of soft material, often lace-trimmed. Worn to cover the hair in privacy of boudoir. Popular during 19th and early 20th centuries.
busby (bŭz'bĭ; *buzz* bi). Tall fur cap, with or without plume, having bag hanging from top over right side. Term incorrectly applied to bearskin.

Busby

calotte (F. kȧ-lŏt; ca lot). Tiny, close-fitting cap, like sectional crown of hat, often having tab at center top. French word for plain skull-cap. Also spelled *calot, callot*.

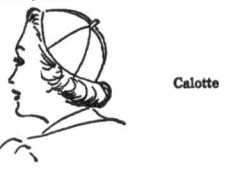

Calotte

calpac (kăl'păk; *cal* pack). Large, black cap, usually of sheepskin or felt, worn by Armenians and other Near Eastern peoples.
camauro (kȧ-mow'rō; cah *mow* ro). Ermine-trimmed, red velvet cap, as formerly worn by popes.
c. of maintenance (măn'tɘ-nɘns; *main* te nance). Low-crowned cap having two pointed ends extending in back; often of scarlet velvet with ermine trim. Carried before English sovereigns at coronation, sometimes before mayors; formerly worn as symbol of high rank or office. Also called *cap of dignity* or *estate*.
catercap (kā'tẽr-kăp; *kay* ter cap). Square cap worn by advanced students. Same as MORTARBOARD.
cerevis (sĕr'ɘ-vĭs; *sare* a viss). Small, visorless, cylindrical cap, similar to modern pillbox, formerly worn by German university students.
cervelière (F. sĕr-vɘ-lyêr; sare ve lyare). Close-fitting steel cap, often worn under helmet or hood of mail during Middle Ages and later.
chapel de fer (F. shȧ-pĕl dɘ fêr; sha pel de fare). Skull-cap of iron or steel, sometimes with brim, as worn in medi-

fāte, făt, dånce, ärt mē, mĕt, hẽr, thêre rīde, rĭd nōte, nŏt, côrn, fōōd, fŏŏt cūte, cŭt, cüré now fĭn(ŋ)ger villa(ɘ) señor pleas(zh)ure

caps (continued)
eval armor with coif of mail. French for cap of iron.
Charlotte Corday c. (shär'lŏt kôr'dā; *shar* lot *cor* day). Soft cap, gathered and

Charlotte Corday Cap

held by ribbon band, with frill framing face and hanging longer in back. Worn by Charlotte Corday (1768-1793) who was guillotined during French Revolution.
chechia (shĕ-shē'ə; she *shee* a). Cylindrical Arab skull-cap with tuft. Adopted also by French soldiers in Africa.

Arabian Chechia

clock-mutch. Old-fashioned cap. Formerly worn by women. So called from *klap-muts*, Dutch word for nightcap.
coif. Close-fitting cap, usually of soft, white cloth, varying in style, of uncertain origin. In Middle Ages, worn as hood-like white cap with extended sides, tied under chin; also, as defensive metal skull-cap under hood of mail. In 16th century, worn under elaborate headdresses; in 17th and 18th centuries, under caps or as cap. Until later 19th century, worn under wig as inner skull-cap by English lawyers and judges. Also, ornamented with hand embroidery, worn, sometimes under hats, by residents of Brittany. Also spelled *quoif*.

14th Century Coif

coiffette (F. kwä-fĕt; kwah fet). Skull-cap of iron. Worn by soldiers during 14th century.
college c. MORTARBOARD.
cornercap. Cap having four, sometimes three, corners. Worn during 16th and 17th centuries with academic or ecclesiastical costume.
cornet (kôr'nĕt; *cor* net). Square, academic cap or MORTARBOARD.

Cossack c. Tall, brimless cap of fur or lamb's wool, formerly worn crushed on head by Russian Cossacks. See also HATS.
coxcomb (kŏks'kōm; *cox* kome). Cap adorned with strip of notched red cloth. Formerly worn by licensed court jesters.
curch or **curchef** (kẽr'chĕf; *ker* chef). Plain, close-fitting cap worn by colonial women in America.
duck-bill c. Cap having long, forward, visor-like brim. See HATS.
dunce c. Tall, cone-shaped cap, often marked with the letter D, for dunce. Originated in schools and worn by students who failed in their lessons.
dust c. Cap made of a kerchief or circle, gathered to head size by elastic run through narrow hem on edge. Worn by women to protect their hair while doing housework, such as cleaning or dusting.
Dutch c. Type of cap worn by women of Volendam, in the Netherlands; made of lace or embroidered muslin, pointed at the top, and flaring away at the sides in two wing-like pieces.
Eton c. (ē'tn; *ee* ton). Close-fitting cap with short visor, as worn by boys at Eton College, England.
fez. Brimless felt cap, shaped like cut-off cone, usually red with hanging black or dark blue tassel; formerly worn by Turks, still worn in parts of Near East. Similar to TARBOOSH.

Turkish Fez

flatcap. Flat, low-crowned cap of varying shape, formerly worn in England.
fly c. Woman's cap with wing-like pieces at sides. Worn during 17th and 18th centuries.
foolscap or **fool's c.** 1. Jester's cap, cape, or hood, often with bells or tassels. 2. Same as DUNCE CAP.
forage c. (fŏr'əj; *for* ij). Small cap worn by soldiers when not in full-dress uniform. Similar to KEPI. No longer worn in U. S. Army.
fore-and-after. Peaked cap worn with peaks over forehead and at back.
galerum (gə-lē'rŭm; ga *leer* um) or **galerus** (gə-lē'rŭs; ga *leer* us). 1. Close-fitting, helmet-like cap of undressed skin or fur. In Roman antiquity, worn by hunters, rustics, etc. 2. Kind of priest's cap.
Glengarry (glĕn-găr'ĭ; glen *ga* ri). Woolen cap, creased through crown from front to back; edges usually bound with ribbon, which ends at back in short streamers. Originally part of uniform of certain regiments of Scotch Highlanders; often having feather tuft; adjusted to head size by lacing at back; worn high in front, sloping backward.

Glengarry

golf c. Man's cap with round flat top, fitted headband, and visor. Usually finished at center of crown with flat button. Worn for golf and other sports, and when motoring.
helmet c. Medium-heavy, knitted cap with turned-up cuff around back and sides of head. Cuff can be turned down and buttoned under the chin. Usually worn by boys.

Boy's Helmet, 1926

house-c. Cap, as worn by students in a university, with emblem or colors of their college or dormitory.
hunting c. Peaked cap, similar in shape to jockey's cap, but often of velvet and stiffened. Worn for hunting.
Joan (jōn; jone). Woman's small, close-fitting cap. Worn in late 18th century.
jockey c. Thin, small, close-fitting cap with long visor, as worn by jockeys; usually in the stable's colors, to match the shirt.
Juliet c. Small, round cap of wide, open mesh, usually decorated with

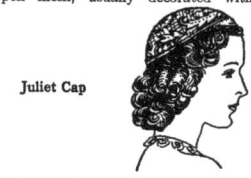

Juliet Cap

pearls or other jewels, similar to that worn on the stage by Shakespeare's Juliet. Worn chiefly for evening.

French Kepi

kepi (kĕp'ĭ; *kep* i). Flat-topped, military cap with horizontal visor, as worn in modern French army.

fāte, făt, dánce, ärt mē, mĕt, hẽr, thêre rīde, rĭd nōte, nŏt, côrn, fōōd, fŏŏt cūte, cŭt, cũre now fin(ŋ)ger villa(ə) señor pleas(zh)ure

Kilmarnock bonnet (kĭl-mär′nək; kill *mar* nock). Broad-topped woolen cap, worn in Scotland.
kulah (kōō-lä′; koo *lah*). Conical cap of lambskin or felt, worn in Persia and India by Moslem monks.
liberty c. Close-fitting, soft cap with elongated crown, usually folded over. First worn by Roman slaves when freed; later adopted by French Revolutionists as symbol of liberty. Compare with PHRYGIAN CAP and PILEUS.
Mary Stuart c. Small cap, usually of delicate fabric and lace, with a peak at center of forehead. Similar to WIDOW'S PEAK.

16th Century Mary Stuart Cap

miter or **mitre** (mī′tẽr; *my* ter). Tall, ornamental headdress with two peaks, worn by church dignitaries. Originally, cone-shaped; gradually changed through the centuries.

Bishop's Miter

mobcap. Woman's cap with high, full crown; often having bands tied under chin.
Monmouth c. (mŏn′mŭth; *mon* muth). Flat, round cap with disk-shaped crown; formerly worn by sailors and soldiers.
montero (mŏn-tā′rō; mon *tay* ro). Hunter's round cap made with a flap.
mortarboard (môr′tẽr-bôrd; *mor* ter board). Close-fitting, round academic cap pointed over forehead, with broad, projecting, square top and a tassel. Also called *trencher*, or *catercap*.
mortier (F. môr-tyȧ; mor tyay). Cap similar in shape to a dentist's mortar bowl. Worn by legal dignitaries in France.
muffin c. Flat, muffin-shaped, woolen cap worn by students at English charity schools; also, fatigue cap worn by certain British regiments.
mutch. Close, linen or muslin cap worn by old women; also, infant's cap or man's head covering.
nightcap. Close-fitting cap, often tied under the chin. Worn in bed to stay the hair or protect the head.
overseas c. Olive-drab, wool cap, having no visor or stiffening, worn overseas by U. S. Army during World War.

Type of Overseas Cap

palisade (păl-ĭ-sād′; pal i *sade*). Cap worn over wire frame in the mornings before commode headdress was arranged.
petasos (pĕt′ȧ-sŏs; *pet* a sos) or **petasus** (pĕt′ȧ-sŭs; *pet* a sus). Close-fitting winged cap as shown on Roman god Mercury.
Phrygian c. (frĭj′ĭ-ən; *frij* i an). Close-fitting cap, taken from Greek representation of cap worn by Orientals, supposed to have been conical in shape. Often identified with LIBERTY CAP or PILEUS.
phrygium (frĭj′ĭ-ŭm; *frij* i um). White Phrygian cap of helmet-like shape, forerunner of the papal tiara. Worn by popes of early Middle Ages.
pileus (pī-lē′ŭs; py *lee* us). Skull-cap or brimless, round, close-fitting cap, sometimes pointed. Made of felt, leather, or wool. Worn in ancient Rome; also by monks. Compare LIBERTY CAP and PHRYGIAN CAP.
sailor c. 1. Cap worn by sailors. Small, stiffened cap similar to that worn by officers, but without visor. 2. Tam-shaped cap with a headband on which there is usually the name of a battleship. Worn by children.
scone c. Broad, flat, round cap with visor, sometimes having crown divided into quadrants. Worn by Lowland Scots. Name derived from scone, round teacake which it resembles.
Scotch c. Brimless cap of thick wool. See BALMORAL. See GLENGARRY.
service c. Round, flat-topped cap, about 3½ inches high, with visor. Worn in U. S. Army when full-dress uniform is not worn.
shako (shăk′ō; *shack* o). High, stiff military cap with a visor and pompon; originally of fur.

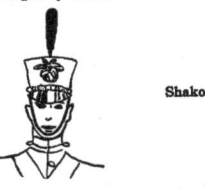

Shako

skull-cap. Tiny, close-fitting cap covering only crown of the head. Originally iron defense for the head, sewed inside cap.
sowback. Scottish term for woman's cap with raised fold running lengthwise.

17th Century Skull-Cap

stocking c. Long, tapering cap of soft fabric, usually knitted, hanging loosely and tipped with tassel or pompon.
taj (täj; *tahj*). Tall, conical cap, a Mohammedan headdress of distinction.

Taj

tam. Short for TAM-O′-SHANTER.
tam-o′-shanter. Cap of Scottish origin, with broad, round, flat top and tightly fitted headband. Usually made of wool and having knot or tassel in center.

Scottish Tam-o′-Shanter

tarboosh (tär-bōōsh′; tar *boosh*). Tall, brimless felt cap, usually red, worn by Moslems, sometimes as the inner part of a turban, sometimes covered by veil. Similar to a FEZ.

Tarboosh

thrum c. Cap knitted from thrum, the extremity of weaver's warp which can not be woven. Worn in England in 18th century, and by workmen in colonial America.
toboggan c. (tȧ-bŏg′ən; to *bog* an). Long, knitted cap with pointed end, having pompon or tassel at tip. Worn by tobogganers. See STOCKING CAP.
trencher or **trencher c.** Same as MORTARBOARD.

fāte, făt, dȧnce, ärt mē, mĕt, hẽr, thêre rīde, rĭd nōte, nŏt, côrn, fōōd, fŏŏt cūte, cŭt, cũre now fin(ŋ)ger villa(ȧ) señor pleas(zh)ure

caps (continued)
tuque (tŭk; tuke). Long, knitted cap, made from bag tapered at both ends and having one end turned inside other. Worn for winter sports by Canadians. Also called *toque*.

Canadian Tuque

watch c. Navy blue, knitted cap worn in inclement weather by seamen in United States Navy.
widow's peak. Cap with point over center of forehead. Originally, worn as mourning bonnet by the widowed Catherine de Medici. Often called *Mary Stuart cap*.
zucchetto (tsōōk-kĕt'tō; tsook ket toe). Small, round, ecclesiastical skull-cap.
capa (kä-pä; cah pah). Spanish word for mantle or cloak.
cap and bells. Cap with bells attached, as worn by court jesters.
cap and gown. See ACADEMIC COSTUME.
caparison (kə-păr'ĭ-sən; ca *pa* ri son). To dress or adorn in showy, sumptuous apparel or ornaments; also, the decorative clothing. Literally, richly ornamental trappings of a horse.

CAPES

cape. Sleeveless outer garment of any length hanging loosely from shoulders; usually covering back, shoulders, arms.
abbé c. (F. ă-bā; a bay). Tiered, above-the-elbow cape, like that worn over abbot's robe.

Abbé Cape

circular. Cape with wide flare, often cut from a circle of cloth. Ankle-length capes, lined with squirrel fur, brightly colored flannel, or surah silk, were fashionable in late 19th century.
huke. Woman's hooded cape of 15th century.
Inverness (ĭn'vẽr-nĕs; *in* ver ness). Sleeveless cape, usually long, fitted closely at the neckline, falling loose and full from the shoulders.
jacket c. Short garment, having front and back, with short cape that suffices for sleeves. Sometimes spelled *jacquette cape*.
mozetta or **mozzetta** (mō-zĕt'ə; mo zet a). Cape with ornamental hood

hanging at back. Worn by certain church dignitaries.

Jacket Cape, 1930's

palatine (păl'ə-tĭn; *pal* a tin). Small shoulder cape or tippet of lace or fur, introduced into France in 1676 by the Princess Palatine.

17th Century Palatine

pelerine (pĕl-ẽr-ēn'; pel er *een*). Tippet or cape, usually waist-length in back, with long, pointed ends in front. Popular in England and colonial America.

19th Century Pelerine

scarf c. Long or short formal cape draped across the back and over the arms. Often worn on the stage by actresses.
talma (tăl'mə; *tal* ma). Long cape or cloak, sometimes hooded, worn in early 19th century. Named for Talma, the French tragedian. Later in 19th century, shorter shoulder capes also called talmas.
tippet. Scarf-like cape of fur or cloth, fastened around neck and hanging down in front.
visite (F. vē-zēt; vee zeet). Light-weight cape or short cloak worn by women in 19th century.
cape coat. Coat with cape attached. See COATS.
cape collar. Short cape. See BERTHA under COLLARS.
cape dress. Dress and cape ensemble. The two garments may or may not be attached, but harmonize in fabric and color. See DRESSES.
capeline (kăp'ə-lĭn or F. kăp-lĕn; *cap* e lin or cap leen). 1. Soft-brimmed hat.

See HATS. 2. Metal head-piece like small skull-cap. Worn by soldiers during Middle Ages. French word meaning hood.
cape net. Stiff cotton net. Same as RICE NET. See NETS.
capeskin. Firm, washable leather. See LEATHERS.
cape sleeve. Loose sleeve of cape-like outline. See SLEEVES.
capitonné (F. kȧ-pē-tôn-nā; ca pee ton nay). Stuffed or padded.
capitonné embroidery. Decorative tufting similar to that used on furniture, but adapted and modernized for use on hats, yokes, panels of dresses, etc., giving quilted appearance. Not really embroidery.
cap of maintenance (măn'tə-nəns; *main* te nance). Cap used as symbol of high rank. See CAPS.
capote (F. kȧ-pōt; ca pote). 1. Hooded cloak. See WRAPS. 2. Mid-Victorian bonnet. See BONNETS.
cappa. Cope or cape worn as part of ecclesiastical or academic apparel.
cappadine (kăp'ə-dĭn or kăp'ə-dēn; *cap* a din or *cap* a deen). Silk floss or waste. See SILK.
cappa magna (kăp'ə măg'nə; *cap* a *mag* na). Ceremonial robe with ermine or silk hood and long, flowing train. Worn by cardinals, bishops, etc.
Capri (kȧ'prē; *cah* pree). Bluish-green color.
Capri blue. Deep, sea-blue color, recalling blue tones seen in Blue Grotto cave of Island of Capri.
capriole (kăp'rĭ-ōl; *cap* ree ole). Formerly, woman's high headdress.
cap sleeve. Sleeve just covering the shoulder. See SLEEVES.
capuce (F. kȧ-püs; ca puce) or **capuchon** (F. kȧ-pü-shôn; ca pu shonh). French word for Franciscan monk's hood or cowl.
capuche (kə-pōōsh' or kə-pōōch'; ca *poosh* or ca *pooch*). Cowl-like hood. See HOODS.
capucine (kăp'ū-sĭn or F. kȧ-pü-sēn; *cap* you sin or ca pu seen). 1. Canary yellow color. 2. Cloak with hood. Also spelled *capuchin*.
capulet (kăp'ū-lĕt or F. kȧ-pü-lā; *cap* you let or ca pu lay). French hood. See HOODS.
caputium (kȧ-pū'shĭ-ŭm; ca *pew* shi um). Hood or hooded cloak. See HOODS.
caracal (kăr'ȧ-kăl; *ca* ra cal). Lynx fur from Asia or Africa. See FURS.
caracul (kăr'ȧ-kŭl; *ca* ra cull). Lambskins obtained chiefly from Russia and north China. See FURS.
caracul cloth. Heavy woolen fabric resembling Persian lamb. Used for women's and children's coats, capes, muffs, stoles.
caramel (kăr'ə-məl; *ca* ra mel). Reddish-yellow or bright tan color.
carat (kăr'ət; *ca* rat). Unit of weight for precious stones, equal to approximately 200 milligrams.
carbuncle (kär'bŭng-kl; *car* bung kl). Cabochon-cut garnet. Formerly, any of several semi-precious stones.

---
fāte, făt, dȧnce, ärt mē, mĕt, hẽr, thêre rīde, rĭd nōte, nŏt, côrn, fōōd, fŏŏt cūte, cŭt, cûré now fin(g)ger villa(ə) señor pleas(zh)ure

carcanet (kär′kə-nĕt; *car* ca net). 1. Ornamental necklace or collar. See NECKLACES. 2. Similar circlet for the hair.
carded silk. Waste silk. See SILK.
cardigan (kär′dĭ-gən; *car* di gan). Semi-close-fitting jacket having a front closing. See JACKETS.
cardigan bodice. Close-fitting, short cardigan. See BODICES.
cardigan sweater. Collarless sweater with front closing. See SWEATERS.
cardinal. Short, hooded cloak. See WRAPS.
cardinal cloth. Red woolen fabric used for robes of certain ecclesiastics.
cardinal red. Bright, rich yellowish red; so called from color of vestments worn by cardinals.
cardinal's hat. Red, brimmed, ecclesiastical hat. See HATS.
carding. 1. Preparing wool, flax, or cotton yarn for spinning by separating and partly straightening fibers, usually on a machine; formerly done by hand, working fibers between two stiff brushes. 2. Roll of wool or other yarn as it comes from carding boards or machine.
carding wool. Same as CLOTHING WOOL. See WOOL.
card strip. Waste cotton left after carding process.
carecloth. Square cloth formerly held over heads of bride and groom during marriage ceremony.
carmagnole (F. kär-mȧ-nyōl; car ma nyole). Jacket, as worn by French Revolutionists. See JACKETS. Also entire costume, including wide black pantaloons, bright-colored waistcoat, high red cap, etc.
carmine (kär′mĭn; *car* min). Rich, intense crimson or scarlet color with purplish cast.
carnation (kär-nā′shŭn; *car nay* shun). Any of various colors of the flower, ranging from light pink to deep red. Old name for flesh color.
carnelian (kär-nēl′yən; *car neel* yan). 1. Variety of chalcedony, from flesh to deep, dull red in color. Used as semi-precious stone in jewelry and for decorating accessories. 2. Flesh-red color.
carnival or **carnaval.** Type of reticella lace. See LACES.
carnival collar. Collar of printed fabric, having deep loops arranged like those on collar of clown's costume. See COLLARS.
caroline (kăr′ō-līn; *ca* ro line). Stovepipe hat. See HATS.
carpetbag. Portable bag with top handle, formerly carried by travelers. So called because first made of carpet material.
carpet slipper. Plain, loose slipper of carpet material. See SLIPPERS.
carpet thread. Strong, durable thread, usually waxed. See THREADS.
carpet or **blanket wool.** Same as MISCELLANEOUS WOOL. See WOOL.
carre (F. kȧr; car). French word meaning breadth or thickness; crown of a hat; shape of a person's back and shoulders.
carreau (F. kȧ-rō; ca ro). French word for check, square, or squared design.

carriage boot. Protective outer boot for women. See BOOTS.
Carrick (kăr′ĭk; *ca* rick). Mantle worn during 1860's. See WRAPS.
Carrickmacross lace (kăr-ĭk-mə-krŏs′; ca rick ma *cross*). Irish needle-point of appliqué or guipure types. See LACES.
carrot color. Red-yellow; color of the carrot.
carry-all. Bag or case holding miscellaneous articles one wishes to carry.
cartisane (kär′tĭ-zăn; *car* ti zane). Strip of parchment wound with silk or metal thread. Formerly used in laces and embroidery to give raised effect.
cartridge plait. Round plait shaped as if to hold a cartridge. See PLAITS.
cartwheel. Hat with large, even brim. See HATS.
casaque (F. kȧ-zȧk; ca zack). 1. Woman's long, mantle-like garment or cassock, usually with large sleeves. 2. Shorter blouse-like garment. See BLOUSES. 3. Also, jockey's jacket. See JACKETS.
casaquin (F. kȧ-zȧ-kăɴ; ca za canh). Woman's blouse, usually fitted, or similar short garment. See BLOUSES.
cascade (kăs-kād′; cass *cade*). Lace or other trimming arranged to fall vertically from neckline or other part of garment in zigzag line.

19th Century
Cascade

casement cloth. Variety of sheer drapery fabrics of silk, cotton, rayon, mohair, or mixture; in any of several weaves and in light, solid, neutral colors. Used for window-length curtains.
Casentino (cá-zĕn-tē′nō; ca zen *tee* no). Coachmen's overcoat of red, lined with green. Worn in the Casentino section of Italy. Adapted for sports wear. See COATS.
casha (kăsh′ə; *cash* a). Soft woolen fabric, similar to flannel, having mixture of Cashmere goat's hair. Used for dresses, blouses, coats.
cashmere (kăsh′mēr; *cash* meer). 1. Fine, soft, formerly costly dress fabric, usually in twill weave. Originally made of yarn handspun from wool of Cashmere goats; now, from soft, native wools. Used for dresses, infants' coats. 2. Soft, fine wool. See WOOL. 3. Article made of cashmere wool, especially shawl as made in India.
cashmere work. Indian embroidery done on cashmere, often with inlaid appliqué. See EMBROIDERIES.
casque (F. kȧsk; cask). Helmet-shaped hat. See HATS.
casquet (kăs′kĕt or F. kȧs-kā; *cass* ket or cas kay). Obsolete term for CASQUE.
casquetel (kăs-kə-tĕl′; cass ke *tell*). Small, light-weight, open helmet having no visor. Worn in ancient armor.

casquette (F. kȧs-kĕt; cass ket). Brimless hat with visor. See HATS.
cassimere (kăs′ĭ-mēr; *cass* i mere). Medium-weight woolen suiting cloth in twill weave, without nap; softer than worsted.
cassinette (kăs-ĭ-nĕt′; cass i *net*). Cloth having warp of cotton, filling of wool or wool mixture.
cassock (kăs′ək; *cass* ock). 1. Ecclesiastical garment of various types: long, close-fitting type worn under surplice and other vestments; shorter, more jacket-like type worn under Geneva gown; apron-like type also known as *skirt cassock.* 2. Long, loose, medieval coat or gown. Worn by both sexes. 3. During 16th century, coat used by foot soldiers. See COATS.

Ecclesiastical Cassock

cast. See COLOR.
Castilian red (kăs-tĭl′yən; cass *till* yan). Brilliant, intense red with yellow cast.
cast off. In knitting, to finish off stitches at end of piece.
castoffs. Discarded clothing.
cast on. In knitting, to put yarn on needle to form beginning stitches.
castor. 1. Light, grayish-brown shade with yellow cast. 2. Beaver hat. See HATS. 3. Heavy, all-wool fabric, similar to broadcloth, but lighter in weight. Used for coats. 4. Soft leather. See LEATHERS.
castor gray. Yellow-green color.
casual. Designed for easy, informal wear; of sports or semi-sports type; as, a casual coat.
Catalin. Trade name for hard, colored, synthetic material. Said to be unbreakable, non-inflammable, and alcohol-, acid-, germ-proof. Used for personal and household accessories.
catalowne (kăt-ə-lōn′; cat a *lone*) or **cataloon** (kăt-ə-lōōn′; cat a *loon*). Woolen fabric. Same as BUFFIN.
catch-stitch. Large, easy cross-stitch. See STITCHES.
catch-stitched seam. Seam pressed open and caught back with catch-stitches. See SEAMS.
catenary (kăt′ĭ-nĕ-rĭ; *cat* e nare i). 1. Shape taken by length of perfectly flexible, fine cord or chain hanging freely between two points of support. 2. Line of cordage on or in fabric in such curve.
catercap (kā′tēr-kăp; *kay* ter cap). Square academic cap. Same as MORTARBOARD. See CAPS.

catgut (kăt'gŭt; *cat* gut). Tough cord made from prepared intestine of certain animals, usually sheep. Used for stringing snowshoe frames, musical instruments, etc.
catskin. Silk hat of inferior quality. See HATS.
catstitch. Same as CATCH-STITCH. See STITCHES.
caubeen (kô-bēn'; caw *been*). Shabby hat. See HATS.
caul (kôl; cawl). 1. Network at back of woman's hat or cap. 2. Network formerly worn to confine hair over head or at back. 3. Net foundation for wig.
caushets. Obsolete term for corsets.
cavalier (kăv-ə-lēr'; cav a *leer*). Characteristic of Vandyke period of dress (1630-40) with its satin doublet and breeches; falling bands; wide lace collars; long, full, slashed sleeves with lace cuffs; broad, generously plumed hats. Term used chiefly of men's apparel, but also of details adapted for women. Also called *Vandyke*.
cavalier boot. 1. High boot with flaring top. See BOOTS. 2. Man's house slipper. See SLIPPERS.
cavalier hat. Large, heavily plumed hat. See HATS.
caxon (kăk'sən; *cax* on). Obsolete term for wig. See WIGS.
ceinture (F. săŋ-tūr; sanh toor). French word for girdle, sash, or belt.
Celanese (sĕl-ən-ēz'; sell a *neez*). 1. Trade name for rayon fiber or fabric made by a firm using the acetate process. See RAYON. 2. Name of a company manufacturing Celanese fabrics. 3. (Not capitalized) Term generally used in U.S.A. to mean acetate rayon.
celeste (sə-lĕst'; se *lest*). French word meaning celestial, heavenly. See SKY BLUE.
Cellophane (sĕl'ō-fān; *sell* o fane). Trade name for thin, transparent, gelatinous composition, tough and waterproof, made in many colors. Used as protective envelope or covering for merchandise, as wrapping paper, for garments; woven into straw-like material for millinery; also used in manufacture of many novelties and novelty fabrics.
Celluloid (sĕl'ū-loid; *sell* you loid). Trade name for hard, transparent, synthetic substance, variously colored to resemble tortoise shell, amber, etc. Used for some notions, toilet articles, novelties, etc.
cellulose (sĕl'ū-lōs; *sell* you loce). Cellulose may be defined as "a compound of carbon, hydrogen, and oxygen, which forms the principal constituent of the cell walls throughout the entire vegetable kingdom." In nature it always occurs in intimate mixture with other substances, which must be removed by suitable processes before the cellulose is useful as a natural fiber (such as cotton, flax, jute, hemp) or as a raw material for the man-made fibers.
cellulose acetate rayon. One of the three types of rayon now manufactured commercially in the U.S.A. Commonly called *acetate rayon*. See RAYON.
center color. Exact center of a color, from which shades, tones, tints are graduated. See COLOR.

cento (sĕn'tō; *sen* toe). Obsolete term for patchwork; also, garment made of patches.
cerevis (sĕr'ə-vĭs; *sare* e viss). Small, pillbox type of student's cap. See CAPS.
cerise (sĕ-rēs'; se *reece*). Bluish-red color, bluer than claret, much bluer than cherry.
cerulean (sĕ-rōō'lĭ-ən; se *roo* li an). Of the color AZURE or clear SKY BLUE.
cervelière (F. sĕr-və-lyĕr; sare ve lyare). Close-fitting steel cap for wear under a helmet. See CAPS.
cestus (sĕs'tŭs; *sess* tus). Girdle, particularly in Greek and Roman mythology. As worn by women of ancient Greece, either narrow cord concealed by chiton, or elaborate belt fastened at waist and hanging down the front.
chain-bag. Same as MESH BAG. See HANDBAGS.
chainette (chān-ĕt'; chain *ett*). Fine, light-weight chain that hangs suspended from both ends.
chain mail. Flexible armor of interlocked metal rings or links.
chain-stitch. 1. Connecting loopstitches made with one thread, resembling links in a chain. 2. Simple loopstitch used in crochet. See STITCHES.
chalcedony (kăl-sĕd'ə-nĭ; cal *sed* o ni). Variety of quartz with wax-like luster, usually pale blue or gray in color. In special colors, known as carnelian, agate, onyx, chrysoprase, etc. Used as ornaments or accessories.
chaldera (Sp. kăl-dā'rä; cahl *day* rah). Old-copper color. See CALDRON. Spanish word for copper kettle.
chalk stripe. White stripe. See STRIPES.
challis or **challie** (shăl'ĭ; *shall* i). Soft, light-weight, plain-woven fabric without gloss, either plain or printed, sometimes figured. Made of fine wool or wool mixture, one of the softest cloths made of wool, or of cotton and rayon. Used for dresses, negligees, sleeping garments. Dates from 18th century. Originally, usually figured in delicate floral pattern.
chalwar (shŭl'wĕr; *shull* wer). Full, ankle-length trousers or wide pantaloons. Worn by Turks. Same as SHALWAR.
chamarre (F. shä-mär'; sha mar). French word meaning lace or embroidery.
chambray (shăm'brā; *sham* bray). Gingham of fine quality, having colored warp, white filling. See GINGHAMS.
chamlet. Early spelling of CAMLET.
chamois (shăm'ĭ; *sham* i). 1. Soft, pliable leather. See LEATHERS. 2. Pale buff or yellow tan color.
Chamoisette (shăm-ĭ-zĕt'; sham i *zet*). Trade name for closely woven cotton fabric, slightly napped by means of emery; used for gloves. Also, glove made of this fabric.
champagne (shăm-pān'; sham *pain*). Light, pale golden shade, the color of the sparkling wine.
champlevé (F. shäŋ-lə-vā; shonh le vay). Inlaid in depressions cut out in the ground. Used of enamel work.
changeable taffeta. Taffeta with warp of one color and woof of another, or

each of several colors, giving different effect in different lights. See TAFFETAS.
Chantilly lace (F. shäŋ-tē-yē; shonh tee yee). Bobbin lace with fine ground and exquisitely outlined pattern. One of the loveliest of all dress laces. See LACES.
chaparajos (Sp. chä-pä-rä'hōs; chah pa *rah* hoce) or **chaparejos** (Sp. chä-pä-rā'hōs; chah pa *ray* hoce). Strong, leather breeches or overalls, usually open at back. Worn by cowboys as protection against brush and thorns. Commonly called *chaps*.
chape. Catch or piece by which a buckle is held to the strap.
chapeau (F. shà-pō; sha po). French word meaning hat.
chapeau à plumes (F. à plüm; a ploom). French phrase meaning hat with plumes.
chapeau bras (F. brä; brah). Small, three-cornered hat. See HATS.
chapel de fer (F. shà-pĕl də fĕr; sha pel de fare). Skull-cap of metal. See CAPS.
chapellerie (F. shà-pĕl-rē; sha pell ree). Hat-making; also used, collectively, of man-tailored hats.
chaperon (shăp'ĕr-ōn; *shap* er ohn). 1. Ancient hood covering head and neck to shoulders. See HOODS. 2. Person accompanying young unmarried woman in public for sake of propriety; usually, older and married.
chaplet (chăp'lĕt; *chap* let). 1. Wreath or garland, usually of flowers, as worn on head. 2. String of beads or similar necklace. See NECKLACES.
chaqueta (chä-kā'tä; cha *kay* ta). Jacket worn by cowboys. See JACKETS.
Charlotte Corday cap (shär'lŏt kôr'dā; shar lot kor day). Soft cap with mushroom crown. See CAPS.
charm. 1. Grace of manner, attractiveness of personality; also, to attract irresistibly. 2. Small ornament or amulet on bracelet, watch-guard, etc.; worn to avert evil or bring good fortune or merely as decoration.
charm bracelet. Bracelet having pendant charms attached. See BRACELETS.
Charmeen (shär-mēn'; shar *meen*). Trade name for fine worsted dress fabric having definite twill.
Charmeuse (F. shär-mēz; shar muz). Trade name for soft, light-weight fabric in satin weave with twilled back, having subdued luster due to spun silk filling. Used for draped dresses, especially for formal gowns.
charm string. Ornamental necklace made of fashionable kinds of buttons strung together. See NECKLACES.
chartreuse (F. shär-trēz; shar truz). Pale yellowish-green shade, color of the liqueur.
chase. 1. To ornament, as a metal surface, by cutting out parts, embossing, etc.; also, a groove or hollow cut out. 2. To set with gems.
chassis (shăs'ē; *shass* ee). Body of an automobile. Term adopted colloquially to mean a woman's figure or the silhouette of a dress.
chasuble (chăz'ə-bl; *chas* a bl). Sleeveless mantle, varying in color. Worn by priests over alb and stole as Mass vestment.

carcanet (kär′kȧ-nĕt; *car* ca net). **1.** Ornamental necklace or collar. See NECKLACES. **2.** Similar circlet for the hair.
carded silk. Waste silk. See SILK.
cardigan (kär′dĭ-gȧn; *car* di gan). Semi-close-fitting jacket having a front closing. See JACKETS.
cardigan bodice. Close-fitting, short cardigan. See BODICES.
cardigan sweater. Collarless sweater with front closing. See SWEATERS.
cardinal. Short, hooded cloak. See WRAPS.
cardinal cloth. Red woolen fabric used for robes of certain ecclesiastics.
cardinal red. Bright, rich yellowish red; so called from color of vestments worn by cardinals.
cardinal's hat. Red, brimmed, ecclesiastical hat. See HATS.
carding. 1. Preparing wool, flax, or cotton yarn for spinning by separating and partly straightening fibers, usually on a machine; formerly done by hand, working fibers between two stiff brushes. **2.** Roll of wool or other yarn as it comes from carding boards or machine.
carding wool. Same as CLOTHING WOOL. See WOOL.
card strip. Waste cotton left after carding process.
carecloth. Square cloth formerly held over heads of bride and groom during marriage ceremony.
carmagnole (F. kär-mȧ-nyōl; car ma nyole). Jacket, as worn by French Revolutionists. See JACKETS. Also entire costume, including wide black pantaloons, bright-colored waistcoat, high red cap, etc.
carmine (kär′mĭn; *car* min). Rich, intense crimson or scarlet color with purplish cast.
carnation (kär-nā′shŭn; car *nay* shun). Any of various colors of the flower, ranging from light pink to deep red. Old name for flesh color.
carnelian (kär-nēl′yȧn; car *neel* yan). **1.** Variety of chalcedony, from flesh to deep, dull red in color. Used as semi-precious stone in jewelry and for decorating accessories. **2.** Flesh-red color.
carnival or **carnaval.** Type of reticella lace. See LACES.
carnival collar. Collar of printed fabric, having deep loops arranged like those on collar of clown's costume. See COLLARS.
caroline (kăr′o-lĭn; *ca ro* line). Stovepipe hat. See HATS.
carpetbag. Portable bag with top handle, formerly carried by travelers. So called because first made of carpet material.
carpet slipper. Plain, loose slipper of carpet material. See SLIPPERS.
carpet thread. Strong, durable thread, usually waxed. See THREADS.
carpet or **blanket wool.** Same as MISCELLANEOUS WOOL. See WOOL.
carre (F. kȧr; car). French word meaning breadth or thickness; crown of a hat; shape of a person's back and shoulders.
carreau (F. kȧ-rō; ca ro). French word for check, square, or squared design.

carriage boot. Protective outer boot for women. See BOOTS.
Carrick (kăr′ĭk; *ca* rick). Mantle worn during 1860's. See WRAPS.
Carrickmacross lace (kăr-ĭk-mȧ-krŏs′; ca rick ma *cross*). Irish needle-point of appliqué or guipure types. See LACES.
carrot color. Red-yellow; color of the carrot.
carry-all. Bag or case holding miscellaneous articles one wishes to carry.
cartisane (kär′tĭ-zăn; *car* ti zane). Strip of parchment wound with silk or metal thread. Formerly used in laces and embroidery to give raised effect.
cartridge plait. Round plait shaped as if to hold a cartridge. See PLAITS.
cartwheel. Hat with large, even brim. See HATS.
casaque (F. kȧ-zȧk; ca zack). **1.** Woman's long, mantle-like garment or cassock, usually with large sleeves. **2.** Shorter blouse-like garment. See BLOUSES. **3.** Also, jockey's jacket. See JACKETS.
casaquin (F. kȧ-zȧ-kăṇ; ca za canh). Woman's blouse, usually fitted, or similar short garment. See BLOUSES.
cascade (kăs-kād′; cass *cade*). Lace or other trimming arranged to fall vertically from neckline or other part of garment in zigzag line.

19th Century Cascade

casement cloth. Variety of sheer drapery fabrics of silk, cotton, rayon, mohair, or mixture; in any of several weaves and in light, solid, neutral colors. Used for window-length curtains.
Casentino (cȧ-zĕn-tē′nō; ca zen *tee* no). Coachmen's overcoat of red, lined with green. Worn in the Casentino section of Italy. Adapted for sports wear. See COATS.
casha (kăsh′ȧ; *cash* a). Soft woolen fabric, similar to flannel, having mixture of Cashmere goat's hair. Used for dresses, blouses, coats.
cashmere (kăsh′mēr; *cash* meer). **1.** Fine, soft, formerly costly dress fabric, usually in twill weave. Originally made of yarn handspun from wool of Cashmere goats; now, from soft, native wools. Used for dresses, infants' coats. **2.** Soft, fine wool. See WOOL. **3.** Article made of cashmere wool, especially shawl as made in India.
cashmere work. Indian embroidery done on cashmere, often with inlaid appliqué. See EMBROIDERIES.
casque (F. kȧsk; cask). Helmet-shaped hat. See HATS.
casquet (kȧs′kĕt or F. kȧs-kā; *cass* ket or cas kay). Obsolete term for CASQUE.
casquetel (kăs-kȧ-tĕl′; cass ke *tel*). Small, light-weight, open helmet having no visor. Worn in ancient armor.

casquette (F. kȧs-kĕt; cass ket). Brimless hat with visor. See HATS.
cassimere (kăs′ĭ-mēr; *cass* i mere). Medium-weight woolen suiting cloth in twill weave, without nap; softer than worsted.
cassinette (kăs-ĭ-nĕt′; cass i *net*). Cloth having warp of cotton, filling of wool or wool mixture.
cassock (kăs′ȧk; *cass* ock). **1.** Ecclesiastical garment of various types: long, close-fitting type worn under surplice and other vestments; shorter, more jacket-like type worn under Geneva gown; apron-like type also known as *skirt cassock.* **2.** Long, loose, medieval coat or gown. Worn by both sexes. **3.** During 16th century, coat used by foot soldiers. See COATS.

Ecclesiastical Cassock

cast. See COLOR.
Castilian red (kăs-tĭl′yȧn; cass *till* yan). Brilliant, intense red with yellow cast.
cast off. In knitting, to finish off stitches at end of piece.
castoffs. Discarded clothing.
cast on. In knitting, to put yarn on needle to form beginning stitches.
castor. 1. Light, grayish-brown shade with yellow cast. **2.** Beaver hat. See HATS. **3.** Heavy, all-wool fabric, similar to broadcloth, but lighter in weight. Used for coats. **4.** Soft leather. See LEATHERS.
castor gray. Yellow-green color.
casual. Designed for easy, informal wear; of sports or semi-sports type; as, a casual coat.
Catalin. Trade name for hard, colored, synthetic material. Said to be unbreakable, non-inflammable, and alcohol-, acid-, germ-proof. Used for personal and household accessories.
catalowne (kăt-ȧ-lōn′; cat a *lone*) or **cataloon** (kăt-ȧ-lōōn′; cat a *loon*). Woolen fabric. Same as BUFFIN.
catch-stitch. Large, easy cross-stitch. See STITCHES.
catch-stitched seam. Seam pressed open and caught back with catch-stitches. See SEAMS.
catenary (kăt′ĭ-nĕ-rĭ; *cat* e nare i). **1.** Shape taken by length of perfectly flexible, fine cord or chain hanging freely between two points of support. **2.** Line of cordage on or in fabric in such curve.
catercap (kā′tẽr-kăp; *kay* ter cap). Square academic cap. Same as MORTARBOARD. See CAPS.

catgut (kăt'gŭt; *cat* gut). Tough cord made from prepared intestine of certain animals, usually sheep. Used for stringing snowshoe frames, musical instruments, etc.

catskin. Silk hat of inferior quality. See HATS.

catstitch. Same as CATCH-STITCH. See STITCHES.

caubeen (kô-bēn'; *caw been*). Shabby hat. See HATS.

caul (kôl; cawl). 1. Network at back of woman's hat or cap. 2. Network formerly worn to confine hair over head or at back. 3. Net foundation for wig.

caushets. Obsolete term for corsets.

cavalier (kăv-ə-lēr'; cav a *leer*). Characteristic of Vandyke period of dress (1630-40) with its satin doublet and breeches; falling bands; wide lace collars; long, full, slashed sleeves with lace cuffs; broad, generously plumed hats. Term used chiefly of men's apparel, but also of details adapted for women. Also called *Vandyke*.

cavalier boot. 1. High boot with flaring top. See BOOTS. 2. Man's house slipper. See SLIPPERS.

cavalier hat. Large, heavily plumed hat. See HATS.

caxon (kăk'sən; *cax* on). Obsolete term for wig. See WIGS.

ceinture (F. săṇ-tūr; sanh toor). French word for girdle, sash, or belt.

Celanese (sĕl-ən-ēz'; sell a *neez*). 1. Trade name for rayon fiber or fabric made by a firm using the acetate process. See RAYON. 2. Name of a company manufacturing Celanese fabrics. 3. (Not capitalized) Term generally used in U.S.A. to mean acetate rayon.

celeste (sə-lĕst'; se*lest*). French word meaning celestial, heavenly. See SKY BLUE.

Cellophane (sĕl'ō-fān; *sell* o fane). Trade name for thin, transparent, gelatinous composition, tough and waterproof, made in many colors. Used as protective envelope or covering for merchandise, as wrapping paper, for garments; woven into straw-like material for millinery; also used in manufacture of many novelties and novelty fabrics.

Celluloid (sĕl'ū-loid; *sell* you loid). Trade name for hard, transparent, synthetic substance, variously colored to resemble tortoise shell, amber, etc. Used for some notions, toilet articles, novelties, etc.

cellulose (sĕl'ū-lōs; *sell* you loce). Cellulose may be defined as "a compound of carbon, hydrogen, and oxygen, which forms the principal constituent of the cell walls throughout the entire vegetable kingdom." In nature it always occurs in intimate mixture with other substances, which must be removed by suitable processes before the cellulose is useful as a natural fiber (such as cotton, flax, jute, hemp) or as a raw material for the man-made fibers.

cellulose acetate rayon. One of the three types of rayon now manufactured commercially in the U.S.A. Commonly called *acetate rayon.* See RAYON.

center color. Exact center of a color, from which shades, tones, tints are graduated. See COLOR.

cento (sĕn'tō; *sen* toe). Obsolete term for patchwork; also, garment made of patches.

cerevis (sĕr'ə-vĭs; *sare* e viss). Small, pillbox type of student's cap. See CAPS.

cerise (sē-rēs'; se *reece*). Bluish-red color, bluer than claret, much bluer than cherry.

cerulean (sē-rōō'lĭ-ən; se *roo* li an). Of the color AZURE or clear SKY BLUE.

cervelière (F. sĕr-və-lyêr; sare ve lyare). Close-fitting steel cap for wear under a helmet. See CAPS.

cestus (sĕs'tŭs; *sess* tus). Girdle, particularly in Greek and Roman mythology. As worn by women of ancient Greece, either narrow cord concealed by chiton, or elaborate belt fastened at waist and hanging down the front.

chain-bag. Same as MESH BAG. See HANDBAGS.

chainette (chān-ĕt'; chain *ett*). Fine, light-weight chain that hangs suspended from both ends.

chain mail. Flexible armor of interlocked metal rings or links.

chain-stitch. 1. Connecting loop-stitches made with one thread, resembling links in a chain. 2. Simple loop-stitch used in crochet. See STITCHES.

chalcedony (kăl-sĕd'ə-nĭ; cal *sed* o ni). Variety of quartz with wax-like luster, usually pale blue or gray in color. In special colors, known as carnelian, agate, onyx, chrysoprase, etc. Used as ornaments or accessories.

chaldera (Sp. käl-dä'rä; cahl *day* rah). Old-copper color. See CALDRON. Spanish word for copper kettle.

chalk stripe. White stripe. See STRIPES.

challis or **challie** (shăl'ĭ; *shall* i). Soft, light-weight, plain-woven fabric without gloss, either plain or printed, sometimes figured. Made of fine wool or wool mixture, one of the softest cloths made of wool, or of cotton and rayon. Used for dresses, negligees, sleeping garments. Dates from 18th century. Originally, usually figured in delicate floral pattern.

chalwar (shŭl'wĕr; *shull* wer). Full, ankle-length trousers or wide pantaloons. Worn by Turks. Same as SHALWAR.

chamarre (F. shȧ-mȧr; sha mar). French word meaning lace or embroidery.

chambray (shăm'brā; *sham* bray). Gingham of fine quality, having colored warp, white filling. See GINGHAMS.

chamlet. Early spelling of CAMLET.

chamois (shăm'ĭ; *sham* i). 1. Soft, pliable leather. See LEATHERS. 2. Pale buff or yellow tan color.

Chamoisette (shăm-ĭ-zĕt'; sham i *zet*). Trade name for closely woven cotton fabric, slightly napped by means of emery; used for gloves. Also, glove made of this fabric.

champagne (shăm-pān'; sham *pain*). Light, pale golden shade, the color of the sparkling wine.

champlevé (F. shäṇ-lə-vā; shonh le vay). Inlaid in depressions cut out in the ground. Used of enamel work.

changeable taffeta. Taffeta with warp of one color and woof of another, or

each of several colors, giving different effect in different lights. See TAFFETAS.

Chantilly lace (F. shäṇ-tē-yē; shonh tee yee). Bobbin lace with fine ground and exquisitely outlined pattern. One of the loveliest of all dress laces. See LACES.

chaparajos (Sp. chä-pä-rä'hōs; chah pa *rah* hoce) or **chaparejos** (Sp. chä-pä-rā'hōs; chah pa *ray* hoce). Strong, leather breeches or overalls, usually open at back. Worn by cowboys as protection against brush and thorns. Commonly called *chaps*.

chape. Catch or piece by which a buckle is held to the strap.

chapeau (F. shȧ-pō; sha po). French word meaning hat.

chapeau à plumes (F. ȧ plüm; a ploom). French phrase meaning hat with plumes.

chapeau bras (F. brȧ; brah). Small, three-cornered hat. See HATS.

chapel de fer (F. shȧ-pĕl də fêr; sha pel de fare). Skull-cap of metal. See CAPS.

chapellerie (F. shȧ-pĕl-rē; sha pell ree). Hat-making; also used, collectively, of man-tailored hats.

chaperon (shăp'ẽr-ŏn; *shap* er ohn). 1. Ancient hood covering head and neck to shoulders. See HOODS. 2. Person accompanying young unmarried woman in public for sake of propriety; usually, older and married.

chaplet (chăp'lĕt; *chap* let). 1. Wreath or garland, usually of flowers, as worn on head. 2. String of beads or similar necklace. See NECKLACES.

chaqueta (chä-kā'tä; cha *kay* ta). Jacket worn by cowboys. See JACKETS.

Charlotte Corday cap (shär'lŏt kôr'dā; *shar* lot *cor* day). Soft cap with mushroom crown. See CAPS.

charm. 1. Grace of manner, attractiveness of personality; also, to attract irresistibly. 2. Small ornament or amulet on bracelet, watch-guard, etc.; worn to avert evil or bring good fortune or merely for decoration.

charm bracelet. Bracelet having pendant charms attached. See BRACELETS.

Charmeen (shär-mēn'; shar *meen*). Trade name for fine worsted dress fabric having definite twill.

Charmeuse (F. shȧr-mēz; shar muz). Trade name for soft, light-weight fabric in satin weave with twilled back, having subdued luster due to spun silk filling. Used for draped dresses, especially for formal gowns.

charm string. Ornamental necklace made of fashionable kinds of buttons strung together. See NECKLACES.

chartreuse (F. shȧr-trēz; shar truz). Pale yellowish-green shade, color of the liqueur.

chase. 1. To ornament, as a metal surface, by cutting out parts, embossing, etc.; also, a groove or hollow cut out. 2. To set with gems.

chassis (shăs'ē; *shass* ee). Body of an automobile. Term adopted colloquially to mean a woman's figure or the silhouette of a dress.

chasuble (chăz'ə-bl; *chas* a bl). Sleeveless mantle, varying in color. Worn by priests over alb and stole as Mass vestment.

fāte, făt, dȧnce, ärt mē, mĕt, hêr, thêre rīde, rĭd nōte, nŏt, côrn, fōōd, fŏŏt cūte, cŭt, cûrl now fin(ŋ)ger villa(ȧ) señor pleas(zh)ure

chatelaine (shăt′ə-lān or F. shȧ-tlĕn; shat e lane or shah tlen). Clasp or chain upon which to hang useful or ornamental articles, such as keys, scissors, watch, etc. Worn at waist by women.
chatelaine bag. Small bag, knitted, beaded, or of leather or fabric, suspended from the belt. Popular about 1900.
chaton (F. shȧ-tôṇ; sha tonh). French word for setting of gem, especially that part of ring in which stone is set; also, stone in a setting.
chatoyant (shă-toi′yənt or F. shȧ-twȧ-yäṇ; sha toy ant or sha twah yonh). Having changeable appearance, as watered silk.
chatta (chă′tə or chă′tä; chat a or chah tah). Word meaning umbrella, as used in India.
chaudron (F. shō-drôṇ; sho dronh). Old-copper color. See CALDRON. French word for copper kettle.
chaussette (F. shō-sĕt; sho set). French word meaning sock, anklet, or understocking.
chausses (shō′sĕz or F. shōs; sho sez or shoce). Tight-fitting breeches, covering hips, legs, and feet. Worn during Middle Ages; often made of linked mail, as part of armor.
chaussure (F. shō-sür; sho soor). French word meaning foot covering of any kind, such as shoe, slipper, boot.
cheap. 1. Tawdry; shabby. 2. A bargain at the price.
chechia (shĕ-shē′ə; she shee a). Cylindrical skull-cap. See CAPS. See HATS.

CHECKS

check. 1. Pattern in squares of any size, woven or applied, resembling checkerboard; also, square in such a design. 2. Fabric having pattern of squares.

Hound's-Tooth Check

broken c. Checked fabric design in which each check is irregular or incomplete rather than square.
glen c. Check design frequently used in tweeds, similar to shepherd's check but in many combinations of color.

Shepherd's Check

gun club c. Check design used frequently in tweeds, consisting of large check over smaller one.
hound's-tooth c. Small, irregular design of broken checks.
overcheck. Pattern of checks in which one color is woven over another.
shepherd's or **shepherd c.** Small, even, black and white check pattern.
cheesecloth. Soft, thin, unsized cotton fabric in plain weave; bleached, unbleached, or dyed. Open weaves called *gauze;* called *bunting* when dyed. Used for fancy dress, experimental draping, curtains, dust cloths, press cloths, etc. Originally used to incase cheese.
chekmak (chĕk′măk; *check* mack). Silk and cotton fabric, from Turkey, interwoven with gold threads.
chemiloon (shĕm′ĭ-lōōn; shem i loon). Woman's undergarment consisting of chemise and drawers in one piece. Word coined from chemise and pantaloon.
chemise (shə-mēz′; shem meez). Loose combination undergarment for women, hanging straight from shoulders, covering torso. Originally, with or without sleeves, worn next to skin; formerly called *shift,* also *smock.*

Brassière Chemise, 1926

chemise dress. Dress hanging straight from shoulders. See DRESSES.
chemise frock. Simple, loose, easy dress. See DRESSES.
chemisette (shĕm-ĭ-zĕt′; shem i zet). Plain or ornamental sleeveless underbodice covering neck, shoulders, and breast; usually made of muslin or lace. Worn by women in late 19th century, generally to fill in neckline of dress. French term for vestee, gilet, etc.
chemisier (F. shə-mē-zyā; sha mee zyay). French word meaning shirtmaker. Often descriptive of details or style of women's blouses.
chenille (shə-nēl′; shen *neel*). French word for caterpillar. 1. Silk, rayon, cotton, wool, or worsted cord having tufted, velvet-like pile protruding all around, similar in appearance to fuzzy caterpillar. Used for filling in cloth; for embroidery, fringes, tassels, etc. 2. Fabric made with filling of this cord. Used for draperies, couch covers, etc.
chenille embroidery. Velvety embroidery of fine chenille. See EMBROIDERIES.
chenille lace. Needle-point with chenille-outlined design. See LACES.
chenille needle. Short, large-eyed needle. See NEEDLES.
chequered chain-stitch. Same as MAGIC CHAIN-STITCH. See STITCHES.
cherry. Bright, clear red shade, color of the ripe fruit.

chesterfield (chĕs′tẽr-fēld; *chess* ter field). Originally, single-breasted, fly-front coat, usually having velvet collar. Now often double-breasted. See COATS.
chestnut. Brown color having yellowish cast.
cheval de frise (F. shə-vălˈ də frēz; she val de freez) or (plural) **chevaux de frise** (F. shə-vōˈ də frēz; she vo de freez). Term applied to crisscross dress trimming with jagged edges, fashionable in 18th century.
chevelure (F. shĕv-lür; shev loor). 1. Hair or head of hair. 2. Obsolete term for wig.
chevener (shĕv′ən-ẽr; shev en er). Person who embroiders clocks and other types of design on hosiery.
cheverel (chĕv′ẽr-ĕl; *chev* er el) or **cheveril** (chĕv′ẽr-ĭl; *chev* er il). Obsolete type of soft, elastic, kidskin leather. Also, elastic, pliant, flexible as the leather.
chevesaile (chĕv′ə-sāl; *chev* e sail). Richly decorated collar. See COLLARS.
cheviot (shĕv′ĭ-ət or chĕv′ĭ-ət; shev i ot or *chev* i ot). 1. Close-napped, rough-surfaced, all-wool fabric in twill weave, similar to serge but heavier and rougher. Originally made from shaggy wool of Cheviot sheep. Used for suits and coats. 2. Stout, moderately heavy fabric in plain weave, made of coarse cotton yarn. Used for shirts, blouses, etc.
chèvre (F. shĕvr; shevr). French word for goatskin, of which handbags are made.
chevreau (F. shĕv-rō; shev ro). French word for kidskin.
chevrette (F. shĕv-rĕt; shev ret). French term for thin kind of goatskin.
chevron (shĕv′rən; shev ron). 1. Type of decoration; strictly, consisting of two or more bars meeting at angle; loosely, V-shaped or zigzag device, as placed on the sleeve or shoulder of garment or used as motif on printed fabric. 2. Obsolete term for glove.
chevron-stitch. Zigzag stitch similar to catch-stitch, but having straight stitch, instead of cross, where diagonal stitches meet. See STITCHES.
chevron weave. Same as BROKEN TWILL WEAVE. See WEAVES.
cheyney (chā′nĭ; *chay* ni). Woolen fabric worn during 17th and 18th centuries. So called for China.
chez (F. shā; shay). French word meaning in or at the home or shop of; as, chez Patou.
chic (F. shēk; sheek). French word meaning originality and style in dress expressed with correct taste.
chicken skin glove. Glove used supposedly to soften and whiten hands. See GLOVES.
chiffon (shĭ-fŏn′ or F. shə-fôṇ; shi *fon* or shee fonh). 1. Soft, delicately sheer fabric in plain weave of silk, rayon, etc., having soft or sometimes stiff finish. Used for dresses, foundations, scarfs, blouses, veils, etc. Often used double. 2. Like chiffon in weave, sheerness, softness, etc.; as, chiffon wool or velvet. 3. Sheer knit fabric, usually silk. Used for hosiery. 4. Any decorative addition to a woman's costume, as a knot of

chiffon batiste

ribbon. French word for rag, scrap, frippery.
chiffon batiste. Finest quality of wool batiste. See BATISTE, 2.
chiffon taffeta. Light-weight taffeta. See TAFFETAS.
chiffon velvet. Light-weight silk velvet. See VELVETS.
chignon (F. shē-nyôṇ; shee nyonh). Knot or twist of hair, natural or artificial, worn at back of head, low or high.

Chignon, 1878

chignon strap. Band, usually of ribbon, looping beneath hair at back, to hold woman's hat in place.
chillo. Cotton fabric in bright colors. Made in India; also made in England for African trade.
chimere (shǐ-mēr′ or chǐ-mēr′; shi *meer* or chi *meer*). Loose, sleeveless, upper robe with large balloon sleeves of lawn. Worn by bishops.
China grass or **straw.** Fibers of ramie plant, stiff and dried. See RAMIE, 1.
China ribbon. Narrow, inexpensive ribbon. See RIBBONS.
China ribbon embroidery. Same as ROCOCO EMBROIDERY. See EMBROIDERIES.
China silk. Thin, transparent, lustrous fabric in plain weave, very light or medium light in weight, of silk or part silk, sometimes colored and figured, with and without stiffening. Used for linings, dress foundations, slips, blouses, infants' wear, box linings, etc. Originally hand-woven of pure silk in China.
China straw. Same as CHINA GRASS.
chin-band or **chin-cloth.** Muffler or band, usually of lace, passing under chin. Worn chiefly to secure headdress, by ladies of 17th century.
chinchilla (chǐn-chǐl′ə; chin *chill* a). 1. Blue-gray fur of chinchilla, the softest, richest, most delicate, and most expensive fur. See FURS. 2. Closely woven double fabric of wool, sometimes part cotton, with both pile and nap, having surface rubbed into tufts or nubs; no longer resembling chinchilla fur. Used for children's heavy coats, trim on coats.
chin collar. Choker collar that flares upward far enough to conceal the chin. See COLLARS.
chiné (F. shē-nā; shee nay). Term used of fabric in which warp threads are dyed, printed, or painted before weaving, producing mottled, variegated effect; manner supposedly Chinese. French word meaning variegated, speckled.
Chinese. 1. Characteristic of Chinese costume. For mandarin, this consisted

of straight coat, fastened at center-front across chest and at underarm; straight, loose sleeves; one or more paneled skirts; rich embroidery in dragon, flower, cloud, wave designs. Ordinary citizens wear shorter coats, trousers for both men and women, slippers. See COOLIE COAT under COATS. See MANDARIN COAT under COATS. 2. As used of color (Chinese red, Chinese blue, etc.), denotes clear, soft depth of tone.
Chinese badger. Long-haired fur of Chinese badger. See FURS.
Chinese embroidery. Satin-stitch embroidery of intricate, often colorful designs. See EMBROIDERIES.
Chinese grass cloth. Same as GRASS CLOTH.
Chinese knot. Compact ornamental knot. See KNOTS.
Chinese mink. Light-yellowish fur of Chinese animal similar to mink. See FURS.
chinoiserie (F. shē-nwä-zrē; shee nwah zree). Chinese motifs, emblems, etc., in decoration; or anything made in style characteristic of Chinese.
chin-piece. Formerly, piece, as of armor, to protect chin. Now a strap to hold hat on.
chin-strap. Strap or band worn under the chin, attached to helmet, cap, hood, or hat. Also, "beauty" strap worn at night, supposedly to prevent double chin.
chintz. Plain-woven fabric sometimes glazed, printed with gay floral pattern in bright colors, often five. Chiefly used for draperies, slip-covers, cushions, etc. Originally, painted or stained calico; mentioned as early as 17th century.
chip. 1. Inexpensive straw. See STRAWS. 2. In jewelry trade, small piece from crystal or diamond, weighing under three fourths of one carat.
chip hat. Hat made of wood or woody chips. See HATS.
chirimen (chǐr′ǐ-měn; *chir* i men). Japanese type of silk crepe. See CREPES.
chiton (kī′tən; *ky* ton). Gown or tunic worn usually next to skin by men and women in ancient Greece. There are

Doric Chiton, 550 B.C.   Ionic Chiton, 600 B.C.

two principal types: (1) Doric, a sleeveless garment of oblong piece of cloth, usually wool, folded over at top to form double covering above waist;

chromo embroidery

pinned at shoulders with ancient brooch. (2) Ionic, a loose gown with sleeves, usually of linen, sewed rather than pinned. Women's gowns longer than those of men. Some fashion writers use the word "chiton" as a synonym for "chemise."
chitterling (chǐt′ēr-lǐng; *chit* er ling). Ruff or frill having compact wrinkled folds resembling crinkled crepe paper; especially frill down front of bodice.
chivarras (chǐ-vär′räs; chi *var* rahss) or **chivarros** (chǐ-vär′rōs; chi *var* roce). Colloquial term in Mexico and southwestern U.S. for leggings.
chiveret (chǐv′ēr-ět; *chiv* er et). Woolen fabric popular in 17th and 18th centuries.
chlamys (klǎ′mǐs; *clam* iss). Short, loose mantle. See WRAPS.
chocolate (chŏk′ə-lət; *chock* o let). Dark color with reddish-brown cast, color of cocoa bean.
choga (chō′gə; *cho* ga). Long-sleeved cloak worn in India. See WRAPS.
choke. Slang term for neckcloth or choker.
choker (chōk′ēr; *choke* er). Something worn closely around neck. 1. Short necklace or jeweled collar. See NECKLACES. 2. Narrow fur piece. 3. Unusually high collar. See COLLARS. 4. High, stiff neckcloth or stock, as formerly worn.
choli or **cholee** (chō′lē; *cho* lee). Short-sleeved bodice or short blouse. See BLOUSES.
chopine (shō-pēn′ or chŏp′ǐn; sho *peen* or *chop* in). 1. Clog or high lift worn under shoe, originally worn in Turkey to increase appearance of height. In 18th century revived by Mme. de Pompadour. 2. Clog combined with shoe, usually in sandal form. See SHOES.
chou (F. shoo; shoo). Soft cabbage-shaped rosette or knot of velvet, satin, ribbon, lace, etc. Used decoratively in woman's dress. French word for cabbage.
chou hat (F. shoo; shoo). Hat with soft, crushed crown. See HATS.
chouquette (shoo-kět′; shoo *ket*). Straw hat. See HATS.
chrisom (krǐz′əm; *cris* om). 1. White baptismal robe, mantle, or cloth. Used for infants as symbol of innocence. 2. Priest's alb or surplice.
chroma (krō′mə; *cro* ma). 1. Color, such as red or blue or green, as distinguished from black, gray, white. 2. Purity of color; color quality of being free from grayness. Often called *purity, intensity*, or *saturation*. See COLOR.
chromatic (krō-mǎt′ǐk; cro *mat* ic). 1. Of or pertaining to color; consisting of color; made in color. 2. Full of color; highly colored.
chromatic circle. Hues graduated in natural sequence around a circle.
chromatic color. Color having clear hue. See COLOR.
chrome leather. Leather tanned by a mineral process. See LEATHERS.
chromo embroidery. Embroidery done over colored paper pattern. See EMBROIDERIES.

fāte, făt, dănce, ärt mē, mĕt, hēr, thēre rīde, rĭd nōte, nŏt, côrn, foōd, foŏt cūte, cŭt, cūré now fin(ṇ)ger villa(ə) señor pleas(zh)ure

huddar (chŭd′ăr; *chud* ar). Hindu shawl. See WRAPS.
hukker shirt. Polo shirt, with short sleeves and open neck. See SHIRTS.
hunari (choon′ə-rē; *choon* a ree) or **chundari** (choon′də-rē; *choon* da ree). Fabric, usually of cotton or silk, figured with tied-and-dyed designs. Used for various parts of costume in India.
hurch embroidery. 1. Elaborate ancient work for church use. 2. Same as GIMPED EMBROIDERY. See EMBROIDERIES.
icisbeo (sĭ-sĭs′bĕ-ō or It. chĕ-chēz-bä′ō; si *sis* be o or chee cheez *bay* o). Bow or knot, usually of ribbon, as formerly worn on cane, fan, etc.
iel or **ciel blue** (F. syĕl; syell). Sky-blue color. From French word for sky, or heaven.
cilice (sĭl′ĭs; *sill* iss). Rough, shirt-like undergarment made of haircloth. Formerly worn by monks doing penance. Also, coarse haircloth, usually of goat's hair.
cimier (F. sē-myä; see myay). Ornament at top, forming crest, of medieval helmet; also, helmet having ornamental crest.
cincture (sĭnk′tŭr; *sink* ture). 1. Girdle, belt, sash, etc., especially as worn on ecclesiastical alb or cassock. 2. Anything that encircles, as bracelet, ring, etc.
cingle (sĭng′gl; *sing* gl). Girdle, sash, belt.
cinnamon (sĭn′ə-mŭn; *sin* a mon). Grayed brown color, slightly reddish.
circassian (sēr-kăsh′ən; ser *cash* an). Fabric of wool and cotton with diagonal weave.
circlet. Ornament in form of small circle, as ring, bracelet, band for head.
circular. 1. In form of circle, round, full. 2. 19th century cape. See CAPES.
circular fulness. Fulness, as in skirt, peplum, sleeve, collar, etc., achieved through cut of fabric, or applied by means of godets, flounces.
circular hose. Knit in tubular shape; not full-fashioned. See HOSE.
circular knit. Made in tubular form on flat or circular machine, as seamless hose, tubular belts, jersey fabric, etc. See KNITTING.
circular skirt. Skirt in circular shape. Circular skirt originally made by cutting waistline hole in center of circle of fabric. See SKIRTS.
circular vamp. Vamp covering front of foot. See VAMPS.
ciré (F. sē-rā; see ray). Used in connection with ribbons, fabrics, laces, etc., that have a shiny effect produced by application of wax, heat, pressure. French word meaning waxed.
ciselé (F. sēz-lā; seez lay). Velvet with cut and uncut loops. See VELVETS.
citron (sĭt′rən; *sit* ron) or **citrine** (sĭt′rĭn; *sit* rin). Greenish yellow, color of citron fruit; *sit* rin). Greenish yellow, color of citron fruit; typical of lemon or lime.
civet (sĭv′ĕt; *siv* et). 1. Substance having strong musky odor. Used in making perfume. 2. Short for CIVET CAT. See FURS.
civet cat. Flat black fur of skunk-like animal, marked with lyre-shaped markings. See FURS.

clad. Clothed. Most often used in uncomplimentary sense; as, shabbily clad, meagerly clad, inappropriately clad.
clair de lune (F. klĕr də lün; clair de loon). Color varying from pale greenish blue to lavender-gray. French phrase meaning moonlight.
clan plaid. Scotch plaid in the distinctive colors of a clan, a family group usually bearing same surname. Same as TARTAN.
claque (klăk or F. klăk; clack). Collapsible hat. See HATS.
claret (klăr′ĕt; *cla* ret). Deep red color of claret or Bordeaux wine.
clasp. Fastening which holds together two parts of anything or two objects; also, to secure with a fastening.
classic. Any wearing apparel in such simple good taste and so becoming that it continues in style in spite of changing fashions.
classical. Having characteristics of ancient Greek and Roman styles of dress; as, classical draperies.
class ring. Ring signifying year of graduation. See RINGS.
classy. Slang term for showy or high-class; of extravagant type.
claw-hammer. Swallow-tailed coat. See COATS.
clay worsted (wŏŏs′tĕd; *wooss* ted). Heavy worsted fabric in flat, diagonal twill weave, looser than serge. Used for men's wear, women's suits. So called for English manufacturer.
cleading (klĕd′ĭng; *cleed* ing). Scottish term for clothing.
clean-stitched seam. Seam stitched and pressed open, then finished by having raw edges turned under, held free from garment, and stitched. See SEAMS.
cleat. One of metal pieces or strips of leather attached to sole of shoe to prevent slipping, provide firm grip.
clew. Ball of yarn or thread.
clientele (klī-ən-tĕl′ or F. klē-äŋ-tĕl; *cly* en *tell* or *clee* onh tell). Following, clients, or customers, in business or profession. French word for body of clients, patrons, patients, or customers.
clinquant (klĭng′kənt or F. klăŋ-käŋ; *clink* ant or *clanh* conh). Glittering, as with gold or silver; gaudily dressed, as in tinseled finery. Also, glitter; showy decoration or dress.
clip. 1. Article of costume jewelry, usually fastening with hinged clasp instead of pin. Made of metal, wood, etc., or synthetic material; usually ornamented. Worn decoratively, fastened to any part of costume. 2. That which is clipped; clipping, as from fabric.
clip-pin. Article of jewelry which may be worn either as pin or separate clips. See PINS.
cloak. Loose outer garment or wrap. Worn by men and women. Name derived from Old French *cloke* or *cloche*, meaning bell, because of original bell-like shape. For types, see WRAPS.
clobber (klŏb′ĕr; *clob* er). 1. English slang term for clothing, apparel. 2. To patch, as clothes or shoes.
cloche (klōsh or F. klōsh; closhe). Close-

fitting hat, the basic hat fashion for more than ten years, beginning early 1920. See HATS. French word for bell.
clochette (klō-shĕt′; clo *shet*). Any small ornament shaped like bell.
clock. 1. Open-work or embroidered decoration on each side of stocking at ankle. Originally intended to hide side seam. Supposedly so called from resemblance in shape to hands of a clock. 2. In 17th and 18th centuries, plaiting on ruff.
clock-mutch. Woman's cap. See CAPS.
clog. 1. Shoe with thick wooden or cork sole. See SHOES. 2. Stout wooden or leather outer shoe. Same as PATTEN.
cloisonné (kloi-zə-nā′ or F. klwä-zō-nā; cloy zo *nay* or clwah zo nay). Inlaid, usually with enamel, in spaces divided off for design. Originally done on precious metals; now abundant, chiefly on brass—buttons, necklaces, bracelets, bric-a-brac, etc.
cloister cloth. Rough, canvas-like drapery material in basket weave. Similar to monk's cloth.
clokey or **cloky** (klō′kĭ; *clo* ki). Americanized spellings of French CLOQUÉ.
cloqué (F. klō-kä; clo kay). French word meaning blistered. Used of dress and coat fabrics with surface irregularly raised in blistered effect; similar to matelassé.
closed feather-stitch. Variety of single feather-stitch. See STITCHES.
close-stitch (klōs; cloce). Same as BUTTONHOLE-STITCH. See STITCHES.
cloth. 1. Fabric, woven, felted, or knitted, made of vegetable, animal, mineral, or synthetic fibers. Commonly used for garments and other covering. 2. Piece of fabric of type, size, texture adapted to certain uses; as, tablecloth, dust cloth, etc.
cloth embroidery. Oriental embroidery on inlaid appliqué. See EMBROIDERIES.
clothes or **clothing.** Any wearing apparel. For types, see SPORTS CLOTHES and DRESSES.
cloth guide. Sewing-machine attachment that is screwed to the base of the machine to guide stitching lines in straight, even, or parallel rows.
clothier. Dealer who makes or sells clothes. More often applied to shop selling men's suits and overcoats.
clothing wool. (klō′thĭng; *clo* thing). Compact, short-fiber wool. See WOOL.
cloth measure. Measure for cloth, in which yard was divided into four quarters.
cloth of gold. Fabric woven wholly or partly of gold metal threads; usually sheer.
cloth of silver. Fabric woven wholly or partly of silver metal threads; usually sheer.
cloth plate. Metal plate on sewing machine, through which needle passes, on which material rests.
cloth stitch. Stitch resembling weaving. See STITCHES.
cloth yard. Yard used for measuring cloth. Now same as standard 36-inch yard; formerly, equal to Scotch ell.

fāte, făt, dánce, ärt mē, mĕt, hēr, thêre rīde, rĭd nōte, nŏt, côrn, fōōd, fŏŏt cūte, cŭt, cûrē now fĭn(ŋ)ger villa(ə) señor pleas(zh)ure

cloud 28 coats

cloud. Large fleecy scarf, very light, loosely knitted. Worn by women as a decorative head covering. Fashionable at different periods since the 17th century.
cloué (F. klōō-ā; cloo ay). Studded with nails.
clout. 1. 17th century spelling of cloud, meaning head scarf. 2. Obsolete term for small piece, fragment, or patch of cloth, leather, etc. 3. Handkerchief; garment; (plural) clothes, swaddling clothes.
clown suit. Baggy costume with trousers and blouse cut in one garment. See FANCY DRESS.
club. Style of dressing hair in clubshaped knot or tail. Fashionable for men in late 18th century.
clue. Variant spelling of CLEW.
clump. Heavy extra sole on shoe, as for rough wear.
Cluny lace (klū'nĭ; cloo ni). Bobbin lace made of heavy linen thread, usually in large, open designs. See LACES.
cluster tucks. Tucks grouped to hold fulness. See TUCKS.
Clytie knot (klī'tĭ; cly ti). Style of arranging hair in knot loosely coiled low on neck. So called from bust of Clytie, Greek nymph, having hair so arranged.
coachman's coat. Heavy doublebreasted coat, usually with large metal buttons. See COATS.
coal scuttle bonnet. Bonnet with pointed head-piece shaped like lip of a coal scuttle. See BONNETS.

COATS

coat. Outer garment worn for warmth, made of fabric or fur, usually fitting upper part of body, extending below hipline, open at front or side, having sleeves. Length and style vary according to fashion.
balmacaan (băl-mə-kăn'; bal ma cahn). Type of loose, flaring overcoat having raglan sleeves. Usually made of rough woolen fabric. So called from Balmacaan, Scottish manor.

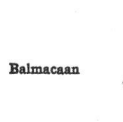

Balmacaan

benjamin (běn'jə-mĭn; ben ja min). Close-fitting overcoat worn by men in early 19th century.
benny. Overcoat. Short for BENJAMIN.
blouse c. Coat with slightly draped effect in the upper part at the waistline made by blousing the coat fabric on the lining. Usually made with kimono sleeve. Popular in 1926.

body c. Close-fitting coat.

Blouse Coat, 1926

box c. Plain, loose coat, usually short, fitted only at shoulders and having a squared, box-like appearance.

Box Coat, 1930's

British warm. Heavy, warm overcoat worn during World War by British army officers.
brunswick (brŭnz'wĭk; bruns wick). Close-fitting riding coat, with collar like man's. Said to have originated in Brunswick, Germany. Fashionable for women in 18th century.
buffcoat. Strong coat made of buffskin, or buffalo leather; especially, a close-fitting short-sleeved military coat worn during Civil Wars in England and by colonists in America.

17th Century Buffcoat

cape c. Any coat having additional cape effect attached for extra protection or decoration or fashion effect.
carmagnole (F. kär-mâ-nyōl; car ma nyole). Short-skirted coat, as worn by French Revolutionists.
Casentino (cä-zĕn-tē'nō; ca zen tee no). Red overcoat, having a green lining; worn by coachmen in the Casentino section of Italy. Adapted for winter sports wear.
cassock (kăs'ək; cass ock). Long, loose, medieval coat worn by both men and women; also, coat worn by foot soldiers during 16th century.

Cape Coat, 1920's

chesterfield (chĕs'tẽr-fēld; chess ter field). 1. Originally, single-breasted, fly-front coat with plain back usually having center seam, notched lapel, and collar, often of velvet. First worn in 18th century by Philip Dormer Stanhope, 4th Earl of Chesterfield; named for him. In 20th century, often made double-breasted and in all overcoat colors. Adapted as tailored coat for women's wear. 2. Four-button cutaway coat of which only top button is fastened. Also worn by and named for Earl of Chesterfield.
claw-hammer c. Colloquial name for swallow-tailed coat, so called from its shape, similar to a hammer with claws for drawing nails.
coachman's c. Double-breasted coat with fitted waistline and wide lapels, in traditional style worn by English coachmen.

Type of Coachman's Coat, 1820's

coatee (kōt'ē; coat ee). Close-fitting, short coat having short skirt, flaps, or tails.
coolie c. Short box coat reaching below waist. Similar in shape to those worn by Chinese and East Indian coolies. Straight or no armhole line.

Coolie Coat

coonskin. Sturdy greatcoat made of raccoon skins.
covert c. (kŭv'ẽrt; cuv ert). Lightweight topcoat of covert cloth, usually unlined.

fāte, făt, dånce, ärt mē, mĕt, hẽr, thêre rīde, rĭd nōte, nŏt, côrn, fōōd, fŏŏt cūte, cŭt, cūre now fin(g)ger villa(e) señor pleas(zh)ure

coats

crispin (krĭs'pĭn;   *criss* pin).   Frock coat having single cape.
cutaway.   Coat having tails or half a skirt portion in the back, the skirt or peplum being cut to taper off from waistline at front to bottom of jacket at back.

Woman's Cutaway Coat, 1900's

dress c.   Coat prescribed by custom for full-dress evening occasions.   For men's wear, cutaway coat having tails.
dust c. or **cloak.**   Same as DUSTER.
duster   (dŭs'tẽr;   *duss* ter).   Lightweight coverall coat or wrap, often of tussore silk.   Fashionable in early 20th century as protection for summer clothes when riding in new open type of automobiles. Also called *dust coat, dust cloak, dust wrap.*

Duster, Early 1900's

frock c.   Man's double-breasted coat with knee-length skirt.   Popular with men of affairs throughout the latter third of the 19th century.
greatcoat.   Heavy overcoat of generous size.   Originally, coat having fur lining.
grego (grē'gō or grā'gō; *gree* go or *gray* go).   Short coat with attached hood, made of thick, coarse cloth.   Worn in eastern Mediterranean countries.
haori (hä'ō-rĭ; *hah* o ri).   Loose, knee-length outer garment or coat having fulness at sides; usually of silk, fastened in front with small silk cords.   Worn by men and women in Japan.
houri-c. (hoo'rĭ or how'rĭ; *hoo* ri or *how* ri).   Kimono-like coat of Turkish origin.
jigger c.   Finger-tip length, semi-tailored sports coat, usually of box type.
jockey c.   Obsolete term for broadcloth overcoat with wide sleeves.
jump.   Coat or jacket, worn by men, reaching to thighs, buttoned down front.
juste-au-corps or **justaucorps** (F.

zhüs-tō kôr; zhoost o core).   Close-fitting, long-skirted coat or doublet worn in 17th and 18th centuries, mostly by men, later by women. French expression meaning exactly to the body.
kooletah (koo'lĕ-tä; *koo* le tah).   Buttonless fur coat, usually of caribou skin, pulled on over head.   Worn by Eskimos.
Macfarlane (măc-fär'lən; mac *far* lan).   Cape overcoat with slit in sides to permit putting hands in pockets of inner garment.

Macfarlane

Mackinaw   (măk'ĭ-nô;   *mack* i naw).   Short, double-breasted coat, thick and heavy, usually of plaid wool.   So called from Mackinac, Michigan, where blankets, clothes, etc., were distributed to Indians in colonial days.   Used for overcoats, jackets.
mackintosh (măk'ĭn-tŏsh; *mack* in tosh).   Outer garment or overcoat made waterproof with India-rubber.
mandarin c.   (măn'də-rĭn; *man* da rin).   Long, loose, richly embroidered silk coat with wide sleeves, such as worn by mandarin, or Chinese official.   Adapted by fashion for ladies' evening wraps.

Type of Chinese Mandarin Coat

mantee.   18th century coat, open from throat, showing stomacher and petticoat beneath.
mousquetaire **c.**   (F.   moos-kə-tĕr; moose ke tare).   Cloth coat with large buttons, trimmed with ribbons.   Fashionable about 1855.
netcha (nĕch'ə; *netch* a).   Coat made of sealskin, as worn by Eskimos.
newmarket (nū'mär-kĕt; *new* mar ket).   Close-fitting coat reaching to floor. Formerly, worn by women as general outdoor coat; by men, as riding coat.
overcoat.   Warm coat, heavier than a topcoat.   Worn especially in winter, over all other clothing.
paletot (păl'ə-tō; *pal* e toe).   Loose

coats

overcoat, now only for women, formerly worn by men also.   French word meaning overcoat.
petersham   (pē'tẽr-shăm;   *pee* ter sham).   Heavy short overcoat made of thick, rough, almost windproof woolen of same name in dark navy blue.   Used in seafaring or for severe weather. Named for Lord Petersham, who introduced it.
pinchback.   Style of coat plaited or otherwise fitted closely to the back.
pink.   Red or scarlet coat, as worn by fox-hunters, often with bright green or tan collars.
polo c.   Loose, tailored coat, single- or double-breasted, belted or not.   Made of camel's hair or an imitation.
polonaise (pō-lə-nāz'; po lo *naze*). Short overcoat, usually fur-trimmed. Worn by men in early 19th century; later, by women.
Prince Albert.   Long frock coat, always double-breasted.   Worn by men. Made fashionable in the U. S. A. through visit of England's Prince Albert in 1876.
raglan (răg'lən; *rag* lan).   Loose overcoat either sleeveless with cape, or with large, full sleeves cut so that seam which joins sleeve to coat runs from armhole into neck.   Named for Lord Raglan, English general.—**raglan-**

Raglan

front c.   Raglan having only front seam.—**two-seam raglan c.**   Raglan having seam in both front and back.—
three-seam raglan c.   Two-seam type having additional seam running down sleeve.
raincoat.   Waterproof coat worn over other garments as protection against weather.

Redingote Costume, 1930's

redingote (rĕd'ĭng-gōt; *red* ing gote). Woman's long, fitted coat, cut princess

fāte, făt, dånce, ärt mē, mĕt, hẽr, thêre rīde, rĭd nōte, nŏt, côrn, fōod, fŏŏt cūte, cŭt, cūre now fin(ŋ)ger villa(ə) señor pleas(zh)ure

coats (continued) style, worn open in front to show dress underneath. Sometimes cut away in front. Originally made with several capes and trimmed with large buttons. French word developed from English words, riding coat.

reefer. Single- or double-breasted, fitted, tailored, over-all coat of sturdy fabric.

Reefer, 1938

reversible c. Coat made either of reversible fabric or of two different fabrics back to back, so that it can be worn with either side out. Often waterproof on one side.
sack c. Short, loose-fitting coat or jacket without waistline seam.
shooting c. or jacket. Short coat or jacket made of strong, heavy material like canvas or drill, with large pockets. Used by sportsmen.
siphonia (sī-fō'nǐ-a; sy *fo* ni a). Light-weight overcoat. Term no longer in use.
slicker. Long, loose coat of waterproof material, especially oilskin or rubber.
spike tail. Slang term for man's swallow-tailed dress coat.
sports c. Simple, tailored coat of casual fabric, such as tweed, with or without fur, in varying styles.
stambouline (stăm-bōō-lēn'; stam boo *leen*). Long, single-breasted coat worn by officials in Turkey on formal occasions.
surcoat or surcot (sẽr'kŏt; *ser* coat). Outer coat or robe of varying types, worn during Middle Ages. Originally, long and fitted with large, long sleeves, frequently lined with fur and richly trimmed; later, shortened. Sometimes sleeveless, with very deep armholes.
surtout (F. sür-tōō or sẽr-tōōt'; soor too or ser *toot*). Man's overcoat cut in style of frock coat.

Swagger Coat, 1930's

swagger c. Easy-fitting beltless sports coat, usually flared.
swallow-tailed c. 1. Fitted coat or jacket with two tails at back. **2.** Full-dress coat worn by men on formal occasions. So called because of two long, tapering ends at back resembling tail of a swallow.
tabard. Sleeveless or short-sleeved mantle or cloak worn by knights over their armor, usually embroidered with the arms of wearer; hence the expression "coat of arms."

Tabard

tail c. Same as SWALLOW-TAILED COAT.
topcoat. Light-weight coat, usually worn over suit in spring and fall. Compare OVERCOAT.
trench c. Loose over-all rainproof coat, with collar and belt of self-fabric, and having many pockets and flaps; usually double-breasted; similar to coats worn by officers in the trenches during World War.

Trench Coat

ulster. Long, loose, protective, practically rainproof coat, sometimes belted at waist, with slit at bottom of skirt in back, closed by button. Worn by both men and women. Originally made of cloth from Ulster, Ireland.

Ulster

ulsterette. Light-weight ulster.
watch c. Heavy windproof overcoat worn in inclement weather, usually by seamen. Also, REEFER or PEA JACKET.
wraprascal (răp'răs-kǝl; *rap* ras cal). Long, loose overcoat fashionable during 18th century.
zamarra or zamarro (Sp. thä-mär'rä; thah *mar* a). Sheepskin coat worn by shepherds in Spain.

coat closing. Lapped closing characteristic of coats; tailored front closing, usually buttoned.
coat cuff. Type of cuff made by turning back end of sleeve. Same as SLEEVE CUFF. See CUFFS.
coat dress. Tailored dress, usually fitted, with coat type of front closing and coat-like lines. See DRESSES.
coatee. Short coat with tails. See COATS.
coat hanger or clothes hanger. Shaped bar of metal, wood, etc., covered or uncovered, having top hook, for holding garments from shoulders.
coat length. Measurement of a coat from top to bottom. See LENGTHS.
coating. 1. Fabric used for making coats. **2.** Finishing process consisting of coating fabrics such as rayon, cotton, silk, etc., with oil, paraffin, rubber, lacquer, or synthetic resins to make them waterproof, heat resistant, etc. Used for raincoats, artificial leather goods, etc.
coat of mail. Garment of chain mail. Worn as defensive armor during Middle Ages.
coat shirt. Shirt, opening all the way down its front length. See SHIRTS.
coat sweater. Sweater that has a front closing of coat type, often with pockets and belt. See SWEATERS.
coattail. Rear flap of coat; especially back skirt on man's cutaway or dress coat.
cobalt blue (kō'bôlt; *co* bawlt). Medium greenish-blue color, richly deep.
cobcab (kŏb'kăb; *cob* cab). Clog-like shoe. See SHOES.
coburg (kō'bẽrg; *co* burg). Thin dress fabric of worsted and cotton or silk, twilled on one side. Formerly, much used for mourning purposes. Named for Coburg, Germany.
cocarde (F. kô-kȧrd; *co* card). Rosette or ornament of ribbon, usually plaited, as worn on hat. French word for cockade.

Cocardes

cochineal (kŏch-ĭ-nēl'; coch i *neel*). **1.** Brilliant scarlet dye, obtained from dried bodies of female insects of this name. **2.** Bright yellowish-red color. Also called *Castilian red*.
cockade (kŏk-ād'; cock *ade*). Rosette or knot of ribbon, often plaited, with ends

cocked 31 **collars**

extending. Used as trimming. Formerly worn on hat to indicate rank, office, or form of service. From French *cocarde*, with same meaning.
cocked. Turned up or tilted at an angle.
cocked hat. 1. Hat worn at an angle. **2.** Hat with turned-up brim. See HATS.
cocker (kŏk′ẽr; *cock* er). High shoe; half boot. See SHOES.
cockle-hat. Hat with shell attached. See HATS.
cocktail dress. Informal but somewhat dressy costume, appropriate for wear in the late afternoon. See DRESSES.
cocoa (kō′kō; *co* co). Dark brown color, slightly lighter than chocolate.
codpiece (kŏd′pēs; *cod* piece). Decorative flap or bag. Worn by men during 15th and 16th centuries to conceal front opening in breeches.
coffer headdress (kŏf′ẽr; *coff* er). Box-shaped headdress of medieval times, worn on top of head, often with hair braided at sides in squared effect.

13th Century Coffer Headdress

coif. 1. Dressed head of hair. **2.** Close-fitting cap of varying styles and uses. See CAPS.
coiffe (F. kwäf; *cwahf*). French word for coif, cap, hood, headdress.
coiffette (F. kwä-fĕt′; *cwah fet*). Iron skull-cap. See CAPS.
coiffeur (F. kwä-fẽr; *cwah fer*). French word for man hairdresser.
coiffeuse (F. kwä-fēz; *cwah fuz*). French word for woman hairdresser.
coiffure (F. kwä-für; *cwah fure*). Style of arranging hair; also, to dress hair.
coin dot. Dot larger than the size of a dime. See DOTS.
coin purse. Small purse with secure closing; often, tiny pouch on rigid frame. Used as container for loose change.
cointise (F. kwăn-tēz; *cwanh teez*). Fanciful piece of apparel, especially scarf. Formerly, worn either for adornment, as over woman's headdress, or for symbol of favor, as over knight's helmet. Old French word for adornment.
coir. Stiff elastic fiber from cocoanut husks. Used in making cordage, cables.
Colbert embroidery (F. kŏl-bẽr; *col* bare). Embroidery with worked background which outlines the unworked designs. See EMBROIDERIES.
colbertine or **colberteen** (kŏl′bẽr-tēn; *col* ber teen). Net-like French lace. See LACES.

COLLARS

collar. 1. Article of dress, separate or attached to garment, worn around neck. Usually of fabric, straight, shaped, or draped; also of other material, as neck-

lace. **2.** In shoe trade, narrow ornamental piece of leather stitched around top of shoe upper.
band. In 16th and 17th centuries, wide ornamental collar or ruff, usually of linen, lace, or cambric; later, turned down over shoulders and called *falling band*.
bertha. Deep collar falling softly from bodice neckline over shoulders. Imitation of short shoulder cape formerly called bertha.

Bertha, 1920's

bib c. Small collar, much longer in front. Worn decoratively over dress.
Buster Brown c. Broad, rounded, starched collar popularized by comic strip character. First worn by small boys; later adapted in fashions for girls and women. Similar to Eton collar.

Buster Brown Collar

cape c. Short cape. Same as BERTHA.
carnival c. Collar of gay, printed fabric with deep loops made of the fabric and arranged similarly to those on the collar of a clown's costume.
chevesaile (chĕv′ə-sāl; *chev* a sail). Richly decorated collar, always attached to garment. Worn during Middle Ages by men and women.
chin c. Choker type of collar that extends upward and flares enough to conceal the chin.

Chin Collar, 1916

choker. Unusually high collar or band.
collaret or **collarette** (kŏl-ẽr-ĕt′; *coll* er *et*). **1.** Small collar, especially of lace, fur, beads, etc., as worn by women. **2.** In colonial America, puff of soft ribbon ending in bow. Worn about throat. **3.** In 16th century, ruching worn inside high, standing collar. **4.** In

Middle Ages, piece of armor to protect throat.

16th Century Collarette

collet (kŏl′ĕt; *coll* et). Small collar or neckband.
convertible c. Straight collar, applied double to normal neckline, to be worn open or closed.

Convertible Collar, Closed and Open

Dutch c. Narrow collar fitting closely around neck, having either pointed or rounded ends. Similar to collar seen in pictures by Rembrandt, Franz Hals, and other great Dutch painters.

20th Century Dutch Collar

Eton c. (ē′tn; *ee* ton). Rather large turned-over collar of stiffened white fabric, as worn, with Eton jacket, by students of Eton College.
falling band. Wide collar turned down over shoulders; usually of linen or other fine fabric, often lace-trimmed. Worn by men during 17th century after accession of Charles I in 1625. Also called *Vandyke* and, in France, *Louis XIII collar*.

17th Century Dutch Falling Bands

fan c. Frilly standing collar at the back of the neck only and flared in the form of a fan.
fanon (făn′ŭn; *fan* un). Wide collar in shape of short cape worn by pope in celebration of Mass.

---

fāte, făt, dånce, ärt mē, mĕt, hẽr, thêre rīde, rĭd nōte, nŏt, côrn, fōōd, fŏŏt cūte, cŭt, cũré now fin(ŋ)ger villa(ə) señor pleas(zh)ure

collars

collars (continued)
fraise (frāz; fraze). Ruff worn during 16th century.
funnel c. Collar flaring outward at the top, fitted snugly at the neckline, and usually opening at the side or back.

Funnel Collar, 1916

galilla. Small, crisp, inside collar, usually of white lawn. Worn as neckline finish standing up beyond collar or neckline of garment. Popular in 17th century for wear with doublets.

17th Century Galilla

Gladstone c. Standing collar having points flaring at the side-front. Worn with a silk scarf tie. Made famous by William Ewart Gladstone when he was Prime Minister of Great Britain.

Gladstone Collar, 1852

johnny c. Small standing collar, from 1 to 1½ inches high, around close-fitting neckline.

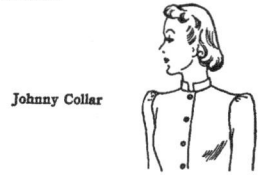

Johnny Collar

little girl c. Narrow, round collar, usually having rounded front ends, similar to PETER PAN COLLAR.
Louis XIII c. Same as FALLING BAND.
Medici c. (mĕd'ĭ-chē; med i chee). Large, fan-shaped collar, wired or stiffened to roll from neck at back, slope toward sides of square front opening. Worn by

women of Medici family ruling Italy in 15th and 16th centuries.

16th Century Medici Collar

moat c. Narrow, standing collar around high, broad, sometimes bateau neckline.

16th Century Moat Collar

mousquetaire c. (F. mōōs-kə-têr; moose ke tare). Turn-over collar of medium width, having front ends pointed, as shown in 17th century mousquetaire costume. Fashionable for women about 1850, usually of linen; popular also in 20th century.
Napoleon c. Straight stand-up collar with a turnover as deep as the collar. Usually trimmed with braid in military style. Invariably worn with wide revers of military type. Favored by Napoleon and men of his period. Revived in women's dress in 1905.
notched c. or notched lapel c. Flat, narrow collar joined to narrow lapels so as to produce notch. Chiefly used on tailored coats and jackets.
Peter Pan c. Youthful, turned-down collar, from 2 to 3 inches in width, having rounded ends in front; sometimes stiffly starched. Named for Peter Pan, the hero in a play of that name by Sir James Barrie.

Peter Pan Collar

piccadilly (pĭk-ə-dĭl'ĭ; pick a dill i). 1. Standing flaring collar worn at back of neck with décolleté. 2. Stiff ruff or collar, usually edged with lace. Worn in 17th century. 3. Man's high wing collar. Worn about 1870.
plain band. Type of falling band without ruffles or lace, worn by Puritans of 17th and 18th centuries.

poets' c. Soft collar attached to the shirt blouse popular during the lives of Lord Byron, Shelley, and Keats.

Poet's Collar, Early 19th Century

poke c. Standing collar having projecting ends.
rabat (F. rá-bá; ra ba). Turned-down collar falling over shoulders, worn by gentlemen in the 15th and 16th centuries. Also, clerical collar, sometimes having short breastpiece.

16th Century Rabat

rabatine (răb'ə-tēn; rab a teen). Collar falling over shoulders as cape or ruff.
rebato (rē-bä'tō; re bah toe). 1. Turned-back collar popular about 1600, sometimes used to support a ruff. 2. Stiff, starched, flaring lace collar worn only at back of neck.
Robespierre c. (F. rō-bəs-pyêr; roe bes pyare). A high turned-down coat collar worn with a frilly jabot and a draped neck-piece finished with a bow. Worn by the French statesman Robespierre about 1790.

Robespierre Collar, about 1790

Roman c. Clerical collar; as, straight plain band of linen or lawn, buttoned in back, or narrow stiff stock with short breastflaps.
ruff. Wheel-shaped plaited collar worn

17th Century Ruff

fāte, făt, dânce, ärt mē, mĕt, hêr, thêre rīde, rĭd nōte, nŏt, côrn, fōōd, fŏŏt cūte, cŭt, cūre now fin(ŋ)ger villa(ə) señor pleas(zh)ure

collars

in 16th and 17th centuries by both men and women. Made of stiff, starched linen or muslin, frequently trimmed with lace. Originally imported from Flanders, as starching was unknown in England until 1564.

sailor c. Collar of two thicknesses of heavy fabric; shaped square in back, narrowing to point of V-neckline in front, as on blouses worn by American sailors. Often trimmed with braid.

Girl's Sailor Collar, 1910

scarf c. Collar that is attached at the neckline and loose in front to lap, drape, or tie.

Shakespeare c. Collar of medium width standing high around neck and flaring away from face. Made of strip of lawn, plaited and stitched in curve and stiffened.

shawl c. Attached collar of rounded, unbroken outline, usually following surplice closing of coat or dress, from waistline up and around the neck.

Shawl Collar, 1920's

standing band. Band of linen stiffened with starch or wire. Formerly worn around neck.

stand-up c. Collar standing upright without fold, varying in width and severity.

surplice c. (sẽr′plĭs; ser pliss). Collar following neckline, which extends from shoulder usually to waistline of opposite side, overlapping in front.

tuxedo c. (tŭk-sē′dō; tuck see doe). Straight collar attached at neckline and down front edges of open-front coat, laid back against garment to form long, flat fold. Usually extends to bottom of garment.

Tuxedo Collar, 1930's

Vandyke c. (văn-dīk′; van *dike*). Large collar of linen and lace, having deep points or scallops on edge. So called because shown in portraits by Van Dyck, the Flemish painter who was the court painter in England during the reign of Charles I. Also called *falling band.*

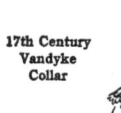

17th Century Vandyke Collar

whisk. 17th century shoulder collar or falling band of varying types, often lace-trimmed.

17th Century Whisk

wing c. Man's standing collar with corners folded down, giving wing-like effect. Worn with full dress and formal daytime dress.

collarband. Band at neckline of garment to which collar is sewn or buttoned.

collar button. Device to button collar to garment, usually man's shirt.

collaret or **collarette** (kŏl-ẽr-ĕt′; coll er et). Small collar or collar-like article of varying types. See COLLARS.

collection. All apparel exhibited at any one fashion showing; as, Vionnet's fall collection. In Paris, spring and fall are the two major periods each year when collections are shown to the trade and to the clientele. Collections shown in between these are called *midseason.*

college cap. Same as MORTARBOARD. See CAPS.

collet (kŏl′ĕt; *coll* et). 1. Circle, rim, or flange, as a ring, in which gems are set. 2. Small collar. See COLLARS.

colletin (kŏl′ə-tĭn; *coll* e tin). Piece of plate armor worn during Middle Ages over neck and shoulders.

colmar. (kŏl′mer; *col* mer). Type of fan fashionable in early 18th century, during reign of Queen Anne.

colobium (kə-lō′bĭ-ŭm; co *lo* bi um). 1. Ancient type of tunic, usually sleeveless. Worn as ecclesiastical vestment before 4th century; replaced by DALMATIC. 2. Similar garment worn by monks, and by kings as coronation robe.

cologne (kə-lōn′; co *lone*). Perfumed liquid composed of alcohol scented with aromatic oils. Used as toilet water by men as well as women. First made at Cologne, Germany, in 1709, and used as perfume. Generally less expensive than perfume. Also called *eau de Cologne.*

colonial. 1. Strictly, characteristic of dress of colonial period of the United States, about 1607 to 1776; may include Puritan, Quaker, and English Cavalier and Restoration styles as worn in different colonies. More generally, costume of late 18th century, with looped-up full skirt, quilted petticoat, tight bodice, low neck; adorned with puffs, laces, ruffles; worn with powdered, high hair dress. 2. Low-cut shoe with buckle. See SHOES.

Colonial Dress

COLOR

Color is what the eye sees, what is reflected in the retina of the eye. The eye can see all the colors of the spectrum when a prism breaks up a ray of light into the colors of which it is composed; it can see color in crystal, in a rainbow, on a color card, in yard goods on a counter, and in apparel in a shop window.

The pigment primary colors are red, yellow, and blue. These can be combined in varying proportions to produce all other colors. Of these, there are dozens of variations, according to which color predominates, such as blue-green and yellow-green, blue-violet and red-violet. In the spectrum and in the rainbow, the various colors appear assembled in the order of their wave lengths; and one color blends into the next. In a color circle, the spectrum colors are arranged in their main groups, which merge from red through orange, yellow, green, blue, indigo, violet, and back to red again.

Color has a language all its own—here only the briefest definitions can be given. Any one desiring a working knowledge of color should study one or more reliable textbooks devoted exclusively to the subject.

color. 1. Quality by which object reflects, transmits, or absorbs light rays, varying in three ways: hue, as red, yellow, blue; value, as light or dark; chroma, as strong or weak according to amount of gray. 2. One of hues of rainbow or spectrum: violet, indigo, blue, green, yellow, orange, red. 3. All the tints, hues, and shades between white and black.

ball park blue c. A clear pastel blue having a violet cast. Color that usu-

fāte, făt, dånce, ärt mē, mĕt, hẽr, thêre rīde, rĭd nōte, nŏt, côrn, fōōd, fŏŏt cūte, cŭt, cūré now fin(ŋ)ger villa(ə) señor pleas(zh)ure

color (continued)

ally dominates a base ball park where men are in shirt sleeves.

binary c. (bī'nə-rĭ; *by* na ri). Secondary color. Made by mixture of two primary colors, as green, which results from mixing blue and yellow.

block c. Colors as applied in block printing.

Boilfast c. Trade term applied to threads that are guaranteed as absolutely fast.

cast. The leaning toward a color, as a gray with a blue *cast*.

center c. Exact center of a color from which white or black is added to make tints, tones, or shades of the given color.

chroma (kro'mə; *cro* ma). 1. Color, such as red or blue or green, as distinguished from black, gray, white. 2. Purity of color; color quality of being free from grayness. Often called *purity*, *intensity*, or *saturation*.

chromatic c. (krō-măt'ĭk; cro *mat* ic). Color having hue, as opposed to the achromatic colors, white, black, and gray, which are neutral and without hue.

complementary c. One of two colors which appear opposite each other in color circle or hue circuit, as red and blue-green, and which form a neutral color when mixed together in certain proportions.

cool c. Hue associated with feeling of coolness, such as tones of violet, blue, and blue-green, with blue predominating, not yellow or red.

coordinated c. (kō-ôr'dĭ-nāt-ĕd; co *or* di nate ed). Colors brought together in harmonious relation.

dark c. Color with more black than hue, as sooty color, seal brown, midnight blue, etc.; color in which eye perceives considerable, not total, lack of hue as produced by addition of black.

deep c. Full, strong hue showing no absence of color, very slight amount of black. Not synonymous with dark.

della Robbia c. (dĕl'ə rŏb'ĭ-ə; *dell* a *robe* i a). Pottery colors having a soft glaze; especially a clear light blue. Named for Luca della Robbia, an Italian Renaissance sculptor and potter, whose terra cotta figures and plaques of madonnas and bambinos are famous for these colors.

dull c. Color lacking in brightness; hue in which the eye perceives quality of grayness.

infra-red c. Designates rays of red that extend beyond the spectrum or out from flame.

light c. Hue in which there is much more white than black; color in which eye perceives considerable, not total, lack of hue, as produced by addition of white.

neutral c. (nū'trəl; *new* tral). Color that has none of the primary colors; color without hue. Twine and natural pongee are neutral.

normal c. Pure center of a hue; foundation color from which tones get darker or lighter, as pure red, yellow, or blue.

ombré (F. ŏŋ-brā; onh bray). Shaded or graduated color, usually going from light to dark tones; color in one range, as from cream to darkest brown or from flesh to darkest red.

pigment. Any coloring material or substance that is used in making colors, such as powders used for making paints.

primary c. Any one of the three foundation colors, red, blue, and yellow, from which all the rainbow or spectrum colors are derived. These are usually classified as red, orange, yellow, green, blue, indigo, and violet.

rich c. Any color conveying full, satisfying, luxuriant impression, as deep scarlet, bishop's purple, etc.

secondary c. Color obtained by mixing two primary colors in equal proportion, as purple, which results from mixture of red and blue.

solid c. Color not broken by design; plain color.

spectrum (spĕk'trum; *speck* trum). The seven rainbow colors: violet, indigo, blue, green, yellow, orange, red; and all the variations between. These colors appear assembled in the order of their wave length when a ray of white light passes through a prism and divides into the colors composing it.

tertiary c. (tẽr'shĭ-ẽr-ĭ; *ter* shi air i). Color obtained by combining or mixing secondary colors, as citrine, a combination of green and orange.

tone. Color quality or value; tint or shade of any color. Any modification of a color in respect to amount of white, black, or gray it contains, or its vividness of hue. A tone may be heightened by the addition of pure color, or subdued by the addition of either white or black.

warm c. Hue associated with the colors of heat, typically fire, sun, blood, etc., such as tones of yellow, orange, red.

color accent. High or vivid color in a design, or a scarf of brilliant hue worn with a dress of solid color or black or white.

colorant (kŭl'ẽr-ənt; *cull* er ant). Something used for coloring fabric or other material, as dye.

color blindness. Inability to distinguish even the primary colors: red, yellow, blue. A few persons are completely color blind, and to them all colors look gray. More persons are partially blind. They can distinguish some chromatic colors, but never in their full value; and see others only as grays.

color card. Card issued periodically by manufacturers of textiles, hosiery, etc., and sometimes by dyers, to acquaint public with season's new colors and names, and show samples of new colors. The Textile Color Card Association of the United States and The British Colour Council of Great Britain are the two foremost sources for official color cards.

color circle. Spectrum colors so arranged as to form a ring around which each color gradually blends into the next.

color cycle. Series of hues graduated in natural order or relationship so that a cycle is completed.

colorfast. Used of fabrics that retain color without perceptible fading after washing or exposure to reasonable amount of light.

color harmony. Pleasing effect resulting from harmonious colors close together.

color scheme (skēm; skeem). Careful selection of becoming colors for a costume, ensemble, or room, to produce any desired effect—dramatic or romantic, cool or warm, restful or stimulating, etc.

COMBS

comb (kōm; cohm). Thin piece, as of shell, horn, metal, wood, plastic, celluloid, etc., having row of teeth on one or both edges. Used for combing, dressing, or decorating hair. First used before 6th century. Also, to disentangle, adjust, lay smooth and straight, as hair or wool.

back c. Comb of varying sizes worn at the back of the head for decoration or to hold the hair.

side c. Comb worn at the side of the head to hold the hair; often decorative.

Spanish c. High comb, usually carved or jeweled, worn by Spanish women as hair ornament, often under mantilla.

combed yarn. Tightly twisted, strong, smooth yarn of long fibers. See YARNS.

combination (kŏm-bĭ-nā'shŭn; com bi *nay* shun). One-piece undergarment. 1. Chemise combined with drawers or pantie. Worn by women. 2. Undervest combined with drawers, as in union suit; latter type also worn by men.

Type of Combination, 1920

combination last. Last varying somewhat from standard. A shoe made on a combination last has a narrower heel or wider toe than the standard. See LAST.

combination-stitch. Back-stitch combined with two or more running-stitches. See STITCHES.

combing. 1. Process of straightening long staple wool into parallel fibers, sometimes used in addition to carding. 2. (Plural) Loose, tangled hair, etc., collected with comb. 3. (Plural) Small wig of combings. See WIGS.

combing wool. Long staple wool. See WOOL.

comely (kŭm'lĭ; *cum* li). Pleasing or fair to look upon. Newspaper writers use word for good-looking woman.

comfort or **comforter.** 1. Thickly padded bedcover, tied or quilted. Also called *comfortable*. 2. Long, narrow woolen tippet, usually knit.

fāte, făt, dánce, ärt mē, mĕt, hẽr, thêre rīde, rĭd nōte, nŏt, côrn, fōōd, fŏŏt cūte, cŭt, cûre now fin(ŋ)ger villa(ə) señor pleas(zh)ure

comfortable. 1. Generously padded bedcover or puff. **2.** Knitted wristlet. **3.** Neck scarf.
comfort shoe. Soft, flexible shoe of a shape to fit comfortably when worn. See SHOES.
comme il faut (F. kŏm ĕl fō; cum eel foe). French phrase meaning as it should be; correct; in proper form.
commercial pattern. Tissue-paper pattern made for sale, as those made by Butterick, McCall, Vogue, etc. See PATTERNS.
commode (kŏ-mōd'; com *mode*). **1.** Headdress, fitting close like a cap over back of head; having strips of lace or self-material, called lappets, hanging at sides or back; built up at front on several forward-leaning tiers of wire. Made of lace, lawn, muslin, etc., usually ribbon-trimmed. Worn during late 17th, early 18th century. Also called *tower*; in France, called *fontange* or *fontanges*. **2.** Dressing bureau; also, small cabinet with wash basin.

17th Century
Commode

common gingham. Gingham of coarse yarns in plain weave. See GINGHAMS.
common-sense heel. Modified heel designed for comfort; similar to Cuban heel. See HEELS.
Commonwealth (kŏm'ən-wĕlth; *com* mon welth). Characteristic of English dress of Commonwealth period; same as VANDYKE and CAVALIER costumes in silhouette, but stripped of ornament and in somber colors to conform with ideas of English Puritans (1649–1660).
compact (kŏm'păkt; *com* pact). Case, usually flat, containing face powder and puff. In addition to face powder, a double compact contains rouge; a triple compact, face powder, rouge, lipstick.
complect (kəm-plĕkt'; com *plect*). Plait together; interweave.
complementary color (kŏm-plə-mĕn'tə-rĭ; com ple *men* ta ri). Any color directly opposite another in the color circle; for example, the complementary color of red is blue-green, which consists of blue and yellow and with red completes the three primary colors. The blue-green of the traffic lights gives a good example of complementary color of red. See COLOR.
complexion (kəm-plĕk'shŭn; com *plek* shun). Appearance or hue and texture of skin, particularly of face.
composé (F. kôn-pō-zā; conh po zay). Composed of, or compound of, several harmonious colors.
composition (kŏm-pə-zĭsh'ən; com po *zish* un). Artificially made substance composed of several, often synthetic, ingredients.

composition button. Button made of synthetic material. See BUTTONS.
composition cloth. Waterproofed fabric made of long flax fibers.
composition dot. Applied dot. See DOTS.
compound (kŏm'pownd; *com* pound). Having extra warp or weft yarns, or both, forming design.
concave curve (kŏn'kāv; *con* cave). Curve rounding inward. See CURVE.
conch hat (kŏnk; conk). **1.** Hat of palmetto leaves. See HATS. **2.** Name given to the hats worn by horses in hot weather.
conditioning (kən-dĭsh'ən-ĭng; con *dish* un ing). **1.** Process of determining percentage of moisture in fibers or fabrics. **2.** Process of treating fibers or fabrics to restore moisture lost in manufacture. **3.** Process of treatment given fibers, furs, etc., in preparation for weaving and dyeing.
cone. 1. Bobbin on which yarn is wound before weaving. **2.** In hat manufacturing: fabric of fur fiber in cone-shape; also, unblocked hat of any type; also, basket-weave straw hat.
coney (kō'nĭ; *co* ni). Alternate spelling of cony. See FURS.
confection (kən-fĕk'shŭn or F. kôŋ-fĕk-syôŋ; con *feck* shun or conh feck syonh). Ready-made clothes or piece of apparel; also, making of ready-made clothes, especially of the frilly, fluffy kind.
confetti colors (kən-fĕt'ĭ; con *fet* i). Mixed colors, usually including blue, red, yellow, green—all the rainbow colors, in fact.
confetti dot. Polka dot used in variegated colors. See DOTS.
confident (kŏn'fĭ-dənt; *con* fi dent). Curl, usually one of several, brought forward over the cheek in front of the ear, as part of 17th century hair arrangement. "You gave your confidence to a woman by whispering to her under her curl."
confirmation dress. White dainty dress, usually of sheer fabric or lace, worn usually by a young girl when she is being confirmed in the church of her faith. See DRESSES.
conformator (kŏn'fôr-mā-tẽr; *con* for may ter). Instrument for taking exact size and shape of objects. Used in fitting or sizing hats.
Congo or Congo brown. Brown earthy color with slightly reddish-yellow cast.
Congo Cloth. Trade name for an all spun rayon fabric of suiting weight. Made 36 inches wide. Used for men's and women's summer suits, shirts, slacks, beach wear, men's caps, ties.
congress gaiter or boot. Shoe with side gusset of elastic, worn by men of affairs. Highly popular in the nineties and in the early years of 19th century. See SHOES.
Conmar. Trade name for a slide fastener.
connaught (kŏn'ôt; *con* nawt). Foundation cloth of cotton fabric used for embroidery.
Consulate (kŏn'sə-lət; *con* sul let). Of

the style of French Consulate (1799–1804) following Directoire style; characterized by long dresses, often white, of simple lines, girdled very high; classic drapery; short sleeves; handsome embroidery; Indian shawls superseding spencers and pelisses; turbans and bonnets; hair dressed high with feathers and fillets.
consumer (kən-sū'mẽr; con *sue* mer). One who buys and uses merchandise. Women are considered the foremost consumers, since they buy, for themselves and their families, 83 per cent of all merchandise manufactured.
consumption (kən-sŭmp'shŭn; con *sump* shun). Using up of goods, food, shelter, clothing, in satisfying human needs.
contemporary (kən-tĕm'pə-rĕr-ĭ; con *temp* o rare i). Existing at same period of time. The short skirt and cloche hat of the early 1920's were contemporary fashions.
Continental hat. Tricorn hat with broad, upturned brim, of type worn by George Washington's Continental Army. Also called *cocked hat*. See HATS.
Continental heel (kŏn-tĭ-nĕn'tal; con ti *nen* tal). High heel. See HEELS.
continental-stitch. Type of tapestry stitches used in needle-point. See STITCHES.
continuous placket. Placket made in fabric or on seam, finished with one continuous strip of material on both edges of opening. See PLACKETS.
contour (kŏn'tōōr; con toor). Shape of the face, head, or body; outline of a figure.
convent cloth. Woolen fabric in plain weave. Used as dress goods; formerly used by the "Sisters" in convents.
convertible collar. Straight collar, applied double, originally so made as to be worn up or turned down.
convex curve. Curve rounding outward; opposite of concave. See CURVE.
cony or **coney** (kō'nĭ; *co* ni). Rabbit skin. Often processed to resemble other furs. See FURS.
cool color. Hue associated with feeling of coolness, with blue predominating. See COLOR.
coolie coat. Short, loose coat, having unshaped armhole. See COATS.
coolie hat. Cloche with brim slanting downward. See HATS.
coon. Shortened form of raccoon. See FURS.
coonskin. 1. Skin of raccoon. See FURS. **2.** Fur coat. See COATS.
coordinated colors (kō-ôr'dĭ-nāt-ĕd; co or di nate ed). Colors harmoniously assembled. See COLOR.
coordination. Assembly or arrangement of parts in suitable relation, as of suit, hat, bag, gloves, to make harmonious or smart ensemble.
coothay (kōō-thā'; coo *thay*). Striped satin fabric made in India.
copa (kō'pə; *co* pa). Sides of crown of hat, especially Panama hat.
copatain (kŏp'ə-tān; *cop* a tain). High-crowned hat. See HATS.

fāte, făt, dánce, ärt mē, mĕt, hẽr, thêre rīde, rĭd nōte, nŏt, côrn, fōōd, fŏŏt cūte, cŭt, cūre now fĭn(ŋ)ger villa(ə) señor pleas(zh)ure

cope. Semicircular mantle or similar robe. See WRAPS.
copenhagen blue (cō-pən-hā'gən; oo pen *hay* gen). Medium light grayish blue.
copintank (kŏp'ĭn-tănk; *cop* in tank). High-crowned hat. See HATS.
copper or **copper red.** Brown color, with dull reddish-yellow cast.
copper lace. Lace of old-copper color. See LACES.
copy. 1. Written matter, usually to be or already published; as, fashion copy. 2. Dress or hat or other garment copied from an original model.
coq feather (F. kŏk; coke). Cock feather. See FEATHERS.
coque (F. kŏk; coke). Loop or looped bow of ribbon. Used as trimming. From French *encoquer*, meaning to twist, fasten.
coqueluche (F. kô-klüsh; oo cloosh). French word for hood or cowl.
coquillage (F. kô-kē-yàzh; oo kee yahzh). Shell-work or decoration in imitation of shells. Used as trimming. French word for shell-fish, shell, or shellwork.
coquille (kô-kēl' or F. kô-kē; oo *keel* or oo kee). Edging or ruching, gathered or fulled in imitation of shell edge. Used as trimming, especially in neckwear, millinery. French word for shell.
coral (kŏr'əl; *cor* al). 1. Branch-like skeleton from the sea, varying in color from near-white to dark lip-red. Used for necklaces, ornaments, jewelry. 2. Color in varying shades and tints; as, pale coral, deep coral, etc.
coral-stitch. Blanket-stitch worked backward. See STITCHES.
corbeau (F. kôr-bō; cor bo). Very dark green, almost black. French word for raven.
cord. 1. String or small rope, composed of several strands twisted or woven together. 2. Rib, like a cord, in fabric. 3. Ribbed fabric, especially corduroy. 4. (Plural) Trousers or breeches made of corduroy.
corded. Ribbed as if with cords or cord-like stripes or lines, as cloth having lengthwise ribs produced by warp; crosswise, by weft; diagonal, by twill weave.
corded seam. Welt seam with covered cord stitched along seam edge. See SEAMS.
cordelière (kŏr-də-lēr'; cor de *leer*) or **cordelière** (F. kôr-də-lyĕr; cor de lyare). Knotted girdle, of type worn by Franciscan friars. Popular during 19th century as trimming on wraps.

Cordeliere

cording. 1. Cable cord covered with bias fabric to make a corded edge or trimming. 2. Rope-like cord, often of silk, used to make loops and trimmings.
cording foot. Sewing-machine foot, having only one prong or side, used for sewing close to edge in which a cord is used.
cordon (kôr'dən; *cor* don). Decorative cord, lace, or braid. Used on costume as fastening; to indicate rank, as badge of honor; or solely for adornment. Also, to ornament with a cordon.
cordonnet (kôr-də-nĕt' or F. kôr-dôn-nā; cor do *net* or cor don nay). Small cord or thread of silk, linen, cotton, etc. Used in fringes, tassels, embroidery; to outline pattern in point lace; to edge lace or millinery braid.
cordovan (kôr'də-vən; *cor* do van). 1. Soft, durable, dark reddish-brown, nonporous leather. See LEATHERS. 2. Dark reddish-brown color.
cord-stitch. Stitch made to resemble raised, twisted cord. See STITCHES.
corduroy (kôr'dŭ-roi; *cor* du roy). 1. Cotton velvet with a wide or narrow wale; usually of mercerized yarn; formed by extra weft or filling, making wales, cords, or ribs. Made in black, white, and wide range of colors; sometimes printed. Used for lounging robes, coats, trousers, slacks, suits, skirts, dresses, etc., especially in sports types. From French *cord du roi*, meaning king's cord; originally used for livery of king's outdoor servants. 2. (Plural) Trousers or breeches of corduroy.
cordwain (kôrd'wān; *cord* wain). Medieval name for CORDOVAN. See LEATHERS.
cordwainer (kôrd'wān-ēr; *cord* wain er). Shoemaker. Originally, worker in cordwain or cordovan leather.
cordy. Type of felt hat. See HATS.
corium (kō'rĭ-ŭm; *cori* um). Armor for upper body, made of overlapping scales or small flaps of leather. Worn by Roman, later by English, soldiers. Latin word for leather.
cork. Porous, light-weight, elastic outer bark of cork-oak tree. Used for thick soles of beach and sports shoes, trimming such as buttons, etc.
corkscrew twill. Fabric, usually woolen or worsted, having spiral twill; woven so that filling is hidden inside.
cornercap. Formerly, academic or ecclesiastical cap. See CAPS.
cornet (kôr'nĕt; *cor* net). 1. Woman's headdress made of delicate material in varying styles, often cone-shaped, usually ornamented with lappets of ribbon or lace. Worn from 14th to 18th century. 2. Part of this headdress, especially a lappet. 3. Square cap. 4. Trumpet-shaped sleeve. See CAPS. See SLEEVES.
corona (kə-rō'nə; oo *ro* na). 1. Circlet or fillet, often of gold, upon ecclesiastical vestment for head. 2. Crown or garland bestowed by ancient Romans in honor of distinguished service. Latin word for crown.
coronal (kôr'ə-nəl; *cor* o nal). Coronet or crown; garland or wreath; circlet suggesting dignity or rank. Also (kə-rō'nəl; oo *ro* nal), pertaining to coronet, crown, etc.

coronation braid (kŏr-ə-nā'shŭn; cor o *nay* shun). Filled cotton cord or braid of irregular thicknesses. See BRAIDS.
coronet (kôr'ə-nĕt; *cor* o net). 1. Ornamental circlet, wreath, etc., for the head. 2. Worn as headdress with formal clothes. 2. Crown of different types denoting various high ranks less than sovereign. Similar to a halo.
corps intime (F. kôr ăŋ-tēm; core anh teem). French expression meaning social coterie or circle of close friends.
corsage (F. kôr-sàzh; cor sahzh). 1. Bouquet of real or artificial flowers worn on the front of a costume, often at the shoulder or waistline. 2. French word meaning waist or bodice of woman's dress. 3. Fitted girdle-like bod-

Corsage Bodice, 1916

ice, shaped to the armhole on one side and slanting down to girdle depth on the other.
corse. Band, as of silk, or ribbon used in making ornamental, often embroidered, vestment, girdle, garter, etc.
corselet (kôr-sə-lĕt'; cor se *let*). 1. Undergarment combining girdle or lightly boned corset and brassière. Also called *foundation* or *one-piece corset*. 2. (kôrs'lĕt; *corse* let) Medieval body armor; also, in 16th century, armor for upper body.
corselet sash. Girdle-like sash. See SASHES.
corset. Smoothly fitted undergarment extending from or below the bust down over the hipline; often stiffened by strips of steel or whalebone, limbered by elastic goring; sometimes tightened by lacing. Worn by women for support and figure-molding. Originally, made in two pieces laced together at front and back. Formerly called *stays*; now usually called *corsets*.
corset bodice. Usually formal bodice or waist part, so draped or shaped as to follow the corset line. See BODICES.
corset cover. Garment to cover the

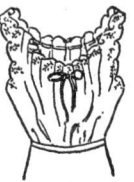

Corset Cover, 1910

corsetière

corset; also, underbodice with built-up shoulders, or camisole.
corsetière (F. kôr-sə-tyêr; cor se tyare). Woman corset-maker; also, one who sells or fits corsets.
corset lace. Narrow tape for lacing corsets.
corset waist. Fitted underwaist, generally buttoned up the front. Usually made with attached supporters or with buttons for supporters. Worn by girls and small women.
cosmesis (kŏz-mē'sĭs; coz *mee* sis). Improvement or keeping up of natural beauty.
cosmetic (kŏz-mĕt'ĭk; coz *met* ic). **1.** Any one of many superficial aids to beauty, applied externally—powder, rouge, lipstick, eye shadow, mascara, etc. Generally used in the plural. **2.** Art of applying cosmetics. **3.** Beautifying; as, cosmetic lotion.
cosmetician (kŏz-mə-tĭsh'ən; coz me *tish* an). One who makes or deals in cosmetics; also, one who applies cosmetics professionally.
Cossack (kŏs'ăk; *coss* ack). In fashion, any influence suggesting costume of Cossacks: For women, long, full skirt, open in front; tight bodice; sleeves, sometimes falling over hands; shawl; headdress of miter type. For men, long circular cape or flared coat; full trousers; white blouse with long, full sleeves; vest; tall fur cap; high boots. Also, the uniform of Cossack cavalry troops, consisting of regular Russian blouse and trousers of dark color, flared fitted coat with open V-neck, flared sleeves, and cartridge plaits at the breast, Cossack fur cap, boots.

Cossack
Costume

Cossack cap. 1. Tall, brimless cap of fur or lamb's wool. See CAPS. **2.** Adaptation of original cap. See COSSACK HAT under HATS.
cossas (kŏs'ăz; *coss* az). Plain cottons from India.
costume (kŏs'tūm; *coss* tume). **1.** Complete dress or apparel, including all outer garments and accessories worn at one time. Also, dress in general; but incorrectly used for a dress. Compare DRESSES. **2.** Type of dress for wear to fancy dress ball. See FANCY DRESS. **3.** Type of dress characteristic of any country, period, class, or calling.
costume jewelry. Colorful or ornate non-precious jewelry designed to complement costume. Often in matching sets of necklace, bracelet, rings, etc. See JEWELRY.
costumer (kŏs-tūm'ẽr or kŏs'tūm-ẽr; coss *tume* er or coss *tume* er). One who makes or deals in fancy dress costumes.
costume slip. Slip designed for wear with particular costume. See SLIPS.
costume suit. Ensemble. See SUITS.
costume velvet. Cotton velvet of good quality. So called because so frequently used for theatrical costumes. See VELVETS.
costumier (kŏs-tūm'ĭ-ẽr or F. kŏs-tū-myä; coss *tume* i er or coss too myay). Costumer; one making, selling, or altering costumes.
costumière (F. kŏs-tū-myêr; coss too myare). Woman costumer.
cot. Sheath for finger. See STALL.
cote. Obsolete term for outer garment or coat.
cote-hardie (kŏt här'dĭ; coat *har* di). Close-fitting, tunic-like garment with sleeves; usually hip-length, buttoned or laced down front. Worn by men in late Middle Ages; sometimes over breastplate of armor; sometimes decorated with coat of arms. Also worn by women.
côtelé (F. kōt-lā; cote lay). Fabric having ribs. French word for ribbed.
coteline (F. cōt-lēn; cote leen). Thin white cotton fabric, usually corded.
cothurn (kō'thẽrn or kō-thẽrn'; *ko* thern or ko *thern*) or **cothurnus** (kō-thẽrn'ŭs; ko *thern* us). Half boot or buskin. See BOOTS.
cotillon (kə-tĭl'yən; co *till* yun). **1.** Black and white striped woolen dress material. **2.** Formal ballroom dance.
coton (F. kô-tôɴ; co tonh). French word for cotton.
cotta. Short ecclesiastical surplice, usually of white linen.
cottage bonnet. Bonnet fashionable in early 19th century. See BONNETS.
cotte (F. kŏt; cot). Garment similar to COTE-HARDIE. French word meaning short petticoat, jacket, coat.

COTTONS

cotton. 1. Soft, downy, fibrous substance attached to seeds of cotton plant, which is spun into yarn and then made into threads or woven into various textiles. **2.** Fabric made of cotton. **3.** Sewing thread spun from cotton. See THREADS.
absorbent c. (ăb-sôr'bĕnt; ab *sor* bent). Cotton batting made highly absorbent by chemical removal of natural oils or fatty matter. Used chiefly for medical purposes.
Egyptian c. Fine, strong cotton of excellent quality, with long, silky staple, naturally off-white in color. Originally grown in Egypt; now also in U. S. Used for knit goods, especially hosiery. Best qualities of Egyptian cotton are the finest, most expensive of all cottons.
macò (mä'kō; *mah* ko). Fine-fibered, long-staple tree cotton, used for hosiery, underwear, etc.
mercerized c. (mẽr'sẽr-īzd; *mer* ser ized). Cotton fiber or fabric treated with caustic solution, making it stronger, more susceptible to dye, and giving it silky luster. Mercerization adds to the beauty of cotton and also makes it slightly more expensive.
sea-island c. Cotton, especially from West Indies, with long silky fibers. Formerly grown on islands along coast of Georgia, South Carolina. Usually a superior grade of cotton.

cottonade. Heavy, coarsely-woven cloth of cotton or cotton mixture. Used for men's sports and work clothes.
cotton back. Fabric woven of mixed yarns, so that cotton shows on back; with some other fiber, silk, wool, or rayon, on face.
cotton batting. Same as SHEET WADDING.
cotton binding. Cotton bias binding. See BINDINGS.
cotton cambric. Same as CAMBRIC, 1.
cotton crepe. Crinkled cotton fabric. See CREPES.
cotton darner. Type of darning needle available in sizes 1 to 10. See DARNING NEEDLE under NEEDLES.
cotton flannel. Durable, soft cotton fabric, used for underclothing, sleeping garments, interlinings. See FLANNELS, 2.
cottonnade (F. kô-tô-năd; co to nahd). French term for cotton cloth; cotton goods.
cotton print. Same as CALICO.
cotton rep. Heavy cotton fabric with ribs, usually horizontal. Used for draperies, children's school clothes, etc.
cotton velvet. Same as VELVETEEN.
cotton wool. Raw cotton.
cotton worsted (wŏŏs'tĕd; *wooss* ted). Cotton fabric made to imitate wool worsted.
couching. Method of embroidery consisting of securing laid threads by taking stitches across them diagonally or crosswise. See EMBROIDERIES.
couching-stitch. Ornamental stitch used to secure laid threads. See STITCHES.
couleur (F. kōō-lêr; coo ler). French word for color.
count. 1. In determining texture of fabric, number of threads or picks to inch; as, fine count, 44-count. Usually called *thread count.* **2.** Of yarn, number of hanks to pound; size, size of fiber.
counter. Piece of stiffened material cut by pattern measurements and used in shoe construction to keep back part in shape. Pasted between lining and outside leather of the quarter. Made of leather of good quality in better shoes; made of fiber or poor leather stiffened with glue in cheaper shoes.
counter book. Catalogue of patterns available for reference at counters in pattern departments of stores; issued by individual pattern companies.
couronne (F. kōō-rôn; coo ron). Ornamental loop for cordonnet edging point lace. French word for crown. See FLEUR VOLANT.
course (kōrs; corse). **1.** In knit goods, crosswise row of stitches, corresponding to weft in woven goods. **2.** Plan of study. **3.** Progress, passage, direction; as, the course of fashion.

---

fāte, făt, dánce, ärt mē, mĕt, hẽr, thêre rīde, rĭd nōte, nŏt, côrn, fōōd, fŏŏt cūte, cŭt, cûre now fin(ŋ)ger villa(ə) señor pleas(zh)ure

court tie. Oxford tie. See SHOES.
couter (kōō'tēr; *coo* ter). Elbow-piece of armor.
coutil (kōō-tĭl' or F. kōō-tē; *coo till* or *coo tee*). Firm, sturdy type of drilling made of hard-twisted yarns, usually cotton, in twill or figured weave. Used for corsets, girdles, etc. French word for drill or ticking. Also spelled *coutille* and *coutelle*.
couture (F. kōō-tūr; *coo* toor). French word meaning sewing or needlework; work, business, or products of a seamstress; seam.
couturier (F. kōō-tü-ryä; *coo too* ryay). French word for male costume designer; usually one who has dressmaking establishment.
couturière (F. kōō-tü-ryêr; *coo too* ryare). French word for woman costume designer. In U. S., the words "couturier," "couturière" are usually used in reference to important dressmakers of Paris.
coverall (kŭv'ēr-ôl; *cuv* er all). One-piece garment worn over a dress to protect it. Women's overalls are often called coveralls.
coverchief (kŭv'ēr-chĭf; *cuv* er chif). Kerchief worn on head as covering.
covered button. Button covered with fabric. See BUTTONS.
coverslut (kŭv'ēr-slŭt; *cuv* er slut). Garment, often apron, worn to hide untidy clothes.
covert or **covert cloth** (kŭv'ērt; *cuv* ert). Durable medium-weight fabric in diagonal twill weave; made of tightly twisted two-ply yarns, one woolen or worsted, the other cotton, silk, or rayon, originally giving cloth finely speckled appearance; hard or soft finished; sometimes waterproofed. Used for suits, coats, raincoats, riding habits. So called because worn in England while riding to covert, or shelter, in fox hunting.
covert coat. Coat of covert cloth. See COATS.
cowboy boots. High-heeled riding boots, often with fancy stitching or trimming on top; usually worn by cowboys. See BOOTS.
cowboy hat. Brimmed felt hat with creased crown; often trimmed with tassel. See HATS.
cowhide (kow'hīd; *cow* hide). **1.** Leather made from hide of cow. See LEATHERS. **2.** Coarse, heavy whip made of braided leather, often rawhide.
cowl. **1.** Monk's hood, usually attached to garment. See HOODS. Also, monk's hooded garment. See WRAPS. **2.** Scottish term for nightcap or other cap worn in

Original Cowl.

Modern Cowl

house.—**c. drape.** Soft fold or drape of self-material at back of neckline similar in effect to monk's cowl dropped over shoulders at back.—**c. neckline.** Soft fold or drape of material at front neckline. See NECKLINES.
coxcomb. **1.** Small strip of red cloth, usually notched to resemble comb of cock, as formerly worn in cap by court jesters. **2.** Jester's cap. See CAPS.
coyote (kī'ōt or kī-ōt'ē; *ky* ote or ky *ote* ee). Fur or pelt of coyote, small wolf of western U. S. See FURS.
coypu (koi'pōō; *coy* poo). Fur of South American rat, plucked like beaver. Usually called *nutria*. See FURS.
crabbing. Process of treating fabric to give particular finish, chiefly to prevent wrinkling after wetting.
crackled. Having effect of fissured or crackled pottery, as lace, silk, net, etc.
crackle net or **crackly net.** Net with mesh of crackle design. Same as CRAQUELÉ NET. See NETS.
crakow (krā'kow; *cray* cow). Shoe with long, pointed toe. See SHOES. Also, elongated toe on such shoe.
crape. **1.** Same as CREPE. **2.** Thin worsted fabric. Formerly used for clerical gowns. **3.** Strip of crape worn as mourning band.
craquelé (F. kräk-lā; *crack* lay). French word meaning crackled.
crash. Any of several coarsely woven fabrics having rough texture due to knotted or uneven yarns. **1.** Linen or cotton cloth of plain weave in varying weights and colors. Used for dresses, blouses. **2.** Art linen, natural, white, or dyed. **3.** Plain-woven cloth of linen or cotton often mixed with jute. Used for curtains. **4.** Absorbent cloth of linen, cotton, or mixture in plain or twill weave. Used for towels. **5.** Coarse cloth of linen with woody fibers, handwoven by Russian peasants. **6.** Novelty wool fabric, so called because of rough texture. Named from Latin *crassus*, meaning coarse.
cravat (krə-văt'; cra *vat*). Necktie or neckcloth; usually, formal scarf folded or tied at front, ends tucked inside coat. Formerly, piece of lace, lawn, or other fine cloth worn about neck by men before introduction of neckties. Highly fashionable during 17th century.
Cravenette (krā-və-nĕt'; *cray* ve *net*). Trade name for waterproof finish given cloth; also, any cloth so treated.
craze. Transient fashion or fad, characterized by quick acceptance and extravagant enthusiasm.
crea (Sp. krā'ä; *cray* ah). Fabric of linen or cotton popular in Spain and Spanish America.
creaser (krēs'ēr; *creece* er). Implement or sewing-machine attachment which creases cloth or leather to make lines as guide for sewing.
crease-resistant. Term used of fabrics, chiefly cotton, linen, rayon, chemically treated to resist wrinkling or recover quickly from wrinkling. See CRUSH-RESISTANT.
creation. Article of apparel of novel or striking

design; garment in which originality is shown.
creedmore. Man's heavy, laced shoe of blucher type. See SHOES.
creeper. **1.** Piece of leather or iron with iron cleats or pieces on the bottom, attached to shoe by strap over foot. Worn to prevent slipping on ice or to keep feet from mud. **2.** Garment like a romper worn by very young children just learning to creep.
crenelated (krĕn'ə-lāt-ĕd; *cren* e late ed). Having series of squared indentations and projections, uniform in size and spacing. Same as BATTLEMENTED.
crénelé (F. krā-nə-lā; cray ne lay). French word meaning crenelated. Past participle of *créneler*, meaning to indent in squares.
Creole (krē'ōl; *cree* ole). Trade name of work shoe. See SHOES.

CREPES

crepe (krāp; crape). Any of various fabrics, usually having crinkled surface, caused by: (1) Way of twisting or slackening warp of filling yarns; (2) novelty weave or calendering; (3) chemical treatment, usually mercerization in sections, causing parts of surface to shrink. Originally, thin, gauzy, silk fabric heavily sized, crimped or creped in drying, first used in black as badge of mourning; in this sense, usually spelled *crape*.
Albert c. Kind of crepe made of both silk and cotton. Fairly heavy. Used in the 1880's for dresses.
Canton c. Soft crepe-woven fabric, heavier, richer-looking than crepe de Chine, having slight cross-ribs caused by method of tightly twisting filling yarns and loosely twisted warp yarns. Favored fabric for dresses; drapes and sews beautifully.
chirimen (chĭr'ĭ-mĕn; *chir* i men). Type of silk crepe of Japanese make. Used for dresses, kimonos, blouses.
cotton c. Plain-woven cotton fabric of various weights, qualities, designs, having crinkled appearance usually produced by twisted yarns. Used for summer dresses, blouses, underclothes, nightclothes, kimonos, children's clothes, etc.
c. de Chine (F. krāp də shĕn; crape de sheen). Lustrous, finely crinkled, washable fabric; plain or printed, usually of silk. Imitations at one time made with silk warp and worsted or other filling. Used for dresses, blouses, lingerie. From the French, *de Chine*, of China.
cotton c. de Chine. Fabric made with cotton warp, spun silk filling, as imitation of, or substitute for, crepe de Chine.
c. lisse (F. lēs; leece). Thin, smooth, glossy silk fabric with feel of crepe. French word meaning smooth, glossy.
Crépella (krā-pĕl'ə; cray *pell* a). Trade name for type of wool crepe. Used for dresses, blouses, etc.
c. meteor (mē'tē-ēr; *mee* tee or). Fine grade of light-weight silk crepe, satin-finished on one side. Used for dresses, blouses, lingerie, negligees.

fāte, făt, dănce, ärt mē, mĕt, hēr, thêre rīde, rĭd nōte, nŏt, côrn, fōōd, fŏŏt cūte, cŭt, cūré now fin(ŋ)ger villa(ə) señor pleas(zh)ure

crinkle cloth. Light-weight cotton fabric with crinkled warp stripes, usually produced by chemical means. Similar to SEERSUCKER.
flat c. Crepe with smooth, soft, flat surface made of silk or other yarns only slightly twisted. Heavier and smoother than crepe de Chine. Used for dresses, blouses, slips, etc.
georgette c. (jôr-jĕt'; jor jet). Sheer, highly creped fabric of fine texture, plain-woven of high-twist yarns; silk, silk and cotton, silk and rayon, or other mixtures. Used for dresses, blouses, gowns, trimming. So called for Mme. Georgette de la Plante, French modiste.
Japanese c. Plain-woven cotton fabric highly creped by twisted filling yarns. Imported from Japan. Used for dresses, kimonos, blouses, smocks, etc.
marocain (mă-rō-kăn'; mar o cane). Ribbed crepe of silk or wool or combination. Used for dresses and for suits of dressmaker type.
mourning c. Dull black crepe, usually silk. Used for mourning millinery, for trimming mourning apparel.
Oriental c. 1. Same as Canton crepe. 2. Hand-woven crepes from China and Japan.
plissé c. (F. plē-sā; plee say). Thin, light-weight cotton crepe in plain weave with permanent puckered stripes, lengthwise of fabric, or allover blistered effect usually produced by chemical means. Similar to SEERSUCKER. Used for underwear, nightclothes, children's garments, men's and women's summer clothes, etc.
satin-back c. Fabric of silk, rayon, or mixture, having crepe face, satin back; made in various weights. Used for dresses, blouses; one side of material often used as trim for other.
Serpentine c. (sẽr'pĕn-tēn; ser pen teen). Trade name for cotton fabric in plain weave, permanently creped in lengthwise grooves. Available in white, solid colors, print. Used for wash dresses, blouses, play suits, nightdresses, etc.
wool c. Sturdy, wiry woolen fabric in various weights and surface effects, with crepy texture due to use of high-twist yarns; use of right- and left-hand twist yarns alternately; or slackening of some warp yarns. Used for dresses, dressmaker suits, blouses, children's clothes. Ideal light-weight woolen for dresses, plaited skirts, etc.

crêpé (F. krĕ-pā; cray pay). French word meaning frizzled,crisped, wrinkled; also, small hair pad or tuft worn by women.
crepe-back satin. Fabric with satin face and crepe back; usually heavier than silk crepe. See SATINS.
crepe de Chine (F. krăp də shēn; crape de shēn). Lustrous, slightly crinkled fabric; usually silk. See CREPES.
crépeline (F. krĕ-pə-lēn; cray pe leen). Thin, light-weight dress fabric of silk or silk mixture. Usually not so good as crepe de Chine, though it is often substituted for it.

crepe lisse (F. lēs; leece). Sheer silk fabric. See CREPES.
Crépella (krā-pĕl'ə; cray pell a). Trade name for a wool dress crepe. See CREPES.
crepe meteor (krāp mē'tē-ẽr; crape mee tee or). Silk crepe, satin-finished on one side, having good draping quality. See CREPES.
crepine (krĕ'pĭn; crep in) or **crespine.** 1. Fringe having wide network at top, knotted or woven. 2. Caul or net for woman's hair, usually woven of gold, silver, or silk threads.
crépon (krā'pɒn or F. krā-pôŋ; cray pon or cray ponh). Crinkled fabric woven with hard-twisted weft yarns, resembling crepe but thicker, firmer. Usually made of silk or silk mixture; also made of rayon, cotton, wool, or combination.
crescent. 1. Raised cordonnet varying in shape, length, thickness. Used in needle-point lace to enclose flat stitches or to join pieces of work together. 2. Ornament or decoration in shape of moon in first quarter.
Cretan-stitch (krē'tən; cree tan). Variation of feather-stitch. See STITCHES.
Crete lace. Loose, colored, bobbin lace. See LACES.
cretonne (krĕ-tŏn'; cre tonn). Strong, medium-weight, unglazed fabric in variety of weaves and finishes, printed on one or both sides in large patterns, usually floral. Made of cotton or linen. Used chiefly for curtains, slip-covers, etc. Probably named for town in Normandy called Cretonne.
crève-cœur (F. krĕv kẽr; crev cur). 17th century name for lovelock worn at nape of neck. French phrase meaning heart-break.
crevette (F. krĕ-vĕt; cre vet). Pinkish color of shrimp. French word for shrimp.
crewel. 1. Worsted yarn, loosely twisted. See YARNS. 2. Short for crewel work.
crewel needle. Needle with long eye, used for making embroidery stitches. See NEEDLES.
crewel-stitch. Rope-like embroidery stitch used in crewel embroidery. See STITCHES.
crewel work. Worsted embroidery in conventional designs on household articles. See EMBROIDERIES.
crew neckline. Round, high neckline, as in a sweater. See NECKLINES.
criarde (F. krē-ärd; cree ard). Stiffened pannier that creaked. See HOOPS.
crimp. To flute or plait finely, often with crimping iron. Also, small fold or wrinkle or series of them.
crimson (krĭm'zən; crim zon). Any of several bright, "live" red colors with bluish tint.
crin (F. krăŋ; cranh). 1. French word meaning coarse hair, especially horse-hair, as woven into various stiff foundation fabrics. 2. Short for CRINOLINE. 3. Heavy silk substance. See SILK.
crinkle cloth. Cotton fabric having crinkled stripes. See CREPES.
crinoletta (krĭn-ə-lĕt'ə; crin o let a). Bustle-like device. See BUSTLES.

crinoline (krĭn'ə-lĭn; crin o lin). 1. Fabric of hair or stiffened silk or cotton, used as a foundation to support the edge of a hem, the top of a sleeve, the brim of a hat, etc.; formerly used for the lower two-thirds of underskirts, to extend skirts. Originally made of horse-hair and linen. 2. Hoopskirt. See SKIRTS. 3. Steel springs or featherbone forming hoop. See HOOPS.
crisp. Light, transparent fabric formerly used for veiling.
crispin (krĭs'pĭn; cris pin). Type of frock coat. See COATS.
crochet (krō-shā'; cro shay). Fancy-work or needlework made by looping any kind of thread or yarn with a crochet needle. Laces and household articles, as well as garments, are crocheted. Also, to make this fancy work.
crochet button. Button mold covered with crochet. See BUTTONS.
crochet cotton. Strong, twisted thread, made in white, black, and beautiful colors; and in many sizes, from 1, the coarsest, to 200, the finest. See THREADS.
crochet hook or **needle.** Hooked needle. See NEEDLES.
crochet lace. Lace made of thread or yarn looped by hooked needle. See LACES.
crocket. Large curled roll of hair worn as part of coiffure by women of the 14th century.
crocodile (krŏk'ə-dīl; crock o dile). Term applied to alligator leather. Not legitimately used in the trade. True crocodile has not been tanned satisfactorily as yet.
croft. To bleach on grass in sun. See GRASS BLEACHING.
croisé (F. krwä-zā; crwah zay). French word meaning twilled.
croisé velvet. Coarse-backed velvet. See VELVETS.
croquis (F. krō-kē; cro kee). French word for quick sketch, rough likeness; used especially of fashion sketch.
cross-basket-stitch. Intersecting groups of parallel threads fastened at intersections by cross-stitches. See STITCHES.
crosscloth. That part of woman's 17th century coif or headdress worn across forehead.
cross-dyeing. Piece-dyeing, when fibers of the fabric react differently to dye. See DYEING.
crossed blanket-stitch. Blanket-stitch worked to form series of crosses above the purled line. See STITCHES.
cross fox. Fur of fox with cross-shaped mark on shoulders. See FURS.
cross Persian. Trade name for fur from sheep with strain of Persian. Not so valuable as true Persian. See FURS.
cross-stitch. Decorative stitch that forms X. Used chiefly for sampler work. See STITCHES.
cross-stitch canvas. Square-mesh canvas on which designs are worked in cross-stitch. See CANVAS.
cross-stitch embroidery. Any embroidery worked chiefly in cross-stitch. See EMBROIDERIES.

cross tucks. Tucks that cross other tucks, thus forming squares or diamond shapes. See TUCKS.

crosswise. Cut across the warp or on a woof thread, making a crosswise line; distinguished from LENGTHWISE and BIAS. Applied to garments so cut; as, crosswise skirt, blouse, yokes, sleeves, front plaits, etc.

crotch. That part of a garment formed by joining of two legs.—**joined leg c.** Crotch formed by joining of leg seams to form closing, as in step-ins.—**pantie c.** Crotch formed by narrow shaped piece set into joining, as in panties, briefs, shorts.—**strap c.** Crotch formed by fabric strip, usually buttoning at front end, joining front to back. Also called *button-tab crotch, French drawer bottom*.

crown. 1. Headdress worn on formal occasions by monarchs and the higher members of the nobility. Also, wreath, decorative circlet, or fillet for head, worn as mark of honor, power, or as reward. 2. Upper portion of hat or other head covering, as distinguished from brim or band. 3. Top part of cut stone or gem, above the edge grasped by the setting. 4. Pointed stitch used in needle-point lace. See PIN WORK. 5. (Capitalized) Trade name for rayon fabric made by firm that uses the viscose process. See RAYON.

Crown Zipper. Trade name for American-made slide fastener, advertised as die-cast rather than molded. See FASTENERS.

crow's-foot. Satin-stitch crossed to form three points with raised triangular center. Used on tailored garments for strength or to provide a finish.

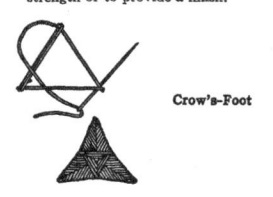

Crow's-Foot

cruche (krōōsh; croosh). Kind of flat curl formerly worn on forehead.

crumenal (krōō'mə-nəl; *croo* me nal). Obsolete term for purse.

crushed leather. Novelty treatment giving to leather a round, slightly bumpy grain similar to blistered fabric. See LEATHERS.

crush hat. Soft or collapsible hat. See HATS.

crush-resistant. Term used of erect pile fabrics chemically treated to make them resist marking, creasing, crushing, and to recover from the effects of pressure or moisture. See CREASE-RESISTANT.

crystal (krĭs'təl; *cris* tal). Variety of transparent, colorless quartz. Used for costume jewelry.

Cuban heel (kū'bən; *cue* ban). Medium high, almost straight heel. See HEELS.

cubica (kū'bĭ-kə; *cue* bi ca). Fine worsted fabric, similar to SHALLOON. Used chiefly for linings.

cubital (kū'bĭ-təl; *cue* bi tal). Sleeve covering arm from wrist to elbow. See SLEEVES.

cubitière (F. kü-bē-tyêr; koo bee tyare). Piece of medieval plate armor worn as guard for the elbow.

cuculla (kū-kŭl'ə; *cue cull* a). Loose, outer garment, usually sleeveless, with opening only for head. Formerly worn as protection for other garments. Similar to monk's SCAPULAR.

cucullate (kū'kŭ-lāt; *cue* cull late). Hooded; covered, as with hood.

cucullus (kū-kŭl'ŭs; *cue cull* us). Hood, often part of cloak. Sometimes made in cap-like shape with long ends that served as scarf to hold it on. Worn by ancient Romans.

cue. Braid of hair hanging down in back, of natural or artificial hair, or part of wig; pigtail. Same as QUEUE.

CUFFS

cuff. 1. Finish for sleeve or glove, for wrist or forearm. 2. Hem-like band on end of trouser leg. 3. Decorative band of leather, wider than collar, sewn around top of shoe. 4. Formerly, glove or mitten.
bracelet c. Cuff of metal, lace, ribbon, or other material, wider than the average bracelet. Worn around the wrist.
double c. Cuff, as on a man's shirt, that has a turn-back, making two thicknesses, usually fastened by cuff links.
French c. Cuff formed by turn-back of broad cuff-band fastened with cuff buttons.
glove c. Added part of long glove covering wrist or forearm; added wrist part of short glove.
mousquetaire c. (F. mōōs-kə-têr; moose ke tare). Deep, wide cuff that flares above wrist, as worn by musketeers of 17th, 18th centuries.
parament (păr'ə-měnt; *pa* ra ment). Ornamental cuff sewn on outside of sleeve, as on 18th century coats.
ruff. Plaited or fluted frill, often stiffly starched, similar to neck ruffs, but worn as cuff.

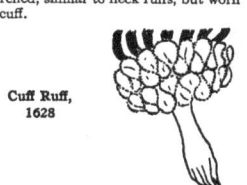

Cuff Ruff, 1628

single c. Cuff, as on a man's shirt, that has no turn-back and fastens with a button.
sleeve c. End of sleeve turned back at wrist, or separate band applied to end of sleeve. Also called *coat cuff*.
cuff link. Fastening device which passes through the two ends of cuff, usually consisting of two decorative buttons connected by shank, bar, screw, or flexible chain.

cuir (F. kwêr; cweer). Beige color having reddish-yellow cast. French word meaning leather.

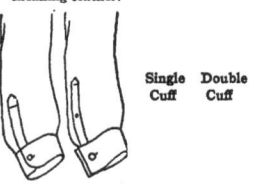

Single Cuff Double Cuff

18th Century Sleeve Cuff

cuirass (kwĭ-răs'; kwi *rass*). 1. Piece of close-fitting defensive armor covering upper body, especially consisting of coupled breastplate and backplate; also, breastplate alone. Originally made of leather. 2. Protective garment for upper body, as jacket or bodice, usually stiff or stiffened.

cuir-bouilli (F. kwêr bōō-ē-yē; cweer boo ee yee). Hard leather, boiled and molded into shape. French phrase for boiled leather. See LEATHERS.

cuisse (kwĭs; kwiss) or **cuish** (kwĭsh; kwish). Plate armor protecting thighs, especially in front.

cuivré (F. kwē-vrā; cwee vray). French word meaning copper colored.

culet (kū'lĕt; *cue* let). 1. Small, flat facet at bottom of cut gem, parallel to table at top. 2. That part of medieval defensive armor covering buttocks.

culgee (kŭl-gē'; cull gee). 1. Jeweled aigret or plume, as worn on turbans in India. 2. Figured silk fabric formerly imported from India.

culotte (kū-lŏt' or F. kü-lôt; *cue lot* or koo lot). Informal trouser-like garment having leg portions that are full and fall together to simulate a skirt. Worn as sports skirt.

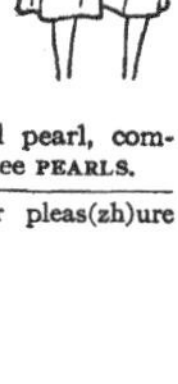

Culotte, 1930's

culture pearl. Cultivated pearl, comparatively inexpensive. See PEARLS.

immerbund

immerbund (kŭm'ẽr-bŭnd; *cum* er bund). Broad fitted sash, worn chiefly by men. See SASHES.

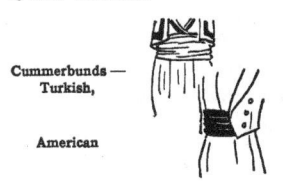

Cummerbunds —
Turkish,

American

iprammonium rayon. One of the three types of rayon now manufactured commercially in the U.S.A. See RAYON.

urch or **curchef** (kẽr'chĕf; *cur* chef). 1. Plain, close-fitting cap. See CAPS. 2. Kerchief-like head covering as worn by Scottish women, instead of cap or mutch.

url. Anything coiled or spiral, especially ringlet of hair; also, to form into ringlets or to make curved.

urling-iron. Metal instrument used, when heated, for curling the hair.

urlpaper. Strip of paper or similar material on which lock of hair is wound to make it curl.

urve. Bend without angles; also, to bend.—**concave c.** Curve that rounds inward.—**convex c.** Curve that rounds outward.

urved needle. Upholstery needle. See NEEDLES.

ushion (kŏŏsh'ən; *coosh* un). 1. Any bag or case stuffed with soft resilient material. 2. Formerly, bustle. 3. Pad for woman's hair.

cushion dot. Dot made by weaving in heavy extra yarns. See DOTS.

cushion-stitch. 1. In embroidery, same as TENT-STITCH, I. 2. Short, straight stitch producing effect of weaving. See STITCHES.

cushion style embroidery. Same as BERLIN WORK. See EMBROIDERIES.

custom-made. Made to customer's special order; cut and fitted to individual measurements, in fabric of suitable color and texture.

cut. 1. Style or manner in which garment is cut and made. 2. Standard length of cloth, varying with different types of fabrics. 3. Decorative slash in a garment.

cutaway. Coat with part of the skirt cut away. See COATS.

cut hose. Hose cut from goods already knit. See HOSE.

cut-off vamp. Vamp reaching to tip of shoe. See VAMP.

cutout. Having part cut away, as cutout

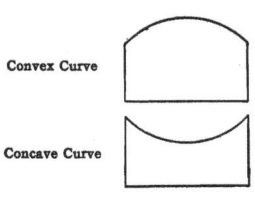

Convex Curve

Concave Curve

shoe; also, something which has part cut away, as a shoe.

cut pile. Term used of fabric with loops, formed in weaving, cut open; distinguished from uncut pile. See PILE.

cutting board. Board on which cloth is laid to be cut in preparation for sewing. Collapsible cutting boards used by women who sew at home.

cutting gauge. Device applied to point of scissors or shears to facilitate cutting cloth in strips of uniform width. Usually included in set of sewing-machine attachments.

cut velvet. Fabric with velvet pattern on sheer background. See VELVETS.

cut work. Eyelet type of embroidery; all openings are neatly buttonholed before they are cut out. See EMBROIDERIES.

cyclamen (sĭk'lə-měn; *sik* la men). Dull blue-red color, redder than plum or prune.

cyclas (sĭk'ləs; *sik* las). 1. Circular robe bordered with embroidery, usually of gold. Worn as outer garment by Roman women. 2. Close-fitting, tuniclike garment or surcoat, often sleeveless. Worn during Middle Ages by knights over armor, sometimes by women.

cylinder silhouette (sĭl'ĭn-dẽr sĭl-ōō-ĕt'; *sill* in der sill oo *et*). Straight up-and-down silhouette. See SILHOUETTES.

cymar (sĭ-mär'; si *mar*). 1. Woman's loose garment or light, scarf-like wrap. 2. Formerly CHIMERE.

Czecho-Slovakian embroidery (chĕk'ō slō-văk'ĭ-ən; *check* o slo *vack* i an). Brightly colored embroidery of geometrical designs. See EMBROIDERIES.

D

lacca silk (dăk'ə; *dack* a). Embroidery silk. See THREADS.

ialmatian (dăl-mā'shŭn; dal *may* shun). Characteristic of costume of Dalmatia, part of Jugoslavia. Consists of long, full skirt; high, round neck; full, usually white sleeves; wide belt; short, open jacket; long apron; lavish embroidery, fringe, metal ornament.

almatic (dăl-măt'ĭk; dal *mat* ic) or **dalmatica.** Long, straight robe with full sleeves, originally Dalmatian. Worn (1) as part of Byzantine costume; (2) by clergy of Western Church for certain ceremonies; (3) by royalty for state ceremonies, as coronations. From Latin *dalmatica*, meaning Dalmatian.

lamascene lace (dăm'ə-sēn; *dam* a seen). Imitation of HONITON, a tapelike bobbin lace. See LACES.

amask (dăm'əsk; *dam* ask). Firm, reversible, glossy fabric of many textile fiber combinations, woven in patterns so that one side has satin warp face designs with filling face background, and the other side is in reverse. Originally, all silk. Modern damasks woven on Jacquard loom. Used for table linens, upholstery, hangings; occasionally, for garments. Named for Damascus, where fabric originated.

damassé (F. dȧ-mȧ-sā; da ma say). Woven like damask; also, damask cloth, especially linen damask.

damassin (dăm'ə-sĭn; *dam* a sin). Damask or brocade with floral patterns woven in gold or silver threads.

dance dress. Youthful evening dress, usually of a bouffant type. See DRESSES.

dance set. Dainty lingerie set consisting of matching panties and brassière.

dancing slipper. Light-weight slipper worn for dancing. Usually of fabric. See SLIPPERS.

Danish embroidery (dăn'ĭsh; *dane* ish). Any embroidery of Denmark, chiefly HEDEBO. See EMBROIDERIES.

dark color. Color deeply darkened in hue by addition of black. See COLOR.

darn. To replace worn threads by weaving in new threads with darning-stitch.

darned embroidery. Embroidery done in variations of darning-stitch. See EMBROIDERIES.

darned lace. Lace with pattern filled in by needlework. See LACES.

darned work. Darned lace or darned embroidery. See DARNED EMBROIDERY under EMBROIDERIES. See DARNED LACE under LACES.

darner. 1. Darning ball or oval implement made of hard wood, ivory, glass, etc. Designed to hold article in rounded shape while being mended; chiefly used in darning socks and stockings. 2. DARNING NEEDLE. See NEEDLES.

darning. Process of replacing worn threads with darning-stitch; also, articles to be darned.

darning cotton. Loosely twisted, soft thread of several strands. See THREADS.

darning needle. Long-eyed needle used for darning. See NEEDLES.

darning-stitch. Stitches so placed as to imitate weaving. See STITCHES.

dart. Shaped tuck taken to fit garment to the figure; as, body dart, hip dart, shoulder dart, etc. Material in tuck sometimes cut away. Also, to take such a tuck.

dart length. Measurement of distance from waistline to fullest part of hips.

daytime dress. Dress suitable for shopping or business wear. Costume between morning and afternoon dress. See DRESSES.

debutante. 1. Girl between the ages of 18 and 20; presumably, one making her debut, or formal entrance into society. 2. Juvenile, youthful. Debutante clothes are those made in sizes 10 to 18.

īte, făt, dȧnce, ärt mē, mĕt, hẽr, thêre rīde, rĭd nōte, nŏt, côrn, fōōd, fŏŏt cūte, cŭt, cūrė now fin(ŋ)ger villa(ȧ) señor pleas(zh)ure

décolletage 42 Dieppe point lace

décolletage (F. dā-kŏl-ə-tázh; day coll e tahzh). Outline of low-cut or décolleté neck or yoke; also décolleté costume. Used in formal evening dresses.

18th Century Décolletage

décolleté (F. dā-kŏl-ə-tā; day coll e tay). Cut very low at neckline, exposing neck and back, or neck and shoulders, as in formal evening dress.

decrease (dē-krēs'; de crease). In knitting, crocheting, tatting, etc., to reduce the number of stitches on the needle. Done chiefly in shaping a garment to measurements. Often accomplished by working two stitches as one.

deep color. Full, strong hue. See COLOR.

deerskin. 1. Skin of deer, made into leathers including BUCKSKIN, ELK, ANTELOPE. See LEATHERS. 2. Garment made of deerskins.

défrisé (F. dā-frē-zā; day free zay). French word meaning uncurled; having come out of curl.

dégagé (F. dā-gȧ-zhā; day ga zhay). French word meaning free, easy.

dégradé (F. dā-grȧ-dā; day gra day). French word meaning subdued, as applied to tones of color.

degumming (dē-gŭm'ĭng; de gum ing). Process of removing natural gum from silk, done before or after weaving or knitting; often, by boiling in soap solution.

delaine (də-lān'; de lane). Light-weight dress fabric, originally woolen. Short for French mousseline de laine, meaning muslin of wool.

delft or **delf** or **delph blue.** Soft, medium blue having no yellow, as used in pottery made at Delft, Holland, in 14th century, or in imitations of it.

Delhi work (dĕl'ĭ; dell i). Rich Indian embroidery done in metal and silk on satin and other fabrics. See EMBROIDERIES.

delineator (də-lĭn'ē-ā-tēr; de lin ee ate er). 1. One who forecasts the fashions. 2. Tailor's pattern for cutting garments of various sizes. 3. (Capitalized) Name of a woman's magazine published for many years by the Butterick Publishing Co.

della Robbia colors (dĕl'ə rŏb'ĭ-ə; dell a robe i a). Pottery colors having soft glaze. Named for Luca della Robbia, Italian Renaissance sculptor and potter. See COLOR.

de luxe (F. də lūks; de lukes). Luxurious; of excellent or highest quality.

demibrassart (dĕm-ĭ-brăs'ērt; dem i brass ert). Piece of armor originally for upper arm. See BRASSART.

demijambe (dĕm'ĭ-jăm; dem i jam). Armor piece for front of leg.

demipauldron (dĕm-ĭ-pôl'drən; dem i paul dron). Small 15th century piece of armor for shoulder, used to join body and arm pieces.

demiseason (dĕm-ĭ-sē'zən; dem i see zon). In-between-season; between previous and approaching season in style. Term applied to costume.

demitoilet (dĕm'ĭ-toi-lĕt; dem i toy let). Semi-formal costume. See DRESS.

demivambrace (dĕm-ĭ-văm'brās; dem i vam brace). Piece of protective armor worn over mail on outside of forearm.

démodé (F. dā-mô-dā; day mo day). Old-fashioned; outmoded; out of style.

denim (dĕn'ĭm; den im). Strong, coarse, washable cotton fabric in twill weave; yarn-dyed, sometimes with white or different colored filling. Used for overalls, heavy wash garments; finer grade, for upholstery, hangings. From French de Nîmes, meaning from Nîmes, a town in France.

Denmark satin. Durable worsted fabric woven with smooth finish in imitation of buff leather. Formerly used for shoe uppers.

dentelé (F. dän-tə-lā; donh te lay). French word meaning notched or scalloped.

dentelle (F. dän-tĕl; donh tell). French word for lace.

dentelle au fuseau (F. ō fū-zō; o foo zo). French term meaning bobbin lace.

dentelle d'application (F. dȧ-plē-kȧ-syôn; da plee ka syonh). French term for lace in which the decoration is sewn to foundation.

dentelle de fil (F. də fēl; de feel). French term meaning thread lace.

dentelle de la Vierge (F. də lȧ vyērzh; de lah vyairzh). Wide DIEPPE POINT LACE, a bobbin lace of Valenciennes type. See LACES.

dentellière (F. dän-tĕl-yēr; donh tell yare). French lacemaking machine that produces braided lace.

deodorant (dē-ō'dēr-ənt; de o der ant). Anything that destroys odors. Cosmetic product for use on the body, chiefly under the arms.

department store. Retail store selling all types of merchandise, including piece goods and notions.

depilatory (də-pĭl'ə-tō-rĭ; de pill a tor i). Preparation that removes superfluous hair.

derby (dẽr'bĭ or British där'bĭ; der bi or dar bi). Man's stiff felt hat. See HATS.

de rigueur (F. də rē-gẽr; de ree gur). French phrase meaning indispensable, required; as, straw hats were de rigueur last season.

dernier cri (F. dẽr-nyȧ krē; dare nyay kree). French term meaning the last word, the latest fashion.

dervish tulle (dẽr'vĭsh tōōl; dur vish tool). Coarse, shiny, stiff tulle. See TULLE under NETS.

déshabillé (F. dā-zȧ-bē-yā; day za bee yay). French form of DISHABILLE, or undress.

design (də-zīn'; de zine). 1. Plan, pattern, or preliminary sketch for something to be done or made; as, design for a dress. 2. Selection and arrangement of parts, ornament, and constructio that form an artistic whole; as, a dres of good design. Also, to make such pattern, plan, or arrangement.

designer. One who designs, by sketch o in material or both, a line of merchan dise, piece of apparel, or accessory.

dessous (F. də-sōō; de soo). Frenc word meaning underclothing.

detached chain-stitch. Same as LAZY DAISY-STITCH. See STITCHES.

detail (də-tāl'; de tail). Particular o minor feature, usually an intricate par of the construction or finishing of . costume or part of costume.

Devonshire lace (dĕv'ən-shēr; dev u: sher). Bobbin lace similar to DUCHESSE Same as HONITON LACE. See LACES.

dhoti (dō'tĭ; doe ti). Long loincloth wrapped around loins, drawn betweer legs, and tucked in at waist; also fabri of which loincloth is made. Worn by Hindu men.

diadem (dī'ə-dĕm; die a dem). Crown or any symbol of royalty worn upon the head.

diagonal buttonhole (dī-ăg'ə-nəl; di ag o nal). Slanting buttonhole cut on the bias. See BUTTONHOLES.

diagonal cloth. Woolen twilled fabric in heavy or medium weight. Used for suits and coats; formerly, for men's clothing. Softer weave used for em broidery ground.

diagonal cross-stitch. Cross-stitch boxed in by vertical stitch connecting the ends. See STITCHES.

diagonal weave. Pronounced twil weave. See TWILL under WEAVES.

diamanté (F. dē-ȧ-män-tā; dee a monh tay). French word meaning set with diamonds; fabric made sparkling with rhinestones, etc.

diamond (dī'ə-mənd; die a mund). Extremely hard, crystalline, precious mineral, usually colorless, but sometimes colored. Cut with many facets and used in jewelry.

diamond couching (kowch'ĭng; cowch ing). Threads couched in diamond pattern. See COUCHING under EMBROIDERIES.

diamond linen. Diaper with diamond design. See DIAPER under LINENS.

diaper (dī'ə-pēr; die a per). 1. Soft, absorbent, cotton fabric, bleached for whiteness. Available in three types: bird's-eye, in dobby weave; diaper flannel, in plain weave; knit diaper, in twill weave. Used for infants' breech-cloths. Also name of the breech-cloth. 2. Fine, figured linen cloth. See LINENS.

diaper flannel. White cotton flannel. See FLANNELS.

diaphane (dī'ə-fān; die a fane). Thin silk fabric with transparent design.

diaphragm (dī'ə-frăm; die a fram). 1. Part of the body from waistline to chest. 2. Part of dress or bodice covering the diaphragm.

dickey. Detachable shirt-front, often with collar. Also applied to various other detachable items of dress.

Dieppe point lace (F. dē-ĕp; dee ep). Bobbin lace made at Dieppe, France. Similar to VALENCIENNES. See LACES.

fāte, făt, dânce, ärt mē, mĕt, hẽr, thêre rīde, rĭd nōte, nŏt, côrn, fōōd, fŏŏt cūte, cŭt, cūré now fin(ŋ)ger villa(ə) señor pleas(zh)ure

imity (dĭm'ĭ-tĭ; *dim* i ti). Fine, lightweight cotton fabric, corded or crossbarred, figured or plain. Used for lingerie, dresses, blouses, aprons, infants' garments.

inner dress. Costume less formal than evening clothes, often having sleeves. See DRESS.

inner ring. Elaborately set ring. See RINGS.

inner suit. Dinner dress having a jacket with sleeves. See SUITS.

ip-dyed hose. Hose dyed and de-gummed after knitting. See HOSE.

ip-dyeing. Process of dyeing after weaving or knitting. See DYEING.

iploidion (dĭp-lō-ĭd'ĭ-ən; dip lo *id* i un). Garment worn by Greek women of classical period; form of the CHITON, with part above waist worn double.

Directoire Costume, 1790's

)irectoire (F. dē-rĕk-twär; dee reck twar). Of the style of the French Directoire (1795–1799); characterized by long, straight skirt, sometimes slit; very low décolletage; small tight sleeves; very high waistline; exaggerated imitation of classic Greek and Roman dress.

iirect printing. Method of dyeing in which each color is applied by separate roller. See PRINTING under DYEING.

iirndl (dĕrn'dl; *deern* dl). Bodice dress with full, gathered skirt, highly popular in 1938. Silhouette similar to that of pioneer women of the U.S.A. See DRESSES.

iischarge printing. Printing piece-dyed fabric with chemical to remove dye in pattern. See PRINTING under DYEING.

iisguise (dĭs-gīz'; dis *gize*). Costume to be worn at a masquerade.

iishabille (dĭs-ə-bĕl'; dis a *beel*) or **déshabillé** (F. dā-zȧ-bē-yā; day za bee yay). Improper or negligent attire.

iisk. Flat, circular hat. See HATS.

iismoded (dĭs-mōd'ĕd; dis *mode* ed). Out of fashion.

iistaff. The feminine side, as of a family; a woman editor, as, Aimee Larkin, distaff of Collier's magazine.

iivided skirt. Garment like skirt in appearance but divided like trousers. See SKIRTS.

iizen (dīz'n; *dis* en). To overdress; to deck out gaudily.

iizenment. Overdressing, especially the wearing of gaudy finery.

ijersa (jĕr'sə; *jer* sa). Woolen fabric used for jerseys.

lobby. Small-figured weave, less intricate than Jacquard. See WEAVES.

lobby loom. Type of drawloom used in weaving figures, originally making use of a boy, the "dobby boy," who sat on top of loom and drew up warp threads to form pattern. Now entirely mechanized and used for less complicated figures than Jacquard.

doeskin (dō'skĭn; *doe* skin). **1.** Leather made from skin of sheep. Used chiefly for gloves. See LEATHERS. **2.** Heavy, napped cotton fabric in twill weave. Used as backing for artificial leathers, sports garments. **3.** Firm, short-napped woolen fabric. Used for men's garments.

dog collar. Wide necklace worn about throat. See NECKLACES.

doll hat. Tiny hat, made in any style, suggesting hat made for doll. See HATS.

Dolly Varden. Name applied to costume consisting of dress with tight bodice; short, quilted petticoat; flowered chintz panniers; large, drooping, flower-trimmed hat—as worn by Dolly Varden, a character in Dickens's "Barnaby Rudge." Also, this type of dress or hat. In fashion about 1870.

Type of Dolly Varden Costume

Dolly Varden pattern. Bouquets of flowers, usually printed on silk and lawn fabrics.

dolman (dŏl'mən; *doll* man). **1.** Long outer garment with close sleeves, open in front; worn by Turks. **2.** Cape-like wrap or coat with the DOLMAN SLEEVE. See WRAPS. **3.** Jacket worn as cloak by hussars. See JACKETS.

dolman sleeve. Sleeve made very wide at armhole, fitted at wrist. See SLEEVES.

domestic arts (də-mĕs'tĭk; do *mess* tic). Household arts; specifically a school course dealing with needlework, dressmaking, millinery, design, color, textiles, clothing, etc.

domestics. Coarse cotton wash goods, originally made in this country. Also, name of store department where bedding and household linens are sold.

domett or **domet** (dŏm'ĕt; *dom* et). Old term for napped fabric with cotton warp and woolen filling, similar to outing flannel.

dominical (də-mĭn'ĭ-kəl; do *min* i cal) or **dominicale** (də-mĭn-ĭ-kā'lĕ; do min i *kay* le). Linen cloth or veil formerly worn by women of the Roman Catholic Church during communion.

domino (dŏm'ĭ-nō; *dom* i no). **1.** Mask or half mask. See MASKS. **2.** Masquerade garb. See FANCY DRESS. **3.** Loose garment with hood, worn by church dignitaries. Also, the hood.

Dom Pedro (dŏm pē'drō; dom *pee* dro). Heavy work shoe introduced by Dom Pedro, of Brazil. See SHOES.

Dongola kid or **leather** (dŏng'gə-lə; *dong* go la). Sheep, goat, or kangaroo skin. See LEATHERS.

dopatta (dō-pŭt'tə; doe *putt* a). Silk or muslin scarf, often interwoven or embroidered with gold or silver threads. Worn by Hindu and Mohammedan men and women in India.

dorado (dō-rä'dō; doe *rah* doe). Yellowish-orange color.

doré (F. dô-rā; dor ray). French word meaning golden or containing gold.

doria (dō'rĭ-ə; *doe* ri a). East Indian cotton fabric, having stripes of different widths.

Doric chiton (dŏr'ĭk kī'tŏn; *dor* ic *ky* ton). Sleeveless Grecian garment. See CHITON.

dormeuse (F. dôr-mēz; dor muz). Nightcap. French word meaning sleeper.

dornick (dôr'nĭk; *dor* nick). **1.** Any cloth made at Tournai, France; especially heavy damask or other fabric for hangings, etc. Word derived from Doornik, Flemish name of Tournai. **2.** Damask-like fabric made at Dornoch, Scotland.

D'Orsay (dôr'sā; *dor* say). Pump cut low at side in curved line. See SLIPPERS.

dossière (F. dô-syêr; doss yare). Part of suit of armor covering the back from neck to waist; back section of CUIRASS.

DOTS

dot. Circle, printed on, woven in, or applied to fabric.

coin d. Dot larger than the size of a dime.

composition d. (kŏm-pə-zĭsh'ən; com po *zish* en). Dot applied chemically to fabric, not woven or embroidered.

confetti d. (kən-fĕt'ĭ; con *fet* i). Dot of polka dot size, used in many colors on one fabric.

cushion d. **1.** Fabric decoration made by weaving in heavy extra yarns and cutting them on the surface to form brush-like dots. **2.** Swivel dots. See SWIVEL under WEAVES.

flock d. Dot applied chemically to fabric, rather than woven or embroidered. Often used on voile. Same as COMPOSITION DOT.

pin d. Smallest dot used.

polka d. (pōl'kə; *pole* ka). Dot of medium size, between pin and coin. Used in allover prints in uniform size and spacing.

swivel d. (swĭv'l; *swiv* l). Type of cushion dot. See SWIVEL under WEAVES.

dotted Swiss. Fine cotton fabric with embroidered, swivel, or chemically applied dots. See SWISS, 2.

double-and-twist. Made up of two or more strands of different colored yarns twisted together. Term used of thread.

double back-stitch. Catch-stitch worked on wrong side of fabric, giving appearance of two rows of back-stitch on right side. Same as SHADOW-STITCH. See STITCHES.

double-breasted (dŭb'l brĕst'ĕd; *dub* l *brest* ed). Said of the front of a garment,

double chain-stitch
usually a coat or jacket, that laps enough for a double row of buttons.
double chain-stitch. Chain-stitch combining two loops. See STITCHES.
double cloth. Cloth comprising two separate fabrics in various weaves, such as twill, satin, Jacquard, etc., woven with two warps and one filling, two fillings and one warp, double filling and double warp, or an additional set of binding threads, so that they are joined together. Used for suits and coats, ribbons, blankets, robes, etc.
double cross-stitch. Canvas stitch in which an ordinary cross-stitch has another made upright on top of it. See STITCHES.
double cuff. Shirt cuff turned back to make two cuff thicknesses, fastened by cuff links. See CUFFS.
double-duty dress. Simple, basic daytime dress that can become an afternoon or a dinner dress by the addition or removal of a jacket. See DRESSES.
double-faced. Applied to fabrics that can be worn or used with either side out.
double-lock seam. Seam stitched straight, then overlaid with zigzag stitch. See SEAMS.
double running embroidery. Type of outline embroidery that is reversible. Same as HOLBEIN WORK. See EMBROIDERIES.
double running-stitch. Two rows of running-stitch worked on same line, with stitches alternating to give a continuous line identical on both sides of fabric. See STITCHES.
double-stitched seam. Seam with row of stitches on right side on both sides of seam line. Same as TOP-STITCHED SEAM. See SEAMS.
double-stitched welt seam. Welt seam with second row of stitching added along top of seam. See SEAMS.
doublet (dŭb'lĕt; *dub* let). 1. Men's close-fitting garment, similar to jacket, with or without sleeves, sometimes having short, skirt-like section; worn from 15th to 17th century. 2. Undergarment quilted and strengthened with links of mail to be worn under armor. 3. Counterfeit gem made of colored glass covered by crystal or real gem stone.

15th Century Doublet

double warp. Two warps in one fabric; also, a fabric having two warps.
dowlas (dow'ləs; *dow* las). Heavy, coarse linen fabric made in France in 16th century; in Scotland and England, in 18th century. Similar to sail cloth.
down. Soft, fluffy feathers on young birds. Also, fine, soft fuzz that grows

under ordinary feathers on adult birds, being especially thick on geese, ducks, and other waterfowl. Used for softest pillows, quilts, padding, etc.
drab. 1. Dull, brownish-gray color. 2. Thick cloth of drab color. Used for rough outer garments, uniforms, etc. From French word *drap*, meaning cloth.
drabbet (drăb'ĕt; *drab* et). Coarse linen fabric of drab color, made in England. Used for smocks worn by workmen, tradesmen, etc.
draft. Outline drawing of a pattern, made usually with ruler, tape, and pencil.
drafting square. Tailor's square having measurements and curves. Designed especially for use in drafting patterns for garments.
drap (F. drȧ; drah). French word meaning cloth.
drap d'Alma (F. dȧl-mȧ; dal ma). French name for type of twilled cloth. See ALMA.
drap d'argent (F. dȧr-zhȯṅ; dar zhonh). French term meaning cloth of silver.
drap de Berry (F. də bĕ-rē; de ber ee). Woolen fabric made in Berry, France. French phrase meaning cloth of berry.
drap d'été (F. dȧ-tā; day tay). Light, twilled woolen fabric. French term meaning cloth of summer.
drap d'or (F. dȯr; dor). French term meaning cloth of gold.
drape. To hang in folds or cover with fabric in loose folds; also, to design garments by this method. Originally, to make cloth or weave.
draped elbow sleeve. Straight, elbow-length sleeve with loose, draped fold at elbow. See SLEEVES.
draped heel. Heel bound to foot with kerchief-like drapery. See HEELS.
draped neckline. Unfitted neckline formed by loose folds of fabric. See NECKLINES.
draped silhouette. Silhouette of softly draped garment, often having irregular hem line. See SILHOUETTES.
draper. Couturier or couturière who designs by draping; skilled dressmaker. Formerly, one who sold yard goods; earlier, one who made cloth.
draper's shop. In 18th and 19th centuries, a shop where fabrics and trimmings were sold, and also where garments were made to individual measurements.
drapery. Fabric hung or draped; loose flowing part of garment. Originally, cloth in general.
drawers. Trouser-like undergarment, worn by both men and women.
drawing string. Same as DRAWSTRING.
drawing thread. Thread sewn through fabric for gathering up fulness; gathering thread.
drawloom. 1. Old type of loom for weaving figured fabrics. 2. Type of damask made on the drawloom.
drawn-fabric stitch. Any stitch used to draw fabric threads together in open-work effect. See STITCHES.
drawn-fabric work. Open-work embroidery. Same as PUNCH WORK. See EMBROIDERIES.
drawn work. Open work made by pulling out threads of the fabric and em-

broidering or hemstitching the edges t form decoration. Sometimes done with colored threads. See EMBROIDERIES.
drawn-work fagoting. Decorativ open-work stitch done in imitation o fagoting over space where threads hav been drawn. See FAGOTING unde STITCHES.
drawstring. String, cord, or ribbon in serted in casing, hem, heading, or eye lets, to draw up fulness. Often used in garments and dress accessories.
dreadnought (drĕd'nȯt; *dred* nawt) Heavy, unattractive, long-napped woolen fabric used for outer garments also, garment made of such material Also called *fearnought*.
Dresden (drĕz'dĕn; *drez* den). 1. Small, delicate flower design in pastel shades printed on warp of fabric before weaving. 2. Fabric so designed, also called *pompadour*.
Dresden point lace. 1. Type of drawn work. 2. Coarse pillow lace. See LACES.

DRESS AND DRESSES

dress. 1. Clothes required by custom or etiquette for certain occasions or times of day. Also called SPORTS CLOTHES. 2. Distinctive or ceremonial attire, as for formal wear. 3. Outer garment worn by women and children, cut in one or more pieces. 4. Clothes collectively. Western dress, as distinguished from Oriental dress, includes coat, hat, trousers, etc., for men; and coat, hat, dress, etc., for women.
afternoon d. or costume. Costume suitable for daytime social functions, more dressy and usually longer than for general wear, more or less elaborate in style and luxurious in fabric, depending on the formality of the occasion.
apron d. Dress having full skirt, open at back in apron style, set on waistband and tied at back. Often worn with sheath type of underskirt.
ball d. Elaborate evening gown suitable for formal social occasion, such as a ball.
basic d. Simple dress which can easily be given variety by wearing it with different decorative accessories at different times.
bloomer d. Child's dress with matching bloomers. For younger children, bloomers are worn under very short dresses.
bungalow apron. Simple, straight-

Bungalow Apron, 1924

fāte, făt, dȧnce, ärt mē, mĕt, hẽr, thêre rīde, rĭd nōte, nŏt, côrn, fōōd, fŏŏt cūte, cŭt, cûrė new fin(ŋ)ger villa(ȧ) señor pleas(zh)urȧ

line dress with kimono sleeves, designed as substitute for house dress. Popular 1910–20.

cancan d. Type of dress worn originally by the cancan dancers in Paris, France, in the middle nineties. Consists of basque bodice with exaggerated sleeves; long, full, plain skirt; and many ruffled petticoats. Inside of skirt has ruffles to match those on petticoat and panties, ruffles being often of plaited lace. The dance is dramatized by the skirt.

cape d. Dress and cape ensemble. The two garments may or may not be attached, but harmonize in fabric and color.

chemise d. (shə-mēz´; shem *meez*). Straight-line dress hanging from shoulder, in imitation of early 19th century French Restoration style. Popular in early 20th century. Also called *tube dress, pillow-slip dress.*

chemise frock. Simple, unfitted dress hanging straight from shoulders. During First Empire, tight-fitting, of sheer material, worn with scant underclothing; as revived in 1924–25, similar in name only.

coat d. Tailored dress, usually fitted, with coat type of front closing and coat-like lines, as in a redingote. Designed for street wear, usually without a topcoat.

cocktail d. Informal but rather dressy costume suitable to wear to a hotel in late afternoon or evening, to private cocktail party, etc.

confirmation d. (kŏn-fẽr-mā´shən; con fer *may* shun). White dress of any conservative style, worn by girl when confirmed in church. Often made with matching or net veil.

dance d. Youthful, not-too-formal evening dress. Often bouffant in style.

daytime d. Costume less elaborate than afternoon dress; less severely tailored than business dress and usually of finer material. Suitable for general town wear, luncheons, lectures, perhaps matinées.

demitoilet (dĕm´ĭ-toi-lĕt; *dem* i toy let). Costume somewhat less elaborate than full dress.

dinner d. Glorified afternoon costume, less formal in fabric and type than evening dress; often long. Has covered shoulders and long or short sleeves on dress or jacket.

dirndl (dẽrn´dl; *deern* dl). Bodice dress, usually in color, especially printed; with full, gathered skirt. Adapted from style worn by Tyrolean peasants. Silhouette similar to that of pioneer women in U.S.A.

double-duty d. Costume, the appearance of which can be changed to suit different kinds of occasions. Often accomplished by omission or addition of jacket.

evening d. Décolleté costume, usually of delicate or luxurious fabric, for evening wear to a dance, concert, theater, or the like.

formal d. Dress worn on full-dress occasions. Evening dress with low décolletage and no sleeves, worn when men wear tuxedo or white tie and tails.

full d. Evening dress, as required by social custom for formal social gatherings. Term chiefly applied to men's evening clothes, essentials of which are white tie and swallow-tailed coat, or "tails." Also, costume prescribed by custom or regulation for certain ceremonies; as, military full dress.

going-away d. or costume. Carefully assembled traveling costume, somewhat more dressy than for ordinary travel. Worn when departure is made an occasion, as for a bridal trip.

house d. Dress suitable for morning wear at home. Usually of gaily printed, washable cotton fabric. Often perky in silhouette, smartly made and trimmed. Also called *home* or *morning dress.*

jumper d. One-piece garment consisting of low-cut bodice in strap-top effect attached to a skirt. Worn with guimpe or blouse.

20th Century Jumper Dress

kimono d. Dress in which the sleeves are cut in one with the body of the dress.

Little Women d. Dress modeled on styles worn by the girls in Louisa May Alcott's book, "Little Women." Made with plain, fitted bodice buttoned up front; long or short, plain sleeves; small, turned-down collar with soft bow tie; full, gathered-on skirt.

monk's d. Dress hanging from the shoulder, cut full and easy through the body, often on the bias. Held at waistline with a girdle or cord belt.

morning d. Glorified house or home dress. Made to look smart even though the fabric is inexpensive. Term preferred by many to HOUSE DRESS.

"Little Women" Dress

Mother Hubbard. Dress usually fitted through the shoulders only; occasionally made over a fitted bodice lining. Originally, for morning wear at home. Later, made of elaborate fabric and worn as tea gown. See SACQUE and WRAPPER.

mourning d. or costume. Garments in dull black fabric, with no more than a touch of white mourning crepe at neckline, and dull black accessories; or costume altogether in white; in either case, without jewelry or ornamentation. Worn during period of mourning for close relative, usually from six months to a year. Designated as *deep mourning.*

—**half m.** Mourning dress with touches of white, gray, or lavender.

night d. 1. Glorified nightgown. 2. Night clothes; any garments worn in bed.

night rail. Dress or robe, unconfined at waist, fastened neatly at neck; worn by women in colonial America during the morning. Made of plainest, drab-best dress material. Literally, a nightgown.

occasional d. Colorful, fairly elaborate dress worn only on special occasion, as to a wedding, a reception, etc.

one hour d. Chemise type of bodice with kimono sleeves and attached straight short skirt, made famous by Mary Brooks Picken in 1924. Could be made in one hour or less.

One Hour Dress, 1920's

Peter Thomson d. One-piece belted dress with plaits from yoke to hem, bodice in exact imitation of a sailor's blouse, with middy collar. Adopted as a uniform by many private schools. Named for its designer, Peter Thomson,

Dirndl, 1930's

fāte, făt, dánce, ärt mē, mĕt, hẽr, thêre rīde, rĭd nōte, nŏt, côrn, fōōd, fŏŏt cūte, cŭt, cūrē now fin(ŋ)ger villa(ə) señor pleas(zh)ure

dresses

dresses (continued) once a tailor in the navy, later in Philadelphia.

Peter Thomson Dress

petticoat d. Dress with decorative petticoat showing beneath hem all the way around.
pillow-slip dress. Chemise dress hanging straight from the shoulder; usually having short kimono sleeves and short skirt. Popular in early 1920's.
sheath gown. Straight, tubular dress, often of firm satin or velvet; usually slashed to the knee to make walking possible. Popular just before 1910. Later developed into the hobble skirt.

Sheath Gown, 1930's

Shirtmaker d. Name registered by Best and Co., New York, for tailored one-piece dress with shirtwaist details.
shirtwaist d. One-piece tailored dress with bodice like a shirtwaist, often tucked, usually belted.

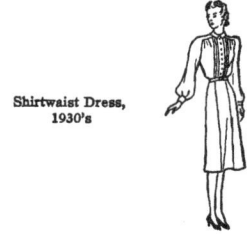

Shirtwaist Dress, 1930's

sleeveless d. Any dress made without sleeves; specifically, a type of jumper dress, not fitted at armhole, worn over blouse.
street d. Simple dress, usually tailored, on the order of DAYTIME DRESS, for general daytime wear on the street.
Sunday-night d. Costume having long or short sleeves, more formal in length than afternoon dress, similar in type to least formal dinner dress. Often gay in color.
transformation d. Costume consisting of slip, coat, tunic, and overdress. Slip may be worn with one or more of the other parts, according to occasion, to transform garment into street, afternoon, or evening dress. Introduced about 1926.
traveling d. or costume. Ensemble, often tailored suit, simple in line, sturdy in fabric, dark in color, suitable for traveling; worn en route.
X-ray d. Dress of transparent fabric. Popular about 1910.

dress clothes. Clothes worn by men or women on formal occasions.
dress coat. Coat for full-dress occasions. See COATS.
dressed kid. Kid with smooth finish. See LEATHERS.
dressed pillow. Pillow for making lace, arranged with bobbins, pins, etc.
dress face. Finish, as of woolen fabric, with pile or nap raised and smoothed all one way, concealing the weave.
dress flannel. Napped woolen fabric. See FLANNELS.
dress form. Papier maché frame in the form of woman's figure. Used for fitting and draping garments. Adjustable forms are made in sections and put together on a metal frame. The form may be extended to bring it to the size of an individual figure.
dress-goods. Fabrics suitable for women's and children's dresses. See GOODS.
dress improver. Hooped pannier, forerunner of the bustle. See HOOPS.
dressing or **dress.** Sizing, starch, gum, or other substance used to stiffen or finish fabric. Also, process of treating cloth with such substance.
dressing case. Case for carrying toilet articles ready for use.
dressing-gown. Tailored robe, sometimes quilted, worn by men and women before dressing or after undressing.
dressing jacket. English term for DRESSING SACQUE. See JACKETS.
dressing sacque. 1. Loose, wrist-length blouse. See BLOUSES. 2. Short, loose jacket. See JACKETS.
dress length. Measurement of a dress from top to bottom. See LENGTHS. Also, length of fabric required to make a dress.
dress linen. Firm linen fabric in plain weave. See LINENS.
dressmaker. 1. Woman who cuts, fits, sews garments, especially for customers. 2. Not severely tailored, but having soft, dressy, or feminine touch; as, dressmaker details, dressmaker suit.
dressmaker-made. Made to individual measurements, but softly draped, usually with feminine details.
dressmaker's dummy. Padded dress form.

duck-bill

dressmaker's gauge. Device, such as the Picken Dressmaker's Gauge, used for marking scallops, width of tucks and space between them, hems, plaits, spacing of ruffles; also, position of buttons, buttonholes, hooks and eyes, and snap fasteners.
dress shield. Crescent-shaped piece, usually made of two layers of fabric with waterproof material between; sometimes made entirely of rubberized silk. Worn to protect clothing from underarm perspiration. Also called *shield*.
dress shield guimpe (gămp; gamp). Guimpe, usually made of net, with dress shields attached.
dress shirt. Man's shirt for evening wear. See SHIRTS.
dress shoe. Shoe for formal wear. See SHOES.
dress suit. Suit worn by men for full-dress evening occasions. See FULL DRESS under DRESS.
dressy. Colloquial term meaning elaborate; smart. Said of garments, apparel in general, etc.
drilling or **drill.** Coarse, firm, linen or cotton twilled cloth, piece dyed, unbleached, or bleached. Light-weight type called *jean* or *middy twill*. Khaki-colored type called *khaki*. Used for men's shirts, middy blouses, coarse outer garments, linings, uniforms, etc.
droguet (F. drō-gā; dro gay). Formerly, any of certain dress materials; chiefly, type of mixed wool fabric of brown and gray; drugget.
dropped shoulder. Extended shoulder line made to reach over upper arm.
drop stitch. Machine knitting of open design formed by dropping certain stitches, that is, by removing certain needles from work at set intervals. See KNITTING.
drugget. Formerly, woolen or mixed fabric, often of brown and gray.
Druid's cloth (drū'ĭdz; *dru* idz). Rough, canvas-like fabric in basket weave. Similar to MONK'S CLOTH.
drumming. Process by which furs are cleaned or softened. See FURS.
dry goods. Merchandise such as textiles, bedding, yard goods, and sewing notions. See GOODS.
du Barry costume. Costume, typical of styles of Louis XV period, worn by Madame du Barry. See FANCY DRESS.
ducape (dū-cāp'; du *cape*). Heavy, corded silk fabric.
duchesse (F. dū-shěs; du shess). 1. Satin in weave. 2. Heavy, firm, soft fabric. See SATINS. 3. Short for DUCHESSE LACE.
duchesse lace. Bobbin lace with tape-like effect. See LACES.
duck. Strong, closely woven linen or cotton fabric in plain weave. Heavy weight, but lighter and finer than canvas. Used for outing shirts, trousers, coats, skirts, middy blouses, small sails, tents, awnings, men's summer suits.
duck-bill. 1. Elongated, visor-like front brim of a hat. See CAPS and HATS. 2. Blunt and square-toed shoe. See SHOES.

fāte, făt, dánce, ärt mē, mĕt, hẽr, thêre rīde, rĭd nōte, nŏt, côrn, fōōd, fŏŏt cūte, cŭt, cûré now fin(ŋ)ger villa(ə) señor pleas(zh)ure

Duck-Bill Bonnet, 1790's

dude. Fastidious or affected man; hence, in western U. S., city-bred person, overdressed Easterner.
duds. Colloquial term for clothing collectively; ragged or cast-off clothing; belongings.
duffel (dŭf'l; duff el). Outfit; equipment, especially clothing, blankets, etc., as for camp.
duffel bag. Sturdy bag carried by sailors and others for personal effects.
dull color. Grayed hue. See COLOR.
dull hose. Silk hose without much shine. See HOSE.
dummy. Model or dress form for displaying garments to customers.
dun. Dull grayish-brown color.
dunce cap. Conical hat worn as mark of stupidity by school children. See CAPS.
dungarees (dŭng-gə-rēz'; dung ga rees). Overalls similar to workmen's, originally made of coarse East Indian cotton cloth called dungaree. Now of denim, etc., and worn for active sports. From Hindu dugri.

Dungarees

dunstable (dŭn'stə-bl; dun sta bl). Plaited straw hat; plait of straw for such a hat. See HATS.
Du Pont Rayon. Trade name for a brand of rayon yarn. See RAYON.
durance (dūr'əns; dure ance). Any

strong fabric similar to LASTING, DENMARK SATIN, etc.
dust cap. Cap made of kerchief or circle, gathered to head size by elastic run through narrow hem on edge. See CAPS.
dust coat or **cloak.** Same as DUSTER. See COATS.
duster. Light-weight, coverall coat. See COATS.
dust ruffle. Ruffle sewn on inside edge of long petticoat or skirt to protect it from hard wear and prevent it from becoming soiled when it touches the floor. Also called balayeuse or sweeper.

Dust Ruffle, 1870's

Dutch blue. Shade of blue lighter and brighter than lightest navy.
Dutch boy heel. Heel similar in shape to that on Dutch wooden shoe. See HEELS.
Dutch cap. 1. Lace or muslin cap with flaring points on each side. Worn by women in Volendam, Netherlands. See CAPS. 2. Adaptation of original Dutch cap, made in hat style. See HATS.
Dutch collar. Narrow, close-fitting, either pointed or rounded collar. See COLLARS.
Dutch cut or **bob.** Haircut in which hair is cut straight around back from lobe of one ear to the other and usually banged in front. See BOBS.
Dutch girl costume. Full skirt with basque bodice, worn with apron, kerchief, cap, and wooden shoes. See FANCY DRESS.
Dutch neckline. Neckline cut about two inches below throat. See NECKLINES.
duvetyn or **duvetine** (dōō'və-tēn; doo ve teen). 1. Formerly, soft twill fabric of wool, with back of mercerized cotton or spun silk. Napped by means of emery cylinder. Used for dresses, suits, coats, etc. 2. Fabric in twill weave with spun silk woof and mercerized cotton warp, napped by emery cylinder. Used for hats, trimmings, etc. Also called silk duvetyn.

dwarf costume (dwôrf; dworf). Costume for Disney version of fairy-tale character. See FANCY DRESS.
dye bath. Any solution prepared for dyeing fabrics.

DYEING

dyeing. Process of coloring fibers or fabrics with natural or pigment dyes, coal tar or aniline dyes. Dyes differ in color fastness, effectiveness on different fibers, reaction to cleaning agents.
batik d. (bä'tĕk; bah teek). Ancient method of applying color designs, in which parts of fabric are coated with wax, only uncovered parts taking dye, on same principle as resist printing. Process repeated for each color in design. Sometimes has crackled effect where streaks of dye were admitted through cracks in wax. Originated in Java. Imitated in modern machine printing.
cross-d. Process of dyeing fabric woven of mixed fibers, which take dye differently. Done with dye or dyes that either give different fibers different colors or color only one.
dip-d. Process of dyeing hosiery and other knit goods after knitting.
piece-d. Dyeing fabric after weaving.
printing. Application of designs to fabric by paste dyes used on blocks, engraved metal rollers, or screens. Process is called block printing and is more expensive if done by hand from carved or engraved blocks. Called direct printing if each color is applied by separate roller on light ground; discharge printing, if solid-color, piece-dyed fabric is printed with chemical paste that removes dye to form pattern and at the same time replaces it with white or a different color; resist printing, if fabric is dyed after printing design in dye-resistant chemical, leaving design clear; screen printing, if design is applied by screen made of bolting cloth on which design has been traced or photographed, each color of design having different screen. See PRINTS.
stock-d. Process of dyeing fibers before spinning.
tie-d. Process of dyeing fabric that has been tied tightly with string in various places, so that tied portions do not take dye, resulting in a design.
top-d. Dyeing over or on top of other colors.
yarn-d. Dyeing of yarn before weaving of fabric.

E

earcap. Cap with tabs or sections that cover the ears. See EAR MUFF.
eardrop. Pendant earring.
earlap. Tab that covers the ear. Same as EAR MUFF.
earlet. Obsolete term for earring.
earlock. Curl or lock of hair worn near ear; also, lovelock.
ear muff. One of pair of adjustable ear coverings, sometimes attached by band or spring. Worn as protection against cold. Also called earlap, eartab.

Ear Muffs, 1938

earring (ēr'rĭng; ear ring). Ornament for ear, with or without pendant; formerly inserted in hole pierced through lobe, now usually screwed or clipped on.
ear shell. Shellfish, iridescent shell of which is used for inlay, buttons, beads, other ornaments. Same as ABALONE.
eartab (ēr'tăb; ear tab). Same as EAR MUFF.
Easter bonnet (ēs'tēr; eest er). First spring hat, especially one bought for wear at Easter time. See BONNETS.

fāte, făt, dánce, ärt mē, mĕt, hēr, thêre rīde, rĭd nōte, nŏt, côrn, fōod, fŏŏt cūte, cŭt, cūré now fĭn(g)ger villa(ə) señor pleas(zh)ure

Eau de Cologne (ō də kə-lōn'; o de co lone). Trade name for COLOGNE. Toilet water lighter than perfume. French term meaning water of Cologne.

ebon (ĕb'ŭn; eb un). Black, color of ebony.

écaille work (F. ā-kī; ai ky) or **écaillé work** (F. ā-kī-yā; ai ky yay). Decorative needlework consisting of pieces of quills sewn on cloth in imitation of fish scales. French words for scale and scaly.

ecclesiastical embroidery (ē-klē-zĭ-ăs'tĭk-əl; e klee zi ass tic al). Elaborate embroidery of sacred motifs. Same as CHURCH EMBROIDERY. See EMBROIDERIES.

échelle (F. ā-shĕl; ai shell). Ladder-like decoration for costume; especially, laced stomacher; sometimes graduated flat bows, larger at top than waist. French word for ladder. Also spelled *eschelle*.

Eclipse Tie (ə-klĭps'; e clips). Trade name for type of tie shoe. See SHOES.

economics (ē-kə-nŏm'ĭks or ĕk-ə-nŏm'ĭks; ee co nom ics or ec o nom ics). As pertaining to merchandising and fashion, the science that makes understandable all essentials affecting production, distribution, and use of material products, such as apparel, cosmetics, home furnishings, etc.

écrasé (F. ā-krȧ-zā; ai cra zay). Term used of fabric having flattened effect. French word meaning crushed.

ecru (ĕk'rōō or F. ā-krōō; ec roo or ai croo). Light tan or beige; the natural color of unbleached linen or hemp.

ecru cloth. Fabric of ecru color, usually of silk.

ecru silk. Unbleached silk. See SILK.

edge. 1. To make a finish on an edge; to apply to an edge; to complete with a border. 2. That which serves as edge trimming or border; edging; specifically, in lace, the outer edge, either CORDONNET or FOOTING. 3. Outside rim of sole of shoe.

edge-stitcher. Sewing-machine attachment for stitching close to a turned edge for joining two edges of lace or fabric, or for applying piping.

edging. Narrow embroidery, lace, or the like, used to finish an edge.

Edwardian (ĕd-wôrd'ĭ-ən; ed ward i an). Characteristic of style in vogue about

Edwardian Costume

1901–10, when Edward VII was king of England, when women's styles showed continued influence of Gibson Girl fashions. See illustration under GIBSON GIRL.

eggplant. Bronze-purple shade, matched to skin of vegetable.

eggshell. Slightly yellowed or stone white color.

eggshell finish. Soft finish, as created on shell of egg by minute depressions and elevations which break up light reflections.

egret (ē'grĕt or ĕg'rĕt; ee gret or egg ret). Plume of an egret or heron. Same as AIGRETTE.

Egyptian (ē-jĭp'shən; e jip shun). Characteristic of dress of people of Egypt. Most distinctive costumes those of ancient period, consisting of white linen loincloth or short skirt for men; straight, narrow, ankle-length tunic and long mantle for women; wigs of human hair or wool, sometimes surmounted by elaborate headdresses; wide, circular collars of fabric or beads; rich jewelry; fabrics of wool and linen, white or brightly colored; sandals.

Egyptian cloth. Sturdy cotton in plain weave. See MUMMY CLOTH.

Egyptian cotton. Long-staple cotton. See COTTON.

Egyptian lace. Knotted lace, often beaded. See LACES.

eiderdown (ī'dēr-down; eye der down). 1. Warm, light-weight, elastic cloth knitted or woven of cotton, wool, spun silk, or mixtures. Has napped surface with fluffy feel on one or both sides. Used for infants' wear, bathrobes, negligees, etc. So called from soft down of eider duck. 2. Down quilt.

eider yarn. Soft yarn. See YARNS.

eis wool (īs; ice). Fine, glossy, wiry woolen yarn. Used for clouds, scarfs, etc. See YARNS.

élan (F. ā-läɴ; ai lonh). Impetuous spirit; ardor; eagerness for action. French word meaning start, rush, dash.

elastic (ə-lăs'tĭk; e lass tic). 1. Rubber fabric, cord, band, or thread. 2. Resilient; springy; flexible; capable of being stretched and then returning to original shape. 3. Woven fabric made stretchable by interwoven threads of India rubber. Used for garters, suspenders, girdles, etc.

elasticised leather. Leather combined with elastic so that it stretches to conform to shape. See LEATHERS.

elastic seam. Seam having elastic inset, as a knitted strip in the seam of a leather or felt coat. See SEAMS.

elastic sewing thread. Thread of covered elastic; used for shirring, decorative stitching, elasticity. See THREADS.

Elbert Hubbard tie. Dark scarf about 9 inches wide and cut on the bias. Tied in loose bow at front neckline. Similar to WINDSOR TIE.

elbow length. Length of arm from shoulder to elbow. See LENGTHS.

elbow sleeve. Sleeve reaching to elbow or slightly below. See SLEEVES.

elegant (ĕl'ē-gənt; ell e gant). Tasteful; rich and beautiful; graceful and refined; as, an elegant costume, in elegant style. Term frequently misused.

élégant (F. ā-lā-gäɴ; ai lay gonh) or **élégante** (ā-lā-gäɴt; ai lay gont). Masculine and feminine forms of French word meaning fashionable person.

Eliottine silk (ĕl'ĭ-ə-tēn; ell i o teen). Knitting silk used for fine bags, men's neckties, etc. So called for Eliot, a writer on needlework.

Elizabethan (ə-lĭz-ə-bē'thən; e liz a bee than). Characteristic of dress worn during period of Queen Elizabeth of England in 16th century, the late Renaissance: wide skirts of rich material over farthingale; low, narrow, corseted waistline, with pointed stomacher; low neckline and large, wire-supported ruff; full, slashed and puffed sleeves; Mary Stuart cap.

Elizabethan Costume

elk. Originally elkskin, but now calfskin or cowhide treated by smoke process. See LEATHERS.

ell. Measure for cloth: 45 inches in England; 39 inches in Scotland. Now little used; 36-inch yard generally accepted.

elongated (ē-lŏng'gāt-ĕd; e long gate ed). Stretched out; made longer.

émail (F. ā-mä-ē; ai my). French word for enamel.

embonpoint (F. äɴ-bôɴ-pwăɴ; onh bonh pwanh). Plumpness, stoutness. From French phrase *en bon point*, meaning in good condition.

embossing (ĕm-bŏs'ĭng; em *boss* ing). 1. Process of raising design from surface, so that it stands out in relief. Usually done by passing fabric between hot engraved metal rollers. Velvet or plush embossed by shearing high pile to different levels or by pressing parts flat. 2. In general, decorating or embellishing with rich ornamentation. 3. Obsolete term for embroidering.

embroider (ĕm-broi'dēr; em *broy* der). To ornament with needlework; also, to form by needlework.

EMBROIDERIES

embroidery. Ornamental needlework consisting of designs worked on fabric with silk, cotton, wool, metal, or other threads, by hand or machine. Two main types of embroidery: Western, including Spanish, Portuguese, Moroccan, Algerian, Hispano, Moresque embroideries; Eastern or Oriental, including Persian, Grecian, Near Eastern, and those from other countries bordering Mediterra-

embroideries

nean. Some named for materials, stitches, or foundations; others named for countries of origin, done chiefly in usual stitches, but distinguished by designs, colors, materials peculiar to region, people, or native way of life.

aloe thread e. (ăl'ō; al o). Embroidery worked in aloe fibers, usually in raised effect.

Anglo-Saxon e. Outline embroidery of ancient Anglo-Saxon times, done with long stitches laid on surface of material and couched with metal or silk threads.

appenzell e. (ăp-ĕn-tsĕl'; ap en tsell). Finest type of drawn-work embroidery, named for town in Switzerland where work originated. Used chiefly on fine handkerchiefs.

appliqué e. (ăp-lĭ-kā'; ap li kay). Embroidery in which one fabric, cut into design, is applied to another by means of concealed or plain or decorative stitches. May be *onlaid*, applied on top of other fabric, or *inlaid*, set in in place of fabric cut away.

Arabian e. (a-rā'bĭ-an; a ray bi an). Oriental embroidery of Arabian origin, characterized by bright colors, geometrical designs, elaborate needlework.

arrasene e. (ăr-a-sēn'; ar a seen). Embroidery worked in arrasene, kind of chenille, to produce velvety effect.

Assisi e. (ä-sē'zē; a see zee). Type of cross-stitch embroidery, having designs left clear, background covered with stitches. Used on banners, table linens, etc.

Ayrshire e. (êr'shēr; air sher). Eyelet embroidery. Same as MADEIRA.

back-stitch e. Ornamental outline embroidery done with back-stitch; same as HOLBEIN WORK, but single-faced instead of double-faced.

batus work. Ancient fancy work ornamented with gold and silver plates attached to fabric by embroidery stitches.

Beauvais e. (F. bō-vā; bo vay). Multicolored, tapestry-like embroidery. Named for city in France where it originated.

Berlin work (bēr-lĭn'; ber lin). Ancient, durable, allover type of embroidery or fancy work in which principal stitch is cross-stitch. Done on canvas. Used during 13th and 14th centuries chiefly for mats, cushions in churches. Also called *cushion style*, *canvas embroidery*, and *canvas work*. Called *Berlin work* since 1820, from use of Berlin wool. In modern canvas work, variety of canvas stitches used in addition to cross-stitch.

black work. Embroidery of black stitches on white fabric.

bonnaz (bŏ-năz'; bo *nahz*). Type of embroidery made on complicated machine invented by a Frenchman, Bonnaz.

Breton work (brĕt'ən; bret on). Ancient peasant embroidery of geometrical and floral designs done chiefly in chain-stitch. Stitches made in colored silk and metallic threads. Also called *Brittany work*, from the place of its origin.

brocade e. (brō-kād'; bro *cade*). Embroidery made by stitching over top of designs of brocaded fabrics.

broderie anglaise (F. brôd-rē äṉ-glāz; brod ree onh glaze). Fine eyelet embroidery. Same as MADEIRA.

Bulgarian e. (bŭl-gā'rĭ-ən; bul *gay* ri an). Oriental type of embroidery, alike on both sides, executed solidly in silk, gold, or silver threads in flat stitches on coarse linen garments of peasants. Used for bright-colored accessories, household furnishings, etc.

bullion e. (bŏŏl'yŭn; *bool* yun). Ancient embroidery done in gold wires. Originated with the Phrygians.

Byzantine e. (bĭz'ən-tēn; *biz* an teen). 19th century appliqué work for bulky materials, combined with decorative stitches.

Californian e. (kăl-ĭ-fôr'nĭ-ən; cal i *for* ni an). Primitive work of pre-Spanish times in California; done with cords of animal substances, fishbones being used for needles. Term more recently used in connection with leather stitching, braiding, etc.

Canadian e. (ka-nā'dĭ-ən; ca *nay* di an). Primitive embroidery of Canadian Indians, done with porcupine quills and strips of animal skins.

candlewick e. Embroidery done with candlewicking and a large needle; worked by taking two or more stitches in the same spot, leaving loops on right side of fabric. Loops are then cut and shaped into small tuft. Used on bedspreads, curtains, etc.

canvas e. or **canvas work.** Any embroidery worked on canvas. See BERLIN WORK.

cashmere work (kăsh'mēr; *cash* meer). Indian embroidery in rich, varied colors, frequently inlaid appliqué, with elaborate needlework almost covering surface of material. Used chiefly in shawls.

chenille e. (shə-nēl'; shen *neel*). Embroidery worked with fine chenille yarn in flat stitches, producing soft, velvety effect. Originated in France.

China ribbon e. Embroidery done with narrow ribbon. See ROCOCO EMBROIDERY.

Chinese e. Single-faced or double-faced embroidery in complicated designs, either shaded or plain, worked in satin-stitch on silk, velvet, etc. Originally, floss and metal threads worked over painted designs on garments, screens, hangings, etc.

chromo e. (krō'mō; *cro* mo). Embroidery done over paper pattern, which is laid on material and covered with satin-stitches, design being printed on paper in colors in which it is to be embroidered.

church e. 1. Symbols, scenes, and figures of religious subjects done in heavy, ancient, elaborate embroidery on altar cloths, hangings, robes, etc. Also called *ecclesiastical embroidery*. 2. Same as GIMPED EMBROIDERY.

cloth e. Oriental work of many pieces of colored cloth joined, as in inlaid appliqué, and stitched with designs.

Colbert e. (F. kôl-bĕr; col bare).

Colored embroidery having designs outlined and left clear, background covered with close allover pattern worked with satin-stitches.

couching (kowch'ĭng; *cowch* ing). Method of flat or raised embroidery, consisting of arranging threads or cords in design upon surface of fabric and securing them with fine stitches, known as *couching-stitches*. Often described according to shape or direction of securing stitches; such as, diamond, basket, wheel, etc.—**blanket-stitch c.** One or more threads laid flat and fastened down by blanket-stitch. Used for borders.

crewel work (krū'ĕl; *crew* el). Embroidery done with crewel yarn, worked in many stitches to form conventional designs. Used for household furnishings.

cross-stitch e. Embroidery of many types and countries, all done in variations of the cross-stitch.

cushion style e. Allover canvas embroidery. Same as BERLIN WORK.

cut work. Open-work embroidery having designs outlined in purl-stitch, with twisted or single bars connecting purled edges and material under bars cut away. From early cut work, lacemaking developed about 12th century.

Czecho-Slovakian e. (chĕk'ō slō-văk'ĭ-ən; *check* o slo *vack* i an). Bright-colored embroidery on linen, worked with cotton, silk, or wool threads in geometrical designs, either by counted stitches or traced patterns.

Danish e. (dān'ĭsh; *dane* ish). Embroidery of Denmark, particularly HEDEBO.

darned e. Embroidery of designs worked in variations of darning-stitch. Used on linen, toweling, canvas, etc.

Delhi work (dĕl'ĭ; *dell* i). Type of Indian embroidery done in chain- and satin-stitches with metal and silk threads on satin and other fabrics.

double running e. Outline embroidery in double running-stitch. Same as HOLBEIN WORK.

drawn fabric work. Open-work embroidery. Same as PUNCH WORK.

drawn work. Open-work embroidery made by removing certain threads of a fabric and interlacing remaining threads with embroidery stitches. Made in three types: simple, embroidered, and tonder, or with color effects. Wide drawn work sometimes called *fagoting*.

ecclesiastical e. (ĕ-klē-zĭ-ăs'tĭk-əl; e klee zi *ass* tic al). Elaborate embroidery for altar cloths, church hangings, etc. See CHURCH EMBROIDERY.

e. on the stamp. Heavily padded embroidery. See STUMP WORK.

English e. Fine eyelet embroidery. Same as MADEIRA.

etching e. (ĕch'ĭng; *etch* ing). Embroidery done in black silk on material on which landscape designs or human figures have been painted with sepia; sometimes in outline, sometimes filled over, closeness of stitches being regulated by darkness of painted surface. Also called *print work*.

embroideries (continued)

eyelet e. (ī'lĕt; *eye* let). Open-work embroidery with floral designs of eyelets. Same as MADEIRA.

fish scale e. Embroidery of flower patterns on silk, satin, or velvet, with colored fish scales covering designs.

flame e. Embroidery in zigzag designs. See FLORENTINE EMBROIDERY.

Florentine e. Type of canvas embroidery in which stitches are worked and shaded up and down in zigzag designs. Also called *flame embroidery*, from its effect. Used for household furnishings.

Geneva e. (jĕ-nē'və; je *nee* va). Embroidery similar to ticking work, done on checked canvas with bands of velvet held down by herringbone and other decorative stitches.

Genoese e. (jĕn'ō-ēz; *jen* o eez). Buttonholed embroidery worked over a cord on linen or muslin, the fabric being cut away from between parts of the design. Used for dress and undergarment trimmings.

gimped or **guimped e.** (gĭmpt; gimpt). 1. Embroidery having design formed by cord or vellum laid on material and covered with gold or silk threads. Also called *church embroidery, laid embroidery*. 2. Embroidery with thin hammered metal plates attached. See BATUZ WORK.

gold e. Elaborate embroidery done with gold threads in outline, flat, and raised designs. Very ancient type of work dating from Biblical times. Usually laid and couched with silk. Used for church hangings, ceremonial robes, etc. Compare BULLION, ORPHREY, and PHRYGIAN EMBROIDERIES.

grass e. Embroidery in satin-stitch made by American Indians, with colored grass for thread; usually done on skins.

Greek e. Type of appliqué in which stitches fastening applied pieces are repeated on ground.

gros point (F. grō pwăṅ; grow pwanh). Canvas embroidery done with larger types of needle tapestry stitches. French term meaning large point.

hardanger e. (här'däng-ẽr; *har* dang er). Norwegian type of needlework in pattern of diamonds or squares, done on coarse linen and open canvas, with part of the material cut and threads between stitches pulled out to form design. Used chiefly for fancy work; occasionally, for blouses, dresses. So called for district in Norway.

Havanese e. (hăv-ə-nēz'; hav a *neez*). Buttonholed embroidery of conventional or geometrical designs worked in colors on heavy materials.

hedebo (hĕd'ĕ-bō; *hed* e bo). Danish form of cut and drawn work in three types, usually in white on white fabric: (1) As done by Danish peasants during 18th and 19th centuries, surface embroidery of conventional floral shapes in chain-stitch with scant drawn work. (2) As done later, embroidered pattern with drawn fillings similar to first type, but having additional cut-and-drawn spaces in squares. (3) As copied in other countries, usually characterized by highly conventional shapes, little surface embroidery, cut instead of cut-and-drawn spaces filled with fancy lace stitches. Originally used by peasants to decorate shirts, underwear, sheets, etc.; now used on collars, doilies, table cloths, etc.

hemstitch e. Type of punch work done in back-stitch made with a large needle, usually a punch-work needle. Stitch is drawn tight to give a hemstitched effect.

Hibernian e. (hī-bẽr'nĭ-ən; hy *ber* ni an). Embroidery in satin- and purl-stitches, done in colors on silk, velvet, or net. Used for cushions, screens, trimmings for garments.

Holbein work (hōl'bīn; *hole* bine). Delicate outline embroidery, alike on both sides, done in Holbein or double running-stitch by means of counted threads on linen. Noted for exact geometrical or conventional designs. Used for samplers, wash linens, garments, etc. Much used in time of the artist, Holbein; so called because often painted by him. Popular in Rumania; often called *Rumanian embroidery*.

huckaback e. Type of darned embroidery done on huckaback toweling, making use of the prominent weft threads in placing the darning-stitches.

Hungarian e. (hŭng-gā'rĭ-ən; hung *gay* ri an). Embroidery of conventional designs done in flat- or satin-stitch on Hungarian peasant garments, linens; characterized by bright colors.

Hungarian point. Canvas embroidery in zigzag designs. Same as FLORENTINE EMBROIDERY.

Indian e. Any embroidery of characteristic Oriental design worked by East Indian natives. Includes cloth embroidery, cashmere work, chain-stitch embroidery, quilting.

Irish work. White eyelet or cut-work embroidery like MADEIRA.

Jacobean e. (jăk-ə-bē'ən; jack o *bee* an). English embroidery of Restoration period; strongly influenced by Oriental work; characterized by central tree design richly ornamented in color with flowers, fruits, birds, etc. Used for hangings, furniture coverings, etc.

Japanese e. Elaborate embroidery worked in satin-stitch with colored silk or metal threads, depicting scenes or forming intricate designs. Also, raised embroidery, padded and shaded.

Jugoslavian e. (yōō'gō-slāv'ĭ-ən; *you* go *slahv* i an). Embroidery of geometrical designs worked chiefly on coarse linen in bright-colored wools with counted stitches—chiefly cross-stitch, slanting satin-stitch, double purl-stitch.

laid e. Embroidery with cord or vellum designs overlaid with stitches. Same as GIMPED EMBROIDERY.

linen e. Chiefly German embroidery, consisting of drawn work on linen with buttonholed designs.

Madeira e. (mə-dēr'ə; ma *deer* a). Embroidery consisting of floral or conventional designs of eyelets punched or cut and then overcast. Used on garments and linens. Also called *broderie anglaise, Ayrshire, English, eyelet*, or *Swiss* embroidery.

Madras work (mə-drăs'; ma *drahss*). Embroidery done in variety of stitches over designs on large, brightly printed silk or cotton handkerchiefs called *Madras*.

Maltese e. (môl-tēz'; mawl *teez*). Embroidery consisting of small tassels worked over surface of heavy materials. Used for curtains, bedspreads, etc.

medieval e. (mē-dĭ-ē'vəl; mee di *ee val*). Bold embroidery of Middle Ages; done in flat stitches couched down by overcasting and worked into figures. Used for hangings. Now imitated by tapestry in panels.

Mountmellick e. (mownt-měl'ĭk; mount *mel* ick). White Irish embroidery done with coarse thread in bold, realistic, floral patterns; often with knitted fringe. Used on linens and other household articles.

needle tapestry work. Canvas embroidery in variety of canvas stitches worked to resemble woven tapestry.

net e. Embroidery of various types done on net ground. See TAPISSERIE D'AUXERRE, TINSEL EMBROIDERY, TULLE EMBROIDERY. Sometimes classed as lace. See BRETON LACE under LACES.

Norman e. Crewel work partly covered with other embroidery stitches.

open-work e. Embroidery with open spaces forming part of design; made by drawing, cutting, or pulling aside threads of fabric.

opus Anglicum (ō'pŭs ăng'glĭ-kŭm; *o pus ang* gli cum). Embroidery of Anglo-Saxon times, done chiefly in split-stitch.

opus pulvinarium (ō'pŭs pŭl-vĭ-nā'rĭ-ŭm; *o pus pul vi nay* ri um). Old name for BERLIN WORK.

Oriental e. (ō-rĭ-ĕn'təl; o ri *en* tal). Types of embroidery made in Eastern countries, especially Chinese, Indian, Japanese, Persian, Turkish. Famous for amount of labor involved, costly materials, boldness of color and design.

orphrey (ôr'frĭ; *or* fri). Elaborate embroidery, usually done in gold or other costly material.

outline e. Embroidery in which design is outlined in color but never filled in.

Paris e. Embroidery done with fine white cord in satin-stitch on piqué. Used for wash articles.

Persian e. (pẽr'zhən; *per* zhan). Any embroidery of Persia; chiefly, geometrical designs on fine linen, designs being completely covered by richly colored filling-stitches and darkly outlined. Also, Persian types of darned work, drawn work, appliquéd, etc.

petit point e. Loosely, any needle tapestry work; specifically, that done in petit point stitch.

Philippine e. Embroidery characterized by dainty floral motifs, done by hand by native women in Philippine Islands. Much used on less expensive lingerie.

Phrygian needlework (frĭj′ĭ-ən; *frij* i an). Ancient embroidery worked with silk and gold threads.
phulkari (pŏŏl′kä-rē; *pool* kah ree). East Indian embroidery of floral pattern.
piqué e. (pē-kā′; *pee kay*). Embroidery worked in white thread on firm material, with corded outlines and various filling-stitches. Used for household linens, children's garments, etc.
print work. Embroidery of black stitches over sepia printed designs. Same as ETCHING EMBROIDERY.
pulled work. Same as PUNCH WORK.
punch or **punched work.** Open-work embroidery made by pulling certain threads of fabric aside with needle or stiletto and fastening them by embroidery stitches. Used chiefly on household linens.—**radio p.** Punch work with round designs, instead of square. Used for solid work, as in designs of tiny baskets, and for corners in embroidery pieces.
Ragusa guipure (rä-gōō′zä gē-pür; rah *goo* za gee pure). Type of cut work. Same as ROMAN CUT WORK.
raised e. Embroidery with raised designs, done in satin-stitch over padding. Used on bed and table linens, for monograms, scallops, etc. Heavily padded embroidery called *stump work*.
Renaissance e. (rĕn-ə-säns′; ren a *sahnce*). Open-work embroidery done in purl-stitch and connected by bars. Similar to RICHELIEU.
Richelieu e. (F. rē-shə-lyē; ree she lyu). Type of cut work, with wide-open designs connected by picoted bars. Done chiefly in purl-stitch on linens. Used for household furnishings.
rococo e. (rə-kō′kō or rō-kə-kō′; ro *co co* or ro *co co*). Embroidery worked with small ribbon often called *China ribbon*.
Roman cut work. Embroidery with open designs outlined with purl-stitches and held together with bars. Similar to RICHELIEU EMBROIDERY. Used chiefly in large centerpieces, heavy table covers. Also called *Strasbourg work*, *Ragusa guipure*.
Rumanian e. (rōō-mā′nĭ-ən; roo may ni an). Outline embroidery. Same as HOLBEIN WORK.
Russian e. (rŭsh′ən; *rush* an). 1. Washable embroidery done chiefly in outline designs on holland. 2. Wool embroidered on cloth over canvas, the canvas later being cut away.
Sabrina work (sə-brī′nə; sa *bry* na). Variety of floral appliqué worked in single or double purl-stitch or chain-stitch. Used for quilts, borders, etc.
Saxon e. Outline embroidery of Anglo-Saxon times. See ANGLO-SAXON EMBROIDERY.
seed e. German embroidery of flowers, done with various seeds connected by stems and leaves of chenille. Formerly used for sachets, handbags, firescreens.
shadow e. (shăd′ō; *shad* o). Type of embroidery worked with catch-stitch on wrong side of transparent fabric. Bermuda fagoting sometimes called *shadow embroidery*.
Sicilian e. (sĭ-sĭl′yən; si *sil* yan). Lace-like embroidery. See SPANISH EMBROIDERY, 2.
smocking. Decorative stitching holding fulness in regular patterns. Used on blouses, children's dresses.
Spanish e. 1. Embroidery of herring-bone-stitches filling design on muslin. Used on wash garments. 2. Lace-like work, in effect like embroidery, made in muslin or cambric by means of braid and closely placed buttonhole-stitches. Also called *Sicilian embroidery*.
Strasbourg work (sträz′bōōr; *strahz* boor). Type of cut work. Same as ROMAN CUT WORK.
stump work or **e. on the stamp.** Embroidery with elaborately stitched biblical or allegorical scenes in grotesque disproportion; often with beads, wire, hair, coral added. Figures in high relief, made by padding or stuffing with horsehair and covering with satin.
Swiss e. Eyelet embroidery. Same as MADEIRA.
tambour work (tăm′bōōr; *tam* boor). Embroidery done on double drum-shaped frame with hooked needle, in stitch resembling chain-stitch. Originally only in Eastern embroideries; now superseded by chain-stitch embroideries.
tapisserie d'Auxerre (F. tȧ-pēs-rē dō-zĕr; ta peece ree doe zare). Embroidery made with Berlin wool on net in satin-stitch. Done in geometrical designs. Used for household articles.
ticking work. Imitation of Oriental embroideries, done on ticking foundation in bright-colored silks, ribbons, and braids. Used for screens, mats, cushions, rugs, etc.
tinsel e. Outline embroidery worked with tinsel on net or other fine, open fabric. Imitation of Turkish metal thread embroidery.
toweling e. (tow′ĕl-ĭng; *tow* el ing). Any embroidery on heavy toweling material. May be drawn, cut, or fringed work, in variety of stitches.
trellis work. Embroidery, similar to ROMAN CUT WORK, made of colored material cut out in designs of flowers climbing over trellis; edged with purl-stitch, decorated with other stitches.
tulle e. (tōōl or F. tül; tool). Simple type of embroidery done with floss silk on tulle, either by darning in counted meshes, or by using embroidery stitches on traced pattern. Formerly used for trimming party dresses.
Turkish e. Embroideries with conventional designs, done on linen or other fine fabric by counted stitches or traced patterns; so worked that there is no wrong side. Done with colored silk or gold and silver thread in various native stitches, or in chain-, satin-, or darning-stitch. Used for garments and household furnishings.
Venetian e. (və-nē′shən; ve *nee* shan). Open-work embroidery with raised designs done in purl-stitches over padding. See ROMAN CUT WORK.
Venetian ladder work. Embroidery consisting of outlining design with two parallel lines of buttonhole-stitches and connecting them with cross-stitches at regular intervals in ladder fashion. Used principally for border work in conventional designs.
Walachian e. (wŏ-lā′kĭ-ən; wol *lay* ki an). Solid embroidery done with single purl-stitch. Used to embroider eyelets and leaves.
white e. Any embroidery on white fabric.
woolwork. Any needlework in which wool yarn is used; especially, wool worked on canvas, producing effect similar to tapestry. See BERLIN WORK. See CREWEL WORK.

embroidery cotton. Thread used in embroidery. See THREADS.
embroidery darning-stitch. Alternating rows of even-basting. See STITCHES.
embroidery eyelet. Oblong or round eyelet worked with close overcasting-stitches. See EYELETS.
embroidery floss or **silk.** Untwisted silk fibers used for embroidery. See THREADS.
embroidery frame. Light-weight frame, often on adjustable stand, for holding material being embroidered.
embroidery hoop. Frame of two hoops, fitting one over other, between which material is held taut while being embroidered.
embroidery linen. Linen suitable for embroidery. Same as ART LINEN. See LINENS.
embroidery needle. Any of various kinds of crewel needles used in embroidery work. See NEEDLES.
embroidery on the stamp. Heavily padded embroidery. Same as STUMP WORK. See EMBROIDERIES.
embroidery scissors. Light small scissors for snipping threads. See SCISSORS.
emerald (ĕm′ĕr-əld; *em* er ald). 1. Precious stone of rich yellow-green color. 2. Vivid yellow-green, color of the gem; as color name, dating from 16th century.
emeraude (ĕm′ĕr-ōd; *em* er ode). Emerald green color. From French word *émeraude*, meaning emerald.
emerize (ĕm′ĕr-īz; *em* er ize). To scratch fabric, usually cotton or wool, with emery-covered cylinder in order to raise nap or give sheen.
emery bag (ĕm′ĕr-ĭ; *em* er i). Small cloth bag filled with powdered emery; an essential for every sewing basket. Used for keeping needles bright and clean.
empiecement (ĕm-pēs′mənt; em *peece* ment). In sewing, an insertion.
emplècement (F. äɴ-pyĕs-mäɴ; onh pyes monh). French term meaning yoke, as of a blouse.
Empire (ĕm′pīr or F. äɴ-pēr; *em* pire or onh peer). Characteristic of costume favored by Empress Josephine during French Empire period (1804–14). Marked by high waistline; décolleté, short bodice; straight, loose skirt; short puff or long sleeves; spencer and redingote; long train from shoulder;

fringe, embroidery, spangles for ornament.

Empire Costume, 1811

Empire skirt. Skirt cut to extend from 2 to 4 inches above normal waistline. See SKIRTS.
emporium (ĕm-pō'rĭ-ŭm; em po ri um). Retail store or bazaar carrying variety of articles. Name formerly given to department store.
empress cloth (ĕm'prĕs; em press). Cloth of wool or wool and cotton, similar to out-of-date fabric called *merino*, but not twilled. Formerly used for women's dresses.
enamel (à-năm'ĕl; e nam el). Smooth, hard composition with glossy finish, applied to surfaces for adornment or as basis for decoration. Used on costume jewelry, other ornaments.
en coquille (F. än kŏ-kē; onh ko kee) French term used of needlework made in shell pattern.
encroaching Gobelin-stitch (ĕn-krōch'ĭng gŏb'ĕ-lĭn; en croach ing gob a lin). Variation of Gobelin-stitch. See GOBELIN under STITCHES.
encrusted (ĕn-krŭst'ĕd; en crust ed). Variant spelling of INCRUSTED.
end. 1. Remnant; fragment of cloth. 2. Yarn of a warp; warp thread.
endimanché (F. än-dē-män-shā; onh dee monh shay). Over-dressed for the occasion. French term meaning dressed in Sunday best; wearing all one's finery.
endment. Small remnant, or end of a bolt of fabric.
engageantes (F. än-gȧ-zhänt; onh ga zhont). Sleeve trimming consisting of deep double ruffles or puffings of self-material, sheer lace, or muslin; usually concentrated at elbow, sometimes hanging to wrist. Also, hanging under-sleeve with lace cuffs. Fashionable part of woman's costume during late 17th century.
engagement ring (ĕn-gāj'mĕnt; en *gage* ment). Ring signifying betrothal. Usually a diamond solitaire. See RINGS.
English embroidery. Fine eyelet embroidery. Same as MADEIRA. See EMBROIDERIES.
English foot. Hosiery foot with separately knit sole. See HOSE.
Enka. Trade name for a brand of rayon. See RAYON.
en pantoufles (F. än păn-tōōfl; onh pahn toofl). French phrase meaning carelessly; in slipshod way; also, informally. Literally, in slippers.

en papillotes (F. än pȧ-pē-yōt; onh pa pee yote). French expression meaning in curlpapers.
enroulement (F. än-rōōl-män; onh rool monh). Roll or coil, especially of ribbon, etc., as used for hat trimming. French word for rolling up.
ensemble (ŏn-sŏm'bl or F. än-sänbl; on *som* bl or onh sonh bl). The entire costume—dress, coat, hat, shoes, bag, etc.; as, one's spring or fall ensemble. Also, harmonious effect in line and color. French word meaning together, at same time. *Tout ensemble* means all together.
ensign blue (ĕn'sĭn; en sine). Dark navy blue color of blue-green hue; almost midnight blue.
en tout cas (F. än tōō kȧ; onh too kah). 1. Combination parasol and umbrella; actually, sunshade which may be used as umbrella. 2. Vanity case. French expression meaning in any case.
entre deux (F. äntr dē; ontr du). Narrow beading or insertion of lace or embroidery resembling hemstitching. Used in seams, especially in handmade lingerie. See BEADING.
envelope bag (ĕn'vȧ-lōp; en ve lope). Handbag of envelope shape. See HANDBAGS.
envelope chemise (ĕn'vȧ-lōp shȧ-mēz'; en ve lope shem meez). Undergarment that combines chemise and drawers in one, with tab that laps over envelope-fashion and buttons. Same as TEDDY.
éolienne (ā-ō'lĭ-ĕn; ee o li an). Plain-woven fabric, usually of silk and worsted or silk and cotton, with filling yarns heavier than warp, giving crosswise corded effect. Similar to poplin, but lighter in weight. Used for dresses, coats, suits, etc.
epaulet or **epaulette** (ĕp'ȧ-lĕt; *ep* a let). Shoulder ornament or trimming designed to give effect of width to shoulder line. Used chiefly on dresses, according to fashion. So called from shoulder badge worn by army and navy officers, consisting of strap ending in fringed pad. Originated as device to hold shoulder belt and protect shoulder bearing musket. From French *épaulette*, diminutive of *épaule*, meaning shoulder.

16th Century Epaulets

epaulet sleeve. Sleeve extended over shoulder. See SLEEVES.
épaulière (F. a-pō-lyēr; ai po lyare). Part of medieval armor worn over shoulder, joining breastplate and backpiece.
ephod (ĕf'ŏd; *ef* od). Ancient ecclesiastical vestment worn by priests.
épinglé (F. a-păn-glā; ai pang glay). Fabric, usually of silk, ribbed or corded in any of several ways. Used for scarfs,

ties, etc. French word for ribbed or corded.
éponge (F. à-pōnzh; ai ponhzh). Soft, loosely-woven, spongy, nubby fabric of cotton, silk, wool, rayon, or mixtures, having looped filling yarns. Similar to RATINÉ. Used for dresses. French word for sponge.
equipage (ĕk'wĭ-pəj; *eck* wi pij). Set or case of small articles for personal use, as manicure set, sewing kit.
ermine (ûr'mĭn; *er* min). White fur with black-tipped tails; winter coat of certain weasels. See FURS.
ersatz (ĕr-zäts'; en *zots*). Term applied to material used as substitute for or in imitation of another; as, ersatz Persian lamb, fabric imitation of the fur. German word meaning substitute.
esclavage (F. ĕs-klȧ-vȧzh; es cla vahzh). Necklace of chains, beads, etc. See NECKLACES.
espadrille (ĕs-pȧ-drĭl' or F. ĕs-pȧ-drē; es pa *drill* or es pa dree). Cheap cotton sandal. See SHOES.
esparto (ĕs-pär'tō; es *par* toe). Coarse cloth made of esparto grass; also, the grass, grown in Spain and Algeria. Used for shoes, cloth.
estameme (ĕs'tȧ-mēn; *es* ta meen) or **estamin** (ĕs'tȧ-mĭn; *es* ta min). 1. Formerly, twilled woolen dress fabric having rough face. 2. ETAMINE.
etamine (ĕt'ȧ-mēn; *et* a meen). Lightweight, wiry, plain-weave fabric, usually of cotton or worsted; similar to bunting and voile, but more open. Used for dresses; formerly used for everything from flags to nun's veiling; first used as filter cloth. Widely used around 1910 for women's skirts that were trimmed with taffeta bands. From French word *étamine*, meaning sieve.
etching embroidery (ĕch'ĭng; *etch* ing). Black stitching on printed design. See EMBROIDERIES.
etching silk. Twisted silk used in needlework, as for feather-stitching, outline embroidery. See THREADS.
etching-stitch. Same as OUTLINE-STITCH. See STITCHES.
etiquette (ĕt'ĭ-kĕt; *et* i ket). Forms, customs, or conventional usages required by good breeding, as observed in social intercourse.
étoffe (F. a-tŏf; ai toff). French word meaning fabric, cloth, goods, material; also, quality, worth.
étoile (F. a-twäl; ai twahl). 1. Star design made by filling in meshes of net foundation. 2. Lustrous satin fabric. See SATINS. French word for star.
Eton cap (ē'tn; *ee* ton). Short-visored cap. See CAPS.
Eton collar. Stiffly starched, turned-over collar. See COLLARS.
Eton jacket. Hip-length jacket with lapels. See JACKETS.
étui (F. a-twē; ai twee). Ornamental case for holding personal accessories, especially, as fashionable during 18th century, thimble, scissors, scent bottle, etc. Often purchased as souvenirs by American tourists in France.
Eugénie (F. ė-zhȧ-nē; u zhay nee). Characteristic of styles worn by Em-

Eugénie hat — press Eugénie during French Second Empire period. See SECOND EMPIRE.
Eugénie hat. Ostrich-trimmed hat. See HATS.
evening dress. Décolleté costume. See DRESSES.
evening gown. Décolleté and sleeveless gown for wear on formal occasions. Same as EVENING DRESS. See DRESSES.
éventail (F. ā-väṅ-tī; ai vonh tie). French word for fan.
Everfast (ĕv'ẽr-fȧst; ev er fast). Trade name for fast-color fabric.
everlasting (ĕv-ẽr-lȧst'ĭng; ev er last ing). Any heavy, durable fabric similar to LASTING, DENMARK SATIN, etc.
exotic straw (ĕks-ŏt'ĭk; ex ot ic). Finely woven straw. See STRAWS.
expensive. 1. Term applied to quality merchandise. 2. Costing more than the average for similar articles.
eyebrow pencil. Cosmetic accessory, shaped like lead pencil. Used to darken eyebrows.

EYELETS

eyelet (ī'lĕt; eye let). Small hole or perforation; also, GROMMET. Used for decoration or lacing purposes.
buttonhole e. Eyelet, first overcast, then worked with single purl-stitch.
embroidery e. Eyelet, either oblong or round, finished with overcasting-stitches very close together.
eyeleteer (ī-lĕt-ẽr'; eye let eer). Sharp-pointed device, as stiletto or bodkin. Used for punching eyelet holes.
eyelet embroidery. Open-work embroidery. Same as MADEIRA. See EMBROIDERIES.

F

FABRIC

fabric. Material from which garments are made. Any cloth, knit, woven, or felted from any fiber, as wool, felt, hosiery, lace, etc. Most fabrics have right side, or face; wrong side, or back. Right side usually folded inside on roll or bolt, for protection in handling.
back-filled f. Fabric sized from the back to give body; usually only in inferior fabrics.
bordered f. Fabric woven or printed with a border that is used as trimming or finish in making a garment.
knitted f. Fabric, such as jersey, knitted by machine, usually a circular machine. See KNITTING.
plain f. Any fabric in plain, satin, or fine rib weave; fabric with little or no texture variation.
reversible f. 1. Fabric that is double-faced and may be used with either side as the right side. 2. Fabric without pile, ply, nap, or pattern running in any one direction. May be used either end up.
self-f. or self-material. Same fabric as the rest of a piece of apparel. Term applied to trimming, etc.; as, bands of self-fabric on a dress, self-facing, self-covered buttons, etc.
fabric count. Same as THREAD COUNT.
fabric weight. Weight in ounces of square yard or running yard of flat, unstretched fabric.
Fabrikoid (făb'rĭ-koid; fab ri koid). Trade name for durable imitation leather, widely used.
face. 1. In dressmaking, to finish an edge by applying a fitted piece or lining of same or other fabric, braid, ribbon, lace, fur, or leather. 2. In making fabric, to dress or finish the surface. Also, surface so treated; usually right side of fabric or leather.
faced. Having separate face formed by second warp or filling; term applied to fabric.
facet (făs'ĕt; fass et). Small plane surface of precious or imitation stone, usually in geometric shape.
Facile-closing handbag. Trade name for closing on handbag that can be opened and closed without clasp or other fastening. See HANDBAGS.
facing. Fabric applied to garment edge, often on the underside. Used as a substitute for a hem; also, for lining on parts of garment that are turned back, such as collars and cuffs.
facing silk. Light-weight, closely woven fabric, often of imitation silk. Used for linings; for concealed facings in garments, especially for facing hems, plackets, etc.
façonné (F. fȧ-sôn-nā; fa son nay). French word meaning figured; used of fabrics, particularly those with scattered motifs woven in.
fad. Minor or short-lived or small fashion.
fadeproof. Same as fast color. See FAST.
fag. 1. Knot or blemish in cloth. 2. End of cloth, rope, yarn, etc., that is coarser, raveled, or worn. Also called fag end.
fagot filling-stitch. Group of parallel stitches tied together at center to form a bundle. Same as BUNDLE-STITCH. See STITCHES.
fagoting (făg'ŏt-ĭng; fag ot ing). 1. Thread, yarn, ribbon, braid, etc., used straight or crisscrossed in open seam to form open-work trimming. See STITCHES. 2. Wide drawn work with threads caught together to form design. See STITCHES. 3. Shadow embroidery, sometimes called Bermuda fagoting. See STITCHES. See SHADOW EMBROIDERY under EMBROIDERIES.
faille (fāl or F. fī; fail or fie). 1. Untwilled, slightly glossy silk fabric in rib weave with light, flat, crosswise grain or cord made by heavy filling yarns. Sometimes faille is stiff; other times, limp with a draping quality. Used for dresses, suits, blouses, children's coats, wraps, slippers, millinery linings, trimmings. 2. Nun's hood; also, veil or scarf covering head and shoulders.
fair stitching. Stitching around sole of shoe, showing on upper side just beyond joining of shoe upper, usually in imitation of stitching that holds a welt.

Falbala

faja (fä'hä; fah hah). Spanish sash. See SASHES.
falbala (făl'bə-lə; fal ba la) or **falbelo** (făl'bə-lō; fal be lo). Festooned or puckered flounce, sometimes in plaited or puffed rows. Popular as dress decoration during 17th century. Originally, same as FURBELOW.
falderal or **falderol** or **folderol** (fŏl'dĭ-rŏl; foll di roll). Trifling ornament; gewgaw; nonsense.
faldetta (fȧl-dĕt'tȧ; fal det ta). Combination hood and cape. See WRAPS.
falding (fŏl'dĭng; fall ding). Coarse cloth of medieval times, or garment made of it.
fall. 1. Ornamental cascade of lace, ruffles, etc., on costume. 2. Non-transparent veil hanging usually from the back of hat down to neck or shoulders. Worn by women. 3. Same as FALLING BAND.
fallal (făl'ăl; fal al) or **fal-lal** (făl lăl; fal lal). 1. Gaudy ornament, trifling trinket, or other bit of finery in dress. In colonial America, full, soft ruffles used in trimming. 2. Affectation or foppishness.
falling band. Large, turned-down collar. See COLLARS.
false front. 1. False hair worn in fringe or bang over forehead. 2. Dickey in the front of a costume.
fan. Flat device mounted on frame, either permanently expanded or capable of being spread open and folded. Made of sheer cloth, or paper, or feathers, etc. Used for fanning; also as a dress accessory, especially with formal costumes. Formerly used by flirtatious women, many of whom could convey messages by means of signs made with the fan, there being a language of the fan just as there was a language of flowers.
fan collar. Frilly, fan-shaped, standing collar at back of neck only. See COLLARS.

FANCY DRESS

fancy dress. Costume representing a nation, class, calling, etc., as worn to costume ball or masquerade party.
Anne Boleyn costume. 16th century costume for Anne Boleyn, one of the six wives of Henry VIII. Consists of full-length robe, with long-sleeved, fitted bodice cut in low, square neckline, and

fancy dress (continued) bell-shaped skirt open from waist to show panel in front; girdle with long ends hanging in front; loose oversleeves of fur; gable headdress.

Anne Boleyn Costume, 1533

ballerina costume (băl-ə-rē'nə; bal a *ree* na). Same as BALLET COSTUME.
ballet costume (băl'ā; *bal* lay). Costume having short, very full skirt of many layers of sheer fabric, secured under basque bodice. Also called *basque* or *ballerina* costume.

20th Century Ballet Costume

basque costume (băsk; bask). Same as BALLET COSTUME.
Bo Peep costume. Costume for nursery rhyme character, having short skirt, bunched tunic of the pannier type, laced black velvet bodice over white muslin blouse, short sleeves, straw hat with streamers. Shepherdess' crook with ribbons as accessory.
clown suit. Full, baggy, one-piece trouser-blouse garment with ruffles at

Clown Suit

neck, ankles, and wrists. Often made of inexpensive cotton cloth, one half plain, one half printed or with motifs appli-

quéd, often in diamonds or disk form. Peaked hat, sometimes trimmed with pompons.
domino (dŏm'ĭ-nō; *dom* i no). Long, loose robe or cloak with adjustable hood, including half-mask. Usually black. Worn as general disguise at masquerades.
du Barry costume. Costume for Madame du Barry, mistress of Louis XV; typical of styles of the period, including fitted bodice with low décolletage, frilled neckline, and short, ruffled sleeves with wide flounces hanging from elbow; full, long skirt open at front to show elaborate panel; frilly, beribboned cap worn over powdered curls.

Du Barry Costume

Dutch girl costume. Dress, usually in Dutch blue, having full skirt and basque bodice sewn together at waistline. Accessories include white apron, kerchief, cap.

Dutch Girl Costume

dwarf costume. Costume for fairy-tale character, consisting of loose belted jacket with square buckle; close-fitting trousers tucked into loose, sock-like shoes; cap, like nightcap, with long

Dwarf Costume

bulbous end; beard; pickaxe—the Disney moving picture version of the costume, as shown in "Snow White."

Harlequin costume (här'lə-kwĭn; *har* le kwin). Costume of pantomime character, Harlequin, consisting of particolored suit of tights, often diamond-patterned, with ruff or ruffle at neck, and a mask. Hat of varying types sometimes worn to complete costume, such as hat with wide cuff-like brim turned up all around, and usually decorated with pompons.
Joan of Arc costume. Costume worn by Joan of Arc, the French heroine. Consists of full, gathered skirt; simple blouse with drawstring at neck; laced bodice; three-quarter sleeves.

Joan of Arc Costume

masquerade costume. Any type of fancy dress worn to a masquerade.
Mother Hubbard costume. Costume for nursery rhyme character, having full-length quilted petticoat; bunched tunic, open in front; muslin apron; laced bodice; sugar-loaf hat; rosette shoes; ruffled sleeves; mitts.
Peter Pan costume. Costume worn by Peter Pan, hero of J. M. Barrie's book and play of same name. As worn by the beloved actress, Maude Adams, short belted tunic covered with leaves, tight knee breeches, pointed shoes, typical Peter Pan collar, small perky hat with feather.

Peter Pan Costume

Pierrette costume (F. pyĕ-rĕt; pyare ret). Costume of female Pierrot, with tight bodice, usually sleeveless; full skirt or peg-top trousers; ruff at neck, sometimes at wrists. Plain or particolored, decorated with pompons. Usually has cone-shaped hat trimmed with pompons.
Pierrot costume (pē'ēr-ō or F. pyĕ-rō; *pee* er o or pyare o). Type of costume worn by jesting character of French pantomime, consisting of loose one- or

fāte, făt, dânce, ärt mē, mĕt, hẽr, thêre rīde, rĭd nōte, nŏt, côrn, fōōd, fŏŏt cūte, cŭt, cûre now fin(g)ger villa(ə) señor plea(zh)ure

two-piece garment with long sleeves, and ruff at neck. Usually white, sometimes with large, black spots. Worn with soft slippers with pompons; and tall toque, with or without brim, having pompon at side.

Pierrette Costume

pirate costume. Costume of various pirate characters, consisting of knee breeches and shirt, with sash at waist; long coat with wide cuffs; high boots with flaring cuffs; bandanna or tricorn hat, or both.
Pocahontas costume. American Indian women's dress, made of deerskin with fringe, decorated with beads. Worn with moccasins, leggings, and belt. Hair worn in long braids, with band around head and feathers for decoration.

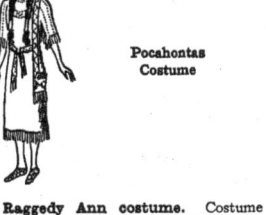

Pocahontas Costume

Raggedy Ann costume. Costume taken from child's story book about a stuffed doll. Consists of bright-colored patched skirt, patched apron, simple white blouse, white socks, and black shoes. Usually worn with ragged woolen wig. Accompanied by Raggedy Andy, dressed in patched and tattered

Red Riding Hood Costume

trousers or overalls of bright blue, little boy blouse, tattered red woolen wig.
Red Riding Hood costume. Costume worn by child in nursery story, consisting originally of a red cape and attached hood, with a drawstring in the casing of the hood, making a ruffle around the face.
Robin Hood costume. Costume of legendary character. Represented as wearing long tights; high, soft shoes rolled over at top; short tunic with wide collar, deeply scalloped around edges and laced up front; peaked hat with feather. Usually in dull, dark green color.

Robin Hood Costume

Santa Claus suit. Belted coat with attached hood; also knickers and leggings. Usually made of red Canton flannel, trimmed with cotton batting to simulate fur.

Santa Claus Suit

Snow White costume. Costume for fairy-tale character, consisting of light, loose, ankle-length skirt; close-fitting

Snow White Costume

dark bodice with pointed waistline and square neck; short puffed sleeves; high standing collar at back of neck; fillet—

as in the Disney moving picture version of "Snow White."
fancy goods. Art needlework and embroideries. See GOODS.
fancy work. Hand embroidery and decorative needlework.
fangled. Gaudily ornamented; showy; faddish. Usually NEW-FANGLED.
fanon (făn'ən; *fan* on). One of various articles carried or worn in celebration of the Mass. Specifically: **1.** The MANIPLE. **2.** Cape-like collar worn by the pope. See COLLARS.
fan plaits. Plaits radiating from a center in fan-like effect. Same as SUNBURST PLAITS. See PLAITS.
fan-tailed. Shaped like open fan or spread of peacock's tail.
fantaisie (F. făŋ-tā-zē; fonh tāy zee). Fancy style or fabric. French word meaning fancy.
farandine (făr'ən-dēn; *fa* ran deen). 17th century fabric of silk mixed with hair or wool.
farmer's satin. Lining material. See SATINS.
farthingale. **1.** Hoop skirt or hoop petticoat. **2.** Device to extend skirt. Much worn in time of Queen Elizabeth. See HOOPS.
fascia (făsh'ĭ-ə; *fash* i a). Band of various widths and types worn by ancient Romans around head, waist, arm, etc.
fascinator (făs'ĭ-nāt-ẽr; *fass* i nate er). Covering for the head, made of silk, lace, net, etc., or of fine yarn knitted or crocheted. Worn by women; later, by children. See CLOUD.

FASHION

fashion (făsh'ən; *fash* un). **1.** Prevailing or accepted style; often embracing many styles at one time. **2.** Particular line or construction, of a garment.
f. bulletin. Special information about significant new fashions, sent from fashion centers or authorities to individuals or firms, or published in newspapers and magazines.
f. clinic. Meeting of group of persons interested in fashion, under direction of a fashion authority, for purpose of presenting and discussing significant fashion trends; clinics usually held at beginning of spring and fall seasons.
f. coordinator. Person who coordinates or harmonizes styles, colors, etc., of articles in various related departments, as in a retail store.
f. cycle. Periodic return of any fashion, such as long skirt or low neck, in form adapted to current mode. Like a pendulum, a cycle usually swings from one extreme to another and back again.
f. delineator (dē-lĭn'ē-ā-tēr; de *lin* ee ate er). Fashion writer or forecaster.
f. dolls. **1.** Dolls dressed in latest styles sent around for display before styles were shown in publications. Common among early American settlers, who received fashion news from France and England. **2.** Miniature mannequins dressed in the newest fashions, on display in piece-goods departments, store windows, etc.

fāte, făt, dånce, ärt mē, mĕt, hẽr, thêre rīde, rĭd nōte, nŏt, côrn, fōōd, fŏŏt cūte, cŭt, cūre now fin(ŋ)ger villa(ə) señor pleas(zh)ure

fashion (continued)
f. forecast. Prediction as to which fashions will be popular during any coming season, based on study of trends and cycles.
f. marks. Raised dots characterizing full-fashioned hose. See HOSE.
f. pattern book. Catalogue of selected pattern designs issued periodically, as Vogue Pattern Book, etc.
f.-plate. 1. Illustrations representing prevailing fashions in wearing apparel. **2.** Person dressed in fashionable clothes, resembling such an illustration.
f. sheet. Booklet of pattern designs issued monthly, as a rule, with descriptions, prices, etc.; usually purchased by the store and distributed free of charge in store.
f. show or **showing** or **presentation.** Exhibition of fashions in any line or lines from standpoint of style; usually in connection with showing the season's new merchandise.
f. trend. Tendency toward any approaching mode; fundamental line along which fashion moves.

fashionable. In accord with the smart prevailing style; modish.
Fashion Aids. Trade name for sewing-machine attachments designed to make it possible and easy for the woman who sews to make fashionable trimmings and finishes.
fashionist (făsh'ən-ĭst; *fash* un ist). Specifically, stylist or fashion coordinator. Loosely, one engaged in fashion work; a term usually disliked by those to whom it applies.
fast. Firmly set, durable, permanent. Said of color or dye that withstands washing and light.

FASTENERS

fastener (făs'ĕn-ēr; *fass* en er). Device that fastens or holds together separate parts.
Conmar. Trade name for a slide fastener.
Crown Zipper. Trade name for American-made slide fastener, advertised as die-cast rather than stamped. Made in many colors, lengths, and types. Used for all types of closings, also for decoration.
hook and eye. Fastener in two pieces, a hook and a loop, which link together to secure the closing on garments. Made of metal or composition.
Koverzip. Trade name for a slide fastener that has the metal part covered with a ribbon or tape.
Kwik. Trade name for a slide fastener.
slide f. Fastener consisting of tape with metal or plastic section through which tab, called a slider, is moved up or down for opening or closing. Provides smooth, secure closing for garments, accessories.
snap f. Fastener in two pieces, disk and spring, which fit together to secure the closing on garments. Made of metal.
Streamline Fastener. Trade name for a slide fastener.

Talon Slide F. (tăl'ən; *tal* on). Trade name for particular type of American-made slide fastener. Made in metal and plastic materials in many styles, colors, and lengths. Used for fastening and for decoration on garments and accessories.

Faust slipper (fowst). Man's house slipper. See SLIPPERS.
favorite or **favourite** (fā'və-rĭt; *fay* vo rit). Lock of hair dangling on temples. Worn by colonial women.
fawn. Yellowish dark tan color of a fawn or young deer.
fearnought (fēr'nôt; *feer* nawt). Heavy woolen fabric used for outer garments. See DREADNOUGHT.

FEATHERS

feather or **feathers.** Part of plumage of birds. Differentiated as quill, or stiff, strong tail or wing feather; and plume, or long, waving feather. Used for decoration in millinery; also for fans, boas, and other accessories according to fashion.
aigrette or **aigret** (ā-grĕt'; ai *gret*). Upright tuft of feathers or plumes which grow on egret, or heron, only during breeding season. Dyed and used as decoration for headdress or hat. Unlawful to bring into U. S. A. Often subject of controversy because, when wild adult birds are killed for their feathers, young are left to starve.

Aigrette, 1890's

bird of paradise f. Long, brilliantly colored plume, often golden orange, from tail or beneath shoulder of full-grown male birds of paradise. Used on hats, for headdresses, etc. Importation into U. S. illegal.
coq f. (F. kŏk; coke). Feather of male domestic bird. Used as trimming in millinery. French word for cock or rooster.
glycerined f. Feather treated with glycerine, having wet appearance.
grebe (grēb; greeb). Smooth, silky, down-like plumage of grebe duck; in color, mostly ivory flecked with brown. Used for millinery.
marabou (măr'ə-bōō; *ma* ra boo). Soft, elongated tail and wing feathers of species of stork. Made into trimmings that sell by the yard at trimming counters; available in black, white, all pastels, and some bright colors. Used on hats, dresses, negligees, etc.
osprey (ŏs'prĭ; *oss* pri). **1.** Aigret plume used on hats. **2.** Artificial plume for millinery trimming.
Ostairette (ŏst-ā-grĕt'; ost ai *gret*). Trade name for imitation aigrette, made of ostrich quill.

ostrich f. (ŏs'trĭch; *oss* trich). Plume-like quill feather from wing or tail of ostrich. Used as hat and headdress ornament; also for fans, capes, etc. Ostrich feathers are worn when fashions are fluffy and elaborate. Often several feathers are carefully glued together as one, to appear abundant. Dyed in all colors and beautifully curled.
paradise f. (păr'ə-dĭs; *pa* ra dice). Same as BIRD OF PARADISE FEATHER.
Featherbone. Trade term for tape made by patented process since 1884, originally as a substitute for whalebone. Made from the stem, shaft, or center of feathers; in several widths and weights; plain or ribbon covered. Used for corset and girdle stays, suspending hoop skirt foundations, tops of sleeves, muff foundations, collar supports. May be bought by the yard at notion counters.
feather cloth. Rough-surfaced cloth woven of wool mixed with feathers.
feather mail. Armor made of feathers. Worn by native Mexicans before Spanish conquest.
feather mosaic (mō-zā'ĭk; mo *say* ic). Overlapping feathers on net or fabric, so arranged as to form a design.
feather-stitch. Blanket-stitches grouped and zigzagged in feather-like design. See STITCHES.
feather work. 1. Same as FEATHER-STITCH. **2.** Same as FEATHER MOSAIC.
fedora (fə-dō'rə; fe *doe* ra). Low felt hat with lengthwise crease in crown; soft, medium brim. See HATS.
fell seam. Flat, sturdy seam with all raw edges concealed. See FLAT FELL SEAM under SEAMS.
felt. 1. Thick, firm-packed, smoothly matted fabric, made of fibers of wool, hair, fur, and cotton, that are carded, hardened, and treated by moisture, heat, and pressure. Sometimes coarsely woven or knitted, then heavily napped and finished smoothly. Used for hats, table covers, pennants, caps, pockets, glove linings, etc. Sometimes made with thick, fur-like finish, and called *fur felt* or *beaver felt*. **2.** Garment, especially a hat, of felt. Hats of felt first made in England at time of Henry VIII.
fent. 1. Formerly, opening or slit, as at neck or placket of garment. **2.** British term for remnant or flawed piece of fabric.
feridgi (fə-rĭj'ē; fe *rij* ee). Long, hooded wrap worn by Oriental women. See WRAPS.
fermail (fēr'māl; *fer* mail). Ancient type of buckle. See BUCKLES.
fern-stitch. Stitch similar to arrowhead-stitch, but with third stitch in each group, forming stem-like line. See STITCHES.
ferret (fĕr'ĕt; *fare* et). **1.** Narrow worsted, silk, cotton, or rayon ribbon or tape for binding, making cockades, rosettes, etc. **2.** Floss silk. — **Italian f.** Ferret made of silk in black, white, and colors.
Ferris waist. Trade name for a corset waist with buttons or tabs for supporters.

---

fāte, făt, dănce, ärt mē, mĕt, hēr, thēre rīde, rĭd nōte, nŏt, côrn, fōōd, fŏŏt cūte, cŭt, curé now fin(q)ger villa(a) señor pleas(zh)ure

ferrule (fĕr'ŭl; *fare* ul). Small end, cap, or ring, often of metal, on tip of umbrella, cane, etc.

feston (F. fĕs-tôn; fess tonh). French word for buttonhole-stitch, especially as used on decorated or scalloped edge.

festoon (fĕs-tōōn'; fess *toon*). Curved garland of flowers, foliage, drapery, etc. Also, fabric hanging in curves between points; as, a festoon of lace or crepe paper.

fez. 1. Brimless felt cap formerly worn by Turks. See CAPS. **2.** Adaptation of Turkish fez. See HATS.

fiber (fī'bēr; *fie* ber). Thread of filament to be spun or woven in making textiles. Fabric fibers include silk, wool, cotton, linen, asbestos, rayon; classified as animal, vegetable, mineral, and artificial, or synthetic.

fiber lace. Lace of banana and aloe fibers. See LACES.

fiber silk. Term applied to artificial or imitation silk; should not be used in describing rayon.

fiber-stitch. Stitch used in bobbin lace. See STITCHES.

fibroin (fī'brə-ĭn; *fie* bro in). Silky ingredient in raw silk. See SILK.

fibula (fĭb'ū-lə; *fib* you la). Ancient type of pin or brooch. See PINS.

fichu (fĭsh'ōō; *fish* oo). Draped scarf or shawl worn about shoulders and tied in knot at breast, with ends hanging down loosely. Also, ruffly draping on bosom of blouse or dress. Word, meaning negligee or careless, first used to describe breaking away from stiff collar of the past.

19th Century Fichu

fig. To dress up; deck out. Also, colloquially, fine dress; array.

figgery. Ornaments; gewgaws.

figured. Marked with pattern or design.

figured weave. Weave which produces design in a fabric. See WEAVES.

filament (fĭl'ə-mənt; *fill* a ment).Thread, or fiber, used as raw material in making textiles.

filament rayon yarn. Rayon yarn, somewhat like silk thread or embroidery silk. See RAYON.

filasse (fĭ-lăs'; fi *lahss*). Vegetable fiber as prepared for manufacture. Distinguished from raw fiber.

filbert (fĭl'bērt; *fill* bert). Pale brown with slightly gray-green cast. Same color as HAZEL. Original name for hazel nut.

filet (F. fē-lā; fee lay). Net lace having square mesh. French word meaning net.

filet lace. Knotted open-mesh lace with darned patterns. Handmade filet lace often used for neckwear, blouse trimmings, etc. Filet net used for dresses, tablecloths, etc. See LACES.

filibeg (fĭl'ĭ-bĕg; *fill* i beg). Modern kilt reaching to knees, as worn by Scotch Highlanders.

filigree (fĭl'ĭ-grē; *fill* i gree). Delicate ornamental open work, especially lacelike jewelry formed of intertwisted delicate wires in gold or silver.

filled gold. Term in jewelry for gold coated over a center of baser metal, as nickel or brass.

filler. Shoe form placed inside shoe to preserve shape while on display.

fillet (fĭl'ĕt; *fill* et). Narrow band or ribbon worn around head or binding hair. Derived from Latin *filum*, meaning thread.

filling. 1. Yarn running crosswise of woven fabric, at right angles to warp, or lengthwise yarn. Yarn carried by shuttle. Also called WEFT, WOOF, PICK, SHOOT. **2.** Substance used to give body to fabric — as starch and china clay for cotton, weighting for silk. **3.** Stitches used in making lace or embroidery, to fill or make more solid the open places in designs.

filling-stitch. Embroidery stitch used to fill in part of design. See STITCHES.

fillip (fĭl'ĭp; *fill* ip). Slight stimulus; exciting or impelling force; as, such and such a thing gives a quick fillip to a fashion.

filo-floss (fī'lō flŏs; *fie* lo floss) or **filo silk.** Very fine, soft embroidery floss or threads. See THREADS.

filoselle (fĭl-ə-zĕl'; fill a *zell*). Silk thread somewhat coarser than floss. See THREADS.

fil tiré (F. fēl tē-rā; feel tee ray). French term for drawn work filled in with delicate needlework. Used on handmade lingerie, etc.

fimble. Male hemp plant, smaller than female but maturing earlier. Also, its fiber.

fin de siècle (F. făn də syĕkl; fanh de syeckl). End of the century; used specifically of end of 19th century.

findings. Threads, tapes, buttons, bindings, hooks and eyes, slide fasteners, Featherbone, belting, braids, and other sewing essentials used in garment making; carried in notion departments.

fine-draw (fīn drô; fine draw). To sew or close up, as a rent or seam, so delicately that joining can not be noticed.

finery (fīn'ēr-ĭ; *fine* er i). Decoration; especially, elaborate clothing or jewelry; fragile, fluffy apparel.

finger. That part of glove which covers finger. Also called STALL.

fingering. 1. Finely twisted woolen yarn for knitting or crocheting. See YARNS. **2.** Serge of coarse texture formerly made in Scotland.

fingerling. Obsolete term for finger covering, thimble, or cover of finger.

fingerstall. Finger covering; glove finger. See STALL.

finger tip. Covering for end of finger, as for protection.

finger-tip length. Length of a coat or other garment which reaches to ends of fingers when arms are hanging. See LENGTHS.

finger wave. In hairdressing, wave pressed in with fingers when hair is wet, and then dried in place.

finisher. Term applied to worker in the apparel trades who finishes, who takes the last final stitches, who checks all work and adds any necessary stitches, paint, gilt, or trimming that completes the work.

FINISHING

finishing. Any of various processes affecting appearance of fabric. Many fabrics pass through a finishing room for steaming, glazing, pressing, or shrinking. **chemical f.** Treatment of woven fabric with chemical for stiffening, filling, softening, bleaching, weighting, preserving, mercerizing, waterproofing, mothproofing, crushproofing, spotproofing, etc.; also, for controlling shrinkage and increasing porosity, as of cottons, and controlling slippage, as of rayons.

mechanical f. Treatment of fabric by mechanical processes including calendering, gassing, napping, shrinking, tentering.

finishing braid. Narrow braid in plain weave, with simple embroidery stitches added for decoration. See BRAIDS.

finnesko (fĭn'ĕs-kō; *fin* ess ko). Boots made of reindeer skin. See BOOTS.

fire opal. Kind of opal with bright, firelike lights in its coloring. Same as GIRASOL.

firmament (fēr'mə-mənt; *fer* ma ment). Obsolete term for jeweled ornament encircling the head.

fishbone-stitch. Series of diagonal single-purl stitches zigzagged across an unmarked line. See STITCHES.

fisher. Durable, dark brown fur of largest of marten family. See FURS.

fish net. Net having very large mesh. See NETS.

fish pearl. Imitation pearl. See PEARLS.

fish scale embroidery. Flower designs covered with fish scales. See EMBROIDERIES.

fish-tail. Shaped like tail of fish; having cut-out V in end.—**f. drapery.** Train, as on a formal gown, shaped like fishtail.

fitch or **fitchew.** Fur of European polecat. See FURS.

five-eighths length. Length of coat or other garment reaching halfway between hips and knees. See LENGTHS.

flair (F. flêr; flare). French word for special aptitude or ability to select or discriminate, as in clothes. It is often said that a woman who dresses smartly and becomingly has a flair for clothes.

flame. Of the color of flames; brilliant scarlet. Also called *flame scarlet*.

flame embroidery. Allover canvas embroidery in zigzag designs. Same as FLORENTINE EMBROIDERY. See EMBROIDERIES.

flandan (flăn'dăn; *flan* dan). Woman's cap-like headdress with long hanging flaps. See PINNER, 2.

FLANNELS

flannel (flăn'l; *flan* el). 1. Soft, light, woolen fabric, slightly napped on one side, in plain or twill weave. Used for shirts, sports clothes, children's clothes, etc. 2. Cotton fabric in plain or twill weave with twisted warp yarn, napped on one or both sides. In plain colors and prints. Also called *cotton flannel*.
baby f. 1. White, soft, all-wool or part-wool flannel in plain or twill weave, yarn- or piece-dyed, with smooth or napped surface. Used for infants' gertrudes, outer garments, coats, etc. 2. Soft twilled cotton flannel with nap, in white or pastel colors. Used for baby wrappers, undergarments, etc.
canton f. (kăn'tŏn; *can* ton). Stout, absorbent, cotton flannel in twill weave with long fleecy nap, usually on only one side. Used for interlinings, sleeping garments, infants' wear, underwear. So called because first made for trade with Canton, China.
diaper f. White cotton flannel, napped on one or both sides, in twill weave. Used for diapers and infants' sleeping clothes.
dress f. Woolen fabric, usually twilled, napped on one side, available in solid colors, plaids, checks, and stripes. Often mixed with cotton; now, also with rayon. Used for dresses, suits, coats, children's apparel, etc.
kimono f. (kĭ-mō'nō; ki *mo* no). Same as FLANNELETTE having printed designs.
ladies' or **lady's cloth.** Obsolete term for fine, slightly napped flannel in plain weave. Copied from cloth used for men's suits and made in lighter weight, hence the name. Used for dresses, suits, women's wear.
outing f. Cotton fabric in plain weave having nap on both sides, made in colors, stripes, and checks. Used for sleeping and infants' garments. Sometimes called *flannelette*.
shaker f. White cotton flannel napped on both sides. Originally made by the Shakers, a religious sect.
shirting f. Woolen flannel in varying weights and colors; plain or twilled.
swansdown (swŏnz'down; *swans* down). Same as CANTON FLANNEL.
twilled f. Any flannel in twill weave.
vegetable f. Fabric of German manufacture, made of pine fiber.
Viyella f. Trade name for part-wool flannel in twill weave, of varying weights and widths. Widely used for shirts, skirts, dresses, sports wear, infants' and children's wear, etc.
Welsh f. Fine flannel, largely handwoven of wool from sheep of Welsh mountains.

flannelette or **flannelet** (flăn-ĕl-ĕt'; flan el *et*). Soft cotton fabric, slightly napped; in white, solid colors, floral designs. Used for baby garments, sleeping garments, kimonos.
flannels. Underclothing or outer garments made of flannel, especially trousers.

flap. Broad, flat, thin part of garment that hangs loose or is attached only by one edge; as, the flap of a pocket.
flapper. Name given to any young woman who wore very short skirts or short, sleeveless dresses, large hats, and the generally exaggerated styles of the 1920's.
flap pocket. Pocket with flap at opening. See POCKETS.
flare. Portion of garment or other apparel that widens or spreads out.

Flare-Back Coat, 1930's

flat. Colloquial term for straw hat. See HATS.
flatcap. Flat, low-crowned cap. See CAPS.
flat crepe. Smooth, soft crepe. See CREPES.
flat fell seam. Flat, sturdy seam. See SEAMS.
flatfold. To fold fabric without making creases; roll without doubling.
flat heel. Broad low heel. See HEELS.
flatiron. Metal implement with handle and approximately triangular, flat, smooth surface for ironing and pressing clothes.
flat knitting. Type of knitting done in flat form. See KNITTING.
flat-lock seam. Seam line in which all raw edges are concealed with the stitches. Made on a machine designed to do flat-lock stitching, which appears as if handmade. See SEAMS.
flat-lock stitch. Zigzag machine-stitch usually used as a seam finish.
flat point lace. 1. Lace without raised work. 2. Sprigs and flowers made separately on pillow. See LACES.
flat-stitch. Variation of satin fishbone-stitch. See STITCHES.
flat-stitched continuous placket. Both edges of placket finished with one strip of fabric or tape so stitched as to lie flat when laundered. See PLACKETS.
flax. Soft, silky fiber of flax plant. Made into thread, or into yarn that is woven into linen. Natural flax, unbleached, makes grayish tan linen. Flax from Ireland, when made into linen, considered whitest and most durable.
flaxen. Of the color of flax; straw-colored; blonde. Said of light, fluffy hair.
Flaxon. 1. Trade name for fine quality of mercerized cotton fabrics, lawn, organdie, voile, etc. Used for blouses, dresses, and lingerie. 2. Cotton fabric in basket weave similar to dimity,

except in finish. Used for dresses and blouses.
fleck. Spot or mark. Also, to spot with variegated dots; to dapple. Black or dark fabric with pin dots of white is often spoken of as snow flecked, or as having a snow fleck.
fleece. 1. Coat of wool covering sheep and similar animals. 2. Textile fabric with soft, fleecy pile. Used for linings. 3. In spinning, a layer of wool or cotton fiber gathered in the carding machine.
flesh. Color of varying pinkish and palest yellow skin tones of the white race. Average flesh color is slightly lighter and pinker than beige.
flesher. Portion of split sheepskin nearest flesh, often tanned with oil to make chamois.
fleshings. Flesh-colored tights. Also, tights in general.
flesh pink. Color name distinguishing those portions of the skin, such as the cheek, having definite pinkish hue.
flesh side. In leather trade, side of hide or skin next to flesh. Distinguished from grain side.
fleur de lis (F. flěr de lē; fler de lee). Iris flower. Also, conventionalized motif of ancient origin used as decorative design. Royal emblem of France. Widely used as a design in fabric, laces, jewelry, etc.

Fleur de Lis Motifs

fleuron (F. flěr-ôŋ; fler onh). Ornament in shape of flower, often at end of an object.
fleur volant (F. flěr vô-lāŋ; fler vo lonh). Ornamental loop for cordonnet in body of point lace pattern. French phrase meaning flying flower. See COURONNE.
flimsies. Colloquial term for women's undergarments of delicate fabric.
float. Warp, filling, or decorative yarn in woven fabric which passes over several other yarns, lies on surface of fabric for some distance, and is then caught in.
floating panel. Additional panel at back or front of a dress, generally hanging loose from waist, sometimes attached to the belt in apron effect.

Dress with Floating Panel, 1922

fāte, făt, dânce, ärt mē, mĕt, hēr, thêre rīde, rĭd nōte, nŏt, côrn, fōōd, fŏŏt cūte, cŭt, cūre now fin(ŋ)ger villa(ɐ) señor pleas(zh)ure

flock. Short fibers of wool, often obtained by shearing nap of fabrics, used to weight low-grade woolens.

flock dot. Dot applied to fabric by chemical means, as in flock-dotted voile or Swiss. See DOTS.

flocket. Long, loose, woman's garment worn in 16th century.

floor length. Length of dress or other garment which just touches the floor. See LENGTHS.

flop. Soft wide-brimmed hat. See HATS.

floral (flō'rəl; *flo* ral). Relating to flowers; as, floral design in lace, floral print.

florence (flŏr'ĕns; *flor* ence). 1. Formerly, woolen fabric made in Florence, Italy. 2. Light-weight silk dress fabric of varying descriptions; SARSENET.

Florentine embroidery (flŏr'ĕn-tēn; *flor* en teen). Type of canvas embroidery in allover design. See EMBROIDERIES.

Florentine leather. Leather decorated with fine tooling, often in gold. Used for hand-bound books; for bags, belts, etc. See LEATHERS.

Florentine neckline. Broad, round neckline; similar to bateau, but not so wide. See NECKLINES.

Florentine-stitch. Upright canvas stitch, usually in zigzag or oblique lines. See STITCHES.

floret (flō'rĕt; *flo* ret). Silk yarn spun from waste. See SILK.

florid brunette (flŏr'ĭd brŭ-nĕt'; *flor* id bru *net*). Person with reddish complexion and dark hair and eyes. See BRUNETTE.

Florodora Girl costume. Full, fluffy skirt; lace-trimmed bodice, with bishop sleeves gathered in at the wrist; and off-the-face picture hat. Popularized by the Florodora chorus in the musical show, "Florodora."

Florodora Girl Costume, 1900

floss silk. 1. Coarse silk fibers. See SILK. 2. Same as EMBROIDERY FLOSS or SILK. See THREADS.

flots. Rows of ribbon or lace placed in overlapping loops.

flounce. Gathered or plaited strip sewn

19th Century Flounces

to garment, lower edge often being left free. Generally worn at bottom of garment, especially on skirt, sleeve, or cape.

flourishing thread (flẽr'ĭsh-ĭng; *fler* ish ing). Linen mending thread. See THREADS.

flowered. Having a floral design; as, a flowered print.

flower toque. Small, close-fitting hat entirely covered with flowers. See HATS.

flue. 1. Fine lint, hair, or downy matter, such as rises from cotton, wool, fur, etc. 2. Feathery fibers extending from each side of shaft of feather or quill.

flushing. British term for coarse, heavy fabric of shoddy. Used for heavy outer garments.

fluting. Plaited ruffle or ruche sometimes inserted as band in garment, especially at neck and sleeves. Originally, made in fine muslin; flutings put in with an iron having ridges, which fluted as it pressed.

fly. 1. Decorative article shaped like a fly, as a pin for the hair or patch for the face. 2. Piece of material, attached by one edge. Especially, piece concealing fastening of garment, as in the fly front of a coat.

fly cap. Woman's cap of 17th and 18th centuries, with wing-like pieces at sides. See CAPS.

fly-fringe. Dress trimming in fashion throughout Georgian era, consisting of tufts of silk matching or contrasting with garment.

flying costume. Costume suited for wear in airplane. See SPORTS CLOTHES.

flying Josie (jō'zĭ; *jo* zi). Lady's riding habit. See JOSEPH.

fly-stitch. Decorative stitch shaped like a fly. See STITCHES.

fob. Watch pocket; also chain, ribbon, or pendant hanging from watch.

foil. Thin tissue-like sheet of metal; as, tin foil, silver foil, etc.

folderol. Variant spelling of FALDERAL.

follette (F. fŏl-lĕt; foll let). Obsolete word for very light fichu.

fond (F. fŏn; fonh). Ground, or honeycomb network, on point and pillow laces, as distinct from the pattern.

fontange or **fontanges** (F. fôn-tänzh; fon tahnzh). 1. Commode headdress. So called in France for Mlle. de Fontanges, who introduced it about 1679. 2. Knot or loop of ribbon usually ornamenting high tiers of commode headdress.

foolscap or **fool's cap.** 1. Jester's cap. See CAPS. 2. Dunce cap. See CAPS.

foot. 1. For types of hosiery foot, see HOSE. 2. On sewing machine, the PRESSER FOOT, CORDING FOOT, etc. 3. Measure of length equaling one-third of a yard, or 12 inches. Used in English-speaking countries.

foothold. Light-weight, low-cut, rubber overshoe with heel-strap instead of heel.

footing. 1. Narrow banding, often of net, used as edge finish. 2. Edge of lace sewed to other fabric.

foot mantle. Formerly, protective covering worn while riding, to prevent soiling the skirt. See SKIRTS.

footwear. Any apparel worn on the feet, as slippers, galoshes, boots, shoes, etc.

forage cap (fŏr'ĕj; *for* ij). Small undress soldier's cap. See CAPS.

fore and aft. In both the front and back.

fore-and-after. 1. Cocked hat worn so that peaks are in front and back. See HATS. 2. Cap having peak at front and back. See CAPS.

forepart. 1. Part of shoe or last from shank forward, including the ball and toe. 2. Type of stomacher worn during 16th and 17th centuries.

foresleeve. 1. Part of sleeve covering forearm. 2. Extra decorative sleeve. See SLEEVES.

forest white. Coarse woolen fabric formerly made at Penistone, England. See PENISTONE.

foretop. Front part of headdress; specifically, top of periwig.

forfar (fôr'fẽr; *for* fer). Coarse, heavy linen fabric, formerly made in Forfarshire, Scotland.

forget-me-not. Soft, medium-light blue color of the forget-me-not flower.

form. A woman's form is her body, specifically from shoulders to hips. See also DRESS FORM.

formal. Worn on full-dress occasions. Said of evening dress with low décolletage, no sleeves. Worn when men wear full dress (white tie and tails) or tuxedo.

formal dress. Dress worn on full-dress occasions. Evening dress with low décolletage and no sleeves. See DRESS.

formality (fôr-măl'ĭ-tĭ; for *mal* i ti). Formerly, formal dress. Often in plural, meaning prescribed costume for associated group of men.

Fortuny tea gowns (fôr-tōō'nē; for *too* nee). Clinging gowns on Grecian lines, slipped over head, with neck opening often gathered by silk cord. Designed by Fortuny, son of the great Spanish painter; made of durable silks; usually plaited their full length; sometimes decorated with stencil designs, beads, or gold and silver tracery. First shown in Paris in 1910.

foulard (fōō-lärd' or F. fōō-lär; foo *lard* or foo lar). 1. Soft, serviceable, washable satiny silk with fine twill; plain or printed, but usually having small figures on dark or light ground. Used for dresses, blouses, lounging robes, ties, scarfs. 2. Soft, fine, mercerized cotton fabric, plain or printed, on twill weave. 3. Handkerchief or kerchief of silk foulard.

foulé (F. fōō-lā; foo lay). Light-weight woolen dress fabric with glossy finish.

foundation (fown-dā'shən; fown *day* shun). 1. Basic underpart over which dress was formerly made; later replaced by separate slip. 2. Short for FOUNDATION GARMENT.

foundation garment. Girdle, corset, or corselet; usually combined with bandeau or brassière.

foundation net. Coarse, stiffened net. See NETS.

foundation pattern. Plain, basic pattern without fulness or designing lines; used for size only. See PATTERNS.

fourchette (foor-shĕt'; foor shet). Small forked piece of leather or other material set in between fingers of glove.

four-gore slip. Slip made of four gores, without underarm seam. See SLIPS.

four-in-hand. Long necktie usually cut on the bias and having an inside padding. Worn tied in a four-in-hand knot at the throat, with ends hanging vertically down front.

fourreau (F. foo-rō; foo roe). French word meaning scabbard or sheath. Close-fitting, sheath-like gown.

fox. Soft, long-haired glossy fur. See FURS.

foxing. Part of shoe that forms or covers lower part of QUARTER. Loosely applied also to the VAMP.

fraise. 16th century ruff. See COLLARS.

frame. 1. The human form. 2. Foundation construction of an umbrella, consisting of ribs, stretchers, etc. 3. Device of various descriptions, made to hold fabric, etc., taut for embroidery, quilting, and other types of needlework.

Franco-Cuban heel. Narrowed Cuban heel. See HEELS.

fray. To wear away or ravel along a worn, torn, or cut edge. Loosely woven or wiry fabrics fray easily.

frazzle. Colloquial term meaning to wear or ravel away; fray. Also, a frayed end. One who looks frazzled is shabby or untidy.

Free Action Sleeve. Trade name for sleeve with length added to the underarm section to allow greater freedom of action for sports, etc. See SLEEVES.

Free-Finger Glove. Trade name for glove design having strip running alongside and continuing around end of each finger, without seam at tip. See GLOVES.

French chalk. Soft, white, absorbent chalk used for absorbing perspiration on hands of those who handle delicate fabrics; for dry cleaning, etc.

French cuff. Double cuff or turn-back of cuff-band. Each cuff usually has four buttonholes, all fastened together with one link. See CUFFS.

French drawer bottom. STRAP CROTCH. See CROTCH.

French fall. Wide-topped boot. See BOOTS.

French fold. Strip of bias fabric first folded so that edges meet at center, then doubled so that side to be stitched is narrower than other. Used as trimming and finishing bands on all types of dress apparel. Not for wash garments.

French foot. Type of hosiery foot with center sole seam. See HOSE.

French gathering. Method of gathering with long stitch on top and short stitch underneath. Gives effect of having less fullness on top, yet fullness underneath is secured.

French or **zephyr gingham.** Fine, soft gingham. See GINGHAMS.

French heel. Curved, high heel. See HEELS.

French hem. Hem having raw edge caught in a tuck on right side. See HEMS.

French hood. Elaborate 16th century hood. See HOODS.

French knot. Ornamental embroidered knot, made by twisting the thread around the needle. See STITCHES.

French merino. Fine grade of merino wool. See MERINO.

French seam. Narrow seam stitched first on right, then on wrong side, concealing raw edges; used chiefly on lingerie fabrics. See SEAMS.

French serge. Finely twilled serge of quality yarns in medium weight. See SERGES.

fret. 1. To decorate with interlacing lines, as of gold or silver. 2. Headdress of net of gold or silver wire worn by women in Middle Ages. 3. To rub or wear away by friction.

friar's cloth (frī'ẽrz; fry erz). Rough, canvas-like drapery material in basket weave. Similar to MONK'S CLOTH.

frieze (frēz; freeze). 1. Rough, shaggy woolen cloth, originally of Irish make, in use for outer garments since Middle Ages. 2. To raise nap on, as cloth; to frizzle or curl. 3. To embroider, as with gold.

frilal (frī-lăl'; fri lal). Obsolete term meaning border of ornamental ribbon.

frill. Narrow ruffle or edging gathered and attached at one edge, left free at other. Used usually as finish for neck, sleeves, etc.

fringe. Border of hanging threads, cords, or tassels. Sometimes made by fraying edges of cloth. Used to give weight to an edge; also to ornament it. Threads of fringes sometimes tied to give variety of effects.

frippery. Tawdry finery; gewgaws.

frisé or **frizé** (F. frē-zā; free zay). Pile fabric with uncut loops, sometimes patterned by cutting some of the loops, by printing, or by using colored yarns. Chiefly used for upholstery.

frisette or **frizette** (frĭ-zĕt'; fri zet). Fringe or bang of hair, frequently curled, worn on forehead.

frisado or **frisado** (frī-zä'dō; fri zay doe). Obsolete napped woolen fabric similar to frieze.

frizz. To curl or crimp hair. Also, the hair so curled.

frizzle. To form crisp small curls; frizz. Also, such a curl or curls.

frock. 1. Dress of any type. Often one of simple style. In fashion language, considered smarter term than dress. 2. Loose outer garment for various purposes, as a tunic or mantle worn by the clergy, loose shirt formerly worn by laborers, frock coat.

frock coat. Man's coat with knee-length skirt. See COATS.

frog. Looped fastening made of braid or cording. Used with a toggle to secure pajama coats, other garments.

froissé (F. frwä-sā; frwah say). French word meaning crushed or crumpled in effect.

front. 1. Partial bodice covering only front or neck; dickey; shirt front; gilet. 2. Piece of false hair worn over forehead. 3. Cravat.

frontage (frŭnt'əj; frunt ij). Incorrect for FONTANGE.

frontlet (frŭnt'lĕt; frunt let) or **frontal** (frŭnt'əl; frunt al). Ornamental band worn across top of forehead, especially hood, projecting over forehead.

frou-frou (F. froō-froō; froo froo). French word meaning a rustling sound, as of woman's silk taffeta dress. Also applied to dress trimmings which might produce such sound, as ruffles, lace, etc.

frounce. Obsolete term meaning to gather, plait, or wrinkle, as fabric; or to curl, as hair. Also, anything gathered, plaited, curled, etc.

frowzy or **frowsy.** Unkempt; slovenly; untidy.

frumpy or **frumpish.** Dowdy; untidy; poorly dressed.

fuchsia (fū'shə; few sha). Purplish-red shade, carefully matched to flower of this name.

fudge edge. Edge of shoe sole stitched and trimmed close to upper.

full. 1. To pucker or make full by gathering the cloth on one side of a seam; as, to full a sleeve. 2. Made with much fabric gathered in in folds. 3. To subject fabric to FULLING.

full bottom. Wig with broad bottom. See WIGS.

full dress. Evening dress; also, costume required for certain ceremonies. See DRESS.

fuller. Literally, one who fulls cloth. Also, one who cleans cloth or clothes.

fuller's earth or **fuller's chalk.** Nonplastic clay, usually in powdered form and of grayish color, used in removing grease and other stains from cloth. Also used for facial mud packs.

fuller's herb. Soapwort, a plant used formerly in removing stains from fabric.

full-fashioned. Knit flat and shaped by dropping stitches. Term applied to hose and underwear. See HOSE.

fulling. Process of shrinking woolen fabric to make it more compact and thicker, by use of pressure, moisture, and heat.

full length. As applied to a coat, length sufficient to reach to bottom of dress. As applied to a dress, length of skirt almost touching the floor. See LENGTHS.

full seam or **trade seam.** Double-stitched seam. See SEAMS.

full vamp. Vamp extending under tip of shoe. See VAMP.

funnel collar. Collar fitted at neckline, flaring outward at top, usually opening at side or back. See COLLARS.

FURS

fur. 1. Hairy coat of certain animals, distinguished from HAIR by being finer, softer, more thickly placed; from WOOL by being less crisp, less curled. Consists of hide or leather; and usually of short, soft underfur and longer, stiffer overfur, top hair, or guard hair. Cured, tanned, dressed, or dyed by various processes to improve appearance, durability, etc., before being manufactured into garments or accessories. 2. Pelt dressed and cut for wear as lining, mark of dis-

tinction, trimming. Garment made of fur; especially, fur collar or neck-piece.
Alaska sable. Incorrect name for SKUNK. No longer legal usage.
Alaska sealskin. Warm, durable, naturally brown fur of seals from islands near Alaska; plucked, dressed, and usually dyed logwood brown, "safari brown," or black.
American badger. Durable fur of badger of western North America. Best of the badger family. Used for trimmings. See BADGER.
American Broadtail. Trade name for processed young Argentine lamb, from one day to nine months old; sheared very close, dyed to imitate BROADTAIL.
American mink. Fur of wild or ranch-bred mink of North America. Ranges in color from pale brown to dark brown, always with darker center-back, and in quality from coarse and flat to full-furred, soft, and silky. Underfur is even and close; guard hair, even and slightly longer. Paler mink often dyed or blended to darker shades. Finest mink, durable and expensive, is found from New York up through Canada.
American opossum. Fairly durable, long-haired, dusty-gray fur of American opossum, having long, creamy-white underfur and darker, silvery-gray guard hair. Sometimes dyed to resemble SKUNK or MARTEN.
American sable. BAUM MARTEN.
antelope. Perishable, short-haired coat of small brown African deer, having no underfur.
arctic fox. Fur of either the white or the blue arctic fox. Most durable of foxes.
arctic wolf. Coarse and durable fur of white wolf of arctic regions, having black-tipped tail.
astrakhan (ăs'trȧ-kăn; ass tra can). Formerly, fur of lambs of karakul or caracul sheep, once obtained from Astrakhan, Russia. Name no longer proper usage for caracul fur.
Australian opossum. Properly, fur of Australian phalanger, an animal of size of large house cat. Fur is thick, durable, fairly long, and crisp-looking. Guard hair is sparse. Underfur is either light brown, shading to silvery gray on top, or rusty brown. Both types have strip of lighter color at outer edge.
baby. Term used to describe smaller and usually finer and softer furs of a species, without reference to age; as, baby fisher, baby Persian.
baby deer. Perishable, short-haired, soft, blue-gray fur of young Alaskan deer. Rare because this animal is under U. S. Government protection.
badger. Coarse, long-haired, very durable fur of small animal inhabiting northern Europe, Asia, and northwestern North America. Underfur is creamy white and long; guard hair, coarse and white with black band below tip. European and Asiatic badger mostly used for brushes.
baum marten (bowm; bowm). Soft, silky, fairly durable, brown fur of European marten. The lighter peltries are usually dyed or blended to sable shades. Sometimes called *beech* or *pine marten*.
bear. Coarse, bushy, sturdy fur of various types of bear, in natural color or dyed.
beaver. Warm, soft, very durable fur of beaver of North America. Peltries range in color from rich, lustrous, golden brown to dark brown. Guard hair is plucked, leaving long, thick underfur. Moist weather causes kinky curls to appear on beaver, but curls are easily removed by an ironing process. SHEARED BEAVER has been more recently introduced.
beaver-dyed cony. Rabbit dyed and plucked to resemble beaver.
beaverette. Beaver-dyed cony, or rabbit fur.
Bessarabian lamb. Coarse-haired, cross-bred type of Persian lamb. Duller, less durable, and with less character than true Persian lamb.
black fox. Fur of red fox, often ranch-bred; during rare periods, fur is pure black. Much so-called black fox is black-dyed fox. Silver fox sometimes called *black fox*.
black muskrat. Fur of muskrat having black back. Chiefly from New Jersey, Maryland, Delaware, Virginia. Used in natural state, never dyed. Of good wearing quality.
bleaching. Process for removing naturally yellowish tinge of all white furs. Dark furs of less expensive types often bleached and then dyed in lighter shades.
blending. Dyeing of surface hairs of paler furs to make them more attractive. Also called *tipping*, *topping*, and *feathering*.
blocked lapin (F. lȧ-păN; la panh). Rabbit fur, closely sheared, dyed, cut, and put together to form effect of blocks or squares, varying in size. Smaller blocks preferred.
blue fox. Rich, lustrous, smoky blue fur of arctic fox, chiefly from Alaska and Greenland. Alaska blue fox is finest. Next in value to silver fox. Often imitated by dyeing white fox.
broadtail. Fragile pelt of stillborn, unborn, or very young Persian lambs. Fur very flat, lustrous, supple; lacks tight curl of Persian lamb, having instead moiré design or galyak effect.
burunduki (bōō-rȧn-dū'kē; boo run *due* kee). Perishable fur of Siberian chipmunk, having more even stripes than American chipmunk — four light, five black. Used for short wraps, trimming Americanization of Russian *burun duchy*, meaning chipmunks. Often incorrectly spelled *baronduki*.
caracal (kăr'ȧ-kăl; *kar* a kal). Reddish-brown fur of African or Asiatic wild cat, having black-tipped ears.
caracul (kăr'ȧ-kul; *kar* a kul). Glossy, curled coat of young lambs obtained chiefly from Russia and North China. Russian caracul is stronger, flatter, more tightly curled, more expensive, heavier, more silky; Chinese caracul, woolier, less expensive, less glossy, less desirable for coats.
chinchilla (chĭn-chĭl'ȧ; chin *chill* a). Perishable, costly, soft fur of chinchilla, small South American rodent, size of large squirrel; now almost extinct. Blue-gray in color, with dark shading.
Chinese badger. Long-haired fur of badger from China, coarser and more wiry than American badger.
Chinese mink. Light yellowish fur of Chinese animal resembling mink. Underfur close and even, with long, silky top hair. Better grades are dyed brown and known in the fur trade as KOLINSKY.
civet cat (sĭv'ĕt; *siv* et). Fairly durable fur of small, skunk-like animal of size of house cat. American species have short, thick, soft, dark underfur and silky, black top hair with white, lyre-shaped markings. Civet cat of Asia and Africa, seldom used in America, is brownish-gray and marked with white spots and stripes.
cony or **coney.** Rabbit fur, especially of rabbit from Europe, Australia, or New Zealand; often processed to simulate more expensive furs.
coyote (kī'ōt or kī-ō'tē; *ky* ote or ky *ote* i). Fur of small wolf, common on western prairies of U. S. In fur trade, usually called *western wolf*, as distinguished from *timber wolf*.
coypu (koi'pōō; *coy* poo). Fur of coypu, or small South American rodent. Same as NUTRIA.
cross fox. Fox fur in tones ranging from yellowish to orange, with a definite brownish-black cross along spine and across shoulders. Pelt may be from red fox which is temporarily marked with cross during certain periods; usually from ranch-bred foxes permanently marked.
Cross Persian. Trade name of fur from sheep with strain of Persian, regardless of country of origin. Generally, this fur is duller, has less character, is less valuable, and does not wear so well as true Persian lamb.
drumming. Process by which furs are cleaned or softened. They are placed with sawdust and heavy pieces of rubber in a metal, wood-lined, rotary apparatus shaped like a drum, with small shelves protruding from the wood-lining. As the drum rotates, the furs and rubber are caught by the shelves, carried along, and then dropped. The rubber pounds the sawdust into the furs, cleaning out excess oil and loose hairs and softening the leather.
ermine (ûr'mĭn; *er* min). Fine, soft, durable white fur with black tail-tips; winter coat of species of weasel of northern Europe, Asia, and America. Russian ermine is best. Skins not pure white are often bleached or dyed. Highly prized, historically celebrated fur once restricted to royalty; still used in coronation robes. Often poorly imitated with rabbit, hare, cat.
fisher. Very durable dark brown fur of largest of marten family, having deep underfur and dark, glossy top hair.

fāte, făt, dănce, ärt mē, mĕt, hēr, thêre rīde, rĭd nōte, nŏt, côrn, fōōd, fŏŏt cūte, cŭt, cūre now fĭn(ŋ)ger villa(ȧ) señor pleas(zh)ure

furs (continued)
Formerly used only for scarfs; now used for garments.

fitch. Long-haired, serviceable fur of European polecat, mostly from Germany and Russia, having creamy-yellow or whitish underfur, long glossy dark guard hair. Dyed platinum, kolinsky, and baum marten shades.

fox. Soft, long-haired, glossy, semi-durable fur of animal of Europe, North America, Asia, Australia; smaller than wolf, and has long, bushy tail. Various types: ARCTIC, BLUE, BLACK, CROSS, KIT, GRAY, RED, SILVER and WHITE FOX.

galyak or **galyac** (găl′yăk; *gal* yak). Very flat, glossy fur derived from lamb, kid, or goat; often of poor quality. Used for trimming. Local word in Bokhara, meaning premature lambs.

genet (jĕn′ĕt; *jen* et). Fur of animal of wild-cat family; sheds easily; light, soft, and semi-durable.

gray fox. Fur of gray-colored fox, chiefly of North America; more coarse and serviceable than most fox fur. Used in natural color and also often dyed to simulate other types.

guanaco (gwä-nä′kō; gwah *nah* ko). Thick, soft fur, naturally fawn-colored, of wild South American animal related to llama and alpaca, but larger. Erroneously called *vicuna*.

hair seal. Fairly durable, spotted, grayish, flat, and wiry fur of seals having no underfur; chiefly from the Atlantic Ocean. Sometimes dyed.

half Persian lamb. Skins of very young cross breed of Persian lambs, chiefly from Rumania and Iraq, having looser curl, coarser hair, and duller luster than full Persian.

hamster. Fairly durable fur of small European animal; flat, yellowish brown, with black markings. Used chiefly for lining men's coats.

Hudson seal. Muskrat with guard hairs removed; fur sheared and dyed black to simulate Alaska sealskin; durable.

Jap marten. Fairly durable, yellowish fur of Japanese marten. Underfur is woolly and long; top hair, rather coarse. Usually dyed sable shade.

Jap mink. Light yellowish mink of Japan, with dark stripe in center-back. Usually dyed to resemble American mink, the fine color and quality of which it lacks. Better grades closely resemble kolinsky.

karakul (kăr′ə-kŭl; *kar* a kul). Skins of lambs first obtained from Karakul, meaning Black Lake, in the Bokhara desert in Russia. Usually spelled *caracul*.

kid caracul. Beautifully marked Chinese kidskins; dyed in many shades; not durable. Incorrectly called *caracul*.

kidskin. Tender, perishable fur of young goats, chiefly from China, Africa, India. Black, gray, or white; some skins beautifully marked. Used in natural shades or dyed for coats, trimming.

kit fox. Durable fur of small fox found in many regions. Underfur is soft and creamy-yellow; top hair is white. Often dyed grayish-blue.

kolinsky (kō-lĭn′skĭ; ko *lin* ski). Fur of Asiatic mink, largely from China and northeastern Russia. Has long, silky top hair, naturally yellowish brown; usually dyed darker. Often called *red sable* and *Tartar sable*.

krimmer. Sturdy pelts of young lambs of Crimea district in Russia; naturally gray, tightly curled fur resembling Persian lamb.

lapin (F. lȧ-păŋ; la panh). Closely sheared, perishable fur of rabbit, chiefly dyed in fancy shades. Black lapin differs from seal-dyed cony, which is not sheared so closely.

Laskin Mouton (lăs′kĭn mōō-tôŋ; *lass* kin moo tonh). Trade name for processed lambskin, with lustrous pile; usually golden brown. Hardy fur; looks and wears like sealskin.

leopard (lĕp′ẽrd; *lep* erd). Fur of large cat from Africa, China, or India. Best grades from Somaliland. Durable, short-haired, wiry, and tawny or buff in color with black rosette markings. There is a pygmy type of Somali, which is smaller, softer, and lighter in color.

leopard cat. Fur of spotted cat chiefly of South America; also, of Africa and Asia. Tawny in color with black spots and grayish underground, having easily shedding top hair.

lynx (lĭnks; links). Very soft, long-, silky-haired fur of North American or European wildcat, varying in color from grayish buff to tawny, with indefinite dark spots and fine streaks. Sometimes dyed a lustrous black.

lynx cat. Fur closely resembling lynx, but shorter, more sandy colored, less durable, and sheds more easily.

Manchurian ermine. Fur of Chinese weasel; larger and somewhat coarser than ermine, and not so durable. Back is pale yellow; sides, creamy white.

marmot (mär′mŏt; *mar* mot). Inexpensive fur of rodent of Europe and Asia, chiefly Russia and China. Seldom used in natural state; usually dyed to simulate mink. American marmot, or groundhog, little used.

marten (mär′tĕn; *mar* ten). Fur of animal from Europe, Asia, and America; larger than weasel, of same species as sable. Has long, glistening guard hair and soft, thick underfur; brown on back, lighter color underneath. Types include BAUM MARTEN, also called *American sable*, and STONE MARTEN.

Mendoza Beaver-dyed Cony (mĕn-dō′zə; men *doe* za). Trade name for rabbit dressed and dyed beaver shade by Mendoza Fur Dyeing Works.

miniver (mĭn′ĭ-vẽr; *min* i ver). Fur of uncertain type used during Middle Ages as trimming on garments. In present English usage, plain white fur, especially ermine.

mink. Thick, soft, durable, brown fur of weasel-like animal of North America, Japan, Russia, China. Has glossy guard hair, darker than underfur, and still darker back stripe; most valuable skins are dark to roots. Best mink from eastern North America.

mink tail. Mink tails, darker and longer haired than the mink and fairly durable, sewn together into plates from which trimmings are made.

mole. Perishable, velvety, soft, lustrous, often iridescent, dark gray fur of very small animal; from Holland, Belgium, France, but chiefly from Scotland.

monkey. Long, silky, very black hair of certain monkeys, chiefly from Ethiopia.

muskrat. Durable fur of North American and Canadian rodent, of the size of small house cat. Has soft, gray underfur and long, glossy, dark brown, water-shedding top hair; often dyed to imitate seal. Pelts usually split into three parts: backs used for natural muskrat, sides for golden muskrat, bellies for silver muskrat. Types in fur trade known as NORTHERN, SOUTHERN, BLACK MUSKRAT.

musquash (mŭs′kwŏsh; *muss* kwahsh). In London fur market, muskrat skins. North American Indian name for muskrat.

near seal. Rabbit fur processed to resemble seal. Same as SEAL-DYED CONY.

northern muskrat. Fur of muskrats with naturally dark brown backs, having high luster when dyed. From any except states far south. Also called *brown muskrat*.

nutria (nū′trĭ-ə; *new* tri a). Fur of South American rat, or coypu, resembling beaver. Stiff, protective, outer hair plucked to leave soft, short, brown underfur; sometimes dyed seal shade.

ocelot (ŏs′ə-lŏt; *oss* e lot). Fairly durable fur of large American spotted cat having variable black markings on tawny yellow or gray ground. Spots usually larger, closer, and more elongated than in leopard.

opossum (ō-pŏs′ŭm; o *poss* um). Long-haired fur of American opossum, dusky-gray in appearance, with whitish underfur and darker, silver-tipped guard hairs. Used natural or dyed to simulate marten or skunk; for sports coats and trimming.

otter. Durable fur of otter, mostly from Labrador and Canadian northwest, brown in color, resembling beaver; similar in characteristics to seal.

paw. Caracul, leopard, mink, Persian lamb, and silver fox paws are used to make garments and trimmings. See PIECED.

pelt. Skin of an animal with the hair intact, as received by the furrier. Term also used of the leather only.

peltry. Skin and hair of an animal as received by the furrier. Also, the place in a fur house where pelts are kept.

Persian lamb (pẽr′zhən; *per* zhan). Skins of very young lambs, chiefly obtained from central Asia, having handsome, durable fur of silky, lustrous hair in a tight, medium-sized knuckle curl. Naturally black or brown or gray; often dyed for uniformity of tone and gloss. See HALF PERSIAN LAMB.

perwitsky (pĕr-wĭt'skĭ; per *wit* ski). Mottled short fur of European and Asiatic polecat. Formerly used for lining coats.

pieced. Made of tails, or paws, or lighter underparts matched and joined. These parts of many peltries are cut out in manufacturing garments. When enough pieces of the same kind have been accumulated, they are matched, sewn into plates, and used to make garments and trimmings, such as mink chevron, milk gill, mink paw, pieced caracul, and pieced Persian coats; mink tail and silver fox tail trimmings; and pieced squirrel and squirrel-lock linings. These are not so valuable, nor do they wear so well as those made of full pelts.

pine marten. European or American marten, larger than stone marten, having soft, dark brown fur, usually dyed to imitate Russian sable. Same as BAUM MARTEN.

plate. Skins or parts of pelts sewn together to make fur for linings, trimmings, or garments.

pointed fox. Fox fur, usually of red fox, dyed black or very dark gray, having white hairs inserted in imitation of silver fox.

pony. Skin of young colt or foal of small stocky breed of horse; strong, with lustrous flat hair; sometimes as beautifully marked as moiré caracul. Often from Russia or South America. Used in natural color or dyed for sports coats.

prime. Term applied to pelts of animals caught at season when fur is in best condition.

rabbit. Fur of animal of various countries; white, gray, brown, blue, fawn, mottled, sometimes black; often used to simulate more expensive furs. Same as CONY.

raccoon (ră-kōōn'; ra *coon*). Durable, long-haired fur of raccoon, chiefly from northern and central United States. Grayish with darker center stripe; off-color skins tipped or dyed, sometimes to simulate skunk.

red fox. Fur of fox from North America, Europe, Asia, Australia; usually ranging in color from pale to deep red. During certain color phases, known as CROSS, SILVER, BLACK FOX, etc.

red sable. Asiatic mink fur. Same as KOLINSKY.

Russian muskrat. Fur of animal smaller than American species; less durable, softer, and silvery gray in color.

sable. Durable fur of the sable, an animal about 18 inches long, from northern Europe or Asia. Very valuable, especially darker skins; Russian sable most valuable of all. Also, lighter colored and somewhat less valuable fur of pine marten of northern North America.

seal. Usually Hudson seal or seal-dyed cony; seldom Alaska sealskin. Not good usage in fur trade. See SEALSKIN.

seal-dyed cony. Fur of large French or Belgian cony, or rabbit, sheared to remove stiff hairs, dyed seal color.

sealskin. Fur of fur seals, mostly from coast of Alaska, after removal of long, coarse guard hairs. Usually dyed brown or black.

sea-otter. Rare and valuable otter fur from north Pacific coast; varying in color from light brown to black; having rich, soft underfur and outer coat of silver-tipped, coarser hairs. Now near extinction.

sheared beaver. Beaver with some of thick underfur sheared away, removing the tendency to curl in moist weather, and making garment lighter in weight and less bulky in appearance. Sometimes called *shaved beaver*.

silver fox. Fur of either common or red fox during rare period when fur is mostly black with guard hairs white-tipped. Chiefly ranch-bred; valuable because of difficulty of imitation.

silver pointed fox. Silver fox peltries that are richly furred, but poorly silvered, enhanced in appearance by gluing in silver hairs plucked from damaged peltries.

skunk. Long-wearing, lustrous fur of North American skunk. Sometimes all black; usually black with short, long, or broad white stripes.

southern muskrat. Fur of muskrat chiefly from Louisiana and Texas, less expensive than other types. Has poorly developed underfur.

squirrel (skwĕr'rĕl; *skwer* el). Soft, fluffy, semi-durable fur of small rodent; best skins from Russia and Siberia, dark gray or dark blue without reddish streaks. If streaked, usually dyed beige, taupe, mink, sable, or summer ermine shade; otherwise, used in natural state.

stoat. English name for WEASEL.

stone marten. Brown fur of marten of Europe and Asia, having whitish underfur; slightly coarser than BAUM or PINE MARTEN.

summer ermine. Fur of brown weasel; also, the beige shade of dye sometimes used to color white ERMINE.

Tartar sable. Asiatic mink fur. Same as KOLINSKY.

timber wolf. Fur of large, grayish wolf of northern U. S. and Canada, as distinguished from WESTERN WOLF or COYOTE.

tipped. When used to describe skunk, means dipped, because entire peltry, leather and fur, is dipped in dye. When used to describe any other fur, means that only top hair has been dyed. Sometimes *topped* or *feathered* used in latter sense.

underfur. Fur underlying longer guard hairs of fur-bearing animal; softer, thicker, and lighter in color.

unprime. Not in best stage or condition; said of furs taken during molting season.

weasel. Short, thick, semi-durable fur of small, slender-bodied animal of many localities; usually reddish-brown on back, white or yellowish underneath. Species of northern Europe and Asia, called ERMINE, white except for black-tipped tails.

western wolf. Fur of coyote or small prairie wolf. See COYOTE.

white fox. Fur of arctic fox in clear, white, winter coat.

wolf. Sturdy, long-haired fur, stronger and less silky than fox, of dog-like animal chiefly from North America; also from Russia and Siberia. Varies in color from nearly white to black; usually yellowish to brownish gray. Used in natural color or dyed to imitate better grades of fox.

wolverine (wŏŏl'vẽr-ēn; *wool* ver een). Durable fur resembling wolf, but coarser. Dark brown in color, with tan stripe along sides.

furbelow (fẽr'bȧ-lō; *fur* be low). Gathered or plaited ruffle; festooned flounce. In broader sense, as "frills and furbelows," any ornamentation of women's dress.

fur cloth. Deep-pile fabric made to resemble different types of fur. Used in place of fur.

fur felt. Deep-napped felt. See FELT.

Fur-Lap. Trade name for ear muffs made of lambskin, having band of fur or metal, or both, which connects the ear laps.

fur set. Collarette and muff to match. Worn by children, and at times fashionable for adults.

fustanella (fŭs-tȧ-nĕl'ȧ; fuss ta *nell* a). Short white skirt worn by men in Greece. See SKIRTS.

fustian (fŭs'chȧn; *fuss* chan). Napped fabric of linen and cotton or linen and wool. Made as early as 12th century.

G

gabardine (găb'ẽr-dēn; *gab* er deen).
1. Firm, twilled, worsted fabric, having fine diagonal rib effect on one side, with surface hard and smooth or soft and dull. Used for coats, suits, uniforms, riding habits, and other sportswear.
2. Softer fabric of mercerized cotton, showing raised rib on right side. Used for sports skirts, coats, suits, etc.
3. Same as GABERDINE.

gaberdine (găb'ẽr-dēn; *gab* er deen).
1. Smock frock or other coarse, loose coat or frock. 2. Medieval Jewish mantle or cloak. See WRAPS. 3. Any covering or protection, as cloak or mantle. See WRAPS. 4. Loose garment, as worn by laborers; also, pinafore. 5. Same as GABARDINE.

gable headdress (gā'bl; *gay* bl). Stiffened, elaborate, hood-like headdress, shaped like a gable, often extending to shoulders. Worn in 15th and 16th centuries, especially by matrons.

gadget (găj'ĕt; *gaj* et). Any contrivance, device, or small article the name of which can not be recalled; often used of something novel.

gadroon (gə-drōōn'; ga *droon*). Inverted fluting, rounded like cartridge plaits; usually short in proportion to width. Used as trimming. Term borrowed from architecture.

Gainsborough hat (gānz'bŭ-rō; *gainz* bur o). Large plumed hat. See HATS.

gaiter. 1. Cloth or leather covering for leg or ankle, buckled or buttoned at the side; often secured by strap under foot. **2.** Ankle-high shoe. See SHOES.

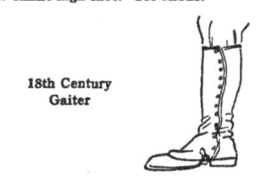

18th Century Gaiter

galatea (găl-ə-tē'ə; gal a *tee* a). Sturdy cotton fabric of superior quality, in satin weave. White, dyed in solid colors, or printed; often striped. Used chiefly for children's play clothes.

galea (gā'lĭ-ə; *gay* li a). Helmet or casque; formerly one of leather as distinguished from one of metal.

galerum (gə-lē'rŭm; ga *leer* um) or **galerus** (gə-lē'rŭs; ga *leer* us). **1.** Wig, as peruke or periwig; also, headdress. Worn by men and women, often as disguise. See WIGS. **2.** Close-fitting cap. See CAPS.

galilith (găl'ĭ-lĭth; *gal* i lith). Hard synthetic material, available in colors. Made into buttons, clips, etc.; used to trim apparel and accessories.

galilla. Small inside collar. See COLLARS.

gallery. In jewelry trade, setting having perforated sides.

galligaskin (găl-ĭ-găs'kĭn; gal i *gas* kin). Long, loose hose or wide breeches. Worn in 16th and 17th centuries. Now, sportsman's leather leggings. Also called *gaskin.*

galloon (gə-lōōn'; ga *loon*). Narrow, tape-like band; either strong lace woven of gold or silver threads on silk or worsted, or ribbon of wool, silk, cotton, etc. Formerly much used for trimming. Also spelled like French word *galon.*

galluses. Suspenders; braces. Term not in good usage.

galon (F. gȧ-lôṅ; ga lonh). French word meaning rich lace, galloon, or officer's stripe.

galon d'argent (F. dár-zhäṅ; dahr zhonh). French term meaning silver lace.

galon d'or (F. dôr; dor). French term meaning gold lace.

galosh (gə-lŏsh'; ga *losh*). **1.** Protective footwear. In modern times, overshoe of rubber or waterproof fabric worn in bad weather. Usually in plural form, *galoshes.* From Middle Ages through colonial days, clog or heavy sole of wood or leather held on by strap or thong over instep. **2.** Strip of material, usually leather, applied around edge of shoe at sole for protection or decoration.

galuchat (gȧ-lu̇'chȧt or F. gȧ-lü-shá; ga *lu* chat or gah loo shah). **1.** Ornamented SHAGREEN. **2.** Kind of sharkskin. See LEATHERS.

galyak or **galyac** (găl'yăk; *gal* yak). Flat, glossy fur of lamb, kid, or goat. See FURS.

gamashes (gə-măsh'ĭz; ga *mash* iz). **1.** British term for gaiters or leggings worn to protect legs. **2.** High boots. See BOOTS. Also spelled *gamoshes, gramashes.*

gambade (găm-bād'; gam *baid*) or **gambado** (găm-bā'dō; gam *bay* doe). Long gaiter, legging, or spatterdash, especially one of a pair attached like stirrups to saddle. Worn as protection from mud.

gambeson (găm'bə-sən; *gam* be son). Coat-like defensive garment of leather or cloth, stuffed and quilted. Worn during Middle Ages; originally, as pad under armor; later, alone.

gambroon (găm-brōōn'; gam *broon*). Twilled fabric of linen, wool, or mixture. Used, especially in linen, for linings.

gamine (F. gȧ-mēn; ga meen). French term meaning tomboy, hoyden; feminine form of *gamin,* a small boy or street urchin. Often used to describe small, vivacious woman of boyish or mischievous type.

gammadion (gə-mā'dĭ-ŏn; ga *may* di on). Ornament formerly used in church embroideries as ecclesiastical emblem. Made by using Greek letter gamma four times in form of cross.

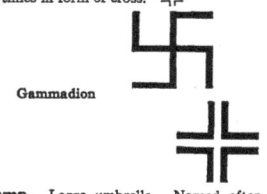

Gammadion

gamp. Large umbrella. Named after Mrs. Gamp, character in Dickens's "Martin Chuzzlewit," who was famous for her bulky umbrella.

gandurah or **gandoura** (găn-dōō'rə; gahn *doo* ra). Shirt-like garment without sleeves. Worn in Near East. From Arabic *ghandurah,* meaning ostentatious dress.

gansey or **gansy** (găn'zĭ; *gan* zi). Type of knitted jacket or jersey. Corruption of GUERNSEY.

gant (F. gäṅ; gonh). French word for glove.

garb. Style of dress; apparel, especially official or otherwise distinguishing costume; also, to clothe or array.

gardebras (F. gȧrd-brä; gard brah). Piece of ancient armor protecting the arm.

garde-collet (gȧrd-kŏl'ĕt; gard *coll* et). In ancient armor, ridge on the PAULDRON to protect the neck.

garibaldi (găr-ĭ-bŏl'dĭ; ga ri *bawl* di). Shirtwaist copied from Garibaldi's shirt; popular in 1860's. See BLOUSES. See SHIRTS.

garland. 1. Wreath or festoon of flowers, leaves, precious stones, etc. Used as adornment. **2.** In Greek and Roman antiquity, headband or fillet, usually of wool. Worn by priests.

garment. Any article of apparel, chiefly one made of fabric.

garmenture. Clothing; dress.

garn. Colloquial British term for yarn or worsted.

garnet (gär'nĕt; *gar* net). **1.** Brittle mineral substance occurring in various colors; dark red transparent variety used as semi-precious stone. Called *carbuncle* when cut in CABOCHON style. **2.** Very dark red color having bluish tint.

garnet work. Ornamentation composed of garnets.

garni (F. gȧr-nē; gar nee). French word meaning trimmed, garnished.

garnish. 1. To decorate, adorn; also, decoration, adornment. **2.** Showy dress or garments.

garniture (gär'nĭ-tŭr or F. gȧr-nē-tür; *gar* ni ture or gar nee toor). Decorative trimming, as on apparel or other articles.

garter. 1. Stocking supporter; either circlet, usually of elastic, worn around leg, or suspended strap with fastener. **2.** In 17th century, small silk sash tied on leg in big bow just below knee.

garter belt. Band, usually of elastic, with attached supporters. Worn around the waist. See BELTS.

garter sew-ons. Short garters used to replace worn garters on corsets and girdles. Available at notion counters.

garter-stitch. Plain knitting stitch. See STITCHES.

gas. In textiles, to singe thread or cloth to remove fuzz. See GASSING.

gash. Scottish term meaning well-dressed; making trim appearance.

gaskin. Short for GALLIGASKIN.

gassing. Finishing process to give smooth surface to cloth and especially to cotton thread. Consists of quickly passing unfinished thread or goods between rollers and over rows of gas flames to singe off fuzz and protruding fiber ends.

gather. To draw up, as cloth on a thread; to full on; also, fashion. Technically, one or two rows of gathering in fabric to draw in fulness. More than two rows called *shirring.*

gathering. Fabric drawn together with thread by hand or by machine, to form fulness; also, act of putting in gathering stitches.

gathering foot. Sewing-machine attachment having a small ridge underneath that pushes the fabric in little plaits under the needle. Used for gathering and shirring fabrics.

gauche (F. gōsh; goshe). Clumsy; uncouth; lacking social graces.

gaucho blouse (gow'chō; *gow* cho). Full, loose blouse. See BLOUSES.

gaud (gôd; gawd). Ornament; bit of finery, as trinket or piece of jewelry. Also, to decorate with gauds; to adorn.

gaudy (gôd'ĭ; *gawd* i). Ostentatious; flashy; showy; especially, without taste.

fāte, făt, dȧnce, ärt mē, mĕt, hêr, thêre rīde, rĭd nōte, nŏt, côrn, fōōd, fŏŏt cūte, cŭt, cûre now fĭn(g)ger villa(ə) señor pleas(zh)ure

gauge or **gage** (gāj; gāige). 1. Standard measure, usually indicating degree of fineness of hose. See HOSE. 2. In sewing, to gather.
gauntlet (gônt'lĕt; *gawnt* let). 1. Glove with wrist portion covering part of arm. See GLOVES. 2. Glove worn in ancient armor. See GLOVES. 3. That part of any glove covering part of wrist.
gauze (gôz; gawz). Thin, transparent, light-weight, but strong fabric in leno weave; loosely woven of cotton, silk, linen, or combination of yarns. Used for dresses, frills, trimmings, curtains, surgical dressings, sanitary goods, etc.
gauze weave. Former name for LENO WEAVE. See WEAVES.
gauzy. Resembling gauze in sheerness, transparency, etc.
gay. Lively in appearance, especially as to color; as, a gay frock. Also, showily dressed.
gear. Apparel; attire; clothing; also, to dress.
gem (jĕm; jem). 1. Jewel, including precious and semi-precious stones, pearls, etc., having value and beauty apart from setting; usually, jewel decoratively cut and polished. 2. Hence, something comparable to precious stone in rareness, perfection, etc. 3. To adorn or embellish, as with gems.
gem stone. Mineral or similar material usable as jewelry when cut and polished.
genapp (jə-năp'; je *nap*). In textile usage, to gas; to singe off loose fibers. See GASSING.
genappe (jə-năp'; je *nap*). Worsted yarn. See YARNS.
genet (jĕn'ĕt; *jen* et). Soft, light fur of member of the cat family. See FURS.
Geneva bands (jə-nē'və; je *nee* va). Pair of cloth flaps, usually of white lawn, at front of collar. Worn as part of clerical dress.
Geneva embroidery. Embroidery on checked canvas. See EMBROIDERIES.
Geneva gown. Long, loose academic gown with large sleeves, used as ecclesiastical vestment.
Geneva hat. Low-crowned, brimmed hat. See HATS.
Genoa lace (jĕn'ō-ə; *jen* o a). Any of several types of lace made in Genoa. See LACES.
Genoese embroidery (jĕn-ō-ēz'; jen o eez). Buttonholed open-work embroidery. See EMBROIDERIES.
genouillière (F. zhĕ-nōō-yêr'; zhe noo yare). Protective knee-piece, separate or attached. Worn as part of medieval armor.
gens du monde (F. zhäṅ dü môṇd; zhonh du mond). People of fashionable society. French phrase meaning people of the world.
georgette crepe (jôr-jĕt'; jor *jet*). Sheer crepe. See CREPES.
German-stitch. Combination of oblique Gobelin- and tent-stitch. See STITCHES.
German wool. Fine, soft yarn of merino wool. Same as BERLIN WOOL. See YARNS.
geta (gĕ'tä; *get* a). Wooden clog shoe worn in Japan. See SHOES.

get-up. General appearance, particularly of dress or costume.
gewgaw. Showy trifle or pretty trinket of little worth.
ghillie. Spelling sometimes used for GILLIE.
Gibson girl. Characteristic of silhouette

Gibson Girl Costume, 1898

or style of dress fashionable in 1890's, as portrayed by Charles Dana Gibson.
Gibson waist. Mannish, tailored shirtwaist, wide at the shoulders. See BLOUSES.
gibus (jī'bəs; *jy* bus). Collapsible hat. See HATS.
gig. To raise nap on fabric, usually woolen.
gigolo (jĭg'ə-lō; *jig* o lo). 1. Smart; chic; fashionable. U. S. usage. 2. A paid escort or dancing partner.
gigot (jĭg'ət; *jig* ot). Leg-of-mutton sleeve. See SLEEVES.
gild. To overlay or coat thinly with gold.
gilet (F. zhē-lā; zhee lay). Sleeveless bodice with decorative front in imitation of blouse. Chiefly worn with suits. French word meaning waistcoat or vest.
gillie (gĭl'ĭ; *gill* i). Sports shoe with fringed lace, usually wound around ankle. See SHOES.
gilt. Gold laid over the surface, as in gilding.
gimcrack (jĭm'krăk; *jim* crack). Trifling ornament; gewgaw.
gimp. 1. Flat, narrow, open-work strip made of twisted strands of silk, wool, cotton, etc., run through with metallic wire or coarse cord. Used as dress trimming. Also, to make or trim with gimp. 2. In lacemaking, coarse thread, usually glazed, which outlines design, slightly raising edges. Also, in general, pattern as distinct from ground. 3. Formerly, neckerchief or stomacher worn by men.
gimped or **guimped embroidery** (gĭmpt; gimpt). Embroidery with attached designs in vellum or metal. See EMBROIDERIES.

GINGHAMS

gingham (gĭng'əm; *ging* am). 1. Firm, light- or medium-weight, washable cotton fabric, yarn-dyed, in plain or fancy weave. Woven in solid colors, stripes, checks, or plaids. Used for dresses, shirts, aprons, children's clothes. 2. Colloquial term for umbrella; especially of cheap fabric.
apron check. Checked gingham; usually in white with any color favored for aprons.
chambray (shăm'brā; *sham* bray). Fine gingham in plain weave with linen-like finish, having colored warp, white filling, white selvage. Used for dresses, aprons, children's clothes. Named for Cambrai, French town where first made to be used for sunbonnets.
common g. Gingham in plain weave, usually finished with starch sizing.
French g. Same as ZEPHYR GINGHAM.
madras g. (mə-drăs'; colloquially, mă'drəs; ma *drahss* or *mad* ras). Gingham made of finer yarn, usually containing greater number of colors than staple or common gingham, woven in various weaves.
tissue g. (tĭsh'ū; *tish* you). Gingham thinner than staple type, often having heavy cord in stripe, check, or embroidered design.
zephyr g. (zĕf'ẽr; *zef* er). Fine, soft-finished gingham in plain weave, having variety of color effects in stripes, cords, checks, plaids, etc.

gipon (jĭ-pŏn'; ji *pon*). Quilted doublet. Worn under or over ancient armor. Also called *pourpoint*.
gippo (jĭp'ō; *jip* o). Short, tunic-like garment.
girandole (jĭr'ən-dōl; *jir* an dole). Pendant piece of jewelry, such as earring, having smaller pendants or cluster of smaller stones around center one.
girasol (jĭr'ə-sŏl; *jir* a sol) or **girasole** (jĭr'ə-sōl; *jir* a sole). Kind of opal, varying in color, having bright, fire-like reflections. Also called *fire opal*.
gird. 1. To encircle, as with cord, belt, girdle, etc.; also, to clothe, as with a garment having a girdle. 2. Obsolete term for girdle; girth; strap.
girdle. 1. Boneless, flexible, light-weight corset, often partly or entirely of elastic. Worn to confine figure, especially through hip line. 2. That which encircles or girds, as a belt, sash, cord, etc., worn around garment at waistline. Also, to bind or encircle. 3. Edge of gem which setting grasps.
girt. Encircled or secured by girdle, sash, etc.; also, to encircle or fasten by girdle.
girth. Measure around body at waistline or top of hips. Also, to encircle, gird, girdle.
glacé (F. glà-sā; gla say). Made or finished with smooth surface in glossy, highly polished effect. Term used of cloth or leather. French word meaning frozen, iced.
Gladstone bag (glăd'stən; *glad* stun). Piece of hand luggage with flexible sides, usually of leather, divided into two equal compartments hinged so as to open flat. Used for traveling, mostly by men. So called for W. E. Gladstone.
Gladstone collar. Standing collar with points flaring at side-front, the type worn with silk scarf tie by William Ewart Gladstone, the famous British statesman. See COLLARS.
glass cloth. Fabric woven of glass fiber.
glass fiber or **silk.** Fine thread or threads formed by winding glass, while in fusion, on rapidly revolving heated cylinders.
glaze. To overlay with thin glossy coating; to render smooth and glossy. Also, glass-like or glossy coating or surface.

---

fāte, făt, dánce, ärt mē, mĕt, hẽr, thêre rīde, rĭd nōte, nŏt, côrn, fōōd, fōŏt cūte, cŭt, cûre now fĭn(ŋ)ger villa(ə) señor pleas(zh)ure

glazed chintz. Chintz having glaze from being treated with paraffin and then calendered.
glazed kid. Chrome-tanned goatskin, glossy but not actually glazed. See LEATHERS.
glazed thread. Thread with sizing. Used for temporary sewing. See THREADS.
glazing. Process, varying according to material, of applying smooth, glossy coating to surface. Also, substance used in glazing; or glaze applied. PATENT LEATHER, example of glazed leather, finished with coats of varnish. GLAZED CHINTZ, example of glazed fabric, treated with paraffin and then calendered.
glen check. Check design similar to shepherd's check. See CHECKS.
Glengarry (glĕn-găr'ĭ; glen ga ri). Small Scottish cap with creased crown. See CAPS.
gloria (glō'rĭ-ə; glo ri a). Closely woven fabric of silk and worsted, silk and cotton, or other mixture in diagonal twill weave. Used chiefly as umbrella cloth. Also called *sanella cloth*.
gloss. Luster or sheen, as from smooth surface; in fabric, often resulting from quality of yarn.
glossing. Giving luster or sheen, as to yarn. With silk yarn, done by stretching and moistening.
glossy. Lustrous; smooth and shining.

GLOVES

glove (glŭv; gluv). Covering for hand, having separate stall or sheath for each finger, which distinguishes it from mitt or mitten; sometimes extending over wrist or arm. Also, to cover or furnish with gloves.
chicken skin g. Glove made of chicken skin. Worn by women while sleeping to soften and whiten hands. Popular as late as early 19th century.
Free-Finger G. Trade name for glove made with strip, or "side-wall," running along both sides and around end of each finger, without seam at tip, instead of the usual fourchette seamed at finger tip. Designed for freedom of action and feeling in fingers, and to prevent wearing out at tips. Made in many color combinations. Also called *three-dimensional glove*.

Free-Finger Glove, 1938

gauntlet (gônt'lĕt; *gawnt* let). **1.** Glove of any material, having widened wrist extension long enough to cover part of arm. **2.** Glove worn in medieval armor; sometimes of chain mail, metal plates, etc., to defend hand; sometimes of leather or other material to prevent chafing under armor.

17th Century Gauntlet

grain g. Glove finished with hair side of leather outward.
half-mitt or **half-mitten.** Type of mitt or mitten extending only to knuckles.
haling hands (hāl'ĭng; *hail* ing). Heavy gloves or mittens, usually of wool, often with leather palms. Worn for heavy work by sailors, working men. So called by American colonists because used for hauling.
mitt. Fingerless glove reaching over wrist, and sometimes arm; fashionable in colonial America. Made of kid or silk or, for summer wear, of lace. Now often made of lace and used as costume accessory.

19th Century Mitt. Modern Mitten

mitten. Warm hand covering, with one sheath for thumb and one for all four fingers. Made of cloth or leather, or knitted of wool.
mousquetaire g. (F. mōōs-kə-tĕr; moose ke tare). Glove with long wrist, having no opening or short lengthwise opening with few buttons. Usually worn loosely crushed down toward wrist.
opera g. Long glove, light or dark in color, sometimes without a thumb.
shooting g. Archer's glove fashioned to protect fingers. Also called *drawing glove*.
shortie. Glove, either slip-on or having one button; extending to wrist or a little beyond.
slip-on. Glove without fasteners, made to extend above wrist and slip on easily.

glove cuff. Part of glove covering wrist or forearm; often an attached cuff section. See CUFFS.
glove silk. Knitted fabric, usually of silk. Used for undergarments, dresses, blouses; formerly, for gloves.
glove or **glover's stitch** (glŭv'ĕrz; *gluv* erz). Stitch used on glove seams. See STITCHES.

glover's needle. Needle having three-sided point. See NEEDLES.
glycerined feather. Feather treated with glycerine for gloss. See FEATHERS.
go. Colloquial term for fad or rage; as, berets are all the go.
goat. Short for GOATSKIN.
goatskin. Leather made from skin of goat. See LEATHERS.
Gobelin (gŏb'ə-lĭn or F. gô-blăṅ; *gob* a lin or go blanh). Superior tapestry of silk and wool or silk and cotton, made since 15th century at Paris or Beauvais factory of Gobelin brothers. Often several generations will work on one piece. Beautiful examples chiefly in museums.
gobelin blue. Greenish-blue color with grayed cast, as seen abundantly in Gobelin tapestries.
Gobelin-stitch. Stitch used in needle tapestry. See STITCHES.
gob hat. Small hat with up-turned brim worn by sailors of U. S. Navy. See HATS.

GODETS

godet (F. gô-dā; go day). Piece of cloth, wider at bottom, set into a garment for fulness or decoration. Usually applied to skirts and sleeves.
rounded-top g. Godet rounded over top rather than pointed.
seam g. Godet, either rounded or pointed at top, stitched in position along one side and other side stitched into seam of garment.
stayed g. Godet secured at top on wrong side by stay of fabric. Used to hold in fulness.

Godey's Lady's Book (gō'dĭz; *go* diz). Periodical dealing largely with fashions, needlework, and etiquette; founded in 1830 by Antoine Godey; published for fifty years; edited until December, 1877, by a most able woman, Sarah Josepha Hale. Famous chiefly for beautiful, colored fashion plates; also, for being first American woman's magazine.
goffer (gŏf'ẽr; *goff* er) or **gauffer** (gŏf'ẽr; *gawf* er). To crimp, plait, flute, or raise in ornamental relief; also, crimping, fluting. From French word *gaufrer*, meaning to figure fabric.
goffered. Having embossed or similar design.
going-away costume. Traveling dress, usually that worn by a bride for the wedding trip. See DRESS.
gold. 1. Precious metal, soft, heavy, and of yellow color. Used in jewelry; made into form of fiber or leaf and used in fabric, lace, accessories, etc. Red gold is reddish yellow or golden; white gold is light yellow color, having no red. **2.** Made of gold. **3.** Gilt; gold leaf or thread; fabric having gold thread in or on it.
gold cloth. Same as CLOTH OF GOLD.
gold embroidery. Elaborate embroidery done with gold thread. Used chiefly for church hangings, ceremonial robes, etc. See EMBROIDERIES.
golden. Having color of gold; made of gold; therefore, very precious.

gold foil

gold foil. Gold beaten or pressed into paper-thin sheets.
gold lace. Lace of gold color, or lace fabric threaded with gold. See LACES.
gold-laced. Ornamented with gold lace.
gold leaf. Extremely thin gold foil. Used for gilding.
gold tissue. Transparent cloth with warp of gold and silk weft. Also made in a cheaper quality, in imitation of metal cloth. Used for overdraping and trimming.
golf cap. Man's sports cap with visor. See CAPS.
golf costume. Costume suited for golfing. See SPORTS CLOTHES.
golf hose. Heavy woolen hose. See HOSE.
golf shoe. Sports shoe, sometimes with cleats on sole. See SHOES.
golf skirt. Heavy, ankle-length wool skirt, having flared bottom emphasized by facing and stitching. See SKIRTS.

GOODS

goods. 1. Merchandise. **2.** Collective term for fabric. Formerly, also called *stuff*.
dress g. Fabrics suitable for making women's and children's dresses. Sold in yard-goods department of a store.
dry g. Materials used for clothing and furnishings. Originally so called to differentiate from wet goods in shipping, such as molasses, oils, liquors, etc.
fancy g. Art needlework, embroideries, stamped linens, and supplies for fancy work.
gray g. Woven or knitted fabrics before being bleached, dyed, or finished.
piece g. Fabrics sold in lengths or from the bolt at piece-goods counters in stores. Same as YARD GOODS.
wash g. Fabrics that may be washed without damage or loss of color.
white g. 1. White fabrics in general, especially white dress fabrics. **2.** Finished products made from white fabric, as tablecloths, sheets, pillowcases, etc.
yard g. Fabric sold by yard or piece. Same as PIECE GOODS.

goose. 1. To repair shoes by renewing soles and part of top at front. **2.** Tailor's heavy smoothing iron. So called because handle resembles neck of goose.
gore. 1. Shaped set-in section, narrowest at top, extending in skirt from waistline to hem; as, front, side, or back gore. Skirts consist of 2, 3, 4, 5, 6, 7, and up to 24 gores. Patterns of skirts are made up of gores. Also, to cut into triangular or tapering shape; to piece, as with a gore. **2.** One of triangular pieces of fabric covering umbrella.
gorget (gôr'jĕt; *gor* jet). **1.** Ornamental, collar-like article of neckwear, full and broad in front; copied from corresponding piece of armor. Popular in 17th century. Also, collar; neck ornament. **2.** Type of wimple consisting of strip of silk or linen cloth wound about throat, covering neck and shoulders, having ends fastened in hair above ears. Worn during 14th and 15th centuries. **3.** Piece of defensive armor covering throat.

17th Century Gorget

goring. 1. Piece of cloth cut in triangular shape to be used as gore. **2.** Elastic fabric formerly used as gore in shoe uppers.
gossamer (gŏs'ə-mēr; *goss* a mer). **1.** Sheer; thin; flimsy. **2.** Thin, soft, gauze-like fabric. **3.** Formerly, outer garment of thin, waterproof fabric. **4.** Light silk hat. See HATS.
Gothic stitch. Connecting loop stitches that form a chain. Same as CHAIN-STITCH, 1. See STITCHES.
gown. 1. Woman's dress of any type; sometimes limited to formal dress or one of elaborate or magnificent style. Also, to clothe, as in gown. **2.** Short for nightgown; also, for dressing gown. **3.** Academic gown or other official or distinctive robe. **4.** Loose garment worn by ancients, as a toga.
Goya (gō'yä; *go* yah). **1.** Used of apparel reminiscent in any way of costumes in paintings by Francisco Goya, especially colors of deep, rich, jewel tones. **2.** Rich, Oriental red.
gradate (grā'dāt; *gray* date). **1.** To shade, as colors or tones of a color, almost imperceptibly one into another; also, to arrange harmoniously, to blend. **2.** Regularly increasing in size.
graduated tucks (grăd'ū-āt-ĕd; *grad* you ate ed). Tucks of gradually increasing size used in series, usually in a skirt, beginning narrow at the top, and each increasing in width until the widest is at the bottom. See TUCKS.
grafting. In knitting and darning, process of fitting small piece of fabric into space and joining it to main piece of material.
grain. 1. Direction of warp and woof threads in fabric; as, the lengthwise or crosswise grain; also, the bias grain, diagonally across the warp and woof. **2.** In dyeing, fiber or yarn, as opposed to woven fabric. **3.** In leather trade, outer or hair side of hide or skin, as opposed to flesh side. **4.** Superficial roughness; granulated appearance.
grained. 1. Dyed in grain; ingrained. **2.** Showing granulated surface.
grain glove. Glove having hair side of leather outward. See GLOVES.
grain leather. Leather made from outer or hair side of skin. See LEATHERS.
granite cloth (grăn'ĭt; *gran* it). Durable, light-weight, hard-finished, pebbly cloth in figured weave. Usually made of worsted yarns; sometimes, of linen. Used for dresses, suits, skirts. So called because rough finish resembles surface of granite.
grass bleaching. Bleaching method in which cloth is exposed to action of sun, air, and moisture by spreading on grass; slower than chemical bleaching, but not weakening to fabric. Also called *crofting*.
grass cloth. Loosely-woven, durable cloth made in Eastern countries of tough grass or vegetable fibers, usually ramie; unbleached, bleached, or dyed. Mostly hand-woven; available in Oriental shops. Launders nicely; perhaps easiest of all fabrics to iron, but wrinkles easily. Used for sportswear, blouses, doilies, lunch cloths, etc. Also called *Canton linen*, *Chinese grass cloth*, *grass linen*.
grass embroidery. Decorative stitching with grass. See EMBROIDERIES.
grass linen. Same as GRASS CLOTH.
gray or **grey. 1.** Color formed by blending of black and white. Also, of color gray; neutral; hueless; dull. Term "in the gray" used of fabric in undyed, unbleached, or unfinished state. **2.** Obsolete term for gray fur, probably of badger.
gray fox. Fur of gray-colored fox. See FURS.
gray goods. Fabric before being bleached, dyed, or finished. See GOODS.
grease wool. Wool with natural oils. See WOOL.
greatcoat. Heavy overcoat. See COATS.
grebe (grēb; greeb). Downy, smooth feathers of grebe duck. See FEATHERS.
grebe cloth. Cotton cloth having downy surface or nap on one side.
Grecian bend (grē'shan; *gree* shan). Name describing tilted angle at which women walked, with body bent forward from hips, when wasp waist and bustles were popular, during 1870's.
Greek. Characteristic of costume worn by Greeks of the classical period (600-146 B.C.); consisting of simple, draped garments fastened by pins, the chief ones being CHITON, or dress; HIMATION, outer garment; and CHLAMYS, or cloak.
Greek embroidery. Type of appliqué. See EMBROIDERIES.
Greek lace. Earliest type of needle-point lace. Developed from cut and drawn work. Same as RETICELLA. See LACES.
green. Color of spectrum between blue and yellow; in general considered similar to but less yellow than hue of fresh growing grass.
green-blue. Color between blue and green.
grège (F. grăzh; grayzh). Color of raw silk. Also called *nutria*, *beige*. French word meaning raw, as silk.
grego (grĕ'gō or grā'gō; *gree* go or *gray* go). Hooded coat. See COATS.
gregorian (grĕ-gō'rĭ-ən; gre *gore* i an). Wig worn in 16th and 17th centuries. See WIGS.
gremial (grē'mĭ-əl; *gree* mi al). Apron, usually of silk or linen. Worn by bishop when officiating. From Latin word *gremium*, meaning lap, bosom.
grenadine (grĕn'ə-dēn; *gren* a deen). Fine, loosely-woven fabric in leno weave, similar to marquisette. Usually made of silk or wool, sometimes mixed with cotton; used for dresses, blouses, etc. In late 19th century, popular over satin. Also made of cotton with swivel dots or figures; used for curtains.

grey Usual British spelling of *gray*.

grillage (grĭl'ĭj; *grill* ij). Barred or grated ground across open spaces of lace design or pattern.

grillé or **grillée** (F. grē-yā; gree yay). Having bars or grating across open spaces in lace pattern. Also, such barred open spaces or GRILLAGE.

grip or **gripsack**. Colloquial term for small piece of hand luggage used in traveling.

gris (F. grē; gree). French word meaning gray.

grisaille (grĭ-zal' or F. grē-zī; gri *zail* or gree zy). Grizzled French fabric of cotton and wool, having figured design. Used as dress goods.

grise (grēs; greece). Expensive kind of gray fur worn in Middle Ages; possibly squirrel or marten.

grisette (F. grē-zĕt; gree zet). 1. French shop girl or working girl. So called because originally dressed in grisette. 2. Coarse gray woolen dress fabric worn by working women in France.

grizzle. 1. Gray hair; gray wig. 2. Color gray; also to make or become gray or grayish.

grizzled. Partly gray; mixed with gray.

grogram (grŏg'rəm; *grog* ram). 1. Loosely woven dress fabric of silk or silk and worsted, having uneven surface; often stiffened with gum. Formerly manufactured in Scotland. Term corrupted from French *gros grain*, meaning large grain, of coarse texture. 2. Garment made of this fabric.

grommet (grŏm'ĕt; *grom* et). Metallic eyelet. Used on sports shoes, sometimes on sports dresses.

grooming. Appearance. Term usually used in a complimentary sense; as, good grooming, meaning being well cared for; dressing carefully and neatly.

gros (F. grō; gro). Fabric of strong texture, especially stout, heavy silk. French word meaning coarse, thick, substantial.

gros de Londres (F. grō də lôṇdr; gro de londr). Glossy, light-weight silk fabric woven with horizontal ribs, alternately narrow and wide, sometimes in different colors or changeable effects. Used for dresses and hats.

grosgrain (grō'grān; *gro* grain). 1. Having heavy crosswise ribs. 2. Stout silk fabric or ribbon, sometimes having cotton filling, corded from selvage to selvage. Cords heavier than in poplin, rounder than in faille. Used for dresses, coats, trimming. French expression meaning large grain or cord.

gros point (F. grō pwăṇ; gro pwanh). 1. Type of Venetian lace. See LACES.

2. Canvas work done with the larger types of stitches used in needle tapestry. See EMBROIDERIES. 3. Type of needle tapestry stitch. See STITCHES.

ground. 1. Background; surface against which decoration of pattern or color shows; as, a dress fabric has a light or dark ground. 2. In leather trade, to prepare surface of hide or skin by scraping flesh side.

grown mohair (mō'hēr; *mo* hair). Hair of grown goats. See MOHAIR.

gruff. Scottish term meaning of coarse texture; coarse-grained.

G string. Strip of cloth passed from front to back between legs, attached to and supported by cord or band around waist. Worn by savages; sometimes by chorus girls.

guanaco (gwä-nä'kō; gwah *nah* ko). Thick, soft fur of animal related to llama. See FURS.

guard hair. Long, protective hair growing up through soft, short hairs of various furs.

guard ring. Close-fitting finger ring, worn above loose ring to keep it from slipping off and being lost. See RINGS.

guernsey (gẽrn'zĭ; *gern* zi). Close-fitting, knitted, shirt-like garment of wool, as worn by sailors.

guide pattern. Pattern of muslin or cambric fitted to individual measurements. Used as a guide in cutting garments. See PATTERNS.

guige (F. gēzh; geezh) or **gige** (gēj; geej). Leather strap which, in ancient armor, held shield of knight.

guilloche (gĭ-lōsh'; gi *loshe*). Ornamental pattern of two or more intertwining curved bands or lines, leaving circular openings sometimes decorated with round ornaments. Often done in braid. Also, to decorate in guilloche. Term borrowed from architecture.

guimpe (F. gămp; gamp). 1. Short blouse, often with sleeves. Usually worn with a pinafore type of dress. See BLOUSES. 2. Chemisette or yoke with high, standing collar; made of sheer lace or fine net. Worn about 1910 to fill in neckline when low-necked dresses were introduced.

Child's Dress with Guimpe, 1911

guimped embroidery. Alternate spelling for GIMPED EMBROIDERY.

guipure (gē-pūr' or F. gē-pür; gee *pure* or gee poor). Heavy lace having no ground, or having designs joined by bars. See LACES.

guipure de Bruges (F. gē-pür də brüzh; gee poor de broozh). Old bobbin lace of tape-like effect. Same as DUCHESSE LACE. See LACES.

guise (gīz; gize). Appearance, as in particular garb or type of costume.

gulix (gŭ'lĭks; *gue* licks). Fine, white linen fabric. Used for shirts. So called for town in Prussia.

gum. Natural substance, gluey when moist, hardening when dry. Found in plants; also, on outside of silk fiber, as deposited by silkworm in spinning cocoon.—**in the g.** In process of manufacture before boiling off of gum or SERICIN. Term used of silk.

gum boot or **shoe**. Rubber boot or shoe. See SHOES.

gum rubber. Pure rubber without any cloth, as in bathing caps.

gun club check. Check design used in tweeds. See CHECKS.

gun metal. Dark, neutral gray, nearly black; color of metal used for making gun barrels.

gunny. Coarse sacking used for rough bags and packing; firmer quality used for curtains. Same as BURLAP.

gurrah (gŭr'ä; *gur* ah). Coarse, thick muslin fabric. Made in India.

gusset (gŭs'ĕt; *guss* et). 1. Triangular, tapered, or specially shaped piece of fabric, leather, etc., inserted in garment, glove, side of shoe, etc., for additional strength, room, or to adjust the fit. 2. Piece of chain or plate mail at joint openings in ancient armor. 3. Scottish term for clock in stockings.

gut. Tough cord used for lacings. Same as CATGUT.

gym shoe (jĭm; jim). Rubber-soled canvas shoe. Same as SNEAKER. See SHOES.

gym suit. Abbreviated suit, often in one piece, consisting of a blouse and bloomers or shorts. Suitable for wear for basketball and gymnasium games and exercises.

gypsy hat. Broad-brimmed hat. See HATS.

gypsy seam. Seam down center-front of a shoe, used in joining the gypsy vamp. See SPLIT VAMP under VAMPS.

gypsy stripes. Stripes in many bright colors. See STRIPES.

gypsy vamp. Shoe vamp with seam all the way down center-front. Same as SPLIT VAMP. See VAMPS.

H

haberdasher (hăb'ẽr-dăsh-ẽr; *hab* er dash er). 1. One who keeps a retail shop selling men's furnishings. 2. Dealer in small wares, as needles, pins, thread, dress trimming; formerly, also hats.

haberdashery. Goods and wares sold in haberdasher's shop; also, the shop.

habergeon (hăb'ẽr-jŭn; *hab* er jun). Jacket of chain or ring mail; shorter, lighter in weight than hauberk. Worn as part of medieval armor.

habiliment (hə-bĭl'ĭ-mənt; ha *bill* i ment). 1. (Usually plural) Dress; attire; costume. 2. Ornament; BILIMENT.

habit. Dress, garb, costume, especially as indicative of particular rank, calling, or pursuit; as, nun's habit, riding habit.

habit-back placket. Placket under meeting plaits, usually used on woman's riding skirt. See PLACKETS.

habit shirt. Type of vestee; woman's garment similar to man's collar and shirt bosom.

habutai or **habutaye** (hä'bōō-tī; *hah boo* tie). Thin, soft, plain-woven, washable silk fabric made in Japan; resembling China silk but heavier, more durable. Used chiefly for blouses, underclothes, sleeping garments. Also called JAPANESE or JAP SILK.

haik (hīk or hăk; *hike* or *hake*). Embroidered white veil worn by women of northern Africa and Arabia. See VEILS.

hair. 1. Single filament or, collectively, entire natural growth on human head. 2. One of thread-like filaments forming characteristic coat of animals; specifically, coat, or hairs collectively, when rather coarse and straight. (When fine and thick, called FUR; when fine, rough-surfaced, kinky, called WOOL.)

haircloth. 1. Stiff, wiry fabric, usually having warp of cotton, sometimes of linen or worsted, and filling of horsehair or camel's hair. Used for stiffening, interlining garments, upholstering. 2. Garment made of haircloth, as hair shirt.

hairdress. 1. Style of arranging hair on head. 2. Formerly, headdress.

hairdresser. One who dresses, curls, cuts, or shampoos the hair.

hairlace. Lace fillet or net for the hair, much worn in 18th century as decoration.

hairline. 1. Very slender stripe. See STRIPES. 2. Cloth, usually suiting in black or dark blue, having narrow stripes, usually in white and of single warp thread.

hair net. Net worn over hair to hold it in place. Manufactured of human hair or silk; single mesh for dress wear, double mesh for service wear.

hairpin. Pin for holding the hair in place. See PINS.

hairpin lace. Insertion lace with looped edges and a firm center, made on a hairpin. See LACES.

hair ribbon. Ribbon worn in hair, usually by children. See RIBBONS.

hair seal. Wiry fur of type of seal having no underfur. See FURS.

hair shirt. Shirt, sometimes loincloth, made of horsehair. Formerly, worn next to skin in penance. Also, any blouse or garment that scratches.

hairwork. Making of various articles, including switches, transformations, etc., from human hair; also, piece when so made. Popular art in 17th century, especially making hair for miniature figures of famous people.

halecret (hăl'ə-krĕt; *hal* e cret). Type of corselet worn in 16th century, especially by Swiss.

half-armor. Armor protecting only part of body.

half back-stitch. Stitch made half as long as a back-stitch on top and slightly longer underneath. May be made more quickly than back-stitch. See STITCHES.

half boot. Short boot. See BOOTS.

half cross-stitch. Needle-point stitch. See STITCHES.

half-hose. Socks, or short hose. See HOSE.

half-mitt. Type of mitt extending only to knuckles. See GLOVES.

half-mourning. Mourning dress relieved only by touches of white, gray, or lavender. See MOURNING DRESS under DRESS.

half Persian lamb. Fur of cross breed of Persian lamb. See FURS.

half-pocket. 1. Small, short pocket, used chiefly for decoration. 2. Ready-made pocket, used to replace worn one in man's trousers. See POCKETS.

half-shirt. 1. Decorative shirt front, similar to vestee. Worn by men and women about 1700. 2. Detachable STOMACHER.

half sleeve. 1. Removable sleevelet for the forearm, usually of lace or sheer fabric, either attached by tapes or held on by elastic at top. 2. Sleeve protector worn by clerical workers. 3. Sleeve of half usual length, as in certain ecclesiastical vestments. See SLEEVES.

half-sole. Extra outer sole extending only to shank of shoe.

half-stitch. 1. In crocheting or knitting, two stitches taken as one. 2. Loose, open stitch used in pillow laces. See STITCHES.

haling hands (hāl'ĭng; *hail* ing). Heavy gloves, as worn by sailors. See GLOVES.

halo beret (hā'lō bĕ-rā; *hay* lo be ray). Off-the-face beret. See BERET under HATS.

halo hat. Hat framing face. See HATS.

halter (hôl'tĕr; *hawl* ter). Strap supporting front of backless bodice. Attached at front neckline and extending around neck. See NECKLINES.

hamster. Flat, yellowish-brown fur, with black markings. See FURS.

hand. Texture or feel of cloth, especially of silk; as, fabric of quality has a good hand, meaning that you can feel the quality or that it will work well in the making.

HANDBAGS

handbag. 1. Soft or rigid bag carried in hand or on arm. Size, shape, handle, etc., depend on fashion. Used by women as container for money and pocket-sized accessories. First popular about 1910. 2. Satchel or grip.

backstrap. Handbag having strap at back as handle.

envelope bag (ĕn'və-lōp; *en* ve lope). Handbag with flap closing, as in ordinary envelope.

Facile-closing (făs'ĭl; *fass* il). Trade name for handbag closing made of metal that can readily be pulled open and snapped shut without clasp or other fastening.

mesh bag. Purse or bag made of flexible fabric of linked wire mesh, often of gold or silver or of plated metal. Sometimes called Whiting bag, from Whiting, a manufacturer of mesh bags.

pouch bag. Handbag of soft material, sometimes draped on rigid frame, sometimes drawn together with a cord.

top-handle bag. Handbag having at top one or more handles, usually straps, by which to carry it.

handcloth. Towel; formerly, handkerchief, napkin.

hand details. Constructive or finishing details made by hand, such as hand-rolled or bound edges, hand shirring or drawn work, fine hand tucks, hand fagoting, embroidery, etc.

hand-drawn. Having threads of different color or texture pulled through drawn-thread space, as in hand-drawn hem.

hand-finished. Made by machine, but with finishing touches applied by hand. Often applied to ready-to-wear.

handkerchief. Piece of cloth of cotton, linen, silk, etc., usually square, varying in size and fabric according to purpose; often decorated with lace, embroidery, monogram, border, etc.; often having floral designs, plaids, stripes, etc., in costume colors. Worn or carried for usefulness or as costume accessory. Finest quality usually has hand-rolled hem.

handkerchief drapery. Drapery, as on garment, consisting of large or small squares of cloth, usually falling in graceful folds.

handkerchief linen. Light-weight linen. Used for handkerchiefs, lingerie, infants' wear, neckwear, dresses, blouses. See LINENS.

handkerchief tunic (tū'nĭk; *tew* nick). Tunic with four points at lower edge. See TUNIC, 2.

hand-knit or **knitted.** Knit entirely by hand, as distinguished from machine-knit.

handmade. Made entirely by hand.

hand-rolled. Rolled by hand, as a hem.

hand-ruffs. Ruffles for wrist, popular during 17th and 18th centuries. See RUFF under CUFFS.

hand-run. Sewn by hand, but with larger, easier stitches than those prescribed for a hand-sewn article.

hand-sewn. Carefully and perfectly sewn by hand.

hang. Way in which a garment hangs on the figure; as, hang of a skirt; the hang of a draped sleeve or collar.

hanging sleeve. Coat sleeve with arm slit. Sleeves hang straight down at sides. See SLEEVES.

hank. Skein or coil of yarn or thread, especially of given length; of cotton yarn, 840 yards; of worsted yarn, 560 yards.

haori (hä'ō-rī; *hah* o ri). Loose, knee-length Japanese coat. See COATS.

hardanger cloth (här'dăng-ēr; *har* dang er). Soft cotton cloth of excellent quality, usually highly mercerized, in basket weave. Used for HARDANGER EMBROIDERY.

hardanger embroidery. Heavy, symmetrical, Norwegian needlework done in elaborate diamond or square pattern. See EMBROIDERIES.

hards or **hurds.** Coarse part or refuse of flax or wool.

hard silk. Silk containing natural gum. See SILK.

harem skirt (hĕr'əm; *hair* em). Full, draped skirt resembling Turkish trousers. See SKIRTS.

harlequin (här'lə-kwĭn; *har* le kwin). Variegated in color; multicolored. From multicolored suit of pantomime character, Harlequin. See FANCY DRESS.

harlequin hat. Hat with wide, cuff-like brim turned up all around. See HATS.
harmonious (här-mō′nĭ-ŭs; har *mo* ni us). Being in harmony; as, a harmonious ensemble; harmonious colors in a print, etc.
harmony (här′mə-nĭ; *har* mo ni). Agreement of different parts or colors, as of costume, making pleasing effect.
harrateen (hăr′ə-tēn; *ha* ra teen). Coarse fabric made of combing wool or hair.
Harris tweed (hăr′ĭs; *ha* riss). Soft, flexible, all-wool, homespun tweed from Harris and Lewis in the Hebrides Islands off the west coast of Scotland. See TWEED.
Harvard cloth or **Harvard shirting** (här′vərd; *har* verd). Twilled cotton fabric, plain or striped; similar to Oxford cloth. Chiefly used as shirting.
hasp. 1. Clasp or fastening, as for box lid, luggage, etc. 2. Spindle for winding yarn or thread. 3. Hank or skein of yarn or thread.

HATS

hat. Shaped head covering having crown and brim or one of the two; made of various materials. Worn by men and women. For other types of headgear, see CAPS, BONNETS, HOODS.
alpine h. Soft felt hat with brim, sometimes peaked crown, and feather, tassel, or brush trim, such as worn by inhabitants of Alps.

Type of Alpine Hat, 1938

bambin h. (băm′bĭn; *bam* bin). Hat with brim rolling away from face, halo-fashion. Taken from Italian word for baby, and so called because circular effect suggests reliefs of heads and figures of babies and madonnas, usually wearing halos, done by Italian sculptor, della Robbia.
beaver (bē′vẽr; *bee* ver). Man's tall hat made of silk imitation of beaver fur. Same as TOP HAT. Highly fashionable in 17th century, when made of beaver fur.
beaverkin. Small beaver hat.
beefeater's h. Brimmed hat, with medium-high, flat-topped crown, worn as part of uniform of British Yeomen of the Guard, often called *beefeaters.* Same uniform has been worn since Middle Ages.
bee-gum h. Colloquial term for high silk hat.
bell-boy or **bell-hop h.** Hat in pillbox shape, usually trimmed with braid. Copy of cap worn by hotel bell boys.
benjy. British slang for straw hat, usually having wide brim.
beret (F. bĕ-rā; be ray). Hat adapted from Basque beret, having round, flat crown of varying width, made of felt or other materials. When worn off the forehead, framing face in halo effect, called *halo beret.* When very flat, similar in shape to a pancake, called *pancake beret* or *pie-pan* or *pie-plate beret.*
beretta (bĕ-rĕt′ə; bare *ret* a). Medium-large draped beret.
Bethlehem headdress. Hat adapted from ancient headdress of women of Bethlehem, Palestine. Shaped like tarboosh and often worn with a veil.

Bethlehem Headdress

Adaptation, 1938

bicorn or **bicorne** (bī′kôrn; *by* corn). Hat with up-turned, two-cornered brim. One style worn by Napoleon. French word meaning two-horned.

19th Century Bicorne Hat

billycock or **billicock** (bĭl′ĭ-kŏk; *bill* i cock). Colloquial British term for round, low-crowned, soft or sometimes hard, felt hat.
boater. Straw hat with straight brim and a ribbon band. Regulation straw hat for men.
bolero h. (bō-lâr′ō; bo *lare* o). Small hat with slightly peaked crown and thick, box-like brim. Originally worn by Spaniards dancing the bolero.
bourrelet (F. bōōr-lā; boor lay). Turban-like hat having thick, rounded edge. Adaptation of ancient bourrelet, twisted scarf or pad.
bowler (bōl′ẽr; *bole* er). Hat similar to derby in shape, often having slightly wider brim with accentuated roll at sides. Worn with formal riding clothes.

Bowler

Breton (brĕt′ən or F. brĕ-tôɴ; *bret* on or bre tonh). Hat with brim rolling upward evenly all around. Originally worn by peasants of Brittany.

Type of Breton Sailor

brimmer. Hat with broad brim.
broadbrim. Hat with very wide brim and low crown, as worn by Quakers. See QUAKER HAT.
bumper brim. Hat having a tubular brim. Size of brim varies. Used on several types of hats.

Bumper Brim, 1938

bycocket or **bycoket** (bĭ-kŏk′ĕt; *by cock* et). Hat with high crown and wide brim turned up in point at front or back. Worn in Middle Ages and 16th century.
cabbage-tree h. Hat having broad brim, plaited or woven from leaf fibers of cabbage tree. Worn in Australia.
caddie or **caddy.** Australian term for slouch hat.
canotier (F. kȧ-nô-tyā; ca no tyay). Hat with straight brim, large or small, and flat crown. French word meaning straw hat, originally as worn by boatmen.
capeline (kăp′ə-lĭn or F. kȧp-lēn; *cap e* or cap leen). Hat with soft, undulating brim, usually wide.
cardinal's h. Red hat with small, rounded crown and broad, flat brim, having specially designed cords and tassels hanging from sides.
caroline (kăr′ə-lĭn; *ca* ro line). High silk hat or stovepipe hat.
cartwheel. Hat with very large, often straight brim of even width; usually having shallow crown.

Cartwheel, 1938

casque (F. kȧsk; cask). Hat shaped like any of various types of helmets. French word for helmet, or armor for the head.
casquette (F. kȧs-kĕt; cass ket). Hat having visor and no brim, similar in shape to man's or boy's cap.

castor (kăs'tēr; *cass* ter). Hat made of beaver or other silky fur or fabric; hence, silk hat. Latin word meaning beaver.

catskin. British slang for inferior grade of silk hat.

caubeen (kô-bēn'; caw *been*). Irish slang for any hat, especially when old and shabby.

cavalier h. Large, heavily plumed hat of type worn by Cavaliers in mid-17th century.

chapeau bras (F. shả-pō brä; sha po brah). Small, three-cornered hat that folds flat and is carried under the arm. Worn as dress hat by gentlemen in late 18th century. Modification still worn as part of full dress in court, diplomatic, and military circles.

chechia (shĕ-shē'ȧ; she *shee* a). Adaptation of cylindrical Arab skull-cap. See illustration of original type under CAPS.

chip h. Hat made of strips or shavings of wood or woody material. Imported from Italy. Highly fashionable in late 18th century. See CHIP under STRAWS.

chou h. (shoo; shoo). Hat with soft, crushed crown. Derived from French word *chou*, meaning cabbage.

Chou Hat, 1938

chouquette (shoo-kĕt'; shoo *ket*). Kind of crocheted straw hat. From French nautical term *chouquet*, meaning cap.

claque (klăk or F. klȧk; clack). Man's opera hat having collapsible crown.

cloche (F. klōsh; closhe). Hat with bell-shaped crown. Often with an even brim turned down; also with short brim back and front, slightly wider at the sides. French word for bell.

Cloche, 1920's

cocked h. Hat having wide stiff brim flaps turned up toward peaked crown. Worn during 18th century.

cockle-h. Hat with cockle shell, sometimes scallop shell. Worn as badge, especially of pilgrim returning from Holy Land.

conch h. (kŏnk; conk). Hat, usually wide-brimmed, made of plaited palmetto leaves. Worn in Bahama Islands.

Continental h. Hat of type worn by George Washington's Continental Army; tricorn hat with broad, upturned brim worn with one point in front.

Late 18th Century Continental Army Hat

coolie h. Hat, generally made in one piece, sloping downward on straight slant, usually from peaked crown. Similar in shape to hats worn by Chinese coolies.

Coolie Hat
Adaptation, 1936

copatain (cŏp'ȧ-tān; *cop* a tain). Hat with high, pointed, sugar-loaf crown.

copintank (kŏp'ĭn-tănk; *cop* in tank). Probably another name for COPATAIN.

cordy (kôr'dĭ; *cor* di). Hat of coarse felt made of wool of inferior quality covered with camel's or goat's hair.

Cossack h. Adaptation of cap worn by Cossacks; usually tall, brimless hat of fur, astrakhan, woolly-surfaced fabric, or felt, somewhat wider at top than at headband.

cowboy h. Hat with high, soft, creased crown; wide brim slightly rolled at sides. Worn by cattle herders, or cowboys, and by vacationists on dude ranches.

crush h. 1. Hat of soft material which can be folded without injury. **2.** Collapsible high hat or opera hat.

derby (dêr'bĭ or British där'bĭ; *der* bi or *dar* bi). Stiff, hard felt hat with round crown and brim curved up at sides. Worn mostly by men.

disk. Hat in shape of disk, made of flat, circular piece of material, generally felt or straw; usually worn tilted at angle over eye, held on by band or snood in back.

doll h. Tiny hat, made in any style, suggesting hat made for a doll; worn far forward on the head and held by a band running around the back of the head. Worn by women.

duck-bill h. Hat having long, forward, visor-like brim; sometimes brim of straw and crown of fabric.

dunstable (dŭn'stȧ-b'l; *dun* sta bl). Plaited straw hat, originally made in Dunstable, England.

Dutch h. Adaptation of Dutch woman's cap, made with pointed crown like the original and turned back off the face, with flare at sides.

Dutch Cap
Adaptation, 1938

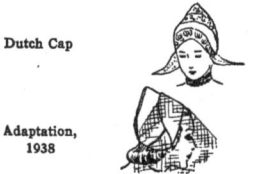

Eugénie h. (F. ē-zhȧ-nē; u zhay nee). Small hat having brim turned up at left; sometimes on both sides; trimmed with ostrich plumes; worn tilted toward right. So called for Empress Eugénie, wife of Napoleon III.

19th Century Eugénie Hat

fedora (fĕ-dō'rȧ; fe *doe* ra). Low hat, usually of soft felt, with crown creased lengthwise; brim originally rolled high at sides. Worn chiefly by men; adapted according to fashion for women.

fez. Adaptation, for women, of Turkish fez cap; made of felt without brim, trimmed with tassel.

flat. Colloquial term for straw hat having low crown and broad brim.

flop. Colloquial term for soft, wide-brimmed hat that flops.

flower toque. Small, close-fitting hat entirely covered with flowers.

fore-and-after. Cocked hat turned so that peaks are worn over forehead and at back.

Gainsborough h. (gānz'bŭ-rō; *gains* bur o). Hat with large, graceful brim,

Doll Hat, 1938

18th Century Gainsborough Hat

fāte, făt, dȧnce, ärt mē, mĕt, hêr, thêre rīde, rĭd nōte, nŏt, côrn, fōōd, fŏŏt cūte, cŭt, curé now fin(ŋ)ger villa(ȧ) señor pleas(zh)ure

hats (continued)

usually turned up on one side, trimmed with plumes. So called from hats in portraits by English painter, Gainsborough.

Geneva h. (jə-nē′və; je *nee* va). Low-crowned hat with wide brim, as worn in 17th century.

gibus (jĭ′bəs; *jy* bus). Man's collapsible opera hat. So called for original maker in Paris.

gob h. Small, close-fitting hat with brim turned up evenly all around, like cap worn by gob, or sailor of U.S.Navy.

Gob Hat

gossamer (gŏs′ə-mēr; *goss* a mer). British term for light silk hat. Originally, trade name.

gypsy h. (jĭp′sĭ; *jip* si). Simple hat with broad brim, varying in type. Worn by women and children.

halo h. (hā′lō; *hay* lo). Hat worn off the forehead, well back on head, acting as circular frame for face. Suggests halo seen in religious paintings.

Halo Hat, 1935

harlequin h. (här′lə-kwĭn; *har* le kwin). Hat with wide, cuff-like brim turned up all around; rather straight at front and back and flaring at the sides. As worn with harlequin fancy dress costume, usually decorated with pompons. See HARLEQUIN COSTUME under FANCY DRESS.

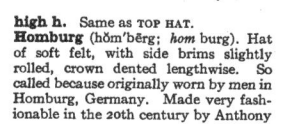

Harlequin Hat

Adaptation, 1938

high h. Same as TOP HAT.
Homburg (hŏm′bērg; *hom* burg). Hat of soft felt, with side brims slightly rolled, crown dented lengthwise. So called because originally worn by men in Homburg, Germany. Made very fashionable in the 20th century by Anthony Eden, at one time Foreign Minister for Great Britain.

Homburg, 1930's

jerry h. British slang term for stiff, round, felt hat.
jockey cap. Woman's hat in imitation of cap worn by jockeys; made with small, close-fitting crown and small, partial brim like a visor. For original jockey cap, see CAPS.
kamelaukion (kăm-ĕ-lô′kĭ-ŏn; kam e *law* ki on). High, brimless hat worn by priests in Orient.
Kossuth h. (kŏs′ōŏth; *koss* ooth). Hat with oval crown, flat top, rolling brim. Popularized in 1851 by Louis Kossuth, Hungarian patriot.
leghorn h. (lĕg′hôrn or lĕg′ērn; *leg* horn or *leg* ern). Hat made of finely plaited straw, naturally butter yellow in color. Frequently made with large, drooping or undulating brim. Named for Leghorn, Italy, place of export.
lingerie h. 1. Hat of lace or embroidery. **2.** Washable summer hat.
Mackinaw h. (măk′ĭ-nô; *mack* i naw). Hat of varying shapes, made of coarse straw. Probably so called for place of distribution in early colonial days, the Indian trading post at Mackinac, Michigan.
marquis (mär′kwĭs or F. mâr-kē; *mar* kwiss or mar kee). Woman's three-cornered hat.
Merry Widow h. Hat with large brim, sometimes 36 inches in diameter, ornately trimmed, often with ostrich plumes. Worn by women in early 20th century. Named for light opera of same name.
Milan h. (mĭ-lăn′ or mĭl′ən; mi *lan* or *mill* an). Hat of fine straw originally manufactured in Milan, Italy. Easily blocked into shape; favored for women's hats.
milkmaid h. Type of garden hat, made of straw, with low crown and broad, slightly drooping brim; tied under chin. Made popular by Marie Antoinette, as affectation of rusticity when she played at being a milkmaid at her model farm.

Type of Milkmaid Hat

mousquetaire h. (F. mōōs-kə-tĕr; moose ke tare). Hat with large, undulating brim, up in front, trimmed with trailing plumes. Worn in 17th and 18th centuries by French musketeers, or royal bodyguards.
mushroom h. Hat with downward curved brim, shaped like mushroom or toadstool; sometimes wider at sides.

Mushroom Hat, 1938

Neapolitan h. (nē-ə-pŏl′ĭ-tən; nee a *poll* i tan). Hat of woven fiber or sheer, lacy, horsehair braid. Originally high and conical in shape, as made in Naples; now, any hat made of such braid.
Nivernois h. (F. nē-vĕr-nwä; nee ver nwah). Small, tricorne hat with low crown, worn by 18th century dandies. Name for Nevers, France.
opera h. Narrow-brimmed hat of dull, usually fine-ribbed silk, with high, semi-round, collapsible crown. Worn by men attending opera. Differentiated from top hat by being dull and collapsible.
pagoda toque (pə-gō′də tōk; pa *go* da toke). Small, brimless hat with crown in pyramid shape, resembling pagoda or sacred Oriental tower.
Panama h. (păn-ə-mä′; pan a *mah*). Light-colored hat of varying type, hand-plaited from young leaves of palm-like tree of Central America; also, machine-made imitation. Worn by men and women in warm climates or weather.
pancake beret. Medium-large flat-topped beret, usually of molded felt.
papal h. (pā′pəl; *pay* pal). Wide-brimmed, low-crowned hat, usually red, trimmed with gold tassels. Worn by pope.
Paris h. High silk hat worn by men.
parson's h. Felt hat with broad, straight brim, low crown. Worn by clergymen.
petasos (pĕt′ə-sŏs; *pet* a sos) or **petasus** (pĕt′ə-sŭs; *pet* a sus). Hat with broad brim and low crown, as shown on god Hermes.
Peter Pan h. Small perky hat with feather, as worn by Maude Adams in J. M. Barrie's play, "Peter Pan."

Peter Pan Hat

picture h. Hat with very large brim, which frames the face; usually having

fāte, făt, dánce, ärt mē, mĕt, hēr, thêre rīde, rĭd nōte, nŏt, côrn, fōōd, fŏŏt cūte, cŭt, cûre now fin(ŋ)ger villa(ə) señor pleas(zh)ure

decorative trimming of ribbons, flowers, plumes, etc.; especially, Gainsborough or similar hat, as seen in famous pictures.
pillbox. Small, round hat with straight sides and flat top, shaped like old-fashioned boxes for holding pills.

Pillbox, 1930's

pith helmet or **h.** Helmet-shaped hat of light weight, made of pith. Worn in tropical regions as protection from sun. Sometimes called *topee* or *topi*.
plateau (plă-tō'; pla *toe*). Flat hat in shape of disk or plate. Usually held on head by band or snood at back.
postilion h. (pŏs-tĭl′yən; poce *till* yun). Hat with high, flat crown and narrow brim, rolled at sides. Copy of type worn by postilion, or guide who rode one of the horses drawing a vehicle.

Type of Postilion Hat

pot derby or **h.** Colloquial term for pot-shaped hat; derby; bowler.
profile h. (prō′fĭl; *pro* file). Hat worn well down over one side of head to frame outline of side face.

Profile Hat, 1938

puggree or **pugree** (pŭg′rē; *pug* ree). Adaptation of PAGRI or PUGGREE, Hindu scarf, as turban-like hat for women.

Hindu Puggree

British Puggree

Puritan h. (pūr′ĭ-tən; *pure* i tan). Black felt hat with broad brim, high, flat crown; trimmed with narrow ribbon crown band, silver buckle in front. Worn in 17th century by New England Puritan men. Adapted for modern women's wear. See PURITAN.
quadricorn h. (kwăd′rĭ-kôrn; *kwod* ri corn). Hat with four points or corners, usually having an upward flare.
Quaker h. Low-crowned hat with large brim slightly rolled at each side, having no adornment of any kind. Worn by Quaker men.
Robin Hood h. High-crowned sports hat, with brim turned up at back and partly on sides, down in point at front; trimmed with high quill. Worn by legendary English outlaw.
rococo h. (rə-kō′kō; ro *co* co). Style of hat worn in Victorian era, usually tipped over face, with brim dipping slightly at front and back; trimmed with flowers of several colors.

Robin Hood Hat

roller (rōl′ẽr; *role* er). Small hat, typically in felt, with narrow, even brim, usually rolled up all around and trimmed with narrow ribbon crown band.
roundlet. Small, round hat worn by men in 18th century. Could be carried

Sailor Hat, 1907

Regulation Sailor, 1938

Short-Back Sailor, 1938

over shoulder by attached streamer.
sailor. Hat with flat crown, and straight brim of varying width. Usually made of straw.
salad-bowl. Hat having deeply rolled brim turned up all around.
service h. Soft, khaki-colored felt hat, with high crown dented in four places and broad, stiff brim. Worn in U. S. Army when full-dress uniform is not worn.
shepherdess h. (shĕp′ẽr-dĕs; *shep* er dess). Shallow-crowned hat with dropped front and back brim and flared sides; worn forward on head, held in place by a ribbon band.
short-back sailor h. Sailor type of hat with very narrow brim or no brim at back and a large, flat, broad, straight sailor brim in front. Often worn tilted upward.
shovel h. (shŭv′l; *shuv* el). Hat with broad brim turned up on each side like a shovel, projecting front and back. Worn by certain clergy.
silk h. High, cylinder-shaped hat with silk-plush finish, used with formal dress by men and by women for formal riding.
skimmer. Flat-crowned sailor, usually of straw, having wide, straight brim. Worn and so-called by students at Eton College.

Skimmer, 1938

slicker h. Waterproof hat with slanting brim that is wider in back than front. Similar to SOUTHWESTER.
slouch h. Soft hat with flexible brim, varying in width.
sombrero (sŏm-brā′rō; som *bray* ro). Hat originally worn in Spain, Mexico, and South America, in varying shapes according to local style. Usually tall-crowned and wide-brimmed. Worn in straw by peasants, in felt by gentlemen. Spanish word meaning hat. As worn by American cowboys, usually called *ten-gallon hat*.

Type of Sombrero

southern belle h. Hat with large, graceful, drooping brim. Often a cape-line, made of leghorn or Tuscan straw with velvet or satin ribbon sash.
southwester or **sou'wester.** Waterproof hat, with brim broader in back to protect the neck. Worn by seamen in

hats (continued)
bad weather. In adaptation for women's wear, brim often turned up in front.

Southwester

stovepipe h. Hat with high crown, especially tall silk hat worn by men on dress occasions.
stroller (strōl'ẽr; *strole* er). Casual, tailored type of hat, mannish in outline, usually of felt. Worn with suits for town and spectator sports wear.
sugar-loaf h. Hat shaped like round-topped cone, resembling loaf shape in which refined sugar used to be made.

Type of Sugar-Loaf Hat, 1780's

sundown. Woman's broad-brimmed sun hat, so called in parts of U. S.
sun h. Broad-brimmed hat, sometimes helmet-shaped, to protect wearer from heat of sun.
swagger h. Informal sports hat with medium-wide brim, usually turned down in front. Often made of felt.
tam or **tam-o'-shanter.** Development of the original tam-o'-shanter into hat of fabric draped over a crown. Use of crown eliminated need for headband. See CAPS.

Tam Hats, 1920's

Tamsui h. (tăm'sŏŏ-ĭ; *tahm* soo i). Hat similar to Panama. Made of plant leaves at Tamsui, in Taiwan (or Formosa).
tarpaulin (tär-pô'lĭn; tar *paw* lin). Wide-brimmed, waterproof storm hat made of or covered with tarpaulin. Worn by sailors, fishermen, etc.
ten-gallon h. Large hat with broad brim, worn by cowboys in western U. S. See SOMBRERO.
topee or **topi** (tō'pē; *toe* pee). Pith hat or helmet worn in India and other tropical countries for protection against heat and glare. Often called *sola topee*, because usually made from sola plant.

Topee

top h. Man's narrow-brimmed hat with tall, cylindrical crown of finely pressed beaver cloth in glossy finish. Also called *beaver, high hat.*
toque (tōk; toke). Small, close-fitting, brimless hat. Formerly, black velvet cap with full crown and small, rolled brim, ornamented with plumes; worn by men and women in France in 16th century.

Toque, 1575

Toque, 1865

tricorn or **tricorne h.** (trī'kôrn; *try* corn). Hat with three-cornered, up-turned brim.

17th Century Tricorn Hat

trilby. Soft felt hat worn in Great Britain.
tub h. Any hat that is washable, especially one made of piqué or similar fabric that will hold its shape without additional stiffening.
turban (tẽr'bən; *ter* ban). Soft hat having fitted crown and narrow, rolled

Turban, French, 1585

Turban, 1870

Knitted Turban, 1926

Open-Crown Turban, 1936

Draped Turban, 1936

Scarf Turban, 1937

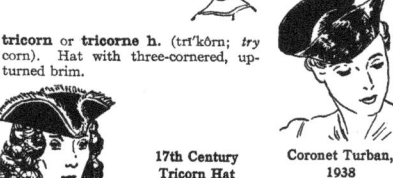

Coronet Turban, 1938

Cuff Turban, 1938

Sikh Turban, 1938

Turban Worn by Dowager Queen Mary of England, 1938

or draped brim, or no brim at all. In 18th century, sometimes called *turbin* and popularly made of gauze and trimmed with feathers. Originally, long strip of cloth or scarf wound around head, part of Oriental headdress.
turban toque. Toque with fabric trimming twisted or folded about it.
vagabond h. Informal hat with brim

of medium width, often turned down. Made of felt or other fabric. Worn with sports clothes.

Watteau h. (wŏ-tō'; wot *toe*). Hat with shallow crown, brim upturned in back, held by bandeau, which is usually covered with flowers. Similar in type to hats shown in pictures by French painter, Watteau.

wide-awake. Soft felt hat with low crown and broad brim.

witch h. Hat with tall, peaked crown, of type seen in pictures of witches. Similar to sugar-loaf hat.

hatband. Band encircling crown of hat; sometimes worn as badge of mourning.

hatbox. 1. Box for a hat or hats, usually deep and round in shape. 2. Box-like piece of traveling luggage, originally designed for carrying hats.

hatchel (hăch'ĕl; *hatch* el). Implement for cleaning flax or hemp, separating coarse parts. Also, to separate coarse from fine parts.

hatching. In tapestry weaving, process or effect of shading color or colors of one part into area of another color.

hat palm. Any of various palms used in making hats.

hat piece. Protective head covering similar to cap, formerly of metal. Worn under hat.

hatpin. Long, straight pin with head, worn for decoration and also to hold hat securely in place by fastening it to hair.

hat-shag. British term for kind of silk plush used for hats.

hatter. One who makes or sells hats.

hatter's plush. Plush, usually of silk or rabbit hair, having long pile or nap pressed very flat, giving shiny, sleek appearance. Used chiefly for men's dress hats.

hatting. 1. Material used for hats. 2. Business of making hats.

hauberjet (hō'bĕr-jĕt; *haw* ber jet). Ancient type of woolen cloth.

hauberk (hō'bĕrk; *haw* berk). 1. Medieval coat of mail similar to a long tunic. Made of ring, or chain mail. 2. Short tunic. Worn formerly by actors.

hausse col (hōs kŏl; hoce coll). 1. Piece of metal in crescent shape formerly worn in front of throat over doublet or coat as protection or badge of rank. 2. Piece of medieval armor to protect part of neck and chest.

haute couture (F. ōt kōō-tür; ote coo toor). Those dressmaking houses, as of Paris, which are most fashionable and important, as Chanel, Patou, etc.

haut goût (F. ō mônd; o goo). Height of style or good taste.

haut monde (F. ō mônd; o mond). High society; often used ironically.

haut ton (F. ō tôn; o tonh). High fashion.

Havanese embroidery (hăv-ə-nēz'; hav a *neez*). Colored buttonholed embroidery. See EMBROIDERIES.

havelock (hăv'lŏk; *hav* lock). Lightweight cloth covering for military cap, usually white and washable, long in back to protect neck from sun. Named for Sir Henry Havelock, 19th century English general.

Havelock

hazel (hā'zəl; *hay* zel) or **hazel nut.** Soft brown shade of reddish-yellow cast, color of shell of ripe hazel nut. Also called *filbert*.

headband. 1. Fillet or band worn around the head. 2. Scottish term for band around top of trousers.

headdress. 1. Ornamental covering for the head. 2. Way of adorning the hair, as with ribbons, flowers, combs, etc.

headgear. Hat; cap; bonnet; headdress or covering of any kind.

heading. 1. Finished edge above a gathering-line. 2. Gathered trimming used as finish, especially at the top of a ruffle.

headkerchief (hĕd'kĕr-chĭf; *hed* ker chif). Kerchief for the head.

headline (hĕd'lĭn; *hed* line). Line just inside hat where brim joins crown.

headpiece. Any covering for the head, especially cap or helmet, as formerly worn in defensive armor.

headrail. Veil or kerchief worn by Anglo-Saxon women as headdress.

head size. Number of inches around crown of head at brow; measurement taken for fitting hats. Most women's hats made in half-inch head sizes, from 21 to 23½.

head veil (văl; vail). Veil worn over head, usually without a hat. See VEILS.

heather (hĕth'ĕr; *heth* er). 1. Purplish blue, the color of heather in bloom. 2. Woolen fabric in heather mixture. 3. Heather mixture.

Heatherbloom. Trade name for mercerized cotton fabric finished in imitation of silk; similar to percaline. Popular for petticoats in early 1900's as a substitute for taffeta.

heather mixture. Combination or mixture of colors in wool fibers so that yarns give flecked appearance, suggesting effect of heather field in bloom, as in Scotland; used chiefly of tweeds and other woolen fabrics.

heaume (hōm; home). Large, heavy medieval helmet. Worn over hood or cap of mail during 13th century.

heavies (hĕv'ĭz; *hev* iz). Colloquial term for heavy underwear.

hedebo embroidery (hĕd'ə-bō; *hed* e bo). Danish embroidery of cut and drawn work. See EMBROIDERIES.

HEELS

heel. 1. Piece beneath back part of shoe, boot, or other foot covering; made of leather, rubber, wood, metal, etc., varying in shape and height. Height measured vertically, at side, just back of HEEL BREAST, from top lift to upper edge of sole, in eighths of inch. High heels first fashionable in late 17th century. 2. Lower back part of hosiery foot.

baby Louis h. (lōō'ē; *loo* ee). Heel like Louis XV heel in shape, but lower in height.

barrel h. Heel of nearly cylindrical shape, somewhat resembling a barrel in silhouette.

boulevard h. (bōō'lə-värd; *boo* le vard). High, covered wooden heel, similar to Cuban, but more shapely and lighter looking.

built-up h. Leather heel composed of separate pieces of sole leather, or lifts, applied separately and fastened together.

common-sense h. Low heel having broad base. So called because of sup-

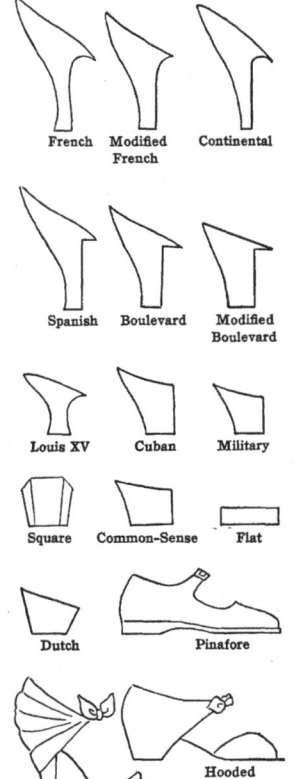

French   Modified   Continental
         French

Spanish   Boulevard   Modified
                      Boulevard

Louis XV   Cuban   Military

Square   Common-Sense   Flat

Dutch   Pinafore

Draped   Hooded

heels (continued)

port it gives and supposed greater comfort.

Continental h. (kŏn-tĭ-nĕn′təl; con ti nen tal). High heel with straight front and slightly shaped back, narrower at base than French heel.

Cuban h. (kū′bən; cue ban). Medium, rather straight heel, without curve of French heel; somewhat narrower at base than flat heel; often of leather.

draped h. Heel bound to foot with kerchief-like drapery covering top of heel and back of foot and tied around ankle.

Dutch boy h. Heel similar in shape to that on Dutch wooden shoe, slanting toward the base. Bottom sometimes shaped like a raindrop.

flat h. Broad, low heel, only slightly shaped at back, usually of leather. Used on women's sports shoes, men's shoes, children's shoes.

Franco-Cuban h. (frăṅk′ō kū′bən; frank o cue ban). Narrow Cuban heel.

French h. Curved, high heel. Usually made of wood covered with leather, having thickness of sole leather; or of wood, with leather top lift at bottom. Sometimes made entirely of leather.

hooded h. Heel covered all in one piece with the back of shoe, without seam or interruption in line. Same piece continues on over instep to serve as fastening.

Louis XV h. (lōō′ē; loo ee). Heel about 1½ inches high, sometimes more, having curved outline, flared at base; placed slightly forward under foot. Popular during reign of Louis XV. Revived as a fashion many times since. Very little used now.

military h. Heel similar to Cuban, but straighter and not so high.

pinafore h. Nearly flat heel curving into very low arch. Used on children's shoes.

Spanish h. (spăn′ish; span ish). High, covered, wooden heel, similar to French, but having straight breast and broader base.

spike h. High heel, higher than French or Spanish, narrow at bottom.

spool h. Heel having wide horizontal corrugations, giving effect like that of old-fashioned spool furniture.

spring h. Low heel in which layer, usually of leather, is inserted between heel seat and heel. Used extensively in children's shoes.

square h. Heel squared off at back so that it has four corners. Sometimes used with squared effect at toe also.

heel breast. Forward face of heel on shoe.
heel cap. Protective covering for heel of stocking or shoe.
heel lift. One of separate pieces, or layers, of sole leather composing leather heel of shoe. — **top l.** Last layer applied in making shoe heel.
heel piece. 1. Heel of shoe or piece added to it for repair. 2. Formerly, armor to protect heel.
heel pitch. Inclination forward, under foot, of shoe heel.

heel plate. Small metal plate attached to bottom of heel as protection against wear.
heel seat. Rounded top of shoe heel, on which foot rests.
heel tap. Lift or piece of leather or metal for heel of shoe.
heliotrope (hē′lĭ-ō-trōp; hee li o trope). Tint of purple-blue; color of the flower.
Hellenic (hĕ-lĕn′ĭk; hel len ic). Classical Greek. Term used in fashion for styles showing classical Greek influence, as in close folds of drapery with sculptured effect of Greek statues. See GREEK.
helmet. Protective covering for the head. As part of ancient and medieval armor and modern military outfit, made of metal.
helmet cap. Knitted cap with cuff around back and sides of head, which may be turned up or down. See CAPS.

HEMS

hem. 1. Finish provided by turning the raw edges under from ⅛ to ½ inch, and then making a second turn to conceal the first. Hem may be secured by hand or machine. 2. Loosely, edge; rim; border.

French h. Finish made by turning the raw edge to wrong side and catching this edge in a tuck which is made on right side and completely conceals the raw edge. Used chiefly on straight edges for fabrics that fray, for inserting embroidery and allover lace bands, and for dropping the hem line of a skirt or unlined cuff.

lingerie h. (F. lăṅ-zhə-rē; lan zhe ree). Tiny rolled, puffed hem, secured by slip-hemming and by overcast-stitches from ⅛ to ⅜ of an inch apart. Used on fine handkerchiefs, neckwear, handmade lingerie, dresses, infants' clothes.

napery h. (nā′pēr-ĭ; nay per i). Hem that, after pressing, appears the same on right and wrong sides. Made by first turning raw edge, then hem, then turning back on the edge, and creasing fabric on the hem line. Hem is put in with fine overhanding-stitches taken through both the turn and the crease. Used chiefly for damask table linens.

rolled h. Very narrow hem made by gently rolling edge of fabric over, securing by slip-stitches under the roll. Practically invisible on the right side. Used on handkerchiefs, lingerie, ruffles, and circular edges, especially in organdie, voile, georgette, etc.

shirt-cuff edge. Double-stitched hem, or two-needle finish, used on tailored lingerie, to give strength to the edge. Used as substitute for trimming.

tucked h. Narrow tuck made near edge in fabric. Material brought over the tuck and felled down to make an edge finish.

hemmer. 1. Sewing-machine attachment for turning fabric under and holding it in a true line under the needle. Every machine has several hemmers, some adjustable for hemming different widths. Also used for felling, sewing on

lace. 2. Person who hems by hand or by machine.

hemming-stitch. 1. Short, slanting stitch. Used where a strong edge, rather than daintiness, is desired. 2. Same as VERTICAL HEMMING-STITCH. See STITCHES.

hemp. Tough, coarse fiber of hemp plant. Used for weaving into coarse fabrics, such as SAIL CLOTH, BALINE, etc.

hemstitch. 1. To make decorative finish, by pulling out number of parallel threads, as at top of hem, catching up an even number of the remaining threads, drawing the thread around them, and securing them by a stitch in the edge of the hem turn. This is repeated for the length of the drawn-thread line. 2. Ornamental needlework so done; also called *hemstitching*. 3. Stitch used to make this ornamental needlework. 4. To puncture fabric with a large machine needle and surround perforation with stitches in imitation of hand hemstitching. See STITCHES.

hemstitch embroidery. Type of punch work done in back-stitch made with a large needle and drawn tight in hemstitch effect. See EMBROIDERIES.

hemstitcher. Sewing-machine attachment with a plunger that holds a large needle which punctures the cloth and embroiders the hole to make it secure. Used also to make picot edges.

henna. 1. Brown color having red-yellow cast. 2. Reddish-orange dye prepared from henna leaves. Used to tint the hair.

hennin (hĕn′ĭn; hen in). High headdress, varying in size and form; sometimes cone-, horn-, or heart-shaped; usually having soft, floating veil attached to apex. Worn by women during 15th century.

Medieval Hennin

henrietta (hĕn-rĭ-ĕt′ə; hen ri et a). Fine, twilled fabric, originally with silk warp and fine worsted filling. Like cashmere, but more lustrous and slightly harder and coarser. Used for dresses and children's wear. Named for Queen Henrietta, wife of Charles I of England.

hercules braid (hĕr′kū-lēz; her cue leez). Corded braid used for trimming. See BRAIDS.

hernani (F. ĕr-nȧ-nē; air nah nee). Type of square-meshed grenadine with wool filling and silk warp.

herringbone-stitch (hĕr′ĭng-bŏn; hare ing bone). Catch-stitch used in embroidery for bands, borders, and filling. See STITCHES.

herringbone weave. Irregular broken twill weave. See WEAVES.
hessian (hĕsh'ən; *hesh* an). Rough, coarse fabric of hemp or mixed jute and hemp. Used for sacking, etc.
Hessian boot. High, tasseled boot. See BOOTS.
Hibernian embroidery (hī-bẽr'nĭ-ən; high *ber* ni an). Colored embroidery in satin- and buttonhole-stitches. See EMBROIDERIES.
hickory. Sturdy, twilled, durable cotton shirting, usually striped in blue or brown and white. Softer and lighter than ticking. Resembles cottonade. Used for shirts, trousers, etc. Often used to describe something that wears endlessly; as, it will wear like hickory.
hide. Raw or dressed pelt — in leather business, pelt of large animal, such as full-grown steer, cow, horse, as distinguished from pelt of small animal, which is called SKIN, and of intermediate animal, called KIP.
high color. Vivid, strong color. Often used to describe naturally red or pink cheeks.
high fashion or **style.** Fashion as adopted by fashion leaders. The smartest of the exclusive current fashions.
high hat. Man's high-crowned hat. Same as TOP HAT. See HATS.
high-low. Laced boot of ankle height. See BOOTS.
high shoe. Shoe reaching above ankle; usually laced or buttoned. See SHOES.
high waistline. Waistline placed on garment above the normal waistline. See WAISTLINE.
hiking costume (hīk'ĭng; *hike* ing). Sturdy sports costume suitable for walking expeditions. See SPORTS CLOTHES.
himation (hĭ-măt'ĭ-ŏn; hi *mat* i on). Ancient Greek mantle. See WRAPS.
hip boot. Boot long enough to reach to the hips. Worn chiefly by fishermen and firemen. See BOOTS.
hip length. Length of coat or other garment which reaches to hip line at its widest point. See LENGTHS.
hive. Straw bonnet resembling a beehive. See BONNETS.
hobble skirt. Very narrow skirt. The accentuated narrowness at the hem made walking difficult. Popular about 1910-14. See SKIRTS.
hobnail. Short nail with large, thick head. Used on heavy shoes and to decorate leather accessories, especially belts.
Holbein-stitch (hŏl'bĭn; *hole* bine). Running-stitch worked twice along same line alternately, to give unbroken line on both sides of fabric. See STITCHES.
Holbein work. Outline embroidery in double running-stitch. See EMBROIDERIES.
hole braid. Bobbin-made braid used in laces. See BRAIDS.
Holland. 1. Form-fitting foundation made by big establishments for special customers. Used as a size guide in cutting and draping to save fittings. Often put on dress form which has been padded to the size of individual's figure. **2.** Closely woven linen fabric originally made in Holland. The first Hollands were made of this fabric. See LINENS. **3.** Linen or fine cotton in plain weave, sized and often glazed. Used now chiefly for window shades. **4.** Finish applied to other fabrics in imitation of Holland.
hollie point lace. Medieval needlepoint church lace. See LACES.
hollie-stitch. Type of buttonhole-stitch. See STITCHES.
Hollywood top. V-top on a lingerie slip, of single or double thickness of fabric. See SLIPS.
Homburg (hŏm'bẽrg; *hom* burg). Soft felt hat with crown dented lengthwise. See HATS.
homecraft. Household or domestic art; craft practiced in the home, as knitting, crocheting, crepe paper work, etc.
home dress. Dress appropriate for wear at home when working. See MORNING DRESS, HOUSE DRESS under DRESSES.
home economics (ē-kə-nŏm'ĭks or ĕk-ə-nŏm'ĭks; ee co *nom* ics or ek o *nom* ics). Science of home management and its relation to family and community life, including the domestic arts and sciences, planning of meals, clothing, housing, budgeting of income, care and education of children, standards of living. Also, course of training in these subjects.
home economist. One versed in the principles and art of home economics.
homemade. Made at home; implying, also, poorly or carelessly made. People who sew are eager to avoid the homemade look.
homespun. 1. Loose, strong, durable woolen fabric in plain or twill weave, usually of coarse yarn, having rough surface. Spun and woven by hand; also imitated by machine. Before the Civil War, practically all people of the U. S. were dressed in homespun. Used now for sports suits, coats, skirts, men's clothes. **2.** Coarse fabric of cotton, linen, jute, or mixtures. Used for drapery, upholstery. Sometimes called *linsey woolsey*, meaning a mixture of linen and wool.
honeycomb smocking (hŭn'ĭ-kŏm; *hun* i kome). Design in smocking made by means of stitches taken on plaits, holding the fulness in a honeycomb effect.
honeycomb-stitch. Connected rows of blanket-stitches so spaced and taken that they resemble a honeycomb. See STITCHES.
honeycomb weave. Weave in honeycomb pattern. See WEAVES.
Honiton lace (hŏn'ĭ-tən; *hon* i ton). Bobbin lace similar to but heavier than duchesse. See LACES.

HOODS

hood. 1. Type of soft head-covering which often fits closely about face and sometimes hangs over back of neck. Worn with many variations in style from 11th century on. Replaced generally by caps and hats in reign of George II. Revived by fashion from time to time for evening, sports, etc. **2.** Scarf-like fold of cloth worn at back of neck of academic or ecclesiastical robe, often indicating rank or degree by its color and fabric. **3.** In hat manufacturing, unblocked hat shape, conical block of fur fiber, or basket-weave straw hat.

Early 18th Century Hood

almuce (ăl'mūs; *al* muce). Cowl-like hood, often fur-lined. Worn by clergy during 13th, 14th, and 15th centuries. Also called *amice* (ăm'ĭs; *am* iss).
babushka (bä'bōōsh-kə; *bah* boosh ka). Hood-shaped head covering with strings of same piece of fabric tying under chin. Often open at back. Worn for sports and dress occasions. Russian word meaning grandmother.

Babushka, 1938

calash (kə-lăsh'; ca *lash*). Hood supported by hoops, to be pulled over head or folded back. Fashionable in 18th century, after introduction by Duchess of Bedford. Copied from folding hood or top of calash or light carriage.

18th Century Calash

capuche (kə-pōōsh'; ca *poosh*). Hood similar to cowl worn by Capuchin monks.

19th Century Capuche

capulet (kăp'ȧ-lĕt or F. kȧ-pü-lȧ; *cap* you let or ca poo lay). Hood worn in

hoods (continued)

southern France, chiefly by peasant women.

caputium (kȧ-pū'shĭ-ŭm; ca *pew* she um). Hood worn by scholars or ecclesiastics.

chaperon (shăp'ẽr-ŏn; *shap* er ohn). Ancient type of hood, covering head and neck, to shoulders. Worn by men and women, nobility and populace, during the Middle Ages and into the Renaissance; also worn with full dress by Knights of the Garter. Superseded by the hat and then allowed to hang around shoulders. Developed into the HUMERAL VEIL.

cowl. Monk's hood, usually attached to great mantle.

French h. Elaborate 16th century hood or cap usually worn back on head to show hair in front, and falling in folds at back and sides.

liripipium (lĭr-ĭ-pĭ'ŭm; lir i *pi* pi um). Hood with peaked top, originally worn by graduates. During development of the garment, peak was made longer and longer, until in 13th century it hung almost to the ground.

15th Century Liripipium

Mazarine h. (măz'ȧ-rēn; *mas* a reen). Type of hood or headdress adorned with lace. Worn about 1700 by the Duchesse de Mazarin.

Nithsdale (nĭths'dāl; *niths* dale). Large riding hood covering the face; worn in 18th century. Named for Countess of Nithsdale.

parka h. Peaked hood with attached scarf ends that are tied around neck for warmth. Worn with winter sports clothes.

Parka Hood, 1938

rayonné (F. rā-yô-nā; ray on nay). Type of hood used in colonial America. French word meaning radiated.

red riding-h. Shirred hood or bonnet of close-fitting, tied-under-the-chin type, usually attached to cape.

riding. Enveloping hood worn while riding in inclement weather.

surtout (F. sür-tōō or sẽr-tōōt'; soor too or ser *toot*). Hood with mantle, worn by women.

Red Riding-Hood, 1908

therese (tē-rēs'; ter *eece*). Large hood worn in late 18th century. Made of thin, gauzy material over frame of wire or whalebone. Name probably derived from Maria Theresa.

hooded heel. Heel covered all in one piece with back of shoe. See HEELS.

hook and eye. Fastener in two pieces: hook and loop. See FASTENERS.

hook-and-eye tape. Tape having hooks and eyes attached. See TAPES.

hookless fastener. General term for SLIDE FASTENER. See FASTENERS.

HOOPS

hoop. Circular band or frame. Specifically: 1. Device for holding embroidery. See EMBROIDERY HOOP. 2. Device of metal, whalebone, or other material, used to expand skirt. Compare BUSTLE.

bearer (bêr'ẽr; *bare* er). Roll of padding worn in 18th century at each hip to raise skirt.

bell-shaped h. Hoops of graduated sizes fastened one above the other, with largest at bottom and smallest at top.

criarde (F. krē-ärd; cree ard). 17th century name for one of stiffened panniers, usually of linen, which made creaking sounds with the least movement. French word meaning noisy, discordant; also gummed or varnished cloth.

crinoline (krĭn'ȯ-lĭn; *crin* o lin). Steel springs forming cage or hoop for extending skirts. Popular in mid-19th century.

Mid-19th Century Crinoline

dress-improver. Hooped pannier, really twin side hoops, or similar device to bunch skirts over hips. Worn by women in late 19th century to improve effect of skirt. Later evolved into bustle.

16th Century Farthingale

farthingale (fär'thĭng-gāl; *far* thing gale). Single hoop mounted on circular piece of material or fastened at waist by tapes. Also, hair-stuffed cushion worn around waist, under the skirt, to extend the skirt.

pannier (păn'yẽr; *pan* yer). Oval wire, straw, whalebone, cane, or wicker hoop extending far out at sides.

18th Century Pannier

hoop petticoat. Petticoat made with hoops to distend skirt. Worn chiefly in 19th century.

hoop skirt. Skirt stiffened with hoops. See SKIRTS.

Hoover apron. Coverall dress with a reversible double front, designed so that when one side was soiled the other clean side could be turned out. Popular during the World War when Herbert Hoover was Food Administrator.

Hoover Apron, 1917

hop sacking. Rough-surfaced cotton, linen, or rayon fabric, of plain weave; usually coarse like original hemp and jute sacking of which bags are made. Used for dresses, coats, suits.

horizon blue (hȯ-rī'zn; ho *rye* zon). Light green-blue shade.

horizontal (hŏr-ĭ-zŏn'tȧl; hor i *zon* tal). Parallel to the horizon, as stripes running crosswise from one side to the other. Distinguished from vertical, or up-and-down.

horizontal buttonhole. Crosswise buttonhole. Most utilitarian buttonholes are cut horizontally. See BUTTONHOLES.

horizontal stripes. Stripes running crosswise of fabric or garment. See STRIPES.

horsecloth. Rough, very heavy woolen dress fabric. So named from the blankets used to cover horses.

horsehair. 1. Hair of a horse, especially of mane and tail, used as fiber for fabric. 2. Fabric of horsehair. Same as HAIRCLOTH. 3. Stiff, loosely woven, transparent fabric of horsehair, used for hats, stiffening, etc.

HOSE

hose. 1. Stockings, or covering for lower leg and foot, usually knit or woven. Formerly not made to cover the foot.

2. Tights, or hose reaching to the waist, formerly fastened to doublet with points. See BOOT HOSE, GALLIGASKINS, TRUNK HOSE.
bed socks. Soft, warm socks, usually ankle-high, often knitted. Worn in bed for extra warmth.
circular h. Hose knit in circular or tubular shape without a seam, often having imitation seams and fashion marks; usually shaped by decreasing number of stitches toward ankle. Hose may become baggy at ankle in wear and laundering.
cut h. Hose made of shaped pieces cut from goods already knit and sewn together, all parts in one piece; or, more often, leg is cut first and foot knitted on. Knit-on method much used in making net or mesh hose; often wrongly advertised as "full-fashioned."
dip-dyed h. Hose dyed and degummed after knitting. Retains more gum than ingrained. Opposite of IN-GRAINED.
dull h. Silk hose that has practically no luster.
English foot. Hosiery foot in which separately knit sole is attached to leg of stocking, eliminating usual center seam on bottom of foot. Used for sports hose. First made in England for soldiers, because of comfort in walking.
fashion marks. Raised dots on full-fashioned hose, near back seam, which indicate where needles have been dropped in knitting operation. Characterized by converging wales or rows of stitches at back of hose.
French foot. Type of hosiery foot having seam continued from back of leg through center of sole. Distinguished from ENGLISH FOOT.
full-fashioned h. Hose knit individually in flat, open piece, beginning at top or welt, with stitches dropped gradually at selvages to shape hose to leg from calf to ankle. Foot is then knitted to leg. Characterized by FASHION MARKS.
gauge (gāj; gaje). Term indicating number of needles used to inch in knitted fabric, especially full-fashioned hose, determining degree of fineness. Hosiery gauge numbers, according to American methods of knitting, usually run from 39, very coarse, to 60, very fine. So-called "100-gauge," sometimes advertised, is on French system, and not nearly so fine as indicated.
golf h. Heavy woolen or other rather bulky socks or stockings. Worn for golf and other outdoor sports.
half-h. Socks or hose covering only half of lower leg. Sometimes made with elastic top.
imitation fashion marks. Marks in the shape of small holes rather than dots. Used on circular-knit and other hose to imitate full-fashioned. Recognized by parallel rows of stitches at back of hose.
ingrain h. Hose knitted from yarn-dyed silk that has retained its natural silk sheen. Highly popular during first 30 years of 20th century.
mock seam. Seam in back of hose, knitted in tube form, made to resemble full-fashioned hose.
ribbed h. Stockings with lengthwise ribs, made in a variety of rib widths. Worn by children; also, for sports, by women and men.
Rograin (rō'grān; *roe* grain). Trade name for hose seamed inside out, having dull surface. Became popular when in-grain stockings became less so.
scogger. Footless worsted stocking. Worn outside shoe in parts of England.
semi-fashioned h. Hose with mock seam to resemble full-fashioned.
sock. Short stocking, or covering for foot and lower leg.
spliced heel. In hosiery, a heel of double thickness.
split-foot h. Black hose having white sole, often of cotton.
split-knee h. Stocking knitted so that the portion where the knee is open, supposedly for comfort and to prevent runs.
vampay or **vamp.** Sock or short stocking, usually of wool. Worn in colonial America, often over other hose.
wale. Lengthwise rib, as in full-fashioned hose.
welt. Reinforced upper part of hose, usually double, sometimes single. Designed for garter fastening.

hose supporter. Clasp attached to elastic that forms a garter.
hosiery (hō'zhēr-ĭ; *ho* zher i). Hose or stockings in general.
hostess gown (hōst'ĕs; *host* ess). Usually, formalized negligee simulating a dress, possibly formal lounging pajamas. Worn by a woman when receiving guests informally in her own home.
hound's-tooth check. Irregular checked pattern. See CHECKS.
houppelande (hoop'lănd; *hoop* land). Full-length, one-piece garment with full and bulky or tight-fitting sleeves, and extremely full skirt with train; worn by women, at first by men also, in 14th and 15th centuries. Skirt and sleeves sometimes lined with fur. Later, belted tightly at normal waistline.

15th Century Houppelande

hour-glass silhouette. Silhouette with pinched-in waistline. See SILHOUETTES.
houri-coat (hoo'rĭ; *hoo* ri). Kimono-like coat. See COATS.
house. Firm or organization making or distributing wearing apparel or dress-making supplies; as, a French house, a dress house, a millinery house.
house-cap. Student's cap. See CAPS.
house-coat. Tailored, one-piece garment, usually of substantial fabric, often cut on princess lines. Handsome

Hour-Glass Silhouette, 1900's

ones often worn as hostess gowns. Popular throughout 1930's.
house dress. Simple home or morning dress. There are more of such dresses made than all other dresses put together. See DRESSES.
household arts. The art, knowledge, and practice of home-making. See DOMESTIC ARTS.
house slipper. Easy, comfortable slipper to wear informally at home. See SLIPPERS.
housewife. 1. The woman of the house; the wife who manages the home. 2. Small container with set of sewing essentials such as needles, thread, scissors, thimble, etc.
how (hŏo; hoo). Scottish term for hood or cap.
huarache (wä-rä'chĭ; wah *rah* chi). Mexican sandal woven of strips of leather, often in light color; sometimes with leather heel straps. See SANDALS.
huarizo (Sp. wä-rē'thō; wah *ree* tho). Soft hair of animal that is a cross between llama and alpaca.
huccatoon (hŭk-ȧ-tōōn'; huck a *toon*). Type of cotton fabric made in Manchester, England, for trade in Africa.
huckaback (hŭk'ȧ-băk; *huck* a back). Absorbent cotton or linen fabric of figured weave, with prominent weft threads. Used for towels, fancy work.
huckaback embroidery. Darned embroidery on huckaback toweling. See EMBROIDERIES.
huckaback-stitch. Surface stitch caught under weft threads of huckaback toweling, often in elaborate patterns. See STITCHES.
Hudson seal. Sheared and dyed muskrat. See FURS.
hue. 1. A color. 2. Attribute of color by which eye normally perceives it to differ from white, black, neutral gray.
hue circuit (sẽr'kĭt; *ser* kit). Color circle.
huepilli (Sp. wĕ-pē'lyē; we *pee* lyee). Mexican woman's blouse. Same as HUIPIL. See BLOUSES.
hug-me-tight. Short, close-fitting jacket, usually knitted or crocheted. See JACKETS.
Huguenot lace (hū'gē-nŏt; *hue* ga not). Mull designs on net. See LACES.

huipil or **huepilli** (Sp. wĭ-pĕl' or wĕ-pĕ'lyĕ; wi *peel* or we *pee* lyee). Mexican woman's blouse-like garment. See BLOUSES.

huke. 1. Hooded cape worn by women in 15th century. See CAPES. 2. Close-fitting garment of Middle Ages, worn by both men and women.

hula skirt (hōō'lä; *hoo* lah). Grass skirt worn by Hawaiian women. See SKIRTS.

hulls. Garments or clothes. From the word *hull*, in its meaning of outer covering.

humeral veil (hū'mə-rəl; *hue* mer al). Veil or scarf matching vestments of Roman Catholic clergy; worn around shoulders at High Mass. Developed from ancient hood, the chaperon, which was superseded by the hat or cap and then still worn but allowed to hang around the shoulders.

Hungarian embroidery (hŭng-gā'rĭ-ən; hung *gay* ri an). Bright-colored embroidery in flat-stitch. See EMBROIDERIES.

Hungarian point. Allover canvas embroidery of zigzag designs. Same as FLORENTINE EMBROIDERY. See EMBROIDERIES.

Hungarian-stitch. Alternating long and short upright stitches used in canvas work. See STITCHES.

hunter or **hunter's green.** Dark, slightly yellowish green.

hunter's pink. Any of various colors used for hunting coats; chiefly, bright red, a little duller than scarlet.

hunting boot. High, laced boot with waterproof sole. See BOOTS.

hunting cap. Peaked cap, similar to jockey cap; usually of velvet. See CAPS.

hunting shirt. Coarse shirt of khaki, leather, etc. See SHIRTS.

hurds or **hards.** Refuse or coarse part of wool, hemp, or flax.

hure. Obsolete word for cap.

hyacinth (hī'ə-sĭnth; *hy* a sinth). 1. Medium lavender-blue color. 2. Transparent reddish or brownish stone, sometimes used as gem.

hyacinth blue. Blue color with purplish tinge, darker than hyacinth.

I

ice creeper. Metallic device attached to shoe to aid in walking on ice.

ice nail. Hobnail on heavy boot to aid in walking on ice.

idiot's delight. Simple type of fancy work made on spool that has four pins (or nails) driven in around the hole at one end. Thread or yarn is looped around pins, and then lifted over each pin in succession, forming long tubular cord which passes down through hole in spool.

ihram (ĭ-räm'; i *rahm*). Garment worn by Mohammedan on pilgrimage to Mecca, consisting of two white cotton cloths without needlework, one wrapped around loins, the other draped over back.

ikat (ē'kät; *ee* kat). Any one of various chiné silk fabrics made in Java, Sumatra, etc.

illusion (ĭ-lū'zhŭn; i *lue* zhun). 1. Kind of tulle, usually made of silk. Used for veils, dresses, trimmings. See NETS. 2. (Capitalized) Trade name for a face powder made by Elizabeth Arden.

imitation (ĭm-ĭ-tā'shən; im i *tay* shun). Likeness having decided resemblance; copy; artificial substitute for something genuine, usually inferior to the original article.

imitation alligator. Leather with stamped markings in imitation of genuine alligator. See LEATHERS.

imitation corded seam. Seam that has both edges turned to same side, then is stitched through the three thicknesses of fabric, giving corded effect. See SEAMS.

imitation fashion marks. Holes in imitation of dots indicating the dropped stitches made in shaping full-fashioned hose. See HOSE.

imitation leather. Fabric processed to resemble leather. See LEATHERS.

imperial (ĭm-pē'rĭ-əl; im *peer* i al). Gold-figured silk fabric said to have been introduced into England from Greece or the Orient in Middle Ages.

import (ĭm'pôrt; *im* port). Merchandise brought in from foreign countries. The most important apparel and accessory items come from France and Great Britain. Short for an imported dress, coat, hat, bag, etc.

imprimé (F. ăṅ-prē-mā; am pree may). French word meaning printed.

improver (ĭm-prōōv'ēr; im *proov* er). Device worn to improve the set of skirt drapery; hoop; bustle. See DRESS-IMPROVER under HOOPS.

in. Fashionable; approved by fashion; in vogue; as, hoop skirts are in again.

inch. Measure of length equal to 1/12 of a foot or 2.54 centimeters. Divided into halves, quarters, eighths, sixteenths, etc.

increase (ĭn-krēs'; in *crease*). In knitting, crocheting, tatting, etc., to add to number of stitches in row, pattern, or round so as to enlarge the piece.

incrusted (ĭn-krŭst'ĕd; in *crust* ed). 1. Inlaid, as lace set into fabric. 2. Studded, as with gems. 3. Overlaid or covered, as with gold.

Indestructible Voile (ĭn-dĕs-trŭk'tĭ-bl voil; in des *truck* ti bl voil). Trade name for type of durable, all-silk voile. Also called *Indestructible Flat Chiffon*.

India cotton. Heavy, figured chintz used as upholstery fabric.

India-cut. Cut in form similar to brilliant, with as little loss in weight as possible. Said of precious stones.

India linon (lĭn'ən; *lin* on). Fine, cotton lawn, closely woven in imitation of linen; slightly sized and usually bleached. Used for children's dresses, aprons, fancy work, waists, lingerie.

India muslin. Fine, soft, cotton fabric in plain weave, originally made in India; also, an imitation of that fabric.

Indian bonnet. Ornamental headdress of feathers, worn by American Indians. See BONNETS.

Indian embroidery. Any of several types of embroidery done by East Indian natives. See EMBROIDERIES.

Indian Head. Trade name for sturdy, firm, cotton material of linen-like weave, made in many lovely colors. Used for work, play, and sports clothing and for home furnishings.

India print. Cotton print in plain weave, with characteristic native pattern hand-blocked in glowing Oriental colors. Also, inexpensive imitations. See PRINTS.

India shawl. Costly shawl of East Indian make, usually of embroidered or figured cashmere. See CASHMERE, 3.

India silk. Thin, soft, plain-woven silk fabric.

indienne (F. ăṅ-dyĕn; an dyen). Printed or painted India muslin, introduced into France from England in 17th century; started tremendous vogue. Variously imitated.

indigo (ĭn'dĭ-gō; *in* di go). 1. Deep, pure violet-blue color. 2. Blue dye obtained from plants or made synthetically. Effective in dyeing many fibers. Also used as a rinse.

individuality (ĭn-dĭ-vĭd-ū-ăl'ĭ-tĭ; in di vid you *al* i ti). Expression of personal taste in dress. In favorable sense, the wearing of distinctive and becoming clothes rather than extremes of fashion.

indument (ĭn'dū-mənt; *in* due ment). Obsolete term for apparel, garment, covering.

influence (ĭn'flū-ĕns; *in* flew ence). Effect on styles, usually modification, due to prominence of some period, country, calling, etc.; as, costume showing Grecian or Cossack influence.

informal (ĭn-fôr'məl; in *for* mal). Suitable for wear on occasions not requiring full dress or formal evening dress; said of dinner dress or the like, worn when men wear business suits. See FORMAL.

infra-red. Red rays such as extend beyond the spectrum of a flame. See COLOR.

infula (ĭn'fū-lə; *in* few la). 1. Scarf-like band, usually of red and white wool, worn across head, with ends hanging free at each side. Adopted by ancient Romans as a symbol, chiefly of religious consecration. 2. One of two tabs at back of bishop's miter. 3. Type of chasuble worn by French and English clergy from 11th to 16th century.

ingénue (F. ăṅ-zhā-nū; an zhay nue). 1. Appropriate for younger woman. Said of style. 2. French word for unsophisticated. 2. Yellowish-green color.

ingrain hose. Lustrous hose knit from yarns degummed and dyed before knitting. See HOSE.

initialed (ĭ-nĭsh'əld; i *nish* ald). Marked with the first letter of a person's given name or full name.

inkle. Broad linen tape; formerly, woolen tape. See TAPES.
inlaid (ĭn-lād'; in laid). Set in, in place of material cut away, so as to form design.
inlay (ĭn'lā; in lay). 1. Ornamental material set into body of surface; also, to set in. 2. In sewing, part turned in at seam.
innovation (ĭn-ō-vā'shən; in o vay shun). Change to something new or novel.
insertion (ĭn-sẽr'shŭn; in ser shun). Narrow lace or embroidery, with plain edge on each side so that it can be set into fabric for ornamentation.
insertion stitch. Any open-seam stitch. See FAGOTING under STITCHES.
inset (ĭn'sĕt; in set). Piece of lace or fabric inserted into garment or other article for decoration or fit.
insignia (ĭn-sĭg'nĭ-ə; in sig ni a). Characteristic mark or emblem distinguishing anything; usually, sign of office or badge of honor.
insole (ĭn'sōl; in sole). 1. Inner or inside sole of shoe, to which upper is stitched and outside sole attached. 2. Separate strip, as of leather or felt, placed inside the shoe for comfort in walking.
inspiration (ĭn-spĭ-rā'shən; in spi ray shun). Origin of the influence affecting or producing a design.
instep (ĭn'stĕp; in step). Part of shoe, stocking, or last which covers upper front part of the arch of the foot from ankle to where it joins toes.
instep length. Length of dress or other garment which ends from 1 to 3 inches above the floor. See LENGTHS.
intaglio (ĭn-tăl'yō; in tal yo). Design in hard material, usually a gem, sunken or hollowed out below the surface.
intake (ĭn'tāk; in take). Point where stitches in knit or woven fabric are decreased, narrowing the fabric.
interlace (ĭn-tẽr-lās'; in ter lace). To lace together cord, ribbon, braid, or thread, usually producing symmetrical design. Also, ornament, as of ribbon, etc., so made.

interlining (ĭn'tẽr-līn-ĭng; in ter line ing). 1. Inner lining, placed in garment between the lining and outer fabric, for warmth or bulk. 2. Cotton or wool fabric used to interline. 3. Padding and lining quilted together.
interweave (ĭn-tẽr-wēv'; in ter weev). To weave together, usually into the texture of a fabric.
in the gray. In undyed, unbleached, or unfinished state. Said of fabric.
intimate apparel. Garments worn next to the body and covered by outer apparel; or garments worn only in the boudoir, as lingerie, negligee apparel, sleeping clothes, etc.
Inverness (ĭn-vẽr-nĕs'; in ver ness). Long, loose, sleeveless cape, fitted at neck and hanging from shoulders. See CAPES.
inverted plait. Plait similar to box plait in reverse. See PLAITS.
inverted-plait placket. Placket concealed under an inverted plait. See PLACKETS.
invest. Almost obsolete term meaning to put on, clothe, or dress.
investiture (ĭn-vĕs'tĭ-tūr; in vess ti ture). Clothing, especially robes of office.
investment. That which clothes; apparel; robes of office.
inweave (ĭn-wēv'; in weev). To weave into fabric as a component part; weave together.
inwrought (ĭn-rôt'; in rawt). Wrought or worked in as a component part.
Ionic chiton (ī-ŏn'ĭk kī'tən; eye on ic ky ton). Loose Grecian gown with sleeves. See CHITON, 2.
Irene Castle bob. Hair cut in manner introduced and made popular by Irene Castle, famous dancer. Worn back off forehead and loosely waved over ears. See BOBS.
iridescent (ĭr-ĭ-dĕs'ənt; iri dess ent). Of changing rainbow colors, as mother-of-pearl.
iris (ī'rĭs; eye riss). 1. Medium lavender-blue color. 2. Changeable, rainbow-like color effect.

Irish crochet. Crocheted lace with shamrock and rose designs. See LACES.
Irish lace. One of laces made in Ireland; especially, crochet lace with shamrock or rose designs surrounded by mesh. See LACES.
Irish linen. Fine, light-weight linen. See LINENS.
Irish poplin. Ribbed fabric, having fine silk warp and heavy worsted filling; originally made in Ireland.
Irish-stitch. Long, upright stitch worked diagonally on canvas. See STITCHES.
Irish work. White eyelet embroidery like MADEIRA. See EMBROIDERIES.
iron (ī'ẽrn; eye ern). Instrument used to smooth garments by means of heat and pressure. Same as FLATIRON.
iron hat. Piece of medieval armor worn to protect the head.
ironing. 1. Process of using heat and pressure to smooth out material. 2. Things to be ironed.
Italian cloth (ĭ-tăl'yən; i tal yan). Cotton- or wool-back satin used for linings. Same as FARMER'S SATIN. See SATINS.
Italian ferret (fĕr'ĕt; fare et). Narrow silk tape. See FERRET.
Italian hemstitching. Drawn-fabric stitch used as seam finish or as embroidery stitch. See STITCHES.
Italian relief-stitch. Single-purl stitches used in flower designs. See STITCHES.
Italian-stitch. Running-stitch done twice on the same line, making a solid line on both sides by filling in spaces ordinarily left between running-stitches. Same as DOUBLE RUNNING-STITCH. See STITCHES.
ivory (ī'və-rĭ; eye vo ri). 1. Hard, opaque substance of fine grain and creamy color, composing tusks of elephants and certain other mammals. Used for various accessories, ornaments, etc. 2. Light cream shade. Old ivory is slightly darker, more yellow.
izar (ĭz'ər; iz er). Piece of white cotton fabric worn as chief outer garment of Mohammedan women. Also loin covering of the IHRAM. Arabic word meaning veil.

J

jabot (zhă-bō'; zhah bo). Frill or ruffle, usually lace or lace-trimmed, worn down front of bodice, and fastened at neckline. Formerly, ruffle on man's shirt bosom.

18th Century Jabot

jabul (Sp. hă-bōōl'; ha bool). Outer garment worn by Philippine women. See WRAPS.
jacinth (jā'sĭnth; jay sinth). Gem stone

of orange color. In ancient times, same as HYACINTH, the gem.
jack. 1. Medieval coat of mail, cheap and coarse. Usually made of two thicknesses of leather, padded or lined with metal. 2. Jacket, or short, fitted garment. See JACKETS.
jack boot. Heavy, all-leather boot reaching above knee. See BOOTS.

JACKETS

jacket. Short, coat-like garment, with or without sleeves, opening down front, usually extending below hips.
acton. Padded or quilted jacket worn under medieval armor to prevent chafing; later, steel-plated jacket.
baju (bä'jōō; bah joo). Short, loose jacket open in front, usually of white cotton. Worn by men and women in Malay countries.
bed j. Short jacket of silk, lace, wool,

or other fabric, for wear over nightdress when sitting up in bed or for warmth when sleeping. Also called bed sacque.

Single-Breasted Jacket, 1930's

20th Century Beer Jacket

beer j. Straight box jacket, often of cotton, like man's work jumper.
bell-boy or **bell-hop j.** Fitted jacket, top-of-the-hip length, having johnny

jackets

jackets (continued) collar and epaulets, decorated with buttons; worn by hotel page boys.

20th Century Bell-Boy Jacket

bietle (bē′tl; *bee* tl). Jacket of deerskin, worn by North American Indian women.
blazer. Light-weight sports jacket, sleeved or sleeveless, semi-tailored, usually in bright color. So called because originally made in brilliant, vertical stripes. Worn as distinguishing garment of school, team, college, or the like, and for general sports wear.

Boy's Blazer

bolero (bə-lĕr′ō; bo *lare* o). Short jacket no longer than normal waistline, with or without sleeves. Worn open in front over bodice or blouse. Spanish in origin.

Type of Spanish Bolero

bush j. or **coat.** Belted, hip-length jacket, usually with two sets of pockets and tailored collar. Made of corduroy and other sturdy materials. Adaptation of hunting coat worn in African bush.

Bush Jacket, 1938

camisole (kăm′ĭ-sōl; *cam* i sole). 1. Short negligee jacket similar to bed sacque, formerly worn by women. 2. Jacket or jersey made with sleeves. Worn formerly by men.
canezou (F. kán-zōō; can zoo). Woman's jacket, often of lace, usually sleeveless.
cardigan (kär′dĭ-gən; *car* di gan). Plain, box-like type of sports jacket or short coat, open or buttoned down front, usually with long sleeves. Made of wool or silk fabric. Named for Earl of Cardigan, early 19th century.
carmagnole (kär-mə-ñōl′; car ma *nyole*). Jacket or short-skirted coat with lapels, wide collar, rows of metal buttons. Worn by Italian workmen in southern France; later adopted by French Revolutionists. Named for Carmagnola, Italy.
casaque (F. ká-zák; ka zack). French term for short jacket worn by jockeys, usually in the bright colors of their stables.
chaqueta (Sp. chá-ka′tà; chah *kay* tah). Heavy jacket, usually of leather. Worn by cowboys, chiefly in Texas.
dolman. Jacket worn as part of uniform by European hussars; fastened across shoulders like cape by chain or cord.
dressing sacque. Loose, wrist-length jacket, usually unbelted. Worn while making toilet. Modern version called *short smock*.
Eton j. (ē′tn; *ee* ton). Straight-cut jacket with broad lapels, open in front, reaching squarely to top of hips, as worn by boys of Eton College, England.

Eton Jacket

hug-me-tight. Close-fitting, knitted or crocheted jacket or shoulder piece; sometimes with sleeves, often without. Worn chiefly for warmth.
jack. Obsolete term for short, tight-fitting jacket.
jazerant (jăz′ẽr-ənt; *jazz* er ant). Jacket made of small, overlapping metal plates fastened into or mounted on foundation cloth. Worn as defensive armor.
jerkin (jẽr′kĭn; *jer* kin). Jacket, short coat, or doublet, sometimes of leather. Occasionally, waistcoat without sleeves.

15th Century Jerkin

jumper. 1. Woman's loose jacket worn over blouse or guimpe. 2. Loose jacket blouse worn by workmen to protect their clothes.
kabaya (kə-bä′yə; ka *bah* ya). Light-weight outer jacket, usually white and of cotton, often lace-trimmed or embroidered. Worn in Java and other Eastern countries, with the sarong.
Lindbergh j. Sturdy, warm jacket similar to Windbreaker, with deep pockets, and fitted waistband and wrists. Favored flying jacket of Colonel Charles A. Lindbergh, who made the first solo flight from West to East across the Atlantic Ocean.

Lindbergh Jacket

lumberjack. Short, straight coat or jacket, originally buttoned, now usually closed by slide fastener in front. Sometimes belted at back, often tightened at bottom line by buckles at sides. First made in imitation of coats worn by lumbermen. Worn by men and boys, and sometimes by women.
mess j. Short, fitted, tailless jacket, usually white. Originally, part of military and naval uniforms only. Now worn by civilians also on semi-formal occasions, usually for dinner, in summer and all year round in warm climates.
monkey j. Short, heavy, snugly fitted jacket. Worn in rough weather by sailors, etc.
Norfolk j. (nôr′fək; *nor* fok). Hip-length, belted jacket, single-breasted, box-plaited front and back.
paletot (păl′ə-tō; *pal* e toe). Close-fitting jacket of contrasting material; during 19th century, worn by women to complete costume.
patti sacque. Short, flared jacket with sleeves. Buttoned in front or back, or both.
pea j. Heavy, warm, woolen jacket, usually loose, short, and double-breasted. Worn by sailors, fishermen, etc.
penelope (pə-nĕl′ō-pĭ; pe *nell* o pi). British term for sleeveless, knitted jacket.
petersham (pē′tẽr-shăm; *pee* ter sham). Heavy jacket of rough-napped, woolen fabric, usually dark blue.
pilot coat or **j.** (pī′lət; *pie* lot). Pea jacket, or heavy, short, woolen coat.
polka (pōl′kə; *pole* ka). Woman's close-fitting, knitted jacket.
reefer. Close-fitting, generally double-breasted jacket or short coat of heavy cloth.
roundabout. Short, close-fitting, waist-length jacket worn by boys, mechanics, sailors, etc.

---
fāte, făt, dănce, ärt mē, mĕt, hẽr, thêre rĭde, rĭd nōte, nŏt, côrn, fōōd, fŏŏt cūte, cŭt, cûré now fin(ŋ)ger villa(ə) señor pleas(zh)ure

sacque or **sack.** Short, loose jacket with sleeves. Worn by women and children.

Bed Jacket, 1930's

shell j. Snugly fitted jacket, short in back. Worn by men on semi-formal occasions instead of tuxedo jacket.
simar (sĭ-mär'; si *mar*). Woman's loose-bodied outer jacket with side flaps or skirts extending to knee. Sometimes longer and worn over petticoat or waistcoat. Worn in 17th and 18th centuries.

17th Century Simar

smoking j. Jacket worn originally by men while smoking; lounging jacket. Often made of velvet or brocaded fabric bound and frogged with braid.
sontag (sŏn'tăg; *sonn* tag). Jacket or cape, either knitted or crocheted, with ends that cross in back. Named for Henriette Sontag, German singer.
spencer. 1. Tight-fitting jacket, often fur-trimmed; worn by women and children in 19th century. **2.** Short jacket worn by men in 19th century.

Spencer, 1802

tabard (tăb'ẽrd; *tab* erd). Formerly, short outer jacket made with or without sleeves. Worn by monks and commoners, especially in inclement weather.
temiak (těm-yăk'; tem *yak*). Eskimo jacket or coat made of bird skins. Worn by both sexes.
vareuse (F. vȧ-rẽz). Kind of loose, rough, woolen jacket worn in southern U. S. Similar to PEA JACKET.
wamus (wŏ'mŭs; *waw* muss). Type of cardigan jacket. Also, outer jacket of coarse, strong cloth, buttoned at collar and wrist bands. Worn in U. S. Also called *wammus, wampus.*

Watteau sacque. Outer jacket with box plait down back, looped pannier-fashion at sides. Worn during 18th century; so called in France.
Windbreaker. Trade name for sturdy, warm sports jacket with fitted waistband.
yellow j. Jacket of golden yellow silk, formerly worn on certain occasions as imperial emblem or conferred as high honor by Chinese ruler.
zouave j. (zōō-äv'; zoo *ahv*). Woman's short jacket with rounded front, made in imitation of jacket of Zouave uniform. Sometimes sleeveless.

jacket cape. Short cape-like garment. See CAPES.
Jacobean embroidery (jăk-ȧ-bē'ẽn; jack o *bee* an). English embroidery with Oriental influence. Has characteristic tree design. See EMBROIDERIES.
jaconet (jăk'ȧ-nĕt; *jack* o net). **1.** Thin, soft, cotton cloth, between cambric and muslin in texture. Used for dresses, infants' clothes, etc. **2.** Cotton fabric glazed on one side.
Jacquard fabric (jȧ-kärd'; ja *card*). Fabric with intricate figured weave done on Jacquard loom. See JACQUARD under WEAVES.
Jacquard loom. Loom having device for figure weaving, consisting of series of perforated cards that pass over rotating prism, allowing warp threads to be raised in such succession as to form pattern indicated by perforations.
Jacquard weave. Figured weave done on Jacquard loom. Used for brocades, damasks, tapestries, etc. See WEAVES.
jaquette (F. zhȧ-kĕt; zhah ket). French word meaning jacket.
jade. 1. Hard, dense gem stone, often highly polished; usually yellowish green in color, but often whitish, pinkish, or dark green. Used for jewelry, accessories, etc. **2.** Any of various shades of green. Also called *jade green.*
jager (yä'gẽr; *yah* ger). Diamond from South African mines of Jagersfontein, blue-white in color, of modern cut.
jam. British term for child's frock.
jama or **jamah** (jä'mȧ; *jah* ma). Long cotton garment worn by Moslems of northern India.
jamb (jăm; jam) or **jambe** (F. zhäɴb; zhomb). Piece of medieval armor worn as protection for leg. Also called *jambeau.*
jamdani (jäm-dä'nē; jahm *dah* nee). Hindu word for figured or flowered muslin.
Jane. 1. False hair worn over forehead. **2.** (Not capitalized) Variant spelling of JEAN.
japan (jȧ-păn'; ja *pan*). **1.** Varnish producing shiny surface, such as Japanese lacquer. Used on wood, metal, leather, etc. **2.** Formerly, silk from Japan.
Japanese. Characteristic of Japanese women's costume. Consists of long, figured garment, the KIMONO; long hanging sleeves; wide padded sash, the OBI; elaborate hairdress with combs and pins.
Japanese crepe. Cotton crepe imported from Japan. See CREPES.

Japanese embroidery. Elaborate silk embroidery in satin-stitch. See EMBROIDERIES.
Japanese or **Jap silk.** Thin, plain-woven silk fabric. See HABUTAI.
Japanese velvet. Velvet with dyed designs. See VELVETS.
japanned leather. Patent leather. See LEATHERS.
Jap marten. Fairly durable, yellowish fur of Japanese marten. See FURS.
Jap mink. Light yellowish mink fur, usually dyed. See FURS.
jardinière (F. zhȧr-dē-nyêr; zhar dee nyare). **1.** Design of many colors, composed of flowers, fruits, and leaves. Also, type of velvet with such designs. See VELVETS. **2.** Pendant ornament on woman's headdress of 18th century. **3.** In French, low ruffle.
jasey (jā'zē; *jay* zee). Colloquial term for wig of worsted. See WIGS.
jaspé (F. zhäs-pā; zhass pay). Having a clouded or streaked blending of colors, as jasper has.
jasper. 1. Green or any bright-colored variety of chalcedony except carnelian. See CHALCEDONY. **2.** Green, red, yellow, or brown variety of opaque, uncrystalline quartz. Used in costume jewelry, etc. **3.** Greenish-yellow color of green chalcedony. Also called *jasper green.*
jasper opal. Yellowish opal similar in appearance to jasper. Also called *jaspopal.*
jasponyx (jăs'pȧ-nĭx; *jass* po nix). Onyx with some or all of its layers consisting of jasper.
jaspopal (jăsp'ō-pȧl; *jasp* o pal). Same as JASPER OPAL.
jaune (F. zhōn; zhone). French word meaning yellow.
Java canvas (jä'vȧ; *jah* va). Coarse, open fabric used as foundation for embroidery. See CANVAS.
Java cotton. Silky vegetable fiber. Same as KAPOK.
Java lizard. Lizard with circular marking. See LEATHERS.
javelle water (zhȧ-vĕl'; zha *vell*). Bleaching solution. Used to remove ink stains and to whiten clothes.
jazerant (jăz'ẽr-ȧnt; *jazz* er ant). Jacket worn as part of armor. See JACKETS.
jean. 1. Heavy, twilled, cotton fabric. Light-weight DRILLING. Used for sturdy working clothes, uniforms, etc. **2.** (Plural) Clothes of this fabric.
jelab (jẽ-läb'; je *lahb*). Wide, woolen blouse or cloak with hood, worn by native Moroccans. Also spelled *jellab, jellib, jellabia.*
jelick (jĕl'ĭk or yĕl'ĭk; *jell* ick or *yell* ick). Turkish woman's garment — either long, tight-waisted coat, open on sides from hips down; or similar looser and wider garment. From Turkish word *yelek.*
jenny. Spinning machine. Short for SPINNING JENNY.
Jenny Lind costume. Fitted bodice with off-shoulder neckline, and bell-shaped hoop skirt often decorated with three graduated ruffles of lace, in the style of 1860; made famous by Jenny

Lind, the popular operatic soprano, known as "The Swedish Nightingale."

Type of 19th Century Costume Worn by Jenny Lind

jerkin (jẽr′kĭn; *jer* kin). Jacket, short coat, or doublet. See JACKETS.
jerry hat. British term for round felt hat. See HATS.
jersey (jẽr′zĭ; *jer* zi). **1.** Plain-knitted, very elastic, ribbed fabric; usually wool or worsted, but also silk, cotton, rayon, etc. Used for undergarments, dresses, suits, coats, sweaters, bathing suits, etc. Also called *jersey cloth*. **2.** Seamless, knitted shirt, pull-over style, worn for active sports. See SHIRTS. Also, any close-fitting jacket, usually of elastic fabric.
jet. 1. Deep black, compact mineral that takes a high polish. Used for buttons, trimmings, mourning jewelry. **2.** Velvety black color of the mineral.
jeune fille (F. zhĕn fē; zhun fee). French expression for young girl. Applied to simple, youthful styles.
jewel (jū′ĕl; *jew* el). **1.** Costly ornament of precious metal, enamel, etc., for personal decoration; usually set with gems. **2.** Precious stone as cut and set for personal wear.
jeweled. Adorned or set with jewels.
jeweling. Jeweled trimming for garment.
jewelry. Real or imitation jewels in general, or collectively; bracelets, necklaces, brooches, etc., either set with jewels or made of stone, metal, crystal, composition, etc. Worn for adornment. — **costume j.** Any jewelry not made of precious stones, usually colorful and showy; designed to complement particular types of costumes. — **novelty j.** (nŏv′el-tĭ; *nov* el ti). Costume jewelry of uncommon design, usually of novel shape, always inexpensive.
jibbah or **jibba** (jĭb′ə; *jib* a). Smock, or long shirt-like garment of similar cut. Probably derived from JUBBAH.
jigger coat. Short, semi-tailored, informal coat. See COATS.

jipijapa (Sp. hē-pē-hȧ-pá; hee pee hah pah). Straw or fiber of Central and South American plant used for making Panama hats. Named for town in Ecuador. Spanish term for PANAMA HAT. See HATS. See PANAMA under STRAWS.
jirkinet (jẽr-kĭn-ĕt′; jer kin *et*). Scottish term for woman's blouse or jacket.
Joan (jōn; jone). Woman's close-fitting cap. Worn in 18th century. See CAPS.
Joan of Arc costume. Costume of French peasant style worn by Joan of Arc, heroine of France. See FANCY DRESS.
Job's tears (jōbz tērz; jobes teerz). **1.** Hard, pearl-like seeds of grass grown in India; used as beads and strung into necklaces. **2.** Greenish grains of chrysolite mineral used as gems.
jockey boot. High leather or rubber boot.¹ Same as TOP BOOT. See BOOTS.
jockey cap. Small, long-visored cap. See CAPS. Also, woman's hat in imitation of original cap. See HATS.
jockey coat. Obsolete term for overcoat. See COATS.
jodhpur (jŏd′pŏŏr; *jode* poor). Shoe for horseback riding. See SHOES.
jodhpurs. Breeches cut full above the knee, closely fitted below, with cuff at ankle, sometimes with strap under foot; designed for horseback riding.

Jodhpurs, 1930's

johnny collar. Small, standing collar. See COLLARS.
joined-leg crotch. Crotch formed by joining of leg seams. See CROTCH.
jonquil (jŏng′kwĭl; *jong* kwill). Bright yellow color matching the jonquil flower. Also called *jonquil yellow*.
joseph (jō′zĕf; *joe* zef). Lady's riding habit, buttoned down the front; popular in colonial America. When worn open, popularly called *flying Josie*. Also applied to other types of coats.
Josephine knot (jō′zĕf-ēn; *joe* zef een). Ornamental knot with ends free for use. See KNOTS.
jours (F. zhōor; zhoor). Open stitches used as fillings in lacemaking.

Jouy print (F. zhōō-ē; zhoo ee). Cotton or linen fabric printed with 18th century French design. See PRINTS.
jubbah (jōōb′bə; *joob* a). Long outer garment worn in Near East. See WRAPS.
juchten (yōōk′tən; *yook* ten). Same as Russia leather, originally bark-tanned calfskin. See LEATHERS.
jugler. Tie string of feathers or fur for woman's bonnet. High fashion during 1880's.
Jugoslavian embroidery (yōō′gō-släv′ĭ-ən; *you* go *slahv* i an). Colored wool embroidery of geometrical designs. See EMBROIDERIES.
Juliet (jū′lĭ-ĕt; *jew* li et). House slipper worn by women. See SLIPPERS.
Juliet cap. Small, round cap of wide, open mesh, usually decorated with pearls or other jewels. See CAPS.
jump. 1. Man's coat or jacket. See COATS. **2.** (Plural) Short stays, or bodice worn in 18th century instead of stays. Also called *jimps*.
jumper. 1. Loose, unfitted garment, usually having boat neck and short kimono sleeves. **2.** Loose jacket-blouse worn by workmen. See JACKETS. **3.** Short, slip-on, hooded garment of fur, worn in arctic regions. **4.** Loose jacket, often slip-on, worn by women. See JACKETS. **5.** Sailor's overshirt, or middy blouse.
jumper dress. Sleeveless, one-piece garment worn with guimpe. See DRESSES.
jumpers. Rompers, or combination waist and bloomers, worn by children.
jupe (jōop or F. zhüp; joop or zhoop). **1.** Inferior linen. **2.** Man's heavy jacket, coat, or tunic. **3.** Petticoat or skirt of dress. **4.** Man's shirt or woman's waist. **5.** (Plural) Stays.
jupon (jū′pŏn or F. zhü-pôṅ; *jew* pon or zhoo ponh). **1.** Fabric with cotton warp and woolen filling, woven on plain loom. **2.** Tight-fitting military garment without sleeves, extending below hips. Part of medieval armor. **3.** Short petticoat or skirt. **4.** Obsolete term for woman's jacket.
jusi (hōō′sē; *hoo* see). Delicate dress fabric of pure silk, not degummed; or silk with hemp or pineapple fibers, made in Philippine Islands. Vegetable fibers are tied, not spun.
juste-au-corps or **justaucorps** (F. zhüs-tō kôr; zhoost o core). Close-fitting, long-skirted coat or doublet of 17th and 18th centuries. See COATS.
jute. Glossy fiber from East Indian jute plant. Used for sacking, burlap, twine. Mixed with silk, wool, etc., in fabrics.

K

kabaya (ka-bä′ya; ka *bah* ya). Lightweight, short coat. See JACKETS.
kaffiyeh (ka-fē′yĕ; ka *fee* yeh). Large, square kerchief; folded diagonally, worn over head, falling to shoulders. Usually of cotton with colorful silk stripes or figures; often tasseled. Worn with AGAL as common head covering of Bedouin Arabs. Also spelled *keffieh, kuffieh, kufiyeh*.
kaitaka (kä′ē-tä-kä; *kah* ee tah kah). Finely woven mantle worn in New Zealand. See WRAPS.
kalamkari (kăl-ăm-kär′ə; kal am *car* ee). East Indian cotton fabrics printed by method in which design is first hand-drawn with pen, and colors are applied by hand afterward.
kalmuck (kăl′mŭk; *kal* muck). Cotton or wool cloth with coarse, hairy nap; also, coarse, dyed, Persian cotton.
kalyptra (ka-lĭp′tra; ka *lip* tra). Veil worn by women of ancient Greece. See VEILS.

kambal (kŭm′băl; *kum* bal). Coarse wool shawl or blanket. See WRAPS.
kamelaukion (kăm-ə-lô′kĭ-ən; *kam* e *law* ki on). Oriental priest's hat. See HATS.
kamik (kă′mĭk; *kah* mick). Eskimo boot. See BOOTS.
kamis (kȧ-mēs′; ka *meece*). Loose shirt or tunic-like garment worn by Orientals. See CAMISE.
kangaroo leather (kăng-gə-rōō′; kang ga *roo*). Fine, tough leather made from kangaroo skin. See LEATHERS.
kapa (kä′pä; *kah* pah). Hawaiian cloth made of bark.
kapok (kā′pŏk; *kay* pock). Mass of silky fibers from a tropical silk-cotton tree. Used as filling for muffs, cushions, pillows, mattresses, etc.
karakul (kăr′ə-kŭl; *ka* ra kul). Variant spelling of CARACUL. See FURS.
kaross (kȧ-rŏs′; ka *ross*). Garment of skins. See WRAPS.
Kasha (kăsh′ə; *cash* a). Trade name for soft silky fabric of wool mixed with goat hair in twill weave. Type of flannel.
Kashmir. Variant spelling of CASHMERE.
Kate Greenaway. Name applied to various children's garments designed by Kate Greenaway, English illustrator, writer, and designer. Styles have characteristics of Empire period, high waistlines, frilled necks and sleeves, bonnets. See BONNETS.

Kate Greenaway Dress, Coat, 1890's

Keds. Trade name for rubber-soled shoes. See SHOES.
kelt. Undyed, homespun cloth, usually black-and-white wool mixture.
kemp. Short, harsh wool. See WOOL.
Kendal or **Kendal green** (kĕn′dəl; *ken* dal). Coarse, woolen cloth, colored green by weavers of Kendal, England. Also, the green color.
Kensington-stitch (kĕn′zĭng-tən; *ken* zing ton). Alternating long and short stitches. See STITCHES.
kepi (kĕp′ĭ; *kep* i). Flat-topped military cap with visor. See CAPS.
Keratol (kĕr′ə-tŏl; *care* a tol). Trade name for type of hard, artificial leather.
kerchief (kĕr′chĭf; *ker* chif). Large square of cloth, usually patterned in color. Worn as head covering or as a neck scarf.
kersey (kẽr′zĭ; *ker* zi). Stout, twilled fabric, with all-wool or cotton warp, closely napped. Like broadcloth, but heavier, because of heavy backing yarn. Used originally for hose; now, for coats, etc.
kerseymere (kẽr′zĭ-mēr; *ker* zi meer).

Kind of woolen cloth. Same as CASSIMERE.
khaddar (kŭd′ēr; *cud* er). Homespun cotton cloth made in India.
khaiki (kī′kĭ; *ky* ki). Japanese all-silk fabric. Used for dresses, blouses, unlined coats.
khaki (kä′kĭ; *kah* ki). **1.** Dark olive-drab color. **2.** Sturdy, twilled cotton fabric of olive-drab color. Used for uniforms, work clothes, riding clothes, etc. See DRILLING.
khirka or **khirkah** (kēr′kä; *keer* kah). Mantle worn by Moslem dervishes. See WRAPS.
kick plait. Plait at side of narrow skirt. See PLAITS.
kid. Leather tanned from skins of goats. See LEATHERS.
kid caracul. Beautifully marked Chinese kidskins, dyed in many shades. See FURS.
kid mohair. Fine hair of young goats. See MOHAIR.
kidskin. Perishable fur of young goats. See FURS.
Kiki skirt. Extremely short, tight skirt. See SKIRTS.
Kilmarnock bonnet (kĭl-mär′nək; kill *mar* nock). Woolen cap worn in Scotland. See CAPS.
kilt. 1. Short, plaited skirt. See SKIRTS. **2.** To plait in folds like those of a kilt.
kiltie tongue. Extended shoe tongue, forming a fringed leather flap over the laces. Used on sports shoes. See TONGUE, 1.
kilting. Series of kilt plaits.
kilt plait. Large, vertical plait lapping over next one. See PLAITS.
kimono. 1. Negligee cut in manner of Japanese kimono. **2.** Garment typical of Japanese costume, made as loose, wide-sleeved robe, fastened around waist with broad sash.

Type of Kimono

kimono dress. Dress made with kimono sleeves. See DRESSES.
kimono flannel. Soft cotton flannel with printed designs. Same as FLANNEL-ETTE.
kimono sleeve. Sleeve cut in one piece with body of garment. Usually short. See SLEEVES.
Kindergarten cloth (kĭn′dēr-gär-tən; *kin* der gar ten). Trade name for stout, smooth-surfaced, closely woven cotton fabric, in plain weave, usually striped. Used for children's clothes.
kinetic silhouette (kĭ-nĕt′ĭk sĭl-ōō-ĕt′;

ki *net* ic sill oo *et*). Silhouette suggesting motion. Achieved by plaits, flared gores, etc. Popularized by Lucien Lelong, Paris couturier, in 1926. See SILHOUETTES.
kip. Raw or dressed pelt of young steer, cow, or horse. In the leather trade, kips weigh from 15 to 25 pounds. Distinguished from SKIN and HIDE.
kirtle (kẽr′tl; *ker* tl). Loose gown or tunic; garment with skirt.
kit fox. Durable fur of small fox. See FURS.
kittel (kĭt′ĕl; *kit* el). White cotton gown worn by orthodox Jews for solemn ceremonies and for burial.
klompen (klŏmp′ən; *klomp* en). Dutch wooden shoes. See SHOES.
knee breeches. Breeches reaching just below knee, usually snugly fitted.
knickerbockers (nĭk′ēr-bŏk-ẽrz; *nick* er bock erz). Loose breeches banded below knee. Worn for sports. Often called *knickers.*

Knickerbockers

knickknack (nĭk′năk; *nick* nack). Small or trivial article, more for ornament than use.
knife plaits (nīf plĕts; nife pleets). Rather narrow plaits, pressed to sharpness. Usually all run the same way around a skirt. See PLAITS.
knitted suit or **sweater suit.** Matching, knitted sweater and skirt, sometimes with jacket. See SUITS.

KNITTING

knitting (nĭt′ĭng; *nit* ing). Process of making fabric by interlocking series of loops of continuous thread or yarn. Done by hand for centuries; later, also by machine. Hand knitting done on straight or curved needles. Stitches are slipped from one needle to the other, each change making one stitch. Also, fabric so made or work to be done by knitting.
circular k. In hand knitting, work done on curved needle by knitting round and round. In machine knitting, type of weft knitting done in tubular form. Sometimes called *tubular knitting.*
drop stitch k. Machine knitting with open design formed by removing certain needles at set intervals.
flat k. Type of knitting done in flat form. Handmade on straight needles by knitting back and forth from side to side. Used for all flat work — scarfs, bedspreads, etc. — also, for sweaters, blouses, and mittens that have a side seam. Machine knitting done flat for many types of garments, notably full-

fāte, făt, dȧnce, ärt mē, mĕt, hẽr, thêre rīde, rĭd nōte, nŏt, côrn, fōōd, fŏŏt cūte, cŭt, cūre now fin(ŋ)ger villa(ȧ) seńor pleas(zh)ure

knitting (continued)
fashioned hose. Flat knitting permits fashioning or shaping of the fabric for fitting purposes or to individual measurements.

milanese k. (mĭl-ə-nēz'; mill a *nees*). Type of warp knitting with two sets of threads knit in diagonal crossing or diamond effect. Almost runproof. Done by machine and used both for undergarments and outer wear in variety of plaids and checks.

overhand k. Style of hand knitting in which one needle is held stationary while the action occurs on the other one.

plain k. Plain hand knitting in the basic stitch. Used for body of plain sweaters, stockings, mittens, etc. Also, simplest form of machine knitting, in which each loop is held by the one above and yarns run across fabric. Will run if a break occurs in any loop. BALBRIGGAN and JERSEY are machine-made examples. Used for both undergarments and outer garments and made in many weights and gauges.

raschel k. (rä-shĕl'; ra *shell*). Type of warp knitting resembling tricot, but coarser. Done by machine in plain and Jacquard patterns, often with lacy effect. Used for underwear.

tricot k. (trē'kō; *tree* ko). Type of warp knitting made either single or double by having one or two sets of threads. Almost runproof in single and absolutely so in double by reason of construction. Made by machine in variety of patterns. Used for dresses, underwear, bathing suits, gloves, hats, etc. Glove silk is example of this weave.

tuck stitch k. Type of circular machine knitting done in variety of patterns and tuck effects by making certain needles pick up more than one stitch at once. Used in undergarments and outer garments, warm pajamas; also used to make imitation fashion marks in hose.

warp k. Knitting in which series of yarns are placed next to each other on different needles and worked lengthwise of cloth in zigzag fashion. Knit flat by machinery.

weft k. Knitting in which one continuous thread goes round and round, crosswise of the fabric, forming a tube, or back and forth, forming flat fabric. Done by hand or machine.

knitting needle. Bluntly pointed rod, available in many lengths and sizes. Used in hand knitting. See NEEDLES.

knit underwear. Underwear knit by machine, either tubular or flat. Made of silk, cotton, wool, rayon, or mixed fibers.

knitwear (nĭt'wêr; *nit* ware). Any wearing apparel knitted by hand or by machine. Mostly used in connection with knitted sportswear.

knop (nŏp; nop). Obsolete word for button; also, a knob.

KNOTS

knot. 1. Tie or fastening in cord, thread, etc., forming a lump. 2. Ornamental bow of ribbon, silk, lace, etc.

Chinese k. Name given to any of several varieties of ornamental knots made of one or two covered cords. Used as trimming on suits and dresses.

Josephine k. Ornamental knot made like a sailor's carrick bend, that is, consisting of two loops so interlaced that the two ends of each loop remain free for use at opposite ends of the knot. Used for trimming.

love k. Decorative knot of ribbon, originally worn as token of love.

lover's k. Ornamental knot of two or more cords intertwined in loops, originally symbolizing constancy of true love.

macramé k. (măk'rə-mā; *mac* ra may). Knot made with two, three, or four threads so that end thread of group encloses the others. Used in MACRAMÉ LACE.

shoulder k. 1. Ornamental knot of ribbon, braid, or lace worn on shoulder in 17th and 18th centuries. 2. Military shoulder ornament of gold wire, worn on certain occasions.

tailor's k. Knot at the end of a needleful of thread. Used by all persons who sew by hand. Made by bringing the thread around the end of the forefinger, crossing the thread, then rolling the thread off the finger with the thumb. The loop thus made is pulled down to form a small, secure knot.

knot-stitch. Basic stitch in which knot of thread is formed on fabric surface. See STITCHES.

knotted work. Lace made by knotting thread. See LACES.

kolinsky (kə-lĭn'skĭ; ko *lin* ski). Fur of Asiatic mink. See FURS.

kolobion (kə-lō'bĭ-ən; ko *lo* bi an). Short-sleeved tunic of ancient Greece.

kooletah (kōō'lĕ-tä; *koo* le tah). Eskimo coat of fur. See COATS.

Kossuth hat (kŏs'ōōth; *koss* ooth). Hat made popular by Louis Kossuth. See HATS.

Koverzip. Trade name for a slide fastener that has the metal part covered with a ribbon or tape.

krimmer. Gray fur resembling Persian lamb. See FURS.

kulah (kōō-lä'; koo *lah*). Cap worn by Moslem monks. See CAPS.

kumbi (kōōm'bĭ; *koom* bi). Silky fiber of white silk-cotton tree found in India. Resembles KAPOK.

kusti (kōōs-tē'; kooss *tee*). Woolen cord worn as girdle by Parsis, a religious sect in India who fled there from Persia to escape persecution in the 8th century.

Kwik. Trade name for a slide fastener.

L

lac (lăk; lack). Substance like resin produced by certain insects cultivated in India and elsewhere. Purified, solidified, and otherwise treated for use in shellac, scarlet dye, lacquer, etc.

LACES

lace. 1. Open-work fabric consisting of network of threads — linen, cotton, silk, wool, rayon, metal, or other fiber — usually having designs worked in or applied. Made by hand with bobbins, needles, or hooks; also by machinery. Used for trimming on lingerie, dresses, suits, coats, etc.; also for entire garments or accessories. 2. String or cord, usually made of leather or fabric, passing through eyelets. Used in shoes, garments, etc., for fastening or decoration. Also, to fasten or draw together with such a string or cord.

Alençon l. (F. à-lôṅ-sôṅ; a lonh sonh). Delicate, durable, needle-point lace, having solid design outlined with cord on sheer net ground; handmade in Alençon, France. Best machine-made imitations have cords run in by hand.

Alençon

allover l. Any wide lace with pattern repeated over entire surface, finished the same on both edges. Used for entire garments or parts.

aloe l. (ăl'ō; *al* o). Fragile lace made from aloe plant fibers in Philippines, Italy, etc.

antique l. (ăn-tēk'; an *teek*). Handmade bobbin lace of heavy linen thread, with large, often irregular, square, knotted net on which designs are darned. Also called *opus araneum* and *spider work*. Imitation antique lace used in draperies.

Antwerp pot l. (ănt'wêrp; *ant* werp). 1. Rare bobbin lace with basket or pot of flowers in its design, the only remnant of the original design representing the Annunciation, or announcement to the Virgin Mary of the incarnation. Formerly much used by Antwerp women as trimming for caps. 2. Needle-point edging.

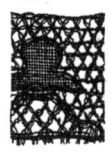

Antwerp Pot Lace

Arabian l. Coarse and heavy needle-point, usually ecru or drab in color, with a heavy, darker cord. Imitations inexpensive, but unsatisfactory. Used for curtains.

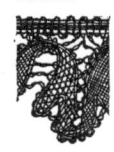

Arabian Lace

araneum l. (ə-rā′nĭ-ŭm; a *ray* ni um). Coarse, open form of darned work. See ANTIQUE LACE.
Argentan l. (är′jĕn-tăn; *ahr* jen tan). Alençon type of needle-point lace, with bolder, flatter, floral pattern, elaborated by open work, and background of strong, open, hexagonal mesh. Used for edging, insertion, banding.
Armenian l. (är-mē′nĭ-ən; ahr *mee* ni an). Handmade, knotted, narrow edging in pointed scallops, each reinforced by loops on one side. Used as edging for lingerie, handkerchiefs, collars and cuffs, infants' wear. Also machine-made.
arras l. (ăr′əs; *ar* ass). Bobbin lace, similar to Lille. Made at Arras, France.
Ave Maria l. (ä′vĕ mə-rē′ə; *ah* vay ma *ree* a). Narrow type of DIEPPE POINT LACE.
baby l. Very narrow lace, used for edging, especially in making layettes and trimming dainty garments for children. Called *baby lace* because extremely narrow width originally confined it to baby caps, baptismal dresses, etc.
Battenberg l. (băt′tĕn-bērg; *bat* en berg). Coarser form of Renaissance lace, made by hand or machine, of linen braid or tape and linen thread brought together to form various designs. Handmade Battenberg used for collars and cuffs; machine-made, for draperies, fancy work, etc.

Battenberg

Bavarian l. (bə-vā′rĭ-ən; ba *vay* ri an). Simple bobbin lace. See TORCHON LACE.
beggar's l. Name given to a type of torchon lace in the 16th century because it was cheap and easily made. See TORCHON LACE.
biliment l. (bĭl′ĭ-mənt; *bill* i ment). Lace, usually of gold threads, ornamented with jewels, as worn decoratively on 16th century headdress.
Binche l. (F. băpsh; bansh). Flemish bobbin lace resembling Valenciennes, originating in the 17th century, and having scroll floral pattern and ground

sprinkled with figures like snowflakes. Widely used for dresses, blouses, and neckwear.

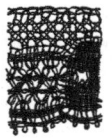

Binche

blonde l. Silk bobbin lace, closely woven, originally in white and cream colors only. In the trade, silk bobbin lace of any color.

Blonde

bobbin l. Untied lace mesh, handmade by means of bobbins worked back and forth over design marked with pins on pillow or cushion. So called to distinguish it from needle-made lace. Also called *pillow lace, bone lace.*
Bohemian l. (bō-hē′mĭ-ən; bo *hee* mi an). Bobbin lace with design in braid or tape effect, imitated effectively by machine. Used for trimming on coarse materials.

Bohemian Lace

bone l. Same as BOBBIN LACE. So called because original bobbins were of bone.
bourdon l. (bŏŏr′dn or F. bōōr-dôṇ; *boor* dun or boor donh). Net lace, having pattern and outer edge outlined with cording.
Breton l. (brĕt′ən; *bret* on). Net having design embroidered with heavy thread, often colored.

Breton Lace

bridal l. Type of reticella or drawn lace, having patterns of coats of arms or initials. Made in Italy during 16th

century. Chiefly used for weddings. Same as CARNIVAL LACE.
Bruges l. (F. brüzh; broozh). Fine, guipure tape lace, similar to duchesse but coarser, made with bobbins. Fine weaves used for dresses; coarse weaves, for curtains and table linen finishes.

Bruges

Brussels l. Now, machine-made net lace, with designs made separately and appliquéd. Formerly, lace with ground made with bobbins around either needle-point or pillow designs. Used for dress trimmings.

Brussels Lace

Buckingham or **Buckinghamshire** l. (bŭk′ĭng-əm; *buck* ing am). Dainty bobbin lace worked in one piece; celebrated for fine, clear ground, with simple pattern accentuated. Made in Buckinghamshire, England, since 16th century. Also laces made by Lille, Maltese, and trolley methods.
bullion l. (bŏŏl′yŭn; *bull* yun). Ancient heavy lace in simple patterns, made with gold or silver thread.
Burano l. (bū-rä′nō; bue *rah* no). Needle-point lace made on the island of Burano, Venice, with square mesh, cloudy effect, and cordonnet not overcast. Similar to Alençon.
buratto l. (bū-rät′tō; bue *raht* toe). Filet type of lace, with two lengthwise threads to each crosswise thread. Design is worked in after ground is woven. Dates back to 16th century. Used chiefly for church and table decorations. Many good machine imitations.

Machine-Made Buratto Lace

carnival or **carnaval** l. (kär′nĭ-vəl; *car* ni val). Type of reticella lace, having heraldic patterns distinctive of owner. Part of trousseau of 16th century brides in Italy, Spain, France; worn afterwards on state occasions. Same as BRIDAL LACE.
Carrickmacross l. (kăr-ĭk-mə-krŏs′; ca rick ma *cross*). Irish needle-point lace made in appliqué or guipure types.

fāte, făt, dånce, ärt mē, mĕt, hēr, thêre rīde, rĭd nōte, nŏt, côrn, fōōd, fŏŏt cūte, cŭt, cūré now fin(ŋ)ger villa(ə) señor pleas(zh)ure

laces

laces (continued)
— **appliqué C.** Lace made by applying designs of sheer fabric to plain, machine-made net, with buttonhole- or chain-stitch, and cutting away material

Appliqué Carrickmacross Lace

around design. — **guipure C.** Lace resembling cut work, with outline of the design worked over foundation of mull or lawn and motifs connected by brides or loops. Used for dresses and trimmings; machine-made type used for curtains.

Guipure Carrickmacross Lace

Chantilly l. (shăn-tĭl'ĭ or F. shäṅ-tē-yē; shan *till* i or shonh tee yee). Bobbin lace with fine ground and designs outlined by cordonnet of thick, silky threads. Closely imitated by machine. Used for dresses and draperies. — **black C.** Expensive but durable variety made of non-lustrous silk.

Chantilly

chenille l. (shə-nĕl'; shen *neel*). Needle-point lace, made in France in 18th century, with design outlined in white chenille on ground of silk net with six-sided meshes.
Cluny l. Bobbin lace like torchon, made of heavy, ivory-white linen or cotton thread, usually with paddle or wheel designs. Machine-made type usually of cotton. Fine weaves used for dress trimming, blouses, and dresses; coarser weaves, for linen trimming, etc.

Cluny

colbertine or **colberteen** (kŏl'bẽr-tēn; *col* ber teen). Coarse French lace, more like net, having open, square mesh. So named for J. B. Colbert, French minister of 17th century.
copper l. Lace of old-copper color.
Crete l. Loose bobbin lace of colored flax with geometrical figures, made on the island of Crete.
crochet l. (krō-shā'; cro *shay*). Lace made with a single thread and a hooked needle called a CROCHET HOOK. The thread is held in one hand; the hook, in the other. The hook picks up the thread, forms one loop and then another, as part of a chain. Thread is picked up again and again by needle to form double and treble stitches. Sometimes designs made separately and applied to bobbin- or machine-made net. Imitations made by machine. See IRISH CROCHET.

Crochet

Damascene l. (dăm'ə-sēn; *dam a* seen). Imitation of Honiton with sprigs and braids of lace joined by corded bars, without needlework filling.
darned l. Term applied to all lace, such as filet, where pattern is filled in by needlework.
dentelle de la Vierge (F. däṅ-tĕl də lȧ vyĕrzh; donh tell de lah vyairzh). Wider type of DIEPPE POINT LACE.
Devonshire l. (dĕv'ən-shēr; *dev* on sher). Honiton lace; formerly, imitations of many other types of lace.
Dieppe point l. (F. də-ĕp; dee ep). Bobbin lace of Valenciennes type, made at Dieppe, France, in 17th and 18th centuries. Narrow type known as *Ave Maria* and *poussin*. Wider type called *dentelle de la Vierge*.
Dresden point l. (drĕz'dən; *drez* den). 1. Type of drawn work made in Dresden, Germany, in 18th century. Ground of fine linen with some threads drawn and others embroidered and interlaced to form square mesh. 2. Coarse modern pillow lace.
duchesse l. (F. dü-shĕs; du shess). Original type of beautiful bobbin lace having delicate, tape-like effect, but not made of tape. Like Honiton, but in finer thread and having more raised work and daintier designs. Used on elaborate dresses, such as bridal gowns. Motifs of duchesse imitated in PRINCESSE LACE. Also called *guipure de Bruges*.

Duchesse

Egyptian l. (ə-jĭp'shən; e *jip* shun). Fine, expensive, handmade, knotted lace, often having beads worked in between meshes. Used for trimming.

Egyptian Lace

fiber l. Frail and expensive lace made of banana and aloe fibers. Used as trimming for sheer fabrics.

Fiber Lace

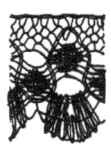

filet l. (fĭ-lā'; fi *lay*). Handmade, open-mesh lace, with patterns formed by filling certain squares of the knotted mesh foundation with darning-stitches. Imitation made by machine. Used for lingerie, linens, neckwear, trimmings; sometimes, for dresses and blouses. Also called *darned filet lace*.

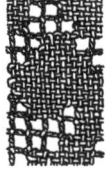

Filet Lace

flat point l. 1. Needle-point lace without any raised parts. Specifically, type of Venetian point. 2. Sprigs and flowers made separately on pillow for duchesse, Brussels, and Honiton. Also called *point plat*.
Genoa l. (jĕn'ō-ə; *jen* o a). Any of several types of lace made in Genoa, Italy, center of lacemaking in 17th century. Term includes pillow and needle-point, gold and silver, bobbin, tape, macramé laces.
gold l. Lace or braid, usually having silk weft threads covered with gilt or gold leaf. Formerly made of gold wire.
Greek l. Heavy needle-point lace. Same as RETICELLA.
gros point (F. grō pwăṅ; gro pwanh). Venetian point lace characterized by raised work, large designs. Also called *gros point de Venise*.
guipure (gē-pür' or F. gē-pür; gee *pure* or gee poor). Lace of heavy material, large pattern, usually either having no ground or having designs joined or held in place by bars or coarse threads; also, having coarse net ground. Originally, kind of lace made with

fāte, făt, dȧnce, ärt mē, mĕt, hẽr, thêre rīde, rĭd nōte, nŏt, côrn, fōod, fŏot cūte, cŭt, cûre now fin(ŋ)ger villa(ȧ) señor pleas(zh)ure

twisted cord which raised pattern into relief. Types include MALTESE and HONITON.

guipure de Bruges (F. də brüzh; de broozh). Same as DUCHESSE LACE.

hairpin l. Lace having looped edges, usually used as insertion. Made on a firm hairpin by winding thread around, then catching the threads together in the center with a crochet hook.

Hairpin Lace

hollie point l. Medieval, needle-point, church lace worked in hollie-stitch with designs of scriptural subjects or religious emblems. After 16th century, used also for wear by Puritans. Originally called *holy point*, from its religious purpose.

Honiton l. (hŏn′ĭ-tən; *hon* i ton). Term now applied to bobbin lace similar

Honiton Lace

to duchesse. — **appliqué H.** Lace for which motifs are made separately and sewed to net ground, which is often machine-made. — **guipure H.** — Lace with round, heavy motifs made up of fine braid, joined by needle-made brides.

Huguenot l. (hū′gə-nŏt; *hue* ga not). Simple imitation lace, with designs cut out of mull and mounted on net.

Irish crochet. Durable, crocheted lace consisting of medallions in rose, shamrock, or leaf design, surrounded by square, chain-stitch meshes, often ornamented with picots, and finished with a scalloped edge. Copy of needle-point lace of Spain and Venice. Best variety made in Ireland; next, in France or Belgium; cheap imitations made in China and Japan. Used as edging, insertion, medallions.

Irish l. Variety of laces made in Ireland. Best known are crochet, net embroideries of Limerick, and Carrickmacross cut work or Irish guipure.

knotted work. Lace made by knotting threads to form patterns, rather than stitching, as in needle-point, or intertwining threads, as in bobbin lace, or looping a single thread, as in crochet. Best example is macramé.

lacis (lā′sĭs; *lay* sis). Old name for square-mesh net foundation on which darned laces are made. Also, lace made on such net.

Lille l. (lēl; leel). Fine, bobbin lace like Mechlin, having patterns outlined with heavy, flat cordonnet. Sometimes dotted.

Lille Lace

Limerick l. (lĭm′ĕr-ĭk; *lim* er ick). **1.** Lace of patterns delicately embroidered on net with darning-stitch. **2.** Machine-made net with applied design of muslin with buttonholed edges. Imitated cheaply but not perfectly by machines. Used for trimming, but expensive.

Limerick Lace

Lisle l. Fine, filmy bobbin lace. Same as LILLE LACE.

macramé l. (măk′rə-mā; *mac* ra may). Knotted lace of Arabian origin, often fringed; woven in geometrical patterns from the selvage down, with many ends knotted together. Silk type used for scarf and shawl ends; coarse, for bedspreads, table covers, etc. Made largely at Genoa, Italy.

Macramé Lace

malines (má-lēn′; ma *leen*). Lace of Mechlin type made at Malines, Belgium. See MECHLIN.

Maltese l. (môl-tēz′; mawl *tees*). **1.** Bobbin lace, originally resembling Mechlin and Val laces in design. **2.** Now, guipure lace with simple, geometrical designs in which the Maltese cross and dots are used.

Maltese Lace

Margot l. (mär′gō; *mar* go). Showy, fragile, modern lace with sketchy design

machine-embroidered in heavy, cotton thread on ground of light-weight, silk net. Used for flounces, ruffles, etc.

Margot Lace

Mechlin l. (měk′lĭn; *meck* lin). Filmy bobbin lace with closely woven design of ornaments and flowers, outlined with a flat, shiny cordonnet. Net ground of six-sided mesh formed with the pattern.

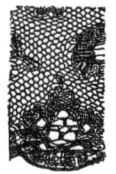

Mechlin Lace

Medici l. (měd′ĭ-chē; *med* i chee). French bobbin lace, often with intricate motifs; similar to Cluny, but of finer thread. Like insertion, but one edge is finished with shallow scallops. Alternates close-woven work with open work.

Medici Lace

metal l. Lace with net foundation on which designs are woven in silver, gold, or copper threads, either by hand or machine.

mignonette l. (mĭn-yŭn-ět′; min yun et). One of first bobbin laces made; light and fine, with open ground, made in narrow widths. Resembles tulle.

Milan l. (mĭ-lăn′; mi *lan*). Tape lace with needle-point mesh and picot edging. Easily imitated by machine. Modern types used as edging and insertion; also as shaped pieces for collars and fancy linens.

Moorish l. Moroccan lace of 16th and 17th centuries, similar to MALTESE LACE.

needle-point l. Lace made entirely with a sewing needle rather than bobbins. Worked with buttonhole- and blanket-stitches on paper pattern.

Northampton l. English 17th and 18th century bobbin lace imitating Flemish designs.

Nottingham l. (nŏt′ĭng-əm; *not* ing am). Any flat lace made by machine in Nottingham, England. Val, Cluny, torchon, curtain laces, etc., and many kinds of net made there.

laces (continued)

opus araneum (ŏ′pŭs ə-rā′nĭ-ŭm; *o* pus a *ray* ni um). Handmade bobbin lace. Same as ANTIQUE LACE.

Oriental l. 1. Machine-made and handmade laces, with design woven through and through the net. Used on dresses, curtains, bed sets, etc. **2.** Costly laces of China, India, Japan, Persia, and Turkey, characterized by originality and boldness of coloring and idea.

orris (ŏr′ĭs; *or* iss). Gold or silver lace in fancy designs popular in 18th century. Word was originally *arras*, from the town of that name in France.

oyah or **Turkish point l.** Turkish crochet lace, sometimes of elaborate design, with flowers in relief. Made with crochet hook and colored silks

Paraguay l. (păr′ə-gwā; *pa* ra gway). Lace made by machine and hand; characterized by spider-web, single-thread effects arranged in wheel designs. Fine types used for dress trimmings; coarser weaves, for fancy work.

Paraguay Lace

parchment l. Lace of raised designs made with parchment strips called CARTISANE.

peasant l. (pĕz′ənt; *pez* ant). Coarse, cheap bobbin lace, made by European peasants. See TORCHON.

Peniche l. Portuguese pillow lace with large mesh ground in black and white.

pillow l. Lace made in either of two ways: pattern worked first and réseau worked in around it; or, made in one piece, on the pillow, with the same threads forming pattern and ground. See BOBBIN LACE.

Plauen l. (plow′ĕn; *plow* en). Lace design embroidered by machine on muslin, net, or other fabric and then chemically treated so that fabric is burnt out, leaving just the embroidered design. By adapting the principles of sewing machine and pantograph (an instrument used for copying), difficult and intricate patterns of real lace are imitated.

Plauen Lace

point d'Angleterre l. (F. pwăŋ däŋ-glə-têr; pwanh donh gla tare). Fine-grounded pillow lace, with designs made with needle or with bobbins and applied to bobbinet. Name is French, meaning English point. Originated in Brussels,

Point d'Angleterre

but was smuggled into England and named for that country to avoid import duty; later, made in England.

point de gaze l. (F. pwăŋ də gäz; pwanh de gahz). Fine Belgian needle-point lace, with delicate flower designs appliquéd on fine bobbin net, which is cut away under the designs.

Point de Gaze

point de Paris l. (F. pwăŋ də pä-rē; pwanh de pa ree). **1.** Narrow bobbin lace characterized by hexagonal mesh and flat design. **2.** Machine-made lace resembling Val lace, but with the design heavily outlined.

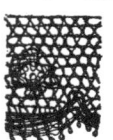

Point de Paris

point d'esprit l. (F. pwăŋ dĕs-prā; pwanh dess pree). **1.** Net or tulle with dots. **2.** Lace with the small oval or square dots first used in Normandy lace. **3.** Small figure in old guipure laces.

Machine-Made Point d'Esprit

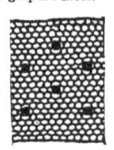

point l. Short for NEEDLE-POINT LACE.
point plat (F. pwăŋ plä; pwanh plah). French term meaning FLAT POINT.
poussin l. (F. pōō-săŋ; poo sanh). Delicate, narrow Valenciennes type of lace made at Dieppe, France. French word meaning chicken. See DIEPPE POINT LACE.
princesse l. (F. prăŋ-sĕs; pranh sess). Very delicate imitation of duchesse lace,

Machine-Made Ratiné

with designs applied to net ground, often by hand.
ratiné l. (răt-ĭ-nā′; rat i *nay*). Machine-made lace with groundwork of heavy loops, similar to Turkish toweling. Used to trim wash dresses of coarse fabric.
real l. Handmade lace other than that which is crocheted or knitted.
Renaissance l. (rĕn-ə-säns′; ren a *sahnce*). Modern lace, having woven tape motifs joined by a variety of flat stitches. Fine type used on dresses; coarser weaves, on draperies.

Renaissance Lace

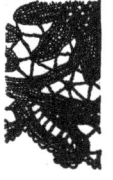

reticella l. (rĕt-ĭ-chĕl′ə; ret i *chell* a). First form of needle-point lace, developed from cut work and drawn work, having geometric designs connected by picoted brides. Later designs had more variety. Used in table linens, for collars, as dress trimmings.

Reticella

Roman l. Needle-point lace of geometric design. Same as RETICELLA LACE.
rose point l. Venetian needle-point lace, having delicate and full designs of flowers, foliage, and scrolls connected by brides, padded buttonholed edges, and string cordonnet.

Rose Point

Saint Gall l. Imitation of Venetian lace, made by embroidering woolen fabric by machine, using cotton or silk

fāte, făt, dánce, ärt mē, mĕt, hêr, thêre rīde, rĭd nōte, nŏt, côrn, fōōd, fŏŏt cūte, cŭt, cūrè now fin(ŋ)ger villa(ə) señor pleas(zh)ure

thread, and then dissolving the wool and leaving only the embroidery.

Saint Gall Lace

Saxony l. 1. Burnt-out laces of Plauen type. See PLAUEN LACE. 2. Embroidered drawn work of 18th century. 3. Curtain lace in imitation of Brussels, with design worked by hand on tambour drum.
Schleswig l. (shlĕs'vĭg; *shless* vig). 1. Danish needle-point of 17th century in fine designs of religious and other emblems. 2. Bobbin lace of 18th century made in Denmark in imitation of Flemish designs.
shadow l. Machine-made lace with flat surface and shadowy designs. Used for dresses and dress trimmings.

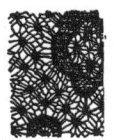

Shadow Lace

Shetland l. Light bobbin lace of Shetland wool. Used for baby covers, etc.
silver l. Lace or braid, usually having silk weft threads covered with thin silver foil or leaf. Formerly made of silver wire.
Spanish l. Any of variety of laces made in Spain. Most commonly known type is lace made of pure silk, with heavy, flat, floral designs held together with varying meshes. Modern varieties often made of rayon. Also, coarse pillow lace of gold and silver threads.
spider work. Heavy bobbin lace. Same as ANTIQUE LACE.
Swedish l. Simple pillow laces of torchon type, made in Sweden.
tambour l. (tăm'bŏŏr; *tam* boor). Lace worked on net ground in chain-stitch. Net is stretched on a tambour frame, or embroidery hoop. Tambour-stitch originally employed in embroidering pattern; now superseded by chain-stitch.
tatting. Knotted lace worked with the fingers and a shuttle, which bears a single thread and forms loops. Made in various designs, most popular being cloverleaf and wheel. Imitated by machine. Used as edging on lingerie and other garments, in fancy work, on linens.
Teneriffe l. (tĕn-ẽr-ĭf'; *ten* er *if*). Lace with motifs of wheels and circles, similar to Paraguay lace. Made chiefly in Canary Islands.
thread l. Lace made with linen, rather than cotton, metal, or other threads.

tonder l. (tŏn'dẽr; *tonn* der). Danish 17th and 18th century lace made of drawn work and embroidery on muslin, sometimes having fine cordonnet.
torchon l. (F. tôr-shôn; tore shonh). Coarse, durable bobbin lace of either linen or cotton thread. Also called *beggar's lace, peasant lace, Bavarian lace.* Fine weaves used on dresses; coarse, in fancy work.

Torchon

trolley or **trolly l.** English bobbin lace, having heavy outline thread and designs of flower sprays, squares, and dots.
Turkish point l. Crochet lace of elaborate floral design. See OYAH LACE.
Valenciennes l. (F. vȧ-läṅ-sĕ-ĕn; va lonh see en). Fine bobbin lace, worked in one piece, in which the same thread forms both ground and design. Designs are flowers or trailing patterns, without raised work or cordonnets, on open and regular mesh. Real lace made of linen; imitation, of cotton. Commonly called *Val.* Exceptionally good imitations are made by machine. Machine-made type widely used on lingerie, children's clothes, wash dresses. Handmade type used on fine handkerchiefs and neckwear.

Valenciennes

Venetian l. Variety of laces made in Venice, including reticella, cut work, drawn work, raised point, flat point, etc. The guipure needle-point lace consists of floral motifs or designs connected by irregularly placed, picoted brides. Used for dress trimmings, table runners, mats, and curtains.

Venetian

warp or **warp net l.** Type of lace in which the design holds ground of warp threads in position. Widely used for filmy curtains.
yak l. 1. Coarse, English bobbin lace made in Northampton. 2. Lace crocheted from yak wool.
Ypres l. (ēpr; eepr). Lace made in imitation of Valenciennes at Ypres, Belgium.

lace pillow. Pillow used in making pillow lace.
lace-stay. Front part of shoe, having eyelets for laces.
lace-stitch. Bobbin lace-stitch. See STITCHES.
lacet (lăs'ĕt; *lass* et). Ornamental braid used as trimming or in fancy work. See BRAIDS.
lacis (lā'sĭs; *lay* sis). Old name for netting or darned lace. See LACES.
lacquer (lăk'ẽr; *lack* er). 1. Type of varnish used on metal, wood, etc., to add luster and provide glossy, hard finish. 2. Bright orange-red color. Also called *lacquer red.*
lacquered (lăk'ẽrd; *lack* erd). Having a hard, shiny surface; covered, or as if covered, with thick varnish.
ladder. Run, or open-work line, in knit fabric, especially stocking.
ladder braid. Bobbin-made braid. See BRAIDS.
ladder-stitch. Embroidery stitch like bar fagoting, or one giving ladder effect. See STITCHES.
ladies' or **lady's cloth.** Fine flannel in plain weave, formerly used for women's dresses. See FLANNELS.
laid embroidery. Embroidery with cord or vellum design covered by gold or silk threads. Same as GIMPED EMBROIDERY. See EMBROIDERIES.
laid-stitch. Long, loose stitch, usually held down by other stitches. See STITCHES.
laine (F. lăn; lain). French word for wool or worsted.
lake. 1. Clear, purplish-red color. 2. Obsolete term for type of fine, white, linen fabric.
lamb (lăm; lam). Fur of any type of lamb. See CARACUL, KRIMMER, PERSIAN LAMB, etc., under FURS.
lamba (lăm'bȧ; *lam* ba). 1. Brightcolored shawl. See WRAPS. 2. Fabric woven of date leaves by African natives.
lamballe (F. läm-bȧl; lam bal). Scarf of silk trimmed with lace, named for the Princesse de Lamballe, friend of Marie Antoinette. Worn just before French Revolution.
lamboys (lăm'boiz; *lam* boiz). Steel skirt extending to knee, worn as part of armor of 15th and 16th centuries.
lambrequin (lăm'brĕ-kĭn; *lam* bre kin). Scarf-like covering worn over helmet as protection from sun and rain.
lambsdown (lămz'down; *lams* down). Heavy, knitted, woolen fabric with thick nap on one side.
lambskin. 1. Leather from skin of lamb not more than two months old. See LEATHERS. 2. Lamb's skin dressed with wool on it; sheepskin of fine texture. 3. Fabric of cotton or wool

with napped, fleecy surface resembling lamb's wool. Used for warm working clothes. **4.** Apron of white leather, worn as emblem of Freemasonry.
lamb's wool. Soft wool of young lambs. See WOOLS. Also, fabric made of it.
lame (lăm or F. läm; lame or lahm). **1.** Gold or silver thread. See THREADS. **2.** Thin metal plate, as of steel for armor.
lamé (F. lȧ-mā; la may). Fabric woven of flat gold or silver metal thread, often brocaded, sometimes mixed with silk or other fiber. Used for evening dresses, wraps, blouses, gilets, etc.
lammy or **lammie.** Sailor's quilted woolen jumper.
lampas (lăm'pəs; *lam* pas). Any fabric of elaborate, ornamental design. Specifically, fabric similar to damask, but in many colors and woven with double warp and filling. Usually silk.
langooty (lŭng-gōō'tĭ; lung *goo* ti). Small loincloth or piece of cloth attached at front of waistband. Worn by East Indian natives of low class.
lansdowne. Fine, wiry fabric in plain weave, with silk warp and worsted filling. Used chiefly for women's dresses.
lap. 1. Part of garment that hangs free or is folded back; tab. **2.** To fold or extend over, as a piece of fabric. **3.** Part of garment covering knees, thighs, and lower part of body. **4.** Folded section of garment used as pocket.
lapboard. Broad, smooth board used by seamstresses, dressmakers, tailors, etc., for working in lap instead of on table.
lapel (lə-pĕl'; la *pell*). Part of garment that turns back or folds over; especially front neckline fold of coat or jacket. Wide lapels called *revers*.
lapin (lăp'ĭn or F. lȧ-păṅ; *lap* in or la panh). Sheared rabbit fur. See FURS.
lapis lazuli (lăp'ĭs lăz'ū-lī; *lap* iss *laz* you li). **1.** Semi-precious stone of deep, rich, blue color. **2.** Blue color of the stone.
lappet. Small lap or flap ornamenting headdress or other garment; especially, one of two strips, usually of lace, hanging at back or sides of commode headdress. Fashionable in late 18th century.
lappet weave. Plain or gauze weave with embroidered pattern. See WEAVES.
lap seam. Unturned seam. See SEAMS.
laqué (F. lȧ-kā; la kay). French term meaning lacquered or varnished.
lark. Pale buff color. Same as PARCHMENT.
larkspur. Light blue color with slight greenish tinge.
larrigan (lăr'ĭ-gən; *la* ri gan). Moccasin type of boot. See BOOTS.
Laskin Mouton (lăs'kĭn mōō-tŏṅ; *lass* kin moo tonh). Trade name for processed lambskin. See FURS.
last. Wooden form or mold, sometimes reinforced with metal, used in shoe construction to give a shoe its shape. Made on standard measurements taken at ball, waist, and instep of foot. Usually designated only by number. — **combination l.** Last that varies in some part from usual standard measurements, as wider or narrower at heel. — **walled l.**

Shoe last having the vamp built over a vertically stiffened piece, or wall, giving boxy effect around toe.
Lastex. Trade name for fine, round, rubber thread, manufactured in strands and wound with cotton, rayon, silk, or wool. Woven into fabrics to give stretch or blistered effect. Knitted into hosiery to serve as garters, into fabric for foundation garments and bathing suits. Also used in dress apparel at waistline, wrists, neck, shoulders, etc.
lasting. Strong woolen fabric used for shoe uppers, covering buttons, etc. See DENMARK SATIN, PRUNELLA, 2.
latchet. Lace, thong, or narrow strap, usually of leather, that fastens shoe or sandal.
lathe (lāth; laithe). Swinging beam on a loom, which carries the reed for separating warp threads and for beating the weft into position in the fabric.
laticlave (lăt'ĭ-klāv; *lat* i clave). Broad purple stripe on Roman tunic. See STRIPES.
lattice basket-stitch (lăt'ĭs; *lat* iss). Embroidery stitch resembling lattice. See STITCHES.
lava-lava (lä'vȧ-lä'vȧ; *lah* vah *lah* vah). Loincloth or waistcloth of printed calico worn by natives of Samoa and other islands in the Pacific.
lavaliere (lăv-ə-lēr'; lav a *leer*). Ornament on chain, worn as necklace. See NECKLACES.
lavender (lăv'ən-dẽr; *lav* en der). **1.** Aromatic herb, leaves and flowers of which are used as perfume. **2.** Bluepurple tint, color of the lavender blossom.
lawn. Fine, soft, sheer fabric, usually cotton, in plain weave, filled with starch or sizing. Often printed after it is woven. Used for handkerchiefs, baby clothes, dresses, blouses, aprons, curtains.
lay. Measure of yarn. See LEA.
layette (lȧ-ĕt'; lay *et*). Complete outfit for newly born child, including clothing, bedding, bassinet, etc.
lay figure. Jointed model of human figure, used in arranging drapery or displaying garments.
layout (lā'owt; *lay* out). Diagram showing arrangement, as of pieces of a pattern on fabric or of type, illustrations, etc., for advertisements, pages, books, or other printed matter.
lazy-daisy-stitch. Elongated chain-stitches grouped to form a daisy. See STITCHES.
lea (lē; lee). Measure of yarn, differing for various fibers: 300 yards for linen; 120, for cotton or silk. Also called *lay*.
leaf. 1. Thin, flat piece, as of gold. **2.** Lap of a garment, as a hat brim; turnback of collar.
leaf green. Any medium green color likened to foliage of trees, varying from yellow-green to darker shades.

LEATHERS

leather (lĕth'ẽr; *leth* er). Hide or skin of an animal, or any portion of it, tanned or otherwise chemically preserved, shrunk, and toughened. Skin or hide of

any beast, bird, fish, or reptile can be used for leather.
alligator (ăl'ĭ-gā-tẽr; *al* i gay ter). Skin of water reptile, having square, box-like markings. Skins of baby alligators usually used for handbags and shoes because of size of markings.
antelope (ăn'tə-lōp; *an* te lope). Fine, soft leather with velvety sheen and texture, made from antelope skins, sueded on flesh side.
antelope-finish suede. Sueded lambskin, goatskin, or calfskin, similar to antelope in finish.
artificial l. (ärt-ĭ-físh'əl; art i *fish* al). Imitation of leather, made by applying nitrocellulose coating to cotton foundation cloth, either firm muslin or heavier, napped material.
boarded l. Leather finished by folding skins grain side in and pressing with a board, repeating operation at close intervals, so that natural grain surface is broken up by close, parallel creases. High-grade, smooth calf frequently finished in this way.
boroso l. (bō-rō'sō; bo *ro* so). Variety of sharkskin, like galuchat in that shagreen armor is left intact in tanning, but with smaller, finer grain. Often imitated by embossing on other types of skin. See SHAGREEN, 2.
box l. Leather given two-way boarding, so that creases run across and up and down. Smooth calf frequently treated in this way. Also see BOARDED LEATHER.
Bucko. Trade name for reversed calf, a sueded leather used on flesh side. So called because of similarity to buckskin.
buckskin. Soft, strong, pliable leather, originally from skins of deer and elk, now also of sheep and calves. Used for shoes, gloves, sometimes clothing; chiefly in white or champagne. Also called *buck* for short.
buffskin. Leather prepared from skin of buffalo dressed with oil, like chamois. Also, skins of oxen, deer, elk, etc., prepared in same way. Also called *buff leather*.
cabretta l. (kȧ-brĕt'ə; ca *bret* a). Skin of cabretta, a hair sheep, finished and used like various types of kid, chiefly in gloves and shoes. Stronger than regular sheepskins, but not so strong as kid leather.
calf or **calfskin.** Strong, soft, supple, fine-grained leather made from skins of cattle a few days to a few weeks old. Takes high polish, as well as dull, or "suede," and patent leather finish. Used for shoes, bags, etc.
canepin (F. kȧn-păṅ; can panh). French word for fine leather, chiefly kidskin, also lamb and chamois skin, as used for gloves.
capeskin (kăp'skĭn; *cape* skin). Firm, washable, glacé-finished leather made from hairy lambskins or sheepskins; originally from Cape of Good Hope in South Africa, now from Russia and other countries. Used especially for street gloves.
castor. Soft, suede-finished kid or goatskin. Used for gloves.

chamois (shăm′ĭ; *sham* i). Soft, strong, pliable leather prepared from skin of chamois, a goat-like antelope, or from processed, oil-dressed and suede-finished skin of sheep, deer, or goats. Skins made into sports clothes, hats, gloves; also used for cleaning purposes.

chrome l. (krōm; crome). Leather tanned by quick mineral process in which skin is treated with chromium salts. Used chiefly for shoes; also, for gloves.

cordovan (kôr′də-vən; *cor* do van). Soft, non-porous, long-wearing, expensive leather made chiefly from part of horsehide butts. Used for heavy, fine shoes, boots, razorstrops. Named during Middle Ages for Cordova, Spain, center for world-renowned tanners.

cordwain (kôrd′wān; *cord* wain). Tanned and dressed goatskin or split horsehide from Spain. Used during Middle Ages for boots of wealthy. Old name for CORDOVAN.

cowhide. Leather from hide of cows. In trade usage, leather made from hides weighing over 25 pounds.

crushed l. Leather processed by novelty treatment giving a round, slightly bumpy grain similar to that of blistered fabric.

cuir-bouilli (F. kwĕr boo-ē-yē; queer boo ee yee). Hard leather, molded into shape while soft from soaking or boiling. Used during Middle Ages for cuirasses and other parts of armor; now used for decorative articles. French phrase meaning boiled leather.

doeskin (dō′skĭn; *doe* skin). Skin of white sheep and lambs, made into leather by formaldehyde and alum tanning process. Used chiefly for gloves.

Dongola kid or **l.** (dŏng′gə-lə; *dong go* la). Skin of sheep, goat, or kangaroo, tanned and finished to resemble French kid.

dressed kid. Kid with smooth or glacé finish, generally on grain side.

elasticized l. (ē-lăs′tĭ-sīzd; e *lass* ti sized). Leather combined with elastic so that it stretches to conform to shape.

elk. Originally, hide of elk, usually treated by smoke process. Now, calfskin, cowhide, etc., treated by smoke to give it color resembling genuine elk. Odor of smoke is characteristic. Used for sports shoes. Genuine elk now called *buckskin*.

Florentine l. Fine tooled leather, often with gold and colored designs, originally from Florence, Italy. Used for belts, handbags, book bindings, decorative accessories.

galuchat l. (F. gȧ-lü-shä or gȧ-lȧ′chȧt; ga loo sha or ga *lu* chat). Kind of sharkskin tanned without removal of hard, pebbly surface. Similar to BOROSO, but with coarser grain. See SHAGREEN, 2.

glazed kid. Chrome-tanned goatskin finished for use as shoe leather; glossy, but not actually glazed. Term derived from mispronunciation of French word *glacé*, simply meaning glossy, as applied to kid.

goatskin. Leather made from skin of goat. Used for gloves, shoe uppers, handbags, etc.

grain l. Leather made from or finished on hair or outer side of skin or hide.

imitation alligator. Leather having square markings stamped on with hot rollers. Much used.

imitation l. Fabric processed to resemble leather.

japanned l. (jə-pănd′; ja *pand*). Varnished leather. Same as PATENT LEATHER.

Java lizard (jä′vȧ lĭz′ẽrd; *jah* va *liz* erd). Lizard from Java, with white, circular markings like smoke rings.

Juchten (yŏŏk′tən; *yook* ten). German word for RUSSIA LEATHER.

kangaroo (kăng-gə-rōō′; kang ga *roo*). Leather made from kangaroo skins, produced exclusively in Australia, largely tanned in U. S. Usually vegetable- or chrome-tanned, sometimes suede-finished. One of the best shoe upper leathers, fine, tough, close-grained.

kid. Shoe leather tanned from skins of mature goats, or glove leather from skins of young goats, wild or domesticated, from India, China, Europe, South America, etc.

lambskin. Skin of young sheep, used in glove leathers.

lizard (lĭz′ẽrd; *liz* erd). Scaly skins of lizards, chiefly from Java and India, tanned into leather. See JAVA LIZARD.

losh hide or **l.** Originally, elk leather. Later, any hide dressed with oil only.

mat kid. Kid tanned by same process as glazed kid, but with dull finish.

mocha (mō′kȧ; *mo* ka). Fine glove leather, soft, supple, and durable; made of skins of hair sheep from Arabia, Persia, Africa. Has suede-like finish on grain side, but is heavier than suede, with finer, closer nap. Named for seaport of Mocha in Arabia, from which first skins were brought. Sometimes made from goatskin.

morocco (mə-rŏk′ō; mo *rock* o). Goatskin, or its imitation in sheepskin, subjected to sumac, chrome, or other tanning process. Originally made in Morocco and stained red.

napa l. (năp′ȧ; *nap* a). Glove leather made by tanning sheepskin or lambskin by a soap-and-oil process. Originally tanned at Napa, California.

ooze l. Suede- or velvet-finished leather, usually calfskin.

ostrich l. (ŏs′trĭch; *oss* trich). Strong, tough, vegetable-tanned leather made from ostrich skins. Identified by quill holes. Used for shoes, accessories, fancy leather goods, etc.

paste grain. Thin leather, as sheepskin, stiffened by coat of paste.

patent l. (păt′ent; *pat* ent). Any leather, cattlehide, kid, calfskin, etc., treated with successive coats of varnish to produce smooth, hard, glossy finish. Used for shoes, handbags, belts, etc.

peccary (pĕk′ə-rĭ; *peck* a ri). Fine-grained, light-weight pig leather of wild boar native to Central and South America. Used for dress and sports gloves.

pigskin. Durable leather of pig's hide, with distinctive marking where bristles were removed. Usually vegetable-tanned. Used for trim and uppers of sports shoes; for handbags, luggage, gloves, belts, etc.

pin seal. Soft, strong leather made from skins of young hair seals. Heavy, natural grain emphasized by tanning and finishing process. Used chiefly in glazed black, also in colors, for handbags, shoes, novelty accessories. Grain imitated on other leathers.

rawhide. Hide that has undergone some preparatory processes but has not been tanned. Used for laces, whips, luggage, etc.

reptile l. Skins of animals that crawl or that move on short legs; including watersnake, python, cobra, boa, alligator, frog. Used for shoes, handbags, etc.

reversed l. (rē-vẽrst′; re *verst*). Leather, usually heavy-weight calfskin, finished on flesh side; more water-resistant than suede. Used for sports shoes.

roan (rōn; rone). Low-grade sheepskin used in some slippers.

Russia l. Originally, bark-tanned calfskin dressed with birch oil, produced in Russia. Now applied to other leathers finished by this process, often colored red and used for purses, etc. Also, a smooth, chrome-tanned leather of similar appearance, generally calfskin or cattlehide, used in shoes for men, women, and children. Also called *Juchten*.

saffian (săf′ĭ-ăn; *saff* i an). Leather made of goatskin or sheepskin tanned with sumac. Dyed in bright colors.

Scotch grain l. Heavy, durable, chrome-tanned leather with pebbled grain, usually of cowhide. Chiefly used for men's shoes.

seal. Soft, strong leather with a natural grain. Made from skins of hair seals obtained chiefly off Newfoundland and Norwegian coasts. Used for luggage, leather accessories.

shagreen (shă-grēn′; sha *green*). **1.** Untanned leather prepared in Russia and Eastern countries from skins of various animals. Given a granulated, pebbly finish and dyed in bright colors, usually green. Used for various household and personal accessories. **2.** Sharkskin, when covered with hard armor of small, close-set tubercles giving appearance of shagreen leather. This surface usually removed in tanning, but left intact in smaller species, as GALUCHAT and BOROSO.

sharkskin. Expensive, durable leather of shark hide. Used for uppers of shoes, particularly for toe caps of children's shoes.

sheepskin. Inexpensive leather prepared from the skin of sheep after removal of wool; sometimes finished to resemble other leathers. Tanned by chrome, alum, or vegetable process. Used for shoe linings, gloves, garments; declining in use for shoes.

skiver (skīv′ẽr; *skive* er). Cheap, soft,

leathers (continued)
grain leather of sheepskin, split, sumac-tanned, and dyed. Used for accessories, hat bands, etc.

snakeskin (snāk′skĭn; *snake* skin). Skin of various snakes, such as boa, python, cobra, watersnake, tanned so as to preserve natural markings, sometimes dyed. Used for shoes, bags, belts, etc.

sole l. Thick, strong leather used in making shoe soles.

suede (F. swäd; swade). Leather, usually made, finished by special process, with flesh side buffed on emery wheel to produce napped, velvety surface. Word means Swedish; so used because velvet finish originated in Sweden. Originally applied to kid, not to calfskin. Used for gloves, shoes, belts, handbags, jackets, etc.

undressed kid. Kid leather finished by suede process on flesh side. Originally much used; now almost entirely superseded by calfskin suede.

veau velours (F. vō və-lōōr; vo ve loor). Soft-finished calfskin, the surface of which has been brushed, rubbed, and worked until it resembles velvet. Used for gloves.

Vici kid (vī′sĭ; *vy* sy). Trade name for bright-finished, chrome-tanned, glazed kid.

wash l. Leather in imitation of chamois, usually made of split sheepskin dressed with oil. Used for cleaning, dusting, etc.

whang l. Calfskin or other strong leather used for lacings, thongs, etc.

white l. Sheepskin or other leather tanned with alum and salt. Colored and used for infants' soft-soled shoes.

leatherboard. Imitation of leather, made of pulp and fiber or various substances molded into board-like shape and glazed.

leather cloth. 1. Fabric with waterproofed surface. 2. Fabric made of leather scraps.

Leatherette (lĕth-ẽr-ĕt′; leth er *et*). Trade name for a paper or cloth imitation of various leather grains and finishes.

leatherine (lĕth-ẽr-ēn′; leth er *een*). Imitation leather made of calico with rubber or rubber substitute coating.

Leatheroid (lĕth′ẽr-oid; *leth* er oid). Trade name for artificial leather made of processed paper and rubber.

Leda cloth (lē′də; *lee* da). Wool velvet, called in French, *velours de laine*.

leg. 1. Part of a garment, as trousers or boot, that covers or partly covers the leg. 2. Joining thread in needle-point lace. See BAR.

leg boot. Boot reaching above ankle. See BOOTS.

leggings. Fitted covering for the legs, usually fastened with a strap over the shoe at the instep, and extending above the knee or to the waist. Worn chiefly by children and made to match a coat or jacket. Also, leg wrapping or puttees, as worn by soldiers and others.

leghorn (lĕg′hôrn or lĕg′ẽrn; *leg* horn or

leg ern). 1. Finely plaited straw. See STRAWS. 2. Hat made of this straw. See HATS.

leglet (lĕg′lĕt; *leg* let). Ring or band formerly worn as ornament on leg just above calf.

leg-of-mutton sleeve. Sleeve shaped like leg of mutton. See SLEEVES.

lei (lā′ē; *lay* ee). Hawaiian garland or wreath made of flowers, feathers, etc.; usually worn around neck.

lemon yellow. Color of lemon fruit, varying slightly from greenish to somewhat redder hue, according to ripeness.

LENGTHS

length. Dimension or measurement from top to bottom; up-and-down proportion, as of coat, dress, sleeve, etc.; direction of the warp in fabric.

coat lengths vary as follows: — **finger-tip.** To ends of fingers when arms are hanging. — **five-eighths.** Half way between hips and knees. — **full-length.** To bottom of dress. — **hip-length.** To hip line at its widest point. — **seven-eighths.** Shorter than dress by a little less than one-eighth of its length. — **three-quarter.** Shorter than dress by one-fourth of its length. — **waist-length.** To normal waistline. — **wrist-length.** To wrist with arm hanging.

dress lengths: — **ankle-length.** To ankle-bone. — **floor-length.** Just touching the floor. — **full-length.** Almost to the floor. — **instep-length.** From about 1 to 3 inches above floor. — **top-of-the-instep.** From 3 to 4 inches above floor.

sleeve lengths: — **bust-length.** In line with the bust line, a little lower than half way between armhole and elbow. — **elbow-length.** Covering elbow bone. — **long.** ½ inch below wrist joint. — **three-quarter.** Ending slightly nearer wrist than elbow.

lengthwise. Cut so that warp threads of the fabric run up-and-down; distinguished from BIAS and CROSSWISE. Applied to garments so cut; as, a lengthwise dress.

leno (lē′nō; *lee* no). 1. Type of weave with paired and twisted warp yarns. See WEAVES. 2. Loose, open fabric in leno weave. Same as MARQUISETTE. 3. Incorrect name for VOILE and SCRIM.

leno brocade. Fabric of leno weave with figure brocaded on.

19th Century Leggings   20th Century Child's Leggings

leopard (lĕp′ẽrd; *lep* erd). Fur of large cat, buff-colored with rosette markings. See FURS.

leopard cat. Fur of small, spotted cat, usually of South America. See FURS.

leotard (lē′ō-tärd; *lee* o tard). Short, close-fitting garment without sleeves, low in neck, fitted between legs. Worn by acrobats, trapeze performers, etc.

lettered silk. Silk fabric decorated by inscription of letters, words, or sentences. Originally, Oriental fabric so decorated.

lettuce green (lĕt′ŭs; *let* us). Light yellowish-green color of the middle leaves of the vegetable. Color of inside leaves is light lettuce; color of outside leaves, dark lettuce.

levantine (lə-văn′tēn or lĕv′ən-tēn; le *van* teen or *lev* an teen). Stout silk cloth in twill weave. First made in the Levant.

leviathan canvas (lə-vī′ə-thən; le *vy* ath an). Coarse, double-thread canvas, so named because of its strength. See CANVAS.

leviathan-stitch. Stitch appropriate to leviathan canvas. Same as DOUBLE CROSS-STITCH. See STITCHES.

leviathan wool. Thick woolen yarn. See YARNS.

levite (lē′vīt; *lee* vite). Polonaise made of muslin or dimity, trimmed or bordered with chintz.

Liberty (lĭb′ẽr-tĭ; *lib* er ti). Trade name for fabrics exclusive with Liberty, of London; notably, fine-textured silks and cottons of excellent quality. See SATINS.

liberty cap. Soft, close-fitting cap. Worn during French Revolution as symbol of liberty. See CAPS.

liberty knot-stitch. Decorative, knotted outline-stitch. See STITCHES.

Liberty pattern. Allover floral print, delicately balanced in color, typical of the designs used by Liberty, of London, for their fabrics.

lid. Slang term for hat.

lift. In shoes, separate, shaped layer of heel; as, a heel of 6 or 8 lifts. See HEEL LIFT.

light. Approaching white in color; pale; said of colors with less intensity of hue than the pure color and nearer to white than black. See COLOR.

light blue. Relatively pale color of greenish-blue hue.

lilac (lī′lək; *lie* lac). Tint of light bluish red, color of lilac flowers.

lilac gray. Pale lavender-gray color.

Lille lace. Fine, filmy bobbin lace like Mechlin. See LACES.

Lillian Russell costume. Elaborate, form-fitting gown with train and enormous hat with plumes. Made famous by the actress Lillian Russell in the late '90's.

lime green. Greenish-yellow color matched to color of the ripe fruit.

Limerick lace (lĭm′ẽr-ĭk; *lim* er ick). 1. Embroidered net. 2. Machine net with applied muslin designs. See LACES.

Lincoln green (lĭnk′ən; *link* un). Dull green color with yellowish tinge.

Lindbergh jacket. Sturdy, warm jacket

with fitted waistband and wrists. Favorite flying jacket of Colonel Charles A. Lindbergh. See JACKETS.

Lillian Russell Costume, 1901

line. 1. Style, outline, or effect given by cut of garment; as, princess line. 2. Merchandise of particular kind or class; as, a manufacturer's line. 3. Obsolete term for linen or flax in any form. 4. Flax fiber from 12 to 36 inches long.

LINENS

linen (lĭn'ən; *lin* en). 1. Strong, lustrous fabric woven of smooth-surfaced flax fibers, usually in plain weave, but often damask, as for table linens. Used, according to fineness of weave and bleaching, for many types of wearing apparel, accessories, household articles, fancy work. 2. Collectively, articles made of linen (now often of cotton).
 art l. Various plain-woven linens, unbleached, ecru, or white. Used for embroidery; also for dresses, uniforms, table linens. Also called *embroidery linen.*
 bandle l. Coarse Irish linen, homemade and handmade, about two feet wide. So called because bandle is Irish measure of two feet.
 book l. Firm linen or cotton fabric, often with sizing to make it stiff. Used in stiffening collars, belts, etc., and in bookmaking.
 butcher's l. Type of bleached crash in plain weave. Originally used for butchers' aprons, jackets, etc.
 diaper l. (dī'ə-pēr; *die* a per). Fine, figured linen fabric, woven in small ornamental patterns, usually of diamond pattern. Used for towels, fancy work, children's dresses, etc. Also called *diamond linen.*
 dress l. Plain, firmly woven linen, in white or colors. Used for blouses, dresses, towels.
 handkerchief l. Sheer, fine linen in plain weave. Used for handkerchiefs, neckwear, blouses, dresses.
 Holland l. Firm, coarse, plain-woven, linen, unbleached or partly bleached, glazed and unglazed; originally from Holland. Used for aprons, furniture covers, window shades, dress-form covers, etc.
 Irish l. Fine, light-weight linen fabric of Irish make, with little dressing; often still hand-woven, grass-bleached. Used for handkerchiefs, collars, etc.
 round-thread l. Soft-finished, plain linen woven of round, hard-twisted yarn. Used for drawn work, hemstitching, hardanger work, because threads are easily drawn.
 sheeting l. Linen used for pillowcases, sheets, towels, table linens.
 spun l. Finest, hand-woven linen, used for daintiest handkerchiefs, neckwear, etc.

linene (lĭ-nĕn'; li *neen*). Substitute for linen, usually of cotton. Like Indian Head, but softer and smooth-finished.
linen embroidery. Buttonholed drawn work on linen. See EMBROIDERIES.
linenette (lĭn-ən-ĕt'; lin en *et*). Cotton fabric made in imitation of linen.
linen straw. Straw with smooth finish. See STRAWS.
linge (F. lănzh; lanzh). French word meaning linen.
lingerie (F. lăŋ-zhə-rē; lanh zhe ree). Women's underclothing; originally of linen, now usually dainty silk and lace-trimmed garments. Term originally borrowed from French language by Sarah Josepha Hale, editor of "Godey's Lady's Book."
lingerie hat. 1. Hat of lace or embroidery. 2. Washable summer hat. See HATS.
lingerie hem. Tiny rolled hem, puffed between stitches. See HEMS.
lingerie tape. Narrow, flat, woven tape. See TAPES.
lingerie trim. Dainty dress trimming, usually neckwear, of delicate texture in white or pastels.
lining (līn'ĭng; *line* ing). 1. Cloth partly or entirely covering inside surface of garment, forming inside finish. In shoes, consists of two parts: inner one of cotton; outer one of leather. 2. Fitted underbodice with sleeves, matching or contrasting with the fabric of the outer waist.
link powdering-stitch. Series of separate loop-stitches. See STITCHES.
linkwork. Fabric composed of metal links interlocked to form mesh.
linon (lĭn'ən or F. lē-nôn; *lin* on or lee nonh). French word for linen lawn. See INDIA LINON.
linsey-woolsey (lĭn'zĭ wŏŏl'zĭ; *lin* zi wool zi). Coarse fabric of linen and wool or cotton and wool, originally made at Lindsey, England. Very popular in American Colonies.
lint. 1. Ravelings or shreds from cloth. 2. Fiber of cotton or raw cotton.
lipstick. Cosmetic paste or cream for the lips, varying in color from white through the reds to dark color; put up and marketed in stick form in small case.
lipstick pencil. Pencil made of hardened lipstick, used to outline the lips after lip rouge is applied with a brush.
lipstick red. Scarlet or crimson color likened to shades of lipstick.
liripipe (lĭr'ĭ-pĭp; *lir* i pipe). Long streamer of gauze or ribbon attached to headdress, often hanging to feet. Worn by men and women in 14th and 15th centuries as part of CHAPERON. Name derived from LIRIPIPIUM, hood with a peak.
liripipium (lĭr-ĭ-pī'pĭ-ŭm; lir i *pi* pi um). Peaked hood worn in medieval period. See HOODS.
liseré (F. lē-zə-rā; lee ze ray). 1. Bright-finished, split-straw braids. See STRAWS. 2. Cord or braid used as binding.
lisle (līl; lile). Made of lisle thread, a fine, hard-twisted cotton, formerly linen. Used chiefly in fine cotton stockings. Named for Flemish town where first made.
Lisle lace. Fine, filmy bobbin lace. See LACES.
lisse (F. lēs; leess). Type of fine gauze used for trimmings, frills, ruching, etc.
list or **listing.** Edge or selvage of textile fabrics.
list work. Type of needlework made by applying list so as to cover or decorate calico or other material.
little girl collar. Narrow, round collar, smaller than Peter Pan or Buster Brown. See COLLARS.
Little Women dress. Simple dress of type worn by the girls in Louisa May Alcott's book, "Little Women." See DRESSES.
liver brown (lĭv'ēr; *liv* er). Dull reddish-brown color.
livery (lĭv'ēr-ĭ; *liv* er i). 1. Characteristic attire or uniform dress, as worn by servants or other class of people. 2. Low grade of wool.
lizard (lĭz'ērd; *liz* erd). Leather made from lizard skins. See LEATHERS.
llama (lä'mə; *lah* ma). Cloth woven from long and woolly hair of the llama.
llautu (lou'tōō; *lou* too). Fringed cord made of vicuña wool, worn about head as sign of nobility by ancient inhabitants of Peru.
loading. Adding any substance to cloth to give it body or weight. See WEIGHTING.
locket. Small, compact case used as container for memento. Worn as ornament, usually on chain around neck.
lockram (lŏk'rəm; *lock* ram). Coarse, cheap linen cloth, formerly used in England.
lock-stitch. Machine stitch having top and bobbin threads that lock together at each stitch. See STITCHES.
logwood brown. Reddish-brown color. Term usually applied to furs.
loincloth. Primitive garment consisting of a piece of cloth worn around loins and hips.
long-and-short-stitch. Alternating long and short stitch. See STITCHES.
long bob. Bobbed hair worn long enough to form curled roll at back. See BOBS.
longcloth. Fine, soft cotton cloth, bleached and gassed but unfinished; similar to calico, but superior in quality. Used for infants' and children's clothes, cotton underwear. So called because one of first fabrics to be woven in long rolls.
long-leg cross-stitch. Cross-stitch with unequal stitches. See STITCHES.
long sleeve. Sleeve which ends ½ inch below wrist joint. See LENGTHS.

long-stitch. Satin-stitch. See STITCHES.
loom. Frame or machine of wood or metal in which yarn or thread is woven into fabric. See DOBBY LOOM, DRAWLOOM, JACQUARD LOOM, WEAVES.
loo mask. Half-mask. See MASKS.
loop. 1. Doubling of a thread, so as to pass through it a needle, hook, or another thread, as in crocheting or knitting. 2. Fold or ring made of ribbon, braid, etc., used as trimming.
loop buttonhole. Loop of crochet, cord, self-fabric, etc., serving as a buttonhole. See BUTTONHOLES.
looped-braid-stitch. Braid-like embroidery stitch. See STITCHES.
loop-stitch. Stitch forming connecting loops. See CHAIN-STITCH, 1, under STITCHES.
loose-bodied. Made to hang loosely without stays; applied specifically to 17th century gowns.
lorgnette (F. lôr-nyĕt; lor nyet). Eye glasses on long ornamental handle, into which glasses fold when not in use. Also, opera-glasses, especially with long handle.
losh hide or **leather.** Oil-dressed leather. See LEATHERS.
loud. Colloquial usage for gaudy or overbright in color; applied to clothing, jewelry, etc.
Louis XIII collar (F. lŏŏ-ē; loo ee). Wide collar turned down over shoulders. Same as FALLING BAND. See COLLARS.
Louis XV heel. Curved French heel. See HEELS.
louisine (F. lŏŏ-ē-zēn; loo ee zeen). Plain, light-weight, durable silk of glossy texture, similar to taffeta. Used for dresses, coat linings, trimmings. Now, no longer on the market.
Louis Philippe. Characteristic of French costume of 1830-48, marked by wide, drooping shoulder accentuated by cape, bertha, or scarf; ruffles, plaits, tucks for ornament; wide-brimmed straw hat with much decoration; wide, banded skirt.
lounging robe. Full-length or knee-length robe, often of flannel, velvet, brocade, frequently lined throughout. Worn by both men and women for lounging and for warmth when indoors.
loup (F. lŏŏ; loo). Half-mask. Same as LOO MASK. See MASKS.
love. Obsolete fabric of thin silk, or border or trimming made of it.
love bracelet. Large link bracelet, often with hearts, Cupids, etc. See BRACELETS.
love knot. Decorative knot of ribbon. See KNOTS.
love lock. 1. Curl or wisp of hair, usually tied with a ribbon, worn hanging over the shoulder by both men and women of cavalier period. Also called *French lock.* 2. In colonial days, long ringlet of hair worn at right temple.

18th Century Love Lock

love ribbon. Narrow, gauze ribbon with satin stripes. See RIBBONS.
lover's knot. Ornamental cord knot. See KNOTS.
low neckline. Décolleté neckline. See NECKLINES.

low shoe. Shoe not extending above ankle. See SHOES.
low waistline. Waistline lower than normal waistline. See WAISTLINE.
lug. 1. Obsolete term for EAR MUFF. 2. (Plural) Colloquial term for dressy or gaudy clothes.
luhinga (lŭ-hĭng'gə; lu *hing* ga). East Indian term for petticoat.
lumberjack. Short, straight coat or jacket, originally buttoned, now usually closed by slide fastener in front. See JACKETS.
lumberjack silhouette. Silhouette of straight over-jacket with waistband, worn over plain skirt. See SILHOUETTES.
lumberman's overs. Boots worn by lumbermen in winter. See BOOTS.
lungi or **lungee** (lŏŏng'gē; *loong* gee). Long cotton cloth worn by Hindus as loincloth, scarf, or turban.
lupis (lŏŏ-pēs'; loo *peess*). Finest grade of Manila hemp weed for weaving into fine fabrics.
luster (lŭs'tēr; *luss* ter). 1. Sheen, gloss, or quality of shining. 2. Poplin-like fabric with lustrous surface, made of silk and worsted. 3. Coarse, long wool having bright sheen.
lustring (lŭs'trĭng; *luss* tring) or **lustrine** (lŭs'trĭn; *luss* trin). 1. Glossy, corded silk fabric, much used for dresses in 19th century. Also called *lutestring.* 2. Shiny fabric of silk, cotton, wool, rayon, or a combination of fibers in satin weave, similar to percaline. Used for linings.
lynx (lĭnks; links). Long-haired fur of North American or European wildcat. See FURS.
lynx cat. Fur similar to lynx, but shorter and less durable. See FURS.
Lyons velvet (lī'ənz; *ly* unz). Velvet with short, silk pile. See VELVETS.

M

macaroni (măk-ə-rō'nĭ; mac a *ro* ni). Nickname for showy, overdressed London fop or dandy. During American Revolution, one of a body of Maryland troops in showy uniforms.

London Macaroni, 1774

Macfarlane (măc-fär'lən; mac *far* lan). Overcoat with cape. See COATS.
machine-made (mə-shēn'māď; ma *sheen* made). Made entirely by machine, as distinguished from handmade and hand-finished.

machine needle. Needle having point and eye at same end, with other end shaped for fastening to needle bar of sewing machine. See NEEDLES.
machine twist. Silk thread for use in sewing machine. See THREADS.
Mackinaw (măk'ĭ-nô; *mack* i naw). Short, sturdy, bulky coat, often with plaid lining. See COATS.
Mackinaw hat. Coarse straw hat of varying shapes. See HATS.
mackintosh. 1. Waterproofed outer garment. See COATS. 2. Rubber-coated fabric, named for the inventor.
maco (mä'kō; *mah* co). Long-staple cotton used in hosiery, underwear, etc. See COTTONS.
macramé or **macramé lace** (măk'rə-mā; *mac* ra may). Bulky, knotted lace, usually fringed. See LACES.
macramé cord. Fine, tightly twisted cord. Chiefly used to make macramé lace.
macramé knot. Knot used in making macramé lace. See KNOTS.
madam. Married or mature woman. Term often used in describing clothes for women over 40 years of age; also, for large women.

madder bleach (măd'ēr blēch; *mad* er bleech). Method of bleaching fabric to secure white background for calico printing. Includes washing, boiling, treating with chemicals.
Madeira embroidery (mə-dēr'ə; ma *deer* a). Embroidery of overcast eyelets on linen or cambric. See EMBROIDERIES.
mademoiselle (F. măd-mwä-zĕl'; mad mwah zel). 1. Young, unmarried woman; a word from the French that is increasingly used to describe smart young girls and women. 2. (Capitalized) Name of a fashion magazine edited to serve fashionable young women.
madras (mə-drăs'; colloquially, măd'rəs; ma *drahss* or *mad* ras). 1. Firm cotton fabric, usually striped. Woven in satin, basket, or figured weaves. Used for shirts, dresses, aprons, etc. 2. Durable, wash silk, usually striped. Used for tailored blouses or dresses and for men's negligee shirts. 3. Figured drapery fabric of cotton or rayon in leno weave. Floating yarns between figures are cut away, giving shaggy appearance.
madras gingham. Gingham of finer

Madras muslin. yarn than ordinary gingham, and usually with more colors. See GINGHAMS.
Madras muslin. Muslin with heavy figures, sometimes colored.
Madras work. Embroidery done over designs on bright silk handkerchiefs. See EMBROIDERIES.
Mae West silhouette. Modified version of Lillian Russell silhouette. See SILHOUETTES.
magic chain-stitch. Chain-stitch with alternate links worked in different colors. See STITCHES.
Magyar (măg′yär; mag yahr). Applied to costumes in bright colors and with detail characteristic of dresses worn by Magyar or Hungarian women; usually having fitted bodice and hip line, with cascading flounces on full, long skirt.
maharmah (mə-här′mə; ma har ma). Muslin cloth worn over head and lower face by Turkish and Armenian women.
mahogany (mə-hŏg′ə-nĭ; ma hog a ni). Dark red-brown color of the finished wood.
mahoitre (mə-hoi′tēr; ma hoy ter). Crescent-shaped padding worn above shoulders in 16th century to increase breadth.
mail. Flexible, mesh-like material made of interlocking metal links or rings. Formerly worn as defensive armor. Worn in combination with plate armor before complete plate armor was used.
maillot (F. mī-yō; my yo). Tight-fitting, one-piece swim suit. French word meaning tights.

Maillot

maison (F. mā-zôɴ; may zonh). French term for house; used in the sense of establishment or business.
maison de couture (də cōō-tür; de oo toor). Dressmaking establishment.
maize. Soft yellow color of the kernels of Indian corn.
make-up. Cosmetics, as powder, rouge, lipstick, mascara, eye shadow, etc. Also, the effect produced by them; as, vivid make-up, accented make-up.
malabar (măl′ə-bär; mal a bar). Cotton handkerchief printed in brilliant colors and designs of East Indian type.
malines or **maline** (mə-lēn′; ma leen). 1. Plain, gauze-like net of silk or cotton, with hexagonal open mesh, usually finished with sizing. Used for neckwear, evening gowns, veiling, and in millinery. 2. Type of flimsy bobbin lace. See LACES.
malo (mä′lō; mah lo). Girdle or loincloth worn by Hawaiian men. Originally of tapa cloth made from bark of trees and dyed brilliant colors; now of brightly dyed cottons.

Maltese embroidery (môl-tēz′; mawl tees). Embroidery of tassels on heavy fabrics. See EMBROIDERIES.
Maltese lace. 1. Bobbin lace like Mechlin and Val. 2. Guipure lace with Maltese cross design. See LACES.
manche (F. mäɴsh; monsh). French word for sleeve.
mancheron (măn′chə-rən; man che ron). False sleeve worn in 16th century. See SLEEVES.
manchette (F. mäɴ-shĕt; monh shet). French word meaning cuff or wristband.
Manchu headdress (măn-chū′; man chew). Headdress typical of Manchu Chinese women. Hair is dressed high on head and shaped into two wing-like pieces at sides. Often glued in place and hung with jewels, coins, beads, flowers, silver ornaments, etc. Varies with status and family of the wearer, and may include metal headband held on by hooks through the ears.

Manchu Headdress

Manchurian ermine. Fur of Chinese weasel; coarser and less durable than ermine. See FURS.
mandarin coat (măn′də-rĭn; man da rin). Long, embroidered coat worn by Chinese mandarins. See COATS.
mandarin color. Orange or reddish-yellow.
mandilion (măn-dĭl′yŭn; man dill yun). Loose outer garment worn in 16th and 17th centuries. See WRAPS.
mandyas (măn′dĭ-ăs; man di ass). Long outer garment similar to cope, worn by clergy of Eastern Church.
manga (măng′gə; mang ga). Mexican coverall cloak similar to poncho. See WRAPS.
manicure scissors. Delicate, sharp-pointed scissors for trimming nail cuticle. See SCISSORS.
Manila hemp (mə-nĭl′ə; ma nill a). Fiber from leaf stalk of plant grown in Philippine Islands. Used in weaving, making cords, etc.
manilla (mə-nĭl′ə; ma nill a). Ring or bracelet of metal, worn on wrist or arm by natives of west Africa.
maniple (măn′ĭ-pl; man i pl). 1. Formerly, ornamental handkerchief carried in hand in celebration of Mass. 2. Now, narrow band matching vestment, worn over left arm by priests at Mass.
mannequin or **manikin** (măn′ĭ-kĭn; man i kin). 1. Model of human figure for display of garments, hats, furs, etc. 2. Dressmaker's assistant who wears new costumes to display them for sale in dressmaking houses, at fashion shows, smart resorts, races, etc. More often called *model*.

mant (mănt; mahnt). Obsolete word for mantilla.
manta (măn′tə; man ta). Coarse cotton cloth used by lower classes of South America for clothing. Also, shawl or other article of clothing made of this cloth.
man-tailored. Made by man tailor or having details of man's tailoring, such as mannish collar, revers, sleeves, etc. See TAILORED.
manteau (F. mäɴ-tō; monh toe). 1. Cloak, cape, wrap, or mantle. 2. Obsolete term for woman's gown.
mantee (măn-tē′; man tee). Coat worn in 18th century. Open in front to show stomacher and petticoat. See COATS.
mantelet (măn′tl-ĕt; man tel et). Small mantle or short cloak.
mantelletta (măn-tə-lĕt′ə; man tel let a). Short robe of silk or wool, without sleeves. Worn by clergy of Roman Catholic Church.
mantilla (măn-tĭl′ə; man till a). 1. Head-covering worn by Spanish women; usually of heavy, black or white silk lace, arranged over high comb, worn off the face or as a veil. 2. Light cloak or cape. See WRAPS.

Type of Mantilla

mantle (măn′tl; man tl). Cloak or loose garment, usually without sleeves. See WRAPS.
mantle and ring. Cloak and ring, worn with veil as religious habit by widows in Middle Ages.
mantua (măn′tū-ə; man tew a). 1. 17th and 18th century fabric, thought to be rich silk from Mantua, Italy. 2. Gown without stays, worn about 1700. Also, robe or overdress, like sacque or loose cloak, usually worn with underdress or over petticoat and stomacher of different color and material.
maquillage (F. má-kē-yázh; ma kee yahzh). French word meaning make-up.
marabou (măr′ə-bōō; mar a boo). Soft tail and wing feathers of African stork. See FEATHERS.
marabout (măr′ə-bōōt; mar a boot). 1. Thrown, or twisted, raw silk. See SILK. 2. Thin, delicate fabric made from it. Used for scarfs, etc.
marble silk (mär′bl; mar bl). Silk fabric having mottled or dappled surface. Made with varicolored filling.
marcasite (mär′kə-zīt; mar ka zite). Glittering mineral, resembling cut steel. Used for jewelry and other ornaments.
marcel (mär-sĕl′; mar sell). Wave given to the hair by means of heated curling irons. Named for Marcel, 19th century French hairdresser. Sometimes spelled *marcelle.*

fāte, făt, dánce, ärt mē, mĕt, hēr, thêre rīde, rĭd nōte, nŏt, côrn, fōŏd, fŏŏt cūte, cŭt, cûrē now fin(ŋ)ger villa(ə) señor pleas(zh)ure

marceline (mär′sə-lēn; *mar* se leen). Thin, fine fabric, usually of silk. Mostly used for linings.
marcella (mär-sĕl′ə; mar *sell* a). Twilled cotton or linen fabric, used for waistcoats, mats, etc.
marechal or **marechale** (mär′ĕ-shăl or mär′ĕ-shăl; *mar* e shall or *mar* e shahl). Kind of scent or perfume, or hair powder scented with it.
Margot lace (mär′gō; *mar* go). Silk net embroidered by machine with cotton. See LACES.
marguerite (mär-gə-rēt′; mar ga *reet*). Waistband or belt popular in 19th century. See BELTS.
Marie Antoinette (F. mȧ-rē ăṇ-twȧ-nĕt; ma ree onh twah net). Having characteristics of court dress of time of Louis XVI, 1780's. Consisted of low bodice with elbow ruffles; huge panniers; long, festooned and draped skirt trimmed with ribbons, flowers, and ruffles; elaborate, powdered headdress; heavily trimmed hat.

Costume of Marie Antoinette

marine blue (mə-rēn′; ma *reen*). Navy blue, purplish or greenish in hue.
marker (märk′ẽr; *mark* er). Sewing-machine attachment that marks a line on fabric by creasing it.
market bleach. Method of bleaching to prepare fabric for market.
marking cotton. Fast-color, cotton thread. Used for marking garments, for basting, and for making tailors' tacks. See THREADS.
marking-stitch. Same as CROSS-STITCH. See STITCHES.
mark-stitch. Method of basting used for marking pattern lines. Same as TAILORS' TACKS. See STITCHES.
mark-up. Trade term, used for the difference between cost and selling price.
marli (mär′lī; *mar* li). Fine net similar to tulle. See NETS.
marmot (mär′mət; *mar* mot). Inexpensive, short, thick fur, usually dyed in imitation of mink. See FURS.
marocain. Ribbed crepe fabric. See CREPES.
maroon (mə-rōōn′; ma *roon*). Dull red color; black mixed with red.
marquis (mär′kwĭs or F. mär-kē; *mar* kwiss or mar kee). Three-cornered hat. See HATS.
marquise (F. mär-kēz; mar keez). Pointed, oval shape of gem, setting, etc.; especially used for diamonds.
marquisette (mär-kĭ-zĕt′; mar ki *zet*).

Soft, light-weight, open-mesh fabric of leno weave. Made of silk or cotton or a combination of the two. Cotton used for curtains; silk, for women's and children's dresses.
marseilles (mär-sālz′ or F. mär-sā; mar *sails* or mar say). Stout cotton fabric in characteristic raised weave, similar to piqué, having the appearance of finest hand quilting. Used primarily for bedspreads and as drapery fabric. First made in Marseilles, France.
marten (mär′tən; *mar* ten). Soft, fine fur of animal related to sable. See FURS.
Martinizing (mär′tĭn-ĭz-ĭng; *mar* tin ize ing). Trade name for process used chiefly on velvet to make it spot-proof, crease-resistant, washable.
Mary Stuart cap. Fabric cap with peak over forehead. See CAPS.
mascara (măs-kăr′ə; mass *ca* ra). Cosmetic preparation for darkening the eyelashes.
mashru (mŭsh′rōō; *mush* roo). Fabric of mixed silk and cotton, originally worn by Moslems. Arabic word meaning lawful; applied to fabric because Moslems may not wear pure silk at prayer.

MASKS

mask. Covering for the face, with openings for eyes and mouth. Worn in classical antiquity as part of theatrical costume; later, as disguise or protection for the face. Worn extensively by women in American colonies in 18th century. Sometimes made of black velvet, held on by silver mouth-piece and worn for protection in winter. Also worn for protection against sun while riding horseback; sometimes made of green silk; also of linen tied on under hoods. In early 1900's, combined with goggles and worn for motoring.

18th Century Mask

domino (dŏm′ĭ-nō; *dom* i no). Mask; especially half-mask worn for masquerades and, during the 17th century, by women and children when traveling, as protection against sun and wind.

17th Century Domino

loom. Silk or satin half-mask reaching only to the tip of the nose. Worn for masquerades or on the stage.
loup (F. lōō; loo). Same as LOO MASK.

masquerade costume (măs-kẽr-ād′; ′mass ker *ade*). Costume for wear to masquerade party. See FANCY DRESS.
masseur (F. mȧ-sẽr; mass ser). Man who massages, that is, rubs or kneads the body, as a health or beauty treatment.
masseuse (F. mȧ-sēz; mass suz). Woman who massages the body.
mass production. Production of apparel or other products in quantity, usually by machinery, for wide, wholesale distribution.
matchcoat. Type of mantle worn by American Indians. See WRAPS.
matelassé (F. mȧt-lə-sā; mat la say). Fabric with raised woven designs in quilted or irregular, blistered effect. Made of wool, silk, rayon, or cotton. Used for suits, coats, wraps, trimmings. Imitated with designs stitched or embossed — not woven in.
material. 1. Substances or parts of which a thing is made or can be made. 2. Fabric; sometimes limited to woolen or cloth stuff.
mat finish. Dull finish, with unglazed, often roughened, surface.
mat kid. Dull-finished kid. See LEATHERS.
maud. Gray plaid used in Scotland as rug or shawl.
mauve (mōv; mohv). Pinkish lilac or delicate purple color.
Mazarine hood (măz′ə-rēn; *maz* a reen). Headdress in fashion about 1700. See HOODS.
McKay (mə-kā′; ma *kay*). Shoe having sole sewn to upper by special process. See SHOES.
Mechlin lace (měk′lĭn; *mech* lin). Bobbin lace with closely woven motifs consisting of ornaments and flowers. See LACES.
medallion (mə-dăl′yən; me *dal* yun). Lace motif, round, oval, hexagonal, or square in shape. Used to ornament linens, lingerie, etc.
Medici collar (mĕd′ĭ-chē; *med* i chee). Large, standing, fan-shaped collar. See COLLARS.
Medici lace. French bobbin lace like Cluny, but with more detail in each motif. See LACES.
medieval (mē-dĭ-ē′vəl; mee di ee val).

14th Century Medieval Costume

Characteristic of dress of the Middle Ages, from about the 5th to the 16th century. During this period, the simple tunics, mantles, and veils worn by women gradually evolved into the elaborate styles of the Renaissance; the surcoat and the houppelande developed, and the hennin superseded the wimple.
medieval embroidery. Ancient embroidery of couching type done in large figures. See EMBROIDERIES.
mélange (F. mā-länzh; may lahnzh). Mixture of colors in weaving; also, mixture of cotton warp and wool weft.
mellay (měl'ā; *mell* ay). Obsolete term for cloth of mixed colors.
melon sleeve (měl'ən; *mell* on). Very full sleeve, often short, shaped like round or oblong melon. Same as BALLOON SLEEVE. See SLEEVES.
melton (měl'tən; *mell* ton). Thick, heavy material, in twill weave, with short, all-wool or cotton warp and woolen weft, finished without pressing or glossing. Nap is raised straight and then shorn to show the weave clearly. Used chiefly for overcoats.
mending tissue. Semi-transparent rubber substance that melts when heat is applied. Used for mending dark silk and woolen materials and for holding hems of men's trousers in position.
Mendoza Beaver (měn-dō'zə; men *doe* za). Trade name for beaver-dyed coney processed by a specific firm. See FURS.
mercer. Merchant who deals in textile fabrics.
mercerize. To treat cotton fiber or fabric, usually under tension, with caustic soda or potash solution for purpose of strengthening yarn or cloth, making it more susceptible to dye, giving it silky luster. So called for John Mercer, 19th century English calico printer.
mercerized cotton. Cotton fiber or fabric that has been mercerized to give luster. See COTTONS.
mercerized cotton thread. Cotton thread with soft, silky finish. See THREADS.
Mercerized Sewing. Trade name for J. & P. Coats and Clark's O. N. T. Boilfast mercerized cotton thread. See THREADS.
merchandising (mẽr'chən-dīz-ĭng; *mer* chan dize ing). Designing, creating, presenting, and promoting merchandise at the right time, at the right place, at the right price, for the right people.
merino (mə-rē'nō; muh *ree* no). 1. Fine wool of merino sheep. See WOOL. 2. Fine, soft dress fabric, resembling cashmere; originally made of the wool of merino sheep. 3. Fine wool yarn for knit goods; or the knit fabric itself, used for hosiery and underwear. See YARNS. — **French m.** Fine woolen fabric made from wool of French breed of merino sheep.
Merry Widow hat. Large, ornately trimmed hat as worn in the musical show, "The Merry Widow," in 1907. See HATS.
merveilleux (F. měr-vā-yẽ; mare vay yuh). Lustrous silk or silk-and-cotton fabric in twill weave; used for coat linings.
mesh. Network, netting, or spaces enclosed by threads.
mesh bag. Purse or handbag of chain mesh. See HANDBAGS.
messaline (měs'ə-lēn; *mess* a leen). Light-weight satin fabric. See SATINS.
mess jacket. Man's short, tailored jacket, usually white and terminating exactly at the waistline. See JACKETS.
metal cloth. Decorative fabric of silk or cotton warp and gold, silver, or copper filling yarns. Used for millinery and trimming.
metal lace. Net with designs woven of metal threads. See LACES.
meteor crepe (mē'tē-ər; *mee* tee or). Silk crepe. See CREPE METEOR under CREPES.
Mexican (měks'ĭ-kən; *mex* i can). Characteristic of Mexican costume, which is the Spanish style of dress combined with the ancient Aztec. Women's costume includes loose, full skirt with starched, lace ruffle; short, sleeveless, cotton blouse; and starched, lace headdress. Also, the Spanish full skirt, which is worn with the mantilla and a high comb. Silver and turquoise jewelry of Indian make worn by both men and women. Men's costume includes white or dark trousers; short, black coat, often embroidered; serape; and ruffled shirt. Now sometimes adapted for women's fashions.
mica (mī'kə; *my* ca). Transparent mineral substance, popularly called *isinglass;* sometimes used for accessories.
Middle Ages. Medieval period of history. See MEDIEVAL.
middy blouse. Slip-on blouse with typical sailor collar. See BLOUSES.
middy braid. Narrow, finely plaited braid; used to trim middy blouses, etc. See BRAIDS.
middy twill. Twilled, cotton fabric like jean; softer than denim. Used for middies, play clothes. See DRILLING.
midinette (F. mē-dē-nět; mee dee net). French term for shop girl or working girl. So called because these girls come out of shops in great numbers at *midi,* or noon, and often make merry in the streets of Paris.
midnight blue. Darkest navy blue.
midriff (mĭd'rĭf; *mid* riff). Same as DIAPHRAGM, part of body between chest and abdomen.
midseason (mĭd-sē'zən; mid *see* zon). Occurring, usually in April and October, between the two big seasonal fashion openings. Applied to the fill-in fashion showings.
mignonette lace (mĭn-yŭn-ět'; min yun et). Narrow bobbin lace. See LACES.
Milanese (mĭl-ə-nēz'; mill a neez). Knitted fabric similar to jersey, but constructed so that it does not ravel. Used for underwear, gloves, hosiery. See KNITTING.
Milan hat (mĭ-lăn'; mi lan). Fine straw hat, made in tailored types or trimmed with ribbon or flowers. See HATS.
Milan lace. Tape lace with needle-point mesh and picot edging. Easily imitated by machine. See LACES.
Milan straw. Closely-woven, fine straw. Used in finest quality of women's hats. See STRAWS.
military. Influenced in style by the uniforms worn by soldiers, or by any detail of such uniforms, either modern or ancient. Braid decoration, epaulets, brass buttons, and helmet-shaped hats are examples of military influence occasionally seen in fashion.
military braid. Flat, tape-like, tailored braid used in rows or on edges as trimming for dresses, suits, etc. See BRAIDS.
military heel. Medium-low, wide heel, similar to Cuban. See HEELS.
milkmaid hat. Type of garden hat, made of straw, with low crown and broad, slightly drooping brim; tied under chin. Originally fashioned for Marie Antoinette. See HATS.
millefleurs (měl'flẽr; *meel* fler). Kind of perfume. French term meaning thousand flowers.
mill end. Mill remnant or short length of fabric.
milliner's fold. Edge of fabric folded four times and thicknesses caught together with slip or basting stitches so no stitches show on right side. Used as an edge finish and for folds in millinery.
milliner's needle (mĭl'ĭ-nẽrz; *mill* i nerz). Long, slender needle for use in millinery; also used as a basting needle. See NEEDLES.
millinery (mĭl'ĭ-nẽr-ĭ; *mill* i nare i). Hats, bonnets, and headdresses of all types worn by women.
mill run. Fabric that has not been inspected at factory or does not come up to standard; usually of secondary quality. Also called *run o' the mill.*
miniver (mĭn'ĭ-vẽr; *min* i ver). Medieval name of a kind of fur. See FURS.
mink. Thick, soft, brown fur. See FURS for MINK, AMERICAN, CHINESE, JAP.
mink tail. Fur of mink's tail, darker and longer than that of the body. See FURS.
mirror velvet (mĭr'ər; *mir* or). Lustrous velvet with pressed pile. See VELVETS.
miscellaneous wool (mĭs-ə-lā'nĭ-ŭs; miss a *lay* ni us). Strong, coarse, long-staple wool. See WOOL.
mission cloth (mĭsh'ən; *mish* un). Rough, canvas-like material. Similar to but less expensive than MONK'S CLOTH.
mistral (mĭs'trəl; *miss* tral). Worsted fabric, with twisted warp and weft threads woven to give a nubbed effect. Used for dresses.
miter or **mitre** (mī'tẽr; *my* ter). 1. Tall, peaked headdress worn by bishops. See CAPS. 2. Woman's headband or fillet. 3. To join fabric or finish a hem at a corner by cutting off triangular piece, turning in raw edges, and sewing together. Method used in putting on lace edges, insertion, etc.
mitt. Fingerless glove. See GLOVES.
mitten. Hand-covering with single stall for all four fingers. See GLOVES.
moat collar. Narrow, standing collar around high, broad neckline. See COLLARS.

mobcap. Woman's cap or headdress, with high, full crown. See CAPS.
moccasin (mŏk'ə-sĭn; *mock* a sin). Leather shoe or slipper of type worn by American Indians. See SHOES. See SLIPPERS.
mocha (mō'kə; *mo* ka). **1.** Fine sheepskin glove leather. See LEATHERS. **2.** Dark, dull, gray brown.
mockado (mə-kā'dō; mo *kah* doe). Fabric thought to be of wool with pile. Worn in 16th and 17th centuries.
mock seam. Seam in circular hose imitating full-fashioned. See HOSE.
mocmain (mŏk'mān; *mock* main). Soft, silky fiber of East Indian tree. Used chiefly for stuffing.
mode. 1. Formal synonym for fashion. **2.** Short for ALAMODE, a light, glossy, silk fabric. **3.** Pale, bluish-gray color, sometimes drab.
model (mŏd'l; *mod* el). **1.** Garment or costume of original design made by designer or dressmaker, to serve as pattern for making copies. **2.** Mannequin. **3.** Person who poses for photographs or sketches to be used in advertising, or one who poses for artist or sculptor.
modesty or **modesty-piece** (mŏd'ĕs-tĭ; *mod* ess ti). Piece of lace or ribbon worn above the breasts, under dresses with lower type of V- or U-neck.
modiste (F. mō-dēst; mo deest). Woman who makes or sells fashionable articles of dress.
mogadore (mŏg'ə-dôr; *mog* a dor). Ribbed silk fabric used chiefly for neckties. Named for Moroccan seaport.
moggan. Scottish term for long stocking without foot; also, knit sleeve.
mohair (mō'hêr; *mo* hair). **1.** Long, lustrous, silky hair of Angora goat. Also, fabric of mohair, as alpaca, cashmere, camel's hair. **2.** Smooth, glossy, wiry fabric of mohair filling and cotton warp in plain or twill weave. Also called *brilliantine, Sicilienne, Sicilian cloth, alpaca*. Used for coats, linings, dresses. **3.** Pile fabric of cut or uncut loops, similar to FRIZÉ, with cotton or wool back and mohair pile. Chiefly used for upholstery. — **grown m.** Hair from older Angora goats. — **kid m.** Fine, silky hair of young Angora goats, finer than that of older goats.
moire (F. mwär; mwar). Watered or clouded fabric, especially silk. Used for coats, dresses, suits, and trimmings. Originally, watered mohair.
moiré (F. mwä-rā; mwah ray). Waved or watered effect on a textile fabric, especially corded silk; produced by passing the fabric between engraved cylinders, which press design in face of material, causing crushed and uncrushed parts to reflect light differently.
mole. Soft, often iridescent fur. See FURS.
mole gray. Dark gray color of mole fur. Same as TAUPE.
moleskin (mōl'skĭn; *mole* skin). **1.** Same as MOLE. See FURS. **2.** Fabric with thick, soft nap resembling fur of mole; especially kind of fustian.
monastic silhouette (mə-năs'tĭk; *mo nass* tic). Silhouette of loose dress hanging from shoulders, with fulness girdled at waistline. Similar to type of monk's robe. See MONK'S DRESS under DRESSES. See SILHOUETTES.

Monk's Robe. Monastic Silhouette, 1938

monkey (mŭng'kĭ; *mung* ki). Long, silky, black hair of certain monkeys. See FURS.
monkey jacket. Short, fitted jacket. See JACKETS.
monk's cloth. Substantial fabric of basket weave with warp and woof threads the same, woven two and two together. Used for sturdy clothes and window hangings.
monk's dress. Dress hanging from shoulder, cut full through the body, belted at waistline. See DRESSES.
Monmouth cap (mŏn'mŭth; *mon* muth). Cap formerly worn by sailors and soldiers. See CAPS.
Monmouth cock. Military cock of the hat. Popular in 17th century. Probably named for Duke of Monmouth.
Monofil. Artificial horsehair used for women's hats. See RAYON.
monogram (mŏn'ə-grăm; *mon* o gram). Initials of one's name used together for decoration.
monotone (mŏn'ə-tōn; *mon* o tone). Sameness of hue; applied to effect of several tones of one color used in weaving or in an ensemble.
monotone tweed. Tweed woven of varying shades of one color. See TWEEDS.
Montagnac (F. mŏn-tå-ñăk; *mon* ta nyack). Trade name for several fabrics; chiefly, soft, curly-napped woolen cloth used for coats.
monteith (mŏn-tēth'; mon *teeth*). Cotton handkerchief, having colored background with white design, made by discharging dye. Name for Scottish manufacturer.
montenegrin (mŏn-tə-nē'grĭn; *mon* te *nee* grin). Woman's fitted outer garment decorated with braid and embroidery.
montero (mŏn-tā'rō; *mon tay* ro). Hunter's round cap. See CAPS.
Moorish lace. Lace similar to MALTESE. Made in Morocco in 16th and 17th centuries. See LACES.
moreen. Coarse, sturdy, cotton, wool, or wool and cotton fabric, with ribbed effect made by fine filling and coarse warp yarns, and often with watered or embossed finish.

morella. Fabric used in 17th century for dresses and drapes.
moresque (mō-rĕsk'; mo *resk*). Decorated or ornamented in Moorish style. Term borrowed from architecture.
morganite (môr'gən-īt; *mor* gan ite). Rose-colored variety of beryl. Used as gem stone.
morion (mō'rĭ-ən; *mo* ri on). Open-faced helmet without visor, resembling hat, worn in 16th century.

16th Century Morion Helmet

morning dress. Glorified house or home dress. See DRESSES.
morning-glory skirt. Skirt fitted at hip line and flared at bottom. Same as SERPENTINE SKIRT. See SKIRTS.
morocco (mō-rŏk'ō; mo *rock* o). Goatskin leather, originally from Morocco. See LEATHERS.
morse (môrs; morce). Clasp or brooch used as front fastening for the COPE.
mortarboard (môr'tĕr-bôrd; *mor* ter bord). Academic cap. See CAPS.
mortier (F. mŏr-tyā; mor tyay). Cap of French dignitaries. See CAPS.
mortling (môrt'lĭng; *mort* ling). Obsolete term for wool taken from dead sheep.
mosaic (mō-zā'ĭk; mo *zay* ick). Fabric design in geometric or curved pattern in imitation of real mosaic work, an inlaid surface decoration composed of small stones arranged to form pictures or designs.
mosaic woolwork. Method of making rugs in which short ends of colored yarn are cemented to canvas. Also called *woolwork*.
moss green. Hue of older gray-green moss or of new, yellow-green moss.
mote. Black spot in yarn or cloth caused by impurity not removed in ginning.
moth ball. Camphor or naphthalene ball widely used for purpose of protecting clothing from moths.
mothproofing. Process used in finishing woolen fabrics, designed to make them mothproof.
Mother Hubbard. Full, loose dress for wear at home. See DRESSES.
Mother Hubbard costume. Costume for nursery rhyme character. See FANCY DRESS.
mother-of-pearl. Hard, iridescent layer on the inside of certain shells. Used for buttons, buckles, inlay for other ornaments.
motif (mō-tēf'; mo *teef*). Unit of design, or figure; repeated to form pattern or used separately as decoration.
motley (mŏt'lĭ; *mot* li). **1.** Variegated in color; composed of different colors. **2.** Woolen fabric of varied colors.

motoring veil. Large, semi-sheer veil to cover the hat and face. See AUTOMOBILE VEIL under VEILS.

mottled. Marked with spots of different shades or colors.

mouche (F. mōōsh; moosh). Small patch, usually black, worn on face as ornament. French word meaning fly.

mouchoir (F. mōō-shwár; moo shwar). French word for handkerchief or neckerchief.

Mountmellick embroidery. White Irish embroidery. See EMBROIDERIES.

mourning crepe (môrn'ĭng; *more* ning). Dull, black, diagonally crinkled crepe, usually silk. See CREPES.

mourning dress or **costume.** In general, dull black clothes, dull black accessories, worn during period of mourning. See DRESS.

mourning veil. Black, semi-transparent veil. See VEILS.

mousquetaire (F. mōōs-kə-têr; moose ke tare). Having real or fancied resemblance to costume worn by French musketeers, or royal bodyguards, from 1622 to 1815. Applied to various articles of dress, such as: cloth coat with large buttons; turnover collar; deep, flared cuff; glove with long, loose wrist; large hat with trailing plume; long, tight, shirred sleeve. See COATS, COLLARS, CUFFS, GLOVES, HATS, SLEEVES.

mousseline (F. mōōs-lēn; moose leen). Fine, soft French muslin.

mousseline de laine (F. də lān; de lain). Wool muslin; light-weight wool fabric, often printed. Used for dresses.

mousseline de soie (F. də swä; de swah). Transparent, gauze-like silk fabric in even weave, with firm finish; often figured. When slightly stiffened, sometimes called *pineapple cloth.* Used for yoke and collar foundations, dresses, and blouses.

mouth veil. Veil draped so as to cover mouth and leave upper part of face uncovered. See VEILS.

moyen-âge (F. mwä-yĕn ázh; mwah yen ahzh). French phrase meaning Middle Ages.

moyle. Type of shoe or slipper. Same as MULE, I.

mozambique (mō-zăm-bēk'; mo zam beek). Loosely-woven dress fabric, having warp of double cotton threads and woolen filling.

mozetta or **mozzetta** (mō-zĕt'ə; mo *zet* a). Cape with hood; worn by higher clergy. See CAPES.

mudguard (mŭd'gärd; *mud* gard). Separate application of leather, either strip or shaped piece, used as trim on shoe. Applied to upper just above sole; sometimes extending all around the foot. First designed to protect upper from dampness.

muff. Separate, pillow-like or tubular covering for the hands, worn for warmth; in fashion since end of 16th century. Made of woolen fabric, feathers, or fur. Now worn chiefly by women and children, but carried by men in U. S. as late as 18th century.

muffetee (mŭf-ə-tē'; muff e *tee*). Short wrist-covering worn by both men and women of 17th century when coat sleeves were short. Also called *wristlet.*

muffin cap. Flat, woolen cap shaped like a muffin. See CAPS.

muffler. Heavy, scarf-like article of dress, worn about the throat.

mufti (mŭf'tĭ; *muff* ti). Ordinary citizen's dress when worn by an officer of the English army or navy instead of his usual uniform.

muga (mōō'gə; *moo* ga). Silk from cocoons of muga moth. See SILK.

mulberry (mŭl'bĕr-ĭ; *mull* bare i). Deep red-blue hue, color of mulberry fruit.

mule. 1. Backless boudoir slipper. See SLIPPERS. 2. Spinning jenny; machine that draws, twists, and winds yarn in one operation.

mull. Soft, sheer, plain-woven, light silk or cotton in white and colors. Term little used in the trade.

mulmul (mŭl'mŭl; *mull* mull). Mull; muslin. Term derived from Hindu word.

multicolored (mŭl'tĭ-kŭl-ērd; *mull* ti cull erd). Consisting of many colors.

multi-strand. Composed of many strands or strings; as, multi-strand necklace.

mummy cloth. 1. Crepe-like cloth of cotton, silk, or rayon and wool. Used for dresses. 2. Sheer, modern cloth, similar to ancient Egyptian fabric. Used as foundation for embroidery. 3. Loosely woven cloth in which mummies were wrapped.

mundil (mŭn'dĭl; *mun* dil). Turban decorated with imitation gold or silver embroidery.

mungo (mŭng'gō; *mung* go). Mill waste from hard-spun or felted cloth. Used in connection with wool, cotton, or better grades of waste in making backing yarns or cheap cloth.

musette bag (mū-zĕt'; mew *set*). Canvas or leather wallet suspended by belt worn over shoulder. Used especially by soldiers.

mush. British slang term for umbrella.

mushroom hat. Hat with brim evenly curved downward. See HATS.

mushru (mŭsh'rōō; *mush* roo). Sturdy cotton-backed satin fabric. See SATINS.

musketeer. Any style resembling costume worn by French musketeers, or royal bodyguards, from 1622 to 1815. Same as MOUSQUETAIRE.

muskrat (mŭsk'răt; *musk* rat). Glossy brown fur of small rodent. See FURS.

muslin (mŭz-lĭn; *mus* lin). Soft cotton fabric of firm, loose, plain weave; bleached or unbleached. Used for dresses, undergarments, sheets, pillowcases, shirts.

muslinet (mŭz-lĭ-nĕt'; muz li *net*). Type of thick muslin or light-weight cotton fabric.

muslin model. Trial garment of muslin made for testing tissue-paper pattern and making any alterations necessary for unusual figures; then used as pattern.

musquash (mŭs'kwŏsh; *muss* kwosh). In London fur market, muskrat skins. North American Indian name for muskrat. See FURS.

mustard (mŭs'tērd; *muss* terd). Yellow-brown shade, color of fresh American mustard sauce.

muster de villers (mŭs'tēr də vĭl'ērz; *muss* ter de *vill* erz). Gray woolen fabric first made at Montivilliers, France; used for clothing from 13th through 16th century.

mutch. Close, linen or muslin cap. See CAPS.

muted (mūt'ĕd; *mute* ed). Subdued or toned down. Often applied to colors.

N

nacarat (năk'ə-răt; *nack* a rat). 1. Bright red-orange color. 2. Fine linen or crepe fabric dyed red-orange.

nacre (nā'kēr or F. nåkr; *nay* ker or nahkr). Mother-of-pearl.

nacré velvet (F. ná-krā; na cray). Changeable velvet with back of one color and pile of another. See VELVETS.

nail. 1. Measure, as for cloth, equaling ⅟₁₆ of a yard, or 2¼ inches. 2. (nā-ēl'; nah *eel*). Arabian sandal. See SHOES.

nainsook (nān'sŏŏk or năn'sŏŏk; *nane* sook or *nan* sook). Soft, light-weight, bleached cotton in plain weave, with soft, lustrous finish on one side; plain or striped. Originally made in India. Used for handmade lingerie and children's garments, especially infants'.

nankeen (năn-kēn'; nan *keen*). Durable, buff-colored cloth, made of Chinese cotton which is naturally brownish yellow. Originally brought from Nanking.

nap. Fuzzy or hairy substance or fibers projecting on some materials, giving downy appearance, forming soft surface, and lying smoothly in one direction. Not to be confused with PILE.

napa leather (năp'ə; *nap* a). Sheepskin or lambskin glove leather. See LEATHERS.

napery (nā'pēr-ĭ; *nay* per i). Linen used in the household, especially table linen.

napery hem. Hem so folded and sewn as to have same appearance on both sides. See HEMS.

napoleon (nə-pō'lĭ-ən; na *po* li on). Top boot designed by Napoleon. See BOOTS.

Napoleon collar. Standing, turned-over collar worn with wide revers of military type by Napoleon and men of his period. See COLLARS.

Napoleonic costume. Type of costume worn by Napoleon. Consisted of tight kneebreeches; square-cut waistcoat; coat cut away from above waistline in front to tails in back; high,

Napoleonic Costume

napping. Finishing process consisting of raising fiber ends of surface yarns on fabrics by means of wire brushes or vegetable burrs, to produce soft, fuzzy finish, as on some flannels, coatings, blankets. Also, fine nap of fur on hat body made of inferior material.
narrowing. Process of working two or more stitches or loops as one, to decrease the size in crocheting, knitting, netting.
natural. Same as FLESH, slightly lighter and pinker than beige. Term also applied to off-white color of fabric in its original state, such as unbleached hemp or muslin.
navy. Medium dark blue color varying from dark reddish blue to dark greenish blue. Ensign, marine, etc., are navy blues.
Neapolitan hat (nē-ə-pŏl'ĭ-tən; nee a *pol* i tan). Hat of lacy fiber or horsehair braid. See HATS.
near seal. Seal-dyed cony. See FURS.
neckband. Band fitting around neck, separate or part of garment; especially, band on shirt to which collar is attached.
neckcloth. Obsolete word for cravat or necktie.
neckerchief (nĕk'ẽr-chĭf; *neck* er chif). Square of cloth, usually patterned, worn around neck. Short for *neck kerchief*.

NECKLACES

necklace (nĕk'ləs; *neck* liss). Ornament worn around neck, usually chain or string of beads or precious stones.
carcanet (kär'kə-nĕt; *car* ca net). Ornamental necklace or collar, usually of gold, jeweled or strung with pearls.
chaplet (chăp'lĕt; *chap* let). String of beads, or similar necklace.
charm string. Ornamental necklace made of fashionable kinds of buttons strung together — cut steel, gilt, gold, silver, smoked pearl, mother-of-pearl, etc. Popular during 1880's.
choker. Band necklace or jeweled collar.
dog collar. Wide necklace, often richly jeweled, worn about throat.
esclavage (F. ĕs-klȧ-vȧzh; *ess klah* vahzh). Multi-strand necklace made of metal chains, beads, jewels, etc. French word meaning slavery.
lavaliere (lăv-ə-lēr'; lahv a *leer*). Or-

nament, usually set with stones, worn hanging around neck, often on chain. Originally, kind of necktie, possibly named for Louise de la Vallière, mistress of Louis XIV.
rivière (F. rē-vyêr; ree vyare). Necklace, especially in several strands, of diamonds or other precious stones. From French *rivière de diamants*, meaning river or stream of diamonds.

NECKLINES

neckline or **neck.** Outline or contour of bodice around the neck.
bateau n. (F. bȧ-tō; ba toe). Boat-shaped neckline, approximately following curve of collar-bone, high in front and back, wide at sides, ending in shoulder seams.

Bateau Neckline, 1920's

boat n. Same as BATEAU neckline.
camisole n. Neckline like that of a camisole top slip, straight above the bust line, with straps over the shoulders.

Camisole Neckline, 1938

cowl drape. Soft drape of self-material at the back neckline.
cowl n. Soft drape of self-material at the front neckline. Such drape at back called COWL DRAPE.
crew n. Round neckline that hugs the throat, as on sweaters worn by college and other boat crews.

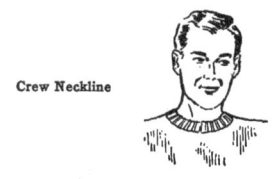

Crew Neckline

draped n. Unfitted neckline formed by loose folds of fabric.
Dutch n. Square or round neckline about 2 inches below throat.
Florentine n. (flŏr'ĕn-tēn; *flor* en teen). Broad, round neckline that extends out over the shoulders, but is not so straight across as the bateau neckline. Much worn during Italian Renaissance.

16th Century Florentine Neckline

halter n. (hôl'tẽr; *hawl* ter). Neckline consisting of strap, rope, or band around neck, attached to backless bodice at the front. Introduced about 1933. Used in sports and evening clothes.

Halter Necklines, 1930's

low n. Neckline cut deep; décolletage.
off-shoulder n. Neckline cut so that neck and upper arms are bare, extending above the bust line, often with a semblance of sleeve draped low on the arm.

Off-Shoulder Neckline, 1938

square n. Neckline of dress or blouse cut to form a square. May be small or extended to the shoulders. Often higher in the back than in the front.
turtle n. (tẽr'tl; *tur* tl). High, turned-over collar that hugs the throat, as on heavy, pull-over sweaters.

Turtle Neck

U-n. Neckline cut in the front in the shape of the letter U.
V-n. Neckline shaped in front like the letter V.
neck-piece. Scarf or boa, usually of fur.

fāte, făt, dȧnce, ärt, mē, mĕt, hẽr, thêre, rĭde, rĭd, nōte, nŏt, côrn, fōōd, fŏŏt, cūte, cŭt, cūré, now fĭn(ŋ)ger villa(ə) señor pleas(zh)ure

neck ruff. Wide, fluffy, light-weight ruff, worn at the neck; usually tied with ribbon.

Neck Ruff, Early 1900's

neckstock. Stiffly folded cravat worn close to the throat, with buckle at back. Worn in 18th and 19th centuries.
necktie (něk'tī; *neck* tie). Narrow band or scarf tied around neck or collar, usually under turnover of the collar.
neckwear (něk'wêr; *neck* ware). Apparel worn at the neck. In the trade, scarfs, collars, ties, fichus, gilets, etc., collectively.

NEEDLES

needle. 1. Small, slender piece of steel used for sewing or embroidery; pierced at one end with hole or eye for carrying thread; pointed at opposite end to facilitate passing through fabric. Needles made of bone and horn at least twenty thousand years old have been discovered. **2.** Instrument with hooked end used for crocheting; long slender rod used for knitting.
beading n. Extremely fine needle for use in sewing on or stringing beads. Size range: from 12, coarsest, to 16, finest.
between. Tailor's needle, short and stubby, for making fine stitches. Size range: from 1, coarsest, to 12, finest.
blunt. Short, thick needle with strong point. Used especially by tailors and glove-makers for sewing heavy fabrics.
bodkin. Blunt needle with large eye. Used for drawing tape, ribbon, etc., through casing or series of eyelets.
calyx-eyed n. (kā'lĭks ĭd; *kay* lix eyed). Self-threading needle, having a fork or notch that opens by an almost invisible slit into the eye. Thread is laid in notch and pulled through into eye. Available in sizes from 1, coarsest, to 9, finest. Used especially by those who can not see to thread an ordinary needle.
candlewick n. (kăn'dl-wĭk; *can* dl wick). Thick needle about 2½ inches long, with large, oval eye. Used in making candlewick embroidery.
chenille n. (shə-nēl'; shen *neel*). Short, sharp-pointed needle with extra large eye for embroidering with heavy or tufted thread. Size range: from 1, coarsest, to 5, finest.
crewel n. Needle with large eye for embroidery threads. Size range: 1, coarsest, to 12, finest. Also called *embroidery needle*.
crochet n. (krō-shā'; cro *shay*). Rod-like, eyeless needle with hooked end, used in crochet work. Made in various sizes, of steel, bone, ivory, etc.

curved n. Needle curved so as to make stitch where straight needle could not be used, as in sewing lamp shades, upholstery, mattresses, etc.
darning n. Long needle with large eye, used for darning. Available in two types: **cotton darner** in sizes from 1, coarsest, to 10, finest; **yarn darner** in sizes from 14, coarsest, to 18, finest.
embroidery n. Sharp-pointed needle with long, wide eye suited for embroidery yarns. See also CHENILLE, CREWEL, SAIL, and TAPESTRY NEEDLES.
glover's n. Needle having three-sided point. Same as SAIL NEEDLE, but shorter in length. Used for sewing gloves and other leather articles.
knitting n. Long, thin, rod-shaped needle made of bone, wood, steel, celluloid, etc., bluntly pointed at one or both ends, sometimes having knob at end opposite point. Also, flexible rod with blunt point at each end, used for circular knitting.
machine n. Needle having point and eye at same end, with other end shaped for fastening to needle bar of sewing machine.
milliner's n. Needle used for basting and for millinery work requiring long stitches. Also called *straw needle*. Size range: 1, coarsest, to 12, finest.
netting n. Needle, varying in length, divided at each end so that yarn may be wound on the needle lengthwise in shuttle fashion, having a small hole for threading. Made of steel, wood, ivory, or bone. Used in making net or mesh.
pack or **packing n.** Large, strong needle used for sewing with packthread, as when doing up packs.
quilting n. Short, sharp-pointed needle designed for making fine stitches. Available in sizes 7 and 8. Used for piecing and quilting bedcovers, etc.
sail n. Long, thick needle with three-sided point. Used for sewing on heavy canvas and for punch work.
sharp. Long, slender needle used for ordinary household sewing. Size range: 1, coarsest, to 12, finest.
straw n. Same as MILLINER'S NEEDLE.
tapestry n. Needle with blunt point and large eye, used for embroidery on canvas. Size range: 18, coarsest, to 24, finest.
wool n. Needle with blunt end and long eye, used for various types of wool work.

needle bar. Bar on sewing-machine which holds the needle.
needle-finished. Term applied to fine, evenly woven fabric finished without sizing, such as handkerchief linen, nainsook, dainty muslins. Some persons wash a fabric before cutting it, to straighten it and to remove sizing in preparation for hand sewing.
needleful. Length of thread for the sewing needle, from 15 to 27 inches long. Shortest lengths used for embroidery; longer lengths, for basting.
needle-point. 1. Needle-point lace. **2.** Stitch used in needle tapestry; or needle tapestry itself.

needle-point lace. Lace made entirely by needlework. See LACES.
needle-point-stitch. Any stitch used in making needle tapestry or needle-point lace. See STITCHES.
needle tapestry work. Canvas embroidery resembling woven tapestry. See EMBROIDERIES.
needle trade. Manufacture of clothing; or any industry in which sewing-machine needle is principal tool.
needlework. All kinds of sewing, knitting, crocheting, embroidery, needle-point, etc.
negligee (něg-lĭ-zhā'; neg li *shay*). Soft, feminine, decorative dressing gown, generally with flowing lines, worn indoors by women. May be held at a waistline with ribbon or sash. Sometimes called *kimono*, which, however, has distinctive style features of its own. Also, any informal attire.
negligee garters. Garters attached to a belt for wear with negligee.
neoclassic (nē-ō-clăss'ĭk; nee o *class* ik). Showing classical Greek influence somewhat modified by the addition of Renaissance or modern detailing.
neora (nē-ō're; nee *o* ra). Shiny, synthetic straw. See STRAWS.

NETS

net or **netting.** Open-work fabric made of thread, twine, etc., with mesh of varying sizes. Used for dresses, veils, trimmings, curtains, tennis nets, fish nets, etc.
blonde n. Washable cotton net, similar to but finer than bobbinet. Used for linings, curtains, etc.
bobbinet (bŏb-ĭ-nět'; bob i *net*). Machine-made net with almost hexagonal meshes. Made of twisted cotton or silk yarn. Originally made by hand, with bobbins. Used for dresses, lace grounds, dress foundations, curtains.
cable n. Cotton net having coarse mesh. Not so satisfactory for curtains as bobbinet, because of stretching in laundering.
craquelé n. (F. kra-kə-lā; cra ke lay). Modern, machine-made net or mesh with threads in a zigzag effect resembling the crackle in glaze of old pottery. Sometimes used in shadow lace of good quality. Also called *crackle* or *crackly*.
fish n. Net, woven or tied, with large, open mesh, similar to but finer than netting used in catching fish.
foundation n. Coarse, stiffened net used in millinery and dressmaking.
illusion (ĭ-lū'zhŭn; i *lue* zhun). Kind of tulle, usually made of silk. Used for veils, dresses, trimmings.
marli (mär'lĭ; *mar* li). Type of gauze somewhat like tulle, used as a ground for lace, embroidery, etc.
rice n. Millinery net of stiff, coarse cotton woven like marquisette. Sometimes called *cape net*. Used for brims and crowns of hats.
tosca n. (tŏs'ka; *toss* ca). Firmly woven, durable net that is more open in design than ordinary bobbinet.
tulle (tōol or F. tül; tool). Fine, fluffy, machine-made net of silk or

nets (continued) cotton, with small meshes. Used in millinery and for trimming dresses and party frocks. One variety called *illusion*. — **dervish t.** Coarse, shiny, very stiff tulle that looks lacquered. Often printed with flowers.

netcha. Sealskin coat. See COATS.

net embroidery. Any type of embroidery done on net ground. See EMBROIDERIES.

netting. Process of making net or mesh.

netting needle. Needle divided at each end. Used in making netting. See NEEDLES.

nettle cloth. Thick cotton material made in Germany as substitute for leather.

network. Fabric of cords, threads, wires, etc., interlaced in open-work surface.

neutral color (nū'trəl; *new* tral). Color without hue. See COLOR.

Neva-wet. Trade name for a process that makes fibers, fabrics, furs, and leathers water- and moisture-repellent; perspiration-, spot-, and stain-resistant; stronger; color-fast.

new abraded yarn. Rayon yarn of a certain type. See RAYON.

new broken filament yarn. Rayon yarn of a certain type. See RAYON.

new-fangled. Faddish; novel. Term used disparagingly.

newmarket. Long, close-fitting coat. See COATS.

nib. Kink or knot in wool or silk fabric.

nightcap. Close-fitting cap worn in bed. See CAPS.

night clothes or **nightdress.** Garments worn while in bed by men, women, children.

nightgown or **nightdress.** Chemise type of garment, sleeved or sleeveless, with soft details, worn while in bed. During mid-19th century, sometimes made top-of-the-hip length.

night-rail. Loose dress worn in morning by women of colonial times. See DRESSES.

night shift. Obsolete term for nightgown.

nightshirt. Tailored nightgown for men or boys, usually just below knee in length.

nile green. Yellowish-green color.

ninon (F. nē-nôṅ; nee nonh). 1. Stout French chiffon, often called *triple voile*. Made in plain weave of hard-twisted yarns, with open mesh. Good quality has clear, transparent surface. Used for dresses, neckwear, fine lingerie, curtains. 2. Light-weight fabric of synthetic yarn. Used for draperies, etc.

Nithsdale (nĭths'dāl; *niths* dale). Kind of large riding hood. See HOODS.

nitrocellulose rayon. Rayon made by a process no longer in use in U.S.A.

Nivernois hat (F. nē-vêr-nwä; nee vare nwah). Hat worn by dandies in 18th century. See HATS.

nœud (F. nē; nuh). Bow or knot of ribbon, as used in millinery or dressmaking.

noil. Short fibers or waste from the manufacture of yarns.

noir (F. nwär; nwar). French word for black.

none-so-pretty. Term used in colonial America for fancy tape.

Norfolk jacket (nôr'fək; *nor* fok). Belted, single-breasted jacket. See JACKETS.

normal color. Foundation color of tone scale. See COLOR.

normal waistline. Line at most contracted part of the body. Also called *natural waistline*. See WAISTLINE.

Norman embroidery. Variation of CREWEL WORK. See EMBROIDERIES.

Northampton lace. English bobbin lace of 17th and 18th centuries. See LACES.

northern muskrat. Fur of brown-backed muskrat. See FURS.

nosegay (nōz'gā; *nose* gay). Posy or small bouquet of fragrant flowers.

nose veil. Short veil. See VEILS.

notched collar or **notched lapel collar.** Collar applied so as to leave notch at joining. See COLLARS.

notion (nō'shən; *no* shun). Small useful article or clever device; any of the items included in notion department of store, as buttons, pins, fasteners, sewing accessories, findings, etc.

Nottingham lace (nŏt'ĭng-əm; *not* ing am). Machine-made lace of Nottingham, England. See LACES.

noué (F. nōō-ā; noo ay). French word meaning knotted or tied. Applied to types of trimming.

novelty (nŏv'əl-tĭ; *nov* el ti). Small personal or household article that is new or unusual.

novelty jewelry. Novel costume jewelry. See JEWELRY.

novelty suiting. Suiting made in variety of weaves and effects. See SUITING.

novelty weave. Variation from the staple weaves. See WEAVES.

nuance (F. nü-äṅs; noo ahnce). Slight shade of difference, as in color, sometimes achieved in costume effects by draping transparent or semi-transparent fabric of one color over another.

nub. Irregularity in yarns from which fabric is woven.

nubia (nū'bĭ-ə; *new* bi a). Soft, light, cloud-like scarf or covering for the head; sometimes of fleecy wool.

nub yarn. Yarn used in weaving chinchilla, etc. See YARNS.

nun's cloth. Bunting; fine, lightweight, woolen fabric in plain, loose weave. Used for dresses.

nun's cotton. Fine, cotton embroidery thread. See THREADS.

nun's veiling. Thin, soft, loosely woven, woolen fabric, in plain weave. Used for veiling, dresses, infants' coats and caps.

nun tuck. Broad tuck on curved line; used chiefly on flared skirt or sleeve. See TUCKS.

nursing basque. Basque with buttoned closings, one on each side of the front.

Nursing Basque

nutria (nū'trĭ-ə; *new* tri a). Fur resembling beaver. See FURS.

nylon. Coined name for new product of chemistry, a synthetic, fiber-forming compound derived from coal, air, water, and other substances. Very tough and strong. Made into bristles, sheets, fabrics, hosiery, plastics, wrappings, etc. Developed by DuPont. Can be spun finer than silk or rayon. Will take dyes used on silk, wool, acetate; and some used on cotton and rayon.

O

obi (ō'bĭ; *o* bi). Broad Japanese sash. See SASHES.

Japanese Obi

oblique Gobelin-stitch (ŏb-lēk' gŏb'ə-lĭn; ob *leek* gob e lin). Variation of Gobelin-stitch. Used in canvas embroidery. See GOBELIN under STITCHES.

oblong cross-stitch. Long, narrow cross-stitch. See STITCHES.

occasional dress (ə-kā'zhən-əl; oc *kay* zhun al). Elaborate or colorful dress for special occasions. See DRESSES.

ocelot (ŏs'ə-lŏt; *oss* e lot). Fur of large American spotted cat. See FURS.

ocher or **ochre** (ō'kẽr; *o* ker). Yellow color similar to or derived from the mineral substance. Used as pigment in paint.

off-color. Not of the natural or normal shade; of an unfashionable color.

off shade. Tone of color slightly different from the clear, true shade of the normal color; as, an off shade of navy blue or forest green.

off-shoulder neckline. Neckline extending above bust line, often with semblance of sleeve draped low on arm, leaving neck and upper arm bare. See NECKLINES.

off-sorts. Wool not up to standard. See WOOL.

oilcloth. Cloth treated with oil or paint to give a patent-leather surface. Used for waterproof table and shelf covering, and occasionally for waterproof jackets, capes, and caps.

oiled silk. Silk fabric coated with chemical having an oil base, as linseed oil; transparent and waterproof. Used for raincoats and capes, bag coverings, etc.

oilskin. Cotton, linen, silk, synthetic cloth, or garment waterproofed by means of oil.

old copper. Dark, dull, reddish brown.

old-fashioned. In outmoded style. Used in reference to dress and manners.

old rose. Soft, dull rose hue made popular during Victorian period. Similar to ashes of roses.

olive (ŏl′ĭv; *ol* iv). Soft yellowish-green color of unripe olive.

olive brunette. Person with dark hair and complexion. See BRUNETTE.

ombré (F. ȯṇ-brā; onh bray). Color term meaning graduated in tone. See COLOR.

omophorion (ō-mō-fō′rĭ-ən; o mo *foe* ri on). Strip of white embroidered silk worn by bishops of Greek Church. Worn around neck, crossed on left shoulder, with ends falling to knee.

one-hour dress. Dress with chemise type of bodice, kimono sleeves, and attached straight, short skirt; made famous by Mary Brooks Picken in 1924; could be made in one hour or less. See DRESSES.

onlaid. Applied on top of other material.

onlay. Decorative material laid on so as to be in relief.

O. N. T. Trade name of first thread having fuzz burned off by gas in finishing. See THREADS.

onyx (ŏn′ĭks; *on* ix). Semi-precious stone, a variety of CHALCEDONY, consisting of layers of different colors. Used for rings, brooches, accessories. Light onyx used for cameos.

ooze leather. Suede- or velvet-finished leather. See LEATHERS.

opal (ō′pəl;! *o* pal). Precious stone that has no one characteristic color, but shows peculiar shifting of delicate colors in changing lights.

open band. 1. Band on a loose sleeve, which does not meet. 2. Twist of yarn or thread spun so that fibers revolve from left to right. Also, yarn or thread so twisted.

open chain-stitch. Chain-stitch in squared effect. Same as SQUARE CHAIN-STITCH. See STITCHES.

opening. 1. Part of garment that opens to permit of garment's being put on, as placket of skirt, neck opening of blouse, etc. 2. Fashion showing of apparel for a new season, especially one of the showings in the houses of the couture; as, the Paris openings, London openings, New York openings.

open shank. Cut away at shank to reveal arch of foot. Applied to shoes.

open-stitch. Any embroidery stitch used for OPEN WORK. See STITCHES.

open-welt seam. Seam finished with a tuck from ¼ to 1 inch wide, made as part of the seam. Often used to panel the front and back of a skirt, or for the bodice seams of a jacket or coat. Same as TUCKED SEAM. See SEAMS.

open work. Work having numerous small openings through the material, as drawn or punch work or lace.

open-work embroidery. Drawn, cut, or punched work. See EMBROIDERIES.

opera cloak (ŏp′ēr-ə; *op* er a). Elaborate evening cloak, usually full length. See WRAPS.

opera glove. Long glove, sometimes without thumb. See GLOVES.

opera hat. Man's tall, collapsible hat, usually of silk faille. See HATS.

opera pump. Plain, untrimmed, classic pump. See SLIPPERS.

opera slipper. Woman's dress slipper or man's house slipper. See SLIPPERS.

opossum (ō-pŏs′ŭm; o *poss* um). Long-haired, dusky-gray fur of the American opossum. See FURS.

opus Anglicum (ō′pŭs ăng′glĭ-kŭm; *o* pus *ang* gli cum). Embroidery in split-stitch done in Anglo-Saxon times. See EMBROIDERIES.

opus araneum (ə-rā′nĭ-ŭm; a *ray* ni um). Handmade lace of linen thread with large mesh and darned designs. Same as ANTIQUE LACE. See LACES.

opus pulvinarium (pŭl-vĭ-nā′rĭ-ŭm; pul vi *nay* ri um). Allover embroidery on canvas, chiefly in cross-stitch. Old name for BERLIN WORK. See EMBROIDERIES.

or (F. ȯr; or). French word for gold.

orange (ŏr′ənj; *or* ange). Reddish yellow; one of the colors of the spectrum.

orarion (ō-rā′rĭ-ŏn; o *ray* ri on). Ecclesiastical stole.

orchid (ȯr′kĭd; *or* kid). Tint of red-purple color, lighter than lilac.

organdy or organdie (ȯr′gən-dĭ; *or* gan di). Crisp, plain or figured muslin in plain weave, slightly stiffened, in white and colors. Used for dresses, aprons, blouses, collars, cuffs, etc.

organza (ȯr-găn′zə; or *gan* za). Sheer, fine, crisp fabric used for diaphanous frocks and as body under delicate sheers.

organzine (ȯr′gən-zēn; *or* gan zeen). 1. Silk yarn used for warp. See SILK. 2. Fabric made by using such yarn.

Oriental crepe (o-rĭ-ĕn′tal; o ri *en* tal). Canton crepe. Also, hand-woven crepes from China and Japan. See CREPES.

Oriental embroidery. Various kinds of embroidery, as made in Eastern countries. See EMBROIDERIES.

Oriental lace. 1. Lace with design woven through and through the net. 2. Laces of Eastern countries. See LACES.

Oriental-stitch. Series of long, parallel stitches intersected by short, diagonal ones. See STITCHES.

Orleans (ȯr′lē-ənz; *or* le ans). Cloth made with cotton warp and worsted filling alternating on surface.

ormuzine (ȯr′mŭz-ēn; *or* muz een). Silk fabric of Persia, now obsolete.

ornament (ȯr′nə-mənt; *or* na ment). Something which adds to the general costume effect, as a medallion or novel pin or jeweled clip worn on a dress.

orphrey (ȯr′frĭ; *or* fri). 1. Elaborate gold embroidery. See EMBROIDERIES. 2. Broad band usually decorated with embroidery in gold or silver thread, used in Middle Ages to adorn priests' albs or knights' robes.

orris (ȯr′ĭs; *or* iss). 1. Gold or silver lace or braid popular in 18th century. See LACES. 2. Upholstery braid. See BRAIDS.

orris root. Root of certain irises used in powdered form for sachets, medicines, dry shampoos, etc.

osnaberg or osnaburg (ŏz′nə-bērg; *oz* na berg). Plain, coarse material woven of flax and tow in loose construction; characterized by rough, uneven yarns. Named for town in Germany where first made. Used for overalls, sacking, curtains, etc.

osprey (ŏs′prĭ; *oss* pri). Term for certain feathers, not really osprey, used as hat trimming. See FEATHERS.

Ostaigrette (ŏst-ā-grĕt′; ost ai *gret*). Trade name for imitation aigrette, made of ostrich quill. See FEATHERS.

ostrich feathers (ŏs′trĭch; *oss* trich). Wing and tail feathers from an ostrich. Often several feathers are carefully glued together as one to give abundant appearance. Dyed in all colors and beautifully curled. See FEATHERS.

ostrich leather. Tough, strong leather made from ostrich skins. See LEATHERS.

otter. Dark brown fur of the otter. See FURS.

ottoman (ŏt′ə-mən; *ott* o man). Firm, plain, heavy fabric having flat, crosswise ribs. Filling of silk, worsted, but usually cotton. Wool ottoman used for dresses, skirts, suits. Silk ottoman used for wraps and trimmings.

ottoman cord. Plain, corded silk fabric.

ottoman rib. Ribbed fabric in which the warp forms the rib.

ouch. Obsolete term for clasp or brooch, jewel setting, or article of jewelry.

outerwear. Clothing, such as coats, suits, sweaters, cardigans, etc., worn over other garments, on the outside.

outfit. Complete ensemble, usually as worn for a particular occasion; as, a sports outfit, skiing outfit, golfing outfit.

outing flannel. Light-weight, napped, cotton fabric. See FLANNELS.

outline embroidery. Embroidery with designs outlined and left open. See EMBROIDERIES.

outline-stitch. Simple embroidery stitch used to outline flowers, stems, etc. See STITCHES.

outsize. Size larger than the regular sizes; generally used for sizes larger than 46 bust. Also applied to hosiery having a top larger than regular.

ouvrage à l'aiguille (F. ōō-vräzh à lä-gwē; oo vrahzh a lay gwee). French word for needlework.

overall (ō′vēr-ȯl; *o* ver all). Any outer garment worn over others to protect them from soil, weather, wear.

overall button. Button, usually of metal, applied to overalls by a special machine. See BUTTONS.

overalls. 1. Loose trousers with a bib and a strap top, made of denim or other sturdy fabric. Worn for decades by workmen. In the 1930's, adopted by women as a work and play garment. **2.** Waterproof leggings.
overblouse. Blouse not tucked in at waist. See BLOUSES.
overcast- or **overcasting-stitch.** Simple slanting stitch used for finishing raw edges, etc. See STITCHES.
overcast running-stitch. Stitch made by overcasting a series of running-stitches. Same as TWISTED RUNNING-STITCH. See STITCHES.
overcheck. Pattern of checks in which one color is woven over another. See CHECKS. Also, fabric so checked.
overcoat. Warm, bulky coat. See COATS.
overcoating. Woolen or worsted fabric of medium or heavy weight used for overcoats.
overdress. 1. Outer dress. **2.** To dress to excess. **3.** Same as TUNIC.
overgaiter. Cloth anklet or spat. Originally used with pumps or other evening shoes in winter. At times fashionable for day dress.
overgarment. Outer garment or dress.
overhanding. Short over-and-over-stitches used to join two edges together; also used in embroidery. See STITCHES.
overhand knitting. Method of hand knitting in which right needle is held as a pencil is held. See KNITTING.
overhand tuck. Tuck sewn with over-handing stitches. See TUCKS.
overlay. Scottish term for neck covering or cravat.
Overlock. Trade name for over-stitch or sewing machine that makes it.
overseas cap (ō'vẽr-sēz'; o ver seez). Small military cap worn by soldiers of U. S. A. in the World War. See CAPS.
oversew (ō'vẽr-sō; o ver so). To sew over and over; overhand.
overshoe (ō'vẽr-shōō; o ver shoo). Foot covering worn over ordinary shoes for warmth or protection. See SHOES.
overskirt. Short drapery worn over skirt of dress. See SKIRTS.
oversleeve. Sleeve worn over another.

Sometimes attached to its mate by a collar piece. See SLEEVES.
over-stitch. Type of finishing stitch, usually made by machine. See STITCHES.
oxford (ŏks'fẽrd; ox ford). **1.** Cotton fabric of small basket-like weave, made of threads equal on warp and woof, dyed before weaving. Used for men's shirts, women's summer sports clothes. Also, cotton print. **2.** Woolen cloth woven of dyed threads, usually black and white, having a flecked appearance. **3.** Low-cut, laced shoe. See SHOES. **4.** Very dark gray color. All named for Oxford University, England, from having been originated or worn there.
oxford blue. Navy blue, slightly reddish in hue.
Oxford gown. Academic gown worn in American colonies on public occasions by men in authority.
oyah lace. Turkish crochet lace in colored silk, with elaborate floral designs. See LACES.
oyster white (oi'stẽr; oy ster). **1.** Gray-white shade with slightly bluish tint. **2.** Off-white.

P

pac or **pack. 1.** MOCCASIN. See SLIPPERS. **2.** Half boot. See BOOTS.
packcloth. Heavy, coarse cotton fabric, as duck or canvas or burlap, used to make packs or to cover them, to make pack soles, etc.
pack duck. Same as PACKCLOTH.
pack needle or **packing needle.** Large, strong needle for sewing packcloth. See NEEDLES.
packthread. Strong, coarse thread or twine. See THREADS.
pad. To round out to a form, as to pad a shoulder or top of sleeve; to stuff or fill in. Also, cushion or small mass of anything soft used for stuffing or padding.
padded shoulders. Shoulder line of a garment thickened or extended by means of inside padding to increase appearance of width or height.
padding. Soft material used to pad or stuff anything; sheets of wool or cotton wadding, cotton batting, etc.
padding cotton. 1. Bulky cotton thread having few twists. See THREADS. **2.** Cotton batting used for padding.
padding stitch. 1. Foundation stitch used for padding under embroidery stitches where a raised effect is desired. See STITCHES. **2.** Diagonal-basting used to hold padding to an interlining.
padou (F. pȧ-dōō; pa doo). Fine narrow silk ribbon or cotton or wool tape.
paduasoy (păd'ū-ȧ-soi; pad you a soy). Strong, rich, slightly corded fabric of heavy silk. Originally made at Padua, Italy. Much worn in 18th and 19th centuries.
paenula (pē'nū-lȧ; pee new la). Ancient Roman mantle. See WRAPS.
page boy bob. Long bob with hair worn almost straight, except for slight curl under at ends. See BOBS.

pagne (F. páñ; panye). Loincloth or short skirt worn by natives of tropical countries.
pagoda sleeve (pȧ-gō'dȧ; pa go da). Sleeve, large at the bottom, fitted at the armhole. From formal costume of the Chinese. See SLEEVES.
pagoda toque. Hat with step-like crown of pyramid shape. See HATS.
pagri (păg'rē; pahg ree). Turban made of narrow strip of cotton or silk 10 to 50 yards long, wound about head, one end left hanging down back. Worn by Hindu men. Originally, badge of subjugation. Hindu word meaning turban.
paillasson (F. pī-yȧ-sôŋ; pie yah sonh). Coarsely woven straw. See STRAWS.
paillette (F. pī-yĕt; pie yet). One of many small glittering disks, usually sewn on fabric to lie flat like fish-scales; spangle.
Paisley (pāz'lĭ; paiz li). **1.** Fine wool fabric of yarn-dyed colors, in many designs, similar to those used for Paisley shawls made in Paisley, Scotland. Used for dresses, shawls, trimmings. **2.** Soft silk print, patterned after the wool fabric. Used for dresses, trimmings, blouses.

Type of Paisley Design

pajamas (pȧ-jä'măz; pa jah maz) or **pyjamas.** Suit consisting of coat or blouse and trousers. Worn for sleeping, lounging, beach wear, depending on the style and fabric; more formally, for afternoon and evening wear at home. Originally, ankle-length trousers worn by natives of India, Persia, etc.
palatine (păl'ȧ-tĭn; pal a tin). Shoulder cape or tippet. See CAPES.
pale. 1. Lacking in depth or intensity of color, as a very light tint of any color. **2.** Obsolete term for vertical stripe.
pale brunette. Person with dark hair, clear complexion. See BRUNETTE.
paletot (păl'ē-tō; pal a toe). Loose coat; also, jacket worn by woman to complete costume. See COATS. See JACKETS.
palisade. Wire holding up hair, part of commode headdress. Also, cap worn over this wire frame. See CAPS.

18th Century Palisade

pall (pôl; pawl). Obsolete term for rich fabric or garment made of it, especially a cloak.
palla (păl'ȧ; pal a). Voluminous wrap worn by women of ancient Rome. See WRAPS.
pallette (păl'ĕt; pal et). One of the round flat plates worn at the armpits as part of medieval armor.

pallium (păl'ĭ-ŭm; *pal* i um) or **pallion** (păl'ĭ-ŏn; *pal* i on). 1. Garment, similar to the himation, worn by Greek men and women over the chiton. 2. White, woolen band in circular shape with pendants, worn by archbishops of Roman Catholic Church on certain occasions.

Palm Beach (päm bēch; pahm beech). Trade name for light-weight fabric in plain or twill weave, with cotton warp, mohair filling. Often striped and in variety of shades. Used for men's and women's summer suits and for slacks. Named for Palm Beach, Florida.

paltock (păl'tŏk; *pal* tock). Short outer garment similar to a jacket, worn by men in 14th and 15th centuries.

paludamentum (pə-lū-də-měn'tŭm; pa lue da *men* tum). Military cloak of ancient Rome. See WRAPS.

pampilion (păm-pĭl'yən; pam *pill* yon). Type of fur trimming for garments, worn in 15th and 16th centuries. Also, coarse woolen fabric.

pan. Flap or tab ornamenting a garment.

panache (pə-năsh'; pa *nash*) or **pennache.** Plume or erect bunch of feathers worn as headdress; originally, as worn on helmets; today, as worn on hats. Also, bunch of tassels or narrow ribbons.

15th Century Panache on Helmet

panache de coque (F. pă-năsh də kŏk; pa nash de coke). Plume of cock feathers.

Panama (păn-ə-mä' or păn'ə-mä; pan a *mah* or *pan* a mah). 1. Fine, hand-plaited straw used for men's and women's hats. See STRAWS. 2. Light-weight fabric, usually of hard-twisted worsted yarn in plain weave, but sometimes of coarser yarn in basket weave. Used in dresses, skirts, suits. 3. Fabric made of cotton warp and double filling, in texture resembling Panama hats. Used for skirts and suits.

Panama cloth. Cotton fabric in close plain weave similar to net. Used in millinery for brims, crowns, etc.

Panama hat. Hat of Panama straw. See HATS.

pancake. 1. Flat surface. 2. Flat hat. 3. Leather scraps pressed and glued to form a sheet; used for insoles, etc.

pancake beret. Broad flat beret. See HATS.

pane. 1. Straight slit in a garment, showing contrasting color beneath. 2. Part or piece of a garment, such as skirt or collar. 3. One of a number of pieces sewn into a garment. Robin Hood's coat shows use of panes of leather. 4. Short for counterpane or coverlet.

panel (păn'əl; *pan* el). Usually the front gore of a dress or skirt, or the center front or back of a dress. May be part of the garment, a full-length gore, as in a princess dress; or it may be applied or allowed to hang free. Used generally as feature of design.

panjam (pŭn'jŭm; *pun* jum). Cotton fabric. Same as PUNJUM.

panne satin (păn; pan). Satin treated by heat and pressure to produce high luster. See SATINS.

panne velvet. Velvet with pile flattened all one way. Used chiefly for trimmings and in millinery. See VELVETS.

pannier (păn'yĕr or F. păn-ñā; *pan* yer or pahn yay). 1. Bouffant drape at the side of a skirt, giving effect of wired pannier. So called because of resemblance to baskets for carrying provisions, etc., usually carried in pairs by horses or mules, one pannier hanging down on each side. 2. Oval-shaped hoop for the side. See HOOPS.

pannier skirt. Skirt arranged over pannier or having applied side fulness or drapery. See SKIRTS.

pannuscorium (păn-ŭs-kō'rĭ-ŭm; pan us *core* i um). Trade name for type of leather cloth used for shoe uppers.

pansière (F. păn-syĕr; ponh syare). Piece of medieval armor made to protect lower front part of body.

pantalets (păn-tə-lĕts'; pan ta *lets*). Long drawers decorated about the ankle with tucks, ruffles, embroidery, and lace, which showed below skirts. Worn by women and children, often as separate frills tied on below knee. Highly popular from 1840 to 1850. Word derived from PANTALOONS.

19th Century Pantalets

pantaloons (păn-tə-lōōnz'; pan ta *loons*). 1. Trousers. During 18th century, closely fitted trousers fastened at calf. Originally, breeches and hose in one garment, introduced by the Venetians. 2. Modern adaptation of pantalets, consisting of long leg portions of sheer fabric fastened at ankle, for wear under hoop skirts or wide flaring evening dresses.

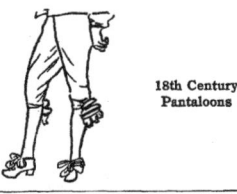

18th Century Pantaloons

pantie crotch. Crotch formed by narrow shaped piece set into joining. See CROTCH.

panties. Short undergarment, having practically no leg portion, fitted snugly at hipline.

Panties, 1930's

pantoffle (păn'tə-fl; *pan* to fl). 1. House slipper. See SLIPPERS. 2. Kind of 16th century patten or overshoe, covering only front of foot, and having deep cork sole. Also see PATTEN.

pantoufle (F. păn-tōōfl; ponh toofl). French word for slipper.

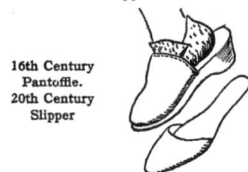

16th Century Pantoffle. 20th Century Slipper

pants. Any type of inexpensive trousers.

pañuelo (Sp. pă-nwä'lō; pa *nway* lo). Kerchief; specifically, square cloth folded to triangle, worn in Philippines as collar or large ruffle.

panung (pä'nŏong; *pah* noong). Long, broad strip of cloth worn by Siamese natives, both men and women, as loin-cloth or skirt. Similar in appearance to knickerbockers.

paon velvet (F. păn; ponh). Velvet similar to panne. See VELVETS.

papal hat (pā'pəl; *pay* pal). Wide-brimmed ecclesiastical hat. See HATS.

paper cambric or **muslin.** Thin, narrow cambric or muslin, glazed and stiffened. Used for linings, etc.

paper cloth. 1. Cloth of bark. Same as TAPA CLOTH. 2. Paper made in imitation of cloth.

paper shears. Pointed shears with long blades. See SHEARS.

papier-maché (pā'pĕr mă-shā' or F. pă-pyä mă-shā; *pay* per ma *shay* or pa pyay ma shay). Strong, light-weight material made of paper pulp mixed with other substances; shaped, usually on molds, into sundry articles, such as dress forms, etc.

papillote (pă-pē-yōt; pa pee yote). French word for curlpaper.

parachute silk (păr'ə-shōōt; *pa* ra shoot). Fine, very closely woven silk fabric in plain weave; used for underwear, blouses, linings, etc.

paradise feather (păr'ə-dīs; *pa* ra dice). Plume from bird of paradise. See FEATHERS.

paragon (păr'ə-gŏn; *pa* ra gon). Cloth similar to camlet, used for common wear in 17th and 18th centuries.

Paraguay lace (păr'ȧ-gwā; pa ra gway). Lace with designs in spider-web effects. See LACES.

paramatta (păr-ȧ-măt'ȧ; pa ra mat a). Light-weight fabric having warp of cotton, filling now of worsted, formerly of silk. Similar to bombazine or merino. Used for dresses.

parament (păr'ȧ-měnt; pa ra ment). 1. Rich, ornamental clothing worn by persons of rank. 2. Ornamental cuff. See CUFFS. Both meanings obsolete. From French parement, meaning ornament.

paraphernalia (păr-ȧ-fēr-nā'lĭ-ȧ; pa ra fer nay li a). Personal belongings, especially ornaments and other dress accessories.

parasisol (păr-ȧ-sī'sȯl; pa ra sy sol). Linen-weave straw. See SISOL under STRAWS.

parasol (păr'ȧ-sŏl; pa ra sol). Small umbrella, often of some decorative fabric, rarely waterproof; carried by women for effect more than as protection against sun. Lace-trimmed or ornate or bright-colored parasol often called sunshade.

parasol skirt. Short skirt with many seams, flared at the bottom in imitation of a parasol. See SKIRTS.

parchment (pärch'mȧnt; parch ment). Pale tan color like that of sheepskin. Also called lark.

parchment lace. Lace made with strips of parchment wound with thread. See LACES.

pareu (pä'rä-ōō; pah ray oo) or **pareo.** Rectangular, figured cotton cloth worn as skirt or loincloth by natives of Pacific islands.

parfilage (F. pär-fē-läzh; par fee lahzh). Unraveling of textile fabrics or other materials into which gold and silver threads have been woven. Fashionable pastime during 18th century.

Paris embroidery. White cord embroidery on piqué. See EMBROIDERIES.

Paris hat. Silk hat. See HATS.

Parisienne (F. pȧ-rē-zyĕn; pa ree zyen). Frenchwoman from Paris. Also, any garment, etc., of French origin, imported from Paris.

parka (pär'kȧ; par ka). Woolen garment, like long shirt with attached hood, sometimes fur-lined. Worn for skiing and other winter sports. Originally, Siberian and Alaskan hooded outer garment made of animal skins.

Parka, 1938

parka hood. Peaked hood with attached scarf ends. Worn with winter sports costumes. See HOODS.

parrot green (păr'ȯt; pa rot). Medium shade of yellowish green; color of green parrot's feathers.

parson's hat. Clerical felt hat with low crown and broad, straight brim. See HATS.

parti-colored (pär'tĭ-kŭl-ẽrd; par ti cull erd). Variegated in color; having a diversity of colors.

parti-striped. Striped in different colors.

partlet (pärt'lĕt; part let). Covering for neck and shoulders, similar to chemisette, usually ruffled, having band or collar. Usually made of linen for women; of richer material, and ornamented, for men. Popular in 16th century.

parure (pȧ-rōōr'; pa roor). Set of ornaments, either trimming for costume, as collar and cuffs, or jewels to be worn together. Used loosely to mean ornaments or decoration in general.

pashm (pŭsh'm; push m). Fleece of Tibetan goat. See WOOL.

passé (F. pȧ-sā; pa say). Old-fashioned; out of date.

passement (păs'měnt; pass ment) or **passament** (păs'ȧ-měnt; pass a ment). Decorative dress trimming of silk, linen, gold, or silver thread. Formerly used as edging on garments.

passementerie (păs-měn'trĭ or F. pȧs-mäṅ-trē; pass men tri or pahss monh tree). Trimmings, especially heavy embroideries or edgings of rich gimps, braids, beads, silks, tinsel, etc.

passing. Smooth thread of silk wrapped with gold or silver strand. See THREADS.

paste. 1. Synthetic composition used in making imitation stones; artificial jewelry. 2. Woman's headdress of 16th century, made of two pieces of stiffened material meeting at center of forehead; worn under hood; adorned with jewels or other decoration.

paste grain. Leather stiffened with paste. See LEATHERS.

pastel (păs-tĕl'; pass tell). Soft, delicate tint or pale tone of a color.

patch. 1. Piece of material, especially cloth. Usually used, when matching original fabric, for mending; when different, for decoration. Also, to mend with such a piece. 2. Piece of silk or court plaster, usually black, applied to face or neck to cover blemish or to heighten beauty; highly popular among women during 17th century.

patch pocket. Pocket applied on outside of garment. See POCKETS.

patchwork. Patches or pieces of fabric, leather, etc., of varying colors, put together to form designs, such as pinetree, nine-patch, etc. Used for the tops of quilts, coverlets, cushions, etc.

patent leather (păt'ȧnt; pat ent). Any of various leathers or imitation leathers with applied smooth, hard, glossy finish. See LEATHERS.

patola (pȧ-tō'lȧ; pa toe la). East Indian silk fabric, especially one made into wedding garment of native woman.

patte (F. păt; paht). Flap, tab, lappet, or strap, whether for decoration or for fastening.

patten (păt'ȧn; pat en). Separate wooden sole on iron rings fastened to boot or shoe by leather straps. Worn to keep feet out of mud. General term for protective foot covering, including PANTOFFLE and CLOG.

18th Century Pattens

PATTERNS

pattern (păt'ẽrn; pat ern). 1. Model for making things, especially clothes. Specifically, guide for cutting all pieces of garments. 2. Dress length, or sufficient material to make a dress. 3. Unit of decorative design; motif. Used singly or repeated.

block p. Pattern of simple design, often of strong, heavy paper, used for size in cutting, or for grading various sizes up and down.

commercial p. Tissue-paper pattern or guide for cutting garments. Made by pattern company. Sold at pattern counters in stores.

drafted p. Pattern drafted, usually for an individual, by means of tailor's square, ruler, or like device, according to a combination of measurements based on rules of proportion.

foundation p. Drafted or commercial pattern of simplest type, with normal seam lines and no fulness or designing lines.

guide p. Pattern of muslin or cambric or similar material, cut from foundation paper pattern and fitted to individual figure. Used as guide for adjusting tissue-paper patterns and for draping, cutting, and fitting.

master p. 1. Basic pattern of a style, from which other sizes are made. 2. Pattern of simple design made as guide for correct size, as a foundation pattern.

transfer p. Commercial pattern having design stamped on paper, ready to be transferred, usually by iron, to the fabric to be embroidered. Sometimes called hot-iron patterns.

triad p. Uncut pattern that has three or more designs for pattern on one piece, the outline of each being indicated by different system of dots or dashes. The desired outline is traced on paper, and this traced pattern is used to cut the garment. Such patterns widely used in Great Britain, as well as in other European countries.

pattern book. Book of selected pattern designs issued periodically. Sometimes called fashion quarterly.

patti sack. Short, flared jacket. See JACKETS.

pattu (pŭt'ōō; putt oo). East Indian homespun wool or tweed; used for shawls, etc.

pauldron (pôl'drȧn; pawl dron). De-

pavé

tachable piece of medieval armor covering shoulder.

pavé (F. pȧ-vā; pa vay). Setting in which jewels are set closely together.

paysan (F. pā-ē-zäṇ; pay ee zonh). French word for peasant.

peach. Tint of tea rose, with a slightly yellow cast; color of the blush side of the ripe peach.

peacock blue. Brilliant green-blue; color between dark centers and yellow borders of spots on peacock's upper tail.

pea green. Medium yellowish green; color of the vegetable.

pea jacket. Heavy, short jacket. See JACKETS.

peanit (pē'nĭt; *pee* nit). Inexpensive straw of exotic type. See STRAWS.

PEARLS

pearl (pûrl; purl). **1.** Hard, smooth, round substance, usually with silvery luster, found within shell of oyster or other mollusk. Used as jewel. Also, imitation of genuine pearl. **2.** Light, warm gray tint, slightly bluish; color of shadow on pearls. **3.** Mother-of-pearl or its color. **4.** Joining thread in needle-point lace. See BAR, 2. **5.** Variant spelling of PURL.

culture p. Pearl grown in oyster shell under controlled, artificially stimulated conditions.

fish p. Imitation pearl used for buttons and ornaments.

Roman p. Imitation pearl made of a glass globe filled with wax and coated with pearly essence.

seed p. Tiny pearl, often used in mass to embroider designs on garments and to make bags, neckbands, ornaments, etc.

Venetian p. (vȧ-nē'shȧn; ve *nee* shan). Imitation pearl made of glass.

pearl button. Button made of mother-of-pearl. See BUTTONS.

pearled. 1. Set or adorned with pearls or mother-of-pearl. **2.** Pearl-like in color or luster.

pearl edge. Narrow edging of small loops, as on ribbon or lace.

pearl gray. Neutral gray. See PEARL, 2.

pearling. Fine, narrow picot edge. Used as finish.

pearly. Of or like pearl.

peasant cloth (pĕz'ȧnt; *pez* ant). Sturdy muslin often dyed or printed in gay colors. Used in the 20th century for beach and play clothes, dirndls, etc.

Type of Peasant Costume

peasant costume. Dress typical of rural peoples; especially those of European countries. Usually colorful and characteristic of the artcraft of the section.

peasant lace. Lace of torchon type. See LACES.

peasant sleeve. Full, loose sleeve. See SLEEVES.

peascod or **peasecod** (pēz'kȯd; *peez* cod). Padded and quilted lower part of doublet, popular in late 16th century. Such a doublet described as *peascod-bellied*.

peau d'ange (F. pō däṇzh; po dahnzh). French phrase meaning parts of an angel. Same as ANGEL SKIN.

peau de cygne (F. pō dȧ sēñ; po de seenye). Soft, lustrous fabric in diagonal weave with prominent cross-thread. Used for dresses, suits, and coats. No longer on the market.

peau de soie (F. pō dȧ swä; po de swah). Firm, soft, durable silk in twill weave with dull, satin-like finish. Made in both single and double face, showing fine cross ribs on one side or both. Used for trimmings, dresses, coats, facings for dress coats.

pebble. To produce a rough, bumpy surface on leather or fabric by graining, finishing, etc.

pebble grain. Surface finish resembling sand or tiny pebbles. Applied to leather and imitation leather by passing it between rollers under pressure.

peccary (pĕk'ȧ-rĭ; *peck* a ri). Fine-grained pig leather. See LEATHERS.

pêche (F. pĕsh; pesh). French word meaning peach-colored.

pectoral (pĕk'tȯ-rȧl; *peck* to ral). Anything worn for ornament, protection, or covering of the breast.

pedal straw (pĕd'ȧl; *ped* al). Straw woven from the foot of stalk. See STRAWS.

pedaline (pĕd'ȧ-lēn; *ped* a leen). Synthetic straw made of hemp fiber covered with Cellophane and woven between cotton threads. See STRAWS.

pedule (pĕd'ūl; *ped* yule). Boot-shaped leg covering of flexible leather, flannel, or other material, worn in ancient and medieval days.

pee. Man's coat or jacket worn during 15th, 16th, and 17th centuries.

peek-a-boo waist. Shirtwaist of eyelet or sheer fabric. See BLOUSES.

peg. Small pointed or tapered piece, as of wood or metal; used to fasten parts of things together, as sole and upper of shoe.

pegged boot or **shoe.** Boot or shoe with sole and upper fastened together by pegs.

peg-top. Wide at top and narrow at bottom. Term applied to trousers, skirts, pockets, etc.; specifically, woman's skirt with bunch or loop of extra material at waistline, popular about 1910. See SKIRTS. Originally, boy's pear-shaped spinning top.

peignoir (F. pā-fĭwär; pay nwahr). Dressing gown or cape. Used in France in place of towel after the bath. Usually made of terry cloth.

pekin (pē'kĭn; *pee* kin). Silk dress material, figured or striped alternately in satin and velvet. Originally made in China.

Pekinese-stitch (pē-kĭn-ēz'; pee kin *eez*). Stitch of looped or braided appearance. See STITCHES.

pelerine (pĕl-ĕr-ēn'; pel er *een*). Waist-length tippet or cape. See CAPES.

pelisse (F. pȧ-lēs; pe leece). Long cloak. See WRAPS.

pelt. Skin or hide of an animal, usually with the fur or hair or wool on it intact, as received by the tanner or dresser. In the fur trade, the raw skin is usually called the pelt only after it has been dressed and prepared for use as fur. The leather side is also called the pelt; as light-weight pelt, meaning thin-skinned.

peltry. Skins, singly or collectively.

pelt wool. Short wool of sheep killed soon after shearing. See WOOL.

pen. Obsolete term for feather or plume; wing feather.

penang (pȧ-năng'; pe *nang*). Cotton fabric similar to heavy-weight percale.

pencil silhouette (sĭl-ōō-ĕt'; sil oo *et*). Straight, slim silhouette. See SILHOUETTES.

pencil stripe. Stripe similar in width to a pencil mark. See STRIPES.

pendant (pĕn'dȧnt; *pen* dant). Ornament that hangs or is suspended, as a lavaliere or dropped earring.

pendeloque (F. päṇ-dȧ-lŏk; ponh de loke). Pear-shaped diamond or other stone, used as a pendant.

penelope (pȧ-nĕl'ȯ-pē; pe *nell* o pee). Sleeveless, knitted jacket. See JACKETS.

penelope canvas. Double-thread canvas. See CANVAS.

Peniche lace. Portuguese pillow lace. See LACES.

penistone (pĕn'ĭ-stŭn; *pen* i stun). Coarse woolen fabric formerly made at Penistone, England. Used for outer garments from 16th to 19th century. Also called *forest white*.

penitentials (pĕn-ĭ-tĕn'shȧlz; pen i *ten* shalz). Colloquial term for garments of black.

peplos (pĕp'lȯs; *pep* los). Wide scarf worn by Greek women in chilly weather.

peplum (pĕp'lŭm; *pep* lum). **1.** Small ruffle, flounce, or flared extension of the costume around hips, usually from bottom of blouse, bodice, or jacket. **2.** Ancient Greek close-fitting gown extending from neck to feet.

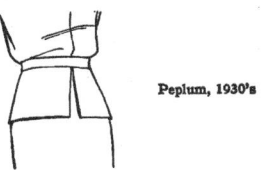

Peplum, 1930's

pepper-and-salt. Effect of mixed pepper and salt given by black and white yarns twisted and woven together.

percale (pẽr-kăl'; per *cal*). Close, firm cotton fabric in plain weave, and in solid colors or prints, usually the latter. Used for wash dresses, shirts, aprons, children's clothes. Perhaps more percale woven than any other fabric.

percaline (pẽr-kǝ-lēn'; per ca *leen*). Fine, thin, cotton fabric in plain weave with glassy surface. Used for linings, petticoats, foundations. Originally used as a substitute for taffeta.

perforation (pẽr-fō-rā'shŭn; per fo *ray* shun). Hole made by punching, boring, etc. Specifically: **1.** Hole in pattern, made in varying sizes to indicate placing of darts or pockets, direction of fabric grain, or the like. **2.** One of many holes, usually made in groups to form designs on shoe uppers, rubber corsets, etc.

perfume (pẽr'fūm; *per* fume). Substance, usually liquid, having a pleasing fragrance; or, the fragrant scent itself. Used chiefly by women. Good perfumes are expensive; Oriental perfumes, most potent. Many designers, especially the French, have perfumes bearing their name, for sale in their own establishments and elsewhere.

period dress. Special style of dress peculiar to particular time in history; as Empire, colonial, etc.

periwig (pẽr'Ĭ-wĭg; *pare* i wig). Wig fashionable in 18th century. See WIGS.

periwinkle blue (pẽr'Ĭ-wĭng-kl; *pare* i wing kl). Medium light blue color with lavenderish tinge. Highly popular in the U.S.A. in the 1920's.

perk. To prink or spruce oneself up.

perky. Trim and jaunty, as a perky bow or hat.

perle or **pearl cotton.** Mercerized cotton thread in many sizes and colors. See THREADS.

permanent finish (pẽr'mǝ-nǝnt; *per* ma nent). Finish of any kind so applied as to last indefinitely, especially after washing.

permanents. Light-weight cotton fabrics that are fast-dyed.

permanent wave. In hairdressing, treatment of the hair by heat, chemical action, steam, etc., to give it a wavy or curled appearance that will last for weeks or months. Those who have their hair water waved after shampooing have generally had a permanent wave.

perpetuana or **perpets** or **petuna** (pẽr-pĕt-ū-ā'nǝ, pẽr-pĕtz', or pǝ-tū'nǝ; per pet you *ai* na, per *pets*, or pe *tue* na). Glossy, durable woolen cloth made in England in 17th and 18th centuries. Similar to lasting. Worn by Puritans in America.

Persian (pẽr'zhǝn; *per* zhan). **1.** Term applied generally to costume of countries east of Mediterranean; characterized chiefly by loose, baggy, gathered-in-at-the-bottom trousers and skirts, and brilliant coloring of costume and ornaments. **2.** Silk, light in color and printed with large flowers. Used for blouses, linings, trimmings. **3.** Thin silk fabric in plain weave, almost transparent. Used for linings, trimmings.

Type of Persian Costume

Persian cord. Corded fabric of cotton and wool similar to rep. Used for dresses.

Persian embroidery. Any embroidery done in Persia or of Persian type. See EMBROIDERIES.

Persian lamb. Skins of very young lambs, having tight curl. See FURS.

Persian lawn. Fine, sheer cotton fabric in plain weave with high luster. Now, practically obsolete. Used for blouses, dresses, neckwear, etc.

persienne (pẽr-zĬ-ĕn' or F. pẽr-syĕn; per zi *en* or pare syen). Cotton, sometimes silk, cloth printed or painted in fanciful designs. Originally made in Persia.

peruke (pǝ-rōōk'; pe *rook*). Wig less cumbersome than the periwig. See WIGS.

Pervel. Trade name for a product made of wood pulp, in imitation of cotton muslin; used for sheets, pillowcases, etc.

perwitsky (pẽr-wĭt'skĭ; per *wit* ski). Mottled short fur of polecat. See FURS.

petal-stitch. Series of chain-stitches with connecting stitches laid in stem-like line. See STITCHES.

petasos (pĕt'ǝ-sŏs; *pet* a sos) or **petasus** (pĕt'ǝ-sŭs; *pet* a sus). **1.** Close-fitting, winged cap. See CAPS. **2.** Low-crowned, broad-brimmed hat. See HATS.

Peter Pan collar. Rounded, turned-down collar. See COLLARS.

Peter Pan costume. Costume worn by Maude Adams when she played the part of the hero in J. M. Barrie's play, "Peter Pan." See FANCY DRESS.

Peter Pan hat. Small perky hat with feather. See HATS.

petersham (pē'tẽr-shăm; *pee* ter sham). **1.** Heavy, rough-napped woolen cloth, usually in dark navy blue. Used for men's heavy overcoats, suitable for seafaring or severe weather. **2.** Heavy jacket of this material. See JACKETS. **3.** Heavy, corded belting ribbon. Used for inner belts, hatbands, hat trimming.

Peter Thomson dress. Tailored, sailor type of dress. See DRESSES.

petite (F. pǝ-tēt; pe teet). French word for small or diminutive. Used of a girl or woman.

petit point (pĕt'Ĭ point or F. pǝ-tē pwăṉ; *pet* i point or pe tee pwanh). **1.** Fine needle tapestry stitch. Same as TENT-STITCH. See STITCHES. **2.** Term used loosely to designate needle tapestry work. See EMBROIDERIES.

petticoat (pĕt'Ĭ-cōt; *pet* i coat). **1.** Woman's underskirt, usually just slightly shorter than outside skirt, ruffled or trimmed. **2.** Formerly, short coat or jacket worn by men. **3.** Wide garment of canvas, oilskin, etc., worn by fishermen. Originally called *petty coat.*

Petticoat, 1890's

petticoat breeches. Short wide trousers trimmed with ribbon and laces, fashionable for men at end of 17th century. Introduced to England from France about 1658.

petticoat dress. Dress with decorative petticoat showing beneath hem. See DRESSES.

petuna (pǝ-tū'nǝ; pe *tue* na). Glossy, durable, woolen fabric. Worn by Puritans in America. Same as PERPETUANA.

philibeg (fĬl'Ĭ-bĕg; *fill* i beg). Scottish kilt. Same as FILIBEG.

Philippine embroidery (fĬl'Ĭ-pēn; *fill* i peen). Embroidery characterized by dainty floral motifs. See EMBROIDERIES.

photographic print (fō-tō-grăf'Ĭk; fo to *graf* ic). Print made from photograph engraved on roller or screen. Popularized for fabric design by Steichen, special photographer for Vogue Magazine in the 1920's. See PRINTS.

Phrygian cap (frĬj'Ĭ-ǝn; *frij* i an). Ancient close-fitting cap. See CAPS.

Phrygian needlework. Ancient needlework with silk and gold. See EMBROIDERIES.

phrygium (frĬj'Ĭ-ŭm; *frij* i um). Helmet-shaped cap. See CAPS.

phulkari (pōōl'kä-rē; *pool* kah ree). **1.** Embroidery made in India. See EMBROIDERIES. **2.** Fabric so embroidered or garment adorned with floral embroidery.

phylactery (fĬ-lăk'tẽr-Ĭ; fi *lack* ter i). **1.** Amulet or charm worn on the person as protection against danger, disease, etc. **2.** Fringe or other border.

picaresque (pĬk-ǝ-rĕsk'; pick a *resk*). Roguish; adventurous. Used to describe swagger fashions.

piccadilly (pĬk-ǝ-dĬl'Ĭ; pick a *dill* i). **1.** Standing collar. See COLLARS. **2.** Formerly, tabbed or scalloped border on collars, doublets, skirts, armholes, worn in 17th century. Also called *pickadil* or *piccadill*. Also, edging of lace or other fine work; high, stiff collar or ruff; stiffened band worn as support beneath collar or ruff. Illustrated under **pickadil**.

pick. 1. Blow driving shuttle across loom, determining speed of loom; as, so many picks per minute. **2.** In determining texture of fabric, number of warp or weft threads per inch. **3.** To

pickadil

throw shuttle, as across loom. **4.** Filling yarn thus carried. See FILLING, 1.

pickadil. Standing collar, usually with scalloped edge.

16th Century Pickadils

Pickelhaube (pĭk′əl-how-bə; *pick* el how ba). German spiked helmet.

picklock. Fine grade of wool from merino and Siberian sheep.

pickover. Floating thread in a weave; one that lies over surface across several threads.

picot (F. pē-kō; pee co). **1.** One of series of loops along selvage of fabric forming finish on one or both sides; also, one of small loops decorating edge of pattern in lace. **2.** Finished edge having tiny points, produced by cutting machine-hemstitching in half.

picoté (F. pē-kō-tā; pee co tay). Made up of picots; edged with picot.

picot-stitch. Stitch forming loops of thread extending below a row of finishing or connecting stitches. See STITCHES.

picture hat. Large-brimmed, extravagantly ornamented hat. The ladies in Gainsborough's paintings wore picture hats. See HATS.

piece. To repair, renew, or add to; to join the parts of; to mend by joining.

pièce de résistance (F. pē-ĕs də rā-zĕs-täns; pee ess de ray zees tahnce). Chief or outstanding feature, as of a costume.

piece-dyeing. Dyeing done after weaving; opposite of yarn-dyeing. See DYEING.

piece goods. **1.** Fabric sold in pieces of fixed length or by the yard. See GOODS. **2.** Name of the department in a store where piece goods are sold.

piecette (pēs-ĕt′; peece *et*). Gusset of a glove.

pied (pīd; pide). Parti-colored; variegated.

pie-pan or **pie-plate.** Beret with very shallow crown. See BERET under HATS.

Pierrette costume (F. pyĕ-rĕt; pyare ret). Costume of female Pierrot. See FANCY DRESS.

pierrot (pē′ĕr-ō or F. pyĕ-rō; *pee* er o or pyare o). Low-cut blouse. See BLOUSES.

Pierrot costume. Type of costume worn by jesting character of French pantomime. See FANCY DRESS.

pigeon's or **pigeon wing.** Loosely curled hair over ear, or wig with such curl. See WIGS.

pigment (pĭg′mənt; *pig* ment). Coloring material of mineral, vegetable, or animal origin.

pigskin. Durable leather from pig's hide. See LEATHERS.

pigtail. Plait of hair hanging down the back; cue or queue.

pigtail braid. Small, round, trimming braid resembling pigtail. See BRAIDS.

pigtail wig. Wig with plaited tail. See WIGS.

piked shoe. Same as CRAKOW. See SHOES.

pilch. Coarse outer garment worn in the Middle Ages and also by primitive people. Made of leather, skins, or fur.

pile. **1.** Fabric surface of closely set threads that stand up and form a uniform and even surface, as in velvet. Made by weaving extra set of warp or filling threads in loops on face of fabric and either cutting loops for cut pile or leaving them intact for loop pile. Distinguished from NAP. **2.** Weave in which yarn is projected from body of cloth in the form of little loops. See WEAVES.

pile-upon-pile velvet. Velvet with designs made by pile of varying lengths. See VELVETS.

pileus (pī-lē′ŭs; pie *lee* us). Soft, close-fitting cap. Same as LIBERTY CAP or PHRYGIAN CAP. See CAPS.

pile weave. Weave in which raised loops are formed. See WEAVES.

pilgrim (pĭl′grĭm; *pil* grim). Cape or ruffle fastened to back of bonnet to shield the neck. Used in 18th century.

pillbox. Small round hat. See HATS.

pillow. **1.** Cushion or stuffed pad used in lacemaking to hold design and bobbins. **2.** Balloon-like silhouettes of sleeves and skirts, called *pillow sleeves* and *pillow skirts.*

pillow bar. Bride or bar made in bobbin lace.

pillow lace. Lace made with bobbins on a pillow. See LACES.

pillow-slip dress. Straight, unfitted chemise dress. See DRESSES.

pilot cloth (pī′lət; *pie* lot). Coarse, strong woolen cloth in dark blue, thick and twilled, having nap on one side. Used for overcoats and sailors' jackets.

pilot coat or **jacket.** Heavy, short coat. See JACKETS.

PINS

pin. **1.** Device used for joining separate pieces; specifically, thin piece of short wire having a head and a sharp point. **2.** Ornament having pin as fastener; as, breastpin or other brooch; fraternity pin or other badge.

baby p. Miniature bar pin. Used for fastening and decoration on infants' clothes.

bar p. Narrow elongated brooch or breastpin with ornamental front; usually, bar of gold, platinum, etc., 2 or 3 inches long, set with gems. First worn on front of sheath gown.

breastpin. Ornamental clasp or pin; brooch.

broach. Same as BROOCH.

brochette. Small brooch.

brooch (brōch; broche). Large ornamental pin or clasp. Usually worn decoratively on dress. Formerly worn on man's hat.

clip p. Article of costume jewelry usually consisting of two clips fastened together to be worn either as pin or, unattached, as separate clips.

Clip Pin, Closed and Open

common p. Pin in sizes 3 to 7: size 3, about 1 inch long; size 7, about 2 inches. Often sold in papers having from 7 to 14 rows and costing from 1 cent to 15 cents each paper, the price depending upon the quality of the pin, the put-up, etc.

dressmaker p. Brass or steel pin in sizes 4, 5, and 6. Sold loose in ¼-, ½-, or 1-lb. boxes. Used for pinning fabrics for cutting and when fitting, same as the common pin.

fibula (fĭb′ū-lə; *fib* you la). Ornamental brooch that fastens like safety pin, though often, as used by Greeks and Romans, in one piece rather than hinged. In use since 2000 B.C. for fastening garments. Sometimes elaborately decorated with designs and figures and made of gold.

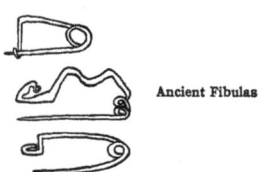

Ancient Fibulas

hairpin. Pin varying in size and shape, usually forked, often decorative; made of enameled steel wire, celluloid, shell, etc. Used to hold the hair in place. In use as ornament in ancient Greece. Then made of metal and ivory and decorated with enamel work, jewels, and tiny sculptured figures. Also worn by Anglo-Saxon women.

hatpin. Long, straight pin, usually having ornamental head. Used on hat as fastening or decoration.

headed p. Pin having a black, white, or colored head, the latter being used chiefly with corsages.

mourning p. Steel pin having a dull, black head. Used for pinning mourning veils on hats on a hat; also, in place of other pins in a costume during period of mourning.

safety p. Pin, similar to clasp, with point which springs into protective guard. Used as fastening.

scarf p. Same as TIE PIN.

stickpin. Long, straight pin having a decorative head. Used as ornament in tie or cravat; sometimes for fastening.

fāte, făt, dânce, ärt mē, mĕt, hēr, thēre rīde, rĭd nōte, nŏt, côrn, fōōd, fŏŏt cūte, cŭt, cūré now fin(ŋ)ger villa(ə) señor pleas(zh)ure

pins (continued)

sunburst. Brooch or pin set with jewels, usually diamonds, radiating from center.

tie p. Decorative pin used to hold scarf or necktie in place.

piña cloth (Sp. pē′ña; *pee* nya). Delicate, soft, transparent fabric, woven, chiefly in the Philippine Islands, from leaf fibers of pineapple plant. Used for sheer shawls, scarfs, handkerchiefs, etc.

pinafore (pĭn′ȧ-fōr; *pin* a fore). Sleeveless apron-like garment worn by a child to protect her dress; garment long romanticized by authors and poets.

19th Century Pinafore

pinafore heel Nearly flat heel used on children's shoes. See HEELS.

pinayusa (pē-nä-yōō′sä; pee nah *yoo* sah). Philippine hemp fabric dyed with native dye.

pin-ball. Small pincushion made in fancy shape over cardboard frame.

pinchback. Coat with fitted back. See COATS.

pincushion. Small cushion into which pins are stuck and kept for use.

pin dot. Smallest dot used as fabric design. See DOTS.

pineapple cloth (pĭn′ăp-l; *pine* app l). **1.** Same as PIÑA CLOTH. **2.** Slightly stiffened MOUSSELINE DE SOIE.

pine cloth. Delicate, transparent fabric made from fibers of pineapple leaf. See PIÑA CLOTH.

pine marten. European or American marten, dark brown in color. See FURS.

pin ground. Ground of a fabric marked with tiny spots like pinheads.

pinhole. Small perforation made by a pin, or any similar perforation.

pinion (pĭn′yŭn; *pin* yun). Shoulder line popular in 17th century, in which shoulder extends over top of sleeve.

pink. 1. Tint of red. Higher color value than flesh; as, pale pink, deep pink, etc. Also, colors of pink, the garden flower. **2.** To cut the edge of cloth, leather, paper, etc., in small notches. **3.** Scarlet coat. See COATS.

pinked seam. Seam having edges notched. See SEAMS.

pinker. Machine operated by crank, having notched or fluted knives for pinking edges; also, a Fashion Aid attachment for the sewing machine, by means of which one can do pinking rapidly and automatically at home.

pinking. Notched edge made in cloth by means of pinker, pinking machine, pinking scissors, or pinking iron. Much used on seams; and on chintz, felt, oilcloth, etc. As applied to shoes, decorative edging in sawtooth design.

pinking iron. Instrument with a sharp end shaped to form notches or curves on the edge of fabric and other materials. A hammer is used to hit the plain top end to cut each scallop or notch or group of notches and scallops.

pinking shears. Shears used for pinking fabrics. See SHEARS.

pinner (pĭn′ẽr; *pin* er). **1.** Small, decorative apron, pinned on at the waist. Worn by parlor-maids. Formerly worn by ladies-in-waiting. In 17th century, child's bib or apron. **2.** Headdress like a cap with long flaps, often pinned on, hanging down on each side. Worn by women during 18th century.

18th Century Pinner

pin seal. Fine-grained, soft leather made from skin of very young seal. Used for bags, wallets, etc. See LEATHERS.

pinson (pĭn′sǒn; *pin* son). Thin, light shoe or slipper. See SHOES.

pin spot. Small spot the size of pinhead, used as pattern on fabric.

pin stripe. Narrowest stripe, often used in fabrics. See STRIPES.

pin tuck. Narrowest tuck. See TUCKS.

pinwheel skirt. Circular type of skirt with flare starting at hips or below and extending to hemline. See SKIRTS.

pin work. Stitches shaped like crescents or points, used in needle-point to lighten effect of raised design or cordonnet edging. Also called *spines, thorns, crowns.*

pioneer woman's costume. Simple costume worn by women who went westward in the covered wagon period of mid-19th century. Consists of skirt of ankle-length, gathered at waistline; plain basque with long plain sleeves; headdress of small sunbonnet type. Illustrated after sculpture by Bryant Baker, costume of which is considered typical.

Pioneer Woman's Costume

pipe. 1. To decorate with piping. **2.** Narrow tube-shaped article; specifically, fluted part of a frill. **3.** In the plural, obsolete trimming for dress, consisting of tubular piece of metal, as gold or silver.

pipe clay. White plastic clay used for cleaning or whitening.

piped seam. Seam having fold of material inserted, which shows as piping on the right side. See SEAMS.

pipe-organ back. Back of skirt with several stiffened gores, widening toward bottom, taped underneath to stand out in rounded effect, vaguely resembling pipe organ. Popular during 1890's.

piping (pīp′ĭng; *pipe* ing). **1.** Narrow bias fold or cord used as finish on edges; any edge extending from another. Extensively used in dressmaking. **2.** Narrow piece of leather, fabric, etc., sewn into seam or on edge of shoe for finish.

piping cord. Finished cord, usually silk, that is applied to an edge.

piqué (F. pē-kā; *pee* kay). **1.** Firm fabric in lengthwise corded effect. Cotton piqué widely used for collars and cuffs, blouses, dresses, skirts, coats, vests, cravats, pipings, etc. **2.** Glove seam in which one edge is lapped over and chain-stitched through the other. **3.** Inlay, as in metal, tortoise shell, etc.

piqué embroidery. Embroidery in white with corded outlines. See EMBROIDERIES.

pirate costume (pī′rȧt; *pie* ret). Costume of various pirate characters. See FANCY DRESS.

pirn (pẽrn; pern). Reed, quill, or the like, used to hold yarn or thread wound about it; also, yarn wound on such a reed or quill.

pirned. Scottish term meaning having colored stripes or brocade.

pirnie or **pirny.** Scottish word for striped woolen nightcap.

pistache or **pistachio green** (pĭs-tăsh′ or pĭs-tȧ′shĭ-ō; pis *tash* or pis *tah* shi o). Pale green, color of kernel of a pistachio nut.

pit. Slang term for pocket.

pitch. Angle at which heel joins sole of shoe.

pith helmet or **hat.** Light pith hat for tropical wear. See HATS.

pizazz (pĭ-zăz′; *pi* zazz). Word coined in the 1930's to express the quality of the unexpected that gives clothes an air, dash, vitality, distinction. Accredited to Harvard University students by Harper's Bazaar.

placard (plăk′ärd; *plack* ard). Stomacher worn in 15th and 16th centuries, usually jeweled.

placcate (plăk′ĭt; *plack* it). **1.** Piece of plate armor worn as extra protection for lower part of breast. **2.** Type of doublet reinforced with steel ribs.

PLACKETS

placket (plăk′ĕt; *plack* et). **1.** Opening in upper part of skirt, in waist part of dress, in neck or sleeve, for convenience in putting garment on. **2.** Formerly, a petticoat or a skirt pocket.

plackets / **platinum**

continuous p. Placket made in center of a gore or on a seam, and finished with one strip of material continued from one side of opening to the other.

flat-stitched continuous p. Type of placket made of a minimum thickness of fabric, and so stitched as to lie flat when laundered.

habit-back p. Type of placket originally used to finish plain back of woman's riding skirt or habit, and having a fly or extension piece underneath the opening. Now used for placket of any fitted skirt.

inverted-plait p. Placket in an inverted plait. Used when skirts are plain around waist and hips and full at lower edge.

seam-p. Placket in seam, made by applying straight strip of fabric to each of seam edges.

short-lapped p. Placket 3 or 4 inches long, cut on lengthwise thread of fabric. Used in full skirts and sleeves, infants' dresses, etc.

tucked-seam p. Placket made on a tucked seam, stitched so that it appears to be a continuation of seam.

welt-seam p. Placket made in imitation of welt seam. Generally used on side opening in gored skirt.

plaid (plăd; plad). **1.** Twilled cotton, woolen, worsted, silk, or synthetic fabric, woven of yarn-dyed fibers, in patterns consisting of colored bars crossing each other to form varied squares. **2.** Square or rectangular garment of tartan worn as cloak by men and women in Scotland. **3.** Cross-barred pattern typical of Scotch plaid.

plaid neuk (plăd nŭk; plad newk). Sewn up corner of plaid. See POCKETS.

plain. 1. Without figure or design; said of fabric. Solid color often called plain color; as, plain blue, etc. **2.** Without extraneous decoration; not luxurious; simple. Also, homely; not beautiful.

plainback or **plainbacks.** Light-weight woolen fabric in plain or twill weave.

plain band. Unornamented falling band. See COLLARS.

plain fabric. Fabric in plain, satin, or fine rib weave, with little or no texture variation. See FABRICS.

plain knitting. 1. Simplest form of knitting. See KNITTING. **2.** Basic stitch used in hand knitting. See STITCHES.

plain seam. Seam stitched and pressed open; raw edges finished by overcasting. See SEAMS.

plain weave. Basic type of weave, with filling thread passing alternately over and under successive warp threads. See WEAVES.

PLAITS

plait (plĕt or plăt; pleet or plate). **1.** Fold of fabric laid back flat, usually lengthwise of fabric. Made singly or in groups for decoration or to hold in width of garment. Also spelled *pleat.* **2.** (plăt; plat) Braid, as of hair or straw. Also spelled *plat.*

accordion p. Narrow straight plaits, from ⅛ to ½ inch wide, resembling creased folds in bellows of an accordion, put in by means of steam.

box p. Combination of two flat folds in opposite directions, with turned-under edges meeting underneath. In series, box plaits form inverted plaits on the underside.

cartridge p. (kär'trĭj; *car* trij). Round plaits formed so as to resemble cartridge belt. Similar to French gathers, but often larger. From ¼ inch to 1 inch in circumference.

inverted p. Plait like box plait in reverse, having fulness turned in. May be in seam, set into garment, or applied.

kick p. Plait used usually at side of narrow skirt to give freedom for walking.

kilt p. Large single vertical fold, covering half of the next fold; used in series all turned one way, as in Scotch kilts.

Scottish Kilt

knife p. Narrow folds turned to one side, set by hand or by means of steam.

simulated p. Line pressed or stitched to imitate the line of a plait, but not constructed like a plait.

sunburst p. Accordion-like plaits that are narrow at top and wider at bottom, thus producing a flare. Fabric plaited on bias so that plaits radiate from a center.

Sunburst Plaits

umbrella p. Flared seams or pressed lines in a skirt or sleeve, placed to imitate the rib lines in an umbrella.

unpressed p. Folds forming plaits that have not been stitched or pressed lengthwise.

Watteau p. (wŏ-tō'; wot *toe*). Box plait at center-back of princess gown, secured from neck to waistline, hanging free from there to bottom of skirt.

plaited stitch. Stitch giving braided effect. See STITCHES.

plaiting (plĕt'ĭng or plāt'ĭng; *pleet* ing or *plate* ing). **1.** Arrangement of fabric in plaits, or folds; or the fabric so treated. Also called *pleating.* **2.** (plăt'ĭng; *plat* ing) Braided fabric or process of braiding. Also called *platting.*

Plaskon (plăs'kĕn; *plass* kon). Trade name for hard synthetic material made

Watteau Plaits, 1745

in many beautiful, enduring colors. May be washed and used indefinitely. Used for buttons, slides, ornaments, dishes, etc.

Plastacele (plăs'tə-sēl; *plass* ta seel). Trade name for shiny transparent plastic. Used as trimming on hats, bags, etc.

plastic (plăs'tĭk; *plass* tic). Substance capable, naturally or by certain method of treatment, of being molded into desired forms.

plastron (plăs'trən; *plass* tron). **1.** Separate or attached front of a woman's dress, extending from throat to waist; so called because of its resemblance to original breastplate of armor. **2.** Shirt bosom, especially one without plaits.

Plastron Worn Inside Laced Bodice

plat. 1. Braid of hair or straw. Same as PLAIT. **2.** Cords braided, as for a belt.

plate. 1. Flat, smooth, thin piece, as of metal. Also, such a piece as used to make up armor. **2.** Skins sewn together, but not completely fitted or finished, for fur linings; also used to make garments or trimmings. **3.** Double edge of hat brim, turned and stitched. **4.** To spin or weave two fibers together so that the finer is on the surface and the poorer is concealed.

plate armor. Armor made of metal plates joined to protect the body.

plateau (plă-tō'; pla toe). **1.** Disk-like hat. See HATS. **2.** Flat piece of fabric or straw, either round or square, used in making hat crowns and toques.

plated. Covered with richer substance; applied to baser metal overlaid with gold, silver, etc.; as, silver plated.

platform sole. Thick shoe sole, usually from ½ inch to 3 inches in depth; often of cork or wood.

platilla (plə-tĭl'ə; pla *till* a). Kind of white linen fabric, originally made in Silesia.

platinum (plăt'ĭ-nŭm; *plat* i num). **1.** Grayish-white precious metal, found in

fāte, făt, dánce, ärt, mē, mĕt, hēr, thêre rīde, rĭd nōte, nŏt, côrn, fōōd, fŏŏt cūte, cŭt, cūre now fĭn(ŋ)ger villa(ə) señor pleas(zh)ure nuggets. Used for fine jewelry, such as rings, pins, etc., into which precious stones are set. **2.** Neutral gray color having a bluish cast. Hair dyed or bleached, or both, to make a silver blonde color. Made famous by the screen actress, Jean Harlow.

platting. Same as PLAITING, 2.

Plauen lace (plow′ən; *plow* en). Lace embroidered on fabric by machine, the fabric being burned out by chemical. See LACES.

play suit. Sports or informal costume in one or more pieces. See SPORTS CLOTHES.

pleasance (plĕz′əns; *ples* ance). Fine quality of lawn used in 15th and 16th centuries for veils, kerchiefs, etc.

pleat. Variant spelling of PLAIT.

pleating. Variant spelling of PLAITING, 1.

plied yarn. Yarn composed of two different fibers. See YARNS.

plimsoll (plĭm′səl; *plim* soll). Term used in Australia for a canvas shoe.

Pliofilm (plī′ō-fĭlm; *ply* o film). Trade name for transparent fabric having rubber base. Said to be water-, dust-, and alcohol-proof and non-inflammable. Used for raincoats, umbrellas, etc.

plissé (F. plē-sā; plee say). French word meaning gathering, plaiting, fold, plait; also, plaited, folded, crumpled, or puckered.

plissé crepe. Seersucker-like fabric. See CREPES.

plover egg (plŭv′ẽr; *pluv* er). Egg-like wooden ball with handle at one end. Used for darning.

plucked wool. Wool from dead sheep. See WOOL.

plug oxford. Oxford with circular vamp. See SHOES.

plum. Deep shade of red-purple or purple-blue; shades of the ripe prune fruit.

plumach (plŏŏ-măsh′; ploo *mash*). Obsolete term for plume.

plumbet (plŭm′ĕt; *plum* et). Obsolete fabric of silk or wool.

plume. Feather or bunch of feathers, especially the longer feathers from the ostrich. Also, any waving ornament resembling feathers.

plumetis (F. plüm-tē; ploom tee). **1.** French term for feather-stitch. **2.** Type of dress muslin.

plumper. Thin, round, light-weight disk used as padding in colonial days in America to fill or "plump" out hollow cheeks.

plus fours. Loose, baggy knickerbockers, reaching well below knee; 4 inches longer, when introduced, than usual length. Worn first in second decade of 20th century by men, for active sports, especially golf.

plush. Rich fabric of wool or cotton, in pile weave, with longer pile than velvet; and coarse back made of cotton, silk, wool, etc. Used for coats, capes, neckpieces, muffs.

plushette (plŭsh-ĕt′; plush *et*). Inferior type of plush.

plush-stitch. Stitch used in Berlin work to make plush-like surface. See STITCHES.

plush velveteen. Plush made of cotton.

pluvial (plŏŏ′vĭ-əl; *ploo* vi al). Long ceremonial robe worn by priests and kings.

ply. Fold or plait; layer or thickness of cloth, as in a collar; twist or strand, as in yarn.

ply weave. Weave with more than one set of warp and filling yarns. See WEAVES.

pneumatic sole (nū-măt′ĭc; new *mat* ic). Shoe sole filled with compressed air, giving effect of platform sole and contributing to comfort in walking.

Pocahontas costume. Costume of American Indian woman. Made of deerskin, fringed and beaded. See FANCY DRESS.

pochette (pō-shĕt′; po *shet*). Handbag. French word meaning little pocket.

pochote (Sp. pō-chō′tä; po *cho* tay). Fiber of the silk-cotton tree, used for stuffing, padding, etc.

POCKETS

pocket. 1. Piece of fabric applied to a garment to form a container. **2.** Small bag used to carry money, jewelry, etc.
flap p. Tailored pocket with flap as finish for opening. Typical of pockets at sides of men's coats.
half p. New ready-made pocket used to replace worn pocket in men's trousers.
patch p. Piece of shaped material sewn, on all but upper edge, to outside of garment. Used on coats and on wash garments, aprons especially.
plaid neuk (plăd nŭk; plad newk). Pocket made by sewing up a corner of the Scottish plaid, which is worn by a garment.
seam p. Pocket, one edge of which is stitched in a seam, as under a front panel. Also, pouch pocket used in side seam of peasant frock or skirt.
slit p. Same as WELT POCKET.
stand p. Pocket opening finished with an upstanding front part.
welt p. Inserted pocket, with edges finished as for a bound buttonhole. Also called *slit pocket.*

pocketbook. 1. Small handbag. **2.** Small case carried in pocket or handbag as container for money.

pocket cascade. Pocket at side of skirt, made within folded and draped section in cascade effect. When used on both sides of a skirt, gives appearance similar to peg-top skirt.

Dress with Pocket Cascade, 1916

pocket handkerchief. Handkerchief of usual size for general daytime wear, fitting easily into pocket or bag.

pocketing. Strong fabric, usually twilled cotton. Used for making inside pockets, especially on men's clothes.

poet's collar. Soft collar attached to shirt blouse. Popularized by the poets Byron, Shelley, and Keats. See COLLARS.

poil. Thread of raw silk used to make core of tinsel.

point. 1. Tapering tip of something pointed; as, pin point. **2.** Tie or lace, as of leather or ribbon, finished with metal tab or aglet at ends. Originally, used to fasten together parts of costume; later, tied in bows for trimming. **3.** One of three lines of decorative stitching on back of gloves. **4.** To insert white hairs into fur pelt. **5.** One of series of needles used in lacemaking. **6.** (F. pwăṉ; pwanh) French word for small stitch or dot used in lacemaking, embroidery, and needlework. Often used for connection between handmade lace. **7.** Short for needle-point.

17th Century Points

point à l'aiguille (F. pwăṉ-tä lä-gwē; pwanh ta lay gwee). French term meaning needle-point.

point appliqué (F. pwăṉ-tä-plē-kä; pwanh ta plee kay). French term meaning appliqué lace.

point à réseau (F. pwăṉ-tä rā-zō; pwanh ta ray zo). French term meaning point lace with net ground.

point d'Alençon (F. pwăṉ d′ä-läṉ-sôṉ; pwanh da lonh sonh). French term meaning Alençon point lace.

point d'Angleterre lace (F. pwăṉ d′äṉ-glə-têr; pwanh dong gla tare). Pillow lace with designs applied to bobbinet. See LACES.

point de gaze lace (F. pwăṉ də gäz; pwanh de gahz). Belgian needle-point appliqué lace. See LACES.

point de Paris lace (F. pwăṉ də pä-rē; pwanh de pa ree). **1.** Narrow bobbin lace. **2.** Machine-made lace like Val. See LACES.

point d'esprit lace (F. pwăṉ dĕs-prē; pwanh dess pree). Net or tulle with dots. See LACES.

point-device (point də-vīs′; point de *vice*). Perfectly costumed, groomed, or made.

pointed fox. Fox fur pointed to imitate silver fox. See FURS.

point lace. Lace made by hand, with a needle. Short for NEEDLE-POINT LACE. See LACES.

point plat (F. pwăṉ plä; pwanh plah). French term meaning FLAT POINT. See LACES.

point Turc (F. pwăŋ tŏŏrk; pwanh toork). Flat, decorative seam finish like hand-stitched double hemstitching, used on expensive handmade lingerie.

Poiret twill (pwä-rā; pwah ray). Fine quality of worsted dress fabric in twill weave; similar to gabardine, but finer. Named for French designer, Paul Poiret.

poitrel (poi'trəl; *poy* trel). 1. Breastplate of armor. 2. Stomacher resembling breastplate.

poitrine (F. pwä-trēn; pwah treen). French word meaning chest or bosom.

poke. 1. Small bag or sack. 2. Projecting front brim of bonnet. 3. Detachable hat brim worn by women in mid-19th century. 4. Obsolete term for pocket. 5. Long, wide sleeve. See SLEEVES.

poke bonnet. Bonnet with rounded front brim. See BONNETS.

poke collar. Standing collar. See COLLARS.

poke sleeve. Long, loose sleeve. See SLEEVES.

poking stick or **iron.** Rod, usually of wood or metal, formerly used to straighten the plaits of ruffs.

Polish (pōl'ĭsh; *pole* ish). High, laced shoe or boot. See SHOES.

polish (pŏl'ĭsh; *pol* ish). 1. Smooth, glossy surface. 2. Preparation used to make a surface smooth and glossy.

polka or **polka jacket** (pōl'kə; *pole* ka). Close-fitting, knitted jacket. See JACKETS.

polka dot. Dot on fabric used in allover pattern. See DOTS.

poll (pōl; pole). Crown of hat or other headgear.

Polo Cloth (pō'lō; *po* lo). Trade name for soft, loosely woven, double-faced camel's hair cloth in twill weave with evenly cut nap. Used chiefly for coats.

polo coat. Tailored coat of camel's hair, or imitation. See COATS.

polonaise (pō-lə-nāz'; po lo *nais*) or **polonese.** 1. Coat-like garment buttoned down front; often short-sleeved, having fitted bodice and cut-away overskirt, usually draped into three wing-shaped festoons. Worn over separate skirt during late 18th century. Named for Polish national costume. 2. Man's short overcoat. See COATS.

18th Century Polonaise

polos (pŏl'ŏs; *pol* oss). High cylindrical headdress seen in Greek representations of certain goddesses.

polo shirt. Informal, washable shirt with short sleeves; often with collarless, round neck. See SHIRTS.

poly-colored or **polychrome** (pŏl'ĭ-krōm; *pol* i crome). Having several or many colors, usually in one costume.

pomade (pə-mād'; po *made*). Fragrant, cosmetic ointment, usually for the hair. From Latin *pomum*, meaning apple, because originally made with apples.

pomander (pə-măn'dēr; po *man* der). Perforated ball enclosing perfume. Formerly worn as an amulet.

pomatum (pə-mā'tŭm; po *may* tum). Perfumed ointment used on the hair.

pomegranate (pŏm-grăn'ĭt; pom *gran* it). Brilliant shade of yellowish red, color of the ripe fruit.

pompadour (pŏm'pə-dōr; *pom* pa dore). Any one of several features of a style attributed to the Marquise de Pompadour, mistress of Louis XV of France, 18th century. 1. Hair dress in which hair is brushed up and back in a full

Pompadour

effect. 2. Silk fabric figured with flowers or bouquets. See DRESDEN. 3. Bodice with low square décolletage. Also certain colors, shoes, laces, caps, aprons, sacques, and stockings of types worn at court of Louis XV, similar to Watteau styles.

Costume of Marquise de Pompadour

pompon (pŏm'pŏn or F. pôŋ-pôŋ; *pom* pon or ponh ponh). Tuft or ball of feathers, wool, ribbon, or the like, usually worn as ornament on hat. Also,

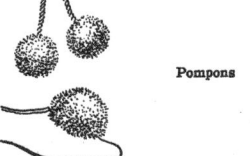

Pompons

tall tuft of wool worn on front of the stiff military headdress known as the shako.

poncho (pŏn'chō; *pon* cho). Straight piece of fabric, usually waterproof, with opening in center for head. Originally, Spanish-American garment. Worn universally, chiefly as raincoat.

pongee (pŏn-jē'; pon *jee*). Thin, soft, undyed fabric in plain weave, made of irregular yarns of silk, cotton, rayon, etc.; smooth or slightly rough in texture; ivory or brownish in color. Originally made in China of silk from wild silkworms. Used for summer suits and coats, dresses, shirts, linings, art needlework. From Chinese word meaning home-woven.

pony. Skin of young pony; used for sports coats. See FURS.

poodle. Formerly, woolly or curly napped fabric, or garment of such fabric. Named for poodle dog.

pope. British term for hosiery size intermediate between standard and outsize.

popeline (pŏp-ə-lēn'; pop e *leen*). Rep having silk warp and wool filling.

poplin (pŏp'lĭn; *pop* lin). Firm, durable, medium-weight fabric in plain weave, with fine cross ribs due to warp threads being finer than weft or filling threads. Made of cotton, silk, or wool, or of silk combined with wool or cotton. Used for dresses, coats, skirts, suits, children's apparel.

poplinette (pŏp-lĭ-nĕt'; pop li *net*). Fabric of wool, linen, or other fiber woven in imitation of poplin.

poppy red. Bright yellow-red color of the poppy flower.

porosity (pō-rŏs'ĭ-tĭ; po *ross* i ti). Quality of being open or having pores or mesh-like spaces; desirable for coolness in summer fabrics. Cottons now finished by certain chemical processes to remove fuzz and make fabric more porous.

portemonnaie (pôrt-mŭ'nā; port *mun* nay). Late 19th century purse carried by women in pocket or muff, never in hand.

porte-train. Petticoat for supporting train of a dress. Worn by women in late 19th century.

Portuguese knot (pôr'tū-gēz; *por* tue geez). Outline stitch knotted at center of each stitch. See STITCHES.

posteen or **postin** (pō-stēn'; po *steen*). East-Indian garment made of leather with fleece left on.

postiche (F. pôs-tēsh; poss teesh). French word applied to transformation, or artificial hair worn to supplement one's own hair.

postilion hat (pōs-tĭl'yən; poce *till* yun). Hat with narrow, rolled brim. See HATS.

posy (pō'zĭ; *po* zi). Single flower or bouquet of flowers.

pot derby or **pot hat.** Pot-shaped hat. See HATS.

pot lace. Rare bobbin lace. See ANTWERP POT LACE, 1, under LACES.

pouch. 1. Small or medium-sized bag or sack, used for carrying things; handbag

pouf in shape of pouch. **2.** To blouse, as part of a garment.
pouf (F. pōōf; poof). **1.** Hair arrangement rolled high in puffs, especially high headdress popular in 18th century. **2.** Any puffed-out part of a dress.

18th Century Pouf

poulaine (F. pōō-lān; poo lane). Shoe with long, pointed toe; or the long toe itself. See SHOES.
poult-de-soie or **pou-de-soie** (F. pōō də swä; poo de swah). Heavy silk of excellent quality with slight rib; used for dresses, coats, vests, cravats, etc. French term for PADUASOY.
pounce. 1. Powder of juniper gum, pipe clay, or charcoal used in preparing material for embroidery, especially for marking designs from perforated patterns. **2.** Perforation or notch made to decorate garment.
pouncet box (powns'ĕt; *pounce* et). Perforated box used for holding and sprinkling pounce. In 18th century, used as a pomander.
pouncing. Rubbing pounce over perforated pattern made according to a design, so that design is transferred through holes to material underneath.
pourpoint (pōōr'point or F. pōōr-pwăṅ; *poor* point or poor pwanh). **1.** Quilted garment, especially doublet of quilted cloth. Worn with armor or civilian clothes from 13th to 17th century. **2.** Obsolete term for quilt for bed.
poussin lace (F. pōō-săṅ; poo sanh). Delicate, narrow lace of Valenciennes type. See LACES.
pouter (powt'ẽr; *pout* er). Term applied to puffed-out effect at the breast, resembling inflated crop of pouter pigeon.
powder. Fine, dry, flour-like substance in varying skin tones, often perfumed, used as a cosmetic; called *face powder*. Originally made from rice flour or starch.
powder blue. Soft medium blue shade.
powder puff. 1. Small pad of soft material. Used for applying face powder to the skin. **2.** Small bellows, used formerly for applying powder to hair or wig.
praetexta (prĭ-tĕx'tā; *pry tex* tah). White robe with purple border. See TOGA PRAETEXTA.
precious metal (prĕsh'ŭs; *presh* us). Rare and valuable metal; especially, gold, silver, platinum.
precious stone. Gem stone of highest commercial value because of purity, rarity, and hardness. Term chiefly designates diamond, emerald, sapphire, ruby, and, though not a stone, pearl.

preen. To dress oneself up; make trim or sleek; to primp in front of a mirror.
première (F. prəm-yêr; prem yare). French term applied to the first showing of anything; as, a fashion première, a cinema première, etc.
pre-shrunk. Term applied by manufacturers to fabric or garment that has been processed and supposedly will not shrink over 3% in either direction under standard wash test or in commercial laundering.
President (prĕz'ĭ-dənt; *prez* i dent). **1.** Trade name for type of fabric with cotton warp and woolen filling, with finish similar to doeskin. **2.** Silk or silk-and-wool fabric in Jacquard weave. Used chiefly for upholstery.
press. To pat gently with a heated iron, without hard pressure; to smooth in a steam press.
press-board. Padded board, a small ironing board, used for pressing fabrics when sewing.
press cloth. Piece of cheesecloth, drill, or unbleached muslin, usually about 12 by 36 inches, used between iron and fabric while pressing garments, etc., to prevent iron from coming in direct contact with material. Used damp on wool, cotton, and linen.
presser bar. Part of knitting machine that closes needle barbs.
presser foot. Sewing-machine foot used for all plain stitching; the foot that holds fabric in position as it passes over the feed-plate.
presser wheel. Wheel in knitting machine having same function as presser bar.
press iron. Flatiron used for pressing.
pretintailles (F. prə-tăṅ-tī; pre tanh tie). Large patterns cut out and laid on dress as trimming, usually in rows. Decoration introduced in 17th century.
pre-war. Applied to fashions having the soft feminine details, such as frills, shirring, ruffles, and lingerie touches, typical of women's clothes just previous to the World War.
price range. Approximate price, defined by top and bottom limit, that one is prepared to pay for any article. Also, grouping of garments or accessories in specified price brackets; as, a price range of $10.75 to $16.50.
prick. To mark, trace, or decorate by making tiny perforations.
pricking wheel. Same as TRACING WHEEL.
prick seam. Glove seam with both edges exposed. See SEAMS.
prick-stitch. Short stitch in heavy material. See STITCHES.
primary color (prī'mẽr-ĭ; *pry* mare i). One of the pigment colors of the spectrum: red, blue, or yellow. See COLOR.
prime. Of the finest quality. Applied to furs of animals caught at season when coat is in best condition.
primp. To dress up, especially in very formal or affected style; to look admiringly at oneself in a mirror.
primrose (prĭm'rōz; *prim* rose). Greenish-yellow or reddish-yellow color.
Prince Albert. 1. Frock coat originating with Prince Albert of England. See COATS. **2.** Man's house slipper. See SLIPPERS.
Prince of Wales. Tongueless, laced oxford. See SHOES.
princess or **princesse** (prĭn'sĕs or prĭn-sĕs'; *prin* sess or prin *sess*). Designating a close-fitting style of garment hanging in unbroken line from the shoulder. See SILHOUETTES.

Princess Dress, 1930's

princesse lace (F. prăṅ-sĕs; pranh sess). Imitation of duchesse. See LACES.
Princeton orange (prĭns'tən; *prince* ton). Brilliant red-yellow color used with black as Princeton University official colors.
prink. To dress up; decorate oneself with fine clothes or jewels; preen.

PRINTS

print. Fabric stamped with design by means of paste dyes used on engraved rollers, wood blocks, or screens. See PRINTING under DYEING.
burnt-out p. Print showing raised designs on sheer ground. Made by printing design with chemical on fabric woven of paired threads of different fibers, then burning out one fiber from the parts printed. Often used on velvet, but also on other fabrics.
India p. Muslin printed with design typical in form and color of those used in India. Genuine India prints are cotton fabrics in plain weave, hand-blocked with native patterns in glowing Oriental colors.
Jouy p. (zhōō-ē; zhoo ee). Cotton or linen fabric printed with modern reproductions of 18th century French prints, often monotone landscape or figure groups in red, blue, or other color on light or white background.
photographic p. (fō-tō-grăf'ĭk; fo to *graf* ic). Printed fabric, the design for which was made from photographs of objects, such as matches, pins, snowflakes, lumps of sugar, etc., and then engraved on screen or roller for printing.
shadow p. or **warp p.** Silk, ribbon, or cretonne having plain filling woven with printed warp, forming indistinct design. Sometimes reversible.
Wedgwood p. Print of white design on colored ground similar to the effect of Wedgwood ware.

printed. Term used of any fabric on which the design is applied by printing process. See PRINTING under DYEING.

fāte, făt, dánce, ärt mē, mĕt, hẽr, thêre rīde, rĭd nōte, nŏt, côrn, fōōd, fŏŏt cūte, cŭt, cūre now fĭn(g)ger villa(ə) señor pleas(zh)ure

printing. Process of dyeing that makes use of engraved blocks, rollers, or screens to stamp design on fabric. See DYEING.
print work. Same as ETCHING EMBROIDERY. See EMBROIDERIES.
privy coat (prĭv'ĭ; *priv* i). Armor of light weight and construction, worn under coat.
processed (prŏs'ĕst; *pross* est). Treated by chemical or mechanical means to render rainproof, shrinkproof, mothproof, etc., or to give certain surface appearance.
profile hat (prō'fĭl; *pro* file). Hat framing side of face. See HATS.
proof. 1. To make impervious to destructive action, as of sun, rain, moths, etc., by chemical or mechanical process. Term applied to fabric. 2. In hat manufacturing, to stiffen by application of heat, after dipping in shellac solution or other medium. Term applied to hoods.
proprietary name (prō-prī'ē-tĕr-ĭ; pro *pry* e tare i). Word or group of words, protected by patent or copyright, designating product or company; for exclusive use of that company, as Talon is the proprietary name of a slide fastener.
prune. Dull dark purple shade like the color of the ripe fruit.
prunell (prŭ-nĕl'; prue *nell*). Heavy, milled cashmere.
prunella (prŭ-nĕl'ȧ; prue *nell* a) or **prunello.** 1. Strong, smooth, worsted dress fabric in twill or satin weave; used for dresses, skirts. 2. Woolen or mixed fabric with smooth surface, popular in 18th and 19th centuries. Used for scholastic and clerical robes, dresses. Heavy grade formerly used for shoe uppers.
prystal (prĭs'tȧl; *priss* tal). Hard, colorless composition; except for cloudiness, similar in appearance to crystal. Used as decorative trim on wearing accessories.
psyche knot (sī'kē; *sy* ke). Knot of hair at back of head, in imitation of hair style of Psyche, a character in Greek mythology, as represented in art.
puce. Dull red-brown color.
pucker. Wrinkle, furrow, or uneven fold in cloth; also, to make such a fold or wrinkle. Usually should be avoided in dressmaking.
pudding sleeve (pŏŏd'ĭng; *pood* ing). Full sleeve. See SLEEVES.
puff. 1. Gathering of fabric, giving inflated appearance. 2. Short for POWDER PUFF. 3. Soft roll of hair used, in hairdressing, under natural hair. 4. Quilting or tufted bed-covering having filling or padding.
puffing. Fabric shirred and made into puffs or rows of puffing for ornamentation.
puff ring. Hollow finger ring. See RINGS.
puff sleeve. Full sleeve gathered or stiffened to stand out. See SLEEVES.
pug. Short cape with hood. See WRAPS.
puggree or **pugree** (pŭg'rē; *pug* ree). 1. Light-weight strip or narrow scarf wound around helmet or hat. Worn by men in India as protection from sun. 2. Hindu turban. See HATS.

puke. 1. Fine-grade woolen fabric used for gowns, hose, doublets, etc., in 15th and 16th centuries. 2. The color puce.
pulicat (pŭl'ĭ-kăt; *pul* i cat). East Indian bandanna, named for a town in Madras province.
pullback. 1. Means of drawing or holding something back. 2. Skirt with fulness held in place at back. See SKIRTS.
pulled wool. Wool taken from dead sheep. Same as SKIN WOOL. See WOOL.
pulled work. Open-work embroidery. Same as PUNCH WORK. See EMBROIDERIES.
pulling-out. Bright-colored lining worn under slashed garment and pulled out through slashes. Worn in Elizabethan period when slashes were profusely used.
pull-on. To be put on by pulling, as a sweater that is pulled on over the head, a glove that has no buttons.
pull-over. Garment that pulls over the head. Usually, blouse or sweater.
pull strap. Small strap of tape or leather at top back of a boot or shoe, for use in pulling it on the foot.
pumice (pŭm'ĭs; *pum* iss). Volcanic glass, pulverized and used for polishing, cleaning, smoothing.
pump. Low-cut slipper without fastening. In 20th century, the classic shoe for smart day wear, made in all heights of heels and in practically all leathers and slipper fabrics.
pump bow. Flat, tailored bow. See TAILORED BOW under BOWS.
pumpkin (pŭmp'kĭn; *pump* kin). Dull, deep orange color like that of the vegetable.
pump sole. Thin single shoe sole with beveled edge. Used on both men's and women's shoes.
punch. To perforate or mark with perforations. Also, any sharp or heavy instrument used for making perforations, as an embroidery punch used in eyelet embroidery.
punch work. Open-work embroidery. See EMBROIDERIES.
punch-work-stitch. Stitch worked with heavy needle on loosely woven fabric on which dots have been stamped to indicate placing of stitches. Two stitches are taken between each pair of dots and pulled tight so that the fabric threads are drawn apart in open-work effect. See STITCHES.
punjum or **panjam** (pŭn'jŭm; *pun* jum). Cotton fabric made in southern India.
punta (pŏŏn'tä; *poon* tah). Straw of upper part of wheat stalk. See STRAWS.
puntilla (Sp. pŏŏn-tēl'yä; poon *teel* yah). Lacework, lace edging, or lacy design. Spanish word meaning little point.
punto (pŏŏn'tō; *poon* to). Italian word for point or stitch. Used in names of laces, as punto a groppo, knotted lace; punto a maglia, darned netting; punto in aria, needle-point lace; punto tagliato, cut work; punto tirato, drawn work.
purdah (pẽr'dȧ; *per* da). Cotton cloth used in India for making curtain or screen of same name, behind which women of a household are concealed from public view.
pure-dye. Term applied to silk that is not artificially weighted more than 10 per cent in colors or 15 per cent in black. Should mean that such silk is washable. See SILK.
purfle (pẽr'fl; *per* fl). To ornament the border of, as with embroidery, metal threads, jewels, etc.; also, any such richly ornamented border or hem.
Puritan (pū'rĭ-tȧn; *pure* i tan). 1. Characteristic of costume worn by Puritans, who belonged to the group that emigrated from England to New England in search of freedom to put into practice the stern and austere religious beliefs which separated them from the English church. For women, costume consisted of close bodice; long, full skirt over homespun petticoat; white apron, kerchief, and cuffs; dark hood or broad hat. For men, plain dark suit with knee breeches; long cloak; broad-brimmed, high-crowned hat; shoes with buckle. 2. Similar to Puritan style by reason of simplicity, soberness of design or color.

17th Century Puritan Costumes

Puritan hat. Broad-brimmed, high-crowned hat. See HATS.
purl or **pearl.** 1. Stitch made by bringing needle out across thread so as to hold it. Also, in knitting, backward stitch or seam-stitch. See STITCHES. 2. Looped edge of embroidery, lace, or galloon, or one of such loops. 3. Fine twisted thread of gold or silver. 4. Kind of 16th century lace. 5. Plait or fold in a garment; especially, fluted part of ruff.
purple. Rich, vibrant color between red and blue.
purse (pẽrs; perce). Small bag or case for carrying money. Originally, pouch bag, usually of fabric, with drawstring; now, handbag or pocketbook.

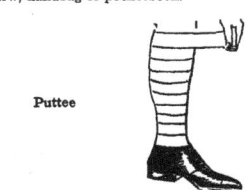

Puttee

fāte, făt, dȧnce, ärt mē, mĕt, hẽr, thêre rīde, rĭd nōte, nŏt, côrn, fōōd, fŏŏt cūte, cŭt, cūrė now fin(g)ger villa(ȧ) señor pleas(zh)ure

purse silk. Thick, twisted silk thread, originally used to crochet or knit silk purses or small reticules. See THREADS.
purse strings. Drawstrings used on pouch purses. Commonly used to mean the finances of the family, as "She controls the purse strings."

puttee (pŭt'ē; *putt* ee). Legging spirally wound around leg from ankle to knee, as worn by soldiers in World War. In recent years, leather leggings and all other leg coverings detached from shoe.
pyjama. British spelling of PAJAMA.

pyrope (pī'rōp; *py* rope). Type of garnet of deep red color known as precious garnet. Used as gem.
pyroxylin (pī-rŏk'ĭ-lĭn; py *rox* i lin). Form of cellulose nitrate, the first plastic made by man. Used for toilet accessories, buttons, ornaments.

Q

quadricorn hat (kwăd'rĭ-kôrn; *kwod* ri corn). Four-cornered hat, usually with an upward flare. See HATS.
Quaker (kwăk'ēr; *quake* er). Characteristic of costume worn by Quaker women. Consisted of plain, simply-made basque dress in soft color, usually gray; gathered skirt, topped by long apron; short-sleeved bodice with white undersleeves; shoulder kerchief. Headcoverings included ruffled cap, and soft hood worn over the cap outdoors; later, stiff beaver hat; still later, stiff poke bonnet. Worn during 17th, 18th, and 19th centuries.

Quaker Costume, 1678

Quaker bonnet. Small, close-fitting bonnet worn by Quaker women. See BONNETS.
Quaker hat. Hat worn by Quaker men, having low crown and wide brim. See HATS.

quality (kwăl'ĭ-tĭ; *quoll* i ti). 1. That property of a thing by which its worth is judged; as, good quality, medium quality, poor quality, or without quality. 2. Coarse tape for strings or bindings. See TAPES.
quarter. Back part of a shoe upper, covering heel, and joined to vamp.
quattrocento (kwä-trō-chĕn'tō; kwah tro *chen* toe). Italian word meaning 14th century. Applied in fashion to apparel showing the influence of Italian Renaissance styles, such as soft, pointed, velvet or lamé shoes and Florentine page boy hair dress.
queue or **cue** (kū; cue). Braid of hair from the back of the head, either natural or part of a wig. Formerly worn by men in China. From French word *queue*, meaning tail.
quiff. British slang for arrangement of hair in which hair is oiled and brushed away from forehead.
quill. 1. Long, stiff, strong feather from wing or tail of a bird. Used chiefly to trim hats. 2. One of rounded folds or ridges of a ruffle; to flute or fold in such ridges.
quilled. Folded or fluted to make quilling.
quilling. Band of quilled material composed of rounded ridges resembling row of quills.
quilt. 1. To sew several thicknesses of fabric or fabric and padding together, through and through; to outline a design in thicknesses of fabric by running-stitches or machine-stitches; to use stitches to block off squares or diamonds in fabric. 2. Bed covering quilted, by hand or machine, through top, filling, and lining; often done in beautiful designs or following the pattern in the quilt top.
quilter. Sewing-machine attachment with guide that is attached to the presser foot to enable one to follow the previous row of stitching and keep the adjoining row an even distance from it. Used for straight lines, diamonds, and squares in machine quilting.
quilting. Fine running-stitches or machine-stitches made through two thicknesses of material with light-weight padding between. Usually a design or pattern is determined upon, and the stitches so placed as to follow the design. Used on quilts, pillows, padded garments, collars, cuffs, etc. See TRAPUNTO QUILTING.
quilting cotton. Cotton batting used as padding in quilts.
quilting needle. Short needle on which a few running-stitches can be made and then the needle pulled through the padded materials easily. See NEEDLES.
quintin. Fine lawn fabric named after town in Brittany.
quirk. 1. Diamond-shaped piece of material at base of thumb or fingers in a glove. 2. Clock, as in hosiery.

R

rabanna (rȧ-băn'ȧ; ra *ban* a). Textile fabric of raffia, made in Madagascar. Used for draperies, curtains, etc.
rabat (rȧ-bä'; rah *bah*). Large clerical collar. Also, turned-down collar worn in 15th and 16th centuries. See COLLARS.
rabatine. Collar worn hanging over shoulders. See COLLARS.
rabbi (răb'ī or răb'ĭ; *rab* eye or *rab* i). Short, bib-like piece of fabric, or rabat, fitted to a collar, as worn by Roman Catholic ecclesiastics.
rabbit. Fur of animal of various countries, often processed to simulate more expensive furs. Same as CONY. See FURS.
rabbit hair fabric. Woolen fabric of various weaves and weights, with rabbit hair woven in, giving it a soft appearance and feel similar to angora.
raccoon (ră-kōōn'; rac *coon*). Coarse, durable fur, usually grayish with darker center stripe. See FURS.
raccroc-stitch (rȧ-krō'; ra *crow*). Stitch used in lacemaking to join net. See STITCHES.
Rachel (rȧ-shĕl'; ra *shell*). Color of tan face powder named after noted London beauty specialist.
rack. Skin of rabbit two months old.
racket. Broad wooden shoe. See SHOES.
radio punch work. Punch work with round designs. See PUNCH WORK under EMBROIDERIES.
radium (rā'dĭ-ŭm; *ray* di um). Smooth, pliable lingerie fabric of synthetic yarn in plain weave, with dull finish and natural sheen of silk. Used for linings, negligees, dresses, etc.
radsimir (răd'sĭ-mĭr; *rad* si mir). Silk fabric, used for mourning dress.
raffia (răf'ĭ-ȧ; *raff* i a). Fiber made from strong palm fiber. See STRAWS.
Raggedy Ann costume. Costume, consisting of patched skirt and apron, simple blouse, white socks, and black shoes, as worn by stuffed doll character in child's story book. Usually worn with ragged woolen wig. See FANCY DRESS.

raglan (răg'lăn; *rag* lan). Loose overcoat, with armhole seams extending from the neck. See COATS.
raglan sleeve. Sleeve with long armhole line extending to neckline. See SLEEVES.
Ragusa guipure (rä-gōō'zä gē-pūr'; rah goo za gee *poor*). Type of cut work. Same as ROMAN CUT WORK. See EMBROIDERIES.
rail or **rayle.** In Old English, a loose garment. In 17th and 18th centuries, a nightgown.
railway-stitch. 1. Series of connected loops of thread. Same as CHAIN-STITCH, 1. 2. Simple crochet stitch. Same as TRICOT-STITCH. See STITCHES.
raiment (rā'mȧnt; *ray* ment). Apparel or clothing in general. Term extensively used in earlier centuries, often in the sense that food and raiment were life's chief essentials.
raincoat. Light-weight coat of waterproof fabric. See COATS.
rainy daisy. Short for rainy day skirt. See SKIRTS.

raised. Having pattern or design in relief. Term used of lace and embroidery.
raised embroidery. Embroidery done over padding. See EMBROIDERIES.
raisin (rā'zĭn; *ray* zin). Very dark, bluish-red color of the dried raisin.
Rajah (rä'jə; *rah* ja). Trade name for strong, rough, compact, silk fabric of plain weave. Made in all colors. Used for dresses, light-weight suits and coats.
rambler-rose-stitch. Uniform stitches bulked around center to form flower. See STITCHES.
ramie (răm'ĭ; *ram* i). 1. Strong, lustrous fiber of Asiatic plant of the same name. Called *China* grass when woven into various fabrics. See STRAWS. 2. Garment made of ramie, as a grass skirt.
ramilie wig (răm'ĭ-lĭ; *ram* i li). Wig with long, braided tail. See WIGS.
rap. Skein of about 120 yards of yarn.
raploch (răp'lŏk; *rap* lock). Scottish term for coarse or rough; also, coarse, rough, homespun cloth of inferior wool.
ras (F. rä; rah). Short-napped fabric. French word meaning smooth, short-napped.
raschel knitting (ră-shĕl'; ra *shell*). Type of machine knitting resembling tricot. See KNITTING.
rash. Outdated kind of cloth of silk, worsted, or a mixture of fibers.
raspberry (răz'bĕr-ĭ; *razz* bare i). Reddish color like that of the fruit for which it is named.
rat. Small pad or roll of hair or the like worn by women, according to the fashion, underneath their natural hair.
ratiné (răt-ĭ-nā' or F. rä-tē-nā; rat i *nay* or ra tee nay). Loosely woven cotton or wool fabric, the weft threads of which are looped to produce rough, uneven weave. Used for dresses and suits.
ratiné lace. Bulky, machine-made lace with looped ground. See LACES.
rational (răsh'ən-əl; *rash* on al). Short, ornamental vestment worn by certain bishops.
rat-tail. Small, firm, round, silk braid. See BRAIDS.
ratteen. Ancient, woolen fabric like frieze.
rattinet. Woolen fabric, thinner than ratteen, but similar.
ravel (răv'ĕl; *rav* el). 1. To pull away the warp or woof threads to make a fringe on the edge of material. Loosely woven material ravels easily. 2. To disentangle or unwind.
rawhide. Untanned, dressed skin. See LEATHERS.
raw silk. Fiber of silkworm cocoons. See SILK.
raw wool. Uncleaned wool as it comes from animal. See WOOL.
ray. Outdated striped cloth.

RAYON

rayon (rā'ŏn; *ray* on). General term used for a number of textile fibers and fabrics made by man. The word *rayon* may be defined as "a generic term for filaments made from various solutions of modified cellulose by pressing or drawing the cellulose solution through an orifice and solidifying it in the form of a filament." There are four different processes for making rayon: CELLULOSE ACETATE, CUPRAMMONIUM, VISCOSE, and NITROCELLULOSE. Nitro-cellulose rayon, the first type of rayon to be spun by Chardonnet in 1884, is now obsolete; but rayon is commercially manufactured today in the U.S.A. by means of the other three processes. The cellulose used by these processes is derived from wood pulp and from purified cotton linters. There are four types of rayon yarn: FILAMENT RAYON YARN, SPUN RAYON YARN, NEW BROKEN FILAMENT YARN, and NEW ABRADED YARN. Rayon fibers may be made fine or coarse, with a high or a dull luster, and in practically endless strands or in short lengths called *staple fibers*.

Each firm manufacturing rayon yarn uses only one process, as a rule; and the names registered by the firm for its products do not apply to rayons manufactured by other firms using the same process. Some firms register a trade name for their rayon yarns, which also applies to all fabrics made from those yarns whether made by themselves or by other firms. There are now many names for rayon yarns and fabrics, and this number continues to increase to such an extent that it is not practical to list all trade names here.

White rayon fabrics are permanently white. Unlike natural fibers whose color must be removed by bleaching, rayon fibers are made white and do not yellow through repeated exposure to light, washing, or cleaning. Dull or glossy rayon fabrics are permanently dull or glossy. This quality is "inborn" and not removed by repeated exposure to light, washing, or cleaning. Like fabrics made of other fibers, the serviceability of rayon fabrics with respect to washing, dry cleaning, color fastness, shrinking, stretching, and wear depends chiefly on the type of fabric, the construction of fabric and garment, and the fastness of dyes used. Properly made rayon fabrics and garments should live up to the claims made for them on tags and in advertisements, and if specified as washable can usually be washed safely and with ease.

Rayon is used in textile merchandise of every description—dress goods, apparel for men and women, underwear, knit goods, linings, and upholstery and drapery fabrics.

Acele (ă-sĕl'; a *seal*). Trade name registered by a firm for the rayon it makes by the cellulose acetate process.
acetate r. or **cellulose acetate r.** (sĕl'ū lōs ăs'ə-tāt; *sell* you loce *ass* e tate). Rayon made from pure cellulose by one of the three processes now commercially used in the U.S.A. Fibers composed of cellulose acetate, a compound of cellulose, which has been coagulated or solidified from its solution through a current of rising hot air. The cellulose used in the cellulose acetate process is derived only from purified cotton linters. Fabrics made from cellulose acetate rayon yarns should not be pressed or ironed with a hot iron.
Bemberg. Trade name registered by a firm for the rayon yarn it makes by the cuprammonium process. The use of this trade-mark on garments or fabrics indicates that Bemberg yarn was used in making the fabric, and is given as a safeguard to the consumer.
Celanese (sĕl'ə-nēz; *sell* a neez). Trade name registered by firm for rayon it makes by the acetate process. Also (not capitalized), term generally used in U.S.A. for acetate process rayon.
cellulose acetate r. Rayon made by one of the three processes now commercially used in the U.S.A. See ACETATE RAYON under RAYON.
Crown R. Trade name for rayon fabrics made by a firm that uses the viscose process. This firm marks its product "Crown Tested Quality" as assurance that it has been laboratory tested and approved.
cuprammonium r. (kū-prə-mō'nĭ-ŭm; cue pra *mo* ni um). Rayon made of fibers composed of regenerated cellulose which has been coagulated or solidified from a solution of cellulose in ammoniacal copper oxide. The cellulose used in the cuprammonium process is derived only from purified cotton linters.
Du Pont Rayon. Trade name for rayon yarns made by a firm that uses both the viscose and the cellulose acetate processes.
Enka (ĕŋ'ka; *eng* ka). Trade name registered by a firm for rayon yarn it makes by the viscose process.
filament rayon yarn. Rayon yarn composed of many fine continuous rayon fibers (called *filaments*) twisted together; smooth in appearance, somewhat like embroidery silk or silk thread.
Monofil. Trade name for artificial horsehair made from viscose rayon fibers, woven into braid, and sewn together to make women's hats.
new abraded yarn. Rayon yarn composed of broken filament yarns.
new broken filament yarn. Rayon yarn composed of cellulose acetate rayon filaments which are run through a machine that converts them into a sliver of long discontinuous filaments, and then drafted and spun into a yarn.
nitrocellulose r. (nī'trō-sĕl'ū-lōs; *ny* tro *sell* you loce). Rayon made by the earliest process, which is no longer used in this country.
Seraceta (sĕr-ə-sē'tə; sare a *see* ta). Trade name registered by a firm for the rayon it makes by the acetate process.
Spun-lo. Trade name registered by a firm for the rayon yarn it makes by the viscose process and also for the fabric made from this yarn.
spun r. Fabric woven from SPUN RAYON YARN, usually in combination with other fibers.
spun rayon yarn. Rayon yarn composed of many short rayon fibers (called *rayon staple fibers*) spun into a continuous strand of yarn, somewhat like linen

rayon (continued)
or woolen or worsted yarns. Sometimes combined with natural fibers to create new fabrics.

Visca. Trade name for rayon fibers spun into artificial straw in various sizes and widths and in two lusters and used for women's hats. Also used for draperies; for decorative effects in woven and knitted fabrics; and as a novelty, in combination with yarns, to take advantage of the brilliance of Visca.

viscose (vĭs'kōs; *viss* cose). Rayon made of fibers composed of regenerated cellulose which has been coagulated or solidified from a solution of cellulose xanthate. The cellulose used in the viscose process is derived from wood pulp alone or wood pulp in combination with cotton linters.

rayonné (F. rā-yō-nā; ray on nay). Kind of hood. See HOODS.

rayon taffeta. Taffeta with rayon filling. See TAFFETAS.

ray-stitch. Straight stitches radiating from a center. Same as SPOKE-STITCH, 2. See STITCHES.

ready-made. Manufactured in a range of sizes, colors, and types and offered for sale, ready to wear; also, apparel so made and sold, as dresses, coats, accessories, etc.

ready-to-wear. Ready-made apparel.

real lace. Handmade lace other than crocheted or knitted, that is, bobbin, needle-point, etc. See LACES.

rebato (rē-bā'tō; re *bah* toe). 1. Turned-back collar. See COLLARS. 2. Stiff, flared collar worn at back of neck. See COLLARS. 3. Support for ruff or piccadilly, as wire framework, cardboard, or stiff material covered with silk or satin.

rebozo (rā-bō'zō; re *bo* zo). Long scarf, plain or embroidered, wrapped around the head and shoulders, sometimes crossed over the face. Worn by rural Spanish and Mexican women.

red. One of the primary colors, seen in the spectrum opposite the violet end; the color of blood.

red fox. Fox fur, usually ranging from pale to deep red in color. See FURS.

redingote (rĕd'ĭn-gōt; *red* in gote). Three-quarter or full-length dress or coat, open from neck to hem, usually belted at the waistline. Worn over a slip or dress. See COATS.

redingote silhouette. Silhouette of figure wearing redingote. See SILHOUETTES.

red riding-hood. Shirred hood or bonnet. See HOODS.

Red Riding-Hood costume. Hooded cape worn by child in nursery story. See FANCY DRESS.

red sable. Asiatic mink fur. Same as KOLINSKY. See FURS.

reed mark. Fault in fabric caused by defect in reed or loom.

reefer (rēf'ẽr; *reef* er). 1. Jacket like a short box coat. See JACKETS. 2. Double-breasted, tailored coat. See COATS.

reel. 1. Spool or other revolving device for winding yarn or thread; also, yarn or thread so wound. 2. In British usage, spool or spindle of wood or cardboard, holding silk or cotton thread. What we call a spool of cotton in the U.S.A. is known as a reel of thread in Great Britain.

reeled silk. Finest grade of silk. See SILK.

regalia (rē-gā'lĭ-ȧ; re *gay* li a). 1. Decorative emblems of royalty or insignia of rank or order. Widely used in official dress of fraternal organizations. 2. Way of wearing such an emblem or similar article over one shoulder and under the arm on the other side, typical of the regal style; as, to wear a decoration regalia-fashion.

regatta (rē-găt'ȧ; re *gat* a). Sturdy, twilled, cotton fabric, usually striped blue and white.

Regency (rē'jen-sĭ; *ree* jen si). Period during which regent governs. 1. Characteristic of French costume of 1715–1723, consisting of dresses of light materials, basque bodices, pagoda sleeves, enormous panniers. 2. Characteristic of English costume of 1795–1820, consisting of long, straight skirts, high waists, low necks, pelisses, shawls, bonnets.

Regency Costumes, French and English

regent pump. Low-cut pump, having vamp and quarter stitched together along vamp line. See SLIPPERS.

regimental stripe (rĕj-ĭ-mĕn'tȧl; rej i men tal). Stripe similar to those on military uniforms. See STRIPES.

reinforce (rē-ĭn-fôrs'; re in *force*). 1. To strengthen, as by binding or facing with additional fabric, or by sewing with two or more rows of stitching. 2. Extra thickness of material or thread around a buttonhole, eyelet, etc.

remmaillé (F. rȧ-mĭ-yȧ; ra my yay). Joined invisibly. Used especially as millinery term to describe braid laced together. French word meaning restitched.

remnant (rĕm'nȧnt; *rem* nant). Leftover piece of cloth; unsold end of piece goods, as advertised in a department store "remnant sale"; piece of more than ½ yard left over from cutting a garment. Pieces of less than ½ yard are classed as scraps.

remodel (rē-mŏd'ȧl; re *mod* el). To make over, renovate, or restyle a garment so as to make it conform with a different model or pattern; to change the style and bring it up to date.

Renaissance (rĕn-ȧ-sȧns'; ren a *sahnce*). Characteristic of styles of 16th century, including huge skirt over farthingale; small, pointed waistline; puffed and slashed sleeves; fitted bodice; wide, plaited ruff. English costume of the period called *Elizabethan*.

Renaissance embroidery. Cut-work embroidery. See EMBROIDERIES.

Renaissance lace. Lace of tape motifs joined by flat stitches. See LACES.

renovate (rĕn'ȧ-vāt; *ren* o vate). To rip, clean, and remake or to put in good condition; as, to renovate a dress.

rep. Firm fabric of cotton, wool, or silk, woven with heavier weft than warp in crosswise ribbed effect. Used for draperies and upholstery; also for skirts, suits, and men's and boys' clothing.

repellent (rē-pĕl'ȧnt; re *pell* ant). 1. Term used of that which repels, but may or may not be proof against; as, a moisture-repellent cloth. 2. Kind of waterproof fabric.

replica (rĕp'lĭ-kȧ; *rep* li ka). Very close copy or reproduction.

repped. Ribbed or corded, resembling rep.

reproduction (rē-prō-dŭk'shȧn; re pro *duck* shun). Likeness or copy, sometimes in another material.

rep-stitch. Canvas-stitch worked vertically. See STITCHES.

reptile leather (rĕp'tĭl; *rep* til). Skins of animals that crawl or move on short legs. See LEATHERS.

réseau (F. rā-zō; ray zo). Groundwork, in lace, of small regular meshes. French word for net or network.

reseda (rȧ-sē'dȧ; re *see* da). French word meaning mignonette. Applied to a grayish green that resembles the color of the flower.

résille (F. rā-zē; ray zee). Net or snood for the hair.

resist (rē-zĭst'; re *zist*). Substance that resists dyes, used in resist printing; applied to cloth in the form of designs, removed after dipping.

resist printing. Printing by applying substance that resists dye to parts of fabric. See PRINTING under DYEING.

resort wear (rē-zôrt'; re *zort*). Clothes designed to be in keeping with social and sports activities of popular place of recreation or entertainment, especially fashionable resort hotel.

Restoration (rĕs-tȧ-rā'shȧn; ress to *ray* shun). Characteristic of dress of the period in England, 1660–85, in which the Stuarts returned to the throne. Marked by use of straight or looped-back skirts; deep, open neck; short sleeves, slit from shoulder; reaction against somberness of Commonwealth.

restyle (rē-stīl'; re *style*). To refashion in new style.

ret. To soak or steep; especially, to soften and help separate fibers, as flax and hemp.

retail (rē'tāl; *re* tail). To sell in small or individual quantity, directly to the consumer; also, such sale. Department stores, specialty shops, and all variety chain stores sell retail.

reticella lace (rĕt-ĭ-chĕl'ə; ret i *chell* a). Needle-point lace with geometric designs and picoted brides. See LACES.
reticulated headdress (rə-tĭk'ū-lat-ĕd; re *tic* you late ed). Headdress characterized by use of the CREPINE over hair padded at sides and veil draped over head and falling to shoulders behind pads. Worn during Middle Ages.
reticule (rĕt'ĭ-kūl; *ret* i cule). Dressmaker type of pouch bag with drawstring top, used during 18th and 19th centuries as carryall for handkerchief, snuff, perfume, needle, thimble, thread, etc.

18th Century Reticule

revered (rə-vērd'; re *veerd*). Worked in kind of drawn work used on linens, handkerchiefs, etc.
revers (F. rə-vēr; re veer). Wide, shaped lapel or lapels. Used on coats, suits, dresses.
reversed leather (rə-vērst'; re *verst*). Leather finished on flesh side. See LEATHERS.
reversible coat. Coat that can be worn either side out. See COATS.
reversible fabric. Fabric that can be used with either end up or either side out. See FABRIC.
reworked wool. Reclaimed wool. See SHODDY under WOOL.
rhason (ra'sən; *ray* son). Long, loose garment similar to cassock. Worn by clergy of the Eastern Church.
rhinegrave (rīn'grāv; *rine* grave). Petticoat breeches; extremely full, skirt-like garment extending to knees, trimmed with ribbons, lace, etc. Worn by men during mid-17th century.
rhinestone (rīn'stōn; *rine* stone). Colorless, lustrous stone made of paste or glass in imitation of diamond.
rhodophane (rō'dō-fān; *roe* doe fane). Technical name of glass fabric developed by French fabric manufacturer, Colombet. It is transparent, brittle, and fragile, but does not shatter. Has been made into hats, bags, jackets, and dress accessories.
rib. 1. Raised ridge, or wale, horizontal, vertical, or diagonal, in textile fabrics, formed by heavier warp or filling yarn. **2.** Vertical ridge formed in knitting.
riband (rĭb'ənd; *rib* and). Ribbon band.
ribbed hose. Hose with lengthwise ribs of varying widths. See HOSE.
ribbing. Arrangement of ribs, as in any ribbed cloth.

RIBBONS

ribbon. Strip of silk, satin, velvet, etc., in various widths, often with a cord finish along both edges instead of selvage.
baby r. Very narrow ribbon, usually satin, in pastel color. Used on infants' and children's garments, lingerie.
belting r. Stiff grosgrain ribbon used for belts and tailored hats, and for support inside skirt waistlines, etc.
China r. Narrow ribbon, usually ⅛ inch wide, woven with plain edge. Popular in mid-19th century; used in CHINA RIBBON EMBROIDERY.
hair r. Ribbon, usually tied in a bow, used to hold the hair in place or worn for adornment.
love r. Narrow gauze ribbon, made in black and white, with thin satin stripes. Formerly worn as mourning band.
watch r. Firm grosgrain ribbon used as a strap for wrist watch.

ribbon wire. Wired tape used in millinery.
rice braid. Braid made to resemble rice grains that are strung lengthwise. See BRAIDS.
rice net. Coarse cotton net. See NETS.
rice powder. Kind of face powder having pulverized rice base. Widely used by women before other face powders were known. Originally put up in small bags and patted on body as well as face. Used especially on arms and neck.
rich color. Full, glowing color conveying satisfying impression. See COLOR.
Richelieu embroidery (F. rē-shə-lyē; ree she lyuh). Type of cut work. See EMBROIDERIES.
ricinium (rĭ-sĭn'ĭ-ŭm; ri *sin* i um). Short, hooded mantle worn during mourning by women of ancient Rome.
rick rack. Flat, woven, zigzag braid. See BRAIDS.
ridicule (rĭd'ĭ-kəl; *rid* i cul). Large pocket worn on women's dresses about 1875 as part of trimming. Forerunner of RETICULE.
riding-habit (rīd'ĭng; *ride* ing). Costume worn for horseback riding. See SPORTS CLOTHES.
riding-hood. Hood worn when riding. See HOODS.
riding-skirt. Medium-short, wraparound skirt worn by women who ride side-saddle.
right-and-left plaid. Plaid with stripes so placed that the weight of the design is to one side, making it necessary in cutting to place all pieces of a pattern to run in the same direction, just as in a napped fabric.
rigolette (rĭg-ə-lĕt'; rig o *let*). Lightweight, scarf-like covering for woman's head; usually knit or crocheted of wool.

RINGS

ring. Circle; especially, circular ornament worn on finger.
class r. Ring with emblem signifying year of graduation from particular institution. Worn on any finger as token.
dinner r. Elaborate jeweled ring. Worn with evening clothes on formal occasions.
engagement r. (ĕn-gāj'mənt; en *gaje* ment). Ring, usually set with solitaire precious stone, as a diamond, given in token of betrothal. In U. S., worn on third finger of left hand.
guard r. Close-fitting finger ring worn above or inside another more expensive or looser ring to keep latter from slipping off.
puff r. Hollow finger ring.
school r. Ring with emblem signifying particular school attended. Worn as token on any finger.
signet r. (sĭg'nĕt; *sig* net). Ring with signet or seal of private or particular type. Worn on any finger.
seal r. Ring having a monogram on emblem engraved on it so that it can make an imprint on sealing wax, etc. Originally used to seal letters and documents.
wedding r. Plain or jeweled circlet, usually of precious metal, signifying married state, placed by husband on finger of bride during wedding ceremony. In U. S., worn on third finger of left hand. Plain wedding ring also worn sometimes by men, in which case it is put on in double ring ceremony during the wedding.

ringhead. Instrument for stretching woolen cloth.
rip. To tear, usually along a line of least resistance, as a seam; also, a place torn or ripped open in a fabric, shoe, glove, etc.
ripping knife. Small knife with hard steel blade. Used to rip stitching in seams or on edges.
ripple cloth (rĭp'l; *rip* l). Woolen dress fabric with long silky hairs on right side. Also called *zibeline*.
Ripplette (rĭp-lĕt'; rip l *et*). Trade name for seersucker.
rivière (F. rē-vyêr; ree vyare). Necklace of precious stones, usually in several strands. See NECKLACES.
roach. Colloquial term for roll of hair brushed upward from forehead.
roan. Low-grade sheepskin. See LEATHERS.
robe. 1. French term for gown or dress. Applied to individual garments, to dress in general, and to loose gowns worn over other dress for ceremonial purposes. **2.** Abbreviation for BATHROBE.
robe de chambre (F. rôb də shäṅbr; robe de shonhbr). Loose morning gown or dressing gown worn by men and women.
robe de noce (F. də nôs; de noss). French phrase meaning wedding dress.
robe de nuit (F. də nwē; de nwee). French phrase meaning nightdress.
robe de style (F. də stēl; de steel).

Robe de Style

robe d'intérieur French phrase meaning bouffant type of frock with tight-fitting bodice and a full and usually long skirt.

robe d'intérieur (F. dăṅ-tā-rē-ēr; danh tay ri er). French phrase meaning hostess gown or robe for wearing in the home.

robe tailleur (F. tī-yĕr; tie yer). French phrase for a simple, tailored frock.

robings. Obsolete term for ornamental parts of a garment, such as lapels, revers, etc.

Robin Hood costume. Costume of legendary character. See FANCY DRESS.

Robin Hood hat. Quill-trimmed sports hat. See HATS.

rochet (rŏch'ĕt; rotch et). 1. Medieval outer garment. See WRAPS. 2. Mantle worn in colonial America. See WRAPS. 3. Close-fitting linen vestment worn by bishops and other prelates.

rocker sole. Shoe sole about ¼ inch thick, having definite upward line at toe and just behind ball of foot. Similar to effect of Dutch KLOMPEN.

rococo (rə-kō'kō or rō-kə-kō'; ro co co or ro co co). 1. Extravagant and exaggerated style, usually consisting of an irregular assemblage of scrolls and conventional shellwork. 2. Style of hat worn in Victorian era. See HATS. 3. Term often applied to over-elaborate decoration not in good taste.

rococo embroidery. Embroidery worked with narrow ribbons. See EMBROIDERIES.

Rograin (rō'grăn; ro grain). Trade name for hose seamed inside out. See HOSE.

rogue's yarn (rōgz; rohgz). Yarn different from others in a fabric, inserted for identification. See YARNS.

rolled hem. Hem made by rolling edge of fabric and securing roll by slip-stitches. See HEMS.

roller (rōl'ēr; role er). Hat with narrow, up-rolled brim. See HATS.

romaine (rō-mān'; ro main). Sheer silk fabric in basket weave, made of fine yarns, having smooth surface and slightly more body than triple sheer.

Roman (rō'măn; ro man). Characteristic of Roman costume; similar to Greek. Consisted of the STOLA, a dress with a flounce at bottom; the ZONA, a girdle; the TOGA, heavy, white mantle draped and pinned; and sandals.

Roman collar. Clerical collar. See COLLARS.

Roman cut work. Open-work embroidery. Designs are outlined with purl-stitches. See EMBROIDERIES.

Roman lace. Needle-point lace of geometric designs. Same as RETICELLA. See LACES.

Roman pearl. Type of imitation pearl. See PEARLS.

Roman sandal. Strapped, low-heeled or heelless sandal. See SHOES.

Roman-stitch. Variation of Oriental-stitch, a series of parallel stitches intersected at center by shorter stitches. See STITCHES.

Roman stripe. Stripe in series of contrasting colors. See STRIPES.

Romany stripes. Bright-colored stripes of varying widths. Same as GYPSY STRIPES. See STRIPES.

Romeo (rō'mē-ō; ro me o). 1. Ardent suitor or beau. 2. Man's house slipper. See SLIPPERS.

rompers. One-piece garment, originated for young children; a combination of waist and short, bloused trousers. Also worn by girls and women for gymnastic work.

Rompers

rond. Beveled strip put on before the heel lifts in shoe manufacture.

rondel or rondelle (rŏn'dĕl; ron del). Round, flat bead.

rope silk. Heavy, silk embroidery thread. See THREADS.

rope-stitch. Overlapped, twisted blanket-stitch. See STITCHES.

roquelaure (rŏk'ə-lôr; F. rôk-lôr; rock a lore or rok lore). Cloak worn in 18th century. See WRAPS.

rosary (rō'zə-rĭ; ro za ri). 1. Chaplet or garland of flowers, especially roses. 2. (Capitalized) String of beads used in a form of religious devotion.

rose. 1. Dull shade of pale, soft red. 2. Ribbon, lace, or jewel in rose shape; worn on shoe, garter, hatband. Favorite ornamentation of 17th century.

rose point lace. Venetian needle-point lace. See LACES.

rosette (rō-zĕt'; ro zet). Ribbon decoration, usually formed in the shape of a rose; used chiefly on women's and children's clothes.

Roshanara (rŏsh-ə-năr'ə; rosh a nar a). Trade name for heavy crepe with crosswise crinkle. Made in silk with satin back.

rouge (F. rōōzh; roozh). 1. French word for red. 2. Any cosmetic for coloring the cheeks or lips red.

roughers (rŭf'ērz; ruff erz). Woolen cloth before fulling, just as it comes from loom.

Rough Rider shirt. Khaki shirt of type worn by Theodore Roosevelt and his Rough Riders. See SHIRTS.

rouleau (F. rōō-lō; roo lo). Roll or fold of ribbon, as for piping. Term used in millinery.

round. 1. Circle. 2. In crochet, tatting, etc., series of stitches worked to complete one circle around the work.

roundabout. Short, fitted jacket. See JACKETS.

rounded-top godet (F. gō-dā; go day). Godet rounded over top. See GODETS.

roundlet. Man's hat worn in 18th century. See HATS.

round seam. Glove seam. See SEAMS.

round-thread linen. Soft, plain linen used in embroidery and fancy work. See LINENS.

row (rō; roe). In crochet, knitting, netting, etc., series of stitches worked from one side to the other of straight piece of work.

rubber. Substance made of the sticky, milky sap of the rubber tree. It is chemically processed when it is known as crude rubber; then treated by various methods to give desired strength, hardness, elasticity, etc. Used in many manufactured articles.

rubber apron. 1. Apron of rubber worn for protection of front of a dress. Same as cotton apron in style, but waterproof. 2. Small, apron-shaped garment of rubber made in flesh color or white; worn under the dress for sanitary purposes.

rubber-coated. Having an inside coating of rubber.

rubber-cored. Having layers of fabric stuck together with layers of rubber between.

rubber-covered. Plated or covered with rubber.

rubberized. Coated or covered with rubber.

rubber-proofed. Waterproofed by being combined with rubber.

rubbers. Low overshoes made of rubber. Worn by men, women, and children as protection against the weather.

ruby (rōō'bĭ; roo bi). 1. Hard, clear, red precious stone; best varieties very valuable. Used in jewelry. 2. Rich, deep, clear red color of the precious stone.

ruche (rōōsh; roosh). Strip of silk, crepe, chiffon, lace, or other fabric, plaited or gathered. Used as dress trimming, usually at neck or wrist.

Plaited Ruching. Ruche, 1900

rudge wash. Kind of kersey made of unwashed fleece.

ruff. Plaited or crimped collar or frill. See COLLARS. See CUFFS.

ruffle. Strip gathered or plaited and used as a trimming or finish, attached so as to leave one or both edges free. Ruffles of lawn and lace on sleeves and shirt fronts worn by men until 19th century.

ruffler. Sewing-machine attachment for making ruffling, plaiting, and frilling.

rug gown. Gown of coarse, shaggy cloth.

rullion (rŭl'yŭn; rull yun). Shoe or sandal of untanned leather. See SHOES.

rumal (rōō-mäl'; roo mahl). 1. Cotton or silk fabric made in India. 2. Kerchief used as headdress by men.

Rumanian embroidery (rōō-mā'nĭ-ən; roo may ni an). Outline embroidery. Same as HOLBEIN WORK. See EMBROIDERIES.

Rumanian-stitch. Series of parallel stitches intersected at center by shorter stitches. Same as ORIENTAL-STITCH. See STITCHES.

rumba costume. Costume consisting of short jacket of bolero style with short, cape-like sleeves, and floor-length skirt that is tightly molded to figure to below hips and from there down is a mass of ruffles. Jacket and skirt do not meet at waistline.

Rumba Costume, 1930's

rumswizzle (rŭm'swĭz-l; *rum* swiz l). Irish material made of imported, undyed wool.
running hem. Inconspicuous stitch used on hems. Same as VERTICAL HEMMING-STITCH. See STITCHES.
running shoe. Soft leather shoe with spiked sole. See SHOES.

running-stitch. Basic sewing stitch; series of short, even stitches, several run on the needle at one time. See STITCHES.
run o' the mill. Fabric not inspected at factory; often sub-standard. Same as MILL RUN.
russel. English woolen twill used for garments in 15th century and after.
russet. 1. Dark reddish or yellowish brown. 2. Coarse, homespun cloth or clothing of a reddish-brown color, formerly worn by country people.
Russia leather (rŭsh'ē; *rush* a). Calfskin or other leather, bark or chrome-tanned. See LEATHERS.
Russian. Characteristic of Russian costume. Men's costume consists of long, belted, full-sleeved blouse of white or bright color, sometimes with band embroidery, usually opening at left side of

Child's Dress Adapted from Russian Costume, 1906

neck; loose trousers, usually tucked into boots; cap or hat, usually of lamb's wool; fur-lined or fur-trimmed coat, often fitted and with flaring skirt. Often adapted in detail for women's fashions. Women's costume includes long, full dress, heavily embroidered or brocaded; sometimes short dress, also decorated; sometimes hand-woven, full skirt with attached, sleeveless bodice; full, long sleeves; embroidered blouse; apron; heavy neck ornaments; elaborate headdress with beads, jewels, embroidery, tassels, ribbons, laces, etc.; wrap and boots like men's.
Russian blouse. Loose, long-sleeved blouse. See BLOUSES.
Russian boot. Boot extending to the calf of the leg. See BOOTS.
Russian braid. Narrow, flat, decorative braid. Same as SOUTACHE. See BRAIDS.
Russian crash. Strong, unbleached linen used for towels, etc.
Russian embroidery. Washable, outline embroidery on Holland; or canvas embroidery in wool. See EMBROIDERIES.
Russian muskrat. Silvery gray fur of Russian muskrat, less durable and softer than that of American species. See FURS.
Russian tapestry. Strong fabric of coarse linen or hemp used in embroidery, for curtains, etc.
rust. Reddish-yellow shade, the color of iron rust.

S

saba (sä-bä'; *sah bah*). Fine Philippine fabric made from fiber of a banana-like plant.
sable (sā'bl; *say* bl). 1. Fur of the sable or marten. See FURS. 2. Black, color of sable. 3. Mourning or funeral garment.
sabot (F. sȧ-bō; sa bo). Wooden shoe, such as worn by peasants in various European countries. See SHOES.
sabotine (săb'ȧ-tēn; *sab* o teen). Makeshift shoe worn by soldiers in World War. See SHOES.
Sabrina work (sȧ-brī'nȧ; sa *bry* na). Type of floral appliqué. See EMBROIDERIES.
sac. French spelling of SACQUE.
sac de voyage (F. sȧk dė vwȧ-yȧzh; sack de vwah yazh). French phrase meaning traveling bag.
sachet (să-shā'; sa *shay*). 1. Dainty ornamental pad or small bag, containing perfumed substance, usually sachet powder or scented cotton. Hung or laid among garments or other articles to be scented. 2. Originally, reticule or other small bag or pouch.
sachet-powder. Perfume in powder form. Used to scent sachets.
sack. English spelling of SACQUE.
sackcloth. Coarse, heavy, unbleached muslin, often used for sturdiest of sports apparel.
sack coat. Short, loose coat. See COATS.
sacking. Coarse, loosely woven cotton fabric, usually less expensive than sackcloth.

sacque. 1. Loose-bodied garment of Watteau type, popular in end of 17th, early 18th century. See WATTEAU SACQUE. 2. Loose, blouse-like garment, often of light color and worn with dark skirt. See JACKETS. Sacque, the form most commonly used, is a pseudo-French spelling from French word *sac*.

Sack, 1938

saddle. Piece of leather on shoe, usually in contrasting color, stitched from forward shank, at one side, over vamp to the other side.
saddle oxford. Oxford type of shoe, having a saddle. See SHOES.
saddle seam. Seam used for joining leather. See SEAMS.
saddle-stitch. Overcasting-stitch used as decoration. See STITCHES.
Safari (sȧ-fä'rē; sa *fah* ree). Copyrighted name given to rich, dark brown color with a bluish cast; applied only to U. S. Government Alaska Sealskin.
safeguard (sāf'gärd; *safe* gard). Petticoat worn outside the dress by women in

colonial America as protection against mud and dust when riding horseback.
safety pin. Utilitarian pin with protective guard for the point. See PINS.
saffian (săf'ĭ-ȧn; *saff* i an). Bright-colored leather. See LEATHERS.
saffron. Reddish yellow, color of dye obtained from a part of the flower of the same name, a species of crocus.
sagum (sā'gŭm; *say* gum). Rectangular cloak worn by Roman soldiers. See WRAPS.
sail cloth. Heavy canvas used for sails, tents, and, in lighter weight, for garments.
sail needle. Needle with three-sided point for use in sewing sail cloth, canvas, etc. See NEEDLES.
sailor. Hat with a flat crown and a brim. See HATS.
sailor cap. Sailor's small, stiff, brimless cap; or child's tam-shaped cap with name of ship on band. See CAPS.
sailor collar. Collar with square back and V-front. See COLLARS.
sailor tie. Shoe with two eyelets and lacing. See SHOES.
Saint Gall lace. Lace made by machine by embroidering a design on woolen fabric, using silk or cotton thread, and then chemically dissolving the wool and leaving only the embroidery. See LACES.
salad-bowl hat. Hat with deeply rolled brim. See HATS.
sallet (săl'ĕt; *sal* et). Simple, lightweight helmet, extended in back over

fāte, făt, dȧnce, ärt mē, mĕt, hẽr, thêre rīde, rĭd nōte, nŏt, côrn, fōōd, fŏŏt cūte, cŭt, cūre now fin(ŋ)ger villa(ȧ) señor pleas(zh)ure

salloo the neck; with or without a visor. Worn during 15th century.

salloo (săl'ōō; sal oo). Red, twilled cotton or calico; used in India, but made in England.

salmon (săm'ən; sam on). Tint of red-orange, color of the fish's flesh.

salon (F. sȧl-ôn; sal onh). French word for drawing room or reception room. Also, a showroom used for exhibition purposes.

salt sacking. Rough, homespun type of fabric in plain weave, of cotton, worsted, or other fibers. Similar in appearance to crash and burlap. Made in summer suiting weights; used for sportswear, summer riding-habits, etc.

Salvation Army bonnet. Black, straw, off-the-face bonnet trimmed with blue silk. Fastened under chin, with ribbon tied in bow at side. See BONNETS.

Sam Browne belt. Broad belt named after British army officer. See BELTS.

samite (săm'īt; sam ite). Rich, lustrous, silk fabric, with six-thread warp; usually interwoven with gold or silver threads. Used during Middle Ages for ornamental cushions, ecclesiastical robes, etc.

sample. One of anything selected from a quantity to show the character of the entire lot. From Latin *exemplum*, meaning example.

sampler. 1. Piece of material on which a detail in construction of a garment is worked out. 2. Piece of needlework, made to practice stitches, to exhibit skill, or to preserve a pattern.

sanbenito (săn-bē-nē'tō; san be *nee* toe). 1. Garment of sackcloth, worn by penitents. 2. Garment of yellow or of black with painted designs, worn by penitents during the Inquisition.

sandal (săn'dəl; *san* dal). 1. Open-shank, strap shoe, often having upper slashed or made of straps. See SHOES. 2. Sole, strapped to the foot. See SHOES. 3. Abbreviated rubber overshoe, usually covering only front of foot, with strap for the heel. 4. Strap or latchet for holding low shoe on foot.

Sanforized. Trade name applied to cotton or linen fabrics shrunk completely, uniformly, and permanently, both in length and in width, so that there will be no further shrinkage in washing beyond ¼ inch to the yard in either direction.

sanitary belt. Belt, usually of elastic, with tabs to which sanitary napkin may be attached. See BELTS.

Sanitized. Trade name applied to process that acts to prevent perspiration odor in fabrics and to make textiles germ-proof, self-sterilizing, antiseptic.

Santa Claus suit. Red flannel coat and knickers, with leggings. Usually trimmed with white cotton batting in imitation of fur. See FANCY DRESS.

sapphire (săf'īr; *saf* ire). 1. Precious stone of rich, transparent blue color. 2. Tone of blue, color of the jewel.

sarafan (sȧ-rȧ-fän'; sa ra *fahn*). National dress of Russian peasant women. Consists of full, gathered or plaited skirt of brocade or other rich fabric, which is usually attached to a sleeveless bodice with high and round, low and square, or other type of neckline.

sarcenet or **sarsenet** (särs'nĕt; *sarce* net). Soft fabric in plain or twill weave; usually of silk. Used for linings, especially in England. Originally from Persia and Byzantium and named for Saracens.

sari or **saree** (sä'rē; *sah* ree). Gauzy fabric draped around the body, with one end thrown over the head; principal garment of Hindu women. Loosely, draping of this kind.

Hindu Sari

sark. Obsolete term for shirt or body garment.

sarong (sä'rŏng; *sah* rong). Long, wide piece of colorful fabric wrapped around waist in skirt-like effect. Worn by the natives of Java, Ceylon, etc.

Sarong

sarpe (särp; sahrp). Ornamental girdle of metal.

sartor (sär'tər; *sahr* tor). Humorous term meaning one who mends or patches; a tailor.

sartorial (sär-tō'rĭ-əl; sahr *tore* i al). Pertaining to the work of a tailor or to men's clothes and grooming in general. Beau Brummel was an example of sartorial perfection.

SASHES

sash. Ornamental band, scarf, strip, or belt worn around waist or over shoulder.

baby s. Ribbon sash tied with bow at back, in imitation of children's style. Popular at end of 19th century.

corselet s. Broad, girdle-like sash, fitted snugly over hips and waistline.

cummerbund (kŭm'ẽr-bŭnd; *cum* er bund). Man's broad sash worn chiefly in India as waistband; in modern dress, arranged in overlapping folds and worn with dinner clothes. From Hindu-Persian word, *kamarband*.

faja (fä'hä; *fah* hah). Bright silk sash worn by Spanish men.

obi (ō'bĭ; *o* bi). Broad sash, usually made of very heavy, stiff silk or satin, brocaded or embroidered in gay colors. Worn by Japanese women.

tapis (tä'pēs; *tah* peece). Wide sash or girdle extending from waist to knee and covering upper part of saya, or skirt. Worn by Philippine women.

tubbeck (tŭb'ăk; *tub* eck). Sash, generally red, worn by Burmese women.

sash blouse. Blouse crossed in front like a surplice, with girdle formed by attached sash pieces. See BLOUSES.

satara (săt'ə-rə; *sat* a ra). Lustrous, ribbed woolen fabric.

satchel (săch'əl; *satch* el). Small piece of luggage, especially pouch-shaped bag, carried in the hand.

sateen (să-tēn'; sa *teen*). Cotton fabric in close satin weave, with lustrous, smooth, satin-like finish. Used for underskirts, linings, dresses, slip-covers, etc.

sateen weave. Weave similar to satin weave. See WEAVES.

SATINS

satin. Silk or rayon fabric, sometimes with cotton filling, having smooth finish, high gloss on face, and dull back. Luster and brilliancy are due to manner of weaving and finish between heated cylinders. Made in many varieties. Used for dresses, blouses, accessories, coats, linings, lingerie, trimmings, etc.

Baronette s. (băr-ə-nĕt'; ba ra *net*). Trade name for rayon fabric in satin weave, with high luster, and sometimes with cotton back. Used for slips, sports dresses, etc.

crepe-back s. Fabric of silk, rayon, or mixture, having satin face and crepe back. Made in various weights. Used for dresses and blouses; one side of material often used as trim for other.

duchesse s. (F. dü-shĕs; doo shess). Highly lustrous, heavy, firm, soft silk fabric. Used for formal dresses, evening wraps.

étoile s. (F. ā-twäl; ai twahl). Satin fabric with lustrous surface. Used for dresses.

farmer's s. Highly lustrous fabric with cotton warp and worsted or cotton filling. Used for linings and petticoats. Also called *Italian cloth*.

Italian cloth. Same as FARMER'S SATIN.

Liberty s. Trade name for soft, closely woven, piece-dyed satin fabric with raw-silk warp and single spun-silk filling. Used for linings and trimmings.

messaline (mĕs-ə-lēn'; mess a *leen*). Soft, light-weight, brilliantly lustrous silk fabric in satin weave; closely woven, usually in solid colors. Used for dresses, blouses, slips, trimmings, linings.

mushru (mŭsh'rōō; *mush* roo). Sturdy cotton-backed satin fabric, often figured or striped. Made in India.

panne s. Satin treated by heat and pressure to produce high luster. Has very smooth, almost waxy surface.

fāte, făt, dånce, ärt mē, mĕt, hẽr, thêre rīde, rĭd nōte, nŏt, côrn, fōōd, fŏŏt cūte, cŭt, cũre now fin(ŋ)ger villa(ə) señor pleas(zh)ure

s. de chine (F. sà-tăṇ də shēn; sa tanh de sheen). Firm silk with satin finish.
s. de Lyon (F. lĕ-ôṇ; lee onh). Satin with ribbed back.
s. merveilleux (F. mĕr-vĕ-yē; mare veh yuh). All-silk, twilled fabric with satin finish.
s. sultan. Silk fabric with satin finish. Made in India.
shoe s. Same as SLIPPER SATIN.
Skinner's s. Trade name for heavy, durable, lustrous satin. Used chiefly for linings and dresses.
slipper s. Strong, durable, closely woven fabric with dull back and semi-glossy face. Used for footwear, evening dresses, wraps.
stovepipe s. Very smooth, lustrous satin. Same as PANNE SATIN.
surf s. Heavy quality of satin.
wash s. Washable, soft, lustrous satin, usually in white or pastel colors. Used for lingerie, neckwear, blouses, dresses.

satin-back crepe. Fabric with crepe face, satin back. See CREPES.
satin de chine (F. sà-tăṇ də shēn; sa tanh de sheen). Silk fabric with satin finish. See SATINS.
satin de laine (F. lĕn; len). Thin, smooth-surfaced cashmere.
satin de Lyon (F. lĕ-ôṇ; lee onh). Satin with ribbed back. See SATINS.
satinette or **satinet** (săt-ĭ-nĕt′; sat i net). 1. Thin or imitation satin. 2. Strong fabric made of cotton warp and woolen or cotton filling. Chiefly used in making trousers. 3. Variation of SATIN WEAVE. See WEAVES.
satin-fishbone-stitch. Slanting satin-stitches worked in fishbone effect. See STITCHES.
satin lisse (F. sà-tăṇ lēs; sa tanh leece). Delicately figured cotton fabric with satin finish.
satin merveilleux (F. mĕr-vĕ-yē; mare veh yuh). Twilled silk fabric. See SATINS.
satin sheeting. Strong, twilled, cotton-and-silk fabric with satin finish. Used in upholstery, embroidery, etc.
satin-stitch. Close, parallel, over-and-over stitches. See STITCHES.
satin stripe. Smooth shiny stripe, usually woven into a crepe or taffeta fabric. See STRIPES.
satin sultan. Silk fabric with satin finish. See SATINS.
satin surah. Highly lustrous type of SURAH.
satin weave. Weaving which produces smooth fabric surface. See WEAVES.
saucer brim. Shallow, upturned hat brim, resembling in shape the saucer used under a teacup.
sautoir (F. sō-twär; so twahr). Long, jeweled chain of gold.
savoir faire (F. sà-vwär fêr; sa vwahr fair). French expression meaning to know how to do. Used to express poise, graciousness, or charm of manner.
Saxon embroidery (săks′en; sax on). Ancient outline embroidery. Same as ANGLO-SAXON EMBROIDERY. See EMBROIDERIES.
saxony. 1. Fabric made from fine wool raised in or near Saxony; especially a kind of flannel, a kind of tweed, and a glossy cloth formerly used for garments. 2. Closely twisted, fine yarn. See YARNS.
Saxony lace. 1. Type of machine-embroidered, burnt-out lace. Same as PLAUEN LACE. 2. Embroidered drawn work. 3. Curtain lace in imitation of old Brussels. See LACES.
say. 1. Gallic mantle of light wool, brightly colored, often brilliantly striped. Finally replaced the Roman toga in fashion and was called *sagum.* Later worn by Robin Hood. 2. Fabric resembling serge.
saya (sä′yä; *sah* yah). Skirt worn by Philippine women. See SKIRTS.
scabbard. Case used to enclose furled umbrella. Also, case in which a sword is carried; usually strapped around waist.
scallop (skŏl′ǝp; *scoll* op). Circular curve or projection, usually made in series along an edge.
scallop buttonhole-stitch. Single- or double-purl-stitch made in scallop design. See STITCHES.
scalloped. Cut into segments of circles at the edge or border.
scallop-finish edging. Edging about ⅝ inch wide, having one side scalloped. Used as a finish for children's underwear and dresses, and for other garments that require frequent laundering.
scapular (skăp′ǝ-lẽr; *scap* you ler). Monk's sleeveless outer garment with cowl, which hangs from shoulders.
scapulary (skăp′ū-lẽr-ĭ; *scap* you lare i). Shoulder strap, as in uniform.
scarf. Wide band of fabric worn loosely in various ways over the shoulders or around the neck.
scarf cape. Long or short formal cape draped across the back and over the arms. See CAPES.
scarf collar. Collar attached at neckline and loose in front in scarf effect. See COLLARS.
scarf pin. Decorative pin used to hold scarf or necktie in place. Same as TIE PIN. See PINS.
scarlet. 1. Intense red-orange color. 2. Scarlet-colored cloth or clothes.
scarpetti (skär-pĕt′tǐ; *scar pet* ti). Shoe worn when rock climbing. See SHOES.
schappe silk (shăp′ĕ; *shahp* eh). Yarn or fabric made from carded spun silk.
Schleswig lace (shlĕs′vǐg; *shless* vig). 1. 17th century Danish needle-point. 2. 18th century Danish bobbin lace. See LACES.
school ring. Ring signifying particular school attended. See RINGS.
schreinerize (shrī′nẽr-īz; *shry* ner ize). To finish fabric, especially cotton, with high luster by type of calendering process making use of steel rollers engraved with fine lines. Finish not permanent.

SCISSORS

scissors. Cutting implement from 3 to 6 inches long, with two blades pivoted on a screw so that the sharp edges face each other, and having ring handles for thumb and finger. Also called *pair of scissors.* See SHEARS.
blunt s. Scissors with ends rounded instead of pointed. May be carried in pocket. Used for cutting paper, string, etc. Often used by children.
buttonhole s. Scissors from 3 to 5 inches long, with blades regulated by a screw. Edges stop short of the pivot, so that a slit can be cut the desired length, without cutting the edge of the cloth.
embroidery s. Light, dainty scissors from 3 to 3½ inches long, used for snipping threads.
manicure s. Delicate, sharp-pointed scissors, sometimes curved at point. Used for cutting nails and cuticle.

scob. Defect in fabric caused by failure of warp to interlace in the weaving.
scogger. Footless worsted stocking. See HOSE.
scone cap. Flat, round cap resembling scone. See CAPS.
scoop bonnet. Bonnet with brim like a scoop. See BONNETS.
Scotch cambric (kăm′brĭk; *came* bric). Fine cotton material like linen cambric.
Scotch cap. Brimless wool cap; also, cap of any of types worn in Scotland. See CAPS.
Scotch cloth. Cheap lawn. No longer in use.
Scotch fingering. Woolen yarn used for knitting. See YARNS.
Scotch grain leather. Heavy leather with pebbled grain. See LEATHERS.
Scotch plaid. Plaid fabric and design originating in Scotland; now used almost everywhere. See PLAID. See TARTAN.
Scottish or **Scotch.** Having style features of national dress of Scotland. Men's costume includes tartan kilt, a full, plaited, skirt-like garment fastened by a belt around the waist and ending above the knees; waistcoat; short coat of velvet or cloth; sometimes a folded plaid worn over the left shoulder, often fastened with large brooch; stockings gartered below the knees and leaving the knees bare; cocked bonnet or tam-o'-shanter with ribbon streamers, sometimes decorated with feather or brooch or both; sporran, a purse of leather or fur, usually fastened by chain around the waist and hanging down at the center-front. Women's costume includes cloth bodice and skirt and tartan shawl.
scratch. Wig covering only part of head. See WIGS.
scratch felt. Cheap wool fabric, woven with long yarns in camel's-hair effect.
screen printing. Process of printing that makes use of screens of bolting cloth for applying designs to fabric. See PRINTING under DYEING.
scrim. Transparent, light-weight, cotton fabric, with open-mesh weave; in white, cream, and ecru. Used for draperies.
scuffer. Children's play shoe. See SHOES.
sea-green. Yellowish green, color of sea water.
sea-island cotton. Long, silky-fibered cotton. See COTTON.
seal. 1. Leather made from skins of hair

seals. See LEATHERS. **2.** Fur, usually Hudson seal or seal-dyed cony. See FURS. **3.** Made of seal leather or seal fur. **4.** Woolen fabric in pile weave in imitation of the fur. Used for coats. **5.** Very dark brown color. Also called *seal brown*.

seal-dyed cony. Processed rabbit fur. See FURS.

seal ring. Ring with emblem engraved on it. Signet ring. See RINGS.

sealskin. Underfur of a fur seal. See FURS.

SEAMS

seam. Joining line where parts of a garment or edges of material are sewed together. Also, the edges of material left after parts are joined, usually on wrong side. Variations include welt, strap, flat-fell, slot, French, etc.

blanket-stitch s. Two edges of fabric joined in an open seam by means of blanket-stitch.

bound s. Seam edge bound with bias binding. Used in tailored garments, unlined coats, etc.

broad-stitched s. Same as top-stitched seam, with additional row of stitching on each side of seam line.

catch-stitched s. Seam which is pressed open and then secured by catching seam edges to fabric by putting needle first in seam edge and then in fabric, using catch-stitches. Used in finishing seams in flannel.

clean-stitched s. Seam stitched and pressed open, with raw edges then turned under about $\frac{1}{8}$ inch, held free from garment, and stitched.

corded s. Seam made same as welt seam, but with covered cord basted along seam edge and stitched in place.

double-lock s. Machine-basted seam overlaid by zigzag stitch that gives strength as well as elasticity. Seam edges are usually pinked. Used on lingerie and other ready-made garments.

double-stitched s. Same as TOP-STITCHED SEAM.

double-stitched welt s. Welt seam with additional row of stitching. Used formerly only on men's clothing.

elastic s. Seam having strip of knitted or elastic fabric set within it for ease of movement. Used chiefly on underwear, boys' and men's Windbreakers, etc.

fell s. Same as FLAT FELL SEAM.

flat fell s. Flat seam so made that the raw edges are turned in and face each other. The seam has two rows of stitching and appears the same on right and wrong sides. Gives flat, sturdy finish. Used chiefly in men's and boys' shirts, slacks, etc.

flat-lock s. Seam made by stitches that zigzag forward and backward across the seam concealing the raw edges and providing a finish. Used on lingerie and other ready-made garments.

French s. Seam made by stitching edges together on right side, trimming off close to stitching, then turning to wrong side and stitching again so as to conceal raw edges. Used on soft, closely woven fabrics.

full or **trade s.** Seam having edges stitched together; then one edge trimmed; and the wider, untrimmed edge turned over it, as in a welt, and stitched. Used on lingerie and other ready-made garments.

imitation corded s. Seam with corded effect produced by basting and then turning both seam edges to the same side and stitching through the three thicknesses of fabric.

lap s. Seam used on heavy, firmly woven materials that do not fray, such as broadcloth. The edges are lapped, basted, and stitched without being turned under.

open-welt s. Same as TUCKED SEAM.

pinked s. Seam that is pinked or notched along edge, as with pinking shears. Used for firm wool and silk fabrics.

piped s. Seam with flat fold of bias or braid inserted so as to show a piping on the right side.

plain s. Seam most commonly used. Stitched on seam line, pressed open, raw edges overcast. When used on plaits and armholes, both edges are overcast together.

prick s. Seam used in gloves; made by laying two pieces together, edge to edge, and stitching with a special machine. Used on men's street gloves; sometimes, on women's.

round s. Seam used in gloves; made by placing two edges together for a narrow seam and stitching over these edges, thus holding the seam and finishing the edges in one operation.

saddle s. Seam made by stitching through and through, with pieces laid edge to edge instead of being lapped. Used in shoemaking.

shirtmaker s. Same as FULL SEAM, but with a third row of stitching. Durable seam that gives longer wear and does not pull out. Used on slips not cut on the bias.

slot s. Plain seam basted and then pressed open, without being stitched. Strip of material then placed over seam on underside and stitched from right side, at even distance on both sides of seam line. The bastings are removed, thus making two facing open welts or tucks.

strap s. Plain seam stitched and pressed open; then bias strip of fabric placed over seam on right side and stitched in place along each edge. Strap seams are often used in firmly woven broadcloth, in which case the raw edges of the strip are cut true and not turned under. On fabric that frays, both edges of the strip are turned underneath and held together with diagonal basting.

tailored fell s. Same as FLAT FELL. Used in making unlined coats and skirts, especially tailored wash skirts.

top-stitched s. Seam that is pressed open, with raw edges pinked or overcast, then stitched from right side on both sides of seam line. Also called *double-stitched seam*.

tucked s. Seam finished with a tuck stitched from $\frac{1}{4}$ to 1 inch from the edge of the seam. Sometimes called *open welt*.

welt s. Seam stitched, one seam edge cut away to within $\frac{1}{4}$ inch of stitching, other edge pressed over narrow seam edge so as to conceal it, and second row of stitching added on right side so as to catch the normal seam.

seam beading. Narrow insertion. See BEADING.

seam binding. Narrow strip of ribbon-like fabric, used for finishing edges. See BINDINGS.

seam blending. Cutting away one edge of a seam to eliminate bulk, as in a welt seam, or cutting away overlapping seams and corners.

seam godet (F. gō-dā; go day). Godet with one side stitched in position in a gore and the other side stitched in a seam of the garment. See GODETS.

seaming. 1. Insertion used to make ornamental seam. Also, braid, lace, gimp, etc., used to cover seams or edges. **2.** Process of making a seam.

seamless shoe. Shoe with a whole vamp, stitched only at the back. See SHOES.

seam placket. Placket on seam, finished by putting strip of fabric on seam edges. See PLACKETS.

seam pocket. Pocket with one side or both sides stitched in a seam of the garment. See POCKETS.

seam-stitch. Knitting stitch. Same as PURL-STITCH, 2. See STITCHES.

seamstress (sēm′strĕs; *seem* stress). Sewing-woman, a woman who stitches and finishes, rather than a dressmaker, who cuts, fits, and makes.

seam tape. Seaming ribbon used as a finish. See TAPES.

sea-otter. Prized fur of otter from the North Pacific. See FURS.

season. 1. Fashion season of several weeks in early spring and early fall when fashions for spring and for fall are being promoted. **2.** Spring and summer season when clothes promoted in the spring showings are worn; fall and winter season when clothes promoted in the fall showings are worn.

secondary color (sĕk′ən-dĕr-ĭ; *sec* on dare i). Mixture of two primary colors. See COLOR.

Second Empire (ĕm′pīr; *em* pire).

Second Empire
Costume, 1860

Characteristic of French dress of 1852–1870. Marked by broad silhouette with close bodice and small waistline; bouffant skirt ruffled and flounced; décolleté neck with bertha or fichu; pagoda sleeves; heavily trimmed bonnet; shawl or mantle.

seconds. Imperfect merchandise, usually sold at reduced rates.

Seco silk. Trade name for combined cotton and silk material in fancy weaves and prints. Used in dresses, linings, curtains.

secque (sĕk; seck). Clog similar to the sabotine. See SHOES.

sectional crown. Hat or cap crown made up of many pieces, usually cut in points that come together in the center.

seed embroidery. German embroidery done with seeds. See EMBROIDERIES.

seed pearl. Tiny pearl. Used in mass for neckbands, purses, etc. See PEARLS.

seed-stitch. Short back-stitch with long under stitch, leaving space between top stitches. See STITCHES.

seerband (sēr'bănd; *seer* band). East Indian term for turban.

seerhand (sēr'hănd; *seer* hand). Type of muslin, of texture intermediate between nainsook and mull.

seersucker (sēr'sŭk-ēr; *seer* suck er). Thin, light-weight washable fabric in plain weave, with crinkled alternate stripes made by making part of the warp very slack. Used for dresses, children's rompers, underwear, men's summer suits.

self. Of the same material as the rest of the piece of apparel; as, self-covered buttons; self-belt; self-fabric; etc.

self-fabric or **material.** Same material as that of the garment. Term often used in connection with buttons or trimmings made of the fabric of the dress. See SELF.

selvage (sĕl'vėj; *sell* vij). Lengthwise edge of woven fabrics, finished so that it will not ravel. Usually cut away in making of garment. Sometimes spelled *selvedge*.

semi-fashioned. Seamed to imitate full-fashioned. See HOSE.

semi-fitted. Clothes fitted so as to conform partly, but not too closely, to the shape of the figure.

semi-made. Term used of dresses cut and partially made; so designed that the purchaser can finish them readily.

semi-sheer. Partially sheer. Triple sheers are semi-sheers. See SHEER.

sendal (sĕn'dăl; *sen* dal). Thin, light-weight silk cloth. Used during the Middle Ages for sumptuous garments.

sennit (sĕn'ĭt; *sen* it). Rough straw used for men's hats. See STRAWS.

sepia (sē'pĭ-ȧ; *see* pi a). Dark, dull brown color, as in rotogravure.

sequin (sē'kwĭn; *see* kwin). Metal disk or spangle used for trimming.

Seraceta. Trade name for a brand of rayon. See RAYON.

serape (sĕ-rä'pä; se *rah* pay). Blanket-like outer garment. See WRAPS.

SERGES

serge (sērj; serj). Popular, soft, durable, woolen fabric; made in great variety. Woven with clear finish in even-sided twill, which gives flat, diagonal rib. Best grades made of worsted warp and worsted or woolen filling. Silk and rayon fibers now also used in manufacture of serge. Used for tailored apparel, such as suits, dresses, coats, shirts, middy blouses.

cheviot s. (shĕv'ĭ-et; *shev* i ot). Heavy, rough serge with pronounced diagonal weave. Originally made of wool of Cheviot sheep. Same as WIDE-WALE SERGE.

French s. Very fine, soft serge that wears well, but looks shiny sooner than other serges. Used for dresses, skirts, suits.

storm s. Light-weight, hard serge with nap; of fine weave, but usually coarser and heavier than French serge. Single yarn used for both warp and filling. Used for dresses, skirts, suits.

Verona s. Thin, twilled fabric of cotton and worsted.

wide-wale s. Serge with pronounced diagonal weave. Sometimes called *cheviot serge*. Used for skirts, suits.

serge de soy (sērj de soi; serj de soy). Material of silk or silk-and-wool mixture. Used in 18th century for men's waistcoats, coats, etc.

sergette. Thin serge.

sericin (sĕr'ĭ-sĭn; *sare* i sin). Gummy substance in raw silk. See SILK.

Serpentine crepe (sēr'pen-tēn; *ser* pen teen). Trade name for crinkled cotton crepe similar to sheer seersucker. See CREPES.

serpentine skirt. Fitted skirt with stiffened flare at bottom. See SKIRTS.

serul (sēr'ŭl; *seer* ul). Bloused pantaloons, ending just below knee and suggesting a bloused harem skirt. Worn in Arabia and parts of Northern Africa.

African Serul

service cap or **hat.** Cap or hat worn in U. S. Army, especially during the World War. See CAPS. See HATS.

set-in sleeve. Sleeve set into armhole. See SLEEVES.

seven-eighths length. Length of coat that is shorter than dress or skirt by a little less than one-eighth of the length from shoulder to hem. See LENGTHS.

sew (sō; so). To make stitches with needle and thread, especially by hand.

sewing. 1. Act of one who sews. 2. Material to be sewed; needlework.

sewing apron. Short apron with pockets made at the bottom for holding sewing supplies. See SEWING HABIT.

sewing basket. Any basket or box made to hold sewing supplies. Same as WORK BASKET.

sewing cotton. Twisted cotton thread. See THREADS.

sewing habit. Short felt apron with compartments and cushion. Designed for use in the Mary Brooks Picken School.

sewing machine. Any machine for stitching; worked by hand, foot, or electric power. The sewing machine has revolutionized the making of apparel and has made it possible for all civilized people to have more and better clothing.

sewing silk. Finely twisted silk thread. See THREADS.

shade. 1. Gradation of color; difference in a slight degree of color quality. Specifically, the dark tone of any color, as it approaches black. Contrasted with TINT. 2. Lace ornament for head, formerly worn by women. 3. Shield worn to protect eyes from light or glare; also, any protection from the sun.

shadow (shăd'ō; *shad* o). 17th century name for a sunshade, either worn on the head or carried in the hand.

shadow embroidery. Embroidery done with catch-stitch on wrong side of sheer material. See EMBROIDERIES.

shadow lace. Machine-made lace with indistinct designs. See LACES.

shadow print. Print done on warp threads of a fabric. Same as WARP PRINT. See PRINTS.

shadow-proof panel. Double thickness of fabric in front or back panel of petticoat or skirt part of slip, to give added protection against transparency of sheer dress.

shadow skirt. Underslip or skirt with broad hem, double skirt, or panel. See SLIPS.

shadow-stitch. 1. Catch-stitch worked on wrong side of sheer material. See STITCHES. 2. In pillow lace, same as HALF-STITCH, 2.

shaft. Rod in a loom. Term used with number to describe weave of a fabric; as, five-shaft satin.

shag. Pile or long nap; also, cloth of silk or worsted, having velvet nap.

shagreen (sha-grēn'; sha *green*). 1. Un-tanned leather with pebbly finish. 2. Sharkskin, when covered with armor of small tubercles. See LEATHERS. 3. Fabric having surface like shagreen leather.

shaker (shāk'ēr; *shake* er). Heavy jersey. Used for sweaters, etc.

shaker flannel. Fine grade of flannel. See FLANNELS.

Shakespeare collar (shāk'spēr; *shake* speer). Collar flaring away from face, as shown in portraits of William Shakespeare. See COLLARS.

shako (shăk'ō; *shack* o). High, stiff, military cap. See CAPS.

shaksheer (shăk-shēr'; shahk *sheer*). Long, full, Oriental trousers worn outdoors by women.

shalloon (shă-lōōn'; sha *loon*). Light-

shalwar weight, loosely woven, woolen fabric in twill weave. Chiefly used for linings. So called because first made in Châlons, France.

shalwar (shŭl′wẽr; shull ware). Oriental trousers; pajamas.

sham. Anything that resembles an article and serves as substitute for it or covers and adorns it; as, a pillow sham.

shank. Narrow part of the sole of a shoe beneath instep, or between heel and ball of foot. Sometimes stiffened by a metal piece called *shank-piece*.

shank button. Button with shank or loop, for sewing button on. See BUTTONS.

Shantung (shăn-tŏŏng′ or, colloquially, shăn-tŭng′; shahn *toong* or shan *tung*). **1.** Plain, rough, washable fabric that is really a heavy grade of pongee. In natural color, solid color, and printed designs. Suitable for sportswear. Named for Shantung, province in China. **2.** Expensive, hand-woven straw of baku type. See STRAWS.

shape. 1. Hat form or frame. **2.** Form or contour. Term applied sometimes to the human figure.

sharkskin. 1. Small pebbly or grained surface, woven in fabric; also, similar surface applied to leather and leatherette. Also, fabric woven with pebbly surface. **2.** Durable leather of shark hide. See LEATHERS.

sharps. Needles for hand sewing. Available in sizes from 1 to 12. See NEEDLES.

shawl. Earliest form of dress; usually straight, square, oblong, or triangular piece of material, worn across shoulders. Still worn by women as covering for head, neck, and shoulders. Later development added sleeves and an opening. Also, shawl worn around waist as a kilt, from which developed the petticoat and then trousers.

shawl collar. Collar and revers cut in one, without notch; usually extending around the neck and lapping shawl-fashion at the waistline. See COLLARS.

shawl material. Silk-and-wool dress fabric, usually with Oriental designs.

sheaf filling-stitch. Embroidery stitch resembling sheaf of grain. Same as BUNDLE-STITCH. See STITCHES.

sheaf-stitch. Open-seam stitch, having appearance of a sheaf. See STITCHES.

sheared beaver. Beaver from which some of thick underfur has been sheared. See FURS.

SHEARS

shears (shẽrz; sheerz). Cutting implement at least 6 inches long, heavier than scissors, having two blades pivoted on a screw so that the sharp edges face each other, and having small ring handle for thumb and bow handle large enough to admit several fingers for greater leverage.

paper s. Pointed shears with long blades. Used chiefly for cutting paper.

pinking s. Shears with notched blades. Used on firmly woven fabrics to pink the edge. Can be used when cutting fabric from pattern and thus save notching seams afterward.

tailoring s. Large, steel shears for cutting heavy, woolen fabrics.

sheath gown (shēth; sheeth). Straight, narrow, close-fitting gown of tube-like silhouette. Popular just before 1910. See DRESSES.

shed. Separation or opening in the warp through which shuttle is thrown in weaving.

sheen. Luster or glistening brightness reflected from surface of fabric.

sheepskin. 1. Leather prepared from skin of sheep. See LEATHERS. **2.** Skin of sheep with wool left on. Used for heavy coats, etc.

sheer. Light-weight, transparent fabric in plain weave, slightly creped; made in varying weights, such as semi-sheer, triple sheer.

sheeting. Muslin, even-weave linen, percale, and crepe de chine woven in widths appropriate for sheets for all sizes of beds; unbleached, bleached, and colored.

sheet wadding (wŏd′ĭng; *wod* ing). Carded cotton, pressed into sheets. Used as padding, especially in the shoulders of tailored garments, for muff linings, quilted robes, etc.

shell button. Hollow button made in two pieces. See BUTTONS.

shell edging. Crochet edging in scallops.

shell jacket. Man's short, fitted jacket. See JACKETS.

shell-stitch. Crochet stitch giving scalloped effect. Used as edging. See STITCHES.

shepherdess hat. Shallow-crowned hat with down-turned brim, flared at sides. See HATS.

shepherd's or **shepherd check** or **plaid.** White-and-black checkered cloth of wool, cotton, or other fiber. Usually in twill weave. Also, the pattern itself. See CHECKS.

Shetland lace (shĕt′lɘnd; *shet* land). Bobbin lace of Shetland wool. See LACES.

Shetland wool. 1. Wool of Shetland sheep. See WOOL. **2.** Fine worsted yarn. See YARNS.

shield (shēld; sheeld). **1.** Crescent-shaped piece of fabric worn to protect clothing from underarm perspiration. Same as DRESS SHIELD. **2.** Broad, plate-like piece of medieval defensive armor. Carried on arm to ward off blows and weapons.

shift. 1. Colonial name for undergarment like a shirt or chemise, usually of fine linen. Often made with long sleeves edged with plaiting. Before 1700, often called *smock*. **2.** Loose dress hanging straight from shoulders, with fulness closely belted at waistline. Similar in silhouette to monastic type. See MONASTIC SILHOUETTE under SILHOUETTES.

shimmy. Colloquial term for chemise.

shingle. Hair cut close to the head, especially in back. See BOBS.

shintiyan (shĭn′tĭ-yăn; *shin* ti yan). Wide, loose trousers worn by Moslem women.

ship tire. Headdress shaped like a ship or with ship-like ornament. Worn by Elizabethan women.

shirr (shẽr; sher). To make three or more rows of gathers.

shirring. Three or more rows of gathers.

shirring plate. Sewing-machine attachment used with the ruffler to shirr fabric by the machine.

SHIRTS

shirt. 1. Loose garment for upper part of body, often having collar and cuffs, and, usually, a front closing. Made of cotton, linen, silk, rayon, or wool. Worn by women for sports. **2.** Sleeveless, collarless undergarment for upper body.

boiled s. Colloquial term for white shirt having stiffly starched bosom. Worn by men for formal dress.

bosom s. Shirt having starched bosom, plaited or tucked, often of different fabric from that of the shirt.

camicia rossa (kä-mē′chä rōs′sä; *ka mee* chah *ross* sah). Red shirt, as worn by Garibaldi (1807–82) and followers.

chukker s. (chŭk′ẽr; *chuck* er). Same as POLO SHIRT.

Chukker Shirt

coat s. Shirt opening all the way down front in coat fashion.

dress s. Man's white shirt for evening wear, usually having starched, tucked, or plaited bosom.

garibaldi (găr-ĭ-bôl′dĭ; ga ri *bawl* di). High-necked, bloused shirt with full sleeves, worn by Garibaldi, the Italian patriot. Adapted for women and popular in U. S. during 1860's.

Garibaldi Shirt

hunting s. Coarse shirt, as of khaki or leather, worn for hunting. Formerly, frontiersman's deerskin jacket.

jersey (jẽr′zĭ; *jer* zi). Sports shirt of knitted silk, wool, rayon, etc.; made in pull-over style, without seams. Loosely, shirt of varying styles, made of any knitted fabric.

polo s. Shirt with short sleeves and often with collarless, round neck; made of soft, absorbent fiber, usually cotton. Worn for active sports.

Rough Rider s. Khaki shirt of type worn by Theodore Roosevelt and his Rough Riders. Made with standing collar, breast pockets with flaps, epaulets; buttoned down front.

Rough Rider Shirt

work s. Sturdy, colored shirt with collar attached.
shirtband. Band of shirt, usually neckband, to which collar is buttoned.
shirt-cuff-edge hem. Double-stitched hem. See HEMS.
shirt frill. Ruffle of cambric used on shirtwaists. Much worn by men in America during colonial period.
shirt front. Shirt bosom; part not covered by coat.
shirting. Closely woven cotton, linen, silk, or rayon fabric used for making shirts.
shirting flannel. Plain or twilled, lightweight, woolen flannel. See FLANNELS.
Shirtmaker. Trade name for tailored shirtwaist type of dress. See DRESSES.
shirtmaker seam. Triple-stitched seam. See SEAMS.
shirtwaist. Mannish, tailored blouse. See BLOUSES.
shirtwaist dress. Tailored dress with bodice like a shirtwaist. See DRESSES.
Shocks. Trade name for sock-like shoes of shirred fabric, with leather soles. See SHOES.
shoddy. 1. Remanufactured wool obtained from discarded and waste woolens. See WOOL. Also, reclaimed silk or rayon waste. 2. Originally, the waste discarded in wool spinning. 3. Any fabric made from or containing shoddy. 4. Not real or genuine; to be avoided.

SHOES

shoe. Properly, foot-covering having sole, heel, upper no higher than the ankle, and some means of fastening. Distinguished from boot by height; from slipper, by fastening. For parts of shoe see: COUNTER, HEEL, QUARTER, SHANK, SOLE, UPPER, VAMP.
alpargata (Sp. äl-pär-gä'tə; ahl par gah ta). Cheap, coarse, Spanish shoe consisting of a foot-shaped mat, or sole, made of hemp or jute rope and an upper of canvas or only of straps. Used as bathing shoe under French name of *espadrille*.
bal. Short for BALMORAL.
balmoral (băl-mŏr'əl; bal *mor* al). Heavy, ankle-high shoe, laced up the front, as distinguished from shoes adjusted by buttons, buckles, etc.; also, as distinguished in pattern from a blucher. Called *bal* for short.

barefoot sandal. Backless, low-cut shoe with open shank and vamp; usually fastened with buckled straps.
baseball s. Shoe of leather or canvas, with cleats on heel and sole to prevent slipping. Worn by baseball players.
bat or **batt.** Woman's heavy, low shoe, laced in front. Formerly worn in England; first sent to New England colonists in 1636.

17th Century Batts

beach sandal. Open sandal made of rubber, cork, wood, or other substance that is not affected by water; often having colorful fabric straps. Used for beach wear.
beaver top. Soft warm shoe with upper of felt or fabric.
bicycle bal (bī'sĭk-l; *by* sic l). Shoe laced far down towards toe, having protective toe cap and leather circles over ankle joint. Originally designed for bicycling; since, used for other outdoor sports.
Blake. Shoe made by sole-stitching method invented by Lyman Blake. Same as MCKAY.
blucher (blōō'chẽr; *bloo* cher). Shoe or half boot with quarters extended forward to the throat of the vamp, inner edges loose, laced across the tongue. Invented by and named for Field-Marshal von Blücher, Commander of Prussian forces at Waterloo.
bracelet tie. Shoe, usually pump-shaped, with ankle strap or straps attached to an extended back piece.
brogan (brō'gən; *bro* gan). Heavy, pegged or nailed shoe, usually ankle-high, often of blucher cut. Worn by workmen. Term sometimes incorrectly used for BROGUE.
brogue (brōg; brohg). Heavy, strong, low-heeled oxford, trimmed with perforations, stitchings, pinkings. Originally, coarse, heelless shoe of untanned hide with hair left on, held in shape with thongs. Worn in Ireland and Scottish Highlands.
buskin (bŭs'kĭn; *buss* kin). Woman's modern low-cut shoe with elastic goring at instep. Also see BOOTS.
cack. Infant's shoe, available in sizes from 1 to 5, with soft leather sole and no heel.
caliga (kăl'ĭ-gə; *cal* i ga). Heavy-soled shoe worn by Roman soldiers.
canvas s. Shoe of canvas with rubber, leather, or fiber sole, as used in playing tennis and in other sports.
chopine (shō-pēn' or chŏp'ĭn; sho *peen* or *chop* in). High lift or clog, resembling short stilt, combined with shoe, usually low-cut in sandal form. First introduced from Turkey.

16th Century Chopines

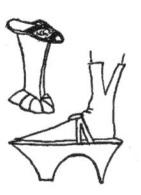

clog. 1. Shoe, usually of sandal type, having wooden or cork sole; worn chiefly on beach. 2. Wooden-soled shoe worn for clog dancing.

Clog, 1938

Clog, 1600

cobcab (kŏb'kăb; *cob* cab). Type of clog shoe. Worn by women in Orient, especially in public baths.
cocker. Obsolete term for high shoe; half boot.
colonial (kə-lō'nĭ-əl; co *lo* ni al). Low-cut shoe having broad tongue outside; properly, extending above the instep, with large ornamental buckle. Worn in colonial America; often without tongue.
comfort s. (kŭm'fẽrt; *cum* fert). Soft, flexible shoe with low heel. Used by elderly people and women needing easy shoes.
congress gaiter (kŏng'grĕs gāt'ẽr; *cong* gress *gate* er). Ankle-high shoe having leather or cloth top, often to match costume; adjusted to ankle by elastic gusset at sides instead of by laces, buttons, etc. Popular in late 19th century. Also called *congress boot*.
court tie (kōrt; cort). Low-cut oxford, usually in patent leather, as prescribed for men's court ceremonial dress in England. Also, women's two- or three-eyelet tie, usually on blucher pattern.
crakow (krăk'ow; *crack* ow). Low shoe of soft material, with long, extremely pointed toe. For ease in walking, toe often fastened to ankle or knee with chain of gold or silver. Worn in England during Middle Ages. So called because supposed to have originated in Crakow, Poland. Same style of shoe known as *poulaine* in medieval France.
creedmore (krēd'mōr; *creed* more). Cheap, heavy, blucher-cut shoe with gussets and laces. Worn by workmen.
Creole (krē'ōl; *cree* ole). Trade name for heavy work shoe with rubber side gorings, resembling congress gaiter.
Dom Pedro (dŏm pĕ'drō; dom *pee* dro). Heavy, one-buckle work shoe, introduced by Dom Pedro, of Brazil.
dress s. Shoe appropriate for wear with formal dress on social occasions.

shoes (continued)

duckbill. Blunt, square-toed shoe worn in England in 15th century.
Eclipse Tie (ē-klīps'; e *clips*). Trade name for woman's one-eyelet tie shoe, with close-stitched throat and pointed tongue.
espadrille (ĕs-pə-drĭl' or F. ĕs-pȧ-drē; ess pa *drill* or ess pa dree). Rope-soled shoe with strap or canvas upper. Used as bathing shoe. Same as ALPARGATA, but French name usually applied to type used for beach wear.

Espadrilles

gaiter (gāt'ēr; *gate* er). Ankle-high shoe, buttoned or having elastic sides; originally, with cloth top. Designed in imitation of shoe with separate gaiter.
geta (gĕ'tȧ; *get* ta). Wooden clog, as worn in Japan. Used for outdoor wear.
gillie or **ghillie** (gĭl'ĭ; *gill* i). Low-cut sports shoe without tongue, having lace often fringed at end, crossed over instep, usually wound around ankle. Scottish term.
golf s. Low-heeled sports shoe, usually oxford, with or without cleats for sole. Used for golf and other outdoor sports.
gum s. 1. Colloquial term for rubber overshoe. 2. (Plural) Sneakers.
gym s. (jĭm; jim). U. S. college slang term for SNEAKERS.
high s. Shoe with upper extending above ankle; often fastened at front with laces, or at side-front with buttons, etc.
jodhpur (jŏd'pŏŏr; *jode* poor). Riding shoe reaching just above ankle; fastened with side buckle.
Keds. Trade name for rubber-soled shoes worn for sports, especially tennis. Made especially for children.
klompen (klŏmp'ən; *klomp* en). Heavy wooden shoes worn by the Dutch; a type of sabot.

Dutch Klompen

low s. Shoe that ends below ankle. Usually called *low-cut*.
McKay. Shoe made by sole-stitching method invented by Lyman Blake. Similar to welt shoe construction, except that outsole, insole, and upper are all stitched together at one time. So called for Gordon McKay who purchased patent rights. Often called *Blake*.
moccasin (mŏk'ə-sĭn; *mock* a sin). 1. Heelless shoe made of soft leather which serves as sole and is turned up at edges and attached to a U-shaped upper piece, or drawn over foot with thongs. As worn by American Indians, ornamented on top. See SLIPPERS. 2. Sports shoe having a vamp like the original moccasin.
nail. Open-toed, flat, heelless Arabian sandal.

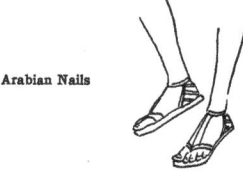

Arabian Nails

overshoe. Shoe of rubber or waterproof fabric worn over ordinary footwear as protection against weather; galosh.
oxford (ŏks'fērd; *ox* ford). Low-cut shoe ending at instep or lower, usually with three or more eyelets, laced and tied across the instep. May also be strapped or buttoned and have any form of vamp or ornamentation. First used in England, more than 300 years ago.
pac or **pack.** Moccasin, without a separate sole, usually of oil-tanned leather.
piked shoe. Same as CRAKOW.
pinson (pĭn'sən; *pin* son). Obsolete type of thin shoe or slipper.
plug oxford. Oxford with circular vamp.
Polish shoe. Front-laced shoe of the regulation height. See BOOTS.
poulaine (F. pōō-lȧn; *poo* lane). Low shoe of soft material, with long, pointed toe; worn in France in Middle Ages. Same style of shoe known as *crakow* in medieval England.
Prince of Wales. Oxford, without a tongue. More often called *gillie*.
racket. Broad wooden shoe, similar to patten. Used in crossing very soft ground.
Roman sandal. Sandal with front composed entirely of straps, equally spaced. Worn by women and children.
rullion (rŭl'yŭn; *rull* yun). Scottish term for kind of shoe or sandal of untanned leather.
running s. Soft leather shoe having spiked sole. Used by athletes.
sabot (F. sȧ-bō; sa bo). Wooden shoe, sometimes carved in one piece. Worn by French, French-Canadian, and other peasants. In recent usage, heavy, wooden-soled shoe with flexible shank. Also called *klompen*.
sabotine (săb'ə-tēn; *sab* o teen). Makeshift shoe of hides and wood worn by soldiers during World War.

Sabots

saddle oxford. Oxford, usually flat-heeled, having a saddle or strip of leather from the shank at each side across the vamp, usually of color contrasting with the shoe color, such as brown on white.
sailor tie. Low-cut shoe with two eyelets and lacing.
sandal. 1. Open-shank, strap shoe, with high or low heel, usually having slashed, braided, or otherwise openworked vamp; sometimes having straps in place of an upper. Made of leather, fabric, or novelty materials. Worn by women and children for sports and street wear; by women, also for evening wear. 2. Footwear consisting only of a sole strapped to the foot, sometimes having a shield for heel and a cap for toe. Worn in various parts of the world from earliest times to the present.

Modern and Early Greek Sandals

scarpetti (skär-pĕt'tĭ; scar *pet* ti). Hempen-soled shoe worn when rock climbing.
scuffer (skŭf'ēr; *scuff* er). Child's sandal-like play shoe, light-weight and flexible, with sturdy sole. Also used for sportswear by adults.
seamless s. Shoe with a whole vamp, stitched only at the back.
secque (sĕk; seck). Shoe like sabotine, but lighter.
Shocks. Trade name for soft sock-like shoes of fabric, shirred over foot with elastic stitching and attached to sturdy leather soles.
shoepack. Shoe shaped like moccasin, made without a separate sole. Much worn during American Revolution.
side-seam s. Shoe having vamp and quarter joined by a seam at each side.
Skuffer. Trade name for special type of child's play shoe, similar to SCUFFER.
sneaker. Laced canvas sports shoe with rubber sole. Used for gymnasium work and for outdoor sports such as tennis.
sock. Low shoe or sandal, especially as worn by actors in Greek and Roman comedies. Similar to BUSKIN.
soft-sole. Soft-soled shoe, especially infant's shoe of soft leather.
solleret (sŏl'ēr-ĕt; *soll* er et). Flexible

steel shoe worn as part of medieval armor.

southern tie (sŭth'ẽrn; *suth* ern). Low-cut shoe with a two-eyelet ribbon tie.

sports s. Shoe for general and spectator sports wear; usually in white and color combinations for outdoor summer wear.

step-in. Shoe with no obvious method of fastening, usually held on snugly by an elastic gore.

stomper (stŏmp'ẽr; *stomp* er). Large, heavy shoe. So called from heavy tread of one wearing such a shoe.

street s. Shoe, usually of low cut and solid construction, suitable for street wear in town. Distinguished from delicate and sports types.

talaria (tə-lā'rĭ-ə; ta *lay* ri a). Winged shoes or sandals fastened at ankles, as seen in representations of the Roman and Greek gods, Mercury and Hermes; also, wings on ankles.

tap s. Shoe specially constructed for tap dancing, with hard sole or with metal plate under toe.

tegua (tā'gwä; *tay* gwah). Buckskin sandal worn by Keresan Indians of New Mexico.

tennis s. Shoe for active sports wear, usually made of canvas with rubber sole and no heel.

tie. Low, laced shoe having three eyelets or less. Usually called *one-eyelet tie*, *two-eyelet tie*, etc.

turn s. Woman's light-weight shoe in which upper is stitched to sole wrong side out before shoe is turned right side out. Process keeps seam from coming through to inner side and chafing foot.

veldschoen (vĕlt'skŏŏn; *velt* skoon). Rough shoe of untanned hide, made without nails. Worn by South African Dutch.

walking s. Comfortable shoe of sturdy material, with low or medium heel; usually a tie.

shoe buckle. Buckle serving as ornament or fastening of shoe. See BUCKLES.
shoe button. Button used to fasten shoe. See BUTTONS.
shoe horn. Shaped piece, as of metal, wood, etc., used to help ease foot into low-cut shoe. So called because originally made from strip of smoothly scraped cow's horn.
shoe-lace. Same as shoe-string.
shoe-latchet. Strap fastening on a shoe.
shoepack. Moccasin-like shoe. See SHOES.
shoe satin. Strong, closely-woven, semiglossy satin. Same as SLIPPER SATIN. See SATINS.
shoe-string. Ribbon, lace, or string for fastening shoe.
shoe-tie. Lace, ribbon, or braid for tying a shoe. Formerly, very showy.
shoe tree. Device used inside shoe or boot to keep it in shape.
shoot. 1. Throw of shuttle across loom; pick. 2. Filling yarn thus carried. See FILLING, 1.
shooter. British colloquial term for black morning coat.

shooting coat or **jacket.** Sturdy, short coat worn by many for sports. See COATS.
shooting glove. Glove used in archery. See GLOVES.
shoppe (shŏp'; shop). Obsolete way of spelling shop. Not appropriate in modern usage, but sometimes seen in names of shops as indication of antiquity.
short-and-long-stitch. Uneven embroidery stitch used as filling. See STITCHES.
short-back sailor hat. Type of sailor hat with brim that is very narrow in back, broad in front. See HATS.
shortie. Wrist-length glove. See GLOVES.
short-lapped placket. Placket 3 or 4 inches long; usually not made in a seam. See PLACKETS.
shorts. Brief trousers, shorts or trunks, shaped with a crotch. Different types worn by men, as undergarment, for sports and beach wear, etc. Also adapted for women and sometimes made with plaits, in a skirt effect. Worn by women on beach or for active sports.

Shorts, 1930's

shot. Of changeable color, usually because warp and filling are different in color; as, shot silk. Term applied to a fabric of mixed fibers, as silk and cotton, dyed in different colors, the cotton being affected by some colors and the silk by others, producing a changeable or mixed effect.
shot silk. Changeable silk fabric, woven with warp and weft of different colors, causing tint to vary.
shoulder (shōl'dẽr; *shole* der). Part of garment covering the shoulder; style or construction of such a part.
shoulder-knot. Ornamental knot worn on shoulder. See KNOTS.
shoulder-puff sleeve. Long sleeve having puff or fulness at shoulder, but fitted from there to wrist. See SLEEVES.
shoulder strap. Shoulder strip of a sleeveless garment, cut in one with the garment or attached. Lingerie shoulder straps usually of ribbon or elastic and ribbon, often adjustable in length; available separately at notion counters.
shovel hat (shŭv'l; *shuv* el). Hat with shovel-like brim. See HATS.
showing. Exhibition of fashions in clothes or accessories, given by the couture or by a smart shop.
shrimp. Yellowish-red tint, color of shrimp when boiled.
shrinkage (shrĭnk'ĕj; *shrink* age). Reduction in size that takes place in fabric when it is washed, dry-cleaned, or submitted to some other treatment.

shrinking. Processes of shrinking woven fabrics by means of steam, cold or hot water, etc., to prevent shrinkage after manufacture into garments.
shroud. Garment to envelop the body for burial.
shuba (shōōb'ə; *shoob* a). Russian overcoat or cloak of fur.
shuttle. 1. Instrument used in weaving, to pass weft thread, or filling, from side to side between warp threads. 2. In a two-thread sewing machine, the device that holds the lower thread and carries it between needle and upper thread to make a lock-stitch. Now largely replaced by round bobbin. 3. Device used in tatting and embroidery to carry the thread.
siamoise (F. sē-ȧ-mwäz; see a mwahz). Silk-and-cotton fabric from Siam; also, European imitation. French word meaning Siamese.
Sicilian embroidery (sĭ-sĭl'yən; si *sill* yan). Lace-like work produced on fabric by means of braid and the buttonhole-stitch. Same as SPANISH EMBROIDERY, 2. See EMBROIDERIES.
Sicilienne (sĭ-sĭl-ĭ-ĕn'; si sill i en). 1. Mohair of coarse weave and wiry finish, with cotton warp and wool or mohair weft. Used for men's and women's light-weight summer coats and suits. Also called *Sicilian cloth*. 2. Fabric made with silk warp and heavier filling of cotton or wool in plain weave, forming crossribs, like a rich poplin.
sideburns. Side whiskers. Common form of the word BURNSIDES.
side comb (kōm; cohm). Comb worn to hold the hair in place at the side, or for ornament. See COMBS.
side-laced. Laced at the side; applied usually to a shoe, laced on either inner or outer side instead of front.
side-seam shoe. Shoe having vamp and quarter joined by a seam at each side. See SHOES.
signet ring. Ring with seal or signet, such as a class ring. See RINGS.
silesia (sĭ-lē'shə; si *lee* sha). Strong, light-weight, twilled cotton fabric like percaline. Used for linings.

SILHOUETTES

silhouette (sĭl-ōō-ĕt'; sil oo *et*). 1. Outline or contour of a figure or costume. The "new silhouette," at the beginning

Silhouettes
1864   1926

silhouettes 132 silhouettes

12th Century	
13th and 14th Centuries	
14th and 15th Centuries	
16th Century	
16th Century	
17th Century Spanish	
17th Century English	
17th Century French	
18th Century Colonial	
18th Century French	
1810	
1860	
1880	
1900	
1912	
1916	
1920	
1924	
1928	
1932	
1936	
1938	
1938	

fāte, făt, dánce, ärt mē, mĕt, hēr, thêre rīde, rĭd nōte, nŏt, côrn, fōōd, fŏŏt cūte, cŭt, cūré now fin(ŋ)ger villa(ə) señor pleas(zh)ure

of any season, means the general contour in fashion at the time, especially as the waistline, skirt length, shoulder width, etc., differ from those of the previous season. **2.** Profile or outline drawing filled in with black.

boxy s. Squared silhouette of straight skirt worn with box coat.

boyish-form s. Straight, uncorseted figure popular in the 1920's. Bust was held in by a boyish-form brassière.

bustle s. Silhouette with exaggerated back fulness directly below waistline drawn back over the bustle. Recurs from time to time in fashion. Very popular in late-Victorian period.

cameo s. Outline of costumed figure seemingly delicately etched, as of woman wearing dainty, lingerie-trimmed dress.

cylinder s. (sĭl'ĭn-dẽr; *sil* in der). Outline of costume that gives effect of a cylinder — round, slender, straight up and down.

draped s. Silhouette of softly draped garment, fitted by draped folds rather than by darts and seams, often having irregular hem line. May be cut from a pattern or draped on the individual or on a dress form.

hour-glass s. Silhouette with tiny, pinched-in waistline, resembling shape of an hour-glass.

kinetic s. (kĭ-nĕt'ĭk; ki *net* ic). Silhouette of gown that gives effect of motion, as by back-swept drapery, plaits that extend out, etc.

lumberjack s. Silhouette of straight over-jacket with waist-band, worn with plain skirt.

Mae West s. Modified version of Lillian Russell costume.

monastic s. Silhouette of dress of monk's dress type, hanging straight from shoulder, with fulness held in by girdle or cord at waistline. Similar in outline to robe worn by monks.

pencil s. Outline of the slimmest, straightest possible costume.

princess or princesse s. (prĭn'sĕs or prĭn-sĕs'; *prin* sess or prin *sess*). Outline of a close-fitting garment in which waist and skirt are made in continuous sections from shoulder to hem. Highly popular during early years of 20th century.

redingote s. (rĕd'ĭn-gōt; *red* in gote). Outline of one-piece garment that opens up the center-front.

skater s. Silhouette of short, wide-flared skirt worn with short jacket, suggesting costume worn by skaters. See SKATING COSTUME under SPORTS CLOTHES.

tubular s. Outline like a tube or pipe, long and straight. Same as PENCIL SILHOUETTE.

Velasquez s. (vă-lăs'kăth; vay *lass* kaith). Lines of dress with tight bodice and skirt that stands out wide at sides; typical of costumes worn by aristocratic Spanish women painted by Velasquez (1599-1660).

SILK

silk. 1. Fine, glossy fiber produced by cultivated silkworm; creamy white in color after gum is removed. Also, dark tan fiber of uncultivated silkworm. **2.** Silk thread. For types, see THREADS. **3.** Fabric made of silk fibers.

boiled-off s. Silk from which natural gum has been removed by degumming process.

cappadine (kăp'ə-dĭn or kăp'ə-dēn; *cap* a din or *cap* a deen). Waste from silk cocoon, or floss taken from cocoon after silk is reeled off.

carded s. Waste silk, usually from imperfect cocoons, carded to be spun.

crin (krĭn or F. krăŋ; crin or cranh). Heavy silk substance taken from glands of silkworm.

ecru s. Unbleached silk, having not more than 5 per cent of original weight removed.

fibroin (fī'brə-ĭn; *fy* bro in). Silky ingredient of raw silk fiber, which is separated from gummy part, or sericin, by boiling water.

floret (flō'rĕt; *flo* ret). Silk yarn or floss spun from waste of the highest grade.

floss s. Coarse, tangled silk fibers on outside of cocoon. Used in making spun silk.

hard s. Silk containing natural gum.

marabout (măr'ə-bōōt; *ma* ra boot). Thrown raw silk that can be dyed without scouring.

muga (mōō'gə; *moo* ga). Silk made from cocoons of Indian moth of same name.

organzine (ôr'gən-zēn; *or* gan zeen). Silk thread composed of several twisted single threads. Used especially for warp in making silk fabric.

pure s. or pure dye s. Unweighted silk; also, silk containing no more than 10 per cent of any other substance, or black silk containing as much as 15 per cent.

raw s. Fiber of silkworm cocoons. Also, silk after reeling from cocoons, before gummy substance, or sericin, is boiled off.

reeled s. Silk filaments unwound from several cocoons and joined to form long, continuous strand. Used in making finest silk fabrics. Also called *thread silk.*

sericin (sĕr'ĭ-sĭn; *sare* i sin). Gummy substance in raw silk fibers, which is extracted from silky ingredient, or fibroin, by boiling water.

s. noil. Short silk fibers and knotty waste from cocoon. Used for inexpensive fabrics.

single. 1. Continuous strand of reeled or spun silk. **2.** (Plural) Such thread twisted, but not doubled, to give more firmness.

sleaved s. Raw silk or floss.

soft s. Silk with natural gum removed.

souple (sōōp'l; *soop* l). Silk yarn or fabric that has been partly degummed to obtain dull finish.

spun s. Short, broken silk fibers and waste from cocoons, carded and spun; less lustrous than reeled silk; makes strong, attractive fabric.

thread s. Same as REELED SILK.

thrown s. (thrōn; throne). Reeled silk processed to make thread suitable for weaving. Chief types are SINGLES, TRAM, ORGANZINE.

tram. Silk thread composed of two or more single threads twisted together. Used especially for filling or weft in best quality silks and velvets. Weaker than organzine.

tussah (tŭs'ə; *tuss* ah). Strong, flat silk fiber, irregular in diameter, naturally brownish in color; produced by uncultivated silkworms, chiefly in India.

weighted s. Silk to which metallic salts of tin or lead have been added. Small amount of weighting is harmless; excessive weighting (50 per cent or more), unless carefully done, is weakening to fabric.

wild s. Commercially valuable silk obtained from larvae of wild silkworms, especially Asiatic silkworms, as the TUSSAH.

yamamai (yăm'ə-mī; *yam* a my). Fine grade of silk fiber produced by silkworm of same name.

silkaline (sĭlk-ə-lēn'; silk a *leen*). Soft, thin cotton material with glazed finish, plain or figured; used for linings, curtains, bedcovers. Does not soil easily.

silkaline thread. High-luster cotton thread, used in embroidery, crocheting, etc. See THREADS.

silk gauze. Thin curtain fabric of silk in plain weave. Also, rayon or cotton fabric in leno weave.

silk hat. High hat with silk-plush finish. See HATS.

silk noil. Short silk fibers. See SILK.

silk serge. Heavy grade of SURAH.

silk tartan. Silk material with tartan pattern.

silver. 1. Precious metal of white or grayish color. Used in jewelry and many accessories. **2.** Neutral gray color suggestive of luster of the metal.

silver cloth. Metal cloth with silk weft and metal warp in silver color. Used for trimmings, evening dresses, wraps.

silver fox. White-tipped, long-haired black fur. See FURS.

silver lace. Lace or braid of silver color. See LACES.

silver leaf. Very thin silver foil.

silver pointed fox. Silver fox peltries to which extra silver hairs have been added in order to improve appearance. See FURS.

silver tissue (tĭsh'ṳ; *tish* you). Sheer metal cloth of silver threads.

silvertone. Velour, velvet, or plush with a shimmering effect, produced by mixing white silk with the stock.

simal (sē'mŭl; *see* mul). East Indian cotton tree which produces fiber resembling kapok, but inferior to it.

simar (sĭ-mär'; si *mar*). **1.** Loose outer garment or robe worn by women; also, chemise. **2.** Woman's jacket. See JACKETS.

simplicity knot-stitch. Two small

back-stitches laid side by side to resemble a knot. See STITCHES.

simulated (sĭm'ū-lāt-ĕd; *sim* you late ed). Having the appearance of something, without the reality; as, a simulated pocket, buttonhole, etc.

simulated buttonhole. Uncut buttonhole, worked to imitate a buttonhole. See BUTTONHOLES.

simulated plait. Line pressed or stitched so as to resemble line of a plait. See PLAITS.

simultaneous contrast (sĭ-mŭl-tā'nĭ-ŭs kŏn'trăst; *sy mul tay* ni us *con* trast). Effect produced when pale and dark colors that are not complementary to each other are used together.

sinamay (sē-nä-mī'; *see nah my*). Stiff, coarse fabric woven from abaca fiber.

sine qua non (sī'nē kwä nŏn; *sy* nee kway non). Latin expression for something indispensable, an absolute necessity.

single. Silk strand or thread. See SINGLE, 1, under SILK.

single-breasted. Closing down the center-front, with lap enough to permit one row of buttons. Said of coats, vests, etc.

single canvas. Plain, open canvas for embroidery. See CANVAS.

single cuff. Shirt cuff that has no turnback; fastened with a button. See CUFFS.

single fagoting (făg'ŏt-ĭng; *fag* ot ing). Fagoting made with a catch-stitch, using one thread. See FAGOTING under STITCHES.

singles. Type of THROWN SILK. See SINGLE, 2, under SILK.

singlet (sĭng'glĕt; *sing* glet). Unlined waistcoat; also, jersey or undershirt of cotton or wool.

siphonia (sī-fō'nĭ-ɑ; *sy fo* ni a). Obsolete term for light overcoat. See COATS.

sisal or **sisol** or **sissol** (sī'săl, sē'săl, sē-säl'; *sy* sal, *see* sahl, *see sahl*). Fine, smooth straw. See STRAWS.

six-cord cotton. Very strong cotton sewing thread of six cords twisted together. Made famous as Clark's O. N. T. and J. & P. Coats Best Six Cord Threads. Manufactured in white and black in a variety of sizes.

size. Measure, or extent of dimensions; as, the size of ready-to-wear garments, pattern size, bust or hip size.

sizing (sīz'ĭng; *size* ing). Finishing process whereby yarns or fabrics are treated with starch, glue, casein, wax, gum, paraffin, clay, or other substances, to give them strength, stiffness, and smoothness.

skater silhouette. Silhouette of short, wide-flared skirt and bolero jacket, suggesting skater's costume. See SILHOUETTES.

skating costume (skāt'ĭng; *skate* ing). Costume for ice skating. See SPORTS CLOTHES.

skein (skān; skane). Definite quantity of yarn, thread, silk, wool, etc., wound on a reel, then taken off the reel, twisted, and looped.

skeleton suit (skĕl'ɑ-tɑn; *skell* e ton). Boy's tight-fitting suit. See SUITS.

sketcher. Fashion artist who makes quick pencil sketches of apparel, to be used as basis for finished drawing or as model for design.

ski costume (skē; skee). Costume for skiing. See SPORTS CLOTHES.

skilts. Short full trousers, half a yard wide at bottom, reaching just below the knee. Worn by country people during American Revolution.

skimmer. Sailor hat with wide brim and exceptionally flat crown. See HATS.

skin. Pelt of small animal, such as goat, sheep, calf, etc., whether green, dry, tanned, or dressed, and with or without hair. In leather trade, untanned skin of steer, cow, or horse. Skins weigh up to 15 pounds, as distinguished from KIPS, weighing from 15 to 25 pounds, and HIDES, weighing over 25.

Skinner's satin. Trade name for heavy, lustrous satin. See SATINS.

skin-tight. Closely fitting.

skin wool. Inferior grade of wool. See WOOL.

SKIRTS

skirt. 1. Part of any garment — coat, dress, etc. — that hangs below waist. **2.** Separate garment covering the body below the waistline. Length varies with fashion. Worn by women and girls.

baby s. Little, short, plaited or flared skirt worn over play or bathing suit.

bell s. Circular-cut skirt, usually held out in bell shape by being lined with stiff cambric and interlined from hem to knee with haircloth; often having pipe-organ back. Fashionable about 1896.

circular s. Skirt made in circular shape, often by use of gores, and hanging in unbroken ripples from waist to hem.

crinoline (krĭn'ɑ-lĭn; *crin* o lin). Hoop skirt extended by crinoline, whalebone, or other stiff material or by steel spring.

divided s. 1. Garment resembling flared skirt, but divided and stitched together to form separate leg sections. Worn beneath by women for horseback riding. **2.** CULOTTE.

Empire s. Skirt cut to extend from 2 to 4 inches above the normal waistline and fitted snugly at the waist.

foot mantle. Outer skirt worn by colonial women to keep the gown clean when riding horseback.

fustanella (fŭs-tɑ-nĕl'ɑ; *fuss ta nell* a). Short, white cotton or linen skirt worn by men in some countries in modern times, as by National Guard in Athens, Greece. Also called *fustanelle*.

golf s. Heavy wool skirt, having flare at the bottom emphasized by a bias facing of the skirt fabric, held in place with many rows of machine-stitching. Skirt originally ankle-length.

harem s. (hêr'ɑm; *hair* em). Softly draped skirt, usually gathered under at bottom to narrow lining, in imitation of Turkish trousers. Fad of about 1910.

Turkish Harem Skirt

hobble s. Very narrow skirt, narrower at the bottom than at the knee, which hinders freedom of movement in walking. Popular about 1910-14.

Hobble Skirt, 1914

hoop s. Crinoline, or skirt held out by framework of hoops made of wire, wood, featherbone, etc.

hula s. (hōō'lä; *hoo* lah). Grass skirt, knee-length or longer, worn by Hawaiian women, notably the professional dancers, known as hula girls.

Kiki s. Extremely tight skirt reaching just to knees. Made popular in 1923 by Lenore Ulric in the play "Kiki."

Kiki Skirt, 1923

Golf Skirt, 1895

kilt. Short, plaited skirt, usually of tartan, extending from waist to knee. Worn by men in Scotland, as part of national dress.

morning-glory s. Gored skirt with

flare at bottom, shaped like the flower for which it is named. Same as SERPENTINE SKIRT.
overskirt. Skirt drapery shorter than dress skirt and worn over it. Often open on left side of front.
pannier s. (păn'yēr; *pan* yer). Skirt having applied side fulness or drapery that extends out, accentuating width of figure. In some periods of fashion, supported with hoops or bustle-like foundations.

18th Century Pannier Skirt

parasol s. (păr'ə-sŏl; *pa* ra sol). Skirt of many gores, cut and stitched to resemble seams in a parasol.
peg-top s. Skirt with deep plaits from waistline to hip, and skirt tapering to almost a hobble skirt. Popular about 1910. Originally, the name of a boy's pear-shaped spinning top.

Type of Peg-Top Skirt, 1910

pinwheel s. Circular type of skirt, with flare beginning at hips or below and definitely flared hem line.
pullback. Style of skirt having fulness drawn back and fastened in festoon or drape. Popular during 1880's.
rainy daisy. Short, tailored walking skirt, popular about 1906. Also worn for roller skating, which was then revived. Short for rainy day skirt.
riding s. Medium-short, wrap-around skirt worn by women who ride sidesaddle.
saya (sä'yä; *sah* yah). Skirt which is tied at waist and extends to ankles. Worn by women in the Philippines.
serpentine s. (sẽr'pən-tēn; *ser* pen teen). Skirt, usually cambric-lined; fitted at hip line; flared at bottom, with extra stiffening. Popular during early 1890's. Also called *morning glory skirt*.
slit s. Skirt having slits, cut upward from bottom, varying in length. Slit first introduced in hobble skirt to aid in walking.
suspender s. (sŭs-pĕn'dẽr; sus *pen* der). Skirt of any type, with straps attached at waist and extending over the shoulders. Straps are usually detachable.
swing s. Skirt cut circular or with many gores, so as to give a swinging motion when the wearer walks. Often made with fulness held in lengthwise lines by tucks, gores, plaits. Popular in 1937, when swing music first became popular.

Swing Skirt, 1926

tie-back s. Skirt drawn backward at hip line, tightly tied back by means of strip of tape or elastic fastened at inside side seams. Fashionable during 1890's.
tiered s. (tẽrd; teerd). Skirt having two or more tiers or flounces or tunics.
trouser s. Tailored skirt, open at the side-front, having matching bloomers or pantalets attached at the waistline. Worn by dress reformers in the 1910 to 1920 period.
tunic s. (tū'nĭk; *tew* nic). Skirt having somewhat shorter overskirt, usually continuation of blouse.

Tunic Skirt, 1930's

two-piece s. Plain, straight skirt with a seam at each side. Also called *twogore skirt*.
wrap-around s. Skirt having two free edges, one of which folds or wraps over the other.
yoke s. Skirt made with piece of material fitted over hips, forming a yoke to which the rest of skirt is gathered or plaited.
Zephyrina Jupon (zĕf-ĭ-rē'nə zhū'pŏn; zef i *ree* na *zhoo* ponh). Hoop skirt with open front, which gave paneled effect. Introduced in Paris in 1868.
zouave (zōō-äv'; *zoo* ahv). Full skirt tucked up at bottom and attached to inside lining. Resembles baggy trousers of uniform worn by French Zouaves.
skirt board. Long, slender ironing board on which to press skirts.
skirt gauge (gāj; gage). Any one of many devices used in dressmaking to mark desired skirt length.
skitty boot. British dialect term for heavy half boot. See BOOTS.
skiver (skīv'ẽr; *shive* er). Cheap, soft sheep leather. See LEATHERS.
Skuffer. Trade name for a play shoe. See SHOES.

skull-cap. Cap closely fitting the crown of the head. See CAPS.
skunk. Fur of North American skunk; all black or black with white stripes. See FURS.
sky blue. Blue of the upper sky at noon of a sunny day in mid-summer.
slacks. Man-tailored, loose-fitting trousers; worn by both men and women as part of casual sports costume.
slack suit. Slacks and matching blouse or jacket worn together.
slash. 1. To cut a slit, as in a garment, usually to show a contrasting color beneath; also, ornamental slit so made. **2.** Strip, usually of tape, worn on sleeve by non-commissioned officer.
slat bonnet. Bonnet having brim reinforced with slats. See BONNETS.
slate. Any one of various grays, similar in color to slate, usually having a slight bluish tone.
slave bracelet. Bracelet of several narrow rings; or one wide band, usually close-fitting. Both types originated with tribal people and slaves. See BRACELETS.
sleave (slēv; sleeve). **1.** To separate, as threads or fibers. **2.** Knotted or untwisted thread; sleaved silk.
sleaved silk. Raw silk or floss. See SILK.
sleazy (slē'zĭ or slā'zĭ; *slee* zi or *slay* zi). Lacking firmness of texture, as a limp, inferior material of loose weave, made with poor yarns.
sleek. Smooth, glossy, or polished.
sleeping bag. Padded bag of canvas or waterproof fabric, in which to sleep out of doors.
sleeping coat. Long coat similar to a pajama coat, which serves as a nightshirt.
sleeping suit. Sleeping pajamas, especially one-piece type without openings for feet. Worn by children.

SLEEVES

sleeve. Part of garment covering the arm.
angel s. Long, wide sleeve, flowing loosely from the shoulder.

14th Century Angel Sleeves

armlet. Small, short sleeve of bandlike shape.
bag s. Sleeve full to below elbow, tapering to wrist, and gathered into wide cuff or plain band. Came into fashion after close of 14th century.

fāte, făt, dănce, ärt mē, mĕt, hẽr, thêre rĭde, rĭd nōte, nŏt, côrn, fōōd, fŏŏt cūte, cŭt, cūre now fin(ŋ)ger villa(ə) señor pleas(zh)ure

sleeves

sleeves (continued)

balloon s. Sleeve cut with extreme rounded fulness from shoulder to elbow; usually lined with buckram or similar fabric. Popular during 1890's. Also called *melon sleeve*.

batwing s. Long sleeve cut deep at armhole, with snug wristband.

bell s. Full sleeve, flaring at lower edge like a bell.

bishop s. Sleeve that is full in the lower part, as in the Anglican bishop's robe, and either loose or held by band at wrist. Widely popular about 1900.

Bishop Sleeves

bracelet s. Sleeve reaching below elbow about halfway to wrist. So called because of a convenient length for the wearing of bracelets.

cape s. Full, loose sleeve, hanging free at front and back of shoulder, like cape. Often cut to extend into the shoulder in raglan or yoke effect.

cap s. Short sleeve just covering the shoulder and not continued under arm.

cornet s. (kôr′nĕt; *cor* net). Trumpet-shaped sleeve ending in low, bell-like flare.

cubital (kū′bĭ-tǝl; *cue* bi tal). Sleeve covering arm from wrist to elbow. From Latin word *cubitum*, meaning elbow.

dolman s. (dŏl′mǎn; *dol* man). Sleeve fitted smoothly into armhole so large as to extend almost to waistline, giving cape-like outline. Often held snugly at wrist.

Dolman Sleeve, 1920's

draped elbow s. Straight, elbow-length sleeve with loose, draped fold at elbow, giving effect of wide sleeve turned back. Worn during 17th and 18th centuries.

Draped Elbow Sleeve

elbow s. Sleeve extending to or slightly below elbow.

epaulet s. (ĕp-ǝ-lĕt′; ep a *let*). Set-in sleeve extended in form of narrow yoke across top of shoulder.

foresleeve. 1. Part of sleeve covering forearm. **2.** Formerly, extra decorative sleeve or partial sleeve that was often removable.

Free Action S. Trade name for type of sleeve, with additional shaped section at the underarm allowing greater freedom of movement.

gigot (jĭg′ǒt; *jig* ot). Leg-of-mutton sleeve.

half s. 1. Removable sleevelet for the forearm, usually of lace or sheer fabric, either attached by tapes or held on by elastic run through a hem at the top. About 1905, worn for warmth with elbow-length sleeves. **2.** Sleeve protector worn by clerical workers. **3.** Sleeve approximately half usual length, as in some ecclesiastical vestments.

hanging s. Coat sleeve with slit in front for the arm itself to come through. Often the arm was covered with an ornate shirt or blouse sleeve. Hanging sleeves, popular in the fifteenth century, hung down at the sides and were often richly embroidered.

15th Century Hanging Sleeves

kimono s. (kĭ-mō′nō; ki *mo* no). Sleeve, usually short, cut in one with the body of the garment, as in a Japanese kimono.

Kimono Sleeves, 1920's

leg-of-mutton s. Sleeve shaped like a leg of mutton; full, loose, rounded from shoulder over elbow, fitted at wrist. Also called a *gigot*.

Middle 19th Century Leg-of-Mutton Sleeve

mancheron (măn′chǝ-rǒn; *man* che ron). False sleeve attached to shoulder top, hanging loosely down back of arm. Worn by women in mid-16th century.

melon s. (mĕl′ǝn; *mel* on). Same as BALLOON SLEEVE.

mousquetaire s. (F. mōōs-kǝ-târ; moose ke tare). Long, fitted sleeve; shirred lengthwise from shoulder to wrist and softly draped.

oversleeve. Sleeve worn over another sleeve. Often of fur. Oversleeves sometimes held together by a collar piece. Abbreviated ones sometimes called HALF SLEEVES.

pagoda s. (pǝ-gō′dǝ; pa *go* da). Funnel-like sleeve broadening toward the wrist; heavily ruffled and showing puffed undersleeve.

peasant s. Long, full sleeve set into dropped shoulder and usually gathered into band at wrist.

poke s. Obsolete type of sleeve, cut long and wide.

pudding s. (pŏŏd′ĭng; *pood* ing). Full sleeve held in at wrist, or above.

puff s. Sleeve gathered and sometimes stiffened so that it puffs out, especially near shoulder.

raglan s. (răg′lǝn; *rag* lan). Sleeve that extends to neckline and has slanting seamline from underarm to neck in front and back.

set-in s. Sleeve, cut separately from waist of garment, sewed in at armhole.

shoulder-puff s. Long sleeve having puff or fulness at shoulder, but fitted from there to wrist. Forerunner of the sleeve with many puffs all along its length, seen in Elizabethan and Renaissance costume.

Shoulder-Puff Sleeve, 1580

sleevelet. Additional fitted sleeve for forearm; usually worn for extra warmth or for protection for sleeve of dress or coat.

three-quarter s. Sleeve ending halfway down forearm, covering three quarters of entire arm.

trunk s. Sleeve wide and full, especially at top; somewhat resembling trunk hose.

undersleeve. Separate sleeve of light material worn under dress sleeve; es-

16th Century Virago Sleeve

fāte, făt, dȧnce, ärt mē, mĕt, hẽr, thêre rīde, rĭd nōte, nŏt, côrn, fōōd, fŏŏt cūte, cŭt, cũré now fin(ŋ)ger villa(ǝ) señor pleas(zh)ure

pecially, sleeve of bright or contrasting color shown through slashes in over-sleeve.
virago s. (vĭ-rā'gō; vi *rah* go). Very full sleeves tied at intervals to form puffs. Worn in 17th century.
winged s. Same as ANGEL SLEEVE.

sleeve cuff. Cuff made by turning back sleeve or applying separate band. See CUFFS.
sleeve length. Measurement of a sleeve from top to bottom. See LENGTHS.
sleeveless. Without sleeves.
sleeveless dress. Any dress made without sleeves; specifically, a type of jumper dress, not fitted at armhole. See DRESSES.
sleevelet. Additional sleeve for forearm. See SLEEVES.
sleeve link. Same as CUFF LINK.
slendang (slĕn'dăng; *slen* dahng). Scarf or shawl draped over shoulders. Worn by women in Philippines.
slenderizing. Made with unbroken lines, usually running lengthwise, designed to make one appear more slender; or of smooth, dark fabrics that achieve the same effect.
sley (slā; slay). 1. Weaver's reed. 2. Movable frame carrying the reed in a loom. 3. To separate fibers and arrange in a reed.
slicker. Plain, sturdy, waterproof coat. See COATS.
slicker hat. Rainproof hat. See HATS.
slide. 1. Clasp or buckle without a tongue. Used as a fastener or ornament on belts, shoe straps, etc. 2. Sliding catch used on a watch chain or cord.
slide fastener. Patented closing device, with teeth attached to tapes in such a way that the two rows of teeth can be drawn together by a slider or separated, to close or open the fastener. Teeth, sometimes called scoops, are made of metal or plastic.
slimpsy. Hanging limply; slimsy.
slimsy. Flimsy, frail, without body. Often used of inferior fabrics.

SLIPS

slip. 1. Underslip usually made the length of the dress with which it is to be worn. Takes place of lining. 2. Undergarment combining corset cover or brassière and petticoat.
bandeau top (băn-dō'; ban *doe*). Top of a slip constructed in the form of bandeau or brassière.
bias s. (bī'ǎs; *by* ass). Slip cut on bias of the fabric. Hugs the figure more closely than slip cut lengthwise and is less likely to show.
bodice top. Straight top of slip, either plain or lace-trimmed.
built-up top. Top of slip having shaped straps cut in one piece with the slip, instead of being straight at top and having shoulder straps.
camisole top (kăm'ĭ-sōl; *cam* i sole). Top of slip finished straight across and having shoulder straps, as in a camisole.
costume s. Slip made to wear under a particular dress, conforming in line, length, style, etc.

four-gore s. Slip made in four gores, paneling front and back and placed so that there is no underarm seam. Similar to princess style in silhouette.
Hollywood top s. Single or double V-top on slip, with fitted, molded bust.

Hollywood Top, 1920's

shadow skirt. Underskirt or slip with broad hem, double skirt, or panel; designed for wear with thin dresses.
slip-cover. 1. Overdress, blouse, or jacket that is designed to be worn over a dress slip or foundation. Several slip covers may be made to wear with one foundation. Compare TRANSFORMATION DRESS under DRESSES. 2. Removable covering for furniture.
slip-on. 1. Glove without fasteners. See GLOVES. 2. See SLIP-OVER.
slip-over. Dress, blouse, or any garment that has no side opening, but is slipped over the head by means of the neck opening. Also called *slip-on.*
slippage. Amount of slipping occurring in fibers or threads of fabric, especially rayon. In 1937, chemical processes for preventing slippage developed for use in less expensive rayon linings, etc.

SLIPPERS

slipper. Properly, any footwear lower than the ankle (excluding rubbers); usually without means of fastening, being merely slipped on the foot.
baboosh (ba-boōsh'; ba *boosh*) or **babouche** (F. bȧ-boōsh; bah boosh). Flat, heelless, Oriental slipper of fabric or leather, having elongated, turned-up, pointed toe. Of Turkish origin.

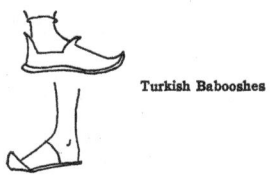

Turkish Babooshes

ballet s. (băl'ā; *bal* lay). Heelless, plain slipper worn by ballet dancers, usually of satin or light-weight kid, with or without reinforced soles and special toe boxing. Usually tied on around ankle with satin ribbon.
bath s. Light, loose slipper, usually backless and heelless; often made of cloth, fiber, or even paper. Used for wear to and from the bath.

bedroom s. Soft, comfortable slipper with flexible sole and usually low heel or no heel. Usually made of felt, soft cotton fabric, or leather.
carpet s. Slipper made of carpet material.
cavalier boot (kăv-ạ-lēr'; cav a *leer*). Soft, ankle-high house slipper, usually having 2-inch, folded collar. Used chiefly by men. So named from 17th century cavalier boot, for which see BOOTS.
dancing s. Any low-cut shoe or slipper worn for social or professional dancing. Usually light in weight.
D'Orsay (dôr'sā; *dor* say). Pump-shaped slipper, low-cut at sides in curves extending to the shank of slipper.
Faust s. (fowst). Man's high-cut house slipper with V-shaped cut on each side and no goring. Similar to ROMEO.
house s. Easy slipper of various materials. Worn informally at home.
huarache (wä-rä'chĭ; wah *rah* chi). Mexican sandal of leather thongs woven in varying patterns. Held on by loose heel straps.

Mexican Huaraches

Juliet (jū'lĭ-ĕt; *jew* li et). Woman's house slipper with high front and back and goring at U-shaped sides.
moccasin (mŏk'ạ-sĭn; *mock* a sin). Soft heelless slipper, of type worn by American Indians. Sole is turned up around foot and joined to U-shaped upper piece. Often ornamented with Indian beadwork. Adapted for wear as house slipper.
mule. Woman's boudoir slipper having high heel but no quarter and sometimes strap at back. Usually made of satin, fine kid, etc.
opera pump (ŏp'ẽr-ạ; *op* er a). Woman's plain, untrimmed pump with high heel. Made of leather or fabric.
opera s. Woman's dress slipper, usually high-heeled. Also, particular type of house slipper for men.
pantoffle (păn'tạ-fĭ; *pan* to fl). Soft house slipper.
Prince Albert. Man's low-cut house slipper, having goring at sides and seam down the front.
pump. Low-cut, thin-soled slipper, gripping foot only at toe and heel, and usually having a whole vamp. First mentioned in 16th century as made with low heels.
regent pump. Two-piece pump, having vamp and quarter joined and stitched along vamp line.
Romeo (rō'mē-ō; *ro* me o). Man's house slipper, often of felt; high-cut at back and front, low-cut at sides.
Sun Shods. Trade name for sandal type of slipper made of two leather

fāte, făt, dȧnce, ärt   mē, mĕt, hẽr, thêre   rīde, rĭd   nōte, nŏt, côrn, foōd, foŏt   cūte, cŭt, cūré   now   fin(ŋ)ger   villa(ạ)   señor   pleas(zh)ure

slippers (continued) strips crossed over the toes and sewed to a sole. Made in Arizona. Worn for sports and informally with play clothes.

Mexican Sun Shods

slipper satin. Strong, durable, closely woven satin. See SATINS.
slipshoe. Obsolete term for loose shoe or slipper.
slip-stitch. Loose stitch concealed between two thicknesses of fabric. See STITCHES.
slit. Long, narrow opening; also, to cut lengthwise or into long narrow strips.
slit fabrics. Term used in the manufacturing trades for bias bindings, pipings, seaming ribbons, etc.
slit pocket. Pocket having narrow welts. See WELT POCKET under POCKETS.
slit skirt. Skirt slit at bottom. See SKIRTS.
slit tapestry. Tapestry slit at place where weft threads of two different colors meet.
sliver (slĭv′ẽr; sliv er). Long, slender piece, especially a loose, untwisted textile fiber.
slop. 1. Any loose outer garment, usually of linen or cotton. 2. (Plural) Short full trousers worn in 16th century by men. 3. (Plural) English term for cheap, ready-made clothing.
sloper. Term used in the dress manufacturing trade for a draper who works without patterns.
slot seam. Seam with additional strip of material stitched underneath. See SEAMS.
slouch hat. Soft hat. See HATS.
slub. 1. To draw out and twist slightly; also, slightly twisted roll of fibers. 2. (Plural) Thick places or lumps in yarn. See YARNS.
slug. 1. Heavy nail used in boot soles. 2. Lint or knot in yarn.
slyders (slī′dẽrz; sly ders) or **slivers** (slĭv′ẽrz; slive ers). 18th century name for overalls.
smallclothes. 1. Close-fitting, 18th century breeches of knee length. 2. Underclothes, especially drawers. 3. Children's clothes.
smart. Having a fashionable appearance; dressed in the mode; chic.
smarten. To spruce up; to make smarter looking.
smicket (smĭk′ĕt; smick et). Obsolete term for woman's smock.
smock. 1. To ornament with smocking. 2. Loose garment like a long shirt, usually with long sleeves and collar and cuffs; worn by artists and by women and girls as a protection for clothes. 3. In colonial days, coarse shirt, usually of heavy linen, worn by farm laborers and workingmen. 4. Before 1700, same as SHIFT.

Smock, 1930's

smock frock. Sturdy garment, similar to a long shirt, worn over other clothes, especially by English field laborers. Often smocked at the top to hold in fulness.

Smock Frock

smocking. Decorative stitching holding fulness in regular patterns, often elaborately done. See EMBROIDERIES. See STITCHES.
smoked pearl. Mother-of-pearl in dark, smoky gray color. Used for buttons, studs, etc.
smoking jacket. Short coat, usually of satin brocade or velvet, worn as lounging jacket. See JACKETS.
smoothing iron. Instrument for smoothing clothes; flatiron.
snakeskin. Tanned skin of various snakes. See LEATHERS.
snap fastener. Metal fastening device in two pieces; sewn separately along opposite sides of openings and snapped together to fasten. See FASTENERS.
snap-fastener tape. Tape, having snap fasteners attached, that may be sewn in openings of garments. See TAPES.
sneaker. Rubber-soled, laced, sports shoe made of canvas. See SHOES.
snip. 1. To cut quickly in a stroke or series of short strokes; as, to snip a seam on a curve to prevent its being puckered. 2. Sample of fabric snipped off.
snippet. Small piece, as if snipped off.
snood. 1. Fillet formerly worn around head by young women in Scotland and considered an emblem of chastity. 2. Small mesh-like skull-cap, or beret; or section attached to back of hat to confine the hair.
snow cloth. Bulky woolen fabric of varying types, especially one with heavy fleece, as blanket fabric, camel's hair, etc. Used for warm winter outer garments, snow suits, etc.

snowshoe. Device for walking on soft snow; usually a light-weight frame with woven center. Worn beneath ordinary shoe, attached by means of thongs.
snow suit. Heavy warm outer suit for wear in winter. For children, made in coat and legging sets or one-piece styles, sometimes with matching cap.
Snow White costume. Fancy dress costume of Disney moving-picture version of fairy-tale character. See FANCY DRESS.
snuff box. Small box, usually ornamental, used for carrying snuff. Highly fashionable during 18th century; worn on the person as an article of jewelry.
soapbark. Bark of South American tree, used as cleansing agent.
soap-fast. Able to resist action of soap; not faded, discolored, or weakened by washing with soap.
sock. 1. Short stocking. See HOSE. 2. Originally, a low shoe or sandal. See SHOES.
socklining. In shoe manufacturing, same as INSOLE, I.
sœurs (sẽrz; serz). French word meaning sisters. Often used in names of dressmaking houses.
softs. Loosely woven or knitted woolens.
soft silk. Degummed silk. See SILK.
soft-sole. Shoe having soft sole. See SHOES.
soie (F. swä; swah). French word for silk.
Soiesette (swä-zĕt; swah zet). Trade name for a soft, highly mercerized cotton material in solid colors and prints. Used for women's and children's dresses, men's shirts and pajamas.
soignée (F. swän-yā; swahn yay). Carefully done; nicely got up; highly finished; well-groomed.
soirée (F. swä-rā; swah ray). Social function held in the evening.
sole. Bottom piece of any kind of footwear. Specifically, part of shoe beneath foot, consisting of outsole or bottom of shoe and, usually, insole.
soleil (F. sō-la-ẽ; so lay ee). 1. Wool fabric in warp twill weave with broken-rib effect, having a high luster. Used for dresses and suits. 2. Soft, silky felt used in millinery.
sole leather. Thick, strong leather. See LEATHERS.
solferino red (sŏl-fĕ-rē′nō; sol fe ree no). Medium bluish-red shade.
solid color. Plain color. See COLOR.
solitaire (sŏl-ĭ-têr′; sol i tare). 1. Gem set alone, especially a diamond; also, ring set with single diamond. 2. Broad black ribbon, worn during 18th century,

Scotch Snood.
Modern Snood

---
fāte, făt, dånce, ärt mē, mĕt, hẽr, thêre rīde, rĭd nōte, nŏt, côrn, fōōd, fŏŏt cūte, cŭt, cūre now fin(g)ger villa(a) señor pleas(zh)ure

close around throat, to protect coat from powdered wig.
solleret (sŏl′ĕr-ĕt; *soll* er et). Steel shoe. See SHOES.
sombrero (sŏm-brā′rō; som *bray* ro). Broad-brimmed hat. As worn by American cowboys, usually called *ten-gallon hat*. See HATS.
sontag (sŏn′tăg; *sonn* tag). Knitted jacket. See JACKETS.
sortie (sôr′tē; *sor* tee). Small knot of ribbon peeping out between bonnet and cap underneath. Worn during 18th century.
soup-and-fish. Slang term for men's formal evening wear.
souple (sōōp′l; *soop* l). Silk yarn or fabric that has been partly degummed. See SILK.
soutache (F. sōō-tăsh; soo tash). Narrow decorative braid. See BRAIDS.
soutage (sōō′tĭj; *soo* tij). Coarse packing cloth or canvas.
soutane (sōō-tän′; *soo tahn*). Cassock worn by Roman Catholic priests.
southern belle hat (sŭth′ẽrn bĕl; *suth* ern bell). Large-brimmed hat. See HATS.
southern muskrat. Fur of muskrat, chiefly from Louisiana and Texas. See FURS.
southern tie. Two-eyelet shoe. See SHOES.
southwester or sou'wester. Broad-brimmed, waterproof hat. See HATS.
sowback. Woman's cap with lengthwise fold. See CAPS.
spagnolet (spă′ñə-lĕt; *span* yo let). 18th century term to describe a gown with narrow sleeves. Derived from French *à l'Espagnole*.
spangle. Small shining disk of metal or other substance. Used to ornament fabric and add glitter to evening garments and accessories.
Spanish (spăn′ĭsh; *span* ish). Having characteristic features of Spanish costume. For women, this includes full skirt; lace-trimmed bodice; fringed shawl; high comb. Dresses for women of upper class, usually black, worn with mantilla of black or white lace. Men's costume consists of dark, tight trousers, slashed below knee; short dark jacket; bright sash; full-sleeved, generally white shirt; flat black hat; head kerchief, wool cap, or other cap. Often adapted in various details in women's fashions.
Spanish comb. High comb worn as hair ornament. See COMBS.
Spanish embroidery. 1. Herringbone stitching on muslin. 2. Designs of muslin, cambric, and braid buttonholed together. See EMBROIDERIES.
Spanish heel. Heel similar to French. See HEELS.
Spanish lace. Any lace made in Spain; usually characterized by flat, floral pattern. See LACES.
sparable (spăr′ə-bl; *spa* ra bl). Small nail used to prevent wearing of soles of shoes.
spare. Scotch term for placket.
sparterie (spär′tẽr-ĭ; *spar* ter i). Straw fabric of esparto grass. See STRAWS.

spat. Short, cloth gaiter, worn over shoe by both men and women; fastened underneath, usually buttoned up the side. Highly popular in late 19th and early 20th centuries. Originally, knee-length gaiter. Short for SPATTERDASH.

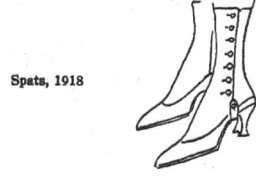

Spats, 1918

spatterdash. Covering for the leg, similar to legging or gaiter. Worn as protection against mud. Compare SPAT.
specialty shop or **store.** Retail store, usually selling a selected line or lines of apparel merchandise limited to one class or related classes; store having fewer varieties of merchandise than department store, but offering special features in its chosen line.
spectator sports clothes (spĕk-tāt′ẽr; speck *tate* er). General term covering simple, tailored clothes suitable for wear by onlookers at sports events.
spectrum (spĕk′trŭm; *speck* trum). The seven rainbow colors: violet, indigo, blue, green, yellow, orange, red; and all the variations between. These colors appear assembled in the order of their wave length when a ray of white light passes through a prism and divides into the colors composing it. See COLOR.
spencer (spĕn′sẽr; *spen* ser). 1. Short jacket, often fur-trimmed. Worn by women and children in 19th century. See JACKETS. 2. Short jacket worn by men in 19th century. See JACKETS. 3. Wig worn in England in 18th century. See WIGS.
sphendone (sfĕn′dō-nē; *sfen* doe ni). Headband or fillet worn by women in ancient Greece.
spider-web-stitch. Crisscross threads held together in center by thread interwoven in spider-web effect. See STITCHES.
spider work. Heavy bobbin lace. Same as ANTIQUE LACE. See LACES.
spike heel. Very high heel. See HEELS.
spike-tail. Slang term for swallow-tailed dress coat. See COATS.
spindle (spĭn′dl; *spin* dl). Slender rod for twisting and winding thread or fibers in spinning.
spine. Pointed stitch in needle-point lace. See PIN WORK.
spinning. Process of making yarn or thread by twisting fibers together. Fine-spun yarns used for high-grade fabrics and laces.
spinning jenny. Machine with many spindles, used in spinning yarns.
spinning wheel. Machine operated by hand or foot, in which a wheel drives a spindle.

spliced heel. Hosiery heel of double thickness. See HOSE.
split-foot hose. Black hose with white sole. See HOSE.
split-knee hose. Stocking knitted so that portion over knee is open. See HOSE.
split-stitch. Outline-stitch in which needle is brought up through thread itself. See STITCHES.
split vamp. Shoe vamp seamed from throat to toe. See VAMPS.
spoke. Bar in drawn-work embroidery formed by wrapping threads with overcast- or buttonhole-stitches.
spoke-stitch. 1. Stitch used in drawn work. 2. Straight stitches placed to radiate from a center. See STITCHES.
sponge cloth. Piece of unbleached duck or drilling or other cloth used to dampen materials while pressing.
sponging. Process of dampening and shrinking wool fabric before making it into garments. Used sometimes to prevent water-spotting.
spool heel. Heel with wide, horizontal corrugations. See HEELS.
sporran (spŏr′ən; *spor* an). Large pouch bag used as purse; made of leather or of skin with fur or long hair left on; often ornamented. Worn hanging from waist in center-front of kilt as part of Scottish national dress.

SPORTS CLOTHES

sports clothes. Wearing apparel of two classifications: (1) Active sports clothes, or particular type of costumes developed for wear by those participating in any sport. (2) Spectator sports clothes, or any simple, tailored attire suitable for onlookers.
bathing suit. Abbreviated one- or two-piece garment of wool, silk, rayon, rubber, cotton; sometimes made with dressmaker details. Worn on the beach or in the water

Bathing Costume, 1909   One-Piece Bathing Suit, 1938

flying costume. Strictly, costume of warm, light-weight fabric suitable for wear while piloting an airplane. Basically consists of trousers tight at the ankle, jacket, helmet, and other necessary accessories. Passengers in a commercial airplane wear any simple traveling costume.

sports clothes (continued)

golf costume. Costume suitable for wear while playing golf. May be one-piece dress designed for freedom of movement; or blouse and short, full skirt, with jacket or sweater; or, depending on the community, slack suit or culotte. Worn with low-heeled shoes, perhaps a sports hat, and possibly gloves.

hiking costume. Simple, sturdy costume for wear on long country walks. May include skirt or culotte or slacks, according to current usage, and sports blouse, sweater, or jacket, in addition to low-heeled walking shoes and other accessories.

play suit. Sports costume consisting usually of shorts with blouse or shirt, sometimes all in one piece; often with separate skirt, sometimes with separate jacket. Used for beach wear, tennis, etc.

Play Suit, 1920's

riding habit. Costume suitable for horseback riding. Basically consists of riding breeches, or jodhpurs, with boots, shirt, and jacket. Type of accessories depends on formality of the occasion.

Formal Riding Habit, 1930's

skating costume. Costume suitable for formal or rink skating on ice. Consists of one or more pieces, as skirt (usually very short and circular, often faced with bright contrasting color) worn with short, fitted or bolero jacket and close-fitting cap, and bright-colored accessories. Ski costume often worn for outdoor skating.

ski costume. Costume made of warm, light-weight, wet-resistant fabric; worn for skiing or other outdoor winter sport. Basically consists of trousers and a jacket-blouse; may include sweater and

Skating Costume, 1938

matching cap, gloves, and other accessories.

Ski Costume, 1938

tennis costume. Costume that is currently fashionable for wear in playing tennis. May be sleeveless, one-piece dress or blouse or shirt or halter-top with shorts or short, full skirt. Worn with soft, heelless shoes.

sports coat. Simple, tailored coat. See COATS.

sports shoe. Shoe for sports wear. See SHOES.

sports suit. Tailored, spectator suit. See SUITS.

sportswear. Originally, term applied only to clothing designed for athletic purposes; later, to apparel worn by spectators at sports events; then widened to include simple, tailored costumes retaining the informality of athletic attire. See SPORTS CLOTHES.

spray. 1. Small collection of twigs, foliage, or stemmed flowers; usually so called only when arranged or worn in horizontal effect. 2. Ornamental design resembling a spray; as, a spray of rhinestones.

sprig. 1. Shoot, spray, or small bunch of stemmed flowers; usually so called only when arranged or worn in vertical effect. Often used for hat trimming. 2. Small ornament, as a jeweled pin, resembling a stemmed flower. 3. Single lace motif, usually a flower or foliage design, made separately and appliquéd to the ground.

spring heel. Low heel used on children's shoes. See HEELS.

spun glass. Fine fibers of glass, drawn out while liquid into thread-like form. See GLASS FIBER.

spun gold or **silver.** Threads of fiber around which have been wound slender, thin, flat strands of silver or gold.

spun linen. Finest, hand-woven linen. See LINENS.

Spun-lo. Trade name for a brand of rayon yarn and fabric made from it. See RAYON.

spun rayon. See SPUN RAYON YARN.

spun rayon yarn. Rayon yarn made by spinning short fibers into continuous strand. See RAYON.

spun silk. Silk spun from short or broken fibers. See SILK.

spur. Pointed metal device fastened to heel of horseman's boot. Used for urging horse by pressure. Formerly, badge of knighthood.

square chain-stitch. Chain-stitches so joined as to give squared effect. See STITCHES.

square heel. Heel cut square at back so that it has four corners. See HEELS.

square neckline. Neckline of a dress or blouse cut to form a square. See NECKLINES.

squirrel (skwẽr′rĕl; *skwer* rel). Soft, semi-durable fur of small rodent. See FURS.

Stafford cloth (stăf′ẽrd; *staff* erd). Trade name for a mercerized, dyed cotton fabric in two-tone effect made by warp and filling of different colors. Used chiefly for hangings.

stall (stôl; stawl). Covering or sheath for finger; finger-piece of a glove.

stambouline (stăm′bōō-lēn; *stam boo* leen). Coat for formal occasions, worn by officials in Turkey. See COATS.

stamin (stăm′ĭn; *stam* in). Coarse woolen fabric, usually red. Used for making undergarments.

stammel (stăm′ĕl; *stam* el). Coarse woolen cloth, similar to linsey-woolsey, usually dyed red. Formerly used for undergarments. Probably same as STAMIN.

stamped velvet. Velvet with figures stamped on by heated dies. See VELVETS.

standing band. Stiff linen band formerly worn as collar. See COLLARS.

stand pocket. Pocket with upstanding welt. See POCKETS.

stand-up collar. Collar standing upright. See COLLARS.

staple (stā′p'l; *stay* pl). 1. Article of merchandise which undergoes little change in style and for which there is constant demand. 2. Fiber of wool, cotton, flax, etc. 3. Average or relative length, quality, fineness, etc., of fibers; as, long-staple cotton.

starch. Liquid preparation used for stiffening cloth or clothes before ironing. Made by mixing starch, a compound found in plants, with cold or boiling water. In using starch mixed with cold water, called *cold starch*, clothes are ironed wet. In using starch mixed with boiling water, called *boiled* or *cooked starch*, clothes are starched and dried and then sprinkled and ironed as usual. Process of starching introduced into England about 1564 from Flanders and extensively used on ruffs.

---

fāte, făt, dánce, ärt mē, mĕt, hẽr, thẽre rīde, rĭd nōte, nŏt, côrn, fōōd, fŏŏt cūte, cŭt, cūrē now fin(g)ger villa(ȧ) señor pleas(zh)ure

star-stitch. Embroidery stitch having shape of eight-pointed star. See STITCHES.
startup (stärt′ŭp; *start* up) or **startop.** Kind of rustic boot. See BOOTS.
stay. 1. To hold in place; to steady or strengthen. 2. That part of a tie shoe which contains the eyelets for lacing.
stayed godet (F. gō-dā; go day). Godet having fulness held in by fabric stay. See GODETS.
stays. Corsets or the pieces of stiffening used in corsets.

18th Century Stays

Steem Electric Iron. Trade name for a large pressing iron with a water compartment that releases steam, dampening and steaming fabric as it presses. Also called *self-dampening iron.*
steeple crown. Peaked hat crown.
steinkirk (stĭn′kẽrk; *stine* kerk). Name given by the French after battle at Steinkirk, Belgium, in 1692, to wigs, buckles, cravats, and other parts of the costume — particularly to cravats negligently knotted, with one end sometimes passed through a buttonhole.

Steinkirk, 1695

stem. Shank of thread made in sewing on a button. Same as THREAD SHANK.
stem-stitch. 1. Slanting overhanding-stitch used in embroidery. 2. Crewel-stitch. See STITCHES.
stencil (stĕn′sĭl; *sten* sil). 1. Piece of thin metal, paper, leather, etc., on which letters or motifs of a design are cut out. These may be applied in color to another surface as often as desired, by brushing, stippling, or sponging paint or ink through the open spaces on the stencil. 2. Pattern or design made by stenciling.
stephane (stĕf′ə-nĭ; *steff* a ni). Headdress resembling coronet, broad over forehead and narrowing on the sides. Worn by ladies in ancient Greece. At first, simple form, fitting head closely; later, standing out from head and elaborately decorated with repoussé figures, birds, fishes, or colored enamel designs.
step-in. 1. Undergarment similar to drawers, but without actual legs. 2. Woman's shoe. See SHOES.
step-in blouse. Blouse attached to step-ins. See BLOUSES.

sticharion (stĭ-kä′rĭ-ən; sti *kay* ri on). Ecclesiastical robe or tunic of white linen; worn in Eastern Church.
stickerei (stĭk′ẽr-ī; *stick* er eye). Braid of even weave, having embroidered, scalloped, or notched edge. See BRAIDS.
stickpin. Ornamental pin. See PINS.
stiffening (stĭf′ən-ĭng; *stiff* en ing). Process of making stiff, or that which serves to do it. Specifically, process of sizing fabric with starch, glue, gelatin, etc., to make it permanently crisp.
stiletto (stĭ-lĕt′ō; sti *let* o). Small, pointed instrument of ivory, bone, or other hard material. Used in eyelet work for puncturing holes in material.

STITCHES

stitch. 1. Single turn or loop of the thread, yarn, etc., made by hand or machine in sewing, crocheting, embroidery, knitting, lace-making. 2. Particular method or style of stitching. All eye-needle types, whether for embroidery, tapestry, lace, or sewing, are based approximately upon the seven basic stitches: running, back, overcast, cross, blanket, chain, knot. Type of design, weight and kind of fabric and thread, length of stitch, and position of thread at right or left of needle provide the many variations.
afghan-s. Simple crochet stitch worked with long, hooked needle to produce a plain design. See TRICOT-STITCH.
appliqué-s. (ăp-lĭ-kā′; ap li *kay*). Any stitch used to fasten applied piece to fabric article or garment.
arrowhead-s. Series of stitches placed to resemble arrowheads, one below the other, all pointing in the same direction. Can be used as border or filling stitch.

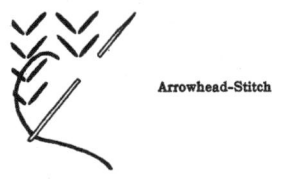

Arrowhead-Stitch

Aubusson-s. (F. ō-bü-sôn; oh boo sonh). Type of needle-tapestry stitch. Same as REP-STITCH.
back-s. Basic stitch, second in importance, from which combination-stitch, seed-stitch, etc., were developed. Made by inserting needle about ⅛ inch back of end of previous stitch and bringing it out about ⅛ inch beyond end. Under stitch is thus twice length of top stitch. Top resembles machine-stitch. Used for strength in plain sewing, also for embroidery.
basket filling-s. 1. Stitch with lengthwise threads alternately passing over and under cross threads, as in darning. 2. Couching stitch worked alternately over and under cords. Used in embroidery.
basket-s. Embroidery stitch resembling series of overlapping cross-stitches, each stitch overlapping the one before by about half. Varies in appearance from close, braid-like line to cross-stitch effect, according to whether stitches are placed close together or spaced. Used as filling or outline where heavy, solid effect is desired.

Basket-Stitch

basting (bāst′ĭng; *baist* ing). Long, loose stitch used to hold fabric in place until final sewing. — **diagonal-b.** Diagonal on top side; short, straight, crosswise stitch underneath. Used to hold two thicknesses of fabric together and to prevent slipping. — **even-b.** Long running-stitches. Used for seams before fitting garment, and for exacting machine work. — **uneven-b.** Twice as long as even-basting, with short stitch underneath and long stitch on top. Quickest method of basting.
blanket-s. Basic stitch, fifth in importance, from which buttonhole-stitch, feather-stitch, etc., were developed. Essential characteristic is single purl, formed by bringing needle out over thread so as to cross it. Blanket-stitch is widely spaced; single-purl buttonhole is the same stitch worked close together. Used for simulated buttonholes, cut work, ornamental edging.

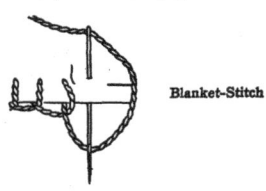

Blanket-Stitch

blind-s. Concealed stitch like slip-stitch, but shorter.
braided-band-s. Embroidery stitch made by weaving threads in diamond shape to fill in band or border.
bredstitch (brĕd′stĭch; *bred* stitch) or **bredestitch** (brĕd′stĭch; *breed* stitch). Old embroidery stitch that appears same on each side of fabric.
brick-s. or **brickwork.** 1. Blanket-stitch arranged to resemble brick formation. Used for bands and borders and for covering large surface. 2. Embroidery stitch in which flat stitches are laid in alternate rows as bricks are laid,

stitches (continued)
end of one stitch coming under middle of stitch above.

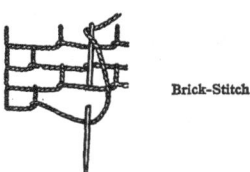

Brick-Stitch

brier-s. (brī'ēr; *bry* er). Type of feather-stitching made to resemble thorns on a stem.
broad chain-s. Same as SQUARE CHAIN-STITCH.
bullion-s. (bŏŏl'yŭn; *bool* yun). Decorative stitch made by twisting needle around thread several times before inserting it into material. Short bullion-stitches sometimes called *knots*.
bundle-s. Group of parallel stitches laid on fabric and tied together at the middle. Sometimes called *fagot filling-stitch* or *sheaf filling-stitch*.

Bundle-Stitch

burden-s. Flat couching.
buttonhole-s. 1. Stitch with a double purl. Used to finish the edges of tailored buttonholes; also, to form a secure edge, as in cut work. Also called *close-stitch* and *feston*. 2. Same as blanket-stitch, but worked close together. Used in laces and open-work embroidery.

Buttonhole-Stitch

buttonhole tied-s. Open-seam stitch made by working from four to six single-purl-stitches on a bar. Used to join ribbons.
Byzantine-s. (bĭz'an-tēn; *bis* an teen). Slanting satin-stitch worked on canvas over four vertical and two horizontal threads in diagonal zigzag pattern.
cable-s. Embroidery stitch of chain-stitch type, differing from ordinary chain-stitch by having small stitch connecting one link to the next.
canvas s. Cross-stitch or any of various stitches used in canvas work.

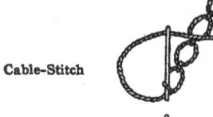

Cable-Stitch

catch-s. Large, easy cross-like stitch made with sewing thread. Used to hold edges too bulky for hem turn, and as finish for seam edges in fabric that does not fray.

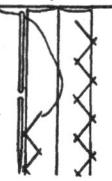

Catch-Stitch

catstitch. Same as CATCH-STITCH.
chain-s. 1. Basic stitch, sixth in importance, from which lazy-daisy and link-powdering were developed. Made of connecting loop stitches that form links, as in a chain. Also called *loop-*, *picot-*, *railway-stitch*. Used in embroidery. 2. In crochet, stitch made by catching thread around hook and pulling it through thread loop, catching thread again to form another loop, and repeating process. There are many other stitches used in crochet that are not given here, since they are all variations of this and are used chiefly in following a pattern.

Chain-Stitch

chequered chain-s. Same as MAGIC CHAIN-STITCH.
chevron-s. (shĕv'rən; *shev* ron). Embroidery stitch made in somewhat the same manner as catch-stitch, but instead of a small cross at each angle, a short, straight stitch covers the joining.

Chevron-Stitch

closed feather-s. Single feather-stitch, always made by putting needle in vertically instead of diagonally.
close-s. (klōs; cloce). Same as BUTTONHOLE-STITCH.
cloth-s. Close stitch, used in making pillow lace, in which threads are woven as in a piece of cloth. Also called *whole-stitch*.
combination-s. Back-stitch combined with two or more running-stitches. Used when more strength is needed than given by running-stitch.
continental-s. Type of stitch used in canvas work; made the same as tent-stitch, but worked on double-thread canvas.

Continental-Stitch

coral-s. Blanket-stitch worked backward with heavy thread and embroidered close together. Used as outline or filling stitch.
cord-s. Fine stitch closely worked over laid thread to give effect of raised line or cord.
couching-s. (kowch'ĭng; *cowch* ing). Overcasting or ornamental stitches taken at regular intervals to fasten down one or more strands of thread, yarn, or cord. Used as ornamental work on dresses, linens, hangings, etc.

Couching-Stitch

Cretan-s. (krēt'an; *creet* an). Variation of feather-stitch made by taking shorter underneath stitch, so that, instead of a straight center line, a braided effect results.

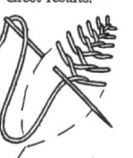

Cretan-Stitch

crewel-s. Outline-stitch used in crewel work. Sometimes called *stem-stitch*.
cross-basket-s. Two groups of parallel threads laid perpendicular to each other

and fastened by cross-stitches where the threads intersect. Used as filling.
crossed blanket-s. Blanket-stitch made so that one stitch slants diagonally to right and next crosses in diagonal slant to the left, resulting in series of crosses above the purled line.
cross-s. Basic stitch, fourth in importance, having many varieties. Made by one stitch crossed over another to form an X. Used on dresses, children's clothes, linens. Also used on canvas in needle-tapestry work, in which each cross is completed before the next is begun.

Cross-Stitch

cushion-s. (kŏŏsh'ən; *coosh* un). 1. In embroidery, same as TENT-STITCH, I. 2. Short, straight stitch producing effect of weaving. Used on coarse canvas; formerly used in embroidery to fill in backgrounds, especially in imitating painted designs. Loosely, any stitch used in canvas work as filling stitch.
darning-s. Stitch done in imitation of weaving, used to reinforce or replace fabric and for allover decoration. Used as a filling stitch in embroidery.
detached chain-s. Same as LAZY-DAISY-STITCH.
diagonal cross-s. Oblong cross-stitch, with a vertical stitch connecting the two ends on the same side of each cross, giving a boxed-in effect.
double back-s. Same as SHADOW-STITCH.
double chain-s. Chain-stitch combining two links or thread loops. Gives a heavier line than single chain-stitch.
double cross-s. Canvas stitch consisting of one ordinary cross-stitch with another made upright on top of it.
double running-s. Running-stitch done twice on the same line to make continuous line on both sides of fabric. Also called *two-sided-stitch*, *Holbein-stitch*, *Italian-stitch*. Used for embroidery and needle tapestry.
drawn-fabric-s. Any stitch producing an open-work effect by drawing fabric threads together in groups to form a design or pattern. Done with coarse needle and strong thread for best results. See ITALIAN HEMSTITCHING, PUNCH-WORK-STITCH.
embroidery darning-s. Even-basting-stitches in alternating rows. Used for filling in bands and borders, etc.
encroaching Gobelin-s. See GOBELIN-STITCH.
etching-s. Same as OUTLINE-STITCH.
fagot filling-s. Same as BUNDLE-STITCH.
fagoting-s. Open-seam stitch similar to single feather-stitch. Used to join ribbons, bands, or folds. Also called *insertion-stitch*. — **Bermuda f.** Fagoting-stitch on the wrong side of sheer fabric. Similar to SHADOW EMBROIDERY.

Fagoting-Stitch

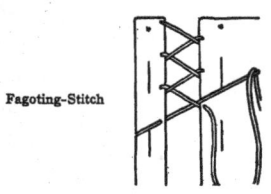

— **drawn-work** or **hemstitch f.** Fagoting done on open sections of fabric from which certain threads have been drawn. Stitches used are of hemstitch type, placed to gather fabric threads in various designs. See DRAWN WORK. See HEMSTITCH. — **single f.** Fagoting made by inserting the needle at right angles to the edges to be joined. — **twisted f.** Fagoting made by inserting the needle parallel to the edges to be joined.
feather-s. Variation of short blanket-stitch, in groups alternating from one side of an unmarked line to the other.

Feather-Stitch

fern-s. Stitch worked on same principle as arrowhead-stitch, but done in groups of three stitches instead of two, so that third stitch of each group forms continuous stem line.
fiber-s. Stitch used in making bobbin lace, for indicating central vein of a leaf design.
filling-s. Any embroidery stitch used to fill in part of a design.
fishbone-s. Embroidery stitch like the backbone of a fish; made with a series of single-purl-stitches worked diagonally and alternately to the left and to the right of an unmarked line. Used as braid or border stitch.

Fishbone-Stitch

flat-s. Stitch worked on same principle as satin-fishbone-stitch, but needle is put in at less of an angle with shorter underneath stitch, giving more overlapping on surface.
Florentine-s. (flŏr'ən-tēn; *flor* en teen). Canvas stitch made upright, usually in zigzag or oblique lines rather than horizontal rows. Stitch usually covers four horizontal threads.

Florentine-Stitch

fly-s. Same as Y-stitch, with shorter tail.
French knot. Ornamental knot made by twisting needle around thread from three to five times and putting needle back at approximately same point as it came through. When the thread is pulled through, a shapely knot is formed. Used for embroidering centers of flowers, etc.

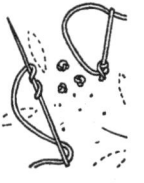

French Knot

garter-s. Usual simple stitch used in hand knitting. Also called *plain knitting*.
German-s. Stitch formed by working long and short slanting stitches alternately across canvas in diagonal line. Used in BERLIN WORK.
glove- or **glover's-s.** (glŭv'ẽrz; *gluv* erz). Stitch made by alternately drawing thread through one side of seam, then other, always from inside outward. Used in sewing seams of gloves.
Gobelin-s. (gŏb'ə-lĭn; *gob* a lin). Canvas stitch laid upright over two horizontal threads and worked horizontally on the canvas. Sometimes called *tapestry-stitch*. — **encroaching G.-s.** Same stitch worked on slant over one vertical and five horizontal threads, with each succeeding row beginning in the same row of squares as the bottom of the preceding row, giving overlapped effect. — **oblique G.-s.** Same stitch worked on slant by laying it over one vertical thread as well as the two horizontal threads.
Gothic-s. Same as CHAIN-STITCH, I.
gros point (F. grō pwăṅ; *gro* pwanh). Needle tapestry stitch as used for canvas work. French term meaning large point.

fāte, făt, dânce, ärt mē, mĕt, hër, thêre rīde, rĭd nōte, nŏt, côrn, fōōd, fŏŏt cūte, cŭt, cūre now fĭn(ŋ)ger villa(ə) señor pleas(zh)ure

stitches

stitches (continued)

half back-s. Stitch similar to back-stitch, but having longer under stitch so that there is space between the top stitches. Not as strong as back-stitch, but gives more strength than running- or combination-stitches.

half cross-s. Stitch used in canvas work, worked diagonally from left to right, the needle being put through from one square to the square immediately below. Usually on double-mesh canvas with trammé laid first.

half-s. 1. In crocheting or knitting, two stitches taken as one to contract edge. 2. In pillow laces, loose open stitch used in delicate parts of design; in contrast to cloth stitch. Also called *lace-stitch, shadow-stitch*.

hemming-s. 1. Quick stitch made with short, slanting stitch on right side and slightly longer slanting stitch on wrong side. Also called *whipping*. 2. Same as VERTICAL HEMMING-STITCH. See under STITCHES.

hemstitch or **hemstitching.** Ornamental stitch, as at top of hem, made by drawing out number of parallel threads and fastening together those remaining in open sections, in successive small groups.

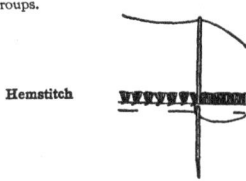

Hemstitch

herringbone-s. Name of catch-stitch in embroidery. Used to form bands, fill borders and motifs. Close herringbone used for heavy stems.

Holbein-s. (hōl′bĭn; *hole* bīne). Same as DOUBLE RUNNING-STITCH.

hollie-s. Type of buttonhole-stitch with a twist. Used in making hollie point lace.

honeycomb-s. Blanket-stitches so connected as to form a honeycomb design. Similar to BRICK-STITCH, 1. Used for filling.

huckaback-s. (hŭk′ə-băk; *huck* a back). Surface stitch darned into the weft threads of huckaback toweling; often placed to form designs or make zigzag borders. Generally in multicolored effects.

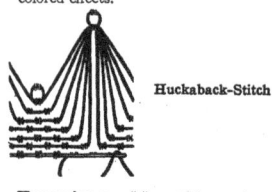

Huckaback-Stitch

Hungarian-s. (hŭng-gā′rĭ-ən; *hung* gay ri an). Alternating long and short upright stitches; worked horizontally on plain canvas. Covers four and two threads.

Hungarian-Stitch

insertion-s. Any open-seam stitch. See FAGOTING, 1.

Irish-s. Long stitch taken in upright direction across several threads of canvas; worked diagonally across canvas. Used in BERLIN WORK.

Italian hemstitching. 1. Drawn-fabric stitch made with alternating vertical and horizontal stitch, forming line similar in appearance to blanket-stitch but with open-work effect caused by use of large needle to punch hole and fine thread to draw fabric threads apart. May be worked in any direction on fabric. Often used as seam-finish on sheer fabrics, in same manner as machine hemstitching, to give flat, strong, decorative finish, for which no preliminary stitching is needed. 2. Same stitch used in embroidery on linen or other fabric for line or for filling, but done on counted threads.

Italian relief-s. Single-purl-stitches used in flower designs to fill in petals and leaves. Often seen in combination with punch work.

Italian-s. Same as DOUBLE RUNNING-STITCH.

Kensington-s. (kĕn′zĭng-tən; *ken* zing ton). Same as LONG-AND-SHORT-STITCH.

knot-s. Basic stitch, seventh in importance. Made by twisting thread around needle in any way that forms a knot in the thread on the fabric surface when the thread is drawn through. See FRENCH-KNOT, LIBERTY KNOT-STITCH, SIMPLICITY KNOT-STITCH.

lace-s. Stitch used in making bobbin lace to fill inside and lighter parts of designs. Also called *half-stitch*.

ladder-s. 1. Embroidery stitch over open seam or drawn or cut-out fabric, resembling fagoting. Done with overcasting, buttonhole-stitch, or catch-stitch. 2. Embroidery stitch with ladder-like effect, generally square chain-stitch.

laid-s. Long, loose stitch laid on surface of fabric; usually held down by stitches worked over it. Used for outline and filling.

lattice-basket-s. Lattice-work embroidery made by laying close, parallel threads and weaving the eye of the needle in and out of these threads as in darning. Used for square, diamond, or basket motifs and border effects.

lazy-daisy-s. Elongated, detached chain-stitches, grouped to form a daisy. Used in embroidery.

Lazy-Daisy-Stitch

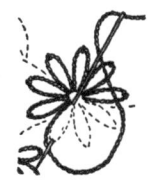

leviathan-s. (lə-vī′ə-thən; le *vy* ath an). Stitch used in canvas work. Same as DOUBLE CROSS-STITCH.

liberty knot-s. Embroidery stitch worked by inserting needle perpendicularly to line to be decorated, carrying the thread around the needle, and then pulling needle through, thus forming a knot. Used for outlines.

link-powdering-s. Series of chain-like stitches not linked together, but completed separately. Usually worked in spaced design. Used for filling. Sometimes called *washable knot-stitch*.

lock-s. Sewing-machine stitch formed by locking top and bobbin threads together at each stitch.

long-and-short-s. Alternating long and short stitches used as a filling- or darning-stitch in embroidery. Also called *Kensington-stitch*.

Long-and-Short-Stitch

long-leg cross-s. Cross-stitch made with one long and one short stitch. Used in linen and canvas embroidery.

long-s. Satin-stitch without padding.

looped-braid-s. Embroidery stitch made by bringing the thread around in a loop and taking one stitch through the loop, length of loop and stitch regulating width of braid. Used chiefly on things that are not laundered.

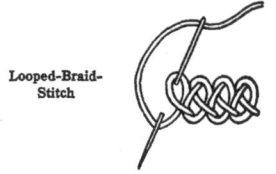

Looped-Braid-Stitch

loop-s. Same as CHAIN-STITCH, 1.

magic chain-s. Chain-stitch worked with two threads of different colors in one needle. Colors made to alternate by looping one thread under needle for one stitch, the other thread for the next stitch.

fāte, făt, dánce, ärt mē, mĕt, hẽr, thêre rīde, rĭd nōte, nŏt, côrn, fōōd, fŏŏt cūte, cŭt, cūre now fin(g)ger villa(ə) señor pleas(zh)ure

Magic Chain-Stitch

marking-s. Same as CROSS-STITCH.
mark-s. Same as TAILORS' TACKS.
needle-point s. 1. Term used to designate any stitch used in needle tapestry. **2.** Any stitch used in making needle-point lace.
oblique Gobelin-s. See GOBELIN-STITCH.
oblong cross-s. Cross-stitch made long and narrow instead of square.
open chain-s. Same as SQUARE CHAIN-STITCH.
open-s. Any embroidery stitch that produces open work.
Oriental-s. Series of long, straight, parallel stitches intersected at center by short, diagonal stitches. Sometimes used as open-seam stitch. Also called *Rumanian-stitch*.

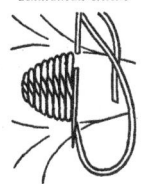

Oriental-Stitch

ornamental buttonhole edge-s. Stitch made by forming series of loops along an edge and working over each loop with buttonhole-stitches. Used to decorate plain edges.
outline-s. Slanting back-stitch used for outlines, stems, and as padding foundation under other stitches. When thread is kept to left of needle, a straighter line is obtained. Shorter stitch is taken and thread is kept to right of needle when broader effect desired. Latter method used in crewel embroidery and known as *crewel-* or *stem-stitch*. Weight in line gained by size of thread and closeness of stitches.

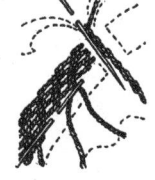

Outline-Stitch

overcast running-s. Same as TWISTED RUNNING-STITCH.

overcast- or **overcasting-s.** Basic stitch, third in importance, from which outline, satin, and many canvas stitches were developed. Slanting stitch used mainly to protect raw edges from raveling or to hold two edges together.
overhanding. Short over-and-over stitches placed close together, with needle always put in vertically. Used chiefly to join selvage or finished edges; also, for eyelets.
over-s. Stitch used to bind raw edge or hem, giving ornamental finish; usually made on sewing machine.
padding-s. 1. Outline-stitch used as filling to form foundation or base over which other stitches are worked. Also, plain stitch laid on fabric as base for raised design. Padding is always concealed by the embroidery stitch. **2.** Diagonal-basting-stitch used to hold padding to an interlining.
Pekinese-s. (pē-kǐn-ēz'; pee kin *ees*). Stitch made by looping thread through a line of back-stitches, couching, or machine-stitches. Used in shading or as outline. Sometimes called *threaded back-stitch*. Illustration shows line made by machine with heavy thread on bobbin.

Pekinese-Stitch

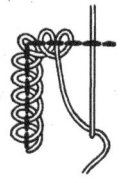

petal-s. Series of chain-stitches laid along one side of a line. Stitches connecting these and forming stem give appearance of outline-stitch.

Petal-Stitch

petit-point-s. (pĕt'ĭ point; *pet* i point). Term from French for TENT-STITCH.
picot-s. (F. pē-kō; pee co). Loop of thread extending down between groups of buttonhole-, blanket-, or crochet-stitches. Used in lacemaking, for decoration, and for edge finishes.
plain knitting. Basic stitch used in hand knitting. Made by putting right-hand needle through first stitch on left-hand needle, throwing thread around point, and drawing loop through, thus transferring stitch to right needle. This process is repeated until all stitches are worked off left needle. Needles are then exchanged in hands and process repeated as before. Stitch may also be made on circular needles or on several small needles used for circular knitting.
plaited s. (plāt'ĕd; *platt* ed). Any stitch giving braided or interwoven effect, as herringbone or basket-weave.
plush-s. Stitch used in Berlin work; made to form loops on surface in plush effect. Loops may be cut and combed or left as stitched.
Portuguese knot. Outline-stitch knotted at center of each stitch. Used as outline.
prick-s. Very short stitch taken in heavy material or where stitches are not to show. Made by putting needle in on right side very close to where it came out.
punch-work-s. Stitch worked on a loosely woven fabric which has been stamped with dots in rows about ⅛ inch apart. Rows of dots must run straight with fabric threads. Horizontal stitches are done first and then connected by vertical stitches, thereby giving square effect. Stitch is always worked from top to bottom.

Punch-Work-Stitch

purl-s. 1. Stitch made by bringing needle through from underside out over thread so as to cross it. Commonly called *blanket-stitch*. Double purl, which is used in making tailored buttonholes, made by throwing thread over needle as it crosses, forming knot or double purl. Commonly called *buttonhole-stitch*. **2.** In knitting, stitch made backward, giving ribbed appearance.
raccroc-s. (rá-krō'; ra *cro*). Very fine stitch used by lacemakers to join net. Done so cleverly that it can not be detected by naked eye.
railway-s. 1. Same as CHAIN-STITCH, I. **2.** In crochet, same as TRICOT-STITCH.
rambler-rose-s. Stitch made by laying back-stitches of bulky thread around and around a center to form a compact flower. Used for clover blossoms, roses, and small flowers.

Rambler-Rose-Stitch

ray-s. Same as SPOKE-STITCH, 2.
rep-s. Canvas stitch worked vertically on double-thread canvas. Covers one

stitches (continued)
horizontal and two vertical threads. Also called *Aubusson-stitch*.

Roman-s. Same as ORIENTAL-STITCH, except that intersecting stitches are shorter and straighter.

rope-s. Overlapped, twisted blanket-stitch used to give rope-like line.

Rumanian-s. (rōō-mā'nĭ-ən; roo *may* ni an). Same as ORIENTAL-STITCH.

running hem. Same as VERTICAL HEMMING-STITCH.

running-s. Basic stitch that is first in importance. Made in series of short stitches of same length, several run on needle at once. Used for seaming, gathering, tucking, quilting, etc.

saddle-s. Simple overcasting-stitch, used as decoration. Often made of narrow strips of leather.

satin-fishbone-s. Slanting satin-stitches worked alternately from side to side and meeting at an angle, the stitches overlapping slightly at center. Gives effect of backbone of fish.

satin-s. Over-and-over stitch laid in straight or slanting parallel lines close together so as to produce a satiny effect. May be worked flat or over padding. One of most widely used embroidery stitches.

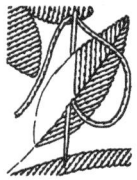

Satin-Stitch

scallop buttonhole-s. Single- or double-purl-stitch made in scallop design, often over padding.

seam-s. Same as PURL-STITCH, 2.

seed-s. Short back-stitch made with long underneath stitch which allows for a space between top stitches. Similar to half back-stitch but irregularly placed. Used for outlining and filling.

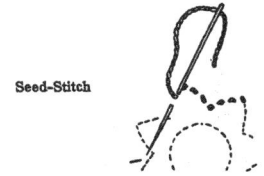

Seed-Stitch

shadow-s. 1. Catch-stitch worked on wrong side of sheer material. Also called *double back-stitch* from appearance on right side. Compare SHADOW EMBROIDERY. **2.** In pillow lace, same as HALF-STITCH, 2.

sheaf-filling-s. Same as BUNDLE-STITCH.

sheaf-s. Open-seam stitch having appearance of a sheaf. Bar threads, which join the two edges, are gathered into groups and tied together with a knot.

shell-s. Stitch crocheted along an edge to produce scalloped effect; made with groups of stitches radiating from certain points placed equal distances apart.

short-and-long-s. Satin-stitches of uneven length put side by side within an outline design so as to form irregular inner edge and even outer edge. Used in half-solid work.

simplicity knot-s. Two small back-stitches laid side by side to resemble a knot. Made of heavy thread. Used for outlines and borders.

slip-s. Loose stitch concealed between two thicknesses of fabric. Made by taking up thread of fabric, then catching needle in hem edge. Used for hems, facings, folds, etc., wherever it is desired that stitches be invisible on right side.

smocking-s. Any one of several decorative stitches used for gathering cloth in regular folds, usually to form honeycomb or diamond pattern.

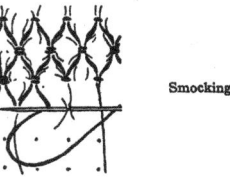

Smocking

spider-web-s. Embroidery stitches so combined as to form open spider web. Made by laying threads in spoke effect over fabric; then, weaving a thread over and under these threads, around and around the center. Used in place of medallions and as a filling in drawn-work corners.

split-s. Long outline-stitch in which needle is brought up through thread itself. Used for stems and outlines and in needle-tapestry work.

spoke-s. 1. Drawn-work embroidery stitch by which threads are held together in pattern resembling spokes of a wheel. **2.** Straight stitches placed so as to radiate from a center. Also called *ray-stitch*.

Spoke-Stitch

square chain-s. Chain-stitch made with slanting underneath stitch instead of straight. Squared effect made by putting needle in at some distance from where it came out instead of in same hole. Also called *open chain-* and *broad chain-stitch*.

star-s. Embroidery stitch in shape of eight-pointed star, made like double cross-stitch.

stem-s. 1. Slanting overhanding-stitch embroidered over a padding thread. Used for fine, definite lines, as in stems. **2.** Outline-stitch used in crewel work; called *crewel-stitch*.

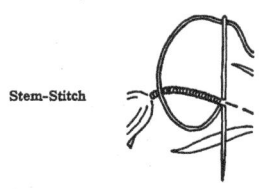

Stem-Stitch

stroke-s. Same as DOUBLE RUNNING-STITCH.

surface darning-s. Stitch laid on fabric with short even- or uneven-bastings. Often used in huckaback work.

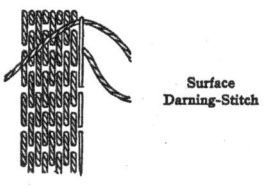

Surface Darning-Stitch

sword-edge-s. Elongated stitch so twisted at top that irregular cross is formed. Used for borders and to soften edges of leaves.

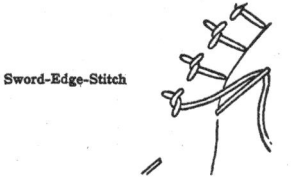

Sword-Edge-Stitch

tailor's tacks. Basting stitches, with large loops left at intervals, taken through two pieces of fabric, then cut apart, leaving threads on both pieces. Used as marking of seam lines and perforations. Also called *mark-stitch*.

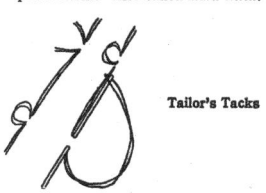

Tailor's Tacks

fāte, făt, dánce, ärt mē, mĕt, hêr, thêre rīde, rĭd nōte, nŏt, côrn, fōōd, fŏŏt cūte, cŭt, cûre now fin(ŋ)ger villa(ə) señor pleas(zh)ure

tambour-s. (tăm′bŏŏr; *tam* boor). Loop-stitch made with crochet needle. Resembles chain-stitch.

tapestry darning-s. Over-and-over stitch giving solid effect in stitches alternating to left and right and so laid as to resemble darned work. Used as border for coarse materials.

tapestry-s. Short, upright stitch used in canvas work to imitate weave in woven tapestries. See GOBELIN-STITCH.

tassel-s. Embroidery stitch in which loops are made and cut to form fringe. See PLUSH-STITCH.

tent-s. 1. Short outline-stitch worked on slanting line. Used for filling in linen embroidery. Sometimes called *cushion-stitch*. 2. Canvas stitch worked on single-thread canvas so that each stitch lies across one vertical and one horizontal thread. When worked on double-canvas, paired threads are separated before working. Can be worked horizontally or diagonally on the canvas. Also called *petit point*.

Tent-Stitch

thorn-s. Embroidery stitch similar in appearance to feather-stitch or fern-stitch, but worked by alternating flat stitches over long laid stitch that forms stem.

threaded back-s. Same as PEKINESE-STITCH.

three-sided-s. 1. Drawn-fabric stitch worked on fine material by using heavy needle to punch hole and fine thread to draw fabric threads apart, giving open-work effect in bands of adjoining triangles. Need not be made to follow grain of fabric. 2. Same stitch worked horizontally on coarse fabric over counted threads, each stitch covering from four to six threads.

tie-s. Stitch made by first taking small stitch, leaving ends of thread several inches long, then tying these in a knot. Used mainly in millinery work; sometimes in dressmaking.

tramé underlay (trăm-a; tram ay). Needle-point stitch made by laying long, parallel threads on narrow mesh of canvas in preparation for stitches that will hold them in place.

Tramé Stitch

trellis-s. Cord-stitch worked in parallel lines, latticed with threads, knotted at each crossing of cord. Used for diamond and square motifs. Also, any combination of stitches so worked as to give trellis-like effect.

triangular blanket-s. Blanket-stitch worked diagonally to form small triangular sections. Used for edging or filling.

tricot-s. (trē′kō; *tree* co). Simple crochet stitch suitable for plain work. Usually done with long hooked needle and fleecy wool. Also called *Tunisian crochet*, *afghan-*, *railway-*, and *idiot-stitch*.

trio filling-s. (trē′ō; *tree* o). One vertical and two diagonal stitches grouped in a design. Also called *thousand-flower-stitch*.

twisted-bar-s. Open-seam stitch made by twisting thread several times around a bar that connects two edges. Space between stitches usually about two-thirds of that between edges. Two ribbons often connected in this manner.

Twisted-Bar-Stitch

twisted chain-s. Variation of chain-stitch made by taking diagonal instead of straight stitch on underside, then bringing thread over needle and around point to obtain twisted effect. Used for trimming on non-washable garments.

twisted running-s. Stitch made by overcasting series of running-stitches so as to produce twined effect. Also called *overcast running*.

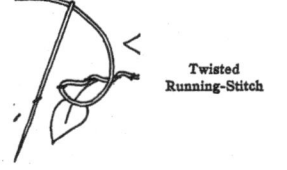

Twisted Running-Stitch

twist-s. Same as CORD-STITCH.

two-sided cross-s. 1. Cross-stitch enclosed on two sides: left side and bottom; so that when it is worked in adjoining rows, cross appears to be boxed in on all sides. Used on loosely woven linen or canvas. 2. Cross-stitch worked so as to appear the same on both sides.

two-sided-s. Same as DOUBLE RUNNING-STITCH.

upright-s. Satin-stitch made vertically in combination with another stitch or as filling-stitch.

vertical hemming-s. Hemming-stitch made perpendicular to hem. Used for inconspicuous hem turn. Sometimes called *running hem*.

washable knot-s. Chain-like stitch used for filling. See LINK-POWDERING-STITCH under STITCHES.

wheat-s. Series of slanting stitches connected at center by means of line of loops. Resembles full wheat ear. Used for border or outline effects.

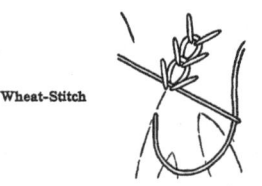

Wheat-Stitch

wheel-s. Stitch used in making design similar to spider's web; done on material, not over space.

whip-s. Short, easy overcasting. Used over rolled edge, drawing up thread to form gathers; or over two selvages laid together to form a flat seam; or to fell down an appliqué edge.

whole-s. Same as CLOTH-STITCH.

Y-s. Decorative blanket type of stitch with each loop fastened down to form series of unconnected Y's.

Y-Stitch

zigzag chain-s. Chain-stitch made by inserting needle at an angle and alternating from side to side.

stitchery. Needlework, including embroidery, tapestry, appliqué, quilting, etc.

stitching. Thread, or the like, applied to fabric to hold thicknesses together or to decorate a surface. Term used chiefly in connection with sewing-machine stitching.

stitchwork. Embroidery.

stoat. English name for WEASEL. See FURS.

stoating. Process of invisibly slip-stitching together two folded-in edges, such as the front facing and top collar of a tailored suit. Also used as method of mending torn goods.

stock. Broad band, soft or stiffened, worn as neckcloth; usually buckled at back. Type of neckwear that followed the cravat.

stock buckle. Buckle formerly used to hold stock. See BUCKLES.

19th Century Stock

17th Century Stomacher

stock-dyeing. Process of dyeing before spinning. See DYEING.
stockinet (stŏk-ĭ-nĕt′; stock i net). Flat or tubular knitted fabric. Used for children's sleeping garments, undergarments, etc.; originally used for stockings.
stocking. General term applied to full-length hosiery, knit or woven. See HOSE.
stocking cap. Long, tapering, knitted cap. See CAPS.
stola (stō′lə; sto la). Long outer garment, usually ankle-length, fastened round the body by a girdle. Characteristic dress of Roman matrons, as toga was of men.

Roman Stola, 2d and 3d Centuries

stole. 1. Long, narrow scarf, usually embroidered and fringed at the ends. Worn over shoulders as ecclesiastical vestment. 2. Shoulder scarf, usually of fur, worn by women as costume accessory. 3. Full-length garment, similar to a stola.

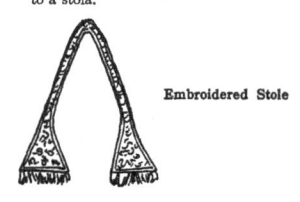

Embroidered Stole

stomacher (stŭm′ək-ẽr; stum ack er)· Decorative article of dress, worn over the breast and reaching to the waist or below, sometimes with the gown laced over it. Usually of stiff, rich material, elaborately ornamented; sometimes padded. Worn by both men and women in 15th and 16th centuries.
stomper (stŏmp′ẽr; stomp er). Heavy shoe. See SHOES.

stone marten. Fur of marten of Europe and Asia. See FURS.
storm boot. Very high shoe. See BOOTS.
storm rubber. Rubber overshoe, high in front to cover the instep.
storm serge. Hard, light-weight serge. See SERGES.
stovepipe hat. Hat with high crown, especially man's tall silk hat. See HATS.
stovepipe satin. Very smooth, lustrous satin. Same as PANNE SATIN. See SATINS.
stowing. Tailoring term meaning to join together so that joining can scarcely be detected. See STOATING.
straight-bodied. Made with stays. Compare LOOSE-BODIED.
strand. Single fiber or filament of yarn or thread; one of several strings, threads, etc., twisted together.
stranding. Coarse cloth formerly used to make cheap blankets called *strands*.
stranding thread. Tailor's thread used in making buttonholes. See THREADS.
strap crotch. Crotch formed by fabric strip joining front to back. See CROTCH.
strapless. Without shoulder straps. Term applied to evening gowns that end just above the bust line, leaving the shoulders and neck bare. Usually held in place by stiffening in the bodice, by adhesive fastening along the top, etc.
strapping. Narrow, machine-stitched band used as finish for seams.
strap seam. Seam with additional strip of material stitched on top. See SEAMS.
strapwork. Interlaced decorative design of bands, fillets, etc.
Strasbourg work (străz′bŏŏr; strahs boor). Same as ROMAN CUT WORK. See EMBROIDERIES.
strass. 1. Paste or brilliant composition substance used in making costume jewelry. 2. Trimming of waxed straw. 3. Silk discarded in making skeins.

STRAWS

straw. 1. Fabric made by braiding, plaiting, or weaving natural fibers (made of stems, stalks, leaves, bark, grass, etc.) or artificial fibers. Used for making hats, bags, shoe uppers, etc. 2. Short for hat made of straw. 3. Light, yellowish-tan shade, color of dried plant fibers.
baku or **bakou** (bä′kŏŏ; bah coo). Fine, light-weight, expensive straw with dull finish, resembling bangkok. Made from fibers of buri palm of Ceylon and Malabar coast.
balibuntl or **balibuntal** or **balibuntal** (băl′ĭ-bŭn-tl; bal i bun tl). Fine, light-weight, smooth, glossy straw woven of buntal, white Philippine fiber obtained from unopened palm leaf stems. Originally, the hat itself; so called because made of buntal at Baliuag in the Philippines.
bangkok (băng′kŏk; bang cock). Smooth, light-weight, dull straw woven of buntal fibers from stems of palm leaves. Named for Bangkok, Siam.
chip. Inexpensive straw, coarsely woven of wood shavings or other woody material cut into strips. Originated in Italy.
exotic s. (ĕks-ŏt′ĭk; ex ot ic). Any smooth, fine, closely woven straw, natural or synthetic.
leghorn s. (lĕg′hôrn or lĕg′ẽrn; leg horn or leg ern). Finely plaited straw made from kind of wheat, cut green and bleached. Named for Leghorn, Italy, where exported.
linen s. Any smooth, closely woven straw with fine, linen-like finish.
liseré (F. lē-zə-rā; lee ze ray). Bright-finished, split-straw braid used in making blocked hats.
Milan s. (mĭ-lăn′ or mĭl′ən; mi lan or mill an). Fine straw, closely woven. Used in finest quality of women's hats. Named for Milan, Italy, where it is manufactured.
neora (nē-ō′rə; ne o ra). Shiny, synthetic straw made by covering ramie or synthetic fiber with Cellophane.
paillasson (F. pä-yà-sôṅ; pah yah sonh). Any coarsely woven straw, natural or synthetic. French word meaning straw hat.
Panama (păn-ə-mä′ or păn′ə-mä; pan a mah or pan a mah). Fine, hand-plaited straw made in Ecuador from choicest leaves of the jipijapa, palm-like plant. Named for Panama, center of distribution for it.
peanit (pē′nĭt; pee nit). Inexpensive straw of exotic type, imported from Java.
pedal or **pedale s.** (pĕd′əl; ped al). Straw woven from the pedal, or bottom, section of grain stalk grown mostly in Italy.
pedaline (pĕd′ə-lēn; ped a leen). Synthetic straw made of hemp fiber covered with Cellophane and woven between cotton threads. Made chiefly in Japan.
punta (pŏŏn′tä; poon tah). Upper section of wheat stalk, bleached, plaited, and used in making hats. Compare PEDAL.
raffia (răf′ĭ-ə; raff i a). Natural or highly colored straw made of strong fibers found in leaf stalks of raffia palm of Madagascar.
ramie (răm′ē; ram ee). Strong, glossy fiber of Asiatic plant. Used to make woven fabrics, hat bodies, nets, laces, etc., and usually marketed as *China grass*.
sennit (sĕn′ĭt; sen it). Braided straw, grass, or fiber used for making hats; specifically, rough straw of Japanese or Chinese manufacture. Used for men's hats.
Shantung (shăn-tŏong′; shahn toong). Expensive, hand-woven buntal fiber straw of baku type, with smooth, even finish. Made in China.

---

fāte, făt, dănce, ärt mē, mĕt, hẽr, thêre rīde, rĭd nōte, nŏt, côrn, fōōd, fŏŏt cūte, cŭt, cūré now fin(ŋ)ger villa(ə) señor pleas(zh)ure

sisal or **sisol** or **sissol** (sī'săl, sē'săl, sē-säl'; *sy* sal, *see* sahl, see *sahl*). Finely woven, smooth, expensive straw, with linen finish; made from sisal, kind of hemp grown mostly in Philippines and shipped to China.

sparterie (spär'tēr-ĭ; *spar* ter i). Straw fabric of esparto grass, used to cover wire hat frames; made in Bohemia and Japan.

tagal s. (tă-gäl'; tah *gahl*). Kind of straw made from Manila hemp. Named for province in Java, where it originated.

toquilla (tō-kē'yä or tō-kēl'yä; toe *kee* yah or toe *keel* yah). Strong, flexible fiber obtained from jipijapa leaves. Used in weaving Panama hats.

toyo (tō'yō; *toe* yo). Shiny, smooth, expensive straw woven from Cellophane-coated rice paper. Similar in weave to Panama. Made in Japan, in Okinawa and Formosa. Japanese word meaning paper.

Tuscan s. (tŭs'kən; *tuss* can). Fine, yellow straw woven from tops of bleached wheat stalks. Often made up in lace-like designs. Named for Tuscany, Italy, from where it originally came.

Visca (vĭs'kə; *viss* ca). Trade name for lustrous, artificial fiber made to resemble straw.

straw braid. Braid of straw varying from ¼ to 3 inches in width. Used in making hats. See BRAIDS.
straw needle. Same as MILLINER'S NEEDLE. See NEEDLES.
Streamline Fastener. Trade name for a slide fastener.
street dress. Simple, tailored dress appropriate for daytime wear for shopping, business, etc. See DRESSES.
street shoe. Trim, medium-weight walking shoe suited for street wear. See SHOES.
stretcher. Frame or any device used to stretch an article or expand it by force, such as shoe, glove, curtain, etc.
string. 1. Small cord, larger than thread. Used in crocheting and knitting, in stringing beads, and as a lace or tie, etc. **2.** Length of warp between beams in a loom. Used as a unit in weaving piecework. **3.** Light beige or light grayed tan shade.
string tie. Very narrow necktie.
strip. Long, narrow piece of cloth, ribbon, etc.

STRIPES

stripe or **stripes.** Line or lines of varying widths printed on or woven in fabric, contrasting either in color or texture with the ground.
bayadere (bä-yä-dēr'; bah yah *deer*). Crosswise stripe, usually in multicolored design.
blazer s. Widely spaced stripes of solid color, as seen in a blazer jacket.
candy s. Stripes of varying widths and bright colors, in imitation of striped candy.
chalk s. White stripe appearing as if drawn with piece of chalk.
gypsy s. Stripes of varying width, in bright colors, usually including yellow, red, green, and blue. Sometimes called *Romany stripes*.
hairline or **hair s.** Extremely slender stripe, often of one warp yarn; usually white, sometimes in color.
horizontal s. Stripes running crosswise of fabric or garment. Worn by tall persons to break the height.
laticlave (lăt'ĭ-klāv; *lat* i clave). Broad purple stripe on front of Roman tunic. Worn as emblem of rank by senators, etc.
pencil s. Stripe as wide as the mark made by a pencil, at any distance from the next stripe in a series.
pin s. Slender stripe, varying from the width of a straight pin to ¹⁄₁₆ inch.
regimental s. (rĕj-ĭ-mĕn'təl; rej i *men* tal). Stripes in even design similar to those used on military uniforms.
Roman s. Stripe of brilliant color, in contrasting series which run crosswise on silk fabrics.
Romany s. (rŏm'ə-nĭ; *rom* a ni). Same as GYPSY STRIPES.
satin s. Stripe of satin weave in fabric of another weave.
tuck s. Heavy stripe woven in sheer fabric.
vertical s. Stripes running up and down fabric or garment. Worn by short persons to give illusion of height.

stripping. In shoe manufacturing, a narrow leather strip used as trimming for shoe.
stroke-stitch. Same as DOUBLE RUNNING-STITCH. See STITCHES.
stroking. Process of laying gathers in tiny plaits by drawing needle between gathers, below gathering thread, and pressing down plaits with thumb.
stroller (strōl'ẽr; *strole* er). Casual, tailored type of hat. See HATS.
stud. Detachable, ornamental button inserted in eyelets for fastening shirt or dress front, or cuff.
stuff. Fabric, without distinctive qualities.
stuff gown. Gown made of stuff, worn by barristers in England.
stump work. Heavily padded or stuffed embroidery. See EMBROIDERIES.
style. 1. Particular cut, design, or type of an article; as, style of a shoe, dress, hat, etc. Also, to give particular cut, design, or other fashion features to an article or group of articles; as, to style a line of coats, hats, shoes, etc. **2.** That which is in accord with favored standards, usually the best in fashion; as, woman of style. **3.** Distinctive or characteristic quality expressing a typical mode; as, Empire style.
style book. Book that describes and explains prevailing styles.
styling. Making a style fashionable; giving to any type of merchandise the fashion essentials of color, construction, silhouette, etc.
stylist. Person who does styling.
stylized. Made to conform to a certain style or to prevailing style.
subarmale (sŭb-är-mā'lē; sub ahr *may*

lee). Coat or garment worn inside cuirass.
subdebutante (sŭb-dĕb-ū-tänt'; sub deb you *tahnt*). **1.** Young girl who is about to become a debutante. **2.** Suitable in style for girl of that age; youthful in style.
succinct (sŭk-sĭŋkt'; suck *sinkt*). Archaic word meaning held in place, as by a girdle. Hence, a close-fitting garment.
succinctorium (sŭk-sĭŋk-tō'rĭ-ŭm; suck sink *tore* i um). Band or scarf pendant to girdle; worn by pope.
suclat (soo-klät'; soo *claht*). East Indian term for broadcloth made in Europe.
Sudanette (soo-də-nĕt'; soo da *net*). Trade name for a fine quality of highly mercerized broadcloth.
suede (F. swäd; swade). **1.** Leather with napped surface. See LEATHERS. **2.** Same as SUEDE CLOTH. **3.** Yellowish-brown color. **4.** To give fabric or leather a napped or suede finish.
suede cloth. Woven or knitted fabric with surface napped and shorn to give appearance of suede leather. Also called *suede*, *suedine*.
suede finish. Finish applied to some wool and cotton fabrics, to make them resemble suede leather.
suedine (swäd-ēn'; swade *een*). Same as SUEDE CLOTH.
sugar-loaf hat. Hat similar in shape to a round-topped cone. See HATS.
suggan (sŭg'an; *sug* an). **1.** Colloquial term in western U. S. for long, woolen scarf. **2.** Irish and Scottish colloquial term for thick bed-quilt or coverlet.

SUITS

suit. Suit for men consists of coat, vest, and trousers. Suit for women consists basically of skirt and jacket or coat; sometimes in three pieces: skirt, jacket, and coat.
costume s. Dress and coat or jacket, designed as an ensemble.
dinner s. Costume worn by women for not-too-formal dining, often a simple dinner dress having a tailored jacket or bolero with sleeves. Also, man's tuxedo.
knitted s. or **sweater s.** Matching sweater and skirt, and sometimes jacket, knitted of wool, bouclé, etc. Ususally of sports or semi-sports type.
skeleton s. Boy's tight-fitting suit, with jacket buttoned to trousers.
slack s. Informal ensemble consisting of tailored slacks and a loose jacket or blouse of matching or contrasting color.
sports s. Sturdy, tailored suit especially adapted as to style and fabric for wear to games, etc.
swagger s. Short, flared, easy-fitting coat and matching skirt of sports type.
town s. Tailored suit, often made of a mannish type of fine-surfaced worsted.

suiting. Fabric having enough body to be tailored nicely; often sturdy, firm cotton. Used for making suits and skirts. Type called *novelty suiting* was originally plain, homespun weave with

sultane rough, irregular filling of different color. Now made in variety of weaves, especially plaid, brocaded, or Jacquard effects.

sultane (sŭl-tān'; sul *tane*). Colonial name for gown with front closing fastened with buttons and loops; worn about 1700. Adapted from the Turks.

summer ermine. Fur of white ermine dyed beige, or brown weasel fur. See FURS.

summer-weight. Light-weight; term applied to clothing, shoes, etc., adapted for wear in warm weather.

sumptuous. Rich; elaborate; elegant. Often used to describe a luxurious costume, especially fur-trimmed one.

sunbonnet. Wide-brimmed bonnet. See BONNETS.

sunburst. Brooch or pin with jewels set in radiating effect. See PINS.

sunburst plaits. Accordion-like plaits in flared effect. See PLAITS.

Sunday best. One's best clothes, as for wear to church on Sunday.

Sunday-night dress. Costume similar in type to least formal dinner dress. See DRESSES.

sundown. Broad-brimmed sun hat. See HATS.

sunfast. Term applied to dyed fabrics that do not fade under a standard test.

sun hat. Hat worn for protection from sun. See HATS.

sunray. Plaits arranged in sunburst effect. See SUNBURST under PLAITS.

sunshade. Same as PARASOL.

Sun Shods. Trade name for sandal type of slipper. See SLIPPERS.

sun suit. Backless play suit, designed to expose much of the body to the health-giving rays of the sun. Worn out of doors by children and young women.

sun tan. Any of various degrees of light brown to which the skin of Caucasian race turns after prolonged exposure to the sun.

supportasse (sŭ-pôr'tăs; sup *pore* tass). Frame of wire used to support ruff.

supporter. Garter; also, elastic foundation garment.

surah (sōō'rə; *soo* ra). Soft, lightweight, twilled fabric of silk or wool. Heavy grade called *silk serge*; high-luster grade called *satin surah*. Used for dresses, blouses, etc.

surat (sōō-răt'; soo *rat*). Cotton fabric of low grade made in India at Surat.

surcingle (sûr-sĭng'gl; ser *sing* gl). Belt or girdle, especially on an ecclesiastical cassock; also, encircled as with a surcingle.

surcoat or **surcot** (sûr'kōt; *ser* coat). 1. Outer coat or robe of varying types. See COATS. 2. Type of tunic or cloak worn over armor from 12th to 14th century; usually emblazoned with coat of arms.

surface darning-stitch. Short, even- or uneven-basting laid on fabric. See STITCHES.

surfle (sûr'fl; *ser* fl). Obsolete term meaning to embroider.

surf satin. Heavy quality of satin. See SATINS.

surplice (sûr'plĭs; *ser* pliss). 1. Garment that overlaps diagonally in front. 2. Loose, white vestment with long, full sleeves; worn by clergymen of certain religious denominations. Originally put on over the head. In 17th century, made open in front so as to be put on without disarranging enormous wigs.

Ecclesiastical Surplice.
Surplice Blouse

surplice collar. Collar following extended neckline that overlaps in front. See COLLARS.

surtout (F. sür-tōō or sêr-tōōt'; soor too or ser *toot*). 1. Man's overcoat. See COATS. 2. Woman's hood. See HOODS.

susi (sōō'sē; *soo* see). Fine cotton fabric having stripes of cotton or silk in contrasting color.

suspender (sŭs-pĕn'dĕr; sus *pen* der). One of pair of straps or bands worn over shoulders to support trousers or skirt; usually buttoned to garment. Generally called *suspenders* or *pair of suspenders*. Also, name sometimes given to garter or supporter.

suspender-belt. Belt combined with shoulder straps or braces. See BELTS.

suspender skirt. Skirt with straps attached at waist and extending over the shoulders. See SKIRTS.

svelt or **svelte** (svĕlt; svelt). Gracefully slender and lithe.

swaddling clothes (swŏd'lĭng; *swod* ling). Bands or first clothes wrapped around newly born infants.

swagger coat (swăg'ẽr; *swag* er). Beltless sports coat. See COATS.

swagger hat. Informal sports hat. See HATS.

swagger suit. Short flared coat and matching skirt. See SUITS.

swallow-tailed coat (swŏl'ō tāld; *swoll* o tailed). Fitted jacket or coat with tails in the back; worn by men on full-dress occasions. See COATS.

swan's-down (swŏnz'down; *swans* down). 1. Fine, soft underfeathers of swans. Used to trim cloaks, dresses, negligees, etc. 2. Fine, soft, thick fabric of wool mixed with silk or cotton. 3. Stout, absorbent, cotton flannel. Same as CANTON FLANNEL. See FLANNELS. Also spelled *swansdown* in second and third meanings.

swanskin. Any of various soft, thick, warm, cotton or woolen fabrics.

swatch (swŏch; swotch). Small piece of cloth used as sample.

swathe (swāthe; swaythe). To bind or wrap.

sweatband (swĕt'bănd; *swet* band). Band placed inside hat where it comes directly in contact with head, to absorb perspiration and prevent its showing through.

SWEATERS

sweater (swĕt'ẽr; *swet* er). Garment, either in jacket or overblouse style, usually knitted or crocheted. Originally, heavy woolen garment worn to produce sweat; later, a sweat shirt.

cardigan s. (kär'dĭ-gən; *car* di gan). Unfitted, collarless sweater of knitted material, buttoning in front and having long sleeves or no sleeves. Adapted from jacket of same name.

Cardigan Sweater

coat s. Substantial sweater that has a front closing of coat type. Tailored on coat lines; often with pockets and belt. Similar to CARDIGAN SWEATER.

pull-over. Sweater of the type that is pulled on over the head. Made with long or short sleeves, or no sleeves.

Pull-Over Sweater

sweater blouse. Short, blouse-like sweater of waist length or longer, with either long or short sleeves. Designed to be worn with a skirt, usually as substitute for other type of blouse.

sweat shirt. Collarless, high-necked, pull-over sweater; often with fleecy inside and fine-ribbed outside. Used by athletes.

20th Century Sweat Shirt

twin s. One of pair of sweaters worn together, usually of matching color, one a pull-over, the other a cardigan.

sweater blouse. Short, blouse-like sweater, often worn as substitute for other type of blouse. See SWEATERS.

sweat shirt. Loose, pull-over sports sweater. See SWEATERS.

Swedish (swēd'ĭsh; *sweed* ish). Characteristic of Swedish costume. Consists of full skirt, plain or banded; fur jacket;

Swedish lace, full-sleeved, white chemisette; wide belt with shoulder-straps, or low, laced bodice; striped or printed, hand-woven apron; kerchief pinned flat; peaked cap with balls on tabs, or tight, embroidered bonnet peaked over forehead.

Swedish lace. Simple torchon lace. See LACES.

sweeper. Ruffle sewn under edge of a long skirt to protect it when it touches the floor. Same as DUST RUFFLE.

swell. 1. Slang term meaning first-rate; excellent; grand. **2.** Stylish; smartly gowned; ultra-fashionable. Not good usage.

swim suit. Plain, close-fitting, one- or two-piece garment. Worn for active swimming.

swing skirt. Circular or gored skirt, cut so as to give a swinging motion when the wearer walks. See SKIRTS.

Swiss. 1. Characteristic of costumes worn in Switzerland, dating from about the 17th century, when laws limiting decoration of dress were relaxed. Costumes vary in different valleys and cantons. Consists, for women, chiefly of full skirt, either long or short; chemisette, with neckline gathered under collar, and full, elbow-length sleeves; bright-colored or figured apron; wide, starched or wired headdress; sleeveless, black velvet bodice decorated with silver rosettes and chains hanging under arms in loops from back to front. Men's dress usually includes knee breeches; full-sleeved, white linen shirt; short jacket or vest; stocking cap or broad-brimmed hat; buckled shoes or sabots. Costume illustrated is from Bern. **2.** Fine, crisp cotton fabric; plain, dotted, or figured; white or colored. Design made by chemical application, swivel, or lappet weaving. Originated in Switzerland. Used for dresses, blouses, curtains, etc.

Swiss Costume

Swiss cambric (kăm'brĭk; *came* brick). Muslin or lawn; used for frills, flounces, etc.

Swiss darning. Darning of thin places on right side of material with stitches like those of fabric.

Swiss embroidery. Eyelet embroidery. Same as MADEIRA. See EMBROIDERIES.

Swiss rib. Knit fabric having two wales, or ridges, alternating on right and wrong sides.

switch. Hair worn to supplement one's own hair for certain styles of coiffure. Consists of separate tress, usually of real hair, secured at one end. Available in many natural hair shades, in single or three-stem styles.

swivel dot. Type of cushion dot. See DOTS. See SWIVEL under WEAVES.

swivel weave (swĭv'l; *swiv* el). Weave having small, woven figures. See WEAVES.

sword-edge-stitch (sôrd ĕj; sord edge). Twisted cross-stitch with elongated stem. See STITCHES.

synthetic (sĭn-thĕt'ĭk; sin *thet* ic). Fabric or other material made by synthesis or the combining of various substances. Usually used as alternate or substitute for genuine or natural material. Term frequently applied to man-made substances and fibers, as rayons, plastics, etc.

syrma (sẽr'ma; *ser* ma). Trailing robe worn by Greek actors in ancient times.

T

tab. Small flap or lappet, sometimes a loop, attached at one side. Used as part of a fastening, as decoration, etc.

tabard (tăb'ẽrd; *tab* erd). **1.** Formerly, short outer jacket. See JACKETS. **2.** Mantle or cloak formerly worn by knights. See COATS.

tabaret (tăb'a-rĕt; *tab* a ret). Strong, silk upholstery fabric with satin stripes.

tabby. Any of several plain-woven fabrics, especially a watered taffeta; also, having a watered appearance; also, to water by calendering.

tabi (tä'bĭ; *tah* bi). Foot covering, similar to a sock, having a thick, slightly stiffened sole and separate stall for large toe. Usually in white cotton. Worn by Japanese.

Japanese Tabis

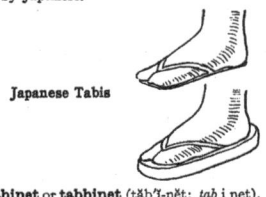

tabinet or **tabbinet** (tăb'ĭ-nĕt; *tab* i net). Poplin fabric, sometimes having watered surface, made chiefly in Ireland; also, dress of this fabric.

tablier (F. tä-blē-ā; ta blee ay). Apron-like part of a dress.

taboret (tăb'ô-rĕt; *tab* o ret) or **tabouret** (tăb'ŏŏ-rĕt; *tab* oo ret). Embroidery frame. See TAMBOUR.

tack. To baste or make quick, sometimes temporary, stitch or stitches; also, a stitch so made.

tacking. Quick sewing, usually with long stitches, done so as not to be conspicuous on right side.

tacky. Colloquial term meaning dowdy, neglected, or shabby in appearance.

taenia (tē'nĭ-a; *tee* ni a). Headband or fillet worn by ancient Greeks.

TAFFETAS

taffeta (tăf'ĕ-ta; *taff* e ta). **1.** Smooth, glossy, silk fabric, in plain weave, alike on both sides; fine, but with considerable body. Formerly, a rich, strong, somewhat stiff fabric; now, pliable and lustrous and made of other fibers than silk. Plain, figured, striped, plaid, or changeable. First used in the 16th century. Used for dresses, blouses, suits, etc. **2.** Dainty; delicate; as, a taffeta complexion or skin.

changeable t. Taffeta having changing color effect; usually made by weaving together yarn-dyed warp and filling of different colors.

chiffon t. Light-weight taffeta of good quality. Soft and lustrous in finish. Used for evening gowns, dresses, suits, blouses.

moiré or **watered t.** Taffeta that has been calendered to give it a watered appearance, the effect changing as the light falls on it.

rayon t. Taffeta made with rayon filling.

wool t. Woolen fabric in close, smooth weave. Used for dresses, skirts, suits.

taffeta weave. Simplest weave, in which filling and warp yarns form even surface. Same as PLAIN WEAVE. See WEAVES.

tag. 1. Rag, tatter, or loose end. Originally, one of the flaps, square or pointed, made by slashing edge or skirt of a garment. **2.** Pendant tassel or strip used as ornament, often bearing a jewel. **3.** Loop for hanging up garment or pulling on boot. **4.** Binding, tube, or point of metal used to stiffen lace or string, to facilitate passing it through eyelet or other opening.

tagal straw (tä-gäl'; tah *gahl*). Straw from Manila hemp. See STRAWS.

tail coat. Man's full-dress coat. Same as SWALLOW-TAILED COAT. See COATS.

taille (tăl or F. tī; tail or tie). **1.** Form or figure; shape of bust. **2.** Waist or bodice; also, its cut or fit.

tailleur (F. tī-yẽr; tie yer). Tailor-made suit or dress. French word for tailor.

tailor (tā'lẽr; *tay* lor). **1.** One who cuts and makes various tailored types of men's and women's clothing, principally, coats, suits, and simple dresses. **2.** To cut or make according to tailor's craft.

tailored. Having simple, trim, fitted lines obtained by careful cutting, seaming, and pressing. Distinguished from DRESSMAKER styling. — **man-t.** Made by a man tailor or characterized by masculine details such as a tailor gives a man's suit.

tailored bow. Flat bow having no wrinkles. See BOWS.

tailored fell seam. Machine-stitched,

tailoring   152   **tasse**

tailored seam, with both raw edges concealed. See SEAMS.
tailoring. Occupation of a tailor; his work or workmanship.
tailoring shears. Large, steel shears. See SHEARS.
tailor-made. Made or as if made by a tailor, with simplicity of cut and trim, careful finishing.
tailors' chalk. Soapstone used by tailors and dressmakers for marking lines on cloth in fitting or altering.
tailor's knot. Knot at the end of a needleful of thread. Used by all persons who sew by hand. See KNOTS.
tailor's tacks. Basting-stitches made through two thicknesses of cloth and then cut apart. See STITCHES.
tailor's twist. Strong silk thread. Same as BUTTONHOLE TWIST. See THREADS.
tails. Colloquial term for swallow-tailed coat, as used by man for full evening dress; also, full dress itself.
taj (täj; tahj). Tall, conical cap. See CAPS.
talar (tā′lẽr; tay lar). Ankle-length robe. From Latin word *talus*, meaning ankle.
talaria (tȧ-lā′rĭ-ȧ; ta *lay* ri a). Winged shoes or sandals. See SHOES.
talaric (tȧ-lăr′ĭk; ta *la* rick). Of the ankles or reaching to the ankles; as, a talaric gown.
talisman (tăl′ĭs-mȧn; *tal* iss man). Charm or amulet; object, often worn on person, supposed to keep wearer from harm and to work wonders.
talma (tăl′mȧ; *tal* ma). Long cape or cloak. See CAPES.
Talon (tăl′ŏn; *tal* un). Trade name for the first well-known slide fastener. See FASTENERS.
tam. Short for TAM-O'-SHANTER. See CAPS. See HATS.
tambour (tăm′bŏŏr; *tam* boor). Original two-piece embroidery frame, usually circular, one part fitting inside the other, holding cloth stretched over the smaller like the parchment of a drum. French word meaning drum.
tambour lace. Lace made by embroidering pattern on net ground. See LACES.
tambour-stitch. Loop stitch made with crochet needle. See STITCHES.
tambour work. Embroidery done on a frame with a crochet needle. See EMBROIDERIES.
tamein (tȧ-mīn′; tah *mine*). Draped garment, similar to Indian sari, worn by Burmese women.
tamis (tăm′ĭs; *tam* iss). Kind of woolen cloth, used for straining foods. Also called *tammy*.
tamise (tăm′ĭs or tȧ-mēz′; *tam* iss or ta *meez*). Trade name for thin woolen fabric.
tammy. 1. Cloth of wool or mixed yarn, sometimes glazed. Used for dresses, linings, etc. 2. Same as TAMIS.
tam-o'-shanter (tăm ō shăn′tẽr; tam o *shan* ter). 1. Scottish cap with tight headband and full, flat top. See CAPS. 2. Development of the original tam-o'-shanter into hat of fabric draped over a crown. See HATS.
Tamsui hat (täm′sŏō-ĭ; *tahm* soo i). Straw hat similar to Panama. See HATS.

tan. 1. Yellow-orange shade, usually neutral in tone. 2. Brownish skin tone resulting from exposure to sun. 3. To treat hides or skins with a tanning agent, often an oak bark called *tannin*, converting them into leather. From Old French word meaning oak or oak bark.
tangerine (tăn′jȧ-rēn or tăn-jȧ-rēn′; *tan* je reen or tan je *reen*). Brilliant yellowish-red color.
tanjib (tŭn-jēb′; tun *jeeb*). Kind of fine muslin made in India.
tap. Half or part of sole for a shoe.
tapa cloth (tä′pä; *tah* pah). Fabric made of steeped and beaten bark of a kind of mulberry tree. Used in Pacific islands. Woven into mats and worn as garments.
tapalo (tä′pä-lō; *tah* pah lo). Scarf of coarse cloth; shawl worn in Spanish American countries.

TAPES

tape. 1. Narrow strip of firmly woven cotton, linen, silk, rayon, etc. 2. In fur trade, to increase the size of a pelt by inserting strips of leather.
  hook-and-eye t. Firm tape to which hooks and eyes are riveted. Used for long substantial closings, as in tight linings and brassières.
  inkle. Broad linen tape. In colonial days, woolen tape used as braid trimming, sewed on in designs.
  lingerie t. Narrow, flat strip of woven fabric run through the eyelets or hems of lingerie. Used as a ribbon substitute to adjust and fasten the garment.
  quality. Coarse tape for strings or bindings, used in 18th century.
  seam t. Seaming ribbon about ½ inch wide; used for finishing the top of hems, sleeve edges, etc.
  snap-fastener t. Firmly woven tape to which snap fasteners are securely anchored.
  twilled t. Sturdy cotton or linen tape, woven in herringbone twill. Used for finishing sturdy garments; for loops on towels, tie strings on aprons, etc.
  weighted t. Closely woven cotton tape to which weights are attached. Used to hold lower edges of garments in place. Made in shot weight type, having shot held within the strip; or in flat weight type, having metal disks attached at intervals of about ½ inch.

tape measure (mĕzh′ẽr; *mezh* er). Tape, usually 60 inches long and from ⅜ to ½ inch wide, divided into inches, half inches, quarter inches, and eighth inches. Used for taking body measurements, for measuring fabric, etc.
tapestry (tăp′ĕs-trĭ; *tap* ess tri). Fabric with pattern woven in by means of colored weft threads. Formerly used extensively as wall hangings. Loosely, any wall hanging. Needle tapestry not a true tapestry, but an embroidery.
tapestry darning-stitch. Over-and-over stitch so placed on surface of fabric as to resemble darned work. See STITCHES.
tapestry needle. Blunt needle with large eye. Used for canvas embroidery. See NEEDLES.
tapestry-stitch. Short upright stitch used in canvas work. See STITCHES.
tape work. Fancy work in which rosettes made with tape are joined with crochet or tatting. Used in making antimacassar sets, mats, etc.
tapis (tä′pēs; *tah* peece). Wide sash or girdle of Philippine women. See SASHES.
tapisserie (F. tȧ-pēs-rē; ta peece ree). French word for tapestry. Also, upholstery or drapery fabric similar to tapestry.
tapisserie d'Auxerre (F. dō-zĕr; doe zare). Embroidery of Berlin wool worked on net in satin-stitch. See EMBROIDERIES.
tap shoe. Shoe with a special toe, used in tap dancing. See SHOES.
tarboosh (tär-bŏŏsh′; tar *boosh*). Brimless felt cap worn by Moslems. See CAPS.
tarfe (tärf; tarf). Obsolete word for brim of hat.
target (tär′gĕt; *tar* get). 1. Obsolete word for small shield or buckler, usually round. 2. Metal ornament, sometimes jeweled, resembling shield. 3. Scottish term for pendant or tassel.
tarlatan or **tarletan** (tär′lȧ-tȧn; *tar* la tan). Thin, open-mesh, transparent muslin, slightly stiffened. Used for stiffening in garments, fancy-dress costumes, Christmas stockings, etc.
tarmosined (tär′mō-sīnd; *tar* mo sind). Obsolete word descriptive of garment made so that it could be worn with either side out.
tarpaulin (tär-pô′lĭn; tar *paw* lin). 1. Cloth, usually canvas, covered with tar or other waterproof material. Used as covering from weather. 2. Apparel made of or covered with tarpaulin, especially a sailor's storm hat. See HATS.
tars or **tarse** (tärs; tarce). Obsolete silk material, thought to be from Tartary.
tartan (tär′tȧn; *tar* tan). Originally, Scotch twilled woolen or worsted plaid cloth, woven in distinctive designs and colors of a Highland clan, and worn only by members of that clan who bear the name of the chief or are related by blood. Relationship may be on the maternal side; but, if the relationship is remote, one is not privileged to wear the tartan, the symbol of the clan. Used for the shawl draped over the shoulders and for the kilt. Now widely used for skirts, suits, coats, shirts. Also, the pattern itself.
tartan velvet. Woven or printed plaid velvet. See VELVETS.
tartarine (tär′tȧ-rĭn; *tar* ta rin). Ancient rich silk fabrics made, supposedly, by the Tartars. Also called *tartarinus*.
Tartar sable. Asiatic mink fur. Same as KOLINSKY. See FURS.
tash (täsh; tahsh) or **tass** (täs; tahss). Fabric of East Indies; made of silk and gold or silver thread.
tasse (tȧs; tass) or **tasset** (tăs′ĕt; *tass* et). One of series of overlapping plates that form a short protective skirt in medieval armor.

fāte, făt, dănce, ärt   mē, mĕt, hẽr, thêre   rīde, rĭd   nōte, nŏt, côrn, fŏŏd, fōōt   cūte, cŭt, cūré   now   fin(g)ger   villa(ȧ)   señor   pleas(zh)ure

tassel (tăs'l; *tass* el). Ornament with threads or cords of silk, wool, rayon, or other fiber hanging in a loose fringe. Usually headed with covered button or mold.
tassel-stitch. Embroidery stitch used to form fringe. See STITCHES.
taste. 1. Individual preference and knowledge as they affect one's ability to discern and apply to one's dress, home, or manner of living that which is harmonious and appropriate. 2. Term used in U. S. for thin, narrow, silk ribbon.
tatting. Knotted lace made by hand with single thread and small shuttle. See LACES
tatting cotton. Mercerized cotton used in tatting. See THREADS.
Taunton (tän'tŭn; *tahn* tun). Variety of broadcloth of specific weight prescribed by law; formerly made at Taunton, England.
taupe (F. tōp; tope). Dark gray; the color of mole fur. French word for mole.
tawdry (tô'drĭ; *taw* dri). 1. Cheap and showy in dress or appearance; without taste. 2. Piece of cheap, gaudy finery or jewelry. Term originally applied to articles bought at a fair held on Saint Audrey's day, and derived from name of saint.
tawdry lace. Obsolete name for type of lace work or braid worn at neck as a tie.
tawing. Kind of mineral tanning in which skins are prepared with alum and other agents.
taxi wrap. Redingote type of coat worn to protect dresses when riding in taxis. See WRAPS.
T cloth. Type of plain cotton cloth marked with T. Made in England and largely sold in Asia.
tea gown. Gown, usually long and of fragile material, in varying styles; glorified boudoir gown. Worn at home, for afternoon tea.
tea rose. Dainty yellowish-pink color, much used for underthings.
teasel (tē'zl; *tee* zl). 1. Bur-like head of the plant commonly called fuller's teasel. Also applied to any contrivance used as substitute. 2. To raise nap on woolen fabric by use of teasel.
teaseling. Process of raising nap on woolen fabric by means of teasels or substitute contrivance. Vegetable teasels considered most satisfactory because they do not break fibers.
teck. Necktie made up in imitation of four-in-hand.
teddy. Abbreviated undergarment that combines chemise and drawers in one, with loose-fitting legs or with strap crotch. Also called *envelope chemise.*
tegua (tā'gwä; *tay* gwah). Buckskin sandal. See SHOES.
temiak (těm-yăk'; tem *yak*). Eskimo jacket or coat. See JACKETS.
temple. Medieval ornament for side of head, often of needlework or jewelry.
tender wool. Wool too weak for combing. See WOOL.
Teneriffe lace (těn-ẽr-ĭf'; ten er *if*). Lace with wheel designs joined together to make doilies, runners, etc. See LACES.

ten-gallon hat. Large, broad-brimmed hat. Popular with men in western and southwestern U.S.A.; also in Mexico and South America. See HATS.
tennis costume. Costume for wear when playing tennis. See SPORTS CLOTHES.
tennis shoe. Usually, canvas shoe with rubber sole. See SHOES.
tensile strength (těn'sĭl; *ten* sil). Breaking strength of a thread or of piece of fabric. Force required to break thread or to pull fabric apart, pulling against either warp or filling threads, is recorded on an instrument in terms of pounds.
tensile top. Dress top or bodice made of fabric woven with Lastex so that it hugs the figure.
tension (těn'shŭn; *ten* shun). Device on sewing machine or loom to regulate tightness, or pull, of thread or yarn.
tenter. Frame with tenterhooks for fastening cloth so that it may be stretched and dried in shape.
tenterhook. Sharp-pointed, hooked nail by which cloth is fastened to tenter.
tentering. Process of stretching fabric after other finishing processes in manufacture. Done on special machine.
tent-stitch. 1. Short outline-stitch used in embroidery. 2. Slanting stitch used in canvas work. See STITCHES.
tenue (F. tē-nü; tuh noo). French term meaning appearance, style of dress, bearing, or manner.
terra-cotta. Varying color of hard-baked clay, usually reddish orange.
terry or **terry cloth.** Fabric woven with raised loop that forms uncut pile. Made of cotton, linen, wool, rayon, or silk, in stripes, checks, plaids, or brocaded effects, as well as in solid colors. In cotton or linen, called *Turkish toweling*. Used chiefly for towels, draperies, bathrobes, beach robes and coats.
tertiary color (tẽr'shĭ-ẽr-ĭ; *ter* shi air i). Color obtained by mixing two secondary colors. See COLOR.
tester. Obsolete word for head-piece of helmet.
tete (tăt; tate). Obsolete word for a woman's coiffure, with hair dressed high and ornamented. From *tête*, French word for head.
tête-de-mouton (F. tăt dē mōō-tôn; tate de moo tonh). 17th century coiffure, with hair arranged close to head in short, thick curls. French for sheep's head, which it resembles.
textile (těks'tĭl; *tex* til). Fabric manufactured by the process of weaving from silk, cotton, linen, wool, synthetic, or other fibers. Also, the material for weaving; as, textile fibers.
texture (těks'tūr; *tex* ture). Surface quality of cloth or manner of weaving.
texturity (těks-tūr'ĭ-tĭ; tex *ture* i ti). Term identifying preshrunk wool, worsted, and mixed fabrics that carry money-back guarantee if shrinkage is greater than 2 per cent. Labeled by Texturity Guild, non-profit corporation.
theatrical gauze (thē-ăt'rĭ-kăl gôz; thee *at* ri cal gawz). Open, light-weight linen fabric in plain weave, stiffened with sizing. Usually inexpensive and avail-

able in wide range of colors. Used for needlework, fancy-dress costumes, draperies. Originally used for stage scenery.
therese (tē-rēs'; te *reece*). Large hood made over frame. See HOODS.
thickset. Cotton material similar to velveteen, principally used in men's working clothes.
thigh boot. Boot extending over thigh. See BOOTS.
thimble. Cap or covering used to protect end of finger in sewing. Usually worn on second finger of right hand. Invented in Holland and introduced into England in 17th century. Most common thimbles are metal, with outer surface pitted so as to keep needle from slipping. Originally called *thumb-bell* because first worn on the thumb. Different countries and different trades have their favorite types of thimble. Many are made of leather, some to fit the palm of the hand; others are leather strips used on two or more fingers.
thimble finger. Second finger on right hand.
thistle (thĭs'l; *thiss* l). Reddish-violet color.
thong. Strip or cord of leather or rawhide. Used for fastening or as a whip.
thorn. Stitch in crescent or point shape, used in needle-point lace. See PIN WORK.
thorn-stitch. Embroidery stitch resembling feather-stitch or fern-stitch. See STITCHES.

THREADS

thread (thrĕd; thred). 1. Slender cord of varying degrees of fineness, produced by twisting together two or more filaments spun from cotton, flax, silk, or other fiber. Used in the construction of garments, for sewing, stitching, embroidering, etc. 2. Any thread-like filament; as, thread of gold. 3. To pass thread through eye, as of needle. 4. To connect by passing thread through; as, to thread beads. 5. Made from or giving appearance of thread; as, thread stockings.
basting cotton (băst'ĭng; *baist* ing). Cotton thread, often glazed, used for basting. Stiffer and not so strong as sewing cotton.
buttonhole twist. Durable, closely twisted thread, usually silk. Used for making buttonholes and eyelets.
candlewicking. Thick, soft, loosely twisted cotton thread of the type used for candle wicks. Used in needlework to make candlewick embroidery.
cannetille (F. kăn-tē; can tee). Gold or silver metal thread twisted spirally. Used in embroidery.
carpet thread. Strong, durable thread, usually waxed. Used for sewing canvas, burlap, and other strong fabrics, as well as carpet, and for sewing on buttons.
cotton. Spool of cotton thread, used for sewing. In some parts of the U.S.A., a spool of cotton is called a *reel of thread*, as in Great Britain.
crochet cotton (krō-shā'; cro *shay*). Strong, glossy, highly twisted, mercer-

threads (continued) ized cotton thread, made in many sizes and colors. Used in crochet work. Also used for embroidery and for decorative machine stitching.

Dacca s. (dăk'ə; *dack* a). Untwisted skein silk for use in embroidery. So called because originated in Dacca, India.

darning cotton. Cotton thread, plain or mercerized, usually of several strands, very loosely twisted; made in black, white, and many colors. Used for mending hose.

elastic sewing t. Covered elastic thread used on bobbin of sewing machine for shirring, for elasticity in seams and stitching, for trimming.

embroidery cotton. Cotton thread of varying number of strands, loosely twisted; available in many colors. Used for decorative needlework. Some known by initials or name of manufacturer, as D. M. C. or C·B or Clark's O. N. T.

embroidery floss or **silk.** Soft, glossy, untwisted silk fibers, raveled or broken off in reeling. Used for embroidery. Also called *floss silk*.

etching silk. Twisted silk thread used in embroidery for feather-stitching, outline work, etc.

filo floss or **silk** (fī'lō; *fy* lo). Fine, soft embroidery thread.

filoselle (fĭl-ə-zĕl'; fill o *zell*). Silk thread, less expensive than floss because spun from coarser material; less glossy, but easier to keep smooth in working. Much used for embroidery and fancy work; also used for textiles.

flourishing t. (flẽr'ĭsh-ĭng; *fler* ish ing). Shiny linen thread used for mending heavy linens and for fancy needlework.

glazed t. Thread with a sizing applied in the finishing. Used for basting and stitches that are to be removed. Sometimes called *starched thread*.

lame (lȧm or F. lȧm; lame or lahm). Gold or silver thread, as used with silk for making braids, metal cloth, etc.

machine twist. Silk thread for use in sewing machine.

marking cotton. Fast-color cotton thread used for marking garments, linens, etc.; also for basting and for making tailor's tacks.

mercerized cotton t. (mẽr'sẽr-īzd; *mer* ser ized). Cotton thread of from two to six strands, with soft, glossy finish. Put up on spools and in skeins in all colors for sewing and embroidery.

Mercerized Sewing. Trade name for J. & P. Coats and Clark's O. N. T. Boilfast mercerized cotton thread, a three-cord thread made in a wide range of colors.

nun's cotton. Fine, white, cotton thread. Used in embroidery.

O. N. T. Trade name, abbreviation of "our new thread," made by the Clark Company. First thread having fuzz burned off by gas in finishing process.

packthread. Strong, coarse thread or twine used for sewing larger packs wrapped in canvas or other material.

padding cotton. Cotton thread of several strands, made in many colors. Used for padding in embroidery.

passing. Smooth, flattened thread made by twisting strands of gold or silver around a strand of silk. Used in embroidery.

perle or **pearl cotton.** Mercerized cotton thread, made in a variety of sizes and colors. Used for needlework, crochet, and knitting. Generally spelled *pearl* in U.S.A.

purse silk (pẽrs; perce). Thick, twisted, silk thread used originally in making crocheted purses, but also for embroidery, knitting, etc.

rope silk. Heavy silk thread formed by many strands of silk spun into threads and twisted together. Used for embroidery.

sewing cotton. Twisted cotton thread, used in varying sizes for ordinary sewing.

sewing silk. Finely twisted silk thread. Used in sewing silk, woolen, and some rayon fabrics.

silkaline t. High-luster, softly twisted, cotton thread made to imitate silk. Used for inexpensive needlework, tacking cotton comfortables, etc.

six-cord cotton. Strong thread with three sets of two strands each, twisted together in smooth, strong, even cord. Made in black and white in many sizes, the finer sizes having the higher size numbers. Used for hand and machine sewing.

stranding t. Tailor's gimp, or a thread, usually linen, twisted and waxed, used to strengthen edge of tailored buttonhole before it is worked.

tailor's twist. Strong kind of silk thread used in tailoring.

tatting cotton. Fine, strong, mercerized cotton thread of crochet thread type used in tatting.

waxed end or **wax end.** Stout thread made of several waxed filaments. Used in sewing leather through prepared holes.

thread-and-needle shop. Retail shop selling sewing and needlework accessories. So called in Great Britain.

thread count or **fabric count.** Number of threads, or picks, per inch of fabric.

threaded back-stitch. Stitch giving looped or braided appearance. Same as PEKINESE-STITCH. See STITCHES.

thread lace. Lace of linen thread. See LACES.

Threadneedle Street. Street in the heart of London, England, where formerly there were many thread-and-needle shops.

thread shank. Shank made by winding thread tightly around the threads used to sew on a button with holes, in order to hold button away from material and allow room to button the garment. Often called *stem*.

thread silk. Silk filaments joined to form continuous strand. Same as REELED SILK. See SILK.

three-dimensional glove. Same as trade-marked "Free-Finger" glove. So called because of inserted "side-wall" piece running around finger from side to side. See FREE-FINGER under GLOVES.

three-piece. Term applied to costume consisting of three separate parts or pieces, as skirt, jacket, and topcoat.

three-quarter length. As applied to a sleeve, length coming slightly nearer the wrist than the elbow. As applied to a coat, length shorter than dress by about one quarter of its length. See LENGTHS.

three-quarter sleeve. Sleeve covering three quarters of arm from the shoulder. See SLEEVES.

three-quarter vamp. Vamp covering three quarters of foot. See VAMPS.

three-sided stitch. Drawn-fabric stitch giving open-work effect in bands of adjoining triangles. See STITCHES.

throat. As applied to a shoe, the point at the instep in front where the vamp is stitched to the rest of the upper.

throatlet. Small, slender neck-piece, as boa or tippet.

throw. 1. Light-weight piece of fabric, as a scarf or shawl, to be thrown across shoulders. 2. Light-weight shawl or blanket. 3. To twist filaments into thread, especially as preparation for weaving.

thrown silk (thrōn; throne). Reeled silk made into thread. See SILK.

thrum. 1. Extremity of a weaver's warp, often 9 inches long, which can not be woven. 2. Cap knitted of such an end. See CAPS.

tiara (tī-ā'rȧ; tie *ay* ra). 1. Crown-like ornament for the head. Worn by women with formal dress. 2. High headdress worn by ancient Persians. 3. Triple crown worn by the pope. 4. Headdress of the Jewish high priest.

Tiara

tiarella (tē-ə-rĕl'ə; tee a *rell* a). Small tiara.

Tibet cloth (tĭ-bĕt'; ti *bet*). Fabric woven from goat's hair. Also, fine woolen material, used for dresses and wraps.

ticking. Strong, firm, cotton cloth in twill weave, with yarn-dyed stripes in various colors running lengthwise on white or colored ground. Sometimes herringbone twill in stripes. Closely woven ticking called *feather-proof* and used for pillow and mattress coverings. When made with printed design, as of floral pattern in striped effect, called *art ticking*.

ticking work. Bright-colored embroidery on ticking ground. See EMBROIDERIES.

ticklenburg (tĭk'lĕn-bẽrg; *tick* len berg). Coarse, mixed linen cloth. Name derived from Tecklenburg, Germany.

tidy. 1. Doily or piece of needlework used on upholstery. 2. Arranged in orderly fashion.

tie. 1. To fasten together by means of string, cord, ribbon, band, or the like. Also, to make a bow or knot in, as hair-ribbon. 2. Anything to be tied when worn, as necktie or shoe-lace. 3. Low, laced shoe. See SHOES. 4. Joining thread in needle-point lace. See BAR.

tie-about. Dress or skirt with overlapping front that ties at the waistline on each side.

tie-back skirt. Skirt drawn and tied back at hip line. See SKIRTS.

tie-dyeing or **tieing-and-dyeing.** Dyeing after portions of fabric have been tightly tied so that they will not take dye. See DYEING.

tie periwig (pĕr′ĭ-wĭg; *pare* i wig). Wig tied with ribbon at back. Same as TIE-WIG. See WIGS.

tie pin. Pin worn on necktie. See PINS.

tier (tēr; teer). One of a series of ruffles, flounces, or bands.

tier (tī′ēr; *ty* er). Term used locally in U. S. for child's pinafore, tied by means of tape or cord.

tiered skirt (tērd; teerd). Skirt having two or more tiers or flounces or tunics. See SKIRTS.

tie silk. Silk fabric, varying in weave and texture, that is resilient, pliable, and firm in tying and knotting. Skein-dyed and not fast color; therefore not practical for all types of apparel. Used principally for men's ties and accessories. Certain types, such as twill or foulard, also used for women's blouses and various accessories, according to the fashion.

tie-stitch. Short stitch with long ends tied in a knot. See STITCHES.

tiewig. Wig tied with a ribbon at back. See WIGS.

tiffany (tĭf′ȧ-nĭ; *tiff* a ni). 1. Flimsy, gauze-like fabric; originally of thin silk, now usually of cotton. 2. In colloquial usage, of fine quality; from Tiffany, an American jeweler.

tights. Garment worn skintight, usually covering hips and legs, sometimes entire body. Worn especially by stage performers. Formerly, close-fitting breeches.

tile red. Bright red-orange color, slightly grayed.

tilleul (F. tē-yĕl; tee yul). Yellowish green, the color of the lime. French word for linden or lime tree.

tillot (tĭl′ŭt; *till* ot). Kind of cloth used for wrapping fabric.

tilter. Petticoat bustle. See BUSTLES.

tilting helmet. Very strong, large helmet, worn for tilting in tournaments of Middle Ages.

timber wolf. Fur of large gray wolf of northern U. S. and Canada. See FURS.

tincture (tĭngk′tūr; *tink* ture). To stain, tinge, or dye. Also, slight cast or coloring.

tinge (tĭnj; tinj). Slight cast or coloring; also, to give color to or modify the tone of.

tinsel (tĭn′sĕl; *tin* sel). 1. Fabric interwoven with bright metallic threads, which produce a glittering surface. Also called *tinsel cloth* or *satin*. 2. Thin, glittering strips of metal. Used to ornament articles of dress and for other decorative purposes. 3. Cheap; glittering; tawdry.

tinsel embroidery. Outline embroidery worked with tinsel on thin fabric. See EMBROIDERIES.

tint. 1. Light tone of any color — one approaching white on the scale; contrasted with SHADE. 2. To color slightly, as a garment or fabric, by dyeing or other means.

tip. 1. To tilt, or a tilted position. 2. End or extremity of anything pointed or rounded, such as piece covering the toe of a shoe, separate from the vamp; upper part of the crown of a hat; end of a feather or tail of fur; etc. 3. Hint, or bit of private information. 4. In fur trade, to stain ends of hair so as to give different or improved appearance. See TIPPED under FURS.

tippet (tĭp′ĕt; *tip* et). 1. Scarf-like cape. See CAPES. 2. Shoulder scarf worn by ecclesiastics. 3. Formerly, long pendant part or accessory of dress, as on hood or cape.

tissue (tĭsh′ū; *tish* you). 1. Sheer, lightweight, open-weave fabric; as, tissue gingham; gold or silver tissue; gauze. Also, gauze-like or sheer; also, to weave or interweave loosely. 2. Ribbon, girdle, or band used to hold helmet.

tissue gingham (gĭng′ȧm; *ging* am). Thin gingham. See GINGHAMS.

tissue paper. Thin, almost transparent paper, much used for patterns and for packing and wrapping delicate articles, gifts, etc. So named because originally used between layers of metallic tissue fabrics to prevent tarnishing. Comes in white, black, and colors. Black used around metal fabric to keep it from tarnishing, and blue to prevent light fabrics from turning yellow.

Titian or **titian** (tĭsh′ȧn; *tish* an). Red or reddish-brown color much used by the painter Titian; usually applied to hair; as, Titian blond.

Titian blond or **blonde.** Person having reddish hair, blue-gray or brown eyes, and medium complexion. See BLOND.

titivate or **tittivate** (tĭt′ĭ-vāt; *tit* i vate). To dress or spruce up. Also, to put on decorative touches.

tobe. Piece of cotton cloth, from 12 to 15 feet long and of various colors, worn as outer garment by natives of Africa.

Tobé. Name of Tobé Toller Davis, one of the first women to do styling in a store. Widely known for her work in merchandising, styling, store promotions, etc. Used in the expressions "Tobé-wise store," "a Tobé formula."

tobine (tō′bĭn; *toe* bin). Heavy silk fabric resembling lustring.

toboggan cap (tȧ-bŏg′ȧn; *to bog* an). Long, knitted cap, worn by men, women, and children when tobogganing. See CAPS.

toe boxing. Stiffened material used to preserve shape of toe of shoe.

toe cap. Piece of leather used to reinforce and decorate toe of shoe.

toe plate. Metal piece attached to sole of shoe at toe, as protection against wear.

toga (tō′gȧ; *toe* ga). Loose Roman mantle of white woolen, originally small and semi-circular; later, an elliptical shape approximately 18½ feet long and 7 feet wide. Doubled lengthwise and draped around body so as to hang in broad, graceful folds, one weighted end being thrown back over left shoulder or across forearm. Originally worn by both men and women; later, only by men.

Roman Toga

toga candida (kăn′dĭ-dȧ; *can* di da). White toga of candidates for office; sometimes whitened with chalk.

toga palmata (păl-mā′tȧ; pal *may* ta). Toga embroidered with palm-branch design; worn for special ceremonies.

toga picta (pĭk′tȧ; *pick* ta). Toga of purple cloth, embroidered in gold; usually reserved for victorious emperors and generals.

toga praetexta (prē-tĕks′tȧ; pre *tex* ta). Toga bordered with purple; worn by young boys, magistrates, priests, high officials in free towns and colonies.

toga pulla or **sordida** (pŭl′ȧ or sôr′dĭ-dȧ; *pul* a or *sor* di da). Mourning toga, dark gray, brown, or black; used also by accused persons and lower classes.

toga pura (pū′rȧ; *pew* ra). Plain white toga, without ornamental border.

toga virilis (vĭ-rī′lĭs; vi *rye* liss). Common toga of plain white, regarded as the manly toga; usually assumed by boys after fourteenth year.

toggle. 1. Rod-shaped button, attached in the middle. 2. To fix or fasten, as with a toggle.

togs. Colloquial expression for clothes, particularly those which, with their accessories, are used for special purpose; as, skating togs.

toile (F. twäl; twahl). 1. French word for cloth; specifically, sheer linen fabric. 2. Fine cretonne with scenic designs printed in one color. See TOILE DE JOUY. 3. Muslin copy of a design, often purchased by firms who wish to copy but not to import original models. Sometimes made by dressmakers to show customers lines in garments that they are prepared to copy.

toilé (F. twä-lā; twah lay). Flower, pattern, or ornament in lace.

toile cirée (F. twäl sē-rā; twahl see ray). French word for oilcloth.

toile colbert (F. kŏl-bĕr; col bare). French word for basket cloth.

---

fāte, făt, dånce, ärt, mē, mĕt, hêr, thêre ride, rĭd nōte, nŏt, côrn, fōōd, fŏŏt, cūte, cŭt, cûre now fin(ŋ)ger villa(ȧ) señor pleas(zh)ure

toile de Jouy (F. də zhōō-ē; de zboo ee). French term for copy of 18th century French print. See JOUY PRINT under PRINTS.

toile de religieuse (F. rē-lē-zhyēz; ruh lee zhuz). French word for nun's veiling.

toilet (toi'lĕt; *toy* let). **1.** Act of grooming one's person, usually including bathing, hairdressing, applying cosmetics, dressing. Also called *toilette*. **2.** Formerly, hairdressing; cloth worn over shoulders while dressing the hair.

toilette (F. twä-lĕt; twah let). **1.** Process of grooming one's person; same as TOILET. **2.** Attire, especially fashionable attire; also, particular costume.

toilinet or **toilinette** (toi-li-nĕt'; toy li net). Cloth used for waistcoats, with wool filling and cotton-and-silk warp.

tomato red (tō-mā'tō or tō-mä'tō; toe *may* toe or toe *mah* toe). Medium yellowish-red color of ripe tomato.

ton (F. tôn; tonh). High mode; prevailing fashion or vogue.

tonder lace (tŏn'dĕr; *tonn* der). Danish drawn work on muslin. See LACES.

tone. 1. Color quality or value. See COLOR. **2.** To accent or subdue; as, to tone up or tone down a design or costume.

tongs. Colonial name for overalls of coarse cotton or linen.

tongue (tŭng; tung). **1.** Strip of leather inside the throat of a shoe, usually under lacing or buckle. **2.** Movable pin in a buckle or brooch, serving as part of the fastening device.

tonlet (tŭn'lĕt; *tun* let). One of horizontal bands used to form short skirt in type of late medieval armor.

tool. Instrument, implement, or other device used in effecting work of any kind, or accomplishing given end.

top. 1. Highest point of anything; uppermost edge or extremity. **2.** Attached or fitted part, as band or turned-over part of top boots; upper of shoe. **3.** Bunch of textile fiber, as flax or wool. **4.** Strand of longer wool fibers. See WOOL. **5.** Headdress popular in late 18th century.

topaz (tō'păz; *toe* paz). **1.** Semi-precious stone, characteristically of varying shades of yellow, although occurring in other colors. **2.** Clear brownish color.

top boot. High, solid-legged or laced boot. See BOOTS.

topcoat. Light-weight overcoat. See COATS.

top-dyeing. Dyeing over one or more colors. See DYEING.

topee or **topi** (tō'pē; *toe* pee). Pith hat or helmet. See HATS.

top-handle bag. Handbag having handle at top. See HANDBAGS.

top hat. Man's tall, satin-finished hat. See HATS.

topknot. 1. Ornamental headdress, as one composed of ribbon, lace, feathers, etc. **2.** Hair arrangement in knot on top of head. **3.** Tuft of hair on top of a person's head at the front.

top lift. Last lift applied to shoe heel. See HEEL LIFT.

top-of-the-instep length. Length of dress or other garment that ends 3 or 4 inches above floor. See LENGTHS.

tops. Buttons finished only on face. See BUTTONS.

tops and drops. Obsolete name for pair of earrings consisting of a top part and attached pendant, or drop.

top-sew. To make hem or seam by means of overcasting or other over-and-over stitch.

top-stitched seam. Seam stitched and pressed open, and then stitched from right side on both sides of seam line. See SEAMS.

toque (tōk; toke). **1.** Small, close-fitting, brimless hat. See HATS. **2.** Pad formerly used when dressing the hair in pompadour style.

toquet (F. tō-kā; toe kay). French word for toque or cap.

toquilla (tō-kē'yä or tō-kēl'yä; toe *kee* yah or toe *keel* yah). Flexible fiber used in Panama hats. See STRAWS.

torchon lace (tôr'shŏn or F. tôr-shôn; *tor* shon or tor shonh). Coarse bobbin lace. Real torchon usually made of linen thread; imitations, of cotton. See LACES.

torque (tôrk; tork). Ancient collar, necklace, armlet, or other ornament of twisted wire, usually gold. Worn by barbaric nations of Asia and northern Europe.

torsade (tôr-sād'; tor *sade*). Ornament resembling a twisted rope or cord. Used as hat trim.

tortoise shell (tôr'tĭs; *tor* tiss). **1.** Mottled brown-and-yellow substance covering the shell of some kinds of turtles. Used in making and trimming various accessories. **2.** Having a mottled effect resembling real tortoise shell.

tosca net (tŏs'kȧ; *toss* ca). Firm, durable net. See NETS.

touffe (F. tōōf; toof). French word for tuft, bunch, or cluster. Often applied to hat trimmings of this type.

toupee (tōō-pē'; too *pee*). Small wig or artificial pad or lock of hair. See WIGS.

toupet (F. tōō-pā; too pay). French word for toupee, forelock, or mass of hair. Also, man of fashion.

tournure (F. tōōr-nür; toor noor). **1.** Petticoat bustle. See BUSTLES. **2.** Poise; graceful manner or distinguished carriage.

tout (F. tōō; too). French word meaning all.

tow (tō; toe). Short, irregular flax fibers separated from line fibers by combing. Not as strong or fine as LINE. Used for less expensive table linens, crash, etc.

tow cloth. Fabric woven of yarn spun from tow.

towel (tow'ĕl; *tou* el). **1.** Cloth used for drying or wiping. **2.** Obsolete word for cloth, especially a piece to be wound turban-fashion around head, or as sash around waist.

toweling. Material for towels, especially that woven in long pieces.

toweling embroidery. Any embroidery on toweling fabric. See EMBROIDERIES.

tower. Woman's high headdress worn in 17th and 18th centuries. Same as COMMODE.

town suit. Tailored suit. See SUITS.

town wear. Type of clothing appropriate for town, as street or business clothes.

toy. 1. Trifling ornament or trinket. **2.** Scottish headdress of wool or linen material, extending down over shoulders; worn at one time by elderly women of lower classes.

toyo (tō'yō; *toe* yo). Shiny, rice-paper straw. See STRAWS.

trace. Obsolete word for braid of hair, or trimming braid.

tracer. Toothed wheel, used for marking. Same as TRACING WHEEL.

tracing braid (trās'ĭng; *trace* ing). Decorative braid, usually sewn on in designs. Same as SOUTACHE. See BRAIDS.

tracing cloth or **linen.** Smooth, transparent cotton or linen cloth, one side of which is sized. Used for making tracings of drawings and designs.

tracing thread. Heavy thread or group of threads used in lacemaking to indicate pattern in outline.

tracing wheel. Sharp-toothed wheel of steel attached to a handle. Used for marking off seam or construction lines prior to sewing. Also called *pricking wheel*, *tracer*.

trade. Manufacturers of garments or accessories, wholesalers, retailers, and all who make their living through the creation or marketing of clothing or allied lines.

trade-mark, trademark. Name or symbol by which a product and its source are identified. The right to the name or symbol is generally acquired by priority of use and protected by registration.

trade name or **trade-mark name.** Name given to an article to distinguish it as produced or sold by particular manufacturer or merchant. May be protected in same manner as trade-mark.

traheen (thrà-hēn'; thrah *heen*). Anglo-Irish word for soleless stocking.

trail. Train of garment.

train. Extended part of dress or skirt which trails at back; cut in one with dress, or separate section attached at waistline or shoulders. For weddings and for state or other very formal occasions, usually carried by attendants; for regular formal social occasions, carried in hand or thrown over arm of wearer while dancing, and sometimes while walking.

tram. Silk thread used for filling. See SILK.

trammé underlay (trăm-ā; tram ay). Needle-point stitch. See STITCHES.

trank. Oblong piece of leather, cut to exact size of glove pattern, from which shape is cut. Also, the shape itself.

transfer pattern. Carbon design that is transferable to cloth by means of a hot iron; or perforated pattern that is transferred by rubbing colored liquid through the perforated design. Stamped pattern, as for embroidery design. See PATTERNS.

---

fāte, făt, dȧnce, ärt mē, mĕt, hēr, thêre rīde, rĭd nōte, nŏt, côrn, fōōd, fŏŏt cūte, cŭt, cûrë now fin(ŋ)ger villa(ȧ) señor pleas(zh)ure

transformation (trăns-fôr-mā′shən; trans for may shun). Hair, made up in pieces of varying shapes, to be worn in addition to natural hair or as a covering for head. Often held in place by an elastic band or flesh-colored adhesives.

transformation dress. Costume consisting of several garments, designed to serve several purposes. See DRESSES.

transparent (trăns-pêr′ĕnt; trans *pare* ent). 1. Thin or fine enough or clear enough not to hide something underneath or behind. 2. Garment of thin, transparent fabric worn over another of velvet, satin, or the like. Popular in 17th century.

transparent velvet. Sheer rayon or silk and rayon velvet. See VELVETS.

trapunto quilting (trä-poōn′tō; trah *poon* toe). Type of quilting in which the design is outlined with a single stitching, and then cotton wadding is drawn or forced in from the back, filling each part of the design separately and giving a rather high relief, instead of a raised outline as produced in Italian quilting.

traveling costume. Costume, often a suit, suitable for wear when traveling. See DRESS.

tread (trĕd; tred). Floor surface of a shoe sole.

trellis-stitch. Parallel lines of cordstitch latticed with cross threads. Also, any trellis-like combination of stitches. See STITCHES.

trellis work. Embroidery similar to Roman cut work. See EMBROIDERIES.

trench coat. Loose, rainproof overcoat having many pockets and flaps. Held at the waistline by stitched belt of self-fabric. See COATS.

trencher or **trencher cap.** Academic cap. Same as MORTARBOARD. See CAPS.

trend. Direction in which fashion is turning. See FASHION.

tresson (trĕs′ŭn; *tress* un). Medieval headdress, or caul, of net work; often richly ornamented.

tressure (trĕsh′ēr; *tresh* er). Obsolete word for headdress; also, coiffure or style of dressing hair. Also called *tressour.*

trews. Close-fitting, one-piece garment consisting of breeches and hose in one piece. Formerly worn by Highlanders and Irishmen.

triad pattern. Uncut pattern, with three or more designs differentiated by different system of dots and dashes in printing the lines. Used widely abroad. See PATTERNS.

triangular blanket-stitch (trī-ăng′gū-lēr; try *ang* gue ler). Blanket-stitch worked diagonally so as to form triangular sections. See STITCHES.

triangular yoke. Yoke with a long point in the center of front or back or both. See YOKE.

tricolette (trĭk-ō-lĕt′; trick o *let*). Knitted fabric resembling jersey cloth, but made of rayon, silk, or cotton.

tricorn or **tricorne** (trī′kôrn; *try* corn). Three-cornered hat having an upturned brim. See HATS.

tricot (trē′kō; *tree* co). 1. Fabric of various yarns, either knitted, or woven so as to give knitted appearance. 2. Soft, ribbed dress fabric of wool or mixture. From French *tricoter*, to knit, derived from town in France where cloth and knitted stockings were first made.

tricotine (trĭk-à-tēn′; trick o *teen*). Soft, firm, worsted fabric, with a narrow, inconspicuous diagonal twill that gives a knitted effect. Similar to gabardine, but with double twill. Used for dresses, skirts, suits, light-weight coats.

tricot knitting. Type of warp knitting, either single or double, made in various patterns. See KNITTING.

tricot-stitch. Simple crochet stitch suitable for plain work. See STITCHES.

trilby (trĭl′bĭ; *trill* bi). Soft felt hat. See HATS.

trim. 1. To decorate; the decoration applied. 2. To make neat or right by clipping or cutting. 3. Neat; in order; of good lines; etc.

trimming. Decoration or ornamental parts; also, act of applying such decorations. Self-trimming is trimming made from the same fabric as the garment.

trinket. Unimportant, valueless piece of jewelry.

trio filling-stitch. One vertical and two diagonal stitches grouped together. See STITCHES.

tripe. Obsolete term for fabric woven like velvet. Now known as VELVETEEN.

triple sheer. Light-weight fabric in plain weave. See SHEER.

triple voile. Stout French chiffon. Same as NINON.

troca (trō′kà; *tro* ca). Any variety of top shell, used in making pearl buttons.

troche (trŏch; trotch). Obsolete word for button set with three or more jewels.

trolley or **trolly lace** (trŏl′ĭ; *troll* i). English bobbin lace having designs of flower sprays, squares, and dots. See LACES.

trollope (trŏl-à-pē′; troll o *pee*). Obsolete word for negligee.

trotcozy (trŏt′kō-zĭ; *trot* co zi). Cowl-like covering used in Scotland to protect head and shoulders while riding.

trotteur (F. trō-têr′; trot ter). French word applied to somewhat plain, substantial costume suitable for walking or other out-of-doors purposes.

trouse (troōz; trooz). Trousers or trews; also, knee-breeches.

trouser (trow′zēr; *trou* zer). 1. Of, for, or pertaining to trousers. 2. Half or one leg of trousers.

trouserettes. Bloomers.

trousers. 1. Outer garment extending from waist to below the knee, covering each leg separately. Worn mostly by men and boys. Formerly, very tight, similar to long hose. 2. Oriental pantaloons, usually very baggy. 3. Pantalets.

trouser skirt. Tailored skirt, open at side-front, with attached matching bloomers or pantalets. See SKIRTS.

trousseau (F. troō-sō; troo so). Outfit for a bride, especially clothing.

Truhu (trū′hū; *true* hue). Trade name for line of washable silks. Used for lingerie, women's blouses, dresses, men's shirts, scarfs.

truncated (trŭn′kāt-ĕd; *trung* kate ed). Shortened, cut off, often squared; as, truncated crown of a hat.

trunk-hose or **trunk-breeches.** Short, full breeches, reaching only to the middle thigh; worn in 16th and 17th centuries.

Trunk-Hose, 1600

trunks. 1. Short, close-fitting breeches worn for various sports, as swimming, running, etc. 2. Same as TRUNK HOSE.

trunk sleeve. Wide, full sleeve. See SLEEVES.

tub or **tubbable.** Said of garment, fabric, etc., that can be laundered without injury.

tubbeck (tŭb′ĕk; *tub* eck). Sash worn by Burmese women. See SASHES.

tube dress. Straight dress hanging from shoulders. Same as CHEMISE DRESS. See DRESSES.

tub-fast. Permanently dyed; said of something that will not fade in washing.

tub hat. Any hat that is washable, especially one made of fabric that will hold its shape without additional stiffening. See HATS.

tubular garment (tūb′à-lēr; *tube* you ler). Dress, suit, or coat, the silhouette of which resembles shape of a tube.

tubular goods or **fabrics.** Fabrics knit or woven in form of seamless tube.

tubular silhouette. Slim, straight-up-and-down silhouette. Same as PENCIL SILHOUETTE. See SILHOUETTES.

TUCKS

tuck. 1. Fold of fabric, as in a garment, stitched in place. Used as decoration, means of holding fulness, or means of shortening or shaping garment. 2. To form tuck or tucks.

cluster t. (klŭs′tēr; *cluss* ter). Tucks in series, either grouped and spaced or used continuously, as at waistline or sleeve.

cross t. Tucks that cross each other at an angle, as at corners of collars, etc. Often in parallel groups crossing each other and forming squared or diamond pattern where they intersect.

graduated t. (grăd′ū-āt-ĕd; *grad* you ate ed). Tucks in series of which each one is smaller than one below. Space between usually equals width of next smaller tuck.

nun t. Tuck of two or more inches in width, placed horizontally on a curve, as in a flared skirt or sleeve. Usually in groups of three, five, or seven.

tucks (continued)

overhand t. Tuck sewn with overhand stitches, often in contrasting color of thread, on right side of garment. Used often on curve or above scalloped edge.

pin t. Tuck of very narrow width.

tucked hem. See HEMS.

tucked seam. Seam finished with a tuck. See SEAMS.

tucked-seam placket. Placket on a tucked seam. See PLACKETS.

tucker. 1. Neck or shoulder covering worn with low-cut bodice in the 17th and 18th centuries. Later, detachable collar or chemisette, usually of thin material. 2. Sewing-machine attachment for making tucks.

tuck-in blouse. Any blouse worn tucked inside the skirt. See BLOUSES.

tucking. 1. Tuck or tucks collectively. 2. Tucked fabric, of cotton, linen, etc., sold by the yard.

tuck-stitch knitting. Circular knitting done in various patterns and tuck effects. See KNITTING.

tuck stripe. Heavy stripe. See STRIPES.

tuft. 1. Small cluster, as of fibers, feathers, etc., close at base and free at top ends; as, tuft of threads used to finish mattress or quilt. Also, in textile manufacturing, one of groups of extra filling yarns which produce looped or pile surface. 2. To fasten padding, as in mattress or quilt, by means of regularly spaced stitches, covered with tufts.

tuftaffeta (tŭf-tăf′ə-tə; tuff taff e ta). Formerly, silk fabric with pattern of tufts or pile.

tuille (twēl; tweel). One of hinged steel plates worn in medieval armor as protection for thighs. Attached, usually by straps, to the TASSES.

tuke or **tewke**. Canvas, or one of various other fabrics used in 15th and 16th centuries.

tulle (F. tül; tool). Fine, small-meshed net. See NETS.

tulle embroidery. Embroidery done on tulle. See EMBROIDERIES.

tum. Term used in woolen manufacture, meaning to subject to rough preliminary carding; to teasel before carding; or to combine several grades or colors.

tunic (tū′nĭk; tew nic). 1. Overblouse or coat, usually to hip line or longer; either

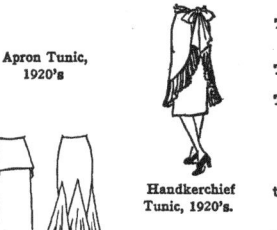

Apron Tunic, 1920's

Handkerchief Tunic, 1920's.

Handkerchief Drapery, 1920's

fitted or gathered at waist, sometimes belted. Has come down through centuries, modified or adapted by fashion. Worn in earliest civilizations, and with a shawl, cloak, or mantle, formed most important article of dress in ancient times. 2. Overskirt part of garment. See SKIRTS. When cut away in back, like an apron, called *apron tunic*. Sometimes made from square of material, with center cut out for waistline, so that outer edge forms lower edge of tunic and corners fall in points. Then called *handkerchief tunic*. 3. Short frock worn by girls and women for active sports. 4. Originally, undergarment reaching to knees or below, with or without sleeves, sometimes girdled. Worn by Roman citizens.

tunica alba (tū′nĭ-kə ăl′bə; tew ni ca al ba). White tunic worn by ancient Romans.

tuque (tŭk; tuke). Canadian sports cap. See CAPS.

turban (tẽr′bən; ter ban). 1. Small, close-fitting hat. See HATS. 2. Moslem headdress consisting of tight-fitting cap with scarf twisted around it. 3. Woman's headdress resembling Oriental turban. 4. Bright cotton handkerchief or bandanna, worn by colored women in America and West Indies.

Moslem Turban

turban toque (tŏk; toke). Toque with fabric trimming. See HATS.

Turkey red. 1. Brilliant, enduring red color produced on cotton by special dye process. Widely used in peasant embroidery, and for decorating pillow shams in the U.S.A. in the 1880's. 2. Fabric dyed this color, formerly imported from Turkey.

Turkey red bleach. Bleaching process undergone by cotton cloth before it is dyed with Turkey red.

Turkish embroidery. Embroidery in colored and metal threads, so worked that it is reversible. See EMBROIDERIES.

Turkish point lace. Heavy crochet lace. Same as OYAH LACE. See LACES.

Turkish or **turkish toweling.** Cotton or linen fabric woven the same as terry cloth, with raised loops on both sides formed by double warp. Used for towels, washcloths, bath and beach robes, etc.

turn. To remodel a garment by ripping and remaking, using opposite side of material.

turn shoe. Shoe with upper and sole stitched together on the wrong side, then turned. See SHOES.

turnover. 1. Trade term applied to the gross amount of sales, usually in comparison to the amount of stock. 2. Local English word for small shawl, worn folded about the shoulders. 3. Part of garment like a collar, which is or may be turned over.

turquoise (tẽr′koiz or F. tōōr-kwäz′; ter koiz or toor kwahz). Mineral which lends itself to high polish, and sky blue variety of which is valued as gem. Also, the color TURQUOISE BLUE. Name derived from Old French word meaning Turkish, because turquoise first came from or through Turkey.

turquoise blue. Greenish sky blue. Also called *turquoise*.

turquoise green. Bluish-green color.

turtle neckline. High, rolled neckline. See NECKLINES.

turtle shell. Mottled brown shell of turtle. Used for accessories. Same as TORTOISE SHELL.

Tuscan straw (tŭs′kən; tuss can). Fine yellow wheat straw. See STRAWS.

tussah (tŭs′ə; tuss ah) or **tussah** (tŭs′ē; tuss eh) or **tussore** (tŭs′ôr; tuss or). 1. Strong, soft, light-weight cloth woven of tussah fiber; usually in natural color because it dyes poorly. Used for summer dresses. Types include PONGEE and SHANTUNG. 2. Strong, flat, silk fiber. See SILK.

tussore (tŭs′ôr; tuss or). Variant spelling of TUSSAH. 2. Sea-shell pink color.

tuta (tū′tə; tew ta). Little-worn, shapeless costume for men or women; designed by Italian artist about 1926 as protest against tyranny of fashion.

tutulus (tū′tū-lŭs; tew tew lus). Coiffure worn by Roman priest and wife, the hair being dressed in cone shape over forehead.

tuxedo (tŭk-sē′dō; tuck *see* doe). Man's correct dress for semi-formal evening occasions, consisting of sack type of coat, often with silk lapels; trousers; black waistcoat; and black bow tie.

tuxedo collar. Straight, flat collar extending around the neck and to bottom of garment on each side. See COLLARS.

tweed. Formerly, all-wool homespun fabric originating in Scotland. Now, rough-surfaced woolen material giving homespun effect, in plain, twill, or herringbone twill weave. Yarn usually dyed before weaving, and tweed woven in two or more colors, in mixed effect, or in check, plaid, or herringbone patterns. Used for coats, suits, and sportswear. Also made in dress weights. — **Harris t.** Soft, flexible, all-wool, yarn-dyed, homespun tweed in heather mixture. So called because originally made at Harris and Lewis in Hebrides Islands, off the west coast of Scotland.—**monotone t.** Tweed of mixed effect produced by weaving together yarns of different shades or tones of the same color.

tweeds. Tweed clothing in general, either for men or women.

twill. 1. To weave so as to produce ribs or diagonal lines; also, the fabric so woven, or the twilled effect which characterizes it. 2. To flute or quill.

twilled tape. Sturdy tape woven in herringbone twill. See TAPES.

twill weave. Weave producing diagonal ribs or lines on fabric. See WEAVES.
twilly. Obsolete kind of coarse woolen material.
twin sweaters. Pair of sweaters, one a pull-over, the other a cardigan, worn together. See SWEATERS.
twist. 1. Number of twists in one inch of yarn. 2. Strong, firmly twisted silk thread used by tailors. See TAILOR'S TWIST under THREADS. Also, tightly twisted cotton yarn.
twisted-bar-stitch. Open-seam stitch with thread twisted around connecting bar. See STITCHES.
twisted chain-stitch. Variation of chain-stitch. See STITCHES.
twisted fagoting. Fagoting made by inserting needle parallel to edges to be joined. See FAGOTING under STITCHES.
twisted running-stitch. Stitch made by overcasting series of running-stitches. See STITCHES.
twist-stitch. Fine stitch worked over laid thread in cord effect. See CORD-STITCH under STITCHES.
twit. Uneven or tangled place in yarn, usually occurring in spinning or drawing.
two-piece skirt. Plain, straight skirt with a seam at each side. Also called *two-gore skirt*. See SKIRTS.
two-sided cross-stitch. 1. Cross-stitch having two sides enclosed, which results in boxed appearance when worked in adjoining rows. 2. Cross-stitch worked so as to appear same on both sides. See STITCHES.
two-sided-stitch. Running-stitch that is worked twice along same line, alternating stitches to give solid line on both sides. See DOUBLE RUNNING-STITCH under STITCHES.
two-toned. Characterized by having one color on one side and a different color on the other. Also, term used to describe color effect of two shades of one color in one article.
Tyrian purple (tĭr'ĭ-ən; *tir* i an). Famous ancient Greek and Roman color of uncertain bluish-red or reddish-blue hue. Supposedly, pigment made from substances in sea-snails.
Tyrolean (tĭ-rō'lĭ-ən; ti *role* i an) or **Tyrolese** (tĭr-ō-lēz'; tir o *leez*). In fashion, applied to garments or accessories giving effect of the costume worn by peasants living in the Tyrol, formerly a part of Austria. Characterized by full skirt, over many petticoats; embroidered apron; embroidered basque or laced bodice; simple blouse; and kerchief. Certain features of men's costume adapted in women's fashions, as the felt hat with tassel or brush; bright, embroidered, woolen vest; bright, embroidered suspenders.

Tyrolean Type of Costume

U

ugly. 1. Unattractive; without beauty. 2. Colloquial term for wired silk shade worn over bonnet to protect face, popular about 1850. Also, any large, ungainly sunbonnet. 3. Strip of cloth, worn as protection from cold, adjusted to leave only eyes, nose, and chin visible. Formerly worn in Canada.
ulster (ŭl'stēr; *ull* ster). Long, loose, heavy coat. See COATS.
ulsterette. Light-weight ulster. See COATS.
ultramarine (ŭl-trə-mə-rēn'; ull tra ma *reen*). Deep blue color with purplish or greenish cast, resembling original pigment made by powdering lapis lazuli. So called because lapis lazuli was first brought from Asia, "beyond the sea."
umber. 1. Dark brown color of umber, or kind of earth; either raw or burnt, latter having a reddish cast. 2. Shade or shadow. 3. Obsolete term for visor of a helmet. Also called *umbrel*.
umbrella (ŭm-brĕl'ə; um *brell* a). Portable shade carried for protection from rain. Consists of collapsible framework of flexible ribs radiating from a handle and covered with waterproof material.
umbrella plaits. Flared seams or pressed lines resembling rib lines of an umbrella. See PLAITS.
uncut velvet. Velvet with woven loops intact. See VELVETS.
underarm. Line on the body from directly under the arm to the waistline. In garments, called underarm section, underarm seam. Line from waistline down is called side seam.
underbody. Underwaist or lining sometimes used in dresses.
underbraider. Sewing-machine attachment that carries the braid. Fabric is placed over the underbraider, with the right side down. Design, which is stamped on wrong side of fabric, is followed in stitching; and the braid is attached underneath, to the right side of the fabric.
underclothes or **underclothing.** Garments worn under other clothes, including those worn next to skin.
undercoat. 1. Coat worn under another. 2. Formerly, petticoat or underskirt.
underdress. 1. To dress less well, or especially less formally, than is customary or required. 2. Garment worn under others.
underfleece. Soft, thick wool underlying outer coat of wool-bearing animal.
underfur. Fur underlying longer guard hairs of fur-bearing animal. See FURS.
undergarment. Garment worn under other clothes.
undergirdle. Belt or girdle worn under or attached beneath outer garment.
undergown. Gown worn under other garment.
underlinen. Underclothes; originally, only those made of linen.
underlining. Lining on underside of a garment or between two thicknesses.
underpropper. Wire arrangement used in 16th and 17th centuries to hold up huge ruffs then worn.
undershirt. Shirt worn under another shirt, usually next to skin.
underskirt. Petticoat worn under skirt.
undersleeve. Separate sleeve worn under dress sleeve. See SLEEVES.
underthings. Underclothes.
undervest. Sleeveless undershirt.
underwaist. 1. Waist worn under another waist or forming the under portion of it. 2. Skeleton waist with buttons at bottom to which other undergarments are fastened. Worn by children and small women.
underwear. Underclothes.
undies (ŭn'dĭz; *un* diz). Lingerie. Short for UNDERGARMENTS.
undress. 1. To disrobe or take off clothes. 2. Loose, informal dress. 3. Ordinary uniform, as distinguished from FULL DRESS.
undressed kid. Kid leather finished by suede process on flesh side. See LEATHERS.
U-neckline. Neckline cut in the shape of the letter U. See NECKLINES.
unfinished. Not processed or subjected to any type of finishing treatment; left as it came from the loom. Term applied to fabrics.
unhair. To remove hair from hides in manufacturing leather.
uni (F. ü-nĭ; oo ni). French term meaning plain weave.
uniform (ū'nĭ-fôrm; *you* ni form). Dress of particular style worn by all members of a group, giving a distinctive appearance; as, a military uniform, a school uniform.
union. 1. Fabric made with warp and filling of different fibers, such as cotton and linen, silk and wool, etc. 2. Obsolete term for fine pearl of large size.
union cord. Round, white cord of linen and cotton thread. Used for laces of stays.
union dye. Direct dye used to color union fabrics.
union label. Trade-mark put on goods manufactured by union labor.
union suit. Undergarment consisting of shirt and drawers in one piece.
unmade-up. 1. Not assembled or manufactured as finished product; said of material. 2. Without cosmetics.
unpressed plaits. Folds forming plaits that have not been stitched or pressed lengthwise.

---

fāte, făt, dȧnce, ärt mē, mĕt, hẽr, thêre rīde, rĭd nōte, nŏt, côrn, fōōd, fŏŏt cūte, cŭt, cûre now fĭn(g)ger vĭlla(ȧ) señor pleas(zh)ure

unprime (ŭn-prīm'; un *prime*). Not in best stage or condition; said of furs taken from animals during molting season. See FURS.
unravel (ŭn-răv'l; un *rav* el). To separate or disentangle, as threads.
untie (ŭn-tī'; un *tie*). To disentangle or loosen parts of something knotted or intertwined.
untrimmed. Not trimmed; without trimming.
untrue wool. Wool fiber of uneven thickness. See WOOL.

up-and-down. Having design or nap that runs one way, usually lengthwise of warp threads.
uparna (ōō-pŭr'nə; oo *pur* na). Silk or muslin scarf, often interwoven with gold or silver threads; worn as shawl or veil by Hindu and Mohammedan men and women in India. Same as DOPATTA.
uplift. Brassière which, by construction, tends to lift and hold up the breasts.
upper. 1. Part of shoe above sole and heel, consisting of vamp, quarter, counter, and lining. **2.** Cloth gaiter.

3. Above the waist or worn over others; said of garments.
upper leather. Leather to be used for shoe uppers.
upright-stitch. Satin stitch made vertically. See STITCHES.
up-swept. Term applied to style of hairdress with smooth, high-swept back and small curls over top of head.
up-to-date. In the style of the present time.
up-to-the-minute. In the very latest style.

V

vagabond hat (văg'ə-bŏnd; *vag* a bond). Brimmed sports hat. See HATS.
vair. Type of squirrel fur used in 14th century as trimming on luxurious robes of royalty and nobility. Symbolically represented on coats of arms.
valance (văl'əns; *val* ance). Band or drapery hanging vertically, as from an edge. Term used chiefly of the finish applied to window drapery; but used occasionally of hat brims and of flaps of leather or metal.
valence (və-lĕn'sĕ; va *len* si). Fabric of silk or silk-and-wool damask.
valencia (və-lĕn'shĭ-ə; va *len* shi a). Fabric having silk or cotton warp and wool filling. Formerly used for waistcoats.
Valenciennes lace (F. và-lôṅ-syĕn' or və-lĕn'sĭ-ĕnz; va lonh syen or va *len* si enz). Narrow, cotton or linen lace; widely used on lingerie, children's clothes, wash dresses. See LACES.
valise (və-lēs'; va *leece*). Piece of informal luggage, usually of leather, carried by hand. Used in traveling.
Val lace. Narrow, cotton or linen lace. Short for VALENCIENNES LACE. See LACES.
vallancy (vă-lăn'sĭ; va *lan* si). Large 17th century wig. See WIGS.
value (văl'ū; *val* you). **1.** Pair return for money spent, or intrinsic worth; also, to estimate the worth of. **2.** Property of color, usually called *brilliance*, which makes it light or dark.

VAMPS

vamp. 1. Part of shoe upper over toe and instep. **2.** Sock worn in colonial America. Same as VAMPAY.
circular v. Vamp covering only fore part of foot, in front of ball.
cut-off v. Vamp extending only to tip of shoe, to which it is sewn. Used chiefly in less expensive shoes.
full v. Vamp extending all the way around under tip to toe and lasted under. Used exclusively in better shoes.
gypsy v. Same as SPLIT VAMP.
split v. Vamp having seam down front, from throat to toe. Also called *gypsy vamp*.
three-quarter v. Vamp extending from inner seam above shank around toe to heel on outer side, covering three quarters of the foot.

whole v. Vamp extending to heel at each side, without seam.
"Y" v. Vamp split into Y-shaped lace stay.

vampay or **vamp.** Sock or short stocking worn in colonial America. See HOSE.
vamped. Patched up; remodeled.
Vandyke (văn-dīk'; van *dike*). **1.** Having features of dress of English period of Stuart kings, often painted by Van Dyck. Women's dress included handsome satin dresses with full skirts open in front; cylindrical bodices with sleeves tight to elbow and falling in streamers from there; broad-brimmed hats with plumes; wide collars having deep-pointed edges. See COLLARS. Men's dress of CAVALIER style. **2.** Certain colors characteristic of Van Dyck's pictures; specifically, dull red and brown.
vanity bag, box, or case. Small container, soft or rigid, in which to carry cosmetic accessories. Used in addition to a handbag for daytime; alone, for evening.
vareuse (F. và-rēz; va *reuz*). Loose, rough jacket. See JACKETS.
varicolored (vâr'ĭ-cŭl-ērd; *vare* i cull erd). Of various colors; variegated.
variegated (vâr'ĭ-ə-gāt-ĕd; *vare* i e gate ed). Marked irregularly with different colored patches.
variety chain store. Store of a chain jointly owned and operated, selling wide variety of merchandise, chiefly in the price range of from five and ten cents to one dollar, as Woolworth's, Grant's, etc.
vat dye. One of a class of dyes that is fast to sun and water.
veau velours (F. vō və-lōōr; vo ve loor). Soft-finished calfskin. See LEATHERS.
vegetable dye. Dye obtained from plants, as distinguished from mineral or synthetic dyes.
vegetable flannel. Fabric of pine fiber. See FLANNELS.
vegetable hair. Fiber of pine, Spanish moss, or other plant, used for weaving, padding, stuffing, and the like.
vegetable ivory. Seed of tropical American palm, used in making buttons.
vegetable leather. Artificial leather made of cotton waste.
vegetable silk. Cotton-like fiber found as seed covering on certain tropical trees. Used for stuffing.

VEILS

veil (vāl; vail) or **veiling.** Piece of fabric, usually thin and light, worn over head or face for ornament, protection, or concealment. One of most ancient articles of feminine attire; part of conventional costume of Anglo-Saxon ladies. Worn chiefly today with, or instead of, hats; and made of net, tulle, or some other transparent, lace-like fabric.
automobile v. Large, plain veil worn over hat and face as protection from dust when automobiles were first used. Also called *motoring veil*.
bridal v. Veil worn by bride during wedding ceremony; usually long, with train.

Bridal Veil, 1930's

haik (hĭk or hăk; hike or hake). White veil, usually embroidered with metallic threads. Worn out of doors by women in northern Africa and Arabia.
head v. Veil worn over head, especially one falling behind.
kalyptra (kə-lĭp'trə; ka *lip* tra). Thin veil worn over head and face by women in ancient Greece.
mourning v. Long, dull black, semi-transparent veil. Worn chiefly by widows.
mouth v. Veil draped across face so as

Mouth Veil, 1937

fāte, făt, dånce, ärt mē, mĕt, hẽr, thêre rīde, rĭd nōte, nŏt, côrn, fōōd, fŏŏt cūte, cŭt, cûre now fin(ŋ)ger villa(ə) señor pleas(zh)ure

to cover the mouth and leave upper part of face uncovered. Worn by women in parts of the Near East.
nose v. Short veil that does not come down far enough to cover mouth.

Nose Veil, 1930's

volet (vo-let'; vo *let*). Short veil of light, filmy material, worn hanging at the back of the head by women of the Middle Ages.
wedding v. Same as BRIDAL VEIL.
yashmak (yäsh-mäk'; yahsh *mahk*). Long, narrow veil with slits for the eyes; worn over face by Mohammedan women. Sometimes made in two pieces and worn over cap.

veining (vān'ĭng; *vane* ing). **1.** Narrow beading joining seams or finishing edges. See SEAM BEADING under BEADING. **2.** Stripe in fabric caused by lapse in warp threads.
Velasquez silhouette (vā-lās'kăth; vay *lass* kaith). Silhouette of tight bodice and wide skirt. See SILHOUETTES.
veldschoen (vĕlt'skōōn; *velt* skoon). Shoe of untanned hide. See SHOES.
vellum (vĕl'ŭm; *vell* um). Fine skin of lamb, kid, or calf, prepared as parchment. Used in lacemaking and embroidery to indicate design.
vellum cloth. Fine, transparent linen or cotton fabric, sized on one side; used for tracing designs.
velours (və-lōōr'; ve *loor*). **1.** Soft, stout, closely woven, smooth fabric with nap, like velvet. Used for coats, suits, capes, dresses. **2.** Velvet-like felt used for both men's and women's hats. **3.** (Capitalized) Trade name for soft-finished calf-skin. French word meaning velvet.
veloutine (vĕl-ōō-tēn'; vel oo *teen*). Corded fabric of merino wool with velvety finish. Used for dresses.
velure (və-lūr'; ve *loor*). **1.** Velvet or similar fabric. **2.** Pad of silk or plush, used to brush silk hats.
velveret (vĕl-vēr-ĕt'; vel ver *et*). Cotton-backed velvet. See VELVETS.

VELVETS

velvet. Fabric with short, soft, thick pile surface of looped warp yarns; and plain back. Made chiefly with silk or rayon pile and cotton back; sometimes all-silk. Ground weave may be plain, satin, or twill. Often woven double, face to face; and, while still on loom, cut apart by small knife with shuttle-like motion. Revolutionized in qualities, textures, and appearance by new weaves and modern methods for waterproofing and making crush-resistant.

Used for dresses, suits, coats, trimmings, and in millinery.
bagheera (bả-gē'ra; ba *gee* ra). Fine, uncut, supple pile velvet with roughish, pebbly finish, which makes it practically uncrushable.
chiffon v. Light-weight, soft, luxurious velvet, with pile pressed flat. Used for dresses, suits, evening gowns, and wraps. Sometimes called *wedding-ring velvet*.
ciselé (F. sēz-lā; seez lay). Type of velvet having pattern formed by contrast of cut and uncut loops. French word meaning chiseled, chased, or embossed.
costume v. Wide cotton velvet of good quality. Better grades have mercerized pile and are durable. Used for suits or coats.
croisé v. (F. krwä-zā; crwah zay). Durable velvet with coarse back, woven so as to hold pile firmly. Used for trimmings.
cut v. Fabric having brocaded pattern of velvet on background of chiffon, georgette, or voile. Used for dresses, blouses, etc.
façonné v. (F. fả-sŏn-nā; fa son nay). Velvet made by burnt-out print method. See BURNT-OUT PRINT under PRINTS.
Japanese v. Velvet with design fixed on it by YUZEN PROCESS, secret dyeing method.
jardinière (F. zhăr-dē-nyĕr'; zhahr dee nyare). Silk velvet with satin ground, patterned with leaves, flowers, etc., in multicolored design, made with pile of varying height and cut and uncut loops.
Lyons v. (lī'ənz; *ly* ons). Rich velvet with short, thick, erect, silk pile; and back of silk, linen, or cotton, which can always be seen from top, through pile. Used for hats and for dresses when stiff velvets are fashionable.
mirror v. Velvet with shimmering appearance. Woven like plain velvet, with pile pressed flat or in different directions. Used for trimming and millinery.
nacré v. (F. nả-krā; na cray). Velvet with back of one color and pile of another, so that it has changeable, pearly appearance. Used for evening gowns, wraps, trimming.
panne v. (F. pän; pan). Velvet similar in appearance to mirror velvet, but with nap all laid flat in same direction.
paon v. (F. päṅ; ponh). Velvet somewhat heavier than panne, with more pile. Pressed flat in same way as panne.
pile-upon-pile v. Velvet with pile of differing lengths arranged so that long pile forms design on short-pile background.
stamped v. Velvet which has had pile crushed by hot dies in order to show pattern or design.
tartan v. Short-napped velvet with tartan plaid designs woven or printed.
transparent v. Light-weight, soft-draping velvet with a silk or rayon back and erect rayon or acetate pile. In solid colors and printed designs. Used for dresses, suits, wraps, etc.

uncut v. Velvet fabric having warp loops left uncut.
velveret (vĕl-vēr-ĕt'; vel ver *et*). Cotton-backed velvet.
wedding-ring v. Velvet so fine that a width of it can be pulled through a wedding ring. Same as CHIFFON VELVET.
Yuzen birodo (yōō'zĕn bē-rō'dō; *yoo* zen bee *ro* doe). Japanese velvet having cut-pile designs made with a chisel over Yuzen process designs.

velveteen. General term for fabrics in which looped weft threads form pile; but usually applied only to cotton velvet with short, close pile. Used for coats, suits, dresses, children's wraps, draperies.
velvet finish. Finish made by grinding or buffing so as to raise a velvety nap. Term applied in leather manufacturing to suedes, etc.
vendeuse (F. väṅ-dēz; vonh deuz). French term for saleswoman.
veneer (və-nēr'; ve *neer*). Layer of finer or more beautiful material on surface of inferior material.
Venetian (və-nē'shən; ve *nee* shan). **1.** Fine woolen cloth in satin weave; having fine diagonal, like covert; sometimes having considerable nap and little twill, like broadcloth; sometimes like whipcord. Used for spring topcoats, suits, in lighter weights, for skirts and dresses. **2.** Closely woven, strong, cotton fabric in satin or twill weave, usually mercerized and dyed in the piece. Has glossy finish imitating silk. Used for linings, skirts, bathing suits. **3.** Domino or other masquerade costume.
Venetian chalk (chŏk; chawk). Soft, white mineral, as steatite or chalk, used to mark fabric in tailoring.
Venetian embroidery. Open-work embroidery. Same as ROMAN CUT WORK. See EMBROIDERIES.
Venetian lace. Variety of laces made in Venice, including reticella, cut work, drawn work, raised point, flat point. See LACES.
Venetian ladder-work. Type of embroidery in which design is outlined with ladder-like arrangement of stitches. See EMBROIDERIES.
Venetian pearl. Imitation pearl made of glass. See PEARLS.
ventail (vĕn'tāl; *ven* tail). Part of helmet, usually below visor, of movable construction to permit passage of air.
verdant green (vẽr'dənt; *ver* dant). Medium yellow-green color.
verdigris (vẽr'dĭ-grēs; *ver* di greece). Bluish or yellowish shade of green, like the color that forms on copper exposed to acid or weather.
verdure (vẽr'jūr; *ver* jure). Tapestry of which design is almost entirely foliage or trees, usually varied with birds, flowers, or animals.
vermilion (vẽr-mĭl'yən; ver *mill* yun). Bright red color varying in tone from crimson to reddish orange.
Verona serge (və-rō'nə; ve *ro* na). Thin, twilled, cotton-and-worsted fabric. See SERGES.

fāte, făt, dânce, ärt mē, mĕt, hẽr, thêre rīde, rĭd nōte, nŏt, côrn, fōōd, fŏŏt cūte, cŭt, cũre now fin(ŋ)ger villa(ə) señor pleas(zh)ure

versicolor (vẽr′sĭ-cŭl-ẽr; *ver si cull er*). Of changeable color; iridescent.
vertical buttonhole (vẽr′tĭ-kəl; *ver ti* cal). Buttonhole made lengthwise of the garment. See BUTTONHOLES.
vertical hemming-stitch. Hemming-stitch made perpendicular to hem. See STITCHES.
vertical stripes. Stripes running up and down fabric or garment. See STRIPES.
vest. 1. Short, close-fitting garment without sleeves; waist-length in back, below waist in front; similar to man's waistcoat or vest. Usually worn with suit. **2.** Extra piece of flat trimming at blouse or jacket front, simulating effect of man's waistcoat. **3.** Short for undervest. **4.** Obsolete term for robe, ecclesiastical vestment, or any outer clothing.
vestee (vĕs-tē′; *vess tee*). Imitation vest or blouse-front worn with a dress or jacket; in particular, bright-colored broadcloth garment without armholes or back, as worn with formal riding habits.

Vestee, 1850's

vestings. Heavy, fancy materials, such as silk piqué, bird's-eye; also highly colored fabrics and those in Persian effects. Used for vests, trimmings, men's ties.
vestments. One of several ritual garments signifying office, especially of the clergy. Outmoded word for any article of dress or clothing.
vichy (F. vē-shē; *vee she*). Cotton fabric woven of threads of different colors. Used for dresses.
vici (vī′sī; *vy sy*). Trade name for type of chrome-tanned, glazed kid. See LEATHERS.
Victoria cage. Trade name for steel skeleton skirt, patented in late 19th century. Worn to distend skirts in hoop or bustle fashion.
Victoria lawn. Fine lawn, as used for bishop's sleeves. Also called *bishop's lawn*.
Victorian (vĭk-tō′rĭ-ən; *vic tore i an*). Characteristic of styles of Queen Victoria's reign, latter half of 19th century. Included wide hoop skirts caught up and flounced, basques, berthas, long sleeves, luxurious fabrics. Later, narrower skirts drawn up over bustle at back, tight jackets, shawls, poke bonnets.

Victorian Costume, Queen Victoria 1872

victorine (vĭk′tō-rēn; *vic tore een*). Woman's fur tippet with long tabs at ends.
vicuna (vĭ-kū′nə; vi *koon* ya). **1.** Soft fabric made from wool of the vicuña, llama-like animal of Andes Mountains. **2.** Imitation of genuine vicuña, usually made from fine merino wool.
Vienna cut. Style of shoe upper in which the only seam is a half-circular one on the outer side of the foot.
vigogne yarn (vē-gōñ′; vee *gon* yuh). Cotton yarn with mixture of wool or wool waste. See YARNS.
vigoureux (F. vē-gōō-rē; vee goo ruh). Fabric having dark and light effect produced originally by process of printing fibers of worsted before spinning yarn.
violet (vī′ō-lĕt; *vy o* let). Clear blue-purple, the color of the flower, varying in depth. French violet is darker and more purple.
violine (vī′ō-lēn; *vy o* leen). Deep blue-violet.
virago sleeve (vĭ-rā′gō; vi *rah* go). Full sleeve tied at intervals. See SLEEVES.
virgin wool. New wool, never used before. See WOOL.
Visca. Trade name for artificial straw used for women's hats. Visca also used, in combination with other fibers, for making fabrics. See RAYON.
viscose rayon. One of the three types of rayon now manufactured commercially in the U.S.A. See RAYON.
visite (F. vē-zēt; vee zeet). Light-weight cape worn by women in 19th century. See CAPES.

visor or **vizor** (vī′zẽr; *vy* zer). **1.** Front part of cap or hat that projects over forehead and shades eyes; also, the separate shade itself with attached headband, as worn for sports. **2.** Movable part of a helmet over the face. **3.** Mask worn to conceal the face.

Sports Visor, 1930's

15th Century Visor

Vitalizing (vī′tăl-īz-ĭng; *vy* tal ize ing). Trade name of process for permanently treating linen and spun rayon to make them resist wrinkling and to give additional life and body to fabric.
vitta (vĭt′ə; *vit* a). Fillet, garland, or headband, especially as worn with religious significance in ancient Greece and Rome.
Viyella (vī-yĕl′ə; vy *yell* a). Trade name of a twill-weave flannel. See FLANNELS.
vizard (vĭz′ẽrd; *vis* erd). Mask or visor.
V-neck. Neckline cut to point in center-front. See NECKLINES.
vogue (vōg; vohg). Mode or fashion.
voile (voil or F. vwäl; voyl or vwahl). Plain, fine, transparent or semi-transparent fabric of cotton, silk, rayon, or wool. Cotton type of two-ply, hard-twisted yarn, dainty and durable. Wool type of hard-twisted worsted yarn. All used for dresses, blouses, etc., varying according to fashion. Cotton and rayon types also used for curtains, etc.
voile de laine (F. vwäl də lān; vwahl de lane). French term for wool voile.
volant (F. vō-läṅ; vo lonh). French word for flounce.
volant piece (vō′lənt; *vo* lant). Piece of medieval armor worn to protect throat.
volet (vō-lĕt′; vo *let*). Short veil of light, filmy material, worn hanging at back of head by women in Middle Ages. See VEILS.
voluminous (və-lū′mĭ-nŭs; vo *lue* mi-nus). Made of much material and full of folds or curves; as, voluminous sleeves or skirts.
voluper (vŏl′ū-pẽr; *vol* you per). Obsolete term for woman's cap, hood, or the like.
vrai réseau (F. vrā rā-zō; vray ray zo). True net ground for lace; specifically, net ground made by needle or bobbins.

W

wad (wŏd; wod). To form into a pad; to stuff or line with padding; also, the pad, or soft, compact mass, especially as used for padding, stuffing, or interlining.
wadding. Any mass of soft, fibrous stuff; especially, sheets of carded cotton. Used to stuff or pad clothing or other articles.

wadmal (wŏd′măl; *wod* mal). Coarse woolen material, frequently hairy, formerly used for heavy, durable garments worn by poor people of Great Britain and Scandinavia. Also spelled *wadmaal, wadmoll, wadmol*.
Waffenrock (väf′ĕn-rŏk; *vahf* en rock). Kind of doublet or tabard worn with armor.

waist. 1. Garment or part of garment covering the body from shoulders to waistline. Usually called blouse or bodice. **2.** Undergarment for children. See UNDERWAIST. **3.** Part of the body between hips and ribs.
waistband. Band, girdle, sash, etc., encircling the waistline; especially band inside the top of a skirt, acting as inner belt.

---

fāte, făt, dânce, ärt mē, mĕt, hẽr, thêre rīde, rĭd nōte, nŏt, côrn, fōōd, fŏŏt cūte, cŭt, cūre now fin(ŋ)ger villa(ə) señor pleas(zh)ure

waist belt. Belt worn at waistline. See BELTS.
waistcloth. Loincloth, the cloth covering the hips and usually extending to the waistline.
waistcoat (wāst'kōt or wĕs'kŏt; *waist* coat or *wess* cot). Garment, usually sleeveless, buttoning in front, extending just below the waistline. Worn under jacket or coat. Also called *vest*. Sometimes worn by women in place of a blouse.

18th Century Waistcoat

waistcoating. Fabric made for waistcoats, especially one patterned in varicolored yarns.
waisting. Material for waists or shirtwaists.
waist length. Length of coat or other garment which reaches to normal waistline. See LENGTHS.
waistline. 1. Line around the part of the human figure between shoulder and hip that is most contracted. 2. Line at which skirt and waist of a dress meet. — **high w.** Waistline above the normal. — **low w.** Waistline below the normal. — **normal w.** Place, just over the top of the hips and below the ribs, where the body is most contracted.
Walachian embroidery (wŏ-lā'kĭ-ən; wol *lay* ki an). Solid embroidery done with single-purl buttonhole-stitch. See EMBROIDERIES.
wale. Ridge, or rib, as in piqué, corduroy, or any twilled fabric; also, the ribs running lengthwise in full-fashioned hose.
walking shoe. Sturdy shoe with low or medium heel. See SHOES.
walled last (wôld; wawld). Shoe last having boxy effect around toe. See LAST.
wallet (wŏl'ĕt; *woll* et). 1. Flat purse or pocketbook, for carrying either paper money or coins. 2. Bag or knapsack used as piece of luggage.
walnut brown (wôl'nŭt; *wawl* nut). Soft, warm, taffy-brown color of English walnut shell.
wampum (wŏm'pəm; *wom* pum). Colorful ornamental beads made of small shells. Used by North American Indians as money or as decoration for apparel.
wampum belt. Belt of wampum. See BELTS.
wamus (wŏ'mŭs; *waw* muss). Cardigan, or heavy outer jacket. See JACKETS.
wardrobe. One's clothes; wearing apparel in general.
warm color. Hue associated with feeling of heat. See COLOR.

warp (wôrp; worp). 1. Lengthwise threads of fabric that form the foundation between which the weft, or filling of cross-threads, is woven. 2. Selvage way of fabric.
warp frame. Machine used in making warp lace.
warping. 1. Thread or threads of warp. 2. Act of laying warp on loom.
warp knitting. Flat machine knitting with threads running lengthwise. See KNITTING.
warp lace or **warp net lace.** Lace with ground of warp threads held in position by design. See LACES.
warp print. Print with design on warp only. See PRINTS.
wash or **washable.** Said of fabric or garment that may be washed without injury.
washable knot-stitch. Series of loop-stitches used as filling. Same as LINK-POWDERING-STITCH. See STITCHES.
wash goods. Fabrics that may be washed without damage or loss of color. See GOODS.
wash leather. Imitation chamois. See LEATHERS.
wash satin. Satin finished for laundering. See SATINS.
wasp waist. Extremely small, slender waistline. Fashionable in late 19th century, when tightly laced corsets were worn.
watch. Timepiece, worn or carried, often in ornamental setting, as pin, bracelet, or ring; or set in article of utility, as handbag or vanity case.
watch cap. Knitted cap worn by men in U. S. Navy. See CAPS.
watch case. Outside covering of watch, or case for holding or keeping it.
watch chain. Chain, usually metal, attached to watch to prevent losing it.
watch charm. Small ornament worn on watch chain.
watch coat. Heavy overcoat worn by seamen. See COATS.
watch paper. Formerly, elaborately cut or printed ornamental paper used inside watch case.
watch ribbon. Firm ribbon used as strap for wrist watch. See RIBBONS.
water. 1. To give cloth a lustrous effect in wavy lines, usually by wetting and calendering. 2. Degree of purity and transparency of a precious stone.
water boot. Watertight boot. See BOOTS.
waterfall. 1. Coiffure similar to chignon. 2. Old-fashioned scarf with long, hanging ends.
waterproof. Term applied to fabric through which water will not penetrate in a standard test, such as a spray of water falling upon the fabric for 24 hours at a rate of 1,000 c.c. (more than a quart) per minute, from a height of 4 feet.
waterproofing. Any of various processes by which cotton, wool, silk, other closely woven fabrics, and leather are made impervious to water, or non-absorbent. Does not change chemical or physical construction of fibers or yarns, and should not alter pliancy of cloth or prevent admittance of air. Done with various insoluble substances such as rubber, gutta percha, oils, fats, varnishes, wax, acids, oxides.
Watteau (wŏ-tō'; wot *toe*). Having certain features seen in costume painted by the French 18th century artist, Watteau. Many of these features called simply *Watteau*. See below.
Watteau back. Back of gown, having fulness taken up in box plait from neck to waistline, and hanging loosely from shoulders.
Watteau bodice. Bodice with low, square or round neckline; short, deeply ruffled sleeves; and many ribbon bows. See BODICES.
Watteau gown. Long, unfitted dress with Watteau back.
Watteau hat. Flat-crowned hat with upturned brim and flower-trimmed bandeau. See HATS.
Watteau mantle. Cape with loose-plaited back. See WRAPS.
Watteau plait. Box plait at center-back of garment. See PLAITS.
Watteau sacque. Short, loose outer garment with Watteau back; looped up at sides. See JACKETS.
wave. 1. Undulating effect of the hair; natural, or artificially produced by hand or machine. 2. Waving, lustrous line in watered cloth; also, pattern formed by these lines.
wave top. Boot top, with double curve, usually higher in front.
wax cloth. Oilcloth or fabric made waterproof with wax or paraffin.
waxed end or **wax end.** Stout thread of several waxed strands. See THREADS.
wear (wêr; ware). 1. Clothing; wearing apparel. Also, adapted to or designed for use as apparel. 2. Impairment due to wearing or other use.
wearing apparel. Clothes or clothing.
weasel (wē'zl; *wee* zl). Short, thick fur of varying color. See FURS.

WEAVES

weave. 1. To form a fabric on a loom by interlacing warp and filling threads, or yarns, either by hand or machine. 2. Particular method used in weaving; as, twill or basket weave.
basket w. Variation of plain weave, made by using two or more warp and filling yarns together, giving appearance of plaited basket.
broken twill w. Irregular twill weave in which the direction of twill is alternated, giving a zigzag effect. Also called *chevron* and *herringbone*, from resemblance to the backbone of a herring.
chevron w. Same as BROKEN TWILL WEAVE.
diagonal w. Twill weave, running on a slant.
dobby w. Weave with small patterns, woven on the dobby loom. Similar to Jacquard, but less intricate.
figured w. Weave which produces design on fabric. When pattern is very intricate, as in damasks, brocades, or tapestries, woven on Jacquard loom;

weaves (continued) when small or simple, as in shirting or corset fabrics, woven on dobby loom.

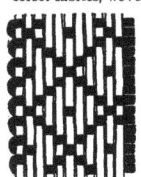

Simple Figured Weave

gauze w. Open, firm weave; now called LENO WEAVE.
herringbone w. Same as BROKEN TWILL WEAVE.

Herringbone Twill

honeycomb w. Weave suggesting honeycomb pattern, having squared and ridged surface. Used for toweling; sometimes, for suiting.
Jacquard w. (jă-kärd'; ja *card*). Figured weave done on Jacquard loom. Used for fabrics having very intricate designs and figures, as brocades, damasks, and tapestries.

Jacquard Weave

lappet w. Plain or gauze weave on which pattern is embroidered while the cloth is being woven.
leno w. Open, firm weave, as in marquisette; produced by intertwining paired warp yarns and passing filling yarns between them. Formerly called *gauze weave*.

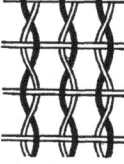

Leno Weave

novelty w. Any of various weaves produced by combination or variation of the staple weaves.

pile w. Weave in which the warp or the filling yarns form loops, either cut or uncut. Warp pile fabrics include plush, velvet, and terry. Filling pile fabrics include velveteen and corduroy.

Pile Weave (Cross-Section)

plain w. The simplest weave, in which each filling yarn passes successively over and under each warp yarn to form an even surface, as in muslin, taffeta, and voile.

Plain Weave

ply w. Weave producing fabric of extra thickness, weight, or warmth by using more than one set of warp and filling yarns.
sateen w. Similar to satin weave, except that the filling threads form the surface.
satinette or **satinet w.** (săt-ĭ-nĕt'; sat i *net*). Variation of SATIN WEAVE.
satin w. Irregular weave in which warp or filling yarns pass over number of yarns of other set before interweaving, forming smooth, unbroken, lustrous surface. Actually, a type of broken twill weave.

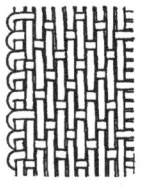

Five-Shaft Satin Weave

swivel w. Weave having small woven figures, usually dots, produced by using extra filling yarns in loom and later cutting away long joining threads between figures.
taffeta w. Same as PLAIN WEAVE.
twill w. Weave having distinct diagonal line or rib, to right or left, due to filling yarns passing over one warp yarn,

Twill Weave

under two or more. Strongest of all weaves. Cotton twills include denim, coutil, ticking; wool twills include serge, gabardine.

Weave It. Trade name for the making of a fabric in darning-stitch fashion on a square frame.
web. 1. Webbing, or any interwoven texture. 2. Textile fabric on a loom or just off a loom. 3. (Plural) Colloquial U. S. name for snowshoes.
webbing. Strong fabric woven of hemp or other material, usually made in narrow strips. Used as support for chair seats, etc.
wedding gown. Gown worn during the wedding ceremony. May be of any style the bride prefers; often of satin, and having train or veil, or both.
wedding ring. Ring signifying married state. See RINGS.
wedding-ring velvet. Fine, light-weight velvet, supposedly so fine that a width of velvet could be pulled through a wedding ring. Same as CHIFFON VELVET. See VELVETS.
wedding veil. Veil worn by bride. See BRIDAL VEIL under VEILS.
wedge-soled. Having a wedge-shaped piece making a solid sole, flat on the ground from heel to toe. Term applied to certain style of shoe.
Wedgwood print. Print of white design on colored ground, similar to the effect of Wedgwood ware. See PRINTS.
weed. Band of black cloth, worn on a man's sleeve or hat as symbol of mourning.
weeds. Distinctive apparel, as worn for mourning or religious purposes.
weeper. Something worn to indicate mourning, as, formerly, white band worn as sleeve cuff, or man's black hatband. Also, usually plural, widow's black veil.
weft. 1. Yarn running crosswise of woven fabric, at right angles to warp, which is lengthwise yarn. Yarn carried by shuttle. Also called *filling*, *woof*, *pick*, *shoot*. 2. Anything that is woven.
weftage. Texture.
weft knitting. Knitting in which thread runs back and forth crosswise of fabric. See KNITTING.
weighted silk. Silk that has had substance added to increase weight. See SILK.
weighted tape. Tape to which weights are attached. See TAPES.
weighting. Process of treating fabric to give it more body and weight; or treating silk yarn to replace loss in weight that occurs when raw silk is boiled to free it from natural gums. Light silks are weighted with sugar; dark ones, with metallic salts and dyes. Term usually applied to "loaded" silks; but cotton and linen may be weighted with sizing, china clay, etc. See PURE SILK under SILK.
weights. Small metal disks of various sizes, pierced so that they can be sewed to lower edge of jackets, coats, panels, and dresses, to hold them in position. Also made in tape strips.

Wellington. 1. Square-topped riding boot. See BOOTS. 2. Similar short boot. See BOOTS.
Welsh flannel. Fine flannel made from wool of Welsh sheep. See FLANNELS.
welt. 1. Strip of material stitched to seam, border, or edge; used in construction of garments for purposes of strengthening or trimming. Often formed by cloth-covered cord, or by hemming edge of cloth over a cord. 2. Strip or flap to be joined to machine-made stockings after forming. 3. Strip of leather stitched to shoe upper, lining, and insole before being attached to outsole. Stitches of latter process usually concealed by means of a channel which is cut in edge of outsole to permit stitching and is then cemented together again.
welt pocket. Inserted pocket. See POCKETS.
welt seam. Seam in which one raw edge is trimmed close to seam line and the other edge is pressed and stitched over it. Used in tailoring. See SEAMS.
welt-seam placket. Placket in imitation of welt seam. See PLACKETS.
wen-chow (wĕn-chow'; wen *chow*). Hat body of Japanese grass, imported from Japan. Lacks luster, but takes dye readily. Used for sports hats.
western wolf. Fur of coyote or small prairie wolf. See COYOTE under FURS.
whalebone. Baleen, the horny substance that takes the place of teeth in whalebone whales. Consists of flattened plates from 3 to 15 feet long, from 250 to 300 of which are found in the mouth of a full-grown whale and which together weigh nearly 1 ton. Now scarce, but formerly much used for stiffening in dresses and corsets.
whang. Leather thong.
whang leather. Leather used for thongs, etc. See LEATHERS.
wheat-stitch. Series of slanting stitches joined by loops, resembling full wheat ear. See STITCHES.
wheel. 1. Circular design in needlework, of various types and patterns. 2. In shoemaking, to make small indentations with wheel, as on upper edge of heel.
wheel-stitch. Stitch used to make spider-web pattern. See STITCHES.
whimsy or **whimsey.** Insignificant accessory, as a miniature fan or handkerchief, etc.; whim; fancy; capricious idea.
whip. 1. To sew with a light overcast- or overhand-stitch; also, stitch so made. 2. Device, usually a lash attached to a handle, for striking a horse. Used as accessory of formal riding costume.
whipcord. Worsted fabric in diagonal twill weave, with strongly marked, round cords, which may be extremely narrow or as wide as ⅛ inch. Used for dresses, skirts, suits.
whipping. Overstitching, either overcasting or overhanding.
whip-stitch. 1. Shallow overcast-stitch. See STITCHES. 2. To sew with shallow overcast-stitches; to whip. Also, something hurriedly put together.
whip thread. Secondary warp thread twined about another warp thread to give additional firmness to fabric, as in leno weaving.
whip yarn. Same as WHIP THREAD.
whisk. 17th century shoulder collar. See COLLARS.
white. Lightest neutral color, containing all rays of the spectrum; the color of snow.
white embroidery. Embroidery in white on white fabric. See EMBROIDERIES.
white fox. Fur of fox from arctic regions. See FURS.
white goods. White fabrics in general; also, finished products of white fabric, chiefly bedding, table linen, etc. White goods sales occur in department stores in January. See GOODS.
white leather. Leather tanned with alum and salt. See LEATHERS.
whiten. To make white or whiter; as, to whiten shoes, to bleach cloth, etc.
whitening. 1. Agent or thing used in making white. 2. In leather manufacturing, the shaving of leather on flesh side to secure even thickness.
white sale. Sale of white goods.
whiteseam. Scottish term for plain needlework.
white sewing. Colloquial expression meaning plain sewing.
whittle. Blanket-like shawl with fringe. Worn in colonial America after 1665.
wholesale (hōl'sāl; *hole* sale). Sale, or pertaining to the sale, of merchandise, usually in large quantity, to retailers rather than to consumers.
whole-stitch. Stitch used in making pillow lace. See CLOTH-STITCH under STITCHES.
whole vamp. Shoe vamp extending to heel at each side. See VAMPS.
wide-awake or **wide-awake hat.** Broad-brimmed felt hat. See HATS.
wide-wale serge. Serge with broad, diagonal weave. See SERGES.
widow's peak. 1. Hair growing in point in center of forehead. 2. Originally, mourning bonnet with a point over center of forehead. See CAPS.

16th Century Widow's Peak

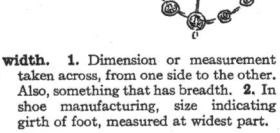

width. 1. Dimension or measurement taken across, from one side to the other. Also, something that has breadth. 2. In shoe manufacturing, size indicating girth of foot, measured at widest part.

WIGS

wig. Head-covering made of false hair interwoven with or attached to a net or cap. Worn to conceal absence or deficiency of natural hair; as coiffure assumed for ornament; as part of theatrical costume; as part of official dress of judges and barristers in England. Modern wig first adopted by Louis XIII to cover his baldness. Wigs made of wool worn by men and women in ancient Egypt.
bag w. Wig having back hair enclosed in a bag, usually of black silk, tied at nape of neck with bow. This bag designed to contain curls of wig and keep the coat from being marked with powder.

18th Century Bag Wig

barrister's w. Wig worn by English barristers, or lawyers, when in court. Of type known as FULL-BOTTOM WIG. BOB WIG also worn in English courts.

Barrister's Wig

bob w. Short wig, usually having bobs, or knots of hair.

Bob Wig

busby (bŭz'bĭ; *buzz* bi). Large, bushy wig.
campaign w. (kăm-pān'; cam *pane*). Wig, usually powdered; made very full, with big curls arranged high on top and long curls hanging toward front. Worn for traveling at end of 17th, beginning of 18th century.
caxon (kăks'en; *cax* on). Obsolete term for wig, especially one that has been much worn.
combings (kōm'ĭngz; *cohm* ings). Small wig made of combings of hair.
full bottom. Wig still worn by English lawyers, and formerly worn by other men. Made long and broad at bottom and with little attempt to simulate real hair. Rows of curls run horizontally around head, and edge is bordered with single curled row; all attached to backing.

wigs (continued)

galerum (gə-lē'rŭm; ga *leer* um) or **galerus** (gə-lē'rŭs; ga *leer* us). Wig somewhat like peruke or periwig. Worn by men and women, often as a disguise.

gregorian (grĕ-gō'rĭ-ən; gre *go* ri an). Type of wig worn during 16th and 17th centuries. So called because supposedly designed by barber named Gregory.

jasey (jā'zē; *jay* zee). Colloquial British term for a wig made of worsted.

periwig (pĕr'ĭ-wĭg; *pare* i wig). Wig, usually powdered and in pompadour style. Fashionable during 18th century.

18th Century Periwig

peruke (pə-rōōk'; pe *rook*). Wig similar to but less cumbersome than the periwig, often made to imitate natural hair. Introduced in 17th century; popular through 18th.

pigeon's or **pigeon wing.** Wig made with loosely curled lock of hair over ear. Worn in 18th century.

pig-tail w. Wig with ends plaited and tied with ribbon. Worn in 18th century.

Ramilie or **Ramillie w.** (răm'ĭ-lĭ; *ram* i li). Wig, bushy at the sides; with long, braided tail on back, tied at top with large bow, at bottom with small bow. Worn in 18th century.

scratch. Kind of wig that covers only part of the head.

spencer (spĕn'sẽr; *spen* ser). Type of wig worn in England in 18th century.

tiewig. Wig tied with a ribbon at back. Also called *tie periwig*.

18th Century Tiewig

toupee (tōō-pā'; too *pee*). 18th century wig with topknot at crown; lock or curl of artificial hair placed at crown of head. Also, small wig used to cover bald spot.

vallancy (vă-lăn'sĭ; va *lan* si). Wig so large as to shade the face; worn in 17th century.

wigan (wĭg'ən; *wig* an). Stiff, canvas-like fabric, usually of cotton. Used to stiffen edges or other parts of garments.

wig block. Round-topped block, used in making or dressing wigs.

wild silk. Silk of wild silkworms. See SILK.

willow. Fabric woven of esparto grass and cotton, similar to sparterie. Used instead of buckram for making foundations of more expensive hats.

14th Century Wimple

Pillbox Hat with Detachable Wimple, 1938

wimple. 1. Piece of cloth wrapped in folds around neck and over head. Worn by nuns. Also worn outdoors by women in general during Middle Ages. Revived at various periods; usually attached to the hat in back and folded around the face. 2. To arrange in plaits or folds, as a veil.

wincey (wĭn'sĭ; *win* si). Fabric woven with cotton or linen warp and woolen filling. Name probably derived from linsey-woolsey.

wind-blown. Descriptive of short haircut with hair arranged to give windblown effect. See BOBS.

Windbreaker. Trade name for a type of sports jacket. See JACKETS.

windclothes. Garments made from windproof fabrics, particularly clothes for Arctic exploration.

Windsor tie (wĭn'zẽr; *win* zer). Scarf of black silk cut on the bias, hemmed on all edges; tied in a loose bow at the front neckline. Worn as necktie. Affected today chiefly by artists. Similar to ELBERT HUBBARD TIE.

wine. Any color resembling color of wines, especially red wines.

wing. Shoulder ornament or knot; small epaulet; also, extended shoulder piece, as on various 17th century garments.

wing collar. Man's collar with folded-down corners. See COLLARS.

winged sleeve. Wide, flowing sleeve. See ANGEL SLEEVE under SLEEVES.

wing tie. Bow tie, especially one with flared ends.

Winterhalter (wĭn'tẽr-hŏl-tẽr; *win* ter hawl ter). Name applied to costumes characterized by off-shoulder necklines,

Type of Winterhalter Costume

corseleted waistlines, crinoline skirts with flounces, as shown in paintings by Winterhalter (1806–73).

wire collar flare. Fine, covered wire used to support women's high, upstanding collars.

witch hat. Hat with brim and tall, peaked crown, of type seen in pictures of witches. See HATS.

witney (wĭt'nĭ; *wit* ni). Heavy woolen fabric, pre-shrunk and napped; produced in Witney, England. Used for blankets and coats.

witzchoura (wĭ-chōō'rə; wi *choo* ra). Mantle with large sleeves and wide collar. See WRAPS.

wolf. Sturdy, long-haired fur. See FURS.

wolverine (wŏŏl'vẽr-ēn; *wool* ver een). Durable fur resembling wolf, but coarser. See FURS.

woof. 1. Yarn running crosswise of woven fabric, at right angles to warp, or lengthwise yarn. Yarn carried by shuttle. Also called *filling*, *weft*, *pick*, *shoot*. 2. Cloth; texture of a fabric.

WOOL

wool. 1. Hair-like covering of sheep and certain other animals, which is one of the principal materials used for clothing. Distinguished from hair by its scaly surface, fineness, and curl; from fur by its crispness and curl. Many types and varieties variously graded, according to fineness, color, length of staple, etc. 2. Fabric or clothing made from wool. 3. Yarn used for knitting or weaving, made from fibers mixed loosely before spinning.

alpaca w. (ăl-păk'ə; al *pack* a). Fine, long, woolly hair of the alpaca, a goat-like animal of South America; naturally black, white, or brown. Superior to ordinary qualities of sheep's wool.

Angora w. (ăng-gō'rə; ang *go* ra). Long, silky, hair-like wool of Angora goat, a type of domestic goat. Used in making mohair.

Botany w. Fine merino wool; originally shipped from vicinity of Botany Bay, Australia.

breech w. Short, coarse wool from hind legs of sheep or goat.

carding w. Same as CLOTHING WOOL.

cashmere (kăsh'mẽr; *cash* meer). Soft, very fine wool found beneath hair of goats of Himalayan region, including Kashmir.

clothing w. (klŏth'ĭng; *clothe* ing). Compact, short-fibered wool with felting properties, suitable for carding and making into woolen cloth. Also called *carding wool*.

combing w. Wool of longer and more valuable fibers, which are combed to straighten them out, short wool being straightened by carding.

grease w. Wool containing natural oils or fats, as it is clipped from sheep. Term "in the grease" used of wool, furs, etc., in natural state, before removal of grease.

kemp. Thick, short, harsh wool that did not mature on sheep. Resists dye.

lamb's w. Soft, elastic wool of lambs

from seven to eight months old. Used in manufacturing textile fabrics.
merino w. (mə-rē′nō; muh *ree* no). Finest wool produced, obtained from merino sheep, a breed originating in Spain.
miscellaneous w. (mĭs-ə-lā′nĭ-ŭs; miss e *lay* ni us). Strong, coarse, long-staple wool, used for blankets, heavy clothing, and carpets. Also called CARPET or BLANKET WOOL.
off-sorts. Wool not up to standard; short, coarse, or stained by-product wool.
pashm (pŭsh′m; pushm). Underfleece of type of goat of Tibet. Used in India for shawls, rugs, etc.
pelt w. Short wool from pelt of sheep killed within three months of shearing; wool from dead sheep.
plucked w. Wool plucked from dead sheep.
raw w. Wool as it comes from the animal.
reworked w. Same as SHODDY WOOL.
Shetland w. Wool of Shetland sheep.
shoddy or **shoddy w.** 1. Remanufactured wool, obtained by shredding discarded woolen, worsted, and knitted garments, mill waste, clippings from tailoring establishments, etc., and converting the fibers into yarn or cloth. 2. Originally, the waste discarded in wool spinning.
skin w. Inferior wool, usually scoured, taken from dead sheep.
tender w. Wool too weak for, or wasting too greatly in, combing.
top. Continuous strand of long wool fibers from which short ones, noils, have been eliminated by combing. After drawing and spinning, it becomes worsted yarn.
untrue w. Wool fiber of uneven thickness caused by poor condition of the sheep.
virgin w. Any wool that has not been used before. Opposed to SHODDY, etc.

wool batiste. Fine, light-weight, smooth wool fabric. See BATISTE, 2.
wool card or **carder.** Hand machine with teeth of bent wire, used in carding wool. Also called *wool comb*.
wool chiffon. Sheerest of woolen fabrics. See CHIFFON.
wool combings. Short fibers removed in combing wool.
wool crepe (krāp; crape). Woolen fabric with crepy texture. See CREPES.
wool-dyed. Dyed before making into fabric. Said of wool.
woolen or **woollen.** 1. Fabric made wholly or in part from short-staple wool. According to U. S. Commercial Standard, the terms "100% wool," "pure wool," or "all wool," may be used only of fabrics containing from 98% to 100% wool. Terms wool, woolen, or worsted may be used to describe fabric containing 95% wool. When wool content is less than 95%, it must be stated as an exact percentage. Most woolens undergo finishing process after weaving, as fulling, calendering, napping. 2. Loose, rough woolen yarn, particularly as used for weaving. See YARNS.

woolenet or **woolenette** (wŏŏl-ə-nĕt′; wool e *net*). Thin woolen fabric.
woolens. Garments made from woolen fabrics, especially underwear.
wool-finished cotton. All-cotton fabric treated to resemble wool.
wool-flock. Lock of wool. Also, cheap grade of wool.
wool grades. Grades of wool fibers according to diameter, classified officially by the U. S. Government. There are now twelve grades, designated by numbers.
woolly or **woollies.** Woolen garment or garments, the plural commonly used to designate underclothing.
wool needle. Blunt needle with long eye. See NEEDLES.
wool shoddy. Reworked wool. Same as SHODDY, or SHODDY WOOL. See WOOL.
wool taffeta. Fine, closely-woven woolen fabric. See TAFFETAS.
wool waste. Fibers and noils that occur as waste in the manufacture of yarns and fabrics.
woolwork. 1. Needlework done in wool on canvas. See EMBROIDERIES. 2. Method of making rugs. See MOSAIC WOOLWORK.
worcester (wŏŏs′tẽr; *woos* ster). Fine woolen cloth formerly made in Worcester, England.
work. 1. To make or decorate by crocheting, knitting, or other type of needlework; as, to work a buttonhole. Especially used of embroidering. 2. Material, garment, etc., upon which one is working. 3. Needlework, or the designs made in needlework.
work bag, basket, or **box.** Small bag or receptacle, usually decorative, to hold needlework, materials for it, etc.
worked buttonhole. Tailored buttonhole, having the edges finished with buttonhole-stitches. See BUTTONHOLES.
workhouse sheeting. Coarse, unbleached twill sheeting.
work shirt. Shirt of durable material suitable for hard wear. See SHIRTS.
worsted (wŏŏs′tĕd; *woos* sted). 1. Firm, strong, smooth-surfaced yarn spun from long-staple, evenly combed, pure wool. Also, loosely twisted yarns for knitting. See YARNS. 2. Any fabric woven from worsted yarn, as gabardine or serge. Named for Worstead, England, where a particular fine wool fabric of that name originated.

WRAPS

wrap. Loose outer garment; originally, one intended to be folded about the person. (Plural) Outer garments in general, worn in addition to regular clothing.
aba or **abba** (äb′ə; *ahb* a). Square mantle of various colors, striped or plain. Worn by Arabs. Usually made of silk for upper classes, of camel's hair for travelers.
abolla (ȧ-bŏl′ə; a *boll* a). Loose cloak fastened at neck. Similar to Greek chlamys. Worn by Roman soldiers.
amictus (ȧ-mĭk′tŭs; a *mick* tus). Toga or other outer garment worn by ancient Romans.

armilausa (är-mĭ-lō′sə; ahr mi *law* sa). Short cloak, early form of surcoat. Worn during Middle Ages.
artois (F. är-twä; ahr twah). Long cloak with lapels and several capes, lowest ending near waistline. Worn by men and women late in 18th century.
balandran (bə-lăn′drən; ba *lan* dran) or **balandrana** (bə-lăn′drən-ə; ba *lan* dran a). Wide, mantle-like cloak or wrap with armholes; worn by travelers in Middle Ages, especially in 13th and 14th centuries.
banyan or **banian** (băn′yən; *ban* yan). Loose wrap, usually brightly colored, sometimes lined so as to be worn either side out. Worn in 18th century in America, especially by Southern planters, as informal or negligee costume. So called from resemblance to body garment worn by banians, caste of Hindu merchants.

18th Century Banyan

bautta (bä-ōōt′tä; bah *oot* tah). Black cloak, having hood that could be drawn over the face.
birrus or **byrrus.** Cloak or cape with cowl-like hood. Worn in bad weather by ancient Romans.

Arabian Burnoose

burnoose or **burnous** or **burnus** (bẽr-nōōs′; bur *noose*). Outer wrap or cloak with hood, woven in one piece, usually

15th Century Capote

fāte, făt, dȧnce, ärt mē, mĕt, hẽr, thêre rīde, rĭd nōte, nŏt, côrn, fōōd, fŏŏt cūte, cŭt, cûre now fin(ŋ)ger villa(ȧ) señor pleas(zh)ure

wraps (continued)
sleeveless. Worn by Arabs and monks. Style fashionable among women in England and America at different periods.

capote (F. kȧ-pōt; ca pote). Long cloak with hood, of varying style. Worn during Middle Ages and later.

capuchin (kăp'ṵ-chĭn; *cap* you chin) or **capucine** (kăp'ṵ-sĭn; *cap* you sin). Dust cloak with hood, usually of gray cashmere or alpaca; often lined throughout with red or striped surah. So called because similar to garment worn by Capuchin monks. Popular during 1880's.

cardinal. Short, hooded cloak, similar to mozetta worn by cardinals. Originally of scarlet cloth. Popular in 18th century.

18th Century Cardinal

Carrick. Fashionable mantle with very wide skirts worn over full-skirted dresses during 1860's.

chlamys (klă'mĭs; *cla* miss). Short, loose mantle, usually oblong in shape, wrapped around the body, fastened in front or on one shoulder; in oldest form, having long, pointed ends. Worn by young men in ancient Greece as outdoor garment; originally, horseman's cloak.

Greek Chlamys, 500 B.C.

choga (chō'gȧ; *cho* ga). Long-sleeved cloak with long skirt, opening down front, fastened above waist. Worn by men of certain classes in India.

chuddar (chŭd'ȧr; *chud* ar) or **chudder** (chŭd'ẽr; *chud* er) or **chuddah** (chŭd'ȧ; *chud* a). Mantle or shawl consisting of strip or sheet of cotton cloth about 3 yards long. Worn by Hindu men; usually wrapped around shoulders, sometimes around waist.

cope. 1. Semi-circular mantle or cloak, originally hooded, fastened only at neckline in front. Worn on ceremonial occasions by priests; also worn as coronation or processional robe, etc., by laymen. 2. Cloak worn by university doctors at Cambridge. 3. Originally, long cape or cloak worn outdoors. From Latin word *capa*, meaning cape.

cowl. Great mantle with attached hood that can be thrown back over

16th Century Cope

shoulders, as worn by old monastic orders.

dolman (dŏl'mȧn; *doll* man). Cape-like wrap with openings for hands or with cape-shaped appendages for sleeves.

Dolman, 1918

faldetta (făl-dĕt'tȧ; fal *det* ta). Woman's outer garment, consisting of cape and hood combined. Worn in Malta.

feridgi (fẽ-rĭj'ē; fe *rij* ee). Originally, a full double skirt, the upper half turned up over the head. Now separated into skirt and cape, pinned together at back waistline. Usually of rich, dark, brocaded material. Also spelled *feridjee*, *ferigee*, *ferijee*.

gaberdine or **gabardine** (găb'ẽr-dēn; *gab* er deen). Jewish mantle or cloak. Worn during Middle Ages. Also, any covering or protection, as cloak or mantle.

himation (hĭ-măt'ĭ-ŏn; hi *mat* i on). Ancient Greek mantle, worn by both men and women; draped in various ways, usually over left arm, across back, under right arm, and again over left shoulder.

Greek Himation, 550 B.C.–300 A.D.

jabul (Sp. hȧ-bōōl'; ha *bool*). Large cloth worn as mantle by women of Philippine Islands; sometimes also draped over head.

jubbah (jōōb'bȧ; *joob* ba). Long outer garment with loose sleeves extending nearly to the wrist. Worn by Egyptians, Arabians, and Hindus.

kaitaka (kä-ē-tä'kȧ; kah ee *tah* kah). Mat of fine-textured material made of flax, usually with ornamental border, worn as mantle in New Zealand.

kambal (kŭm'bȧl; *kum* bal). Coarse shawl or blanket of wool worn in India.

kaross (kȧ-rŏs'; ka *ross*). Square, rug-like garment made of skins. Worn by natives in South Africa.

khirka or **khirkah** (kĕr'kȧ; *keer* kah). Garment like a robe or mantle that is worn by dervishes in Moslem countries. Originally made of shreds and patches.

lamba (lăm'bȧ; *lam* ba). Bright-colored shawl or mantle, often striped, woven by Madagascan women.

mandilion (măn-dĭl'yŭn; man *dill* yun). 1. Full, loose outer garment reaching about to mid-thigh; with or without sleeves. Worn by soldiers in 16th and 17th centuries. 2. Similar garment worn by New England colonists; lined with cotton and fastened at neckline with hooks and eyes.

manga (mäng'gȧ; *mahng* ga). Garment similar to poncho, formerly worn in Mexico.

mantilla (măn-tĭl'ȧ; man *till* a). Light cloak or cape of silk, velvet, or lace. Worn by women.

mantle. Cloak, usually without sleeves, worn over other garments.

matchcoat. Mantle or wrap of fur or coarse woolen cloth, worn by American Indians.

opera cloak. Elaborate or luxurious loose cloak or wrap worn for attending opera or formal evening parties.

paenula (pē'nū-lȧ; *pee* new la). Long, heavy mantle or cloak of wool or leather, without sleeves, frequently hooded. Worn by poorer classes in ancient Rome.

palla (păl'ȧ; *pal* a). Square of heavy cloth draped and worn as loose outer garment by women of ancient Rome.

Roman Palla, 1st and 2d Centuries

paludamentum (pȧ-lū-dȧ-mĕn'tŭm; pa lue da *men* tum). Large, loose mantle worn by Roman emperors and generals.

pelisse (F. pȧ-lēs; pe leece). Long cloak, open down front; often with round collar. Originally of fur, or lined or trimmed with fur, and worn by both sexes. Later, of silk or cotton, and worn by women and children.

18th Century Pelisse

18th Century Roquelaure

pug. Obsolete short cape with hood attached; usually made of silk, velvet, or other rich fabric.
rochet (rŏch′ĕt; *rotch* et). **1.** Outer garment, usually short-skirted, worn in Middle Ages. **2.** Long woolen mantle trimmed with fringe, brought to colonial America from Devon or Cornwall. Also called *rocket*.
roquelaure (rŏk′ē-lōr or rōk′lôr; *rock* e lore or *roke* lor). Cloak of heavy materials, often fur-trimmed, lined with bright-colored silk. Worn in 18th century. Length varied from knee to floor. Often with cape. Named for Duke of Roquelaure.
sagum (sā′gŭm; *say* gum). Cape or rectangular cloth fastened at right shoulder, worn by Roman soldiers in war time.
serape (sĕ-rä′pā; se *rah* pay). Blanket-like garment worn as outer garment by Mexicans and Latin Americans. Also called *sarape*.

taxi w. Sheer redingote type of coat to be worn over dresses to protect them when riding in taxis.

Watteau mantle. Cape with loose-plaited back of type painted by French artist, Watteau.
witzchoura (wĭ-chōō′rə; wi *choo* ra). Mantle having large sleeves and wide collar, worn in first part of 19th century.
wrap-around. Garment, or part of garment, to be wrapped around person, sometimes loosely, sometimes snugly, as skirt or girdle. See SKIRTS.
wrapper. Originally, loose, informal garment for casual wear at home. Revived in 1939 as a new fashion growing out of the monastic silhouette. Made in all fabrics and for all occasions, usually with belted or girdled waistline.
wraprascal (răp′răs-kəl; *rap* rass cal). Long, loose coat. See COATS.
wreath (rēth; reeth). Garland, as of intertwined flowers or leaves. Worn as crown or chaplet.
wrinkle (rĭnk′l; *rink* l). Crease; slight fold; small ridge or furrow, as in cloth.
wristband. 1. Band on a sleeve at the wrist. **2.** Useful or ornamental band or bracelet worn on the wrist.
wrist fall. Pendant frill or ruffle of lace or other fine material, attached to sleeve at wrist.
wrist length. Length of coat or other garment, taken with arms hanging at sides, which reaches to wrist. See LENGTHS.

Wrapper, 1901    *Wrapper, 1938*

wristlet. Band, as of fabric, metal, leather, or other material, worn on wrist as ornament or protection. Also see MUFFETEE.
wrist watch. Small watch on bracelet or strap. Worn on the wrist.
wyliecoat (wī′lĭ-kōt; *wy* li coat). Scottish petticoat or undervest. Also, a nightdress.

X

X-ray dress. Dress of transparent fabric. See DRESSES.

Y

yak lace (yăk; yack). **1.** English bobbin lace. **2.** Crocheted wool lace. See LACES.
Yale blue. Medium blue color like that used on emblems of Yale University.
yamamai (yăm′ə-mī; *yam* a my). Fine grade of silk fiber. See SILK.
yard. Unit of measure equaling 36 inches, or 3 feet. American yard, not fixed by government standard, supposed to be infinitesimally longer than standard established by English government.
yardage. 1. Extent of a thing measured in yards; the total number of yards. **2.** Yard goods.
yard goods. Piece goods. See GOODS.
yardstick. Stick one yard long, used in measuring cloth.

YARNS

yarn. Term applied to the product of any spinning mill whether the basic fiber be wool, cotton, linen, silk, rayon, or other fiber. Yarns are used for weaving, knitting, and crocheting. They are continuous strands of spun fibers — animal, mineral, vegetable, or man-made. Yarn is to be distinguished from *thread*, which is made up of several yarns twisted together, usually to produce strong strands for sewing purposes.
alaska. Yarn made of long-staple cotton and carded wool.
Berlin wool. Fine worsted yarn made from wool of merino sheep of Saxony or other German state. Used for fancy work. Also called *German wool*.
bourette or **bourrette** (F. bōō-rĕt; boo ret). Yarn of various fibers, having unevenly spaced nubs or knots.
combed y. Long fibers separated from shorter fibers, laid parallel to each other, and made into tightly twisted, strong, smooth yarn.
crewel (krōō′ĕl; *crew* el). Worsted yarn, slackly twisted, used for embroidery and fancy work. Formerly used for fringes, laces, etc.
eider y. (ī′dĕr; *eye* der). Soft yarn made from fine wool. Used for knitting.

eis wool (īs; ice). Fine, glossy, woolen yarn.
fingering. Finely twisted woolen yarn of medium weight, used for knitting and crocheting.
genappe (jə-năp′; je *nap*). Smooth worsted yarn. Used with silk in fringes, braids, etc. So called for Genappe, Belgium.
leviathan wool (lə-vī′ə-thən; le vy ath an). Thick woolen yarn made up of many strands. Used in embroidery.
merino (mə-rē′nō; muh *ree* no). Fine wool yarn. Used for knit goods.
nub y. Yarn with frequent twists or knots. Used for weaving chinchilla, ratiné.
plied y. (plīd; plyd). Yarn composed either of two different fibers, as silk and cotton, or of two fibers of the same kind, one twisted and one not twisted.
ply y. Yarn made up of several strands twisted together.
rayon y. Yarn made of continuous filaments of rayon fiber twisted together.

fāte, făt, dȧnce, ärt   mē, mĕt, hēr, thēre   rīde, rĭd   nōte, nŏt, côrn, fōōd, fŏŏt   cūte, cŭt, cüre   now   fin(ŋ)ger   villa(a)   señor   pleas(zh)ure

yarns (continued)
— **spun rayon y.** Yarn made of short lengths twisted together in spinning machines. Used in same types of weaving as cotton, linen, silk.
rogue's y. (rōgz; rohgs). Yarn of different fiber, color, or twist, inserted into material for purpose of identification.
saxony (săks'ən-ĭ; *sax* on i). Closely twisted, fine yarn of wool from Saxony, Germany. Used for knitting, etc.
Scotch fingering. Loose, woolen knitting yarn.
Seraceta (sĕr-ə-sē'tə; sare a *see* ta). Trade name for type of cellulose acetate yarn.
Shetland wool. Thin, fine worsted with slight twist, made of wool of Shetland sheep.
slub y. Yarn with irregular texture due to unevenness in the woof threads.
vigogne y. (vē-gŏn'yŭ; vee *gon* yuh). Cotton yarn containing small percentage of wool or wool waste.
woolen y. Soft, fuzzy, uneven yarns made from shorter fibers lying crosswise in all directions, carded but not combed before spinning. Used in soft surface fabrics, such as blankets and some flannels.
worsted y. (wŏŏs'tĕd; *woos* ted). 1. Firm, smooth, strong yarn made from long wool fibers that have been combed to remove short fibers and laid parallel before spinning. Used for weaving worsted fabric, usually clear-patterned, hard-surfaced, long-wearing cloth. 2. Loosely twisted yarns for knitting.
zephyr y. Fine, soft worsted or woolen yarn. Used for knitting and embroidery.

yarn count. 1. Number of hanks per pound; also, size of fiber. 2. Same as THREAD COUNT.
yarn darner. Darning needle. See NEEDLES.
yarn-dyeing. Dyeing, as yarn, before weaving. See DYEING.
yashmak (yăsh-măk'; yahsh *mahk*). Long, narrow veil worn by Mohammedan women. See VEILS.
yelek (yĕl'ĭk; *yell* ik). Turkish woman's garment of coat type. See JELICK.
yellow. Primary color, seen between green and orange in the spectrum; pure, light golden color.
yellow jacket. Yellow silk jacket formerly worn in China as emblem of rank. See JACKETS.
yellow ocher. Dull yellow-tan color.
yoke. Fitted portion of a garment, usually over shoulders or hips, to which the rest of garment is sewed. — **triangular y.** Neck yoke with long point in center of the front or back, or both; often extending to the waistline.
yoke skirt. Skirt that has yoke fitted over hips. See SKIRTS.
youthen (yōōth'ən; *you* thin). To make or become youthful in appearance.
youthful. Suitable for or becoming to a young person.
Ypres lace (ēpr; eepr). Lace made at Ypres, Belgium. See LACES.
Y-stitch. Embroidery stitch resembling series of Y's. See STITCHES.
Yuzen birodo (yōō'zĕn bē-rō'dō; *yoo* zen bee *ro* doe). Japanese velvet with cut-pile design. See VELVETS.
Yuzen process. Japanese secret dyeing process used on painted silks and velvets, forming clear, bold designs in rich colors.
"Y" vamp. Shoe vamp split into Y-shaped lace stay. See VAMPS.

Z

zamarra or **zamarro** (Sp. thä-mär'rō; tha *mar* ro). Sheepskin coat. See COATS.
zanella cloth (ză-nĕl'ə; za *nell* a). Twilled fabric used in umbrellas. Same as GLORIA.
zenana (zĕ-nä'nə; ze *nah* na). Lightweight striped fabric with quilted appearance. Used for women's dresses. Originally, women's quarters in an East Indian or Persian house.
zenith blue (zē'nĭth; *zee* nith). Medium light-blue color with slight lavender cast.
zephyr (zĕf'ẽr; *zeff* er). 1. Any article of apparel made of very light material; specifically, athlete's light-weight jersey. 2. Short for ZEPHYR CLOTH, ZEPHYR YARN, etc.
zephyr cloth. Thin, fine cassimere used for women's clothing.
zephyr or **French gingham.** Fine, soft, needle-finished gingham. See GINGHAMS.
Zephyrina Jupon (zĕf-ĭ-rē'nə zhū'pŏn; zef i *ree* na; zhoo ponh). Hoop skirt with open front. See SKIRTS.
zephyr shawl. Soft, light-weight shawl of cotton and worsted, usually embroidered.

zephyr shirting. Soft, gauze-like flannel with warp of silk.
zephyr yarn. Fine worsted or woolen yarn. See YARNS.
zibeline (zĭb'ə-lēn; *zib* e leen). Thick woolen fabric having nap of long, silky hairs. Same as RIPPLE CLOTH.
zigzag. Line running in angular turns alternating from side to side. Used as decorative unit in many types of work. Characteristic of certain weaves.
zigzag chain-stitch. Chain-stitch worked at angle, alternating from side to side. See STITCHES.
zigzagger. 1. Sewing-machine attachment used for stitching appliqué, joining lace and insertion to fabric, joining seams in lace, ribbon, etc. 2. One who operates a zigzagger.
zimarra (zĭ-mär'ə; zi *ma* ra). Type of cassock worn in house and street by priests of Roman Catholic Church.
zip. 1. Colloquial term for life, dash, sparkle. 2. To move quickly; to close with a slide fastener.
Zipper. Trade name copyrighted by rubber manufacturer for galoshes fastened with slide fastener. Frequently used, but not correctly, for any slide fasteners in garments and accessories.
zircon (zẽr'kən; *zer* con). Crystalline mineral, transparent varieties of which are used as gems. Occurs in reddish, brownish, colorless, pale yellow, and smoky varieties.
zona (zō'nä; *zo* na). Latin word for belt or girdle.
zonar (zō'när; *zo* nar). Belt formerly worn by Jews and Christians of the Levant. See BELTS.
zone. Obsolete term for girdle, belt, cincture.
zoster (zŏs'tẽr; *zoss* ter). Belt or girdle worn in ancient Greece. See BELTS.
zouave (zŏō-äv'; zoo *ahv*). Full skirt resembling trousers of French Zouaves. See SKIRTS.
zouave jacket. Woman's short jacket. See JACKETS.
zucchetto (tsŏŏk-kĕt'ō; tsook *ket* o). Ecclesiastical cap. See CAPS.
Zulu cloth (zōō'lōō; *zoo* loo). Twilled fabric of close weave, used as foundation for crewel or outline embroidery.

ILLUSTRATION INDEX

	PAGE
Abbé Cape	22
Aglets, 16th Century	1
Aigrette, 1890's	56
Alençon	86
Alpine Hat, Type of, 1938	70
Amice, Ecclesiastical	2
Angel Sleeves, 14th Century	135
Angelus Cap	19
Anne Boleyn Costume, 1533	54
Apron Tunic, 1920's	158
Arabian Lace	87
Arrowhead (Tailor's Finish)	3
Arrowhead-Stitch	141
Ascot Tie, Man's	3
Babooshes, Turkish	137
Babushka, 1938	77
Baby Stuart Cap, 17th Century	19
Bag Wig, 18th Century	165
Baguette-Cut Stones	4
Baldric, 18th Century	5
Balkan Blouse, Type of	9
Ballet Costume, 20th Century	54
Balmacaan	28
Banyan, 18th Century	167
Barrister's Wig	165
Barrow-Coat, Type of	5
Basket-Stitch	141
Basque Beret	19
Basque Bodice, 19th Century	10
Bateau Neckline, 1920's	102
Bathing Costume, 1909	139
Bathing Suit, One-Piece, 1938	139
Battenberg	87
Batts, 17th Century	129
Bavolet, Evening	19
Bavolet, Peasant	19
Bearskin	19
Bed Jacket, 19th Century	83
Beer Jacket, 20th Century	81
Bell-Boy Cap	19
Bell-Boy Jacket, 20th Century	82
Bertha, 1920's	31
Bethlehem Headdress. Adaptation, 1938	70
Bicorne Hat, 19th Century	70
Biggin	19
Binche	87
Biretta, Priest's	19
Bishop Sleeves	136
Blanket-Stitch	141
Blazer, Boy's	82
Blonde	87
Blouse Coat, 1926	28
Bob Wig	165
Bohemian Lace	87
Bolero, Type of Spanish	82
Bolero Blouse, 1926	9
Bonnet, 1865	10
Boots, 1625	11
Bouffant Skirt, 1930's	12
Boulevard Heel	75
Boulevard Heel, Modified	75
Bowler	70
Box Coat, 1930's	28
Boyish Bob, 1926	9
Bretelles, 20th Century	14
Breton Lace	87

	PAGE
Breton Sailor, Type of	70
Brick-Stitch	142
Bridal Veil, 1930's	160
Brother-and-Sister Clothes	15
Bruges	87
Brussels Lace	87
Buffcoat, 17th Century	28
Buffont, 18th Century	15
Bumper Brim, 1938	70
Bundle-Stitch	142
Bungalow Apron, 1924	44
Buratto Lace, Machine-Made	87
Burnoose, Arabian	167
Busby	19
Bush Jacket, 1938	82
Buskins, Early Greek	11
Bust Extender, 1909	16
Bust Forms, 1938	16
Buster Brown Collar	31
Bustle Silhouette, 19th Century	16
Buttonhole-Stitch	142
Cable-Stitch	142
Cabochon Shapes, Buckram	17
Cabriolet, 1810	10
Calash, 18th Century	77
Calotte	19
Camisa Blouse, 19th Century	9
Camisole Neckline, 1938	102
Cap with Flaps, 1525 and 1938	19
Cape Coat, 1920's	28
Capote, 15th Century	167
Capuche, 19th Century	77
Cardigan Sweater	150
Cardinal, 18th Century	168
Carrickmacross Lace, Applique	88
Carrickmacross Lace, Guipure	88
Cartwheel, 1938	70
Cascade, 19th Century	23
Cassock, Ecclesiastical	23
Catch-Stitch	142
Cavalier Boots, 1625	11
Chain-Stitch	142
Chantilly	88
Charlotte Corday Cap	20
Chechia, Arabian	20
Chemise, Brassière, 1926	25
Chevron-Stitch	142
Chignon, 1878	26
Chin Collar, 1916	31
Chlamys, Greek, 500 B.C.	168
Chopines, 16th Century	129
Chou Hat, 1938	71
Chukker Shirt	128
Clip Pin, Closed and Open	111
Cloche, 1920's	71
Clog, 1600	129
Clog, 1938	129
Clown Suit	54
Cluny	88
Coachman's Coat, Type of, 1820's	28
Coal Scuttle Bonnet, 19th Century	10
Cocardes	30
Coffer Headdress, 13th Century	31
Coif, 14th Century	20
Collarette, 16th Century	31
Colonial Dress	33

172

ILLUSTRATION INDEX

	PAGE
Combination, Type of, 1920	34
Commode, 17th Century	35
Common-Sense Heel	75
Concave Curve	41
Continental Army Hat, Late 18th Century	71
Continental Heel	75
Continental-Stitch	142
Convertible Collar, Closed and Open	31
Convex Curve	41
Coolie Coat	28
Coolie Hat. Adaptation, 1936	71
Cope, 16th Century	168
Cordeliere	36
Coronation Braid	13
Coronet Turban, 1938	74
Corsage Bodice, 1916	36
Corset Cover, 1910	36
Cossack Costume	37
Couching-Stitch	142
Cowl, Modern	38
Cowl, Original	38
Cretan-Stitch	142
Crew Neckline	102
Crinoline, Mid-19th Century	78
Crochet	88
Cross-Stitch	143
Crow's-Foot (Tailor's Finish)	40
Cuban Heel	75
Cuff, Double	40
Cuff Ruff, 1628	40
Cuff, Single	40
Cuff Turban, 1938	74
Culotte, 1930's	40
Cummerbunds—Turkish, American	41
Cutaway Coat, Woman's, 1900's	29
Décolletage, 18th Century	42
Directoire Costume, 1790's	43
Dirndl, 1930's	45
Doll Hat, 1938	71
Dolly Varden Costume, Type of	43
Dolman, 1918	168
Dolman Sleeve, 1920's	136
Domino, 19th Century	98
Doric Chiton, 550 B.C.	26
Doublet, 15th Century	44
Draped Heel	75
Draped Turban, 1936	74
DuBarry Costume	54
Duchesse	88
Duck-Bill Bonnet, 1790's	47
Dungarees	47
Dust Ruffle, 1870's	47
Duster, Early 1900's	29
Dutch Cap. Adaptation, 1938	71
Dutch Collar, 20th Century	31
Dutch Girl Costume	54
Dutch Heel	75
Dwarf Costume	54
Ear Muffs, 1938	47
Edwardian Costume	48
Egyptian Lace	88
Eighteenth Century Silhouettes, Colonial and French	132
Elbow Sleeve, Draped	136
Elizabethan Costume	48
Empire Costume, 1811	52
Epaulets, 16th Century	52
Espadrilles	130
Eton Jacket	82
Eugenie Hat, 19th Century	71
Fagoting-Stitch	143
Falbala	53

	PAGE
Falling Bands, 17th Century Dutch	31
Farthingale, 16th Century	78
Feather-Stitch	143
Fez, Turkish	20
Fiber Lace	88
Fibulas, Ancient	111
Fichu, 19th Century	57
Figured Weave, Simple	164
Filet Lace	88
Fishbone-Stitch	143
Flare-Back Coat, 1930's	58
Flat Heel	75
Fleur de Lis Motifs	58
Floating Panel, Dress with, 1922	58
Florentine Neckline, 16th Century	102
Florentine-Stitch	143
Florodora Girl Costume, 1900	59
Flounces, 19th Century	59
Fourteenth and Fifteenth Century Silhouette	132
Free-Finger Glove, 1938	66
French Fall Boots, 17th Century	11
French Heel	75
French Heel, Modified	75
French Knot	143
Funnel Collar, 1916	32
Gainsborough Hat, 18th Century	71
Gaiter, 18th Century	64
Galilla, 17th Century	32
Gammadion	64
Garibaldi Shirt	128
Gauntlet, 17th Century	66
Gibson Girl Costume, 1898	65
Gibson Waist, Early 1900's	9
Gladstone Collar, 1852	32
Glengarry	20
Gob Hat	72
Golf Skirt, 1895	134
Gorget, 17th Century	67
Guimpe, Child's Dress with, 1911	68
Hairpin Lace	89
Halo Hat, 1935	72
Halter Necklines, 1930's	102
Handkerchief Drapery, 1920's	158
Handkerchief Tunic, 1920's	158
Hanging Sleeves, 15th Century	136
Harem Skirt, Turkish	134
Harlequin Hat. Adaptation, 1938	72
Havelock	75
Helmet, Boy's, 1926	20
Hemstitch	144
Hennin, Medieval	76
Herringbone Twill	164
Himation, Greek, 550 B.C.—300 A.D.	168
Hobble Skirt, 1914	134
Hollywood Top, 1920's	137
Homburg, 1930's	72
Honiton Lace	89
Hood, Early 18th Century	77
Hooded Heel	75
Hoover Apron, 1917	78
Hound's-Tooth Check	25
Houppelande, 15th Century	79
Hour-Glass Silhouette, 1900's	79
Huaraches, Mexican	137
Huckaback-Stitch	144
Hungarian-Stitch	144
Ionic Chiton, 600 B.C.	26
Irene Castle Bob	9
Jabot, 18th Century	81
Jacket Cape, 1930's	22

ILLUSTRATION INDEX

	PAGE
Jacquard Weave	164
Jenny Lind, Type of 19th Century Costume Worn by	84
Jerkin, 15th Century	82
Joan of Arc Costume	54
Jodhpurs, 1930's	84
Johnny Collar	32
Juliet Cap	20
Jumper Dress, 20th Century	45
Kate Greenaway Dress, Coat, 1890's	85
Kepi, French	20
Kiki Skirt, 1923	134
Kilt, Scottish	113
Kimono, Type of	85
Kimono Sleeves, 1920's	136
Klompen, Dutch	130
Knickerbockers	85
Knitted Turban, 1926	74
Lazy-Daisy-Stitch	144
Leggings, 19th Century	94
Leggings, 20th Century Child's	94
Leg-of-Mutton Sleeve, Middle 19th Century	136
Leno Weave	164
Lille Lace	89
Lillian Russell Costume, 1901	95
Limerick Lace	89
Lindbergh Jacket	82
Liripipium, 15th Century	78
"Little Women" Dress	45
Long-and-Short-Stitch	144
Looped-Braid-Stitch	144
Louis XV Heel	75
Love Lock, 18th Century	96
Macaroni, London, 1774	96
Macfarlane	29
Macramé Lace	89
Magic Chain-Stitch	145
Maillot	97
Maltese Lace	89
Manchu Headdress	97
Mandarin Coat, Type of, Chinese	29
Mantilla, Type of	97
Margot Lace	89
Marie Antoinette, Costume of	98
Mary Stuart Cap, 16th Century	21
Mask, 18th Century	98
Mechlin Lace	89
Medici Collar, 16th Century	32
Medici Lace	89
Medieval Costume, 14th Century	98
Middy Blouse, 1920's	9
Military Braid	13
Military Heel	75
Milkmaid Hat, Type of	72
Miter, Bishop's	21
Mitt, 19th Century	66
Mitten, Modern	66
Moat Collar, 16th Century	32
Monastic Silhouette, 1938	100
Monk's Robe	100
Morion Helmet, 16th Century	100
Mouth Veil, 1937	160
Mushroom Hat, 1938	72
Nails, Arabian	130
Napoleonic Costume	102
Neck Ruff, Early 1900's	103
Nineteenth Century Silhouettes—1810, 1860, 1880	132
Nose Veil, 1930's	161
Nursing Basque	104

	PAGE
Obi, Japanese	104
Off-Shoulder Neckline, 1938	102
One Hour Dress, 1920's	45
Open-Crown Turban, 1936	74
Oriental-Stitch	145
Outline-Stitch	145
Overseas Cap, Type of	21
Paisley Design, Type of	106
Palatine, 17th Century	22
Palisade, 18th Century	106
Palla, Roman, 1st and 2nd Centuries	168
Panache on Helmet, 15th Century	107
Pannier, 18th Century	78
Pannier Skirt, 18th Century	135
Pantalets, 19th Century	107
Pantaloons, 18th Century	107
Panties, 1930's	107
Pantoffle, 16th Century	107
Paraguay Lace	90
Parka, 1938	108
Parka Hood, 1938	78
Pattens, 18th Century	108
Peasant Costume, Type of	109
Peg-Top Skirt, Type of, 1910	135
Pekinese-Stitch	145
Pelerine, 19th Century	22
Pelisse, 18th Century	169
Peplum, 1931's	109
Periwig, 18th Century	166
Persian Costume, Type of	110
Petal-Stitch	145
Peter Pan Collar	32
Peter Pan Costume	54
Peter Pan Hat	72
Peter Thomson Dress	46
Petticoat, 1890's	110
Pickadils, 16th Century	111
Pierrette Costume	55
Pile Weave (Cross-Section)	164
Pillbox, 1930's	73
Pillbox Hat with Detachable Wimple, 1938	166
Pinafore, 19th Century	112
Pinafore Heel	75
Pinner, 18th Century	112
Pioneer Woman's Costume	112
Plain Weave	164
Plastron Worn Inside Laced Bodice	113
Plauen Lace	90
Play Suit, 1920's	140
Pocahontas Costume	55
Pocket Cascade, Dress with, 1916	114
Poet's Collar, Early 19th Century	32
Point d'Angleterre	90
Point de Gaze	90
Point de Paris	90
Point d'Esprit, Machine-Made	90
Points, 17th Century	114
Poke Bonnet, 1846	11
Polonaise, 18th Century	115
Pompadour	115
Pompadour, Costume of, Marquise de	115
Pompons	115
Postilion Hat, Type of	73
Pot Lace, Antwerp	86
Pouf, 18th Century	116
Princess Dress, 1930's	116
Profile Hat, 1938	73
Puggree, British	73
Puggree, Hindu	73
Pull-Over Sweater	150
Punch-Work-Stitch	145
Puritan Costumes, 17th Century	117
Puttee	117

ILLUSTRATION INDEX

	PAGE
Quaker Costume, 1678	118
Rabat, 16th Century	32
Raglan	29
Rambler-Rose-Stitch	145
Ratiné, Machine-Made	90
Redingote Costume, 1930's	29
Red Riding-Hood, 1908	78
Red Riding Hood Costume	55
Reefer, 1938	30
Regency Costumes, French and English	120
Regulation Sailor, 1938	73
Renaissance Lace	90
Reticella	90
Reticule, 18th Century	121
Rick Rack Braid	13
Riding Habit, Formal, 1930's	140
Robe de Style	121
Robespierre Collar, about 1790	32
Robin Hood Costume	55
Robin Hood Hat	73
Rompers	122
Roquelaure, 18th Century	169
Rose Point	90
Rough Rider Shirt	129
Ruche, 1900	122
Ruching, Plaited	122
Ruff, 17th Century	32
Rumba Costume, 1930's	123
Russian Costume, Child's Dress Adapted from, 1906	123
Sabots	130
Sack, 1938	123
Sailor Collar, Girl's, 1910	33
Sailor Hat, 1907	73
Saint Gall Lace	91
Salvation Army Bonnet. Adaptation, 1938	11
Sandals, Modern and Early Greek	130
Santa Claus Suit	55
Sari, Hindu	124
Sarong	124
Sash Blouse, 1917	9
Satin-Stitch	146
Satin Weave, Five-Shaft	164
Scarf Turban, 1937	74
Second Empire Costume, 1860	126
Seed Stitch	146
Serul, African	127
Seventeenth Century Silhouettes, English, French, Spanish	132
Shadow Lace	91
Shako	21
Shawl Collar, 1920's	33
Sheath Gown, 1930's	46
Shepherd's Check	25
Shirtwaist Dress, 1930's	46
Short-Back Sailor, 1938	73
Shorts, 1930's	131
Shoulder-Puff Sleeve, 1580	136
Sikh Turban, 1938	74
Silhouettes, 1864 and 1926	131
Simar, 17th Century	83
Single-Breasted Jacket, 1930's	81
Sixteenth Century Silhouettes	132
Skating Costume, 1938	140
Ski Costume, 1938	140
Skimmer, 1938	73
Skull-Cap, 17th Century	21
Slat Bonnet, Mid-19th Century	11
Sleeve Cuff, 18th Century	40
Slipper, 20th Century	107
Smock, 1930's	138
Smock Frock	138

	PAGE
Smocking	146
Snood, Modern	138
Snood, Scotch	138
Snow White Costume	55
Sombrero, Type of	73
Soutache Braid	13
Southwester	74
Spanish Heel	75
Spats, 1918	139
Spencer, 1802	83
Spoke-Stitch	146
Square Heel	75
Stays, 18th Century	141
Steinkirk, 1695	141
Stem-Stitch	146
Step-In Blouse, 1920's	9
Stock, 19th Century	148
Stola, Roman, 2nd and 3rd Centuries	148
Stole, Embroidered	148
Stomacher, 17th Century	148
Sugar-Loaf Hat, Type of, 1780's	74
Sunbonnet, Early 19th Century	11
Sunburst Plaits	113
Sun Shods, Mexican	138
Surface Darning-Stitch	146
Surplice Blouse	150
Surplice, Ecclesiastical	150
Swagger Coat, 1930's	30
Sweat Shirt, 20th Century	150
Swing Skirt, 1926	135
Swiss Costume	151
Sword-Edge-Stitch	146
Tabard	30
Tabis, Japanese	151
Tailored Bow	12
Tailor's Tacks	146
Taj	21
Tam Hats, 1920's	74
Tam-o'-Shanter, Scottish	21
Tarboosh	21
Tent-Stitch	147
Thirteenth and Fourteenth Century Silhouette	132
Tiara	154
Tiewig, 18th Century	166
Toga, Roman	155
Top Boots, 1789	12
Topee	74
Toque, 1575	74
Toque, 1865	74
Torchon	91
Tramé Stitch	147
Trench Coat	30
Tricorne Hat, 17th Century	74
Trunk-Hose, 1600	157
Tunic Skirt, 1930's	135
Tuque, Canadian	22
Turban, 1870	74
Turban, French, 1585	74
Turban, Moslem	158
Turban Worn by Dowager Queen Mary of England, 1938	74
Turtle Neck	102
Tuxedo Collar, 1930's	33
Twelfth Century Silhouette	132
Twentieth Century Silhouettes—1900, 1912, 1916, 1920, 1924, 1928, 1932, 1936, 1938	132
Twill Weave	164
Twisted-Bar-Stitch	147
Twisted Running-Stitch	147
Tyrolean Type of Costume	159
Ulster	30

ILLUSTRATION INDEX

	PAGE
Valenciennes	91
Vandyke Collar, 17th Century	33
Venetian	91
Vestee, 1850's	162
Victoria, Queen	162
Victorian Costume, 1872	162
Virago Sleeve, 16th Century	136
Visor, 15th Century	162
Visor, Sports, 1930's	162
Waistcoat, 18th Century	163
Watteau Plaits, 1745	113
Wheat-Stitch	147
Whisk, 17th Century	33
Widow's Peak, 16th Century	165
Wimple, 14th Century	166
Winterhalter Costume, Type of	166
Wrapper, 1901	169
Wrapper, 1938	169
Y-Stitch	147

Printed in the USA
CPSIA information can be obtained
at www.ICGtesting.com
LVHW051115040124
767941LV00003B/58